# The Church of God

## Body of Christ
## and
## Temple of the Spirit

by Louis Bouyer,
of the Oratory

translated by
Charles Underhill Quinn

FRANCISCAN HERALD PRESS
1434 WEST 51st STREET • CHICAGO, 60609

*The Church of God* by Louis Bouyer, translated by Rev. Charles Underhill Quinn from the French *L'Eglise de Dieu,* Paris: Les Editions du Cerf, 1970. American edition published with permission. Copyright © 1982 by Franciscan Herald Press. All rights reserved. No part of this book may be reproduced, stored in retrieval system, or transmitted, in any form or by any means, electronic, mechanical, photocopying, recording or otherwise, without written permission of the Franciscan Herald Press, 1434 West 51st Street, Chicago, Illinois 60609.

**Library of Congress Cataloging in Publication Data**

Bouyer, Louis, 1913–
   The Church of God, Body of Christ, and Temple of the
Spirit.

   Translation of L'Église de Dieu, corps du Christ et
temple de l'Esprit.
   1. Church—History of doctrines.   I.   Title.
BX1746.B62713     262'.009     80-19347
ISBN 0-8199-0777-4

NIHIL OBSTAT:
   Mark Hegener O.F.M.
   *Censor*

IMPRIMATUR:
   Msgr. John R. Keating, S.T.L., J.C.D.
   *Administrator, Archdiocese of Chicago*

May 10, 1982

MADE IN THE UNITED STATES OF AMERICA

# Contents

## Part II
## An Essay on Doctrinal Synthesis

# Preface

Even before the beginning of the twentieth century, people spoke of the "Century of the Church." The early unfolding of modern "ecumenism" (of Protestant origin), as well as the currents of thought that developed in Eastern Orthodoxy and Catholicism, seem to have verified this prediction throughout the first half of this century, particularly since the First World War. Then John XXIII convoked a council. By the very fact that it became a reality, and through its reverberations, it could seem to have accomplished something beyond all expectation—and results that to some extent were a complete surprise.

This is not true only because of the major place in the council of the Church's reflection upon herself. The direct concern of the constitution *Lumen Gentium* was ecclesiology. But there are other texts—some of them doctrinal, such as the constitution *On the Sources of Christian Revelation* or that on the liturgy, or the more pastoral decrees on ecumenism, the governing of dioceses, or the missions on which are no less concerned with the same question. However, this is not to diminish their value but to emphasize the obvious: first by its convocation, then by the Spirit that dominated its debates, the council constituted an ecclesiological event whose import far surpasses what it was able to accomplish by itself.

By the same token, with all that it produced or gave rise to, the council can be understood and fairly evaluated only if it is put into the context of an entire movement: the Church's rediscovery of herself. This movement began during the first half of this century, and an evolution of minds in the nineteenth century had prepared the way. Without suspecting it, the French Revolution had started it off, with its overturning of accepted spiritual and cultural values. But once we try to analyze this renewal of the Church, however closely it may be bound to the historical context of the nineteenth century, it appears to be the progressive resolution of a crisis situation: the great crisis of the Protestant Reformation and the reactions produced by it in Catholicism, which can hardly be reduced merely to what has been called the Counter Reformation.

It seems, then, that any study of the modern problem of the Church, as we have come to posit it, must begin with awareness of the ecclesiological implications and consequences of the religious crisis of the nineteenth century. Yet it is obvious that the Reformation, so active a force during this time, cannot be explained without a correct view of the conditions laid down for it by the Middle Ages. And again, we cannot understand the Middle Ages, particularly in regard to the idea "Church," if we do not understand what Christian antiquity both bequeathed and created.

Even a sketchy history of ecclesiology must therefore provide a foreword to any modern ecclesiology, if we want it to proceed from a critical view of the materials and manifold influences that have come together in its preparation. Again, we must not forget that, in every age, we cannot separate the ecclesiological problem from the theological problem in its entirety, nor from the whole complex of social ideas and realities to which are bound, ineluctably, the reality of the evolvement of the Church and the notions that Christians have formed of it. Hence the immeasurable importance for our problem of studies like that of Troeltsch on the social ideas of Christian churches and groups.[1] A number of these analyses are debatable, but no work of the same type has broached the subject on the same scale or with comparable sources at hand. From the moment of its publication, this fact was never better seen than by such a well-informed and circumspect Catholic thinker as Friedrich von Hügel.[2]

This, therefore, involves recapitulating the many centuries of the Church's existence, beginning with the reflections that this experience has not ceased to elicit. In addition, this must be done in the light of the discussions and decisions of the Second Vatican Council and in consideration of the complex situation that resulted from it. It is with this in mind that we have sought to work out a coherent view of the Church within God's plan, as we have discovered it in his Word.

Needless to say, it was long before the council—even before anyone spoke of it—that this problem had been at the center of our research and meditation. Readers who are familiar with our work on the Virgin Mary, *Le Trône de la Sagesse,* may remember that it was to have been followed by another volume, dealing precisely with the Church, before still another work on the created universe. Consequently, for many years our thoughts have been oriented toward what the fathers of the Church called the Christian *oikonomia.* The works were to have proceeded from anthropology, concentrated on the person of Mary as the type of Christian perfection, to sociology, in order to end with the cosmology of Christianity. It is the central volume of this trilogy that we present today.

It is central because of its place in the development of our reflections, but it is clear that in this we are merely part of our own time. For the subject is also central in the preoccupations of Christians of our age. We will not hesitate, then, to say that here will be found the heart, as it were, of our Christian experience and of all the thoughts it gives rise to in us.

Yet this centrality of view supposes a prior vision of the Christian personality in its eternal vocation, as we tried to sketch in *Le Trône de la Sagesse* and which, perhaps, we shall one day take up again in a broader perspective. But it is also situated within the heart of an interpretation of the meaning of the world, of divine creation, of its fallen and redeemed history in accord with the fullness of the plan of creation and salvation. This is the object of the third volume of our attempt at a synthesis of the Christian *oikonomia,* which will be devoted to the cosmos: within the perspectives of this divine glory, in the biblical sense, of which the world is to be the effulgence *ad extra,* just as the Divine Word is its glow *ad intra.*

As a matter of fact, this last work has been long in progress in an effort to come to grips with the unfolding of Christian revelation and its interpretation, along with a philosophical reflection upon the totality of the experience of man when left to his own devises and his own lights, at least as they appear to be. The central intent of this study has to be a Christian interpretation of what is called the "modern scientific vision of the world." Even if we are a long way from following Fr. Teilhard de Chardin in all his conclusions, we shall join him in the *Problematik,* which he managed to make famous. To be more precise, we agree with A. N. Whitehead in believing that modern science has become a typical product of that encounter of human research with Christian revelation to explain the rational order of the world that is supposed by our science and that it can be conceived only in a climate of thought which, if not Christian, is at least dependent upon Christianity or results from it. Yet the development in science and technology which is its inevitable result, albeit a product that reacts against its own source, has yet to be fully achieved (and undoubtedly never can be). A Christian interpretation of it ought to come down to a criticism of the present moment through a philosophy enlightened by the total experience of Christian man. In this way it might sketch the needed complement to what we have discovered, as well as the rectification of our undertaking as proposed by revelation—which is itself at the very source of Christianity.

However provisional such an attempt might be in essence—an attempt at a critical synthesis of the experience and (within that experience) of the total awareness of a humankind receptive to biblical faith—an exploration of Christian tradition seems to us to be much vaster and more profound than it is in our silly "cosmology" manuals. At the same time, such an attempt ought to be receptive not only to the heritage of the thinkers of antiquity (without whom modern thought would be incomprehensible) but also to the attainments of the great contemporary cosmologies, such as those of Alexander or Whitehead, as well as the phenomenologies of science or the whole of human existence, in which science is merely a part or a fragment. In an investigation of these latter disciplines, and each in his own way, Wittgenstein was perhaps the most ingenious originator and Minkovski a more modest pioneer, even though he opened complementary channels that are undoubtedly no less important.

Whatever the vastness of the investigation we have undertaken, a synthesis of this type, we believe, can be nothing but intensely personal. Ultimately, it is only by our discovery of ourself that we are finally able to discover the world, just as we cannot discover it in depth if we do not dedicate ourselves totally to our research: "We philosophize only with our whole soul." Even if we go no further than a simple outline with this aim in mind, it would undoubtedly be better to use our last bit of effort, seated in our coffin, to close the cover before the ink dries.

Before we get to that point, however, we should like to deliver three other volumes which would bring us from the *oikonomia* we have briefly described to theology in the most proper sense of the term: in the sight of God within the faith. This "economy" presupposes theology, but theology can develop dialectically only in favor of an interpretation that is consequent upon this economy within the context in which revelation has been inscribed.

In other words, we do not believe that man can arrive at knowledge of himself, either as person or society, nor can he know the universe of his total experience, without knowing or, rather—within the context of Pauline *epignosis*—"acknowledging and recognizing" God in Jesus Christ. Therefore, only an essay of Christology (inseparably a theology of the Word, of revelation of the word of God in Jesus Christ, and a hermeneutics of history in general and biblical and Christian history in particular) can give the preceding studies their central perspective. That means raising our vision through our own experience and transcending to its supreme object. This object then reveals itself as the subject which is, at once, quite different from and quite close to what we might call another experience in which our experience is contained: the experience of the Source Being and the supreme end upon which our own being depends.

But in Jesus Christ this divine subject and the human subject become one, and their union in Christ is but the principle of a union which is to become universal. This oneness is revealed to us by the Divine Spirit, who is both its motor and its term. Thus our Christology ought to reach its end and completion in pneumatology. Indeed, both of them will have to be transcended (together with our entire vision of the creative and saving economy) in the unfathomable vastness of the deity, in the luminous darkness of the source of all things: the invisible Father, "from whom all fatherhood, in heaven as on earth, derives its name."

Shall we ever be able to reach the end of this double trilogy, some of whose parts are well advanced, and all the others are, at best, in the outline stage? That is obviously God's secret, and (we must admit) we have many times been tempted to fear we have too long delayed in its undertaking. We have expended our strength on other tasks, called for by circumstances, and it seems to us that their fruit has been quite meager, despite their considerable volume. On the other hand, these manifold tasks, called for by needs in the Church to which we felt we had a duty to bring some personal contribution, however modest, have reenforced us with a pastoral experience without which, we believe, the work of a theologian is a mere sham, devoid of living content.

In what we have done so far in our task, as well as in what we hope to accomplish relatively soon, the interest and sympathetic criticism that so many readers (often unknown to us) continue to give will, as always, be our best support. Throughout one's existence, a vocation like the one we felt we heard drives one more and more to solitude. This "loneliness," which is the test and also the reward of the man of prayer, would merely be cause for anguish in the writer unless he felt surrounded by the invisible presence of those to whom he is writing. May those many friends who—at times simply and movingly—showed their brotherly interest and concern find assurance here of all the courage they need to carry on.

At this point, may they also allow him to tell them in a few words how much he is indebted to still others, who have been and remain the chief people to awaken or give stimulus to his meditation.

Without speaking here of those he has never known (except through their writings), he must mention those who were first to lead him toward the view of the Church expressed in this present book, whether from Protestantism, Anglicanism, or Orthodoxy: above all, Oscar Cullmann, Arthur Michael Ramsey, Sergie Boulgakoff, and Vladimir Lossky. (The latter two, when still with us, would have surely disagreed with each other, but in the Father's house they must be having a brotherly discussion!)

Within Catholicism, I have shown elsewhere what I owe to that prodigious Christian Socrates, Dom Lambert Beauduin. And to respect his wish to remain in anonymous seclusion, I also cite a "monk of the Eastern Church," who seems to have furnished living demonstration of what I affirm about the profound unity of Catholicism and Orthodoxy. Although I am an Oratorian (which ought not imply an *anima naturaliter jesuitica*), I owe more than I can say to Frs. Guy de Broglie and Henri de Lubac (however much they might smile at their being put together—and not only by me). After monks and Jesuits I must mention two Dominicans, whom I cannot separate in the gratitude I owe them: Fr. Dumont, who has the wisdom to write much but to publish little, but whose influence is unbounded, and Fr. Congar, who writes a great deal, but before whom I feel (with all my books) like a dreamer. I am far from agreement with Fr. Congar on all he writes, but forty years of unclouded friendship (even though we have been on the verge of becoming hot headed) have made our discord, at least for me, a most enriching concord. "In conclusion, may I be allowed this unaccustomed effusiveness: a work like this, which I am giving to the public, has put me in a position to affirm, perhaps better than anyone else, that in ecclesiology (however broadened) Fr. Congar has not only read, digested, and rethought everything, but has elic ited, or at least understood and encouraged, almost everything of value that has been done in this area over the last half century.

When I think of the difficulties of every kind, particularly health, and of the years "in captivity" (I'm not speaking only of OFLAG) over which his colossal work, with such profound roots, was shaped (tirelessly, if sometimes impatiently), my admiration, respect, and affectionate gratitude are beyond expression. The "Boar of the Ardennes" is not only a recluse (like me) but the preeminent recluse—even though he wants to be, above all, "a man for others." I will be wary of provoking his anger (which might be well deserved) by pretending to be part of his band, but I am happy to end this preface by acknowledging all I owe him.

*Paris, Jan. 10, 1970*

# Notes

1. Ernst Troeltsch, *Die Soziallehren der christlichen Kirchen und Gruppen,* published in 1911 and reproduced in the first volume of his complete works.

2. See his remarks in *Eternal Life* (Edinburgh, 1912), p. 199. We had completed the first part of our work when Fr. Yves M.-J. Congar published the first volume of his monumental study on the history of Catholic ecclesiology, *L'Écclesiologie du haut Moyen-Age. De saint Grégoire de Grand à la désunion entre Byzance et Rome* (Paris, 1968). We are happy to point out the profound convergence between his views and ours. His other volume, *L'Église de saint Augustin à l'époque moderne,* came to us while we were correcting our proofs.

# Part I
# The Church in Christian Experience and Reflection

# Chapter 1
# The Church of the Fathers

One of the major changes produced during the nineteenth century and somewhat enlarged at the beginning of the twentieth is that a view of the history of the ancient Church, built up gradually by Protestant scholars, has been considerably modified by Protestants themselves.[1] Harnack can be considered the last great defender of this historical concept, even though he transformed it to the point of changing it into something radically different. On the other hand, it should be pointed out that his major opponent, Alfred Loisy, who was to come to the fore in Catholicism (with his book *L'Evangile et l'Eglise*),[2] may have denounced with rare insight certain insupportable *a prioris* that Harnack unconsciously endorsed in his *Essence of Christianity*[3]—a prisoner of various presuppositions on which this typically Protestant history of the Church was built. (Harnack's synthesis of these presuppositions was merely a final phase.)

This may be summed up in a simple formula: Protestant history of the Church opposed primitive, evangelical, and apostolic Christianity to the Church of the Fathers, the latter looked upon as at least the seed of later Catholicism. Loisy skillfully demonstrated that the characteristic elements of this Catholicism were present in the New Testament, and this is something that Harnack himself did much to bring to light. But Loisy was no less persistent in seeing a cleavage between this Catholicism, which could be called apostolic (in the sense that it was the work of the apostles, beginning with St. Paul), and Jesus.[4] The difference was that for Loisy, then under the influence of the "eschatological" school (which was to find its greatest representative in Albert Schweitzer),[5] the primitive Gospel had nothing to do with the interior, humanist, and spiritualist Gospel described by Harnack in *The Essence of Christianity*. Rather, the primitive Gospel was the proclamation of a sudden and definitive coming of a Kingdom of God that was quite foreign to this world and swooped upon it only to do away with it. Loisy dispelled the dream of a premature liberal Protestant Jesus, but he preserved the idea of an opposition between Jesus and the Church that succeeded Him. Yet Loisy recorded the fact that this Church, in its essential elements, did not appear after apostolic Christianity, outside the New Testament, but rather within the New Testament through the induction of the apostles into the *de facto* situation created by the delayed *Parousia*: "They were expecting the Kingdom of God, and it was the Church that came."

Despite the differing positions that were (and still are) held since this controversy began at the beginning of the twentieth century, there is hardly any Protestant historian today who does not acknowledge at least this fact: the later writings of the New Testament, as well as the pastoral epistles attributed to St. Paul, attest to an organized Church, authoritatively preaching a definite interpretation of the Gospel and convinced of having and communicating its spiritual content in sacramental rites that were interpreted realistically, i.e., as containing in a certain way what they signify. And in one sense this was, essentially, what the Church of the Fathers was to remain. On the other hand, this view and this reality, to say the least, began to appear in the major Pauline captivity epistles, and the first features can be seen in the earlier epistles. The only fundamental element of Catholicism which does not seem to have appeared in apostolic times, but to have come slightly later, is the concrete form that was to be assumed by the hierarchy of ministries, centered locally on the "monarchical" episcopate.[6] All the more reason, therefore, to say that the idea of seeing the episcopate itself, in its totality, as centered in the Bishop of Rome evolved very gradually.[7] Yet even contemporary Protestant theologians who most strongly stress the relative slowness of both these developments have little difficulty finding at least their roots in the New Testament. The monarchical episcopate was at least made possible by the establishment of locally responsible ministries under apostolic authority, as can be seen from the pastoral epistles. Papal authority is not without its remarkable prehistory in Peter's authority within the apostolic community.

We may assert substantially today, as an uncontested fact, that the Church of the Fathers succeeded in a practically homogeneous fashion that Church which appears to take form in the unfolding of the New Testament, and which, in an overall perspective (whatever one might say of some few elements), is already given there in its entirety.

Among the fathers, this view of the Church was certainly lived in a very conscious way. But for a long time, it does not seem to have been the object of any theological synthesis. The consciousness of the Church, then, is a living and precise consciousness, but it is not (or is only barely) a reflex consciousness. In the fathers we can find numerous treatises or sermons on the Divine Persons, on the Incarnation, and (with less technical precision) on the Redemption, and even on the sacraments, but it would be difficult to find there even one work that could be considered simply a study on the Church as such. St. Augustine's *City of God,* which undoubtedly comes closest to it, is much more a study of the Kingdom of God in history, in which there is at most a tendency (not exclusively his) to identify the Church with this kingdom, even though with him this identification is far from absolute.

We should make a serious mistake were we therefore to deduce that the Church had merely secondary importance in patristic times. The contrary is closer to the truth: it is because they placed the Church everywhere, in their faith and in their life, that the fathers did not feel the need to devote special study to it. The Church in this regard is nothing more than a particular case of a general rule: just as an organism is not sensitized to the function of one of its organs until the organ is disturbed or confused by some cause, the realities and truths of the Christian faith became the object of systematic developments or definitions only after they were questioned in one way or another.

However, it would be a gross error to think that the Church or her members voiced nothing interesting or precise about her before these crises or that she or her members have said everything that could be said about her, once these crises happened.[8]

What is perhaps most striking to us today, when we look at the Church at this period, is the way in which she seemed to bring about the union of factors that seem to us to be opposed to one another, if not even contradictory:

1. The unity, and more precisely the unicity, of the universal Church and her manifestation—indeed her fundamental realization—in the local church
2. The sense that this unity is a gift of the Spirit, and the spontaneous certitude that she is no less—quite the contrary—a visible, tangible unity, asserted not only in common institutions but in a whole community of life in which these institutions are the organ
3. The hierarchy and the full association of all the laity with the life of the Church
4. The sense of a living tradition and the attachment to Scripture
5. The sacramental and liturgical life and the most interior personal life
6. The unity of a defined faith and the liberty and variety of its expressions and systematizations

7. Especially, perhaps, a very powerful sense of salvation and divine election as a grace given to the Church, as distinguished from "the world"
(even her opposition to the world), and a missionary activity which is
not only tireless in its efforts, indefinitely fertile in its resources, but has
an efficacy that seems hardly believable to us

It is worth examining each of these points in detail.

## I. The Universal Church and the Local Church

That the Church is one everywhere in the world where she exists, and that
there can be but one Church, is, as Dom Christopher Butler put it in his book
*The Idea of the Church,*[9] such a well-established conviction in the Church of
the Fathers that most heretics who have separated from her took this idea with
them. In a general way, none of them claimed the right to a private church,
different from that of the basic group; all upheld, with Catholics, that there is
only one universal Church by that name—but, obviously, their own!

This universal view is found in *The Shepherd of Hermas* in a popular form,
with the tower built from different stones, which are men. Once these stones
were polished and assembled by angels, there were no longer even cracks
between them: the tower, built by the side of the waters (symbolizing baptism), seems to be built of one solid block.[10] But this image of a perfectly
joined building does not express the whole reality to the onlooker. The
Church, therefore, will appear to the onlooker as a personal being, a being
that is already old but without age, or rather a being of eternal youth.[11]

However, the epistles of Ignatius of Antioch give particularly convincing
and far from isolated evidence that this one Church is, first of all, the local
assembly of the faithful, grouped about the bishop united with his *presbyterium,* organized by the service of the deacons. It is especially the
eucharistic assembly that manifests this.[12] The word "manifest" is insufficient, however. What constitutes the Church as one living temple of God, like
the tower of Hermas, is precisely this eucharistic assembly at which all receive the divine teachings from the bishops and the priests, at which all pray
together, offer together through the ministry of the deacons, and receive
together the "food of immortality" which constitutes all into one body, the
Body of Christ, for a common life of communicative charity, in unceasing
thanksgiving.[13] The same idea can be found in Justin[14] and Irenaeus,[15] and
even, fully, into the fifth and sixth centuries with possibly the most hellenized
of fathers, the Pseudo-Areopagite, in his description of the *synaxis.*[16]

The point is that the Christian, wherever he goes—like Ignatius going from church to church; from Syria, where he was bishop, to Rome, where he was to die; in churches where no one knew him and where he knew no one and, like Abercius many years later, and so many others—is received as if he were at home and still finds the same Church.[17] This is expressed in the oldest form of solemn concelebration, in which bishops from churches, near or far, celebrated the Eucharist together and asserted and actualized the communion of their local churches in the one Church.[18]

## II. Unity of the Spirit and Visible Unity

This unity and unicity are constantly explained to us as the unity of a unique love, the *agape* of God, poured into our hearts by his Holy Spirit, as St. Paul says in a text that is often repeated and commented upon.[19] But this very interior outpouring of the Spirit and the *agape* is expressed in the unity of defined faith, of hierarchy, and of sacramental communion. And, again, what expresses it is as well conceived as the means given from on high, whereby the Spirit and love are poured out. Nevertheless, all of that flourishes in mutual love, concretely expressed everywhere by the community of life of Christians who never hesitated to place their possessions in common as well as their spiritual charisms, and throughout the world by the same charity, the same exchanges from one church to another and among all the churches.[20] At this stage, what is undoubtedly the earliest assertion we have of a preeminence of the church of Rome was expressed quite naturally in this phrase: "The Church that presides in charity."[21]

## III. Hierarchy, Charisms, and Laity

On the other hand, within each church are definite functions which quickly became organized on practically the same model and were bestowed for life on particular individuals by the laying on of hands and prayer: episcopate, presbyterate, and diaconate (leaving aside the other more or less variable or temporary functions, such as that of the *didascalus*). There is also a flowering of manifold charisms in the whole body of the Church: visionary and prophetic gifts, varied *dynameis* of healing, or other miraculous manifestations. We are persuaded—and when we don't seem to remember it sufficiently the authorities forcefully remind us—that all these gifts must be used in the service of charity, and therefore unity. But we must emphasize that exactly the same thing is said about the stable functions, beginning with that of the bishop, and that it is by an optical illusion that certain Protestant historians thought they could discern in the early Church an opposition between the regular and the charismatic ministries. Rather, it would seem that an undue transfer of recent situations to the Church of the Fathers has been made by speaking simply of tensions in this regard.[22]

There is no question that conflicts arose at times. But they were as much conflicts among the "ministers" as between the "ministers" and the "charismatics"—when they were not simply conflicts among the "charismatics" which provoked the intervention of the authorities! And even when there was a *de facto* conflict between the hierarchy and the "charismatics," it was never seen as a conflict *in principle:* it was always over precise objects—a conflict between authorities and "charismatics" precisely like those that occurred occasionally (for analogous motives) among the authorities or the "charismatics" themselves.[23]

The case of the Corinthian community, in which the "charismatics" seem to have exhibited an endemic exuberance and turbulence, is very revealing. No more than St. Paul before them, St. Clement and the Roman presbyters, as they stepped in, did not seem to be animated by any wish to repress or throttle "charisms." Like the Apostle, these men were concerned only with reminding us that the "charisms," to the extent they were authentic or faithfully exercised, could be exercised only in the service of charity, and therefore of unity. The exercise of the "charisms" must never disturb the exercise of those ministries which were more stable by nature. But the unity they favored, and never ceased to explain in detail, has nothing to do with an authoritarian militarism. As they say explicitly, it is an organic unity in which no one can be passive, where all the "laity" have a role equivalent to the role of the priests in the Old Covenant, but a role in which everyone, in his place within the totality, exercises his own activity for the good of all to its fullest extent.[24]

It is important to emphasize that this question of "charisms" and "ministries" did not assume specific importance in the first generations of the Church as we might tend to believe. Renewed in the fourth century, monasticism did little more in this area than it did in the earlier centuries. Indeed, we must not forget that from its very beginnings monasticism was essentially a charismatic movement. Nor can we forget that it has so remained (for all practical purposes) as long as it has been a living reality, both in the West and in the East.[25] In this regard, nothing has been more characteristic than the reaction of the episcopate. From the first beginnings of monasticism with St. Athanasius, the reaction has been positive.[26] Far from wishing to stem the sudden expansion of this movement, the early bishops, as a group, made the closest alliance with it. The result became the universal custom in the East of choosing the bishops from among the monks, while at the same time in the West there was a constant tendency to "monasticize" all the clergy, at least those in major orders. We might even wonder if this reaction, as positive as it may have been in principle, did not go too far (even with St. Basil), to the point of such a *de facto* institutionalization of monasticism as to cause it to lose its essential and original character.[27] Whatever may be said about this unforeseen consequence, the primary principle is too important not to be given full exposure: far from seeing any opposition in the early Church between "charism" and stable "ministry," her instinctive reaction was to consider as self-evident that the highest "ministries" were normally to be bestowed on those who gave evidence of the most noble "charisms."[28]

However, this would be to restrict the problem too greatly and put further in the past the modern optical illusion of which we have spoken, which reduces the relationship of the hierarchy within the totality of the body of the Church, in the Church of the Fathers, to the relationships between the "ministries" and the more or less extraordinary or exceptional "charisms."

Here we are touching on a matter which goes far beyond the problem we have been studying: practically, for all the fathers, priesthood in the Church is universal, in the sense that the life of the whole Body and each of its members (in particular) is a priestly life. This must be understood in what is an obviously twofold sense, but basically (as we shall understand it when we speak of the sacraments and their connection) with the whole of Christian life within the Church. On the one hand, in the eucharistic assembly all people are priests in the eyes of the fathers. The liturgy of the community is a collective act, which therefore does not mean that everyone had, or could have, the same function, without distinction, but rather that everyone had a "service" or special "ministry" that was equally sacred. When they prayed, offered, and communicated, the faithful (the laity) participated in an essential fashion in the sacred action and thereby performed a priestly task. From St. Justin to St. Gregory the Great, and even in the Epistle of Clement of Rome before them, this was formulated in the most express terms.[29] The comparison Clement made between the differing duties of the Old and New Covenants is especially expressive. For him, the faithful of the New Covenant do not correspond to the laity of the Old, but rather *to the priests*. In the sense that the laity could have existed in the old People of God, they were no more in the new People, where *all* are priests.

With the same authors, however, beginning with Clement himself, these statements unabashedly come close to no less categorical statements on the special function of the bishop as high priest.[30] Without him, the collective priesthood could not be exercised, since it can be exercised only within the body in which the bishop has the indispensable role of head. Without the bishop, who presides over the spreading of the word and the eucharistic consecration, no one could pray, offer, and communicate.

Outside the eucharistic assembly, on the other hand, what all accomplish is extended to the whole of life. For all, this whole life becomes eucharistic because, in its entirety, it must be illuminated by the properly eucharistic act of thanksgiving and saturated by the transfiguring *agape* which has its source within it.[31] But here again the indefinitely varied initiatives through which each of us is called to witness, through our words and our whole life, to the specifically priestly grace given to all, must be coordinated within the cohesion preserved by all with the pastoral function of the ministerial priesthood. St. Ignatius was not the only one to stress this point. Indeed, just as Christians always present themselves to the world as one body, even when they act as individuals within this body, the internal unity of the Spirit and of love remains inseparably the unity with the bishop and his presbyterium.[32]

## IV. Tradition and Scripture

Just as the life of the individual Christian can never be isolated from that of the Church, to which it is bound organically, and just as the life of each local church can never be separated from the life of the one and unique Church, the life of the universal Church can never be limited to the present generation. The Church is present, in her sameness and totality, in every generation, but she is always the Church of the Apostles, the Church founded upon them by Christ himself.

This is affirmed by tradition. In the way the fathers understood the word, tradition is above all (if not exclusively) something objective: what is handed down.[33] Therefore, tradition is first of all the rule of faith, the synthetic statement of what every Christian, and the whole Church, at all times must believe, what Vincent of Lérins described in his famous phrase: "*Quod semper, quod ubique, quod ab omnibus creditum est.*"[34] However, tradition is also the Scripture; the Old Testament first of all, but also what it gradually came to constitute in a defined canon in the New Testament: what the apostles had expressed, fixed into an "inspired" Scripture on equal footing with the Scripture of Israel, together with the Gospel of Christ which he himself proclaimed and of which he is the object. Again, it is the organized and organic life of the Church in her hierarchical structure, as well as in all her sacramental and, especially, eucharistic liturgy. And beyond and within all this, it is the incarnate life of charity, the life of the Spirit, the Spirit of God, in this entire body, which is the Body of Christ. All this is tradition, because all of it has been received and handed down: received from the apostles, who received it from Christ, who received it from the Father.[35]

But all of this, which once and for all was received and transmitted initially in and by Christ, never ceases to be received and transmitted. And if it is true—according to the formula of Vincent of Lérins—that what is transmitted is always what has been transmitted from the beginning, it is no less true and hardly less important to add that this is also transmitted, at every stage, just as it has been from the beginning in Christ: that is to say, not as a dead letter but as the Spirit of life, which is equally life giving. In this sense, which is no longer objective but subjective, tradition is nothing more than the continuity of the life of the Church in all her members, as a life that is always living and lived in the present.[36] Yet it must immediately be added: it is a life lived in them and by them, but in no way a life which would be proper to them on their own, of which they would be the source, indeed the masters. It is the life of the Spirit, a life given by Christ which never ceases to be his very own, in a transcendent and exclusive sense, even when it is communicated and effectively shared.[37]

The result is that tradition is always new and always the same. There are elements of it which, even in their materiality, once they have reached the maturity of their development, are no longer susceptible to change, as is the case with the books of Holy Scripture, first with the Old Testament and then with the New.[38] To a certain extent, this is also true with the "kernel" of the symbols of faith, even though they are susceptible to precision and, as well, to the multiplication of their formulas.[39] This is true with the hierarchical structure of the Church, at least in its essential elements, although, like Scripture itself, it took some time for them to be differentiated and defined.[40] It is true again with the substance of liturgical and sacramental life, although the same development is manifested even in the most basic elements and their whole overlay of secondary formularies and rites may profoundly differ from one local church to another and, at the same time—at least to the end of the period under consideration—be in a state of continual elaboration.[41]

But within the heart of living tradition, as with every living being, is a continuity and a necessary complementarity between what no longer changes, beginning with a more or less brief period of maturation, and what never ceases developing and diversifying. All this merely makes a tradition in which everything holds together.

With this in mind, we can understand that the problem "Scripture or tradition," or even "Scripture *and* tradition," has never been posited as it has come to be in modern times.[42] For Scripture and tradition never appear as two autonomous factors, or even as correlatives, whether as a cooperation or as an opposition. When the ancients spoke of "tradition," Scripture was always included (whether this meant the Old Testament tradition as the only extant tradition or the tradition of both testaments, which came somewhat later). Indeed, it was within tradition that Scripture arrived at its formation, that it was progressively acknowledged and formally accepted. It is perfectly precise to the extent that it became formalized and was acknowledged, that it came to be not only central but basic. Even though from the outset there were no precise technical formulas, an inspiration of a unique quality and immediacy was acknowledged. But this is never reached, never even conceived, apart from the totality of tradition, whose central kernel it enlarged. Actually, it is only in this way that Scripture can have meaning for those who read it, a meaning that has not been externally superimposed but coincides with the *nous Christou* which inspiration has deposited there once and for all.

As Irenaeus said when spontaneously expressing the sense of Scripture in tradition, which was the understanding of the entire ancient Church: heretics can display astonishing knowledge of Scripture and no less astonishing virtuosity in synthesizing its basic principles, but they do this in the manner of mosaic makers, who shamelessly reuse the colored cubes that had formed the King's portrait to shape an ordinary, popular image. Only those who live within the Church, who bear within themselves the *hypothesis pisteos* (i.e., the living schema of her faith), can rediscover and release within the Church the only true *eikon basilike*.[43]

## V. Sacraments and Interior Life

In the ancient Church, this leads directly to the ever fertile alliance between the sacraments and the most interior and personal spiritual life. The realism of the fathers' notion of the sacraments is one evidence of this. For them, the sacraments do not only effect what they signify, but (as Dom Odo Casel was right in maintaining) they are not limited to the understanding that is manifested in the interpretation of various recent Catholic theologies.[44] Not only do the fathers believe that the sacraments communicate grace *ex opere operato* (a later term)—not only do they believe that the Body and Blood of Christ are given to us objectively in the Eucharist, in such a way that the words

"This is my Body, this is my Blood" are to be understood in a sense that is obviously mysterious but, at the same time, absolutely real—but, according to their interpretation, there is a great deal more: the whole mystery of Christ, the mystery of his death and resurrection, and the mystery of our salvation in its eschatological fullness. The phrase *"quotiescumque hoc perficitur opus redemptionis exercetur,"*[45] from the Leonine Sacramentary, could be countersigned by the whole of patristics, including those fathers whose predilection for symbolism is most noticeable, such as Origen or Augustine. With them this symbolism is realistic, and does not confuse the sign with the thing signified, but always refers to (or rather acknowledges) the presence of the thing beneath the sign.[46]

And yet we could not wish for more assertive expressions than those in each line of the catecheses of the early Church[47] on the necessity of faith so that these realities become our own, nor on the necessity of faith (that faith which is at the origin of the most personal assimilation of the mystery of salvation) as imparted by the Church in the presentation of the sacraments to the faithful.

Undoubtedly, the expression "sacraments of the faith" must not be interpreted in the fathers in a subjectivist or even a directly subjective sense.[48] In this expression, the faith in question is the objectivized faith in the Gospel proclamation of the Christian mystery, as formulated particularly in the baptismal symbols. But there is no less doubt that, for them this objective faith cannot be separated from its "real apprehension" (as Newman would have said) by the faithful. Indeed, if the "sacraments of the faith," in their understanding of the term, are given to us, it is so that our most personal faith might grasp the reality of the mystery or, rather, let itself be penetrated by it, so that our whole life might be transformed by it. This is exactly what Augustine means when he declares to the neophytes that they receive the sacrament of "themselves" in the Eucharist i.e., they receive the body of the dead and risen Christ so that they themselves might become "the body of Christ" in the totality of their lives, transformed by charity.[49]

It is thus that tradition is received and can then be transmitted or handed down by us, not as some inert material which we pass on from hand to hand but as a seed of life, as communicated acts, as a fully fructifying life, to those who receive it. And it is precisely the faith, as understood by the fathers—that faith that seizes hold of one's whole being and hands it over to the efficacy of the creative and salvific Divine Word—which is the unique and the necessary principle of their salvation, of their life "in Christ." Through faith thus opening itself to what comes to it in the sacraments, the world of the new creation becomes our world, the world in which we are re-created.

This leads us directly to the relationship between the Church and the world as seen by the fathers. But before we get to that point, let us consider one consequence they drew from the preceding for the unfolding of the life of grace in the various members of the Church.

## VI. Unity and Diversity

For them, it was not only in the equally necessary diversity and community of the "charisms" and "ministries" that catholic unity was asserted in the Church. It was also, and to no less an extent, in the diversity and community of the most subjective modalities of this life of grace, adapting itself in each of us to our own peculiarities (which we might well call natural) but also transforming them totally.

The faithful are taken into the Church as they are, with all they have and are, and all are received on an equal basis. Just as the ancient opposition between Jew and Greek was dispelled in this context, so was the opposition between barbarians and Hellenists (i.e., all cultural differences)—between men and women, rich and poor, masters and slaves. Once people were received, it was only from sin that they must be purified; sin aside, everything else they brought with them was welcomed. Still, all were renewed in such a way that otherwise natural clashes became harmonies whereby each person enriched everyone else, all of whom profited in turn. "Everything is yours," provided you are Christ's just as Christ is God's. Certainly the remodeling that each and every one of us must undergo to reach this point is complete. Everyone must learn to die to himself in order to be in Christ and to live for others. But nothing substantial is ultimately lost or cast aside. On the contrary, everything is reborn to new life.

Perhaps even more than the distinction between rich and poor or master and slave, the distinction between the knowledgeable and the ignorant is typical of this unlimited diversity that is welcomed by the Church. Yet it is only she that can accomplish the metamorphosis to this point. "Scientific faith" can be alive only because of the faith of the poor in spirit. Its spirit is rich only in faith; otherwise it goes astray. But the faith of the learned, on the other hand, will justify, defend, and especially fortify and enlighten the faith of those who are less well instructed.[50]

Hence it follows that if there is but one spirituality in the Church, the spirituality of the Gospel, it will be affected by all the varied aspects of the human experience. Yet this happens in such a way that no experience can be isolated from others, nor can it be subjected to—any more than it could impose—non-Gospel contraints. One of the most austere monks, Paphnutius, at the Council of Nicaea defended the sanctity of marriage,[51] and perhaps the major part of Origen's *Contra Celsum* is a justification of the faith of simple people—by the most ingenious mind in Christian antiquity.[52]

This applies directly to the form of each individual's life in the Church and leaves its imprint on the forms of the Church's collective life. What is more one or unifying than life in the Eucharist, as the primitive Church conceived and lived it? Yet what astonishing diversity among the formularies and even the eucharistic liturgies was accepted from one church to another and in the same church, even long after the celebrants' freedom of improvisation had been stopped![53]

Still more surprising is the explicitly admitted variety in local formulations of the same faith, as long as they were convergent. And it was not by chance or independent trial-and-error experimentation that people arrived at statements of the same basic truths in various places. Read only St. Athanasius' *De Synodis* (he was the most unbending defender of the faith of Nicaea) and one is surprised by the liberal attitude with which he welcomed opposing approaches to the same faith, as long as they claimed to be equivalent and complementary.[54] What is possibly most surprising in this respect is what strikes us least, because we have become too used to it: the primitive Church allowed and preserved—intact—four statements from the Fourth Gospel which are profoundly different (even if they are reconcilable since they are equally and inseparably inspired). One has to spend many hours poring over such data (they are innumerable) and to have looked deeply into the unifying paradox before one can understand how patristic and how typical of the early Church is the famous phrase: *"In necessariis unitas, in dubiis libertas, in omnibus caritas."*

## VIII. *The Church and the World*

But it is in relation to the Church and the world that this spontaneously synthetic character of the life and the consciousness of the primitive Church is most striking, for it is in this area that such a synthesis could seem to us modern thinkers to be impossible and even inconceivable. As long as persecution or its threat hovered over the Church of the Fathers, the Church, with disconcerting facility, united separation from the world and openness to the world, flight from the world (even radical condemnation of the world) and love of the world. Like her Master, the Church seems to have instigated hatred of the world only so she could tell it: "When you have lifted me up [on the cross], I shall bring all men to me."

At this time, entrance into the Church through baptism meant not only giving up the world, which could be taken as metaphorical, but, as well, a *de facto* break which made one an outlaw and a candidate for martyrdom.[55] And this condition of the Christian in the world was so well inculcated by the Church as the natural condition that, when the world ceased to weigh heavily upon Christians, it was the most generous of them who bore the responsibility. The appearance of monasticism in the fourth century cannot be otherwise explained.[56]

All the baptismal catecheses we have spoken about are, from beginning to end, nothing more than detailed affirmations of the completely renewed view of life that is imposed on the new Christian by his entrance into the Church, with its corollary: an unending struggle against "the spirit of the world."[57]

Yet, curiously, there has never been another age in the life of the Church when she has been so missionary toward the world, through the "witness" of each Christian as well as the "preaching" of the whole of Christendom. And the adaptation, range, and efficacy of this witness and preaching are attested to by the most astonishing fact in all of Christian history: after the initial setback (a relative setback) with those who seemed to have been so well prepared to welcome the Christian message (i.e. the Jews), there was rapid and widespread success with those who apparently had no preparation to accept it (the Greeks and the hellenized Romans). And as if this were not enough, the same thing happened again, apparently with the same facility, with all the barbarians who appeared on the scene in succession.[58]

To attract the world to herself in such a way, it was necessary that this Church (who marked herself off from it and fiercely defended herself against it, more than ever before) appear to this same world, as diversified as the latter was, in astonishingly complete accord with its needs! The only thing that can explain this paradox, which is more disconcerting than all the rest, is the striking modality the primitive Church witnessed to: living a reality which she herself possessed, far more than being possessed by it. This is a gift of God—not only a gift God gave her but a gift in which he gives himself. This explains how harmony is achieved between "not of the world" and "all things to all men," in the unshakable assurance of "all are yours" and "all become one with you." "You no longer belong to yourselves," for "you are Christ's and Christ is God's."[59]

# Notes

1. On all that follows, see F. M. Braun, *Aspects nouveaux du problème de l'Église* (Fribourg–Lyon, 1942).
2. Alfred Loisy, *L'Évangile et l'Église* (Paris, 1902).
3. Adolf von Harnack, *Das Wesen des Christentums* (Leipzig, 1900).
4. The post-Bultmann school still tries to maintain this, especially Conzelmann, for whom Luke would be primarily responsible for this *Frühkatholizismus* (cf. his book on the theology of St. Luke, *Die Mitte der Zeit,* published in 1953). Other contemporary Protestant exegetes, such as those of the Scandinavian school since Anton Fridrichsen, are the first to point out the artificiality of this opposition between this *Frühkatholizismus* and Jesus: the result of a doctrinal *a priori* that is belied by the facts and the texts.
5. See especially his *Vom Reimarus zu Wrede* (1st ed., 1906).
6. For this problem, see below, pp. 318ff.
7. Also see below, pp. 456ff.
8. The best summary of the contemporary texts on the Church can be found in the two-volume work of G. Bardy, *La théologie de l'Église de saint Clément de Rome à saint Irénée* (Paris, 1945) and *La Théologie de l'Église de saint Irénée au concile de Nicée* (Paris, 1947).
9. B. C. Butler, *The Idea of the Church* (Baltimore–London, 1962), which criticizes the recent defense of the inverse thesis by Anglican Canon Greenslade in his book *Schism in the Early Church.*
10. *The Shepherd of Hermas,* Vis. III and *Simil.* XIX.
11. Ibid., Vis. II and III.
12. See especially the epistles to the Philadelphians, 1:2; to the Ephesians, 5:1; to the Romans, 2:2.
13. Cf. Philadelphians 4, and Ephesians 20:2.
14. *First Apology,* 65–67, P.G. 6, col. 428ff.
15. *Adversus Haereses,* 4, 17, 5.
16. *Hierarchia ecclesiastica,* ch. 3.
17. A. Abel, "Étude sur l'inscription d'Abercius," in *Byzantion, op. cit.* (1926), 3:321ff.
18. Cf. below, pp. 298ff.
19. Romans 5:5.
20. See the reassembled texts in J.-A. Moehler, *L'Unité dans l'Église* (Fr. tr.; Paris, 1938), pp. 6ff.
21. Superscription of the epistle of Ignatius to the Romans.
22. This is still true of a recent study that is as remarkable as that of H. von Campenhausen: *Kirchliches Amt und geistliche Vollmacht* (Tübingen, 1953).
23. This comes to light from a reading of the epistle of Clement of Rome to

the Corinthians, when we do not wish to introduce some preconceived idea into it.

24. Cf. especially ch. 40ff. of the epistle of Clement.

25. See our *Spiritualité du Nouveau Testament et des Pères* (2d ed.; Paris, 1966), p. 395.

26. See the epistle of Athanasius to the monk Dracontius, who refused the episcopate, P.G. 25, col. 524ff.

27. Again, cf. our *Spiritualité du Nouveau Testament et des Pères*, p. 412.

28. Characteristic of this viewpoint is an author as late as Pseudo-Dionysius; for him, not only was the ideal bishop what we would call today a charismatic, but the validity of sacraments given by a bishop who wasn't a charismatic became at least questionable. Cf. *Epist*. VIII; P.G. 3, col. 1092 B. The same conviction is found again during the time of Symeon the New Theologian, and has never completely disappeared from Eastern tradition.

29. Cf. Clement of Rome, epistle to the Corinthians, 41.

30. See the following paragraphs in the epistle of Clement.

31. See especially Justin, *First Apology,* 13; P.G. 6, col. 345.

32. Ignatius of Antioch, *Magnesians,* 6,1, and Ephesians 4. Cf. *Smyrniots,* 7,1 and 8,1.

33. This is properly the meaning of *paratheke,* but it is also found applied to *paradosis.* See the articles on these two terms in *A Patristic Greek Lexicon,* ed. G. W. H. Lampe (Oxford, 1965), fasc. 4.

34. Vincent of Lérins, *Commonitorium,* 2; P.L. 50, col. 639.

35. See Yves M.-J. Congar, *La Tradition et les Traditions* (Paris, 1960), vol. 1, especially pp. 42ff.

36. Cf. Hippolytus of Rome, *Philosophoumena,* 1, praef. 6, with Congar's commentary, op. cit., pp. 52 and 102.

37. This is a point rightly emphasized by Moehler.

38. On this point, O. Cullmann is evidently right. Although New Testament scripture has fixed a central traditional nucleus in an expression of definitive value, the early Church, in canonizing the books of the New Testament, never deduced that the living tradition of what makes up its very content had ceased to have or would no longer have any importance. Cf. O. Cullmann, *La Tradition, problème exégétique, historique et théologique* (Neuchâtel–Paris, 1953), pp. 44ff., and Congar, op. cit., pp. 53ff.

39. See J. N. D. Kelly, *Early Christian Creeds* (London, 1950).

40. Cf. as early as Clement of Rome (Epistle to the Corinthians, 42:4 and 44:2).

41. See our study, *Eucharistie, théologie et spiritualité de la prière eucharistique* (2d ed.; Paris–Tournai, 1968), pp. 137ff.

42. Damien van den Eynde, *Les Normes de l'enseignement chrétien dans la littérature patristique des trois premiers siècles* (Paris: Gembloux, 1933).

43. Irenaeus, *Adversus Haereses,* 1,1, 20 and 1,4 *in toto.*

44. Above all, *Le Mystère du culte dans le Christianisme* (Fr. tr.; Paris, 1946, and 2d ed., greatly enlarged, Paris, 1964).

45. In this exact form, the formula is found in the Secret of the 9th Sunday after Pentecost in the missal of St. Pius V, but it comes directly from the *Sacr. Leon.*, no. 25.

46. Cf., for example, St. Augustine, *Tract. in Joannem,* tr. 80, 3; *Enarrationes in Psalmos,* in Ps 73:2.

47. See the book of Louis Villette, *Foi et Sacrement* (Paris, 1959).

48. The excellent study, mentioned in the foregoing note, is not entirely unscathed, perhaps, by this error.

49. Cf. Augustine, *Serm.* 272; P.L. 38, col. 1246.

50. Again, this is one of the points so excellently illustrated by Moehler in *L'Unité dans l'Église*; cf. the cited Fr. tr., pp. 128ff.

51. Socrates, *Hist. eccl.,* book 1, ch. 11; P.G. 67, col. 101ff.

52. Especially 3, 54ff.; *Sources chrétiennes,* no. 136, pp. 126ff.

53. Cf. note 41.

54. P.G. 26, especially col. 776AB. See our commentary in *L'Incarnation et l'Église-Corps du Christ dans la théologie de saint Athanase* (Paris, 1939), pp. 20ff.

55. Nothing is more characteristic in this regard than a reading of the account of the martyrdom of Daniel's companions, which was always done at the end of the baptismal vigil in the early Church.

56. See our *La Vie de saint Antoine* (Paris, 1950) and our *Spiritualié du Nouveau Testament et des Pères,* pp. 368ff.

57. This is very noticeable in the *Catecheses* of St. John Chrysostom, published by Fr. A. Wenger in *Sources chrétiennes,* no. 50.

58. See A. von Harnack, *Mission und Ausbreitung* (1st ed.; Berlin, 1902).

59. 1 Corinthians 3:22–23.

# Chapter 2
# The Transition from the Fathers to the Middle Ages

## I. A Church of Numbers or a Church of Believers?

From the age of persecution, the problem of the relationship of the Church to the world was to introduce the first problems into the notion that the Church had of herself. And the reversal of the situation that was to make the Church, which yesterday was an outlaw and persecuted, into a privileged body within the state would become (if that is possible) a still more difficult trial for ecclesiology, possibly because it was more insidious. Things may be summed up by saying that the Church had everything to gain from a situation in which the world pretended to ignore her, while allowing itself gradually to be won over by her. Beyond a certain hostility, the Church would cease to be able to react positively to it, while giving unmistakable signs of disintegration once she no longer had to collide with the world. It seems that we have here a particularly striking verification of the law Arnold Toynbee described as the evolution of societies and the civilizations that are bound up with them.[1]

The first great heresies the Church had to face, the so-called Gnostic heresies, not only did not disturb her functioning but it seems we may say they contributed toward her development and made people more clearly aware of what she is. Some historians may have tended to exaggerate this influence, as if the struggle with heretical Gnosticism caused the appearance of an episcopate (which has been rather incorrectly called "monarchical" and the appearance of a definite rule of faith (not to speak of the canon of the Scriptures).[2] In fact, all of this was present (at least germinally) before the paroxysm of the Gnostic crisis, but it can be acknowledged that the reaction it caused had the effect of accelerating the development of these various principles.

It was the setbacks of the especially violent persecutions in the middle of the third century that were to determine the appearance of the first heresies or schisms that were aimed directly at the very nature of the Church. More generally, they also gave rise to the controversies that related to the validity of sacraments given by heretics or schismatics.

Behind the schism of Hippolytus (the same was true later with Novatus, Novatian, and Donatism), we must acknowledge a hesitation between two possible attitudes, especially in regard to Christians who had fallen into a sin as grave as denial of faith. These attitudes call for two ecclesiologies, and this hesitation was to have repercussions on the validity of the orders received in schisms or heresies, which were themselves the consequences of the different attitudes adopted toward the problem of the *lapsi*. In the muddle caused by the urgency and delicate nature of the problems that had arisen, we can see curious inconsistencies, as when the laxist Novatus and the rigorist Novatian came together in common cause, or when bishops who favored an understanding policy toward the *lapsi* (this was the case of the African bishops who surrounded St. Cyprian) showed themselves more intractable than their more rigorous colleagues (such as the Romans) when the question was the validity of baptisms or ordinations performed outside the Church.[3]

However confused this problem may be, beneath it all is one of the problems that has most violently divided the Protestant churches of today. The problem is also behind the Jansenist controversy and behind two more and more clearly opposing parties, even in the Catholic Church today, on the question of the "discipline" of the sacraments. This problem may be formulated in a few words if we accept the terminology forged by nineteenth-century Protestantism: Must the Church, as willed by Christ, be a "multitudinist" Church or a Church of "professing" members?[4] In other words, should one admit as members of the Church only those who profess her faith formally and accept all practical consequences in their whole life, or should one retain within the Church all those who have at least belonged to her through baptism and do not formally reject her faith, even if they seem lukewarm in their practical conformity?

There is no doubt that the trend in the early centuries was much more toward a Church of the professing. But once there was a prolonged cessation of persecutions, the exigencies became less urgent. The result became visible in the alarming number of defections (even among the clergy) when persecution started again in a particularly severe form.

From the time of the Peace of Constantine, the trend from a professing to a multitudinist Church accelerated. As we have mentioned, monasticism appeared in many regards as a compensatory movement—not so much, as people have sometimes thought, that it created a kind of superchurch (with Christians who were more exacting than others toward themselves) within the Church. It was to have this understanding of itself only in the latter phases of its decadence, with the inevitable result of a dangerous acceleration of the masses to a multitudinist Church of the most lax type. But at its beginnings, since monasticism was a lay movement, not separated from the body of the laity, monasticism played a fermenting role that carried far beyond its original framework.[5]

Along with the more or less sectarian movements of the Middle Ages, many modern thinkers have tended to see in the practice of the baptism of infants (a general practice by the fifth century) a decisive factor in the wholesale transition from a Church of the professing to a multitudinist Church. Hence the reaction of the Baptists (i.e. the Anabaptists), who generally go hand in hand with modern efforts to reconstitute churches of the professing and are able to link up (by necessity) with them.[6]

In fact—without denying a certain general relationship between both—the data of history, whether ancient or modern, do not seem completely to justify such fixed theories. We have seen a number of communities that were fervent and exigent in their way of being Christian that retained these characteristics for generations, even though they practiced infant baptism. On the other hand, communities that accepted only adult baptism more than once reached a point of unexpected laxity in their discipline and the clarity of their faith.

Beyond the inevitable "risk" of infant baptism (no one can foresee what the further reactions will be—nor is the risk absent in adult baptism, at least when it is not postponed to the deathbed, as was at times the case in antiquity), infant baptism presuppose exigencies on the part of the child's family that are more difficult to impose and even less possible to assure than when they are directly involved in an adult candidate.

But the really decisive factor in the transition from a professing to a multitudinist Church seems to have happened right after the Peace of Constantine: the rapid and possibly ineluctable creation of a social compulsion in favor of Christianity, as opposed to the various risks its profession had previously exposed the baptized. This more general phenomenon of the attenuation (even the total extenuation) of freedom in adhering to the Church was to be decisive in bringing about this reversal.[7] And, we must emphasize, this could have gone hand in hand with the continuous practice of adult baptism. For example, when Charlemagne had all of Widikind's Saxons baptized *en masse,* the fact that they were adults did nothing toward putting things in order.

## II. *Ambiguities in Augustinian Ecclesiology*

Quite another problem, still unresolved and even less understood, was introduced into the honored equilibrium of early ecclesiology at the end of the patristic era. Like the preceding problem, it was to weigh heavily upon all the developments of the Middle Ages and their consequent backlash. Despite the fact that the foregoing problem was always present and aggravating, it seems no less evident that this second problem was ultimately to play the central role by provoking the slow cracking and ultimate disrepair of the ancient edifice.

This problem is a particular aspect of what has been called the "hellenization of Christianity." More precisely, it is the inevitable result of a massive inpouring of Platonism into Christian anthropology and therefore sociology. In the West, it is obviously St. Augustine who was primarily responsible for this, even though he was merely the particularly brilliant heir of a tendency that appeared long before him and that, at least in the East, would have many extensions, none of which would be beholden to him. Yet it is true that, with Augustine this tendency was to bring out certain of its ecclesiological consequences. And they were to reappear most forcefully even many years after him, always within the context of an Augustinianism *redivivus.*[8]

With Augustine, as with Plato, the soul is pure spirit, which of itself has no bond with the world of bodies. Its spiritual activity tends to be conceived as all the more pure and intense to the extent that it is freed and disengaged from the body. Yet we must not forget that Augustine fully admits God's creation of matter and the union of body and soul as resulting from the creative act and not from the fall of the soul. But it seems hard to contest that the practical consequences of this admission were quite restricted, in his spirituality at least, by half-conscious residues of his previous Manichaeanism. It is true even when he reacts (as in his *Retractationes*) against the primary tendency of his Platonism, which he had carried forward (e.g., in his *Soliloquies*) to a radical intellectualization of the spiritual life, practically identical to Platonic contemplation. The mystical moralism of his theology of charity was gradually to detach him from this, but traces remained.

The repercussion on ecclesiology of this anthropological orientation is especially felt in the developments, however admirable, of the view of Christianity that runs through his *Enarrationes in psalmos*.[9] His whole interpretation of the psalms is dominated by the twofold Pauline analogy between the union of Christ and the Church and the Bridegroom and the Bride—the head with the body. But the ecclesiology that devolves from it is quite different from that of St. Paul by its ultraspiritualism. However Christological this ecclesiology is in seeing the total Christ in the Church (*Unus Christus amans seipsum*), it is certainly not bereft of all realism, but its realism is purely the realism of charity. It is in the moral consequences that the mystical identification of Christ with our brothers and his family must be seen in each of us. He almost completely ignores the realization of this identification in the concrete Church.

Surely the sacraments, and especially the Eucharist, are occasionally brought up, with excellent formulas, and Augustine, like Origen, unquestionably takes them in a very realistic sense. Just as baptism unites us with the dead and risen Christ, the Eucharist nourishes us with his presence. But, even more than with Origen, what occupies Augustine's attention here is above all the symbolism, and in the specific case of the Eucharist the symbolism of the union of all, expressed by the fact that the grains of wheat make one loaf of bread. More than any other father, he represents in this line of thought the tendency that achieves full flower in Hugh of St. Victor, who, for example, under the same word, *sacramentum,* confuses all Christian symbolisms, whether or not they are sacramental in the strict sense. From him the Middle Ages borrowed the definition of a sacrament as "a visible sign of an invisible grace," which abstracts completely from the sacrament as an existential event in which this grace is not merely described or recalled but actually communicated.

Finally, the only aspect of the Church as Bride and Body of Christ (so frequently mentioned in the *Enarrationes*) is that of a communion or fellowship in grace which is identified with the pure dissemination of charity in souls. Only this aspect is retained. The Bride becomes as heavenly as her Bridegroom, which is a rather dangerous idealization, while the "body" is so spiritualized that what is corporal about it can no longer be seen.

However unconsciously, this inevitable impression, which is found in the *Enarrationes* and also in the *Tractatus in Johannem* and the commentaries on the great Pauline texts, must have reacted on the reading of the *City of God* throughout the Middle Ages. Its reading tended to produce an interpretation that was more "Augustinian" than the meaning Augustine wanted to give it.

What is this "city of God" to which the book owes its title? In Augustine's thought it is no longer the Church as such—any more than the state as such is the "city of the devil." As defined by the book, both cities are basically eschatological, though they are continually built, throughout the course of history, in an incessant tangle, amid unceasing conflicts, until the final separation. One is founded upon the love of God, pushed to self-contempt; the other on the love of self, pushed to contempt of God. Hence, through an inevitable reversal, an ultraspiritualization of the Church, passing into the ranks of a pure object of faith—but, by the same token, becoming lost in the invisible. The expression and the idea of an "invisible Church" would certainly have been rejected by Augustine as absurd. But it is possible to think they may have been the practically ineluctable products of some of the most authentic elements of the original Augustinianism.

Although this is a questionable compensation, it is true that Augustine supplied a massive counterweight to this frantic spiritualization of the Church, identified with the sole communion of grace in charity. This counterweight might be called his ecclesiastical polity, as it was developed particularly (if regretfully) in his conflict with Donatism.[10] The stress on the aspect of authority, an authority that imposes itself morally from a numerically defined unanimity, is the first element that strikes us in Augustine's practical ecclesiology. It resulted in the celebrated phrase *"Securus judicat orbis terrarum."*[11] One can escape the problem by saying that the unanimity that judges here is unanimity in love; however, it is defined explicitly only as being a mass. And the ambiguity reaches its fullness only when Augustine breaks with his scruples and prior reticence and accepts, and then defends, the intervention, *manu militari,* of the public authority to impose the decisions of the ecclesiastical authority.[12]

Although we have merely sketched the theory, we have reached a practical notion of the Church as not only an authoritarian power, but possessing an authority that is defined in terms of material extension and, without hesitation, relying on the sword. Here, then, we see the Church bursting into two Churches, as it were: one is quite spiritual and interior, stressing only the communion of grace in charity and escaping into the invisible, on the glorious pretext of being a pure object of faith; the other, firmly constructed, is aware of her authority and the strength that this authority represents through her spread throughout the world, but also dangerously tractable to the use of this world's arms in order to assert herself.

These elements of Augustinianism and the developments to which they gave rise lead us straight into the Middle Ages.

## Notes

1. A. Toynbee, *L'Histoire, un essai d' interprétation* (Fr. tr.; Paris, 1951), pp. 74ff.

2. This is the case particularly with Harnack, especially in the work mentioned above (ch. 1, n. 58).

3. On all this, see A. Fliche and V. Martin, *Histoire de l'Église* (Paris, 1935), 2:189ff. (by J. Lebreton).

4. We are thinking here particularly of the studies of G. Frommel and H. Bois (especially Bois' book *Le Réveil du Pays de Galles*), which owe a great deal to the distinction made by Troeltsch between what he calls "the Churches" and "the sects."

5. See our *Spiritualité du Nouveau Testament et des Pères,* pp. 385 and 395.

6. See Troeltsch, op. cit., section 4 of ch. 3, devoted to the Baptist movement in early Protestantism.

7. See T. M. Parker, *Christianity and the State in the Light of History* (London, 1955).

8. On this point, see especially the volume devoted by Troeltsch to the ecclesiology of St. Augustine: *Augustinus, die christliche Antike und das Mittelalter* (Munich, 1915).

9. The principal ecclesiological texts of the *Enarrationes* will be found in E. Mersch, *Le Corps mystique du Christ* (Louvain, 1933), 2:94ff. Also *Le Visage de l'Église* (choice of texts) by H. Urs von Balthasar, in the Camelot and Grumel translation (Paris, 1958).

10. Cf. the texts mentioned by Congar, *L'Ecclésiologie du haut Moyen Age* (Paris, 1968), pp. 104ff.

11. *Contra epist. Parm.,* 3,4; P. L. 43, col. 101.

12. On all this, see Batiffol in *Le Catholicisme de saint Augustin* (Paris, 1920), vol. 1.

# Chapter 3
# The Medieval Church in Byzantium and in the West

It would be erroneous to believe that in this or any other area the Middle Ages represented a deliberate departure from the position of the Church of the Fathers. In the East, especially, it lived on in a conviction that it was merely an extension of it.[1] And even in the West, where a break from this tradition is possibly more visibly marked, we can find, to the end of the Middle Ages, apparently unchanged survivals of the patristic Church.[2]

To be precise, we might say that the Church of the Fathers lived on in the Middle Ages, and the living *awareness* of what the Church is and signifies continued to wilt, while the fissures that became visible at the end of the patristic age were becoming the first breaks with that tradition and the preparation for those that were to come afterward.

## I. Caesaro-Papism and Papo-Caesarism

It is typical that the first great ecclesiological rupture which was to separate East and West, then progressively alienate them from one another, was in the context of this contact between the Church and the world in which the first hesitations and incertitudes had been sketched. Nothing gives greater evidence of this than the major reproaches exchanged by the Christians of East and West even today on the level of ecclesiology. According to the polemic of Catholics of the West, the weakness that separated the Orthodox of the East from them has been called "caesaro-papism."[3] On the other hand, the Eastern Orthodox turn the accusation against Catholics of the West and reproach them, symmetrically, for having succumbed to "papo-caesarism."

However, it might be worthwhile to point out that these two formulas, which were a subject of dispute between Catholics and Orthodox, are the discovery of Protestant authors. It seems that the term "caesaro-papism" was coined by Mommsen,[4] and that Hobbes gave the celebrated description of the papacy as "the ghost of the Roman Empire, seated upon its tomb."[5] We must immediately add that impartial history refuses to give literal endorsement to either judgment.

An idea that is still too facilely admitted by Western historians (and not only Catholics) says that the emperors of Byzantium came to arrogate to themselves or to exercise in fact a quasi-papal authority over the Eastern Church. This is an obvious exaggeration. On the contrary, one reading of the *Epanagoge* is enough to convince one that the Byzantine East devised a very precise systematization of coordination between the power of the emperor and the hierarchy (essentially that of the "ecumenical" patriarch). Actually, the imperial authority was formally excluded from involving itself in any properly ecclesiastical domain, and especially in the definition of dogma.[6] Allowing the possibility of nomocanonical legislation by the emperor is not in any way a contradiction of this principle; it is understood that the emperor alone, with this expedient in mind, could assure the practical application of these canonical principles, defined solely by the authority of the bishops and the councils. Whatever interferences to which this cooperation could have given rise, caesaro-papism, even reduced to discipline and not doctrine, expresses something that has no exact correspondence with reality.

The same must be said about the converse accusation, brought against the West, of papo-caesarism. Even those popes who in the second half of the Middle Ages claimed possession of "two swords" (i.e. spiritual and temporal authority) never tended in principle to confuse the two authorities (the simple distinction between the two swords precludes the supposition). They did not claim to wield the temporal or the spiritual sword but only to direct their use—to the point of reserving to themselves the granting of the benefice to the lawful receiver.[7]

However much these expressions may seem like caricatures, it is impossible to deny that they represent, if not a tendency, what might at least be called a revealing temptation of either the West or the East. It is certain that the Byzantine East became progressively accustomed to allowing the imperial power (which in principle had become Christian) to exert influence on governing the Church, which, as we shall see from the controversies of monotheism and iconoclasm, carried heavy weight in the solution of even purely dogmatic questions.[8]

Two factors seem to have played at least a "casting role" in this regard. The first was the customary presence in the East (in Byzantium, as the New Rome) of the Christian emperor. From the Age of Constantine, a text like Eusebius of Caesarea's *De laudibus Constantini* is quite revealing.[9] Even before the facts corresponded or were able to correspond to the theory, the official conversion of the Roman Empire soon created the idea that the body of the Church and the body of the empire were identical, since the whole empire in principle had come to the faith through the conversion of its head.[10] From this idea stemmed the term *isapostolos* (equal to "the apostles"), given to Constantine, as well as the title *hiereus* of his successors.[11] Hence the restoration, or transposition, of the old religious value to the imperial dignity. Caesar was no longer divinized but was acknowledged (in exchange) as the preeminent manifestation of Christ in this world, insofar as Christ is the Logos through whom and in whom creation subsists. Eusebius said the imperial authority was an epiphany of this cosmic role of the Logos, which goes hand in hand with a transfer to the Roman Empire, as the universal empire, of the Old Testament theology of the People of God, with the emperor becoming a superior equivalent of the king of Israel, as the "anointed one" of the Lord and therefore the truly "messianic" icon of Christ himself.[12]

It might be said that this is an encounter between a realized eschatology, tending to confuse the Christian empire with the Kingdom of God, and a consecutive regression of the New Testament vision of the People of God that tends to confuse this idea with the vision of it in the Old Testament. Yet this regression is not complete inasmuch as a vivid awareness was preserved of the transition from a particular people to a universal principle, even though some maintained that the law of which the monarch was both the expression and the guardian was no longer the law of Moses but the law of the Gospels. However, there is no doubt that the codes of Theodosius and Justinian, even in the way they attempted to translate the Gospel injunctions into law, involve a regressive confusion of the two covenants.

If we want a revealing test of this intertwining of realized eschatology and a return to the literalism of the Old Testament, it would suffice to look at another book that is only somewhat later than that of Eusebius: Cyril of Alexandria's commentary on Isaiah. For Cyril, the messianic prophecies seem to find their fulfillment in the Christian empire, even though this empire seemed to him to be a new Israel distinguishable from the old only by its universalization, which went hand in hand with acknowledgment of the King-Messiah who now appeared on earth, whose vice-regent was now the emperor.[13]

The second factor, which permits this ideology to be expressed in the facts without eliciting much resistance, is the very thing which might have seemed to have preserved the Church from the fatal danger of equally fallacious identifications, and this is the customary recruiting, from very early times, of the bishops of the East from the ranks of the monks. In principle, this assured the "spiritual" character of authority in the Church, but it soon resulted in an implicit resignation of ecclesiastical authority as authority. The monk-bishop was to become typical in the Eastern Church, and even in times of decadence he had the advantage over his Western colleagues of remaining a hierarch, a doctor of the faith, and especially a priest. This, certainly, was worth more than the portion of the "lords," who in theory (but rarely in reality) were "spiritual," which so many bishops of the West had become. But with a kind of monastic passivity, the monk-bishop resigned himself to surrendering almost the total jurisdictional aspect of his pastoral responsibility into the hands of the emperor.[14]

In the West, evolution took the opposite direction. There again, two major factors appear. The first was the absence of imperial authority and the second was the presence of the Roman See.

Yet to maintain, as people have that the popes' sense of universal responsibility was merely a doctrinal result of the fact that they came to play the role in the West of the absent emperor (as his replacement) is a historical misconception. During the time the imperial authority (though far away) was recognized, if not always as very effective, in the West, and by a pope who saw himself as the emperor's subject, who held views about him and the empire that were practically indistinguishable from those of his Eastern colleagues, the doctrinal claim of the preeminence of the Holy See was expressed with a precision that has never been surpassed. Interestingly enough, the later definitions, including those of the First Vatican Council, have never recaptured this concept in its entirety. And such assertions, even if they never found a precise echo in the East at that time, never seem to have given rise to unrest or disquiet. It goes without saying that we want to speak here of Pope St. Leo and his teaching on the role of the Bishop of Rome.[15]

Even if he does not provide all of its later terminology, there is no doubt that the entire teaching of the First Vatican Council was already substantially there, particularly since Leo refers to the universal and sovereign authority of the Bishop of Rome over the Church, and over the other bishops, with all its consequences for the power of determining orthodox doctrine without the possibility of appeal to any other authority on earth. And, we must add, Leo went even further than the definitions of the First Vatican Council when he said that the authority of bishops is entirely in the authority given to Peter by Christ (which was the common feeling of the fathers, as illustrated even by one whom some see as the theoretician of an antipapal "episcopalism," St. Cyprian[16] *and* to the successors of Peter in the Roman See.[17]

Yet, for St. Leo, this assertion did not seem to imply any queasiness about the direction of the affairs of the universal Church by a general council, such as that of Chalcedon. On the contrary, he was in favor of this, and it is not apparent that the Eastern bishops of the time saw any threat in his teaching to their authority, exercised individually or at the council. They must have been no less unaware of what have been called the "Roman claims" of Leo, since the claims appear in the *Tome* to the Antiochians which the bishops themselves enthusiastically canonized. The explicit sense of their acclamation, "Peter has spoken!" (after they read the *Tome*), must not be pressed too far, but the least that can be said is they had neither scruple nor hesitation in using such an expression in response to a pontiff who so clearly asserted himself as the successor of Peter, as the head of the church of Rome, but—first of all—as the head of the whole Church.[18]

In fact, more than a century later the repetition of analogous assertions (though less keen in their form) by Pope Gregory the Great was expressly understood to uphold, and not in any way constrain or restrain, the power of bishops in general. And here, on the pope's part, we do not have merely a rhetorical affirmation. It is the expression of a total policy in which Gregory (probably the first in the West) was to enter the conflict with the general tendency of the civil authorities to reduce the bishops' role to the simple function of officers of the royal power, entirely dependent upon it.[19]

We must also be aware that we are now at the first decisive turning point in the history of Western ecclesiology. Not only was Gregory not tempted to attribute to himself a quasi-imperial authority, it is certain that he always considered himself to be, like Leo, a citizen of the Roman Empire, which was considered to be unchanged under the authority of the monarch of Byzantium. No more than he, we cannot refuse to look at the facts that he knew only too well. By this time in the West, when the various local authorities of "barbarian" origin persisted in considering themselves (or rather claiming to be) simple legates of the imperial authority, this claim was a fiction. On the other hand, intervention by these authorities in ecclesiastical affairs paid no mind to the nuances which were always respected, at least formally, by the Byzantine Empire. Not content with choosing the bishops, the Eastern princes gave this dignity to certain officials of their retinue who had little of the ecclesiastical about them, intending to use them as simple subordinates.[20]

It was precisely to fight this confusion and to uphold, or rather reestablish, an episcopate that was a true arm of the Church that Gregory claimed independence from the state, along with supremacy in the Church for the authority of the Roman Pontiff. Nothing clarifies this point more than his conflict with the patriarch of Constantinople, when the latter began to claim the title "ecumenical patriarch." Gregory in no way reproached him for attributing to himself a role which belonged only to the Bishop of Rome; on the contrary, he reproached him for arrogating to himself an authority which the pope refused to claim for *him*self. Although nothing was said expressly (doubtless because Gregory did not wish directly to challenge the interference of the imperial authority), it is clear that Gregory could not admit any sort of primacy to any bishop, whether of Old Rome or New Rome, because his see corresponded geographically with the seat of the empire.[21]

The reason for this was that intrusion in the Church of an authority that was shaped upon secular authority (and all the more strongly if it flowed from this) reduced and distorted episcopal authority. The authority that Gregory wanted to exercise was not of this kind; like every form of episcopal authority, it was authority of a ministerial order. In addition, the only one who can claim authority over the bishops is one who can understand this authority solely as that of a *servus servorum Dei*—in other words, an authority, as Gregory said explicitly, whose nature does not curb the authority of the other bishops but rather upholds it.[22]

Yet between the time of Leo and Gregory we have two texts—one Western, one Eastern—which demonstrate that even when there was affirmation on both sides of the distinction between the two functions or powers, the spiritual and the temporal, the West tended to subordinate the second to the first while, in the East, the second tended to monopolize the reality of the first.

In his letter to Emperor Anastasius in 494, Pope Gelasius I asserted: "*Duo quippe sunt quibus principaliter mundus hic regitur: auctoritas sacra pontificum et regalis potestas.*"[23] But he added that the princes were no less dependent on the pontiffs for all that referred to salvation, and it is clear that this included the way in which they performed their functions.[24]

The *Novella VI* of Justinian, of March 6, 535, declares: "*Maxima quidem in hominibus sunt dona Dei a superna collata clementia sacerdotium et imperium, illud quidem divinis ministrans, hoc autem humanis praesidens ac diligentiam exhibens.*"[25] But from this is immediately drawn the supposed duty of the prince to intervene to have the *vera Dei dogmata* and the *sacerdotum honestatem* respected.[26]

With Leo III and the imperial coronation he granted Charlemagne on December 25, 800, a second turning point was reached. However, it is uncertain whether Leo had a clear idea of the consequences of his intervention, or—even more—of the later interpretations that might be given them. After a period of complete anarchy in the West in both Church and state, when the papacy had been degraded by and become the plaything of the factions, and by the unworthy occupants these factions brought to the See of Peter, Charlemagne's intervention was decisive in helping the papacy reestablish itself. The pope probably had nothing else in view in placing the crown on Charles' head than to give him the recognition of the Church and to acknowledge the support Charles promised him in return. But perhaps he assured himself in advance against any attempt by Charlemagne or his successors to transform this chance support into a kind of permanent protection. On the other hand, Charles' repugnance in accepting the empire through this expedient must be explained by fear of the implications the Church could derive from this coronation and, through it, the difficulties with Constantinople which would be its immediate consequence.[27]

However we may wish to understand Leo III's action, it constitutes a precedent that would encourage succeeding pontiffs to formulate new claims over the centuries.

Gregory VII's reform appeared as a return to the ecclesiastical policy of Gregory I in circumstances that were analogous but possibly even more grave. This time the pope opposed an explicit claim by the princes to give investiture to the prelates within a context which seemed, in effect, to signify complete assimilation, not only of jurisdiction but of every episcopal function, to civil control. But the limits to which his struggle with Henri IV was to bring him produced a new fact that had far greater import than anything done by the other Gregory. And undoubtedly involuntarily, it transformed the whole sense.

The pope's deposing of the emperor at this stage did not imply a direct assertion of a quasi-imperial power by the pope. It appeared only as an exceptional measure, justified by reasons that were quite Augustinian. It was only *ratione peccati* that the pope intervened to remove the crown from a person who had made himself unworthy of it by his abuse of power and especially by his encroachment upon the jurisdiction of the Church.[28]

Yet the intense political activity that Gregory VII deployed to have Christendom ratify his action prepared the way, despite his intentions, for the last and most serious turning point. By an effort which was aimed only at keeping ecclesiastical authority free of the meddling of the secular authority—and without knowing or wanting it—he laid the groundwork for assimilation of the ecclesiastical authority to a higher-order secular authority.[29] This became an accomplished fact when Innocent III claimed possession of the two swords for pontifical authority (at least in principle): possession of secular authority in addition to the supreme ecclesiastical authority.

Thus this theory of a necessary union of the two authorities approximates what was characterized by the Byzantine *Epanagoge*. However, from this union is now deduced not only the dependence of the secular authority but identification of the source of secular authority with the supreme ecclesiastical authority.[30]

On first sight, this was an absolute victory of the spiritual authority over the temporal; but like so many "absolute" victories it was to be a Pyrrhic victory. This is true not only or especially because of the easily foreseeable reactions that such a doctrine would produce; it is more profoundly true because of the deep alteration that would almost immediately result for the spiritual authority. With the papacy claiming to act directly on the temporal sphere, and in a position—if not directly to control it—at least to impose its own direction on it through the choice and behavior of docile princes, the papacy was inevitably led to enter that sphere and, sooner or later, be absorbed by it. The theoretical supremacy of spiritual authority that Innocent III asserted was to have an unexpected but probably unavoidable consequence in its *de facto* secularization. This was to be the case with such pontiffs as Alexander VI and (perhaps even more) Julius II.[31]

These developments in the West involved the papacy in a complex concept of spiritual authority vis-à-vis its relationship with the temporal authority; and even before the issue came to term, a major event revealed the breach that had been formed by the ecclesiastical mentalities of the East and the West. We mean what happened in 1054—an event that Western historians came to call the "Greek Schism" and Easterners the "Latin Schism." According to most historians, it is clear that this breach was far less important as a departure point for what happened later than as a revelation of a misunderstanding that already obtained between the two halves of the Church, in which there was no inkling of opposition between "Catholicism" and "Orthodoxy."[32] The unilateral development of principles between such role-conscious popes of antiquity as Leo and Gregory I and so intelligent and informed an Easterner as Photius posed no necessary antinomy;[33] nevertheless, both sides reached a point at which mutual misunderstanding became a kind of inevitable fatality. What is most striking in the conflict between Cardinal Humbert, the papal legate from Moyen-Moutiers, and the patriarch Michael Caerularius is that both wanted practically the same thing and were seeking to bring it about, along lines that would have seemed to Theodosius the Studite normally convergent but, to them, seemed mutually exclusive.[34]

Like Michael, Humbert was desirous of promoting a reform of the Church, and especially a reform of the episcopal function which would restore its full spiritual authenticity. But Humbert was incapable of seeing it in terms other than those laid down by the reform of Gregory VII, whereas Michael followed another line of thought, the *Epanagoge,* interpreted in a Byzantine framework that had become limited and narrow. It might be said that both men had become prisoners of what modern Orthodox call *phyletism*—i.e, confusion of ecclesiastical institutions with a particular cultural totality that has developed to the point of appearing to have become one with it. Michael Caerularius was undoubtedly persuaded to preserve the tradition of the old imperial, ecumenical Church, but he was unable to distinguish it (as Photius did, without difficulty) from a Byzantine Church that had become provincial. For his part, Humbert may have confounded fidelity to the ecclesiastical ideal, inherited from Gregory I, with the typically Latin and medieval forms, based on the developments of Gregory VII's reform.

Hence the extravagant "catalogues of errors" they sent to one another and their mutual thundered excommunications. However wounded was his pride (more ethnic than personal) and whatever the general misunderstanding manifested by Michael Caerularius, we must admit that the fool's crown goes to his antagonist. Not only did this bizarre Roman legate misinterpret and exceed his powers by proclaiming an excommunication, he acted in the most contradictory fashion by claiming to issue a papal judgment in the name of a pope who was already dead—in conditions in which, even from his own point of view, he no longer had competence or power.

This quarrel between two equally irascible and excessive prelates would have had but little consequence if it were not evidence of a mutual lack of understanding that analogous events would contribute to making less and less remediable.

## II. Secularization of Ecclesiastical Authority in the West

But we must return to what we have emphasized: the evolution of the West was not simply the evolution of the papacy, it was even more, an evolution of the concept and reality of spiritual authority in general, above all in its relationship with the temporal authority.

We have seen how, in the Latin Middle Ages, the evolution of the papacy, intended to thwart a general evolution of the episcopate, was absorbed by and within the temporal power, and (contrary to its intentions) allowed itself to become involved in this process. Now we must take a closer look at this evolution in the totality of the episcopacy of the West.

Throughout the whole of the Latin Middle Ages the episcopacy was the object of more or less constant pressure from the temporal authority, which tended to absorb and assimilate it. The best-intentioned bishops, such as the popes, sought to safeguard their independence by equiping themselves with temporal authority, but they too were brought to an equally disastrous result. After all is said and done, they achieved the very result they tried to avoid: secularization of their authority.[35] The bishops, like the papacy, were not primarily intent upon freeing themselves on the political level from the secular authority by asserting their possession of a higher, spiritual authority; even more, they sought to endow themselves with an economic basis for independence by accruing the possessions of the Church.[36] Both motives or inserts are inextricably bound together, but the economic effort became more and more imperative—to the same extent that the nobility during the decline of the Middle Ages saw itself threatened by the rise of the wealthy merchant class. In the sixteenth century, bishops and popes became important organizers and beneficiaries of a fiscal system that had become more and more outrageous—much more than "lords," whose titles were their only claim to spirituality.

The same thing happened with the great Orders, and first with the monastic orders that (strange to say) had benefit of the Gregorian Reform and its successive revivals. From the beginning of the twelfth century, the riches of Cluny gave rise to the reaction of Cîteaux, but it did not take even a century before Cîteaux became worse than Cluny had ever been. The thirteenth-century Religious (the mendicants) in turn were victims of the process. To maintain their independence from temporal power and riches, they too turned to power and riches, and did not take long in succumbing.[37] Cathedral or monastic churches, provided with endowments and exemptions to escape dependence on the laity, were soon coveted by secular people, who accepted or sought ecclesiastical functions only to accede to the worldly benefits associated with them.

Hence an episcopate or the most prominent sees, such as the papacy itself, were practically in the hands of the great noble families or the wealthy middle class, who had little interest beyond the concomitant political power and benefices. A typical consequence of this state of affairs was that some episcopal sees, such as Strasbourg during the whole of the fifteenth century, never had an incumbent who took the trouble to be consecrated (only one, throughout this period, went so far as to be ordained a priest). In these circumstances, the episcopal functions of ordination and (much less regularly) confirmation were still exercised but by auxiliaries who were deprived of any jurisdictional or pastoral function. Monks, who were consecrated titular bishops, generally left their monastery only once or twice a year for those liturgical functions that could not be avoided. At the end of the Middle Ages there were many areas where the episcopacy appeared only as a survival, shared between a bishop-with-title, who was nothing more than a nobleman in spirit, with very secular concerns, and a titular bishop, who was was merely an episcopal workman, recalled from retirement just long enough to administer a sacrament.[38]

To understand the ease with which the Protestant churches were able to forgo the very idea of bishops, we must be aware of this situation. And to understand the conciliary crisis at the end of the Middle Ages, we must see it against this background. But we must also add the correlative evolution, even when antagonistic, of civil and ecclesiastical law.

Over the course of the thirteenth century in the West, with Raymond of Peñafort and Gregory IX, canon law attained, if not codification (which came only in the twentieth century for tbe Latin Church), at least a systematization.[39] On first sight, this "autonomous" canon law seems radically opposed to the confusions of the nonocanonical legislation of the East. In the West, in the sphere of the law, was to come the analogue of what we have already observed on the factual level. The attempt of the ecclesiastical authority to free itself from the secular was to make it once again and unconsciously, model itself after the latter.

This century's great monarchs of the West, such as Philip the Fair, and its lawmakers saw a rediscovery of the Roman law of the empire, and an attempt was made to transpose and apply it in favor of royal authority.[40] It was in opposition to (and therefore in relation to) the newly conceived notion of royal authority that the canonists, more and more, developed their notion of spiritual authority. Hence a peculiar crossfire resulted. St. Thomas, in his *De Regimine principum,* not only looked upon the spiritual authority as a *ministerium* but tried to apply this notion to thc authoiity of the Christian prince.[41] On the other hand, the royal lawmakers soon defined the authority of the king as a *dominium,* i.e., a real ownership over goods and the lives of his subjects. For their part, the canonists tended more and more to define spiritual authority (revindicating its increasingly threatened independence) as a pure *potestas* which slipped ever so gradually into a *dominium.*[42] The moralists persisted in teaching that popes and bishops should comport themselves as "servants" of all, but they themselves came imperceptibly to define by this term simply the virtuous way in which they exercised their authority, without concern about that authority itself.[43]

The first sign of this deterioration became evident in the conflict between popes and councils, and the election of rival pontiffs merely furnished an occasion for it to explode at the time of the Great Western Schism. Harmony between a collegial authority of the whole episcopate and the central authority of the Roman Pontiff was no longer conceivable once all authority was interpreted as *dominium* and no longer as *ministerium*. On one hand, the pope could be looked upon as above and beyond the body of bishops, who held merely a derived (i.e. delegated) authority of his own, or, on the other hand, he could see himself reduced to merely a proxy of the power of the council. As long as people remained within the confines in which authority was understood at this time, there was no logical possibility other than this mutually exclusive conciliarism or papalism.[44]

We see this more or less primitively expressed in the many tracts (on both sides) to which the controversy gave rise and multiplied in the fourteenth, fifteenth, and even sixteenth centuries. These were the first tracts *De Ecclesia,* but they dealt only with the hierarchy, which was looked upon primarily as a *potestas*.[45]

It must be pointed out that it was at this time that the word "hierarchy," introduced in the fifth and sixth century by the Pseudo-Dionysius, first took on the meaning that we are accustomed to give it today. This meaning has become so natural and obvious to us that we regularly project it into their reading of the writings of the Pseudo-Dionysius, without suspecting their total misconception of its true sense. For him, "hierarchy" had an essentially dynamic meaning, extending on the level of creation the "thearchy" of the Divine Persons. This had nothing to do with a division of the Church (or the universe, in the case of the "heavenly hierarchy") between masters and subjects, in which the former were the only ones who were active and the latter were purely passive and dependent. Quite the contrary. As Dionysius understood the hierarchical principle, it meant that the most exalted beings in nature and grace could possess what they received (the divine *agape*) only by communicating it. And Dionysius specified that this communication's agent, whoever he might be, far from being removed from his most lowly participants, as a screen between them and the divine source, produced immediate contact between each person and the divine gift. Consequently, in accordance with their individual response to the gift received, the least in the hierarchy could be raised as high as the most exalted, and even higher.[46]

But from this time on, when the word "Church" was mentioned people basically understood the clergy and especially the bishops. The subalternate grades were no longer looked upon except as depending totally upon the higher grade. They shared in the gifts of that grade only by belonging to and depending upon it in the strictest sense, and by being passive in their relationship to it. The result was a distinction like that between the "teaching Church" (the bishops and, ultimately, the Sovereign Pontiff) and the "taught

Church," or, correlatively, "active infallibility," reserved to the first category in its isolated state, and "passive infallibility," possessed by the second category, as the term indicates, only to the extent of its subjection to authority.

Only one work of the fifteenth century escapes these schemas: the *De Concordantia catholica* of Cardinal Nicholas of Cusa. Having made the transition from conciliarism, whose harmfulness he strongly felt, to a much deeper and nuanced papalism than that of the curialist theologians and canonists, he attempted to reconcile the two antagonistic theses in a superior synthesis. Undoubtedly for him, the whole Church is "implicated" in the pope, but the pope remains inconceivable outside the whole body of bishops of the Church, that is, as the *explicatio* of the divine plan.[47]

Unfortunately, although Nicholas of Cusa's treatise was bound up with an ingenious philosophy, it was too personal and esoteric, and had little influence. Canonists and theologians on both sides generally used it in opposing one another.

## III. *The Origin of Anticlericalism and Religious Individualism*

A reaction, or rather series of reactions, began to be manifested at this time against views of the Church that reduced her either to a dictatorial monarchy or an aristocratic oligarchy. We can see the trend with Occam,[48] Wyclif,[49] Jerome of Prague,[50] and Jan Hus.[51] These reactions varied between a more or less anarchical democracy (which was to result in the birth of a number of sects, such as the Moravian Brethren, the Waldensians, and the Brethren of the Free Spirit) and an evangelism which, with ecclesiastical properties, gave authority over the People of God to the princes.[52] There is no need to underline the fact that these reactions prefigured the different "churches" of the Protestant Reformation in the following centuries.

More generally, the beginning of the thirteenth century (if not the end of the twelfth) saw the rise of the bourgeoisie, the wealthy middle class, which supported the emancipation and consolidation of royal power. This gave the secular segment of Western Christendom a consistency and self-awareness that was quite new. And it coincided with a period in which the laity, in accordance with the system of contemporary clergy, for all practical purposes ceased to be considered an integral part of the Church.

Hence the beginning of a spontaneous liaison between the self-assertion of the laity and a more or less latent anticlericalism and, on a deeper level, a feeling of frustration or, worse, hostile indifference on the part of the laity, even (and especially) when people were most religious, to the Church, which they identified with the clergy, and more particularly with an overbearing hierarchy.[53]

Even if these conditions did not create it, a spirit of subjectivist individualism in every area, especially in religion, became more and more noticeable. We could be tempted to explain this individualism by the alteration in the idea of the Church which we have just described and the feeling of alienation from it that gradually took hold of the laity as a consequence. The layman no longer felt at home in a Church that was integrally clericalized, and he became less and less able to draw support for his piety from a kind of worship whose forms and language (by this time Latin had ceased to be commonly used) were those of an exclusively clerical culture. Of necessity, even when he did not feel the need to leave the Church, he turned in upon himself to obtain the spiritual nourishment the Church denied him. Hence this subjectivist individualism.

Such an explanation would be simplistic, if only because the clergy themselves seemed as affected as the laity by this new spirit, to the point that one could easily turn the explanation around and see in medieval individualism a tendency that began with the clergy. There was neo-Aristotelianism, inherited from the Arabs; the revival of abstract mysticism with the Rhenish thinkers; and even before these developments the sentimental devotion of St. Bernard to Christ's humanity, as well as that of those who followed him, including the author of *The Imitation* (not to mention the Franciscans).

If these developmental factors were not the only causes of this individualism, they were, in the domain of religion, the most important ones, and it is undeniable that the clerical milieu was the major contributor to their development. Speaking more broadly, we may say that the "secular" universities (which, of course, were no less clerical at the time), which arose around the cathedral churches, along with those orders which were the first to make their presence felt in them; Canons Regular, Dominicans, Franciscans, Carmelites, and later the Brethren of the Common Life (in opposition to the monasteries and their schools, where patristic Christianity and its Christian culture survived) were the chief centers of this new religious culture.[54] Again, we must put into proper perspective, behind these city schools (with their fresh spirit), the great phenomenon (typically urban as well) that was to play such a major role in the revolutions of the sixteenth and even the eighteenth centuries: the rise of a new class that was equally alien to the peasantry and the old nobility, i.e., the city bourgeoisie, which had made the rapid transition from manual trade to big business.[55] Possibly this factor is the most important, since it represents the emergence of a class without a given structure, from the viewpoint of medieval society, and owes everything to its individual qualities of enterprise and tenacity. The growing place it occupied among the clergy, long before it was admitted through another shift to a possible equality with the lords (who began to decline as the bourgeois class rose), might even explain, to a large extent the facile victory of this individualism in the clerical mentality.

Beyond this, we must not forget the pressure from still existent elements of the old Celtic cultures (and to a certain extent those of the Germans as well) for which the Christianized Graeco-Latin humanism of the Church fathers substituted itself, even though it was never able to stifle it completely.

All these factors (and undoubtedly others that are less easy to discern) fed this individualism and subjectivism which began to appear at the turn of the first millennium in the West and which, in the sixteenth century, seemed to break down all barriers. But it is only too certain that the weakening and internal withering of the old consciousness of the Church gave them practically free rein.

Yet we must not reach too hasty a conclusion: that, with free examination and research into unprecedented religious experiences, the sixteenth-century Church was ready to topple into the Protestant Reformation. Were we to think so, we would be yielding to a twofold simplification of the reality. We would misunderstand everything about the ancient Church that survived in the sixteenth century (and would continue to survive much later) and everything that Luther retained of it and even rediscovered.[56]

## Notes

1. See our *La Spiritualité orthodoxe et la spiritualité protestante et anglicane* (Paris, 1965).

2. Dom Jean Leclercq has demonstrated the survival of the patristic mentality in what he called ''monastic theology,'' in contradistinction to medieval Scholasticism. Cf. *L'Amour des lettres et le désir de Dieu* (Paris, 1957), pp. 179ff.

3. For the present state of discussions on this point see Congar, op. cit.

4. No one seems to have paid much attention to the history of this term, which is absent from even the principal theological dictionaries.

5. Hobbes, *Leviathan,* part 4, ch. 47.

6. Louis Bréhier, *Le Monde byzantin,* vol. 2: *Les institutions de l'empire byzantin* (Paris, 1949), pp. 444ff. The text of the *Epanagoge* will be found in P. Zapos, *Jus graecoromanum* (Athens, 1931), 2:236ff.

7. See H.-X. Arquillère, *L'Augustinisme politique* (1st ed.; Paris, 1934; repub. in 1955).

8. See Congar, op. cit., p. 350.

9. P.G. 20, col. 1315ff. See also "Vita Constantini" at the beginning of the same volume. Among the numerous commentaries that these texts have given rise to during the past years, we mention N. H. Baynes, *Eusebius and the Christian Empire* in *Annuaire de l'Institut de philologie et d'Histoire orientales* (Brussels, 1934), 2:13ff; H. G. Opitz, "Euseb von Cäsarea als Theolog," in *Zeitschrift für Neutestamentliche Wissenschaft* (1935), 34:1ff.; H. Eger, "Kaiser und Kirche in der Geschichtstheologie Eusebs von Cäsarea," in ibid. (1939). 38:97ff.; F. E. Cranz, "Kingdom and Polity in Eusebius of Caesarea," in *Harvard Theological Review* (1952), 45:47ff.

10. See the typical Eastern texts mentioned by Congar, op. cit., p. 356.

11. See Louis Bréhier, "Hiereus kai Basileus," in *Mémorial Louis-Petit* (Paris, 1948), pp. 41ff.

12. Abundant study has been given to this influence of the Old Testament on Irish and Carolingian Christianity (cf. Congar, op. cit., pp. 251–252), but much less attention has been given to the amalgam prior to the Old Testament notions and the sacral notion of the Roman Empire. Yet this can be seen even in Eusebius, and becomes more obvious still in the work of Cyril of Alexandria (mentioned in the following note).

13. P.G. 70, especially col. 448Dff.

14. See the study of Dom Th. Strottman, "L'Épiscopat dans la tradition orthodoxe," in *L'Épiscopat et l'Église universelle* (Paris, 1962), pp. 309ff.

15. Trevor Jalland, *The Life and Times of Saint Leo the Great* (London–New York, 1941), pp. 64ff. and 303ff.

16. See the preface of Pierre de Labriolle to his translation of St. Cyprian, *De l'Unité de l'Église catholique* (Paris, 1942), pp. xviiiff.

17. See the texts mentioned and commented on by Jalland, op. cit., pp. 64ff.

18. Ibid., p. 293.

19. See the first two chapters of vol. 5 of Fliche and Martin, op. cit. (Paris, 1938), by René Aigrain and Louis Bréhier.

20. As Aigrain shows (op. cit., pp. 155ff.), the secular founders of churches (in the temporal order) tried throughout the whole of the seventh century, despite the councils, to turn them into transmittable family property.

21. On this point see Congar, op. cit., p. 347, especially note 93.

22. *Epistula ad Eulogium Alexandrinum,* P.L. 77, col. 933C, or *Monumenta Germaniae historica,* ep. 2.

23. Found in C. Mirbt, *Quellen zur Geschichte des Papsttums und des römischen Katholizismus* (5th ed.; Tübingen, 1934), no. 187.

24. Again, see Congar's commentary, op. cit., pp. 254ff.

25. *Corpus Juris civilis,* III, 35ff, in Mirbt, op. cit., no. 202.

26. F. Dvornik, *Byzance et la primauté romaine* (Paris, 1964), p. 62.
27. See E. Amann, *L'Époque carolingienne,* vol. 6 of Fliche and Martin, op. cit. (Paris, 1937), pp. 153ff.
28. See vol. 8 of Fliche and Martin, by Fliche (Paris, 1964). Cf., in a rather different sense, Arquillière, op. cit.
29. Fliche, op. cit., 8:179ff.
30. On the work of Innocent III, see what Fliche himself has to say at the beginning of vol. 10 of Fliche and Martin, op. cit. (Paris, 1950), pp. 11ff. Cf. the remarks of G. Le Bras, *Institutions ecclésiastiques de la chrétienté médiévale,* ibid. (Paris, 1964), 12:571ff.
31. Cf. the observations of J. Lortz, *La Réforme de Luther* (Fr. tr.; Paris, 1970), 1:30ff.
32. See *1054–1954. L'Église et Les Églises, Études et travaux offerts à Dom Lambert Beauduin* (Chevetogne, 1954), and especially the study of P. Congar, *Neuf cents ans après,* pp. 3ff.
33. The works of Dvornik have shown that Photius in reality (unlike the legend that has been perpetuated down to our own day) in no way rejected the papacy, but even admitted its claims within the framework of what was a typically Eastern ecclesiology. See particularly his major work, *Le Schisme de Photius, histoire ou légende* (Paris, 1950). Photius' responsibility in the composition of the *Epanagoge* is admitted by most contemporary historians. Again, see Dvornik, *Patriarch Photius in the Light of Recent Research* (Munich, 1958), p. 51.
34. Theodore the Studite is possibly the most remarkable example of a completely Eastern theologian who, nonetheless, makes his own practically all the theology of the Roman See that was developed in the West at the end of the patristic era. See S. Salaville, "La primaute de saint Pierre et du Pape d'après Thédore le Studite, in *Échos d'Orient* (1914), 17:23ff.
35. Cf. Lortz, loc. cit., at n. 31.
36. Le Bras, loc. cit., at n. 30.
37. For what concerns the mònks, see Dom Philibert Schmitz, *Histoire de l'ordre de saint Benoît* (Fr. tr.; Maredsous, 1948), 3:3ff.
38. Cf. the pages of R. Aubenas in vol. 15 of Fliche and Martin, op. cit., pp. 313ff., and vol. 14 (by E. Delaruelle, E.-R. Labande, and P. Ourliac), pp. 900ff.
39. See Le Bras, op. cit., pp. 63ff.
40. P. Fournier, "Un tournant de l'histoire du droit, 1060–1140," in *Revue de l'histoire du droit français et étranger* (1917), 41:129ff.
41. Ed. R. M. Spiazzi (Rome, 1954), pp. 257ff.
42. Cf. C. G. Mor, "Le droit romain dans les collections canoniques des Xe et XIe siècles, in *Revue de l'histoire du droit français et étranger,* 4th series (1927), 6:512ff., and G. Le Bras, *Le droit romain au service de la domination pontificale,* in ibid. (1949), 27:337ff.

43. On this subject see Congar's two studies, *La hiérarchie comme service selon le Nouveau Testament et les documents de la Tradition* and *Quelques expressions traditionelles du service chrétien,* in Congar and Dupuy, *L'Épiscopat et l'Église universelle* (Paris, 1962), pp. 67ff.

44. On medieval conciliarism and its developments, see Dom Paul de Vooght, "Le conciliarisme aux conciles de Constance et de Bâle," in *Le Concile et les Conciles* (Chevetogne–Paris, 1960), pp. 43ff., and O. de la Brosse, *Le Pape et le Concile* (Paris, 1965).

45. Typical is the work H.-X. Arquillière, edited under the title *Le plus ancien traité de l'Église: Jacques de Viterbe, De Regimine christiano (1301–1302)* (Paris, 1926).

46. See our *Spiritualité du Nouveau Testament et des Pères,* pp. 480ff. and 496ff.

47. E. Vansteenberghe, *Le cardinal Nicolas de Cusa, l'action, la pensée (1401–1464)* (Paris, 1920), pp. 52ff. It is possible to connect it with the *Oratio synodalis de primatu* of John of Torquemada (ed. E. Candal, *Concilium Florentinum,* IV, 2).

48. Cf. V. Martin, *Les origines du Gallicanisme* (Paris, 1939), 2:32ff., and B. Tierney, "Ockam, Conciliar Theory and the Canonists," In *Journal of the History of Ideas* (Jan. 1954).

49. See H. B. Workman, *John Wyclif. A Study of the English Mediaeval Church* (Oxford, 1926), 2 vols.

50. R. R. Betts, "Jerome of Prague," in *University of Birmingham Historical Journal* (1947), 1:51ff.

51. See P. de Vooght, "L'hérésie de Jean Huss," in *Hussiana* (Louvain, 1960).

52. On all these movements, see especially Gioacchino Volpe, "Eretici e moti ereticali del XI al XV secolo, nei loro motivi e referimenti sociali," in the June, August, and October 1907 issues of *Rinnovimento,* as well as Troeltsch, op. cit., section 9 of ch. II.

53. See G. de Lagarde, *La naissance de l'esprit laïque au déclin du Moyen-Âge* (Saint-Paul-Trois-Châteaux, 1934), vol. 1. Five other volumes have appeared since 1934, the last in 1946.

54. The best analysis of the spirit of this age is still J. Huizinga, *Le déclin du Moyen-Age* (Fr. tr.; Paris, 1932).

55. See B. Groethuysen, *Origines de l'esprit bourgeois en France. I. L'Église et la bourgeoisie* (Paris, 1927).

56. The entire subject of this chapter has been treated by Fr. Congar in *L'Église de saint Augustin à l'époque moderne* (Paris, 1970). We saw this work only after we had composed our own. On this medieval period in particular, one will find a much more detailed justification of viewpoints in Congar, very close to what we propose here.

# Chapter 4
# Reformation Churches and Ecclesiologies

## I. *The Church in Luther's Thought*

### A. Preservation of the Renewed Primitive Church

If we are to make the transition to the Church and the ecclesiology of the Reformation, the first thing that must strike us, despite what one might customarily think, is what Luther and Lutheranism preserved from the medieval Church and what thereby survived in his thought of the Church of the Fathers. Harnack went so far as to say that the Lutheran Church would never be more than a superficially modified Catholic Church.[1] The scorn in his judgment cannot be denied, but a fact is stated. In the first period, when Luther composed the major part of his most decidedly reformation-oriented works, it is obvious that he never dreamed of founding a new church, or even substantially modifying the Catholic Church. Even in 1520, the year he was condemned by Leo X, his *Treatise on Christian Freedom,* which teaches the universal priesthood of the laity, emphasized that this teaching was not to interfere with the traditional structure of the Church or, especially, the ministerial priesthood of bishops and priests.

This attitude, which was to persist at least subliminally with Luther even during the succeeding years, when he seemed to be departing from it, was thought to be the result of a merely instinctive conservatism. This is a rather simplistic view. Rather, we should say that from the beginning Luther—and a number of Lutherans with him—kept one point in common with a number of

Catholics (even those of a "reforming" tendency) who refused to break with the traditional Church. If the contemporary ecclesiology (which gave them support and whose evolution we have followed) made them uneasy, many positive elements of the primitive Church nevertheless persisted. They may have vaguely perceived her spiritual riches, even if they were no longer fully capable of defining her. From the moment that a precise threat of a break in this continuity presented itself, as these elements disintegrated, a reflex held them back, which was much more than mere conservatism, in the strict sense of the word.

But saying this does not get to the heart of the question. Aulén demonstrated all that Luther owes to Christian humanism and especially to the rediscovery of the patristic doctrine on redemption.[2] It can be upheld with good arguments that, by the same means, he had at least begun to rediscover something of the Church of the Fathers and that his conflict with the authorities, which he soon found himself engaged in, would never completely do away with this incipient discovery. In this regard, another theologian and historian, a Swede, Y. Brilioth, pointed up the importance of Luther's 1514 sermon on the Eucharist. The whole vision of the Eucharist as proposed to us here, is Augustinian, though not exclusively, and it joins to the individual presence of Christ in each local celebration the presence of his whole mystical body, still on earth or already in the heavenly homeland.[3] One text fully justifies Brilioth when he maintains that Luther's attachment to traditional liturgical forms (undoubtedly connected with the importance that his spiritual formation in this tradition had for his most personal experience) also reflects a renewed sense of the community aspects of ancient tradition. In other words, if Luther had not entered into outspoken and bitter conflict with the representatives of authority in the Church of his time, the first impulse of his reformation would have tended much more toward a "return to the sources" of traditional ecclesiology than to a new church and a new ecclesiology.

## B. The Invisible Church

This conflict was to introduce a second phase into his ecclesiology which, at first sight, seems quite the opposite of the first. Not only did he appeal from the visible hierarchical and authoritarian Church to the invisible Church of the *communio sanctorum,* but the *De captivitate babylonica* was to stigmatize the whole of traditional Catholicism as a radical corruption of the Gospel. But here again a closer look is appropriate. The *De captivitate* is first of all directed at a sacerdotal and sacramental organization of the Church which is absorbed within a system of domination, and in turn tainted by filthy lucre. In it, priests are described as traders in grace, having reserved its transmission to themselves for purely self-interested aims. Beneath this is an outline of opposition to a magical notion of the sacraments which looks upon them as mere channels of grace and not as the sacraments of faith. But it would be too literal an understanding of these prophet-type denunciations to see a church that could dispense with all institutional forms in the very spiritual church he preached, in opposition to a Church that was materialistic in two ways: by the superstition of the people and its exploitation by the clergy for lucrative purposes. Here we have nothing more than a resurgence of the first Augustinian notion of the Church as essentially a community of faith in grace, a resurgence that was the successor to many others, but which in Luther's thought, even at this time, implied no more than it did with Augustine: the complete liberation of the institutional Church that many medieval sectarians had already advocated.

The Reformer's immediate reaction upon his return to the Wartburg shows this quite well, when he discovered (with Carlstadt and the first Anabaptists) the consequences that they drew from his teaching, particularly reduction of the Eucharist to a simple fraternal banquet that no longer had anything sacramental about it.[4]

## C. The Church in the Power of the Princes

A third phase stands out in the vacillations of his ecclesiology. For most historians, this phase has remained the determining one. Indeed, it is this phase in which the Lutheran Church, at least in Germany, was to know the institutionalization that was to mark it throughout the *Kirchenrecht* of later years. But we must point out that here, for Luther himself, we have nothing more than a tentatively grasped expedient in unforeseen circumstances, where he was much more concerned with providing for immediate needs than with acting in accordance with systematic principles. Here again is the analogy with St. Augustine, but now it is the St. Augustine of the fight with the Donatists. In a word, it came down to the Church's reliance on the secular power. But there is this difference, that, with all properly ecclesiastical authority in default, the secular authority would not be called upon only to bolster the spiritual authority but to substitute itself for it.

At first sight, we seem merely to have fallen back into the same situation that Gregory VII wanted to oppose: the Church in the power of the laity—and in this case the power of the princes. Luther went so far in this direction that he did not hesitate to give the Christian prince the title and function of *Summus episcopus,* and even to involve him in drawing from this title all the consequences for an authoritarian reorganization of the Church.

Yet we must look carefully at the circumstances in order to measure the exact import of this appeal. At this time, Luther found himself suddenly at an *impasse*. On one hand, the legitimate ecclesiastical authority seemed to him to have deserted the cause of the Gospel by condemning him. On the other hand, his eager disciples applied his principles with a one-sided logic that was always deeply antipathetical to him, not so much because of his supposed conservatism as because of more complex considerations (which we have already tried to analyze). Luther remained infused with a notion of the Christian people identified, in principle, with the Church as being built on earth, which is more a legacy of the patristic era than of the Middle Ages (when it merely survived). He turned to the Christian prince in this danger, in a manner that was not basically different from what many bishops had done before him, from Constantine to Charlemagne.

To interpret it suitably—as shocking as this recourse may seem to us, when we consider it in the abstract—we must understand the notion of the Christian prince that had been worked out by the patristic period and the Middle Ages and, also, be mindful of the specific person whom Luther had in mind.

From the first point of view (as paradoxical as this may appear), even the princes who since the thirteenth century had taken the notion to themselves (forged by imperial Roman law)—of sovereign power as a *dominium* exercised over one's subjects and all their goods, both cultural and material—continued to consider themselves the "anointed" of the Lord in the manner of David. Whether or not they were consecrated (as was the case with the emperor or the king of France), they considered themselves ecclesiastical persons, exercising a consecrated power and, for this reason, a power that was sanctioned by the Church's purposes; and they were generally acknowledged to be such. Consequently, for them to act more or less directly in the ecclesiastical domain, provided this was within limits that were religiously justified or justifiable, was not so much an irregular intrusion as exercise of an inalienable responsibility.[5]

Undoubtedly, if Constantine had behaved as a *Summus episcopus,* it was in minimizing his role as an "external bishop." But—and this was the concrete situation—if the "internal bishops" showed themselves to be failing in the exercise of their mission, did not the "external bishop" have the right and even the duty to exercise a substitute function which had become necessary? In an Augustinian context, all authority appeared as a mere element of the carnal condition of mankind and, consequently, the spiritual authority could not be adequately differentiated from the temporal authority; and in the context of the Middle Ages, the spiritual authority, in its great efforts to maintain its autonomy, had completed the assimilation. Thus the step seemed doubly facilitated, and it appeared ineluctable when it came to questions of person.

If Luther had many illusions about the princes of his time, he was the first and (a little later) the most eloquent in denouncing them. But at a moment when all the drawbacks to which his step would lead him had not yet appeared, he did not need to have illusions about the temporal Christian princes to expect their spiritual concerns to be more authentic than the concerns of the spiritual authorities. There was never any question, for example, that Philip the Wise (who was his protector) had stronger Christian concerns than Albert of Brandenburg, the scandalous archbishop of Cologne, whose speculations on indulgences set the Reformation in motion.

We must go even further. It is not an exaggeration to say that, failing the bishops, Luther turned to the princes to put the organization of the Reformation in their hands, not so much to oppose the bishops who had sided against him as in despair of getting help from those who were ready to follow him. Most of the time, these transitions to the Reformation simply allowed them to proceed to a legal secularization, corresponding to a *de facto* secularization which had long preceded it. Even when they flaunted sentiments of piety, and even to the extent that these were sincere, purely ecclesiastical affairs were no more a concern of theirs at this point than before. It might seem obvious that nothing more need be asked of these great lords, lords of a domain that was originally "spiritual"—and often much less—than of temporal lords. To understand this, we recall what we have said about the *de facto* state of the episcopate, especially in Germany, as early as a century before the Reformation.[6]

## D. Attempts at Restoration of an Independent Church

The appeal to the princes allowed the Reformer to stop the development of sectarian movements and supplied support without which he would have been unable to organize his reformation, between the opposition of the Catholic hierarchy and these disintegrating movements. But he did not need much time to measure to what extent this subservience (which at the moment had been the only hope for what he was doing) could become paralyzing. Because Luther was unable even to hope to break the new chains that had been forged for him and for the church that had been transformed under his influence, the last part of his life was marked by groping attempts to restore, in more or less traditional paths, a relative autonomy of the church, if not with regard to the state at least within the state. We thus reach a fourth and last Lutheran ecclesiology, which in many respects is merely a reconstitution and restabilization of elements of traditional ecclesiology.

A significant fact of this latter period is the consecration of three bishops which Luther attended in 1542 and 1544. It would be impossible to find a more significant indication of both his wish to return to the church that had become Lutheran a traditional structure, of which circumstances in Germany had deprived her, and the *ersatz* character of this reconstitution. What could an episcopate be, deprived of the historical bond with the apostles, except a simple organ of "superintendence" or ecclesiastical "inspection," not only subject to the only existing authority (that of the princes) but completely dependent on it? Indeed, this is what the clerical functionaries gradually became, who afterward were established throughout Lutheran Germany. And it was to this (with little difference) that the other improvised "bishops" were reduced, whom Bugenhagen was to set up in Denmark, in a movement that subsequently spread to Norway. The only church that passed over into Lutheranism and in which bishops continued the "Catholic" episcopate was the Church of Sweden and its offspring in Finland.[7]

Yet there is no question that if circumstances had been propitious in Germany, a reformation that made as little modification of traditional institutions as did the Swedish Reformation would have corresponded to Luther's first plan and satisfied the most conscious (though unsystematic) desires of reconstruction of his last years.

In the successive "confessions of faith" and articles or formulas of concord, whereby the Lutheran party strove to define itself after the Diet of Augsburg in 1530, a notion of the church as visible and structured began to be formed and systematized. It was the immediate work of Melanchthon but the elements were very much Luther's, and Luther made the work his own without hesitation. It is the famous formula according to which the true Church is found wherever the authentic word of God is preached and the sacraments of the Gospel are faithfully administered.[8] This formula could be interpreted in a traditional Catholic sense. Obviously, the crux is to know whose prerogative it is to define the authentic word of God and, correlatively, what the sacraments of the Gospel are. The lasting tendency of Lutherans, and of Luther himself in this last phase, was to reduce the sacraments to baptism and the Eucharist (still interpreted in a sense that was practically Catholic), and to add to them, as appendix to the first and gate to the second, what his catechisms called "the Power of the Keys," i.e., penance. But, while retaining a ministry with sacerdotal functions and even ordination to this ministry by the laying on of hands, which was called "evangelical," Luther and Lutherans always manifested a characteristic hesitation between its restabilization in a traditional spirit and refusal to see a properly sacramental element in it which would be constitutive to the Church, faithful to her institution by Christ.

This "braking" action in Lutheranism seems to be the result of two factors.

The first is the devolution of Church authority to the secular authority, which now was impossible to change. Obviously, the second is the "radical" interpretation of the universal priesthood which Luther reached, in what we have described as the second and ultraspiritualizing phase of his ecclesiology, which left almost no room for a return to the traditional view of the ministry. But behind these two immediate causes is the outline of an episcopate that was completely degenerate in its exercise, a legacy of the late Middle Ages, particularly in Germany. This fact was too facilely persuasive in showing the impossibility of restoring the episcopate to its original spirit.

From this fact a consequence has never been drawn explicitly, by Luther or his successors, but it became evident during the last years of his life and has never ceased being determinative in the German Lutheran churches. It is this: since authority in the church in administrative and even legislative matters had been given to the prince (later to the state), doctrinal authority, which the prince was not concerned with exercising (any more than he had the means to do so), rested for some time on the "prophetic" personality of a reformer, then fell to the universities. Certainly the word of God alone is proclaimed sovereign for everyone, whether princes or peoples, popes or bishops. But particularly with the growing insistence that characterizes the work of the aging Luther to position his reformation on a systematic pedagogy, on the basis of the "little" and "great" catechisms, determination of what is or is not the word of God passed inevitably to the colleges and universities where pastors and schoolmasters were trained.[9]

This was not as new as one might think. With their privileges of pontifical exemption and their capacity of conferring degrees that gave authority to teach publicly in the Catholic Church, the medieval universities, under the guise of preparing and helping the bishops in their doctrinal task, had reached the point, more or less, of substituting themselves for the bishops. While the bishop in the early Church was *ex professo* a doctor of the faith, the medieval bishop in many cases was just capable of countersigning the teaching of specialists, so recognized by their peers. At the councils of Constantinople and Basel, university theologians even managed to have themselves admitted with a deliberative voice, just as previously their faculties were accustomed to drawing up censures which often were of much greater weight than those of individual bishops, even when they were assembled in local councils. In this, all Lutheranism did, then, was bring a long-standing procedure to its final consequences.[10]

Furthermore, the point is of much more general import and can bring the best conclusion to these notes on Lutheran ecclesiology. Once again, coming from Luther's hands (and following Harnack's notion), the Catholic Church remained what it had always been, but modified in a rather superficial way. Again, we must add that all of these modifications had also been made from time to time (at least in outline) in the Church of the Middle Ages. We might simply wonder whether most of them, in what was intended to be a movement of reformation through a return to the Christianity of the Apostles, did not represent the final consequences of the medieval degradations of the institutions or concepts of Christian antiquity.

## II. The First Protestant Sects

This is a point on which the propagators of sectarian movements, which Luther fought, were right, and they appealed from what he had effected to his principles, interpreted in a way which was not his. For them, there was merely a substitution of a neo-popery for the old variety, which was scarcely better, and possibly worse, than the official popery.

Catholics were not long in drawing from such declarations the conclusion that the sects were the logical conclusion of Lutheranism or Protestantism in general. To our own day, this has been a theme of Catholic polemics, that the chain-splitting of the Church into indefinitely multiplied sects is an inevitable product of Protestantism and is therefore condemned by the facts.

We must admit that these are simplistic views. In the first place, what is striking in the sectarian movements that arose first among the Lutherans (such as Anabaptism) and then among the other major Protestant churches is that they are hardly different from other movements of this type that abounded throughout the Middle Ages. Their only point in common with the Protestant movement is the theme of a return to the Gospel and the purity of the primitive Church—the theme of all the medieval sects (and many related heresies, at least since Montanism). Even when the sects go back to more specific themes of Luther or the other reformers, such as justification by faith or the sovereignty of the Scriptures, they did not make them the core of their teaching, or they gave them a sense that was no longer that of the mainline Protestants. To the Scripture theme is always added the at least implicit idea of an immediate inspiration of believers. And justification by faith is transformed into a sanctification of these believers, which was often supposed to be sudden and total and, in any case, was always required from those who wished to belong to a sectarian church.

It is on this point that the cleavage between the reformers, especially Luther, and the sectarians is total. According to Luther, justification by faith immediately implies that the Church is a Church of sinners—sinners who are undoubtedly pardoned but sinners nonetheless. On the other hand, all sectarians have this common point, that they want to be churches of saints.

Furthermore, we must differentiate two varieties among the sects. The most widespread and most common are without intellectual concerns and facilely dismiss as a threatening corruption any kind of scientific theology. The "saints" are to look for an "evangelical" simplicity which does not tolerate a critical or rational spirit.[11] Side by side with this principal variety, which is eminently represented by Anabaptists, another type of sectarianism soon appeared. Between the two, exchanges were constant but their spirits remained profoundly different and even hostile. The other type is merely a resurgence of the heretical *gnosis* of antiquity. It is not by claiming a more intense religious experience, or a purer life, that this type is differentiatcd, but by claiming a "higher knowledge," in which confused speculations and ambiguous mysticism search endlessly for new syntheses.

The latter conventicles flourished in sixteenth-century Germany and seventeenth-century England, and in the eighteenth century acquired new efflorescence, particularly because of Jakob Boehme. They had considerable influence on many intellectual and even political movements, from Freemasonry to Romanticism, and the German Idealist philosophy of Hegel and Schelling owes them a great deal. But they seldom spread to the popular movements; rather, like all Gnostic sects, they appealed to circles of "initiates" rather than the church at large.[12]

The case was quite different for sectarian movements of the first kind, even when theologians or churchmen were at their head, as with Carlstadt and the first Anabaptists. They sought a resurrection of the early Church as represented in the Acts of the Apostles, interpreted by a popular imagination which is attached to the extraordinary gifts of the Spirit, to the strict separation of believers and nonbelievers, to spiritual and material communism, within an apocalyptic expectation of the Kingdom of God on earth. In early Anabaptism, all this was conveyed by a real revolution that tended toward, and for a time achieved (on a local basis), the overthrow of all society. Hence the violent reactions of Luther and many other men of church or state who were very far from his notions.

This first eruptive and massive form of Anabaptism was soon succeeded by a second, more peaceful wave that was more durable. For the revolutionary violence that claimed to transform everything around it was substituted the marginal life of small groups of "elect" in an atmosphere of the "upper room." Their propaganda was tireless but without restrictive claims, and they preferred to remain the "little flock" in order to persevere in a complete unity of vision and life.[13] Baptism was given solely to adults; thus it was repeated (hence the name Anabaptists, "rebaptizers"), and it signified for all these sectarians that there is no true Christian other than one who embarks, without turning back on a life transformed by his acceptance of the Gospel. Such a person was thus introduced into the society of the "saints" on earth.

We have now returned to the strictest form of the "church of the professing," and it is not astonishing that it indignantly rejected the Lutheran Church, which in its growing connection with the state seemed to be mired in the worst confusions of the "multitudinist church." In this sectarian church, the universal priesthood is realized literally: each father of a family is the priest of his home and each can exhort his brothers and preside at the Common Supper in the general meetings. Only gradually and reluctantly did these groups, in order to survive, provide themselves with a rudimentary organization and more or less regular pastors.[14]

## III. The Reformed Churches before Calvin

The sects that were attached to Protestantism, even when they were more or less profoundly influenced by it, did not really belong to it. It cannot be said that they proceed from Protestantism—except that the disturbance caused by the Reformation encouraged their multiplication. But once again, in their depth, they correspond to the type of earlier sects, and the Protestant reformers, beginning with Luther, were correct in seeing them as the greatest threat to their work. Also, it is not astonishing that, as a whole, they were even more rigorous than the medieval Inquisition in attempting to suppress them *in ovo*. In fact, Luther pushed the secular power to the point of real extermination of sectarians.

These sects must be sharply differentiated from the churches that sprang from the Reformation—that, while acknowledging what they owed to Luther's impetus, refused to accept his reorganization of the Church. This refusal is understandable when we observe (as we have done) the improvised, chaotic, and ultimately incoherent character of the ecclesiology—or rather successive ecclesiologies—that Luther sketched out, without reaching a satisfactory synthesis.[15]

These other churches, which had arisen in the area of the Rhine Valley, therefore called themselves "Reformed" but did not endorse the attribute "Lutheran," accepted by the churches that subscribed to the Augsburg Confession and the pertinent formularies. Catholics got the habit of calling them "Calvinists," which, rightly, they more or less categorically rejected. This nomenclature was a fundamental error, for the most typical notions of Calvinism, such as twofold predestination or a "dynamic" notion of the sacraments, were never more than the product of a minority school, except for a time in a few countries such as Scotland or the Netherlands. It is nevertheless true that Calvin rescued most of these churches from a crumbling provincialism by endowing them with a structure, the system that is called "synodal presbyterian." But we must emphasize that this system was put into practice in many places where people never accepted Calvinism in general or even Calvin's fundamental ecclesiological ideas. Conversely, some churches were founded, such as the English Independents and the American Congregationalists, that followed theological Calvinism quite strictly for several generations but never accepted Calvin's church structure.

To understand Calvin's ecclesiology and his later avatars throughout the history of the Reformed churches, we must be aware of the situation in which these churches found themselves before the influence of Calvin's ecclesiology made itself felt. These churches cannot be assigned a unique origin: their parent is neither a local group nor (even less) an individual. They arose spontaneously and rather simultaneously under similar influences in a number of more or less independent cities, such as those that were founded in the sixteenth century in great number all along the Rhine. It may be said that they began by reflecting the culture of the middle class, to the extent that, even when they were provided an organization that was autonomous from that of the cities, they continued to bear the mark of the municipal councils from which they arose.

In a good number of the Rhenish cities there had been a long period of confusion between spiritual and temporal authority, and for many years the bishops were their lords. When the middle-class representatives came to the fore, either through negotiation or violence, and obtained more or less complete freedom on the political plane, it seemed quite natural to arrogate to themselves spiritual independence as well. The confusion maintained between the two powers by the bishops, who sought at times (quite late into the sixteenth century) to regain an undivided totality of power, made no small contribution to the confusion of the middle-class representatives.

These middle-class milieus, particularly in these regions, were saturated with Humanism, but the biblical and religious Germanic Humanism of which Erasmus is the most famous representative. An "interior religion," expressed in individual and social life that was impregnated with the evangelical spirit—a religious moralism that saw Christ as the model of perfect humanity rather than as the Savior—is what they sought confusedly and what Reformed Evangelism brought them.

Its spirit is best expressed by Zwingli, the Zurich reformer, even though his radicalism (which was moderated in practice by extreme political prudence) sometimes caused timid or less simplistic spirits to fall back.[16] What in one sense was still quite medieval and even Constantinian in Zwingli's views on the Church was that he did not seem to see in it anything other than the civil community, envisioned in its religious aspect. The "magistrate" (i.e., the local government), practically independent of any authority, imperial or otherwise, was indistinctly the authority for both the Church and the state. In a "Reformed" city, it goes almost without saying, he found the inspiration of his politics, both spiritual and temporal, in the word of God—"naturally," as the local preacher interpreted it.

The idea of a universal Church was not abolished, but he saw this as nothing more than the free fraternization of local communities. In such a vision of a humanized and rationalized "Gospel"—in which, if we speak of "justification by faith," as Luther did, we see only personal conviction of the truth of the Gospel as a perfect law—it follows that the sacraments were deprived of any supernatural sense that they preserved with Luther. They were now nothing but *verba visibilia,* a kind of parable in action, and it would be pure superstition to look to them for a special presence of divine grace or, even more, the real Body and Blood of Christ. This was the most salient point by which these Reformed differentiated themselves from Lutherans and, since the famous but fruitless Marburg Colloquy between Luther and Zwingli, the stumbling block in all efforts at rapprochement.

On the other hand, Zwingli emphasized the social character of the "Supper," particularly as a festive celebration of the local community, reaffirming that it finds its basis in the common acceptance of the Gospel.[17] Hence the frequently emphasized paradox that in Zurich, even today (it seems), many habitual non-churchgoers are regular communicants. The three or four yearly celebrations are nothing more than occasions for getting the community together, and it is a duty whose performance is as patriotic as it is religious.

Such was the situation and state of mind at the end of the third decade of the sixteenth century in most of the cities that had gone over to the Reformation in areas north of French- and German-speaking Switzerland, as well as in Alsace. Faced with the overheated conventicles of the Anabaptists, whom they pursued with no less rigor than Luther had done, there was an obvious danger that these churches might dissolve into provincialism and evaporate the positive content of their Christianity.

## IV. Calvin's Ecclesiology

Vigorous correction of this situation was the work of Calvin;[18] but recent studies show all that his work owed to a precursor: Bucer, the Strasbourg reformer. Bucer instituted a compromise between Lutheranism and the "Sacramentarians" of Switzerland, such as Zwingli and Oecolampadius, and did not limit himself to combining subscription to the Augsburg Confession with a much more symbolic interpretation of the sacraments and liturgical forms that was much freer of medieval tradition than Luther's. More precisely he worked in the spirit of Luther to endow the Protestant Church with her own proper structure. Defining his function in a quasi-episcopal manner, he completed the ministry of pastors with "elders" (lay delegates) for administration of the church, in accordance with an increasingly systematic discipline, and "deacons" who were dedicated to charitable service. Later he went so far as to reintroduce—under the name "confirmation"—a personal profession of faith by young Christians who, with their first communion, were preparing for accession to the role of responsible members of the church.

During his first stay in Geneva, Calvin had employed himself unsuccessfully in imposing a discipline of this kind, requiring the faithful not only to accept a definite faith but rigorous principles of Christian life. The people of Geneva, unwilling to follow him in these requirements, had sent him into exile. He went to Strasbourg, and during his stay there adopted many ideas and initiatives of Bucer, from which he constructed the first and undoubtedly the firmest theoretical-practical ecclesiological system that historical Protestantism has ever had.

In many respects, Calvin remained much closer to Luther than did the other reformers. Justification by faith in the grace of God alone was for him, as for the German Reformer, the key to authentic reformation. However, his jurist's realism contributed mightily to the synthesis he worked out between this fundamental assertion and the complementary assertion of the effective sanctification of the justified person, as the result and necessary sign of his justification. On the other hand, if he did not accept (any more than Bucer did) the very evident sacramental realism of Luther, maintaining Zwingli's assertion that since the risen body of Christ is in heaven it could not come down again to earth, he manifested a lively concern with keeping the substantial reality of the sacraments. Hence the idea that they are pledges of God's grace, given by God himself, although they cannot contain it, but are given in such a way that they raise us through faith to heaven, where Christ's Blood purifies us in baptism, while Christ nourishes us at the Supper with his flesh and thus makes us his mystical body in the Church.

The first edition of the *Institution chrétienne,* written at Strasbourg in 1536, considered the Church merely under the aspect of the invisible Church, the heavenly community of the elect whom God alone knows. But he asserts, in line with Luther and Melanchthon, the earthly presence of this Church, attested by the purely proclaimed word and the purely administered sacraments. The later editions, however, extended these few notations, so that the last edition devotes a quarter of its development to the Church and the sacraments. And this progression went directly to the theological and practical definition of the Church in her visible aspect. She is called "our Mother," engendering us to the faith through the word and the sacraments that accompany it. The ministry, which we are told is instituted by Christ, and which comes closer and closer in Calvin's terms to a properly sacramental institution, is described as the means whereby this "motherhood" is exercised.

Through an exegesis that was personal to him, which we cannot begin to discuss here, Calvin saw its fullness in the pastoral function, combining preaching of the word and administration of the sacraments. He insists upon the collegial character of this ministry, and all its members act together as so many instruments (necessarily united among themselves) of Christ alone. To this he added the ministry of the "presbyters" or "elders," who are responsible laymen associated with the pastors in management of the Church, and that of "deacons," who are ministers of the charity of the Church. In his thought, the "doctors" seem to constitute a special category of ministers of the word, dispensed from pastoral responsibilities in order to deepen the study of Scripture and the systematization of doctrine.

But perhaps the most interesting point in this system, compared to the directions the churches of the Reformation seemed to have taken, is that all of this organization presupposes a radical autonomy of the Church with respect to the state. Calvin railed tirelessly against the pernicious confusion into which the medieval Church had fallen by making bishops temporal lords, but he was no less fearful of putting management of the Church back into the hands of the "magistrature." Undoubtedly, he did not abandon the Constantinian idea of a Christian state in which all members are, at the same time, members of the Church. Of very undemocratic inclinations, he did not envision an election of elders, as was later the practice in the Reformed churches. He conceded designation of these elders to the magistrature. He even admitted, as fully in the nature of things, that state functionaries could at the same time exercise the functions of elders or deacons. But he emphasized that in this case they must radically differentiate between their civil and their ecclesiastical functions. As for management of the church and all the procedures it required, only the "consistory" (the assembly of pastors and elders) was competent to make decisions. Beyond the local church he envisioned "synods," formed from delegates from the consistories, on either the regional or the national level, for deciding common problems. But in no case could the magistrature, as such, involve itself in this governing process.

On the other hand, the competence of the consistory was not restricted to church affairs in the narrow sense of the word. It had the duty to obtain from individual believers an explicit confession of faith, which it had authority to define and specify, and to apply a discipline of Christian life to which all had to submit. It was the duty of the magistrature to enforce the application of this discipline. Certainly, Calvin did not admit that he was thereby resubordinating the magistrature to the ecclesiastical authority. Both had distinct and independent powers, but both were subject to the sovereign authority of the word of God. And since it was the role of the church, and especially the pastors, to teach it, and of the consistories and synods to formulate its confession and draw from it the practical applications on the disciplinary level, one reached, if not the equivalent of the medieval doctrine of the two swords, something close to the theory that Bellarmine was soon to formulate for Catholics: the "indirect power" of the Church over the state.

In fact, the history of Calvin's activity in Geneva was a history of his efforts to impose his ideal of a Christian city on stubborn magistrates. And when we see that the regimentation of the population at which it was aimed fell far short of his ideal, we measure the extent to which this independence of the state versus the church remained relative in Calvinist perspectives.[19]

All this brings us back to an ideal of a "Church of the professing." But the Church, as conceived by Calvin, is what it is not by virtue of a sectarian illuminism but by an authoritarian pedagogy: the discipline which remained the backbone of all the more or less Calvinish churches.

We must specify one final point, the position of the Church vis-à-vis the episcopacy.[20] Calvin's thought on this subject seems to have fluctuated and to have ended indecisively. The best modern Protestant interpreters of his doctrine are divided on the profound sense of his orientation. For Auguste Lecerf, for example, Calvin intended only a plural episcopacy, belonging equally to all the pastors who together possessed in fullness the ministry of the word and the sacraments. For Jacques Panier, on the other hand, Calvin became more and more oriented toward a stable ministry of presidency over church councils, consistories, or synods by pastors who had general responsibility for local churches. The only thing he would have rejected was a monarchical notion of the exercises of such an episcopacy, exclusive of the collegiality between the pastors and the collegiality extended to the elders.

The fact is that Calvin accepted an organization of this type in the Reformed Church of Hungary and advised it for Poland. But even though he exercised more than episcopal power, not only in Geneva but over the churches that adopted his teaching, he did nothing to perpetuate it in Geneva or establish it elsewhere, with the exception of Hungary and Poland.

An even more marked divergence between what must be called his neo- and his traditional Catholicism is his interpretation of the apostolic succession. For him, it is a succession in the transmission of true doctrine, and only that. This suffices, and the historical succession in the transmission of the ministry adds nothing to it. The Church of today is apostolic or it is not, depending upon whether it teaches the doctrine of the apostles and therefore reproduces the organization of the Church which Calvin thought he saw in the New Testament. Any other kind of continuity seemed bereft of importance for him. He insisted upon the laying on of hands on new ministers by their colleagues, but rejected the sacramental in this. His notion of the sacraments denied that anything was transmitted. Here, as in the Supper and baptism, each person receives *with* the sign, but not *in* it (nor properly speaking *by* it), directly from on high, the grace of the Spirit.

Again, all the notions by which Calvin strongly reinforced the elements received from Bucer were far from universally admitted by all members of the Reformed churches! But the synodal-presbyterian organization that he forged, with the radical independence it assured the church with respect to the state, became universal with them, to the point of formation of churches that were called "independent" or "congregationalist."

But before these churches made their appearance, a third ecclesiastical system was designed among Christians whom the Reformation separated from Rome: that of the Anglican Church.

## V. *The Anglican Church*

The genesis of Anglicanism (the word appeared only in the nineteenth century, in the circle of F. D. Maurice) was even less systematic than the ecclesiology (or ecclesiologies) of Luther. However, from a situation that seemed so complex as to defy analysis at the end of the sixteenth century, the genius of Hooker drew a logical system that was less rigorous than the Calvinist system but had an organic cohesion that was no less remarkable. One school was to work it out further at a later date—the Caroline Divines—in ways that are not always identical, although their homogeneity is undeniable.[21]

The first separation of the Anglican Church was a royal schism, caused by the purely personal and dynastic motives of a sovereign who, a few years before, had received from the Holy See the title "Defender of the Faith" for his polemic with Luther and who, throughout his life, never ceased persecuting with utmost rigor the first English Protestants (as well as Catholics) who refused to follow his will. Yet Henry VIII could not have achieved his goals if he had not chosen as archbishop of Canterbury, in the person of Cranmer, a churchman who, like Zwingli, was secretly married and shared most of Zwingli's ideas, especially on the Eucharist. Cambridge, where Cranmer was trained before he traveled on the Continent and became familiar with the most extreme "reforms," had been a center of radical Reformist ideas. With Cranmer at the head of the Church of England, these ideas spread underground, to such an extent that at the death of the king, and under his successor Edward VI, who was surrounded by men who had been won over to these ideas, its Catholic facade crumbled suddenly and the church seemed to veer toward the extreme forms of Protestantism. It is enough to compare the first Prayer Book (1549), in which Cranmer's ideas can be seen only vaguely (particularly in the eucharistic liturgy), with the second (produced three years later) to measure the extent of the movement.

Nevertheless, the mass of the faithful remained attached to the traditional forms and beliefs, while most of the clergy was won over to a Reformism that was much more moderate than that of its official leaders. Most of the bishops were also in this position. And in the singularly complex personality of Cranmer, an atavistic taste for tradition put a brake on the radicalism of his principles. Consequently, when after only a few years of royal Protestantism a Catholic monarch, in the person of Mary Tudor, returned to the throne, the Catholic reaction had little difficulty winning out. However, the rigorousness of the repression under Mary did a great deal more for the popular success of Protestant propaganda than the favor of her intermediary reign did for the Catholic cause. When Elizabeth acceded to the throne, she found religion in England in a state of division and anarchy. Queen Elizabeth (and her government) might have leaned toward a Humanist and Reformist Catholicism if the uncomprehending policy of Rome (which was not satisfied with the repression of Mary) had not turned her away from it definitively. Therefore, while safeguarding surface continuity with the restored Catholicism of Mary Tudor and Cardinal Pole, she attempted, through broad compromises, to reconcile the different Protestant tendencies that were sufficiently moderate to lend themselves to it. In addition, she returned to her father's policy of using the church by attaching it to herself as a factor of national unity and royal domination.

But between Edward and Elizabeth, the predominant type of Reformed influence from the Continent had changed. For the Zwinglianism that accommodated itself to medieval forms was substituted a more or less strict Calvinism with which the majority of Protestant agitators, who had returned from exile, were impregnated. For these people, Cranmer's "reform" was merely a sketch of a reformation. For a church whose structure and ritual were still more or less Catholic a new church would be substituted, totally remade from top to bottom on the Calvinist model. Two theologians and polemicists, Cartwright and Travers, popularized this model, and hardened and absolutized its lines. For this first form of Puritanism, the church (as conceived by Calvin) and its discipline (whose framework he had traced) became a fundamental and unquestionable exigency of the word of God.

These ideas found their first opponent in Archbishop Whitgift, even though he was deeply penetrated by Calvinist ideas. But at the end of the century these notions met a refutation that was much more definite: an ingenious, positive construction that constituted the first attempt to make Anglicanism something other than an unstable political compromise between irreconcilable tendencies. This new ideal of a Reformed Catholic Church was the theme of the great work of Hooker: *The Laws of Ecclesiastical Polity.*

Hooker too had been profoundly influenced by Calvin, particularly in the former's teaching on the sacraments. The "dynamic virtualism" that Hooker taught proceeds directly from Calvin, while, paradoxically, Hooker is distinguished by more realism, a more patristic Christology (as far from Calvinist Nestorianism as from Lutheran Monophysitism), and a more pronounced "spiritualism." (The body in the Eucharist is, for him, the "mystical" body of Christ, not his real body, and this "mystical" body, again for him, and in opposition to Calvin, is not the visible but the invisible Church.)

But this in no way prevented him from seeing the logician-like and antihistorical character of Calvin's ecclesiology. Compared with Travers, who presented this ecclesiology and the disciplinary program that followed from it as taken directly from Scripture, Hooker without hesitation responded that this is pure illusion. Correctly interpreted, Scripture says nothing of the sort. Travers' is a mental construct, artificially superimposed on the texts, and Hooker thus concluded that the ideal of the Reformer (i.e. returning to the purity of the primitive Church) must be adopted by the Church of England, but that the new models that people were proposing or wanted to impose on him were no more in conformance with this ideal than the model presented by the Roman Church.

He went further. The whole undertaking was to draw from Scripture, and from Scripture alone, a perfect and immutable model of the Church, which to him seemed condemned, not only in its first results but in its principle. According to Hooker, this was a complete misunderstanding of the true importance of Scripture. Its sovereignty is not crowned by setting it in such isolation. All one does is see it from a wrong perspective and therefore become incapable of understanding it. Scripture did not exist before the Church, like a treatise that designed its structure in advance and a code that would answer all questions before they were posed. However directly and uniquely inspired by God Scripture is, it appeared within the existing Church. It is in the "interior" of her tradition, then, that it must be read, and by appealing not only to a simple passivity in its hearers and automatically applying ready-made recipes, but to their reason nourished by a total experience and called to assimilate itself to and be applicable to a life whose conditions constantly change the truth as formulated at a certain moment—a function of conditions that are its own.

The Church, then, is not a fictional being that men must change from its present state in order to make it conform to a model that was given once and for all, or in such a way that all it must do is conform to immutable oracles. The Church is a living being, to which the Son of God gave life in incorporating himself in humanity in order to incorporate humanity in him. It is a matter of receiving it from him just as it has come down from him to us. No reformation, however corrupt the Church may be supposed to be, can substitute another church. All it can do is return the Church to greater fidelity, to its true nature. This must be done in the sovereign light of the word of God, expressed in the Scriptures. But again, it must be interpreted by the whole of Church tradition, which is not the simple, passive reception of truth but its rational assimilation in the most lofty sense of the word—by the whole body from which we proceed. Our own reflections, enlightened by the Spirit of God, cannot cut us off from it, however critical they must be.[22]

Over the course of the first half of the following century, after Hooker, the Caroline Divines developed this Anglican attempt to create a reformed Catholic Church. However, the antagonistic development of Protestant tendencies in England—and no less, perhaps, the political clumsiness of Charles I and Archbishop Laud—were to put a check on this effort. It seemed definitively abolished with the triumph of Cromwell and his Roundheads. But once again, developments in Protestantism and Cromwell's triumph of Puritanism (if it *was* a triumph) resulted in a form that was quite different from that of Cartwright and Travers.

## VI. *Independent and Congregationalist Churches*

The parliamentary burghers of London were faithful to the Calvinist Presbyterianism that had won the day in Scotland, but Cromwell's Roundheads had gone further. Moreover, there had appeared in the Presbyterianism of Cartwright and Travers the first indications of a metamorphosis of the ecclesiastical ideal of Calvin, despite the hardening and absolutization of the system we have pointed out. By opposing this system, Hooker had signified a tendency to go beyond it. This was expressed in the productions and activities first of Robert Browne and then Henry Barrow, the "fathers" of what was to be called Congregationalism.[23]

In this new system, the ministries of pastors, elders, and deacons were preserved. But, as Troeltsch says, if the pastors and the elders keep the government of the church, its authority belongs solely to the totality of the community. All major decisions were reserved to the community. In turn, this supposes two things: the radical or basic independence of each local church and, because each local church is composed of adult Christians, the members' capability of assuming their full responsibilities within it. Synods are accepted in principle to coordinate the activity of the local churches, but the posited church remains essentially the local church, and only it can decide what it will accept or reject.

Although the Congregationalists retained baptism of children, it seems unquestionable that a strong influence of Baptist sects was exerted upon them.

A major consequence of Congregationalists' insistence on the authority of the local community was the tendency to accentuate not only the independence of the church with respect to the state but a separation that was much more rigorous than Calvin had envisioned, although these communities had long retained a strict Calvinist doctrine that a number of Presbyterian churches did not long retain or ever accepted.

Browne became reconciled with the Elizabethan church and Barrow was executed somewhat later. Their disciples emigrated to Holland, where they regrouped under the direction of Robinson at Leiden. From there, under James I and with his support, they prepared for the mass departure which was to end in the installation of Congregationalism in New England, following the voyage of the Pilgrim Fathers on the *Mayflower*.

A form that was close to Congregationalism proper, but more fluid in acceptance of the framework of a state church and admission of laymen as preachers, was that of the Independents. They came to power in England with Cromwell and took possession of a great number of Anglican parishes. But more interested in the moral exigency of Puritanism than in any of its ecclesiological conceptions or its prophetic illuminism, they were the first Protestants to tolerate the existence of churches of different types (with the exception of Catholics and conservative Anglicans). At the end of the Commonwealth, they melted into the Presbyterian or Congregationalist groups, the basic elements of what was called, with the restoration of the Stuarts, Nonconformity. Besides these Nonconformists, who regained a foothold in England, the Presbyterians and Congregationalists acquired various radical forms of renovated Baptists. The Baptists, who took the title General Baptists at their beginning, were nothing more than Congregationalists, installed in Amsterdam under the leadership of John Smyth, but they fraternized with members of a moderate form of primitive Anabaptism, called Mennonite. In fact, they remained a particular type of Congregationalists, not illogically adopting the "sole baptism" of adults while diluting their original Calvinism (first of all on predestination). Returning to England in 1611 under the leadership of Helwys and Marton, part of this community formed the nucleus of the General Baptists, who in the following years, particularly in America, became widespread.

But more radical forms of Baptists continued to develop, particularly in the Anglo-Saxon world, that were closer to the sect than to the church. The first were the Particular Baptists, who separated from the Independents on the issue of baptism of adults, while retaining a strict doctrinal Calvinism. But later there were movements that were clearly sectarian, such as John Lilburn's Levellers, Gerard Winstanby's Diggers, and many others.

## VII. The Methodist Church and the Free Churches

Toward the middle of the seventeenth century—if we leave aside these marginal sects (which continued to proliferate, rather than disappear or melt into one another)—the ecclesiological evolution of Protestantism appeared to be complete. Finally, however, it gave place—not to a great number of divided churches (as Catholics complacently imagine)—but to four great types of churches that were relatively homogeneous and quite distinct from the sects that surrounded them (as continually surrounded the Catholic Church in the Middle Ages): the Lutheran, Reformed Presbyterian, Anglican, and Congregationalist churches (the General Baptists were merely a variety of Congregationalists, halfway between a church and a sect). These churches, depending upon their principles, had local variations and more or less autonomous governments, but there was always complete intercommunion among them and a broad measure of cooperation. Each represented a real ecclesiastical unity, corresponding to a well-defined ecclesiology.

The later history of Protestantism was marked by the appearance of a supplementary type; but strictly speaking, it is much more a question of accidental separation than creation of a truly new type. Obviously, we are speaking about the Methodists. Unlike the first Calvinists, who formed Presbyterianism, and their successors, who created Reformed Congregationalism, the Methodists had no particular ecclesiology as a point of departure and no desire to found a new church. Their initiator, John Wesley, an Anglican priest, was attached to the most traditionalist principles of Anglicanism, but the spiritual and missionary awakening that he was to create met, at first, an almost total lack of understanding in his own church, at least from the authorities. Then, despite Wesley, Methodism separated from the church.[24]

More than by organization, the Methodist churches in the period of their greatest vitality were distinguished by a collective pedagogy, destined (as much as possible) to make a church of professing members from a multitudinist church. Contrary to primitive Calvinism, this was not the doing of any authority but came from a cooperation of "classes" that brought groups of Christians of good will together around a nucleus of more mature Christians. But in its branch that had emigrated to America, the Episcopalian branch, the church that resulted from the separation was merely a rubber stamp of the Anglican Church. Even in England, the Methodists installed themselves in a practical compromise between moderate Presbyterianism and Congregationalism, while preserving a strong nostalgia for the structure and worship forms of Anglicanism. Today in England, in particular, it is not surprising that Methodism is considering reintegration in the Anglican Church.

The same is valid for the other "free churches" that the same movement of "awakening" (or analogous movements) created from the different Reformed churches, especially the Presbyterians in France and Switzerland. They were the products of renewed efforts to re-create churches of "professing" members within the churches that had become *de facto* "multitudinist." The apathy of the mother church brought them, despite themselves, to form a Free Church which was more or less modeled on the structures of the original church. With time, the movement made its way within this church as well, while the church that had separated from it returned, by the force of events, to a multitudinist type. Then, because circumstances no longer justified the separation, it was reabsorbed, except for a few hold-outs who almost invariably turned to the sect. This is what happened in Scotland with most of the Presbyterian Free churches and in France with the Evangelical Reformed Church and the Free Reformed churches. This process is not without interest, however—to the extent that it led ancient churches to certain more or less felicitous syntheses of ecclesiological principles that were more complementary than exclusive.[25]

## Notes

1. Because it is impossible to give even an elementary bibliography on Luther and the Reformation in this space, we limit ourselves to the best Catholic work on the subject, J. Lortz, *La Réforme de Luther* (Fr. tr.; (Paris, 1970), 2 vols.

2. Gustaf Aulén, *Christus Victor* (Fr. tr.; Paris, 1949). See the chapter on Luther.

3. Yngve Brilioth, *Eucharistic Faith and Practice, Evangelical and Catholic* (London, 1930), pp. 94ff.

4. It must be noted that the three preeminent Reformation treatises of Luther were written practically together and published a few months apart, in 1520. But while the last one to be published expresses a spirituality that accepts the forms of the traditional Church (*Christian Freedom*), the second (*De captivitate Babylonica*) confuses these forms and their state of corruption at that time, while the first one (*Letter to the German Nobility*) hints at the recourse that would be made to the princes.

5. See Congar, op. cit., pp. 292ff.

6. On this point see Lortz, op. cit., vol. 1, ch. 3, par. 6 and 7.

7. See Lortz, op. cit., vol. 2, part 2, ch. 4. On the Reformation in Sweden, see ch. 4 of book 1, by E. de Moreau, in vol. 16 of Fliche and Martin, op. cit. (Paris, 1950).

8. The formula was already found in the "Articles" of Suabia (1529); cf. the Weimar ed. of *Lutherswerke*, 30, 3:86ff. The last developments of Luther's thought on this subject are in his treatise *On the Council and the Churches* (1539); *Werke*, 50:488ff.

9. Although the drama of Luther seems to us to be one of a religious genius, harmed by an insufficient critique of the instruments of thought which

the late Middle Ages had handed down to him, we must never forget that he was a professional theologian and his Reformation, with the 95 theses of Wittenberg, began in 1516 as a Scholastic dispute.

10. On the development from the Middle Ages of the tendency of the universities to take the place of the bishops as the *ecclesiastical* magisterium, see Congar, *L'Église de saint Augustin à l'époque moderne,* pp. 241ff.

11. Despite his taste for Bohemian esotericism, Gottfried Arnold, in the eighteenth century, presented the radical expression of this tendency in his *Unparteyische Kirchen-und Ketzerhistorie* (Leipzig, 1699).

12. See the studies of A. Koyré, *Mystiques, spirituels, alchimistes du XVIe siècle allemand* (Paris, 1955).

13. A good synthesis of these different forms of Anabaptism will be found in J. Lecler, *Histoire de la Tolérance au siècle de la Réforme* (Paris, 1955), 1:201ff.

14. On all the preceding, see Troeltsch, op. cit., the first paragraph of section 4, ch. 3.

15. See our *La Spiritualité orthodoxe et la spiritualité protestante et anglicane* (Paris, 1965), pp. 108ff.

16. On Zwingli and Zwinglianism, see the two articles in *Dictionnaire de Théologie Catholique,* the first by L. Cristiani and the second by J. V. M. Pollet; see also J. Courvoisier, *Zwingli* (Geneva, 1947).

17. See Brilioth, op. cit., pp. 153ff.

18. There is not enough space here to give an inclusive bibliography on either Calvin or Luther, but on the particular point of Calvin's ecclesiology, we must mention the excellent work of A. Ganoczy, *Calvin, théologien de l'Église et du ministère* (Paris, 1964). Its only defect is that it does not treat the important problem for Calvin's perspectives on the relationship between the Church and the state. On this point, the study can be completed by Troeltsch, op. cit.; again, section 3 of ch. 3 merits very careful reading.

19. On all this, see P. Imbart de la Tour, *Les Origines de la Réforme,* vol. 4: *Calvin et l'Institution chrétienne* (Paris, 1935), pp. 98ff.

20. Ganoczy, op. cit. (pp. 386ff.), sheds special clarity on this point, which is studied too little by other authors.

21. On the beginnings of Anglicanism, see Philip Hughes, *Reformation in England* (3 vols.; London–New York, 1951–1954). On Hooker and the Caroline Divines, see G. Tavart, *La poursuite de la catholicité* (Paris, 1965).

22. The best edition of Hooker's *The Laws of Ecclesiastical Polity* is still Keble's three-volume work (1836). On Hooker, see also J. S. Marshall, *Richard Hooker and the Anglican Tradition* (London, 1963).

23. On the origin of the Congregationalists and the Independents, see Troeltsch: the paragraph on what he calls the "Free Churches" in section 3 of ch. 3, as well as divisions VII and ff of the paragraph devoted to the Baptist movement in general, in section 4. For later Congregationalism, especially in

New England, see Perry Miller, *The New England Mind,* vol. 1: *The Seventeenth Century* (New York, 1939).

24. The few pages given by Troeltsch to Methodism in his study of the "sects" are insufficient. For English Methodism, are *The Nature of the Christian Church according to the Teaching of the Methodists* (London, 1937), and for American Methodism, see *Doctrines and Discipline of the Methodist Church* (Nashville, 1960).

25. On the recent history of the Free Churches, see A. Vidler, *The Church in an Age of Revolution* (London, 1961), pp. 56ff., 169ff., and 133ff.

# Chapter 5
# The Catholic Church in the Seventeenth and Eighteenth Centuries

## I. *The Church of the Catholic Reformation and the Counter Reformation*

Parallel with the ecclesiological evolution of Protestantism, we must see what reactions were provoked in the Catholic Church by the disturbance of the Reformation. It is a commonplace of too many manuals to assert that this reaction is entirely found in what is usually called the Counter Reformation, understood as a purely disciplinary and moral reformation, accompanying a simple contraction of medieval Catholicism into an authoritarian papacy.

Having been assured by the Council of Trent of her monarchical power, and imposing it through such compliant instruments as the Jesuits and the Inquisition, the essentially papalist Church, which the curial canonists and theologians of the Middle Ages fostered, would have had her claims accepted without any concession other than return to greater integrity and fervor. This view of things, and above all of the Council of Trent and its consequences, was popularized by two historical accounts of this assembly that have long remained classic: the ultramontane view of Pallavicini and the anticurialist view of Paolo Sarpi. For the last fifty years, however, the "scientific" view of Mgr. Jedin has dissipated—if not destroyed—this simplistic view of the Counter Reformation period.[1]

This is not to say that there is no correspondence between events at the end of the sixteenth and the beginning of the seventeenth century and the long-accepted description of the Counter Reformation, but such correspondence is only part of the overall picture and perhaps not the most important part. If one is to grasp the work of the Council of Trent, nothing would be more mistaken than to see it as merely the success of purely reactionary ideals of reform that had become the ideals of Paul IV. If such a current had made itself felt, it was to a great extent held in check by a very different current which flowed back to the reformist Humanism that antedated the Protestant Reformation and within which it had its source. To put everything in one sentence: If certain men at the Council of Trent thought the movement that resulted in the Protestant Reformation was false in principle, there were at least as many influential men who thought that the movement ought to be corrected and deepened, insofar as the Reformation had led it astray. The Jesuits, who have so often been described as the major supporters of the so-called Counter Reformation, were dependent upon so many elements of this reforming Humanism that we are often surprised to see how many positions they supported and orientations they encouraged that were close to what we see among their Protestant contemporaries. It has been observed—perhaps ironically—that nothing was closer to Calvin's Geneva than the Jesuits' Paraguay, or how the pious meditations of Baxter, the great Puritan spiritual thinker, astonishingly resembled the *Exercises* of St. Ignatius—so closely that it is hard to be convinced that they proceeded from the same sources and not from deliberate imitation.

This is also conveyed in ecclesiology. The Jesuit cardinal, Bellarmine, reinstated and perfected a theology of the pontifical supremacy which owes much to medieval curialists. However, many parts of their theology had irreversibly been allowed to lapse, and Bellarmine's synthesis is profoundly different. If the supremacy of the spiritual over the temporal power has been maintained, their infrangible distinction, nonetheless, is clearly asserted. Any direct power over temporal things is denied to the spiritual authority. It is granted only an "indirect power," which can operate within these limits to suspend or withdraw the authority of a sovereign who violates the rights of the spiritual power. Yet even in this case this indirect power could not permit the spiritual authority, even that of the Sovereign Pontiff, to substitute itself for it, or even to substitute someone other than the regular successor of the legitimate authority.[2]

Similarly, if the possibility of radical origin for the power of the bishops in the power of Peter, as it subsists in his successors (according to the ancient doctrine of St. Leo), is not dismissed, the conclusion that was drawn by many medieval curialists, that the bishops are only vicars of the Sovereign Pontiff, is rejected as a heresy.[3]

The Church, it is true, is defined by criteria that are chiefly external, in which profession of the true faith, administration of the sacraments instituted by Christ, and submission to the Sovereign Pontiff are (or seem to be) put on the same plane.[4] But the Bellarminian ecclesiology cannot be called, purely and simply, *the* ecclesiology of the Council of Trent, except in all that it gives up, at least tacitly, of a certain kind of medieval papalism—any more than it can be described as the type of ecclesiology that would be enforced after the council.

In those milieus that were most penetrated with the need for a Catholic reformation, following the line traced by the Council of Trent, medieval conciliarism was hardly less modified than the papalism it opposed. But it subsisted, and even revived with singular vigor, in the various forms of Gallicanism or Febronianism in the eighteenth century.[5]

The Gallicanism of the theology faculty of Paris, eminently represented by André Du Val at the beginning of the seventeenth century, no longer questioned the pontifical monarchy, understood at least in the sense that the papacy is of divine institution and pope is the only visible head of the Church. Yet he attempted to maintain for the episcopacy, and especially for ecumenical councils, an authority which is not simply derived from that of the pope. On the other hand, royal Gallicanism aimed at the first of the four articles of the famous Declaration of 1682, which expressly rejects even the Bellarminian theory of indirect power. But those who asserted the second article, while extending its interpretation of the superiority of a council over the pope (upheld at Constance and Basel, where it was issued), even beyond extraordinary cases, such as the Great Schism, felt obliged to begin with acknowledgment of the pontifical *plenitudo potestatis*. Conversely, the fourth article, while granting the pope the "principal share" in decisions touching on faith, and recognizing the bishops' universal authority, maintained that these decisions could not be irreformable: "*nisi Ecclesiae consensus accesserit.*" All explanations of these formulas seem contradictory. Their apparently decisive assertions betray a deep uncertainty.[6]

It is reflected in the attitude of the French bishops of the time toward the Holy See, and Bossuet's attitude is typical. Depending on the circumstances, he passed from the most Gallican assertions to laughable declarations, where he speaks of himself as "prostrate at the feet of Your Holiness, while remaining attached to the breasts of the Roman Church."[7] Behind these fluctuations were conflicting ambitions: the desire to favor the royal politics and the wish not to be cut off from hopes of the cardinalate. But they would not have been possible without the sense of an unresolved complexity of the problems in question.

A more profound illustration is given by the attitude of the Port Royal groups on these questions. Without reservation, they applauded the doctrine expressed by Saint-Cyran in his *Petrus Aurelius,* in which he vigorously opposed the assertions of certain English religious that exalted the immediate dependence of the Holy See against the authority of the ordinaries. But once an affair such as the *Régale* appeared, people hurried without reservation to the side of the Holy See, opposing the inroads of the royal authority in spiritual matters.[8]

On the surface, we remain on both sides of the issue of an ecclesiology of power which was not perfectly harmonized in either direction. But we must see behind these fluctuations an undeniable emergence of a renewed sense of the Church which goes beyond such a narrow point of view.

The biblical and patristic renaissance that distinguished the seventeenth century in France, as it had a century earlier in Spain, resituated this question of *potestas* in a much broader context, which the Middle Ages had mostly neglected. Undoubtedly, this is the most positive aspect of the work of the Council of Trent, where it is shown to be most dependent on reformist Humanism (chiefly Spanish at the time but also Italian, with such people as Sadolet, Seripando, Contarini, and Morone from the preceding epoch).[9] The bishop reappeared as, above all, the doctor and the priest, and from this fact his pastorate was no longer reduced to a simple problem of authority. The example of such prelates as Charles Borromeo or Blessed Bartholomew of the Martyrs is of more importance here than the doctrinal syntheses which were still developing.

The same thing prevailed on the second-rank level of the priesthood, the presbyterate. Richer's affirmations on the divine institution of pastors, to an extent that restricted the authority of the bishops themselves, even though these affirmations were reasserted up to the time of the Synod of Pistoia (not to mention the Civil Constitution of the Clergy at the beginning of the French Revolution), were scarcely followed. But what is much more significant is a renewal of the spiritual sense of the priest's consecration and the spiritual, intellectual, and moral exigencies it implies.[10]

The same is also true for the other statements of Richer or Marcantonio de Dominis, and Marca, who was somewhat influenced by him and which were to reappear with the parliamentary Gallicanism of the eighteenth century. They go back to Occam's theses on the authority that belongs properly only to the whole body of the faithful, of which episcopal or papal authorities are only an emanation.[11] Their echo was most limited. But much more important is the revived sense among a number of the laity of their belonging to the Church, which is not merely passive submission to authority but the necessarily personal assimilation of the doctrine, drawn from the very sources of the divine word and tradition, and implementation through living faith of the means of grace, with the responsibilities that flow from them. The impassioned interest that affected an entire cultivated laity in the debates on grace and on severe or lax morality, even if it lapses (as was the case so many times in antiquity) into a superficial taste for quibbling and pettifoggery, is indicative of a renewed sense of the fact that Church matters are not merely matters for the clergy.

## II. Jansenism, Febronianism, and Josephism

This rekindled sense of an equality between responsible hierarchy and laity, though on different levels, is the undeniable positive element of even such tendencies or movements as Febronianism or Josephism. For as long as the reality of this elementary equality is misunderstood, we cannot understand why so many churchmen and faithful, whose consciences and spiritual and theological culture were incontestable, were so little disposed to combat them, and even thought they could join them without scruples.

Behind these movements, and at least as part of their prehistory, there is unquestionably Jansenism. It is hard to deny its negative aspects and deeply disturbing consequences. But it is impossible to ignore its complexity and not see the authentic quality that is intermingled in it, without which this movement could not have experienced success or lasted, despite deterioration and decomposition that accelerated at the very moment of its greatest success, to the middle of the eighteenth century.[12]

The word "Jansenism" has been used to lump together so many incoherent things that we must specify, when we use the word, what we intend to designate. If it is a question of the doctrine on grace and predestination that is summed up in the five propositions of the constitution *Cum occasione,* it is certain that such a doctrine was never taught by those who were called Jansenists before the time of Quesnel. All the people of Port Royal rejected it. Saint-Cyran, who received one of the first copies of Jansenius' treatise only on his deathbed, was never interested in its elaboration. In fact, he was skeptical about the possibility of producing a systematic speculative doctrine from the texts of St. Augustine, and skeptical about pastoral interest in such a project. For his part, the great Arnauld always adhered to a strictly Thomistic theology, while Nicole held a doctrine on grace and human freedom that was different from the Molinism of his Jesuit adversaries but practically its equivalent.

If we were to ask what these men had in common, we should have to resolve two points, which seemed to them to be closely connected. The first, which they owed chiefly to Saint-Cyran but also to St. Charles Borromeo and to many others before and after him, in the tradition of reformist Humanism, was admiration for the Church of the Fathers and the desire to see an equivalent of it revived in the contemporary Church. The second, in the same line, was the design to give not only the clergy but the best of the laity a positive and exigent Christian ideal. Again, the tendency toward a Church of "professing members" was a common point of all branches of reformism at this time, as at many others. What was called their rigorism was merely a hardening of this tendency, which polemics would of course reinforce. We must observe, however, that Arnauld's *Treatise on Frequent Communion* was in no way intended to be a polemical writing against this practice but, on the contrary, an attempt to connect it with an overall renewal of Christian life.

We must emphasize that all of this went far beyond the milieu of Port Royal and those more or less strict followers of Augustine to whom "Jansenism" may be applied more or less correctly. A good number of Jesuits in particular, before and during the controversies which were to follow, represented fundamentally analogous tendencies. Even Bourdaloue defended a concept of Christian ethics that was much more rigorous than the Jansenist-tending Massillon or even a Port Royalist like Nicole.

The real conflict, in which Jansenius' theories on grace were long merely a pretext or side issue, was caused by exasperation and tension between these and other tendencies that had belonged to the Counter Reformation, properly speaking, from its beginnings. But they took a systematic form only at this time, and first of all within the Company of Jesus; they were the doing of only a few people. Since Luther's time, the other tendencies appeared in a personality like that of the nuncio Jérôme Aléandre, combining Humanism, which if it was not pagan was at least secularized, with a fundamentally authoritarian ecclesiastical conservatism. In a world transformed by the enthusiastic rediscovery of pagan antiquity and by the new secularist ideal that was based on it, there was the desire to go to greatest lengths to keep within the Church all those who shared this new spirit, by asking them in return to accept her authority and her structures without argument. Within bounds, they therefore left to the men of the Church not only every decision but every preoccupation concerning the form and content of the Church, and all striving toward Christian perfection. Provided the laity gave them the homage of fidelity and unconditional loyalty, they would grant them the broadest possibilities in accommodating to the new world that had appeared. Once again, this tendency was not that of all the Jesuits, and especially when it reached the extremes that are called "laxist," it involved many others in the Catholic

Church. But a conflict broke out between the French Jesuits who were oriented in this direction and the people of Port Royal, who favored the opposite orientation, on the spiritual direction to be given to the most distinguished laymen. Every attempt at resurrecting the Church of the Fathers, and consequently every tendency toward a Church of the Professing, seemed to be the exclusive doing of theologians or spiritual directors who were more or less Augustinian and, finally, Jansenists. Conversely, the tendency toward a "worldly" Church and the effort to "modernize," with its "multitudinist" orientation, appeared to be the work of the Jesuits and their friends.

The major disadvantage of the interminable debate that was to ensue was, again, the opposition of actions and beliefs that were more complementary than contradictory, such as the Church's fidelity to her origins and permanent principles and her "opening out" to the changes of a world in transformation. Perhaps even more serious was the simplistic consequence: identifying, first abusively, fidelity with rigorism; then "opening out" with laxism; and then, in the confusion and violence of polemics, almost simultaneously attacking and upholding each side.

Still, the values represented by both orientations did not lose their beneficence, but they became progressively altered and warped in view of these artificial oppositions, and by the very people who became their champions. The political and cultural aspects of the quarrel ended, as often happens in such cases, in unperceived exchanges of original positions. The eighteenth-century Jansenists exchanged the moderate ultramontanism of their great ancestors for a more and more secularizing Gallicanism. For their part, the Jesuits passed from being the defenders of reconciliation with their time, as in the preceding century, to seeming to be the most rigid defenders of the *ancien régime*.

Nevertheless, the liturgical movement was manifested by the often very positive reforms of the liturgies of the dioceses and the great religious orders, and by a great popular effort for the improvement of the faithful. Even though it was often wrongly called "Jansenist" by its opponents, the movement contributed to one of the most positive rebirths of the understanding of the Church as a community of worship and of tradition as the life of the truth, not only in the heart but precisely in this community. What was achieved in his parish of Asnières (near Paris) by a pastor such as Fr. Jubé seemed to anticipate the best of present-day reforms in their material aspect and even in their spirit.[13]

As can be seen particularly through a study of diocesan rituals, this liturgical renovation was understood as the kernel of a pastoral renovation, renewing the faithful's sense of actively belonging to the Church. It is in connection with all of this that the notion of the Church as the Mystical Body of Christ experienced its first revival in modern Catholicism. At times the notion was altered, as in the decisions of the Synod of Pistoia, by the ideas of Richer or by Gallican concepts. But we find, even in propositions that were condemned by the bull *Auctorem fidei*, because their contexts exposed the notion to the risk of misinterpretation (as did the many propositions of Quesnel which were condemned in the bull *Unigenitus* for analogous reasons), many developments and applications of this notion that the Second Vatican Council revived almost word for word in a context which separates them from these ambiguities.[14]

Similarly, Febronianism undeniably enveloped a very elevated sense, profoundly nourished by patristic sources, of the responsibilities and essential functions of the episcopacy. But unfortunately it became involved in too negative an ultramontanism and catered to the illusion of the most religious Gallicans: recourse to support by the secular authorities could contribute to the desired restoration of the episcopacy more surely than harmonization with the Roman supremacy even though free of the unfortunate secular implications to which the papalism of many curialists of the Middle Ages had enticed it. Josephism, which was much less a definite system than a complex political theory in which secretly antagonistic factors were associated, is far from having only negative aspects. It expresses a deep sense of the educative role of the clergy and hierarchy, and favors rebirth of a traditional and especially patristic culture, together with a properly pastoral theology.[15]

The chief weakness of all these movements was acceptance of the Church's subjection to secular authorities, who persisted in proclaiming themselves Christian and deriving from this their "right" to intervene in the most properly ecclesiastical affairs, at the very moment they were becoming penetrated by secularizing notions and practices. In connection with this, the traditional role of the papacy, as the defender of the entire ecclesiastical organization in its autonomy and radical independence with respect to the temporal, was more and more misunderstood.

On the other hand, the missionary direction of the Church and (for this direction to be real) the need to combine it with awareness of the varied and changing conditions of the world in which the Church was to spread (i.e., a disposition of generous welcome to everything positive in it) were factors of no less importance. Here again, dangerous confusions and facile simplifications at times were the price that was paid for this optimism and generosity (as in the unhappy affair of the Chinese rites, whose complexity has been honestly and impartially analyzed by Fr. Henri Bernard-Maître). But the frantic anti-Jesuit spirit of certain opponents was no less unjust in this respect than the blanket condemnation, under the rather vague accusation of Jansenism (or Gallicanism), of the achievements we have mentioned.

What was lacking in the Catholic Reformation and its sequels, which were much further reaching than the way the Counter Reformation is commonly understood (although they were divided by unfortunate and in great part artificial oppositions), was a sufficiently synthetic view of tradition; and the confusions that typify the Reformation in general, both Protestant and Catholic, do not allow us to escape this criticism. "Authority" and "freedom" were looked upon as opposite terms, and the same is true of the role of the Roman Pontiff and that of the bishops. Behind these oppositions was not the simple universality of the Church (seen too often as a simple uniformity), which is opposed to local insertion and actualization (seen simply in terms of autonomy); again, tradition was seen only as immutability that was opposed (on both sides and in every confrontation) to an opening to the world, which was poorly differentiated from a simple, compromising accommodation.

The violent crisis caused by the French Revolution was needed for these confusions (on one hand) and the resulting oppositions (on the other) to burst forth and the real syntheses to be sought. Yet it was in the eighteenth century that this reexamination of the problems began, in a line of endeavors whose origins go back at least to the end of the sixteenth century.

## Notes

1. H. Jedin, *Geschichte des Konzils von Trent* (Freiburg im Breisgau, 1949), vol. 1.

2. See his treatise *Controversia de Summo Pontifice,* book V, ch. VI and VII, in the Vivès ed. of *Opera omnia* (1870), 2:155ff.

3. Op. cit., book II, ch. XXXI; ibid., 1:614.

4. *De Conciliis et Ecclesia,* book III, ch. II.

5. On Gallicanism after the Council of Trent, especially, in France, see A. G. Martimort, *Le Gallicanisme de Bossuet* (Paris, 1953).

6. Martimort, op. cit., pp. 17ff.

7. Ibid., p. 356.

8. See J. Orcibal, *Jean Duvergier de Hauranne abbé de Saint-Cyran et son temps (1581–1638)* (Louvain, 1947) and *Louis XIV contre Innocent XI* (Paris, 1949).

9. Cf. with Jedin, op. cit. (esp. pp. 31ff.), M. Bataillon, *Erasme et l'Espagne* (Paris, 1937), and G. Alberigo, *I vescovi italiani al Concilio di Trento* (Florence, 1959).

10. On Richer, see V. Martin, *Le Gallicanisme et la Réforme catholique* (Paris, 1919), pp. 361ff.

11. M. de Dominis, *De republica ecclesiastica, libri X* (3 vol.; London,

1617–1622), and P. de Marca, *De Concordia Sacerdotii et Imperii* (Paris: Baluze, 1663).

12. See the remarkable summation of Louis Cognet, *Le Jansénisme* (Paris, 1961).

13. We have been able to consult the work, which unfortunately has still not been published, of Michel Arveiller, "'Jubé, curé d'Asnières,'" an exhaustive study of this too-little-known personality.

14. For example, no. 2615 of Denzinger-Schönmetzer, *Enchiridion symbolorum et definitionum,* on the Church as the mystical body of Christ.

15. All the studies on Febronianism and Josephism produced to the present are too sensitive to the ultramontane reaction of the nineteenth century. Nevertheless, see the chapters devoted to these movements at the end of vol. 19 of Fliche and Martin, op. cit. (Paris, 1956), by E. Preclin and E. Jarry, pp. 769ff.

# Chapter 6
# First Prefigurations of the Church's Awakening

In the first generation that followed the Protestant Reformation there was no lack of good minds to judge that many of the conflicts that had abruptly erupted—first between Catholics and Protestants, then among Protestants themselves and among Catholics—were perhaps not irreconcilable. Unfortunately, what ruined such efforts over two centuries (in addition to impassioned intransigences) was an incapacity to differentiate the real reconciliatory syntheses from simple political compromises. The interlacing of temporal interests with spiritual problems unhappily played a part, in the direction of artificial reunions and unjustifiable divisions.

## I. First Attempts at Ecumenism

The "colloquies" between Catholics and Protestants, encouraged by Charles V, were far from mere attempts at repairs that would be wholly political.[1] The emperor, whose Christian convictions were sincere and whose religious posture was more than honorable, even after he clashed with the stubbornness of Luther and his first adversaries at the Diet of Worms, persisted in feeling that the declared oppositions were not absolutely irreconcilable. For a long time, this was the feeling of excellent minds on both sides, although it was more widespread among reformist Catholics than among the Protestant reformers. The final failure of the Colloquy of Regensburg was not due solely to the powerful political interests which, on both sides, prevented a fragile accord from developing. The mutual concessions that Melanchthon or Bucer, on one side, and Seripando or Contarini, on the other, were ready to make rested on attempts at insufficient theological conciliation. The most typical was the notion of twofold justification, proposed by Seripando, which did not go to the heart of the problem and was unable to satisfy the staunchest intellects on either side.[2]

Later, when the first vigor of the Protestant movement was exhausted and men were somewhat placated, while the internal contradictions of Protestantism were beginning to show themselves to be irremediable, the same kind of attempts at "getting together" was revived, such as the meeting between Bossuet and Leibnitz or the probably more interesting meeting between Bishop Spinola and the Protestant theologian Molanus. But the former went no further than a diplomacy of chiefly political aims or a philosophy that was at once too ambitious and too conscious of the spiritual realities in question. The latter encounter, despite a better theological effort, did not get to the root of the oppositions.[3]

Similar endeavors also were undertaken in which theological perspicacity was not negligible, although elements of political intrigue played too prominent a part and the endeavors were doomed from the start. This is true of the efforts of the Jesuit Possevino in Scandinavia and Russia, the Franciscan Santa Clara in England, and the Gallicans Ellies du Pin and Girardin with the archbishop of Canterbury, William Wake—as well as the liturgist Jubé,[4] of whom we have already spoken, who with this aim in mind made a trip to Moscow. But rather than the properly political intrigues in these common opposition to ultramontanism vitiated the undertakings from the outset. Nothing seemed more surely to condemn these endeavors at reunion than proclaiming the formal divisions, then trying to overcome them artificially.

Further efforts, with mutual explanations and understanding, were untainted. They were often undertaken by sincere converts whose experience with both sides convinced them that the most positive statements of either side were not, perhaps, mutually exclusive. This was the case in France in the seventeenth century with Pellison and in Germany in the preceding century with Gropper. The same thing happened in England with some Catholic-minded Anglicans (whom Mgr. Nédoncelle has studied).[5] But in all these cases the endeavors at rapprochement failed in the face of the call to brute force by others. It was thought that the opposition could be surmounted more easily this way, but the differences were merely exacerbated.

If one element contributed to deferring reconciliations that were not mutual resignations, it was the temptation of the secular authorities to resolve by force the divisions that the theologians were not successful in healing. The revocation of the Edict of Nantes, the Dragonnades of Louvois or Gustavus Adolphus, and repeated attempts by the Hohenzollerns to achieve, through decisions by the authorities in their states, a union at least between the Reformed and the Lutherans had no other result than to inflame the conflicts and make their resolution more hopeless.

It seems that nothing could materialize from all this until a totality of maturations and crises on both sides could lead to a full revival of all the problems, allowing and then obliging the deepest presuppositions to be defined in this context. In this regard, two factors had a determining influence on both sides. One was the religious awakening among Protestants of the eighteenth century, which has been given the name Pietism but goes far beyond what is ordinarily understood by that term. The other was the French Revolution and what followed it, which obliged Catholicism to undertake a purification imposed by circumstances. Thus on both sides, people were forced into constructive self-criticism which, to this time, they were unable or unwilling to undertake.

## II. Pietism

Pietism was a reaction against the great secularization that Protestantism experienced after the disappointing conclusion of the Thirty Years' War, when the principle *cuius regio huius religio* stabilized the divisions that the appeal to force had proved incapable of reducing. But it was also an endeavor to disengage Protestant religious life from a theology that had hardened into polemics, within Protestantism itself and between Protestants and Catholics.[6]

The sources of the movement, as we see them intermingled with its initiator, Spener, are complex and contradictory. The deep interiority of the warm Christocentric devotion with which the English Puritans had unconsciously metamorphosed their Calvinism passed into Holland with the refugees who were banished by the policy of the Stuarts, and it played its part in this. In addition was the mystical orientation of a great part of Catholic devotion during the Counter Reformation, particularly along the line of Quietism and especially that of Fénelon and his followers. Its primary basis, however, is found in a transformation, at first pastoral and then theological, of German Lutheranism. Johann Arndt and Johann Gerhard had been its chief artisans a generation before.

Arndt's *True Christianity*, one of the century's most influential works on spirituality, had integrated Calvinist "sanctification" with Lutheran "justification" and thereby conferred upon it a significance of mystical interiority. Thus "justification by faith" became the principle of a transformation of the heart of man by the indwelling of Christ the Savior. Gerhard provided theological systematization on the basis of a development of Lutheran sacramentalism, nourished by a reading of the Greek fathers and restoring "Christ in us" to its prominence within the Christian ideal, without in any way damaging the "Christ for us," that is, the objective redemption by the cross, the object of faith.

All of this was merely an interpretation of Luther the theologian by Luther the pastor: of the commentary on Romans by the catechism of the Reformer. But it was evidently a reinterpretation that again immersed Lutheran spirituality in the unbroken line of the New Testament tradition of the fathers. Consequences on the ecclesiological level could have been considerable. They would have been even greater, perhaps, if Spener, though influenced by the theology of Gerhard and his school, had not, from pastoral concern, relied on Arndt, who was above all a pastor.

In fact, Spener was discouraged, even disgusted, by contemporary Lutheran theology, which had sunk more and more into a polemic-oriented scholasticism that Arndt had earlier deplored. From the very beginning of the Pietist movement, he endeavored to develop it, not counter to theology but as much outside it as possible. Yet, influenced in great part by Baxter and the Puritan spiritual leaders of his school, he did not see the spiritual renewal as a renewal of individuals alone but of fervent communities—not opposed to the churches or seeking to be free of them but endeavoring to revitalize them from within. It is in this sense that his formula *ecclesiolae in Ecclesia* must be understood.

With some of his disciples, such as Francke and the Halle school, these *ecclesiolae* rapidly turned into sects, since the church offered them little more than a material framework. In the Pietism of Würtemberg, on the contrary, through the ecclesiastical realism of its promoters and the interest they brought to bear on a solid biblical theology, these same *ecclesiolae* were a ferment of renewal for the whole life of the church. With Francke, and no less with Arnold and Zinzendorf, the disdain for (or simple ignorance of) theology-oriented Pietism became a religious emotionalism that grew more and more heated. With Francke, it turned into simple psychologism (reproduction, through an artificial pedagogy, of an experience of "conversion," fixed in his description once and for all and following that of the initiator). With Zinzendorf, this became an emotional and Illuminist mysticism; with Arnold, a doctrinal esotericism, combined with a mystical eroticism.

But for individuals who had a solid theological culture and a surer Christian instinct, Pietism was the path to a very positive spiritual liberation, outside the narrow-mindedness of the Protestant syntheses of the seventeenth century. The finest example of this is undoubtedly a great spiritual power, on the border of the Netherlands and Germany, the mystic Tersteegen. Another case—of a depth and purity that was less authentic but whose influence was to be extraordinary—was that of John Wesley.

Touched by Pietism while under the influence of the Moravians, who had become disciples of Zinzendorf (whom he had met while going to America for a first and unsuccessful missionary endeavor), Wesley might be thought to have narrowly moralizing first fervor of his traditionalist Anglicanism. Instead, a warm, simple, deeply evangelical and missionary Christianity was substituted, and all that was lacking to draw a real ecclesiological renewal from a dying Christianity was the precision of solid theological thought.

Despite his neuroticisms and eccentricities, and even the infantilism of his improvised theological essays, Zinzendorf followed an analogous path. He went much further in the preciseness of his views about a renovated church, although the handicaps of his personality prevented him from emerging from an inconsistent utopianism.

It may be said that Wesley, in his revivalist activity, did a great deal of ecumenism in the sense that we understand the term today, although he was too poor a theologian to realize this or to make it into a theory. For his part, Zinzendorf sketched a primary theory, which (to speak truly) was completely chimerical, on the basis of an activity that was not unproductive but quite disordered.

Above all, both of them had this in common: they did not envision the spiritual renewal of the Christian individual outside a living community, a community of life, which sustains and propagates life. This is all the more remarkable since they were fortified with Lutheran personalism. For both of them, "justification by faith" had the same importance, as if to place the principle of all forms of Christianity in an immediate relationship of each believer with Christ, a basic and irreplaceable element of any Christianity worthy of the name. But both of them interpreted "justification by faith" not in a forensic sense but in the sense of transformation, at least in the bud, of the Christian's whole being. They nourished this conviction with many borrowings, made without false shame, from the treasury of Catholic tradition.

And neither of them for an instant thought to oppose this experience to life that is integrated in a community. On the contrary, they did not conceive it *except* within community life. Each refused to seek this community of life with Christ elsewhere than in the traditional Church, as they knew her (Anglicanism or strongly sacramental Lutheranism). They abhorred the idea of sectarianism, which did not interest them in the least. Both wanted the Church to revive her awareness of her significance and her nature through the "awakening," the "conversion," of individual Christians, and for this awakening to work its full effect.

In fact, as we have seen, the lack of understanding by the Anglican authorities, as well as his weak theology, brought Wesley, quite against his intentions, if not to effect at least to prepare for a supplementary schism. On the other hand, Zinzendorf very consciously wanted to make the community of his Moravian brothers, integrated within the Lutheran Church and under his influence, the instrument for a reunion of all opposing churches into one. But the "religion of the heart," around which he sought to work out this rallying together, came from pious ideas that were mixed with excessive sentimentality, which ended in inconsistent lucubrations.

Both men prepared a spiritual milieu without which the new theological syntheses, which in the nineteenth century opened the way for a solid ecclesiological renewal, could not have arisen, and therefore for an ecumenism that went beyond insufficient compromises and unrealistic utopias.[7]

Of the first two endeavors at a genuinely renewed ecclesiology, emerging from the confusions and contradictions into which the Middle Ages had gradually sunk and from which neither Protestantism nor reformist Catholicism was able to free itself, one began its formation in Anglicanism but led its author to Catholicism, without in any way making him abandon what the Reformation had given him. This was the case with Newman. The other attempt, that of Moehler, developed within a Catholicism that was heir to the best reformist tradition and went beyond its internal contradictions. But this endeavor would probably not have seen the light of day without the initial shock of Protestant influences. And the Protestantism from which Newman took his first and richest spiritual intuitions was the direct heir of Wesley. Similarly, the Protestantism to which Moehler owed so much had emerged from Pietism and more precisely from the personal influence of Zinzendorf.

These two facts are most significant. But their import is greatly enhanced when we realize the more general fact that the whole of ecumenism, and more generally the Protestant ecclesiastical awakening in the nineteenth century, came from movements that were quite different from Pietism or Wesleyan Methodism. In fact, they soon opposed or criticized them roundly; yet they would not be conceivable without the "prehistory" that these other movements constituted.

# Notes

1. See Otto von Habsburg, *Charles-Quint* (Paris, 1967), especially pp. 98ff.

2. H. Jedin, op. cit., 1:3ff.

3. Cf. G. Gaquère, *Le dialogue irénique Bossuet-Leibniz* (Paris, 1966), and G. Haselbech, "Der ireniker P. Christoph Rojas y Spinola," in *Katholik,* new series, vol. 12 (1913), as well as C. J. Jordan, *The Reunion of the Churches* (1917).

4. Possevino has not received the study he deserves (see, however, the article of J. Ledit in *Dictionnaire de Théologie catholique*). On Francis à Santa Clara (Ch. Davenport), see the volume of M. Nédoncelle in the following note, pp. 87ff. For Jubé, see n. 13 of ch. 5. The correspondence of Wake and the Gallicans was studied in greatest detail by Norman Sykes, *William Wake, Archbishop of Canterbury (1657-1737)* (2 vols.; Cambridge, 1957), 1:252ff.

5. M. Nédoncelle, *Trois aspects du problème anglo-catholique au XVIIe siècle* (Paris, 1951).

6. The study of A. Ritschl, *Geschichte des Pietismus* (Bonn, 1880-1886), has not been replaced. Unfortunately, it is vitiated by a hostile prejudice.

7. Again, see our study, *La Spiritualité orthodoxe et la spiritualité protestante et anglicane,* especially pp. 240ff.

# Chapter 7
# The Ecclesiology of Moehler

Before he became their colleague, J. L. Moehler had Drey and Hirscher as teachers at the Catholic theological faculty at Tübingen.[1] Undoubtedly, their teaching was marked by Josephism, but they displayed its most positive aspects, and it contained the principle for a renewal of all theology. Also, history had major importance in their notion of Christianity. For Drey, the whole of Christian dogmatics had to be synthesized, not by starting from some abstract notion but around the evangelical reality of the Kingdom of God. Hirscher was essentially a moralist, anti-Jesuitical and anti-Scholastic, and taught a Christian ethic that strove to emerge completely from casuistry to propose a positive Christian ideal.

Moehler later reacted against the anti-intellectualism of Hirscher, but there is no doubt that the romantic vitality of the two men's notions and their strong sense of history remained at the base of all his ideas.

It was precisely for a scientific teaching of ecclesiastical history that his teachers attempted to prepare him. After his ordination and one year as a parish priest, Moehler returned to Tübingen, where he spent two years as a repetitor; then, before he received the chair that was destined for him, he was given a travel scholarship, which allowed him to become informed on all research studies in German theological centers, both Protestant and Catholic.

## I. The Influence of Schleiermacher and Neander

During this travel, his stay in Berlin was decisive. He took courses from Marheinheke on the comparative study of confessions of faith of the various churches, from which he got his idea for his *Symbolik*. But he was especially marked by the teaching of Schleiermacher, and even more by the historian Neander (a convert from Judaism).

If Pietism and everything connected with it is a disconcerting perplexity, its ambiguity is not less in the personality and work of Schleiermacher. This disciple of the Pietists, formed by the Moravians and then a student at Halle (the university where Francke's influence dominated), became the "father" of Protestant liberalism and represents the form that is most "liberated" from any form of traditional dogma. Yet the Protestant theologian who reacted most vigorously against this orientation, Karl Barth, was no less categorical in underlining the irreversible turn that Protestant thought took with Schleiermacher, and the undeniably positive aspects of his work.[2]

Although Schleiermacher had almost completely dissociated himself from Lutheran orthodoxy, the piety of the Moravians left an indelible mark on him. Faced with the rationalism of the *Aufklärung,* he asserted the *sui generis* character, irreducible to the reasoning reason, of the "religious sentiment." He defined it as a "sentiment of dependence" upon the All, which is unity, but it is not easy to say whether in his thought the All is a transcendent of God, considered in his immanence in the world, or simply the world seen as spiritual unity.

In any case, this "sentiment of dependence," however personal its experience may be in each person, is inseparably a religious and a community sentiment, since it attaches us to the One which is also the All. Irreducible to reason, for that very reason it is inaccessible to expression or rational communication. It is expressed and communicated only in symbols, which are the dogmas as well as the rites. But they express only the collective religious experience of a given community and therefore have no absolute value, even though they are indispensable to the religious life.

Obviously, all this is marked with subjectivism, and even a pantheist-tending agnosticism (which need not be emphasized), which could have no final effect other than precipitating the dissolution of traditional Christianity in Protestantism. Yet many minds, beginning with Moehler, retained from this teaching some positive elements, which, freed from their subjectivist and monist envelope, lent themselves to a revival of the understanding of Christianity.

The first of these elements, faced with the ambient Rationalism, is the strongly expressed distinction between the irrational, which is merely subrational, and what eludes the reason in the religious fact because it goes beyond it—without, however, contradicting it. This absolutely *sui generis* character, not simply of the "sentiment" but of the "religious fact," was the first lesson Moehler drew from Schleiermacher.

Secondly, even on the level of "sentiment," into which Schleiermacher withdrew, religion appeared in his teaching as having to be, without contradiction, both intensely personal and essentially communitarian. Hence the possible resurrection of an organic idea of the Church, in which she ceases to appear as a simple external authority that compresses the individual. She can again become a body, to which he belongs and outside which his most intimate life cannot blossom.

Finally, without falling into Schleiermacher's anti-intellectualism and agnosticism, Moehler, like many other auditors of Schleiermacher, discovered (thanks to him) the prime importance of the symbol in expressing a religious truth that transcends the human mind without emptying it of mystery. But with Moehler, and increasingly so, the symbol was not the simple expression of an experience in its subjectivity but of the Divine Fact itself, which it grasped.

These decantations were prepared by the other teachings Moehler followed at Berlin, those of Neander. Neander had already applied them to the study of the Church as a historical reality and, more precisely, the preeminent reality of Christian history.

Until Neander, Church history was most often a simple history of events, councils, striking personalities, and institutions. Neander, however, intended to make all reality the history of the Church herself—a community of life, the commonly lived experience of Christian truth over the centuries. This intuition gripped the mind of young Moehler and gave him the principle for his own synthesis of the Church.

## II. Unity in the Church

This phrase appeared a few years later, in 1825, as the title of his book (*Die Einheit in der Kirche*), and it was the departure point for the ecclesiological renovation that would end with the Second Vatican Council. The correct title is not "The Unity *of* the Church," as in the first French translation of the book, but "Unity *in* the Church."[3] That is, unity is not considered a simple external aspect of the Church but as essential to its nature.

In fact, this ecclesiology is quite pneumatological. From the earliest pages, Moehler says he considers indisputable the foundation and original organization of the Church by Christ. He proposes to study how this institution has, as its goal and effect, the expression and communication of the life of the Holy Spirit in souls. It is not that he believes the unity of the Church is purely an object of faith; quite the contrary. He wants to show how the concrete, phenomenal Church visibly manifests this spiritual and, more precisely, supernatural unity. It is not only a question of the unity of subjective life shared by Christians, but the transcendent unity of the life of the Spirit of God in them. But he wants to show how this unity is affirmed in them in effective realization by the Catholic Church—in the community of charity, in the "love of God poured into our hearts by the Holy Spirit." (It is superfluous to emphasize how radically new this notion is with respect to the formation of medieval and postmedieval ecclesiology.)

Still more profoundly—and here Moehler shares the views of Drey on the idea of the Kingdom of God as the departure point for the systematization of Catholic dogma—it is essential that Christian truth be the truth of divine charity communicated to men. Conversely, this evangelical truth can be preserved and propagated only where there is living charity.

The Church, then, is essentially the realization of this divine life, which in its depth is the divine love communicated to mankind by the Holy Spirit. It is from this fact that the evangelical truth is bound up with the Church, that she alone can have the truth within herself and communicate it by extending herself to men.

Two parts follow in this development. The first considers "spiritual unity" in itself. The second studies the realization in "organic unity."

## III. *Spiritual Unity*

The first chapter of the first part is titled "Mystical Unity." Moehler starts from this principle: the Christian faith is above all faith in the communication of the divine life in the Holy Spirit, life which is love. The faith under this aspect, one could say, is merely a progressive awareness of the life of the Spirit living in us through charity.

Hence it follows that one cannot receive the Spirit without tending to communicate it in love. Even if some (like St. Paul) receive the communication of the Spirit directly, they can keep it within themselves only by adhering to the body where it lives, for the Spirit is love.

Thus the notion of tradition is introduced. Moehler defines it as fundamentally that pouring out of the Spirit which is the same in everyone and unites all in itself. Hence this formula:

> Each individual must accept in himself through a personal religious experience the holy life which exists in the Church. He must transform and make truly his own in his own contemplation the

religious experience of the community. He must finally allow to be created and developed in him a completely holy life, in accord with the dispositions that his knowledge of Christianity will have called forth.[4]

What follows stresses the inseparability of an authentic knowledge of God and the quality of being rooted in holiness, that is, fellowship in charity.

All this had been fashioned in Greek patristics, particularly by Clement of Rome, Ignatius of Antioch, Clement of Alexandria, and Origen, of whom Moehler quotes the most characteristic texts. It follows from this, Moehler shows, that the propagation of Christian truth and conversion to Christianity, according to the fathers (among others), are not the fruit of reasoning or human wisdom but of the witness of life, eliciting desire to share this life, and leading toward association with it. In this perspective, he emphasizes, the fathers gave the name "true philosophy" not simply to Christian teaching but to the whole of Christian life.

Still following the early Christians, Moehler says the moral decadence of men led them into the initial error of idolatry. The conclusion is: "The unity is essentially in a life created immediately and continually by the divine Spirit, who wishes that it be maintained and perpetuated by the power of mutual love."[5] From all this results, first of all, the inseparable conjunction of faith with charity. This is why we learn nothing about Christ except through the Church, and we cannot experience his life except in the Church, the community of believers. The unity, holiness, and truth of the Church are therefore one reality, seen under its different aspects.

The second chapter is a more particular examination of "the unity of teaching." The basic, underlying idea of this chapter brings us close to Schleiermacher: the faith exists as a fact of the interior life before it is expressed in formulas, whatever they may be. Moehler expresses this idea in a phrase of which he is fond and uses frequently: "Christ in the hearts before being in the written Gospel." This is why the Church alone, in which Christ lives through his Spirit, correctly interprets the Scriptures that speak of him.

In this regard, all churches can be only an extension of the primitive Church—that of the apostles—whose Spirit has been communicated to them conjointly in truth. The Spirit, abounding in the Church, keeps what she believes alive in such a way that the faith of each person is enlightened and fructified only in the joining of all, for as Moehler says: "The totality of the gifts of the Spirit is only in the totality of believers."[6] This is why the early churchmen identified error with innovation, insofar as it is a separation from what is held by all as a whole.

At this point he made a first analysis of tradition. "Tradition," he says, "consists in the Gospel preached since the Apostles." It is precisely the Gospel in souls. It is only in the second stage that tradition becomes fixed in writing, and following these writings allows following the continuity of tradition.

On the other hand, tradition, even so expressed, can never be understood, except within the Church.

Tradition does not prove; it is content with showing up error that is foreign to it—a simple innovation.

Behind the external tradition, then, "the identity of the awareness of one of her members, a determined group a diocese with the awareness of the whole Church."[7] He is more specific: "In the manner of an inner impulse, the love *in Christo,* by the Holy Spirit, unites each believer with the totality of other Christians (and this Christian unity can be discovered either in an experience or in an intuition or contemplation); this same love binds the Christian to all the past generations, hence the same need to feel in harmony with the past, and it does not rest until it is perfectly assured of this identity" between his faith and the faith of all time. This comes through the study of written tradition.

Moehler introduced a new idea here, underlining the point that tradition is not transmitted by a simple passive reception. The Spirit that is in us is the same Spirit that was in the first Christians; therefore external faith (i.e. received from them in the expressions they gave it) is only a beginning. It must extend into personal assimilation, which is the work of the Spirit in us. Hence the very important conclusion: "The faith is therefore not a blind submission to an authority, as the heretics of the 2nd century claimed. But it asserts itself as having its own authority within. Its harmony with the faith of all ages is a necessary consequence of Christianity."[8] Thus "fantastic and selfish demonstrations are contrary to the ever real awareness of Christianity; they are therefore also contrary to the awareness of the individual Christian."[9] Yet this Christian "has at his side the uninterrupted belief of the entire Church as the historical basis of his feeling."[10]

But the continuity of transition, once it is understood this way, can no longer be simply static. "The vital interior unity must be safeguarded, otherwise it would not always be the same Christian Church; but the awareness of the Church can grow, and her life always develops further by becoming more precise, she blossoms forth in becoming more and more clearly present to herself. It is in this way that the Church reaches adulthood; she becomes the adult Christ."[11]

This leads to the problem of the relationship between tradition and Scripture, considered as "the written Gospel." A new description of tradition follows because of this problem. The principle is revived that Scripture, the written Gospel, is posterior to the living and preached Gospel, and derived from it. Hence it follows, once again, that any interpretation of the Scriptures will be rejected if it is not in conformity with the living tradition that subsists necessarily, substantially the same, in the life of the Church after the composition of the written Gospel as before.

"Since tradition is [therefore] the expression of the Holy Spirit giving life to the community of the faithful, [an expression] which comes down the centuries... , Holy Scripture (for its part) is the embodied expression of the same Holy Spirit at the beginning of Christianity, by means of the Apostles endowed with a special charism. Scripture in this respect is the first member of written tradition." But "since Scripture has been taken from the living tradition... one cannot prove by Scripture that tradition must not contain what is not in this same Scripture."[12] In favor of the contrary opinion, Moehler refers to declarations of Scripture itself (e.g., Jn 20, 30, 31 and 21, 24, 25).

On one hand, the result is that Scripture alone, as dead letter, cannot be sufficient for a Christian. To receive its content, he must exercise his faculties, and not in isolation but within the living tradition. On the other hand, he needs Holy Scripture, and more generally the whole of written tradition, to achieve awareness of the identity of his Christian awareness with that of the centuries.

In this context, the question Must tradition be coordinated with or subordinated to Scripture? appears bereft of meaning, denoting a false view of their relationships. The same is true of the idea that one should retain from tradition only what is also in Scripture.

On the other hand, there are no points that can be proved by Scripture alone and others by tradition alone. What is proved by Scripture is proved only by Scripture as part of the whole of tradition. Conversely, "without Holy Scripture considered as the most ancient incarnation of the Gospel, the Christian doctrine could not have been preserved in all its purity and simplicity."[13] But "without a steady tradition, we would be lacking the profound meaning of the Scriptures, for without intermediary members we could not understand the bond of things among themselves."[14] It seems that this last formula must be understood in the sense of St. Irenaeus, who tells us that the correct bond between the statements of Scripture can be established only from the "hypothesis of faith" that the Church bears within herself.

The conclusion of his chapter is that the Gospel in the heart (before the written Gospel) fortifies the necessary attachment of the Christian to the *person* of Christ (in contradistinction to his teaching) and to his brothers in Christ.

The next two chapters verify and apply these principles to the concrete historical reality. The first does it *a contrario,* by studying heresy, considered as a "multitude without unity." It is in effect, according to Moehler, a simple product of the egotism of a thought that is coming apart. Claiming it is based directly on the Scriptures, it alters their meaning. Finally, having corrupted their content, it ends by formally contradicting them.

Faced with this, the true Church reflects the "unity" that affirms itself "in the multitude."

In the last chapter of his first part, Moehler revives and extends the analysis he had made of the handing on of tradition, not by simple passive acceptance but by living assimilation. According to him, man has a radical capacity for knowing, but according to the fathers, this is not fulfilled outside the revelation of Christ and the grace of the Spirit. On one hand, it may be said that Christianity and Christianity alone responds to the profound needs of man. But on the other, it must be said that it alone makes these needs clear by fulfilling them.

This brings Moehler to the formation of what he calls the "philosophy of the faith," starting with the definition of *gnosis,* given by Clement of Alexandria, as "truth conscious of itself" or "perception of truth by itself."[15] By making the faith explicit, then, *gnosis* reconstructs it insofar as this faith lives in us. In this philosophy of the Christian, Moehler distinguishes what he calls a "mystical theology," which is content with contemplating its harmony without seeking to analyze it, and a "speculative theology," which is involved in this analysis.

The primary justification for this undertaking is defense of the faith, not only against external opposition but anything that could alter it in us through pernicious confusions.

The result is an authentic *gnosis* only on the basis of faith and within a fellowship that is forever abandoned to the *gnosis* of the most scientific and the faith of the most simple faithful. Moehler sees the same necessary interdependence between the lives of ascetics and those of Christians who remain in the world as between the blessing of creation and the necessity of the cross.

Behind these harmonies he rediscovers the affirmation, already stated, that the truth of Christianity can never be limited to the realization of it that each person can attain personally. Hence, in order to reach a higher form of it, whereby we will be fully ourselves but only within and with the whole Church, our need to rid ourselves of a base form of freedom which separates and encloses us within our limitations.

Indeed, the Church and the Church alone effectuates harmony within the inevitable and necessary diversity. Everything that is good in each sect must be found again in her, but without its concomitant negative aspects.

Moehler sees a particularly striking manifestation of this harmony on the liturgical level. Community of worship throughout the Church, far from establishing a paralyzing uniformity, comes from the variety of complementary local rites.

No longer on the spatial but on the temporal plane, we now look more to the early centuries for an eternal model of the Church, which she can inherently reproduce. What the apostles established must be extended in the fertile harmony of this diversity, which alone can explicate its richness.

## IV. Organic Unity

The second part of the volume shows more definitely how the spiritual unity of the Church is conveyed on the phenomenal level in organic unity. As Moehler states it, it is first of all the unity of the local church around the bishop. From here he goes to the unity among neighboring churches, realized in the metropolitan see, and finally to the whole Church and the universal episcopacy. It is at this point, as a conclusion, that the significance of the pontifical primacy appears.

The first chapter of the second part therefore studies "unity in the bishop." The departure point is the fact that supernatural love, the charity communicated by the Spirit, needs to be incarnated in one body of Christians, brought together in one, given place.

Yet from apostolic times, we see, these local communities were formed around men who were placed there by the apostles, first to extend the apostles' activity and then to replace them when they were gone. Thus, when the apostles were no longer there, the bishops (only one in each church) appeared aware that they were succeeding to the apostolic authority through their authority, as we see with Ignatius and Irenaeus. Moehler does not spend much time on the historical conditions in which this succession came about. For him, what is essential is the significance of this episcopacy, exercised by one bishop in each church, once it had been set up. This is how he understands it:

> As soon as the holy principle, the form of unity, has become active in the souls of the faithful, they feel so attracted and so directed toward the union of all that their inner desires are satisfied only when they see their unity represented and concretized in an image. For a given place, the bishop is this visible image of the invisible union of all Christians. In him is personified the love of the members for one another; he is the manifestation and the living center of the Christian sentiments aspiring to unity. And

since these sentiments can be unceasingly contemplated in the bishop, he is the actualized and fully conscious love of Christians. He is also the pre-eminent means of maintaining and preserving it in unity.[16]

But this could be understood as if the bishop were only an emanation and, in some way, a delegate of the local community. Moehler foresaw this interpretation and discarded it. Christians' common life in love does not come from their own substance. It is completely supernatural in its origin and nature. It is the life of *divine* love, which only the *Holy Spirit* can give. Although the role of the bishop is to express the love which makes the life of the community, it can exist only by a positive disposition of apostolic origin and by the gift of the Spirit which is bound up with it.

Nevertheless, to those who do not yet live in the Spirit, the authority of the bishop appears to be in the realm of the law; he is there only to teach them what they are to become. They must therefore see in him the terminus toward which their common life tends. Since he is closer to perfection, his activity no longer appears as law to them but as the "free actualization of man who has become *spontaneously active* in the Holy Spirit."[17]

The bishop therefore responds to the need for the Spirit in the community, thanks to a gift by the Spirit to the community.

The unique priesthood of the bishop is not in opposition to the universal priesthood of the faithful. The latter priesthood becomes a reality only through the integration of each person within the community, and the bishop receives a special gift to assure this total unity.

But the result is that the activity of the bishop, far from reducing the community to simple passivity, cannot be exercised except in concert with the common activity. Indeed, the goal of his activity is the activity of all together. It cannot be exercised against the community or, even less, outside it, but always in it, for it exists only for the community.

Yet unity in charity for any particular community within the one Church cannot be closed within this community. Local communities are called to meet their neighbors—to exercise, with respect to them, the same charity that makes their own interior life. Hence the role of the metropolitans, which Moehler examines in the following chapter.

In appearance, the function of the metropolitan arose from fortuitous circumstances that led the local communities to draw nearer one another around a center. But the function nevertheless corresponds to a basically spiritual necessity: that fellowship in love which must be the accomplishment of communities as well as individuals.

Chapter III treats the vision of the unity of the episcopacy, corresponding to the ultimate universality of charity. Indeed, this cannot be limited to the relationships between communities that are bound by the inevitable material fact of proximity. It is an intrinsic requirement of this love that comes in us with the Holy Spirit that we share in unity all his gifts with all Christians, even those whom we would not otherwise meet if the internal requirement of love did not impel us to them.

Here, rightly, Moehler insists on constant communication of the various churches among themselves, which is characteristic of the Church of the Fathers. What happens to each part is consciously interpreted by this part, and by all others, as affecting the whole. For all parts are conscious of living in the same faith in the same redemption, of having one sole hope, and of living all this through the same sacraments, which unite everyone despite distances.

This unity of the Church in the faith, in the objects and the sacraments of the faith, is preserved and maintained by the unity of the episcopacy. Penance, as practiced and understood by the primitive Church, implied that the reconciliation of men with God also brings reconciliation of men among themselves.

But this is above the manner of episcopal consecration that affirms this unity. Each bishop must receive his consecration from at least three bishops, representing the entire episcopal community. The bishop's consecration appears as a consecration in unity by unity itself.

Moehler concludes this chapter by remarking that this union and this unity of the episcopacy give greater radiance to the personality of each bishop by interesting him in and associating him with the life of the whole.

The last chapter turns to the Roman primacy, within the same perspectives on the universal unity of the episcopacy. The primacy of Peter in the apostolic college shows that primacy is a basic element in the constitution of the Church. Yet the universal primacy of a bishop among other bishops can manifest itself only progressively, for, we must emphasize, it found a reason to be exercised only from the moment the Church was in dispersal and needed to be reunited.

The central importance of Rome is not, he remarks, that it can, by itself, explain that the primacy was recognized in the Bishop of Rome. On the contrary, his very primacy led Peter to settle in Rome, as the place from which the primacy that had its principle in him could best be exercised.

Beginning with this fact, the natural connection among the churches and the internal impetus of this common life in love, proceeding from the Spirit, led to the growing precision of the role of the Bishop of Rome.

The conclusion of the last chapter, and the book, is that the forms of unity always appear according to its needs, although they are, like unity itself (in the service of which they are exercised), the gift of the Spirit.

## V. *Critique of* Unity in the Church

Moehler's presentation of the Church appeared so very new, even though it was based on patristics, that it disconcerted many and produced vehement criticism. Moehler was fully aware that he treated only one aspect of the Church, which moderns too often overlook. A few years before he published *Unity in the Church* he had given a classical course in ecclesiology, and the first words of *Unity* specify that he presupposed that the readers would know the classical aspects. Yet he soon felt the necessity of showing more explicitly the linking of his pneumatological ecclesiology with Christology and, at the same time, insisting on the historical continuity of the Church with the person and work of Christ. He was also acutely aware of possible ambiguities in many of his expressions, which were influenced by Schleiermacher. All this is manifest in the notes that M. Geiselmann, the last editor of *Die Einheit in der Kirche* and *Symbolik*, discovered.[18]

These complements and minor alterations suggest the necessary complement of a pneumatological ecclesiology by a Christological ecclesiology—two other chief self-critiques.

Moehler realized he had too narrowly considered the end to which the Church tends, or, if one prefers, the final state which must be hers. Undoubtedly, this state is germinally present in the Church of today, but only partially and inchoately. The Church is not a sphere of the world in which sin no longer exists, abolished in perfect charity. If it were, the Church would already be the realized Kingdom of God. It is, instead, the sphere in which the struggle against sin is pursued: the preparation for the Kingdom.

Hence it follows that the institutions of the Church cannot be considered simply an expression of, or even the concrete realization of, life in the Spirit, but first of all as a means of grace, of channels whereby this life comes to us.

All of this was brought up by Moehler a few years later and developed in his *Symbolik*,[19] in which he opposed the Catholic notion of Christianity to the Protestant notion. Against Schleiermacher and religious romanticism in general, he emphasized (in second place) the ambivalence of the community. Yet it must be noted that *Unity in the Church,* despite the place it gives the "vitalist" and "organicist" ideas then in fashion, is very firm on the personalism of Christian life. There was no question of the Christian's simply melting into the whole; on the contrary, he is to develop his personality by integrating it in the totality of the Church. *Symbolik* therefore specified that it is not simply as a community that the Church is the fullness of life in love. There are communities that corrupt or oppress the individual. The Church gives life its fulfillment insofar as she is the community of *divine love*, animated not by a *Volkgeist* but by the Spirit of *God*.[20]

However, as he specified a little earlier, the Church cannot be defined solely as the Communion of Saints. She is not the actualized Kingdom but a trainer in holiness, in view of the Kingdom to come.[21] The same important passage specifies that she is such insofar as she is the continued incarnation of the Redeemer. She merely extends the redemptive cross in mankind, so to speak—*Ut opus redemptionis perenne redderet*.[22]

Hence the importance and the true sense of the expression "Body of Christ" as applied to the Church: it is applied to her as to an institution created by him, in which his incarnation is analogically extended.[23]

The result is that the Spirit in the Church is manifested, above all, in the preaching of men sent by Christ and their celebration of the sacraments he established.[24]

Man, then, enters the Church to be liberated from what prevents him from being himself. But this liberation cannot be achieved or begun except by submission to the community.[25] Again, it is necessary that a divine, not a human, authority govern it. This is why the authority of Christ is extended in the authority of those whom he established over the Church.[26]

The unity of the Church comes, then, both from the institution by Christ *and* the continued presence of the Spirit.[27]

Within this perspective, the hierarchy in general and the primate in particular were no longer seen as resulting from a need and immanent impetus of the Spirit but as proceeding from the historical Christ. The pope, thus, appeared no longer as the *crowning* but as the *basis* of unity.[28] The gifts of the Spirit, nevertheless, are freely communicated to all, but they are coordinated with the authority that alone is in charge of transmitting the truth and salvation.[29]

In his total synthesis, Moehler never revived these pneumatological and Christological aspects of the Church. But one would be wrong if he therefore thinks *Symbolik* represents a step backward with respect to *Unity in the Church*, or that it brought up nothing essential. When we carefully reread the first of these two works, we see signs of each complement that are developed in the second work.

## VI. *Moehler's Influence*

Moehler's influence was slow in penetrating the Scholastic statements of Catholic ecclesiology, but it was very noticeable in the school of Roman theologians who prepared the First Vatican Council. Perrone, a professor at Gregorian University from 1824 to 1863 and rector until 1876, mentions only *Symbolik* in his chapter "De Ecclesiae constitutione." But later, Moehler's influence seems to be broader on Passaglia, Schrader, and Franzelin. It combines with the great seventeenth-century treatises of Petau and Thomassin on positive theology to revive utilization of the Greek fathers.

Passaglia is perhaps most interesting in this regard, first by the statement that a theology of the Church must start from the different biblical images which are applied to it. He also stresses the necessity of combining a view of the Church that starts from within with the view that is constructed on external notes.

For his part, Franzelin revived Moehler's idea of the Church as a continued incarnation. He built his synthesis on the two complementary notions of the Church as the Body and the Bride of Christ.

Finally Schrader, in composing the schema *De Ecclesia* for the First Vatican Council, proposed to define the Church as the *Corpus mysticum Christi*. However, this schema was only discussed by a commission of fathers who did not fully understand it.[30]

It was only in the twentieth century, with the Second Vatican Council, that Moehler's ideas received the attention they deserve. Still, it can be wondered if the pneumatological element has yet acquired in customary teaching of Catholic theology, whether official or not, the full place that Moehler gave it from the start.

## Notes

1. On the present state of research on Moehler, see the study of J. R. Geiselmann, which appeared in the collective work *L'Ecclésiologie au XIXe siècle* (Paris, 1960), pp. 141ff.

2. See H. Bouillard, *Karl Barth* (Paris, 1957), 1:153ff.

3. The more exact French translation appeared in 1938 as the second volume of the *Unam Sanctam* collection of Fr. Congar. It is the work of Dom André Lilienfeld, which we shall refer to as *U.E.*

4. *U.E.*, p. 12.
5. *U.E.*, p. 20.
6. *U.E.*, p. 31.
7. *U.E.*, p. 38.
8. *U.E.*, p. 70.
9. Ibid.
10. *U.E.*, p. 41.
11. *U.E.*, p. 42.
12. *U.E.*, p. 49.
13. *U.E.*, p. 52.
14. Ibid.
15. *U.E.*, p. 120.
16. *U.E.*, p. 171.
17. *U.E.*, p. 176.
18. See Geiselmann, op. cit., pp. 158ff.
19. Moehler produced five editions of his *Symbolik*, from 1832 to 1838. The French translation of Lachat, which at times omits whole paragraphs, is very deficient.
20. Par. 37.
21. Par. 32.
22. Ibid.
23. Par. 53.
24. Par. 57.
25. Par. 37.
26. Ibid.
27. Ibid.
28. Par. 43.
29. Par. 48.
30. R. Aubert, "La géographie ecclésiastique au XIXe siècle," especially pp. 36ff., in *L'Ecclésiologie au XIXe siècle*.

# Chapter 8
# The Ecclesiology of Newman

Another body of ecclesiological work, perhaps of no less import than Moehler's, was sketched out in England at about the same time, in complete independence of Moehler though under analogous influences: the work of Newman. Newman's thoughts are not conveyed in a systematic work but in a series of complementary essays. On many points they cross-check with Mochler's work and complete it.

Worked out within Anglicanism and then in the Catholic Church, which he joined in 1845, Newman's ecclesiological research was pursued in both churches in continuous fashion. It can be said he "transferred" to the Catholic Church because he recognized that the Church he had sought to revitalize in Anglicanism existed, in fact, only in Catholicism. However, much time was needed for Catholics to accept the vision of the Church that he, like Moehler, developed from a study of the fathers—but Newman's thought, which was deeply impregnated by biblical culture, had hardly any equivalent among nineteenth-century theologians.[1]

## I. Newman and the Oxford Movement

The genesis of Newman's thought, particularly on the ecclesiological plane, can be understood only within the context of the Oxford Movement, whose leader he had become at the very moment he was separating from it.

In many respects, the Oxford Movement can be considered a revival, after two centuries, of Catholic tradition in Anglicanism, of which Hooker was the initiator and which continued with the Caroline Divines. Abruptly interrupted by the failure of the policies of Charles I and Laud, this movement may seem to have been uprooted by Cromwell's Commonwealth; however, this was not the case. In isolated cases, such as that of Jeremy Taylor, who took refuge in his "Golden Grove," it had been kept alive, though more or less secretly. On the continent, among the *émigrés,* Cosin and others developed it forcefully. With the return of the Stuarts, it was revived in the Church of England; but a blow that may have seemed fatal was dealt it by the fall of the Stuarts under James II. Its adherents' fidelity to the dethroned monarch and their refusal to swear allegiance to William and Mary excluded them from the official English church and obliged them to continue clandestinely.

Yet these "Nonjurors" had descendants. It may be that the circumstances that led them, sometimes despite themselves, to maintain and develop the Catholic tradition in groups that were free from the "guardianship" of the state prepared the way for their distant successors to espouse a policy of independence from the state, which was to be the new and possibly most characteristic trait of the Oxford Movement from its beginnings.

The immediate origin of this movement was the policy the British government took to suppress a series of episcopal sees in the established Anglican Church in Ireland, which Newman's friends in England denounced as an intolerable intrusion by the state in the affairs of the church. As a reaction, they asserted the profound autonomy of the church with respect to the state, even when the church found herself bound to the state through circumstances. In the Church of England, this was the occasion for a hardy renaissance of the idea of the continuity of the Anglican Church with the primitive Church through the apostolic succession of Anglican bishops. The Tractarian Movement followed upon this. Under the impetus of Newman, and with the collaboration of Keble, Froude and Pusey, it revived the theses of the Caroline Divines and the Nonjurors, although the former developed them much further than had been foreseen. The result was an astonishing reanimation of traditional Catholicism in Anglicanism. Yet without the deep traces left in the Church of England by the Wesleyan Movement, this revival would not have had the spiritual and intellectual fullness that was to characterize the Oxford Movement. Like Newman, Pusey owed it a great deal.

Newman had awakened, at age fifteen, to a personal spiritual life through the influence of Mayer, one of the "Evangelicals" who had kept the best of Wesleyanism alive (i.e. the need for personal consecration, without reservation, to the God of the Gospel, revealed in Christ, by and for the testimony of his followers). Hence an at least implicit notion of the Church persisted; in which the religious individual could neither remain passive under grace nor surrender to its power except within the community of believers.

The second generation, with Ward and the Oakeleys, tended to turn the movement to a pure and simple assimilation by Anglicanism of the notions and practices of the contemporary Catholic Church, and therefore in the direction of a narrow anti-Protestantism. On the other hand, Newman, even after his conversion to Catholicism, remained faithful to the ideal of a church returning to its original model and never adopted a simply anti-Protestant attitude, which was typical of a Counter Reformation spirit.

It goes without saying that this instinctive refusal won Newman even less comprehension in the Church he joined than he had experienced in the one he left. But this is precisely what gives his work an import that goes considerably beyond the circumstances in which it originated and developed.

The notion that Newman fashioned for himself of this Catholic attitude, which is truly faithful to the whole of tradition and constitutes the real answer to the difficulties raised by the Protestant Reformation, is fully expressed in his *Lectures on Justification,* to which we will return. But his properly ecclesiological ideas are clarified in a series of other works.

We must familiarize ourselves with a number of parochial sermons which he developed for his congregation of St. Mary's, not in a systematic form but with great richness—his vision of a church that had been brought to full awareness of herself. Other works, in which more technical statements can be found of his thoughts on such a church, are his lectures in *Prophetical Office of the Church,* the fifth and last of his Oxford University sermons, and his *Essay on the Development of Christian Doctrine,* which returns to one of his major themes. All these works are from his Anglican period, but he republished them when he became a Catholic, after adding a series of notes to *Prophetical Office* which specified the points on which his thought had consequently evolved. We must also mention the short "Catholic work," *On Consulting the Faithful in Matters of Doctrine,* which developed a theme he had only hinted at in *Prophetical Office,* as well as the preface he wrote at the end of his life for the republication of this volume and related texts (under the title *Via Media*).

Again, none of these texts is a total synthesis of the "problem" of the Church; but they develop a series of closely coordinated points in his thought that study this problem, which are no less important than Moehler's.

## *II. The People of God in Newman's* Sermons

To our knowledge, no study has yet been made of Newman's Anglican sermons from the viewpoint of his doctrine on the Church.[2] This is regrettable, for they contain abundant matter on this subject and furnish an essential basis for understanding the most theological developments of his other works.

Indeed, the sermons show the importance that Newman, because of his meditation on Scripture, attached to the biblical notion "the People of God." The Church of the New Testament always appeared to him to be in discontinuous continuity with Israel (this paradoxical formula seems the only way to describe the situation). Thus the progressive formation of Israel prepared for the Church of Christ. In both, human history sketches the evolvement of a providential line—a "God party," as Newman might say—which is differentiated and separated from mankind in general, only to become capable of renewing it entirely. In the New Covenant, as in the Old, the regrouping can be made only on the basis of purification; judgment is not set against salvation but is its inevitable counterpart. This regrouping is a "remnant," and a remnant apparently deprived of all hope of ultimately "winning out," that carries the destiny of the whole, which it will finally make triumph. The Christian Church, beginning with Christ himself, understands herself in this way, as the materialization and fulfillment of the people born of Abraham, although she had broken from them. And the Church of the New Covenant, in turn, will make the transition to the Church of Eternity only by a similar development, marked by the cross and by division, in order to achieve, only in the Kingdom, the definitive peace and glory of the Resurrection.[3]

With Newman, this vision is nourished by the exegeses of the fathers, especially those of Alexandria. Long before such contemporary critical studies as those (especially) of Fr. de Lubac, Newman saw profound theological truth behind their allegories, which at first sight seemed disconcerting, and how essential this truth is for Christian theology and, above all, for the awareness the nascent Church had of herself by reading the Scriptures in the light of Christ.[4]

The Church as materialization and fulfillment, and again as preparation and promise—the Church necessarily becoming, an unbreakable unity in which she never ceases dying and being reborn; and finally the Church structured by the progressive realization of her destiny, but composed of the ineluctable conjunction of multiple individual destinies, in which no one has a role that is indifferent or simply passive—these are only a few basic teachings of these texts.[5]

As has been shown in the admirable anthology of Fr. Przywara, S. J., *A Newman Synthesis,* this biblical vision of the life of the Church and the Christian could be summed up, according to Newman, by the title of the famous essay of Miguel de Unamuno, "La Agonía del Cristianismo" (i.e. the struggle to the death, which is also a struggle against the death of Christianity), despite the constant serenity of Newman's thought. This explains the irritation that the work and the person of Newman have always caused in Christians who are too facilely optimistic, whether "integralists" like W. G. Ward or "progressive" like Charles Kingsley. On all these ecclesiastic triumphalisms, as with all naively euphoric "openings to the world," Newman's lucidity will always have the effect of corrosive irony. There is hardly another Catholic theologian who so completely escapes Barth's reproach of wanting to substitute a *theologia gloriae* for the *theologia crucis.* Certainly, glory is always present in Newman, however hidden it may be in the cross, which explains his basic serenity. On the other hand, contrary to Barth, he never allows hope to separate itself from the mystery of the cross: even in his eschatology, there is no automatic, complete restoration.

## III. *The Tradition of the Church according to Newman's* Prophetical Office

Again, it is in the context of these sermons that Newman's more technically theological texts on the Church must be placed to understand their exact import. *The Prophetical Office of the Church* centers on a view of tradition in the Church which is expressed *ex professo* in one masterful page, but it dominates the work and, we might say, all of Newman's ecclesiological thought and ecclesiastical activity.[6]

In *Prophetical Office,* tradition appears as substantially one, though it manifests itself in a double form or, rather, double aspect. There is "prophetical tradition," as he calls it, which is basic. It is the life of truth in the whole Church, in all her members, which never develops in isolation in either but in the union of all. But great or lesser holiness, the gifts of grace or nature that are unequally distributed, produces the phenomenon that she has her particular development in each Christian as well. The life of the body exists only in the members, but there is no one in whom the Church develops independently from her development in all the others. This vast totality, which is complex and diverse, is the fruit of the Spirit in new humanity, even though, inevitably, many dregs are mixed in. The prophetic tradition is continually exposed to alteration or corruption—and nevertheless, so to speak, is fructified by being frittered away infinitely.

The constant task of reassembling it while disassembling it, and also differentiating its authentic interpretation from what has no right to this title, belongs to the "episcopal tradition." Yet this tradition is not different from the prophetic tradition; it cannot even be distinguished from it. Immersed in it, it only authenticates, with the authority that belongs to the successors of the Apostles alone, what at a particular time must be taken from it to distinguish what is essential from secondary or questionable proliferations. Again, it is not capable of exhausting its richness and the variety in its definitions, which, to be correctly understood, demand to be replaced in this vast context, outside of which they would lose their meaning.

The most eminent representatives of the *episcopal* tradition are also the most eminent representatives of the *prophetic* tradition. But in this regard it cannot be said they enjoy a particular charism as bishops. The definitions they canonize, the broadest expressions (e.g. the liturgies) they accredit with their authority, may very well not be their own, personal work. Indeed, in contradistinction to the apostles, whose successors they are (but not their replacements), no charism of inspiration is attached permanently to their function. Their charism pertains only to judging about the faith, that is, expressions of the faith that have normative value. But it is only in constant connection with the whole life of the body, of which they are the guides, that their function can be exercised; therefore always in the interior of this body.[7]

Fr. Henry Tristram (in the article "Newman" in *D.T.C.*, signed "Bacchus et Tristram") deserves credit for being the first to point out the central importance of this view in Newman's work. Newman would have given him fundamental complements in the study *On Consulting the Faithful,* which, at the time, exposed him to the worst misunderstandings of theologians, who were not at all open to these perspectives.[8]

## *IV.* The Laity and the Faith of the Church

In this work, Newman derived support from Pius IX's consultation of the bishops preceding the definition of the Immaculate Conception of the Virgin in 1854. Underlining the fact that the pope asked the bishops to inquire into the general feeling of the faithful about this belief, Newman emphasized that this inquiry was merely an application of a constant practice of the Church.

Her definitions are never mere oracles of authority, falling from on high on a crowd of unprepared and passive subjects. Always, she merely defines a belief which already exists, in the whole body of the faithful, even though its expression has been more or less latent. They thus verify the constant principle that the faith is never the faith that is imposed by an authority, cut off from a body it dominates, in a simply external fashion, but the faith of the whole Church. If this is the case even for definitions of the truths of faith, the Church, for an even stronger reason, cannot, in matters that touch more particularly on the laity and their life in the world, govern them and ignore their experience. Quite the contrary. The Church can govern them only by paying closest attention to their experience.

There is hardly any need to emphasize how far ahead Newman was of what has since been called "the promotion of the laity." He had written his article at a moment when he was concerned with providing the Catholic laity, called to exercise great responsibilities in the world, with a training that could prepare them for their task. He wanted to attract attention to the impossible state the Church was in with respect to working in this direction without their collaboration. But it would singularly restrict the import of his analysis if we reduce it to recognition of an activity that is proper to the laity simply with respect to the world.

As important as this problem was in his eyes, it could not be resolved if one did not, first of all, acknowledge that the laity in the Church, and even those in the sacred domain of the faith, have a role that goes beyond passive acquiescence. He went so far as to recall how the history of Arianism, which he had studied closely, irrefutably shows that in certain crises the episcopal hierarchy, divided or frightened, can keep quiet or speak too clearly (even if, thanks to God's providential care of his Church, it never came to their formally canonizing error). In such cases, he dared say, we observe a temporary suspension of episcopal authority. Then—as the Arian crisis showed between 331 and ca. 375—it is the testimony given to the truth by the totality of the faithful which maintains it, toward and against everyone, until the hierarchy again understands and canonizes this belief of the lowliest members.

It does not seem that Catholic theology has ever gone so far, and with such sure discernment, in affirmation of the active role of the whole body of the Church in the living preservation of the faith. But few theologians at this time were prepared for the agonizing revision it required in certain representations of the *Ecclesia docens,* in contradistinction to the *Ecclesia discens.* Did not these two aspects unconsciously form two distinct churches (so to speak), one purely active and the other purely passive, that were merely set side by side?

## V. *The Life of Faith in the Church:* Essay on Development

This calling up of the life of truth in the whole Church, as Newman understood it through a theology replete with an incomparable historical sense, is clarified by remarks he formulated in the first part of his fifth and last Oxford University sermon. Indeed, he shows that the truth in the word of God is not communicated to us in a technical, philosophically worked-out form. It is proposed to us immediately, by divine revelation in figurative expressions that are directly accessible to the believing assent of the most simple minds. These figures permit us to understand the objects of the faith as living realities which our conceptual analysis cannot exhaust, but through these basic expressions the faith adheres to its objects from the outset, as through a vital communion. Analysis will specify and conceptually articulate this grasp, without dispelling its mystery. Dogmatic definitions judge the substantial conformity of these constructions to the goal of faith. But no more than the theologies they sift through the judgment of faith, the most authentic definitions, even if they preserve us from interpretations of the divine word that would disfigure it, cannot exhaust the content of the statement of the objects of faith made by this word. Therefore, definitions can never simply be substituted for it. Indeed, they never cease being dependent on and referring to the content.

Newman's *Grammar of Assent* justifies this presentation of the status of revealed truth in the Church and in the heart of the faithful by developing it in concrete examples. It draws the major distinction between a simple *notional* grasp of statements of the faith and the *real* grasp, which is that of the faith itself and which, beyond the statements, is indispensable but always deficient, and which alone reunites the believer with the object of faith in its mystery.[9]

We have traced the final step of the *Essay on Development* through which Newman's spirit came to the Catholic faith. And this work goes back to the general theme of the fifteenth sermon, while shedding many of its secondary aspects. However, it does not merely develop this theme of doctrinal development, which was central in this sermon; it adds essential complements.[10]

However much the *Essay* concentrates on the doctrinal problem, it does not separate it from the totality of the development of the Church. This leads Newman to specify that the doctrinal developments proceed not simply from previously explicated doctrinal data but just as much from what implicit truth there may be in the behavior of the Church and Christians in the moral, ascetical, liturgical, and institutional orders. The truth of Christianity, because it is a truth inseparable from life, cannot be expressed simply side by side with life, but only in connection with it.

Later, Newman was to observe how much the importance of this problem of development in doctrinal matters (which he emphasized) was in accord with a general movement of thought at this time. He pointed out the convergence of his views with certain ideas of Coleridge, though he did not seem to become aware of this until long after the composition of the *Essay*. This parallelism is not surprising when we observe the extent that both men benefited from a long, meditative reading of Hooker, with whom the idea of development in the Church seems prophetic—by contrast with the theological staticity of most religious thinkers of the seventeenth century.

Newman also brought up the parallelism of his research with Darwin's in biology. Since the end of the century, many have grasped this analogy, but they drew an interpretation of the *Essay* which compromised it with the cause of Modernism. This interpretation is a complete misconception (which unfortunately is not dissipated by all of Newman's exegetes). Nothing can be more contrary to the faithful interpretation of the *Essay* than to see in it an apology for a theological evolutionism. In this regard, the utilization of Newman by Catholic theologians—even those far removed from Modernism, particularly but not exclusively Mariologists—in favor of a proliferation of dogmas, identified purely and simply with "dogmatic progress," is no less a misconception. Newman, like the fathers who inspired him, beginning with St. Athanasius and the Cappadocians, never tired of recalling that the Church does not dogmatize for pleasure; she does so only when constrained by the necessity of opposing heretics. But the multiplication of formulas that inevitably results is a mixed blessing. It fragments a truth that is one, and to retain that truth in its unbreakable unity, it may be necessary to return to formulas that were set forth in the purity and simplicity of the immediate expressions of the divine word.

It can be said that "development" for Newman is what "community" was for Moehler. Newman did not undertake a defense of development as such, any more than Moehler wanted to defend community, no matter what its sense.

As a historian, Newman considered development in the Church, even on the level of doctrine, an undeniable fact. But he verified that this phenomenon is but one particular case among many. He emphasized that all doctrine that lasts over generations is subject to this law. With penetrating insight, he examined many examples other than Catholic doctrine, notably Calvinism. But the question he posed with respect to Catholic developments is their legitimacy. In other words, the simple fact of manifest development cannot justify Catholic doctrine as it is presented to us after 2,000 years of Christianity. It is demonstration (supposing it is possible) of the fact that this development—and this development alone, among all the developments presented by all the Christian churches—is the legitimate development. This is to say, it is a question of determining which developments respond to the internal exigencies of the authentic, living truth of faith and which, on the other hand, are a debasement or corruption of it.

This comes down to justifying the role exercised in the Catholic Church by the *episcopal tradition* within the *prophetic tradition,* as judge and guardian of the prophetic tradition. And this corresponds exactly to what Moehler meant when he insisted on the importance of written tradition in allowing the faithful, and the Church herself, at all times to verify the coincidence of their consciousness of the truth with that of the whole Church since the beginning. Every effort in the *Essay,* therefore, is exerted to show the "notes" by which authentic development is differentiated from nonauthentic development. We shall limit ourselves to recalling them briefly, as Newman set them down.

The first note may be considered to encompass all the others, and it is related more to the Church herself than to her doctrine. It is the preservation of the original type throughout all developments. The Church of the New Testament and of the Fathers, Newman observes, is one, and conscious not only of her unity but of her uniqueness and her ability to speak with authority in the name of the One who sent her. Only the Catholic Church presents this fundamental character.[12]

The second note details and deepens the first; it is the "conservation of principles." The great New Testament statements on the redemptive Incarnation, the Resurrection, and the Last Judgment, together with the sacraments that bring us the very content of these saving mysteries, and acceptance of the apostolic authority and ministry as coming from Christ himself—all this is still the basis of present-day Catholicism, as it was for the primitive Church.[13]

Then comes the "power of assimilation." At this point it becomes apparent that humankind is not the subject of static conservatism. The whole reality of the Church—and all her constitutive principles—is not afraid of facing up to the world or mingling with it. In the encounter, this prevails over all the forces of opposition or dissolution, so that everything that is positive in the realities the Church meets in the world is in turn accepted, and transfigured, by the Christian spirit.

On the other hand, heretical systems are obliged to close themselves off from the world in order to survive and develop, as in a laboratory retort, or they allow themselves to break up and, finally, assimilate by contact. The evolved forms of liberal Protestantism may retain the "cover" of Christian formulas, but they no longer express anything but the content of philosophies of the time.

The authentic Christianity of the Church, on the contrary, has taken possession of human philosophies and refashioned them in order to render them useful in expressing Christian dogma.[14] Authentic developments can be difficult to foresee before the event; but once they appear, it is always possible to establish a logical bond between them and prior formulations or realizations. All of this, both the old and the new, adheres to the particular time or period.[15]

Furthermore, very few developments that on first sight seem to be novelties without precedents are impossible to anticipate. It was only at Nicaea that a definitive formula left no room for ambiguity on the divinity of Christ, but equivalent affirmations are found from the time of the first Christian generations, even though they do not have the clarity or precision they were later to acquire. The same is true for dogmas and realities whose definition apparently was long delayed, such as the papacy; yet St. Leo, in the fifth century, spoke no less strongly on the matter than the so-called ultramontane theology of the nineteenth century.[16]

Furthermore, legitimate inventions are recognized as enlightening and strengthening what has gone before, not as diminishing or altering. Far from voiding and replacing old formulas, the new formulas presuppose them and support and assure their permanent efficacy.[17]

Newman's last note, like the first, observes the chronic energy of both true development and the type that has been preserved down to our own time. Whereas schisms and heresies have periods of sudden development and maturity, then an apparently irremediable decline (when they do not disappear altogether), the vitality of authentic development is nourished by the very difficulties it encounters, surmounts them, despite temporary setbacks or fluctuations, and is apparently unexhausted and inexhaustible.[18]

These seven notes do not claim to be exhaustive. In the view of demonstration by "convergent probabilities," explained in detail by the *Grammar of Assent,* they must be considered a body of signs that are sufficient for the faith, for free adhesion of the mind under the influx of grace from the Divine Spirit, and they are fully rational.[19]

# VI. *The Preface of* Via Media

The Church's visibility and unity, however real, are not dispensations from faith, properly so called; they require faith. This is pointed up by several of

Newman's finest analyses, which are introduced in the preface to the *Via Media,* where, at the end of his life, he reproduced (with autocritical notes) his *Prophetical Office.*[20] Here—even more than with *Essay on Development*—misunderstandings and misconceptions have accumulated. In the notes he added to *Prophetical Office,* Newman refuted certain accusations he had earlier brought or written against the Catholic Church—on the whole, formal accusations of doctrinal errors. But these notes, in general, retract nothing of *other* criticisms that bear on the specific behavior of Catholic authority or rather widespread tendencies among Catholics in devotion or political action. In an annexed document in the second volume, Newman reproduced a series of retractions, aimed especially at the papacy, which he felt in conscience obliged to make public, after a fresh examination of the facts, even before his conversion.

It is legitimate to infer that the book's other, often very harsh criticisms were not expunged or refuted because, at the end of his Catholic life, as at the time of his conversion, they seemed to him well founded. This inference or implication is abundantly verified by his correspondence (which will soon be published in its entirety). Thus the object of his preface was to explain these facts. But the explanation—contrary to what too many hasty apologists suppose—was certainly not, in Newman's mind, a justification.

The principle developed by the preface is that the prophetical office of the Church is but one of her offices, to which must be joined the function of government and the priestly office, which Newman extends to everything in the liturgical or devotional domain. According to Newman, possession by the true Church of a principle of doctrinal infallibility, attached to imperative definitions of the faith (unless we posit a chimerical supposition of absolute wisdom and perfect holiness in all holders of Church authority—and, it might be necessary to add, in the entire body of the faithful), cannot anticipate every shift in the exercise of these diverse functions. Yet such shifts are always the result of sin and human weakness and, particularly, insufficient lucidity in those who possess authority. Infallibility can therefore be considered normal in the conditions in which God willed to bring about mankind's salvation, that is, not through incessant miracles but by taking men as they are, including those to whom he entrusted the highest responsibilities. Undoubtedly, his providence always preserves the Church from foundering definitively, and this is why she is assured of infallibility—but only in this very restricted sense: that she will never, as a body, formally profess an error that is destructive of the faith or, consequently, that her responsible leaders would impose it with authority. This allows for all sorts of deviations in the masses and even positive wrongdoing by the leaders.

If all this is normal in this very precise sense, it must in no sense be considered normative. Because all these imperfections, which can be very serious, are the result of sin or (at least) insufficient wisdom, they must unceasingly be overcome by the holiness that is associated with attempts of critical lucidity—a critique that is undoubtedly constructive and unflinching. This, we may say, is the meaning of most of Newman's activity once he became a Catholic.

His preface is aimed not at an ideal description of the functioning of the Church but at defining the precise point at which an effort of purification must be undertaken, as well as constantly renewed endeavor at reforms. To do this, the Church should not be mesmerized by details or strike out blindly in every direction. It must propose to reestablish (insofar as possible) the always unstable balance and cohesion between its complementary functions of government, doctrinal teaching, and sacral activities. This balance is never completely attained and is constantly threatened; it is in the nature of things that this be so. But it is a basic requirement of Christianity that this situation be constantly borne in mind, so that this balance is constantly reestablished—not haphazardly but in accordance with a coherent view.

This preface is not, then, a justification of the Church in her empirical state, at whatever period in her history, but the outline of a program to be revived and unceasingly pursued in a Church which, to be the true Church of Christ, remains no less an *Ecclesia ex hominibis* and therefore the *Ecclesia semper reformanda.*

Whatever the intentional discretion with which Newman expressed himself in this preface, our interpretation is the only one that is consistent with the general argument, or verified by the whole direction of his written works and his entire life in Catholicism.

## Notes

1. On Newman's life, The most thorough work at present is Meriol Trevor, *Newman* (2 vols.; London, 1962). A synthesis of the most up-to-date research on Newman's thought will be found in Louis Cognet, *Newman, ou la recherche de la vérité* (Paris, 1968).
2. *Parochial and Plain Sermons* (8 vols.; London, 1834– , and republication by Copeland in 1868); also *Sermons on Subjects of the Day* (London, 1843, republished by Copeland in 1869). On Newman and Scripture, see J. Seynaeve, *Cardinal Newman's Doctrine on Holy Scripture* (Louvain, 1953).
3. Cf. nos. 8, 20, 21 of vol. 2 of *Parochial and Plain Sermons;* nos. 1, 2,

3, 4, 5, 16, 17 of vol. 3; nos. 7, 8, 10, 11 of vol. 4; nos. 10, 13, 16 of vol. 6; no. 9 of vol. 7; nos. 3 and 4 of vol. 8; and most of *Sermons on Subjects of the Day,* especially nos. 12–18.

4. We know the famous passage from the *Apologia* on the effect produced on him by his reading of the Alexandrine fathers (pp. 26ff. of the Longmans ed.). Also, we must not forget that *Tract 89* was composed by his friend John Keble on this subject, the allegorical exegesis of the fathers.

5. Cf., with several of the texts mentioned, nos. 19–25 of *Sermons on Subjects of the Day* and, in *Parochial and Plain Sermons,* nos. 2, 4, 10, 22 of vol. 2; nos. 14 and 15 of vol. 3; nos. 6, 7, 19, 20, 22 of vol. 4; nos. 1, 11, 12 of vol. 5; and nos. 9, 14, 17 of vol. 6.

6. Published in 1837, the *Prophetical Office of the Church* was republished by Newman in the first volume of *Via Media* in 1877, with an introduction and notes that we shall mention further on. Newman's teaching on tradition, which perhaps finds its most important expression in this work, has been studied by G. Biemer, *Überlieferung und Offenbarung. Die Lehre von der Tradition nach John Henry Newman* (Freiburg im Breisgau, 1961) (a work invaluable for the texts it brings together but spoiled by a few gross material errors, such as attribution to Newman of a book of Manning!), and J. Stern, *Bible et Tradition chez Newman* (Paris, 1967) (a particularly interesting work in ch. 5 and 7, which retrace the genesis of the idea of development in Newman and endeavors to interpret it exactly).

7. *Via Media,* 1:249–251. Cf. *Apologia,* p. 112 in the Longmans ed. (1902).

8. Republished by J. Coulson (London, 1961).

9. *An Essay in Aid of a Grammar of Assent* (1870).

10. *An Essay on the Development of Christian Doctrine* (1845).

11. It is curious that, up to now, no one seems to have located this source, yet it is enough to read the third book of *The Laws of Ecclesiastical Polity,* particularly the conclusion, for this to become evident (cf. also ch. IV). It is true that Hooker, in what concerned him, excluded as a principle of development what he considered to be doctrine that is necessary for salvation; but according to him, all the rest, including the basic structure of the Church, is subject to it. What is more, the problem of book III, even then, was Newman's problem: How differentiate authentic developments from those which are not? It is clear that Hooker is also the source of analogous ideas that are found again in Coleridge.

12. P. 171 of the Longmans ed.

13. Pp. 178ff.

14. Pp. 185ff.

15. Pp. 189ff.

16. Pp. 195ff.

17. Pp. 199ff.

18. Pp. 203ff.

19. The best interpretation of Newman's idea of development, restored to the body of Newman's thought, still to be that of J. H. Walgrave, *Newman, le Développement du Dogme* (Tournai-Paris, 1957). The brilliant essay of N. Lash, "Second Thoughts on Walgrave's 'Newman' " (*Downside Review* [Oct. 1969], p. 339), gives an interesting glimpse of the most recent discussions on the problem and demonstrates that Newman did not treat all aspects of it (which had never been his intention). But to us, he does not seem to have grasped as exactly as Walgrave how the question is situated within Newman's thought, or, even less, perceived the exact import of the dogmatic formulas according to Newman.

20. See above, n. 6 of this chapter.

# Chapter 9
# The Awakening of the Church and Nineteenth-Century Protestantism

The Oxford Movement,[1] by which Newman was led to rediscover the Church, was not a unique or isolated phenomenon in the nineteenth century in the churches of the Reformation. In the Lutheran world in particular, but not exclusively, there was hardly a country where more or less analogous movements did not arise. Other than in Anglicanism, these movements did not go as far, perhaps, or as quickly recover various elements of Catholic tradition. On the other hand, because they were less "reactionary" than the first generations of Anglo-Catholicism of the nineteenth century, they were more often more positive in reconciling the best of the Protestant Reformation with Catholic tradition.

It is also true that, more than the Oxford Movement, these other movements continued the religious renaissance that was bound up with Pietism and went beyond it—even if, too soon, they criticized the latter's insufficiencies.

All these movements, as well as the Oxford Movement, owe a great deal to the general atmosphere of Romanticism, particularly its "rehabilitation" of the Middle Ages and, more generally, its reaction against the individualism and rationalism of the Enlightenment. This can be understood all the better since Romanticism, in its Germanic or Anglo-Saxon forms, had sources in common with Pietism, even though Pietism was not always its immediate source.

## I. Grundtvig and Danish Lutheranism

This connection is particularly evident in Nicolai Frederik Grundtvig, a Danish thinker and churchman, who was virtually a contemporary of Kierkegaard, even though his name is practically unknown outside his native country, where he had much influence.[2]

Grundtvig had been brought from rationalism to living faith through a typically Pietist conversion. But this, in a renewed Lutheran orthodoxy, caused him to rediscover the Church as the sole teacher of the faith and her sacraments as the faith's necessary nourishment. For him, it was confession of the faith of the Church, expressed chiefly in the Apostles' Creed, the baptismal creed, which is the only possible basis of the Christian's faith. Scripture itself, far from being abandoned to individual exegesis and its dangers, can be read with profit only in this light. This is the essential thesis of his book against liberal theology, *The Reply of the Church*. Thus the Church must be the educator not only of individuals but of Christian peoples, and must inspire their whole life.

A poet of a popular inspiration that was hardly less fertile than that of the Wesley brothers, though superior in quality, Grundtvig had a lasting influence on the Danish church by his *Salmbog* (a combination prayer book and hymnal). His influence on this church extended the renewal of the Christian community in a renovation of all the traditional popular culture and the first movements of "social Christianity" of the nineteenth century.

He went to England at the time the Oxford Movement was entering its period of crisis and conflict with the Anglican authorities, and he felt a large sympathy for its inspiration, though he criticized Anglo-Catholics for what seemed to him a simple Romanizing reaction, a search for "papist" authority without the pope.

## II. Henric Schartau and Swedish Lutheranism

Less brilliant but hardly less interesting is another Scandinavian personality, who belonged to an earlier generation, and one whom the church of Sweden can claim as the first pioneer of what was to be called the Ecclesiastical Awakening. We are speaking of Henric Schartau, whom the Swedish archbishop, Yngve Brilioth, compared to Wesley, although he added that if

Wesley could call the world his parish, Schartau would have said *his* parish was the world.[3]

Schartau too was a convert from Pietism. But a distinctive characteristic of his conversion was that it came during a traditional Lutheran service, during the liturgical recitation of the confession of sins, followed by the collective absolution, in the "fore-mass" that Olaus Petri translated and elaborated in the sixteenth century. As he said, he suddenly received the words of the priest as "the words of Jesus, the promise of Jesus, the assurance of Jesus, based on the redemption by his blood."

This conversion was caused by the influence of the Moravian disciples of Zinzendorf, and it was nurtured by this influence. But all his work as a preacher and pastor integrated him to a renovated vision of the traditional Church, in which he inculcated the reciprocal duty of the Church: to proclaim the Gospel of salvation in its liturgical and sacramental celebration, to assimilate this doctrine of life in a participation that is both communitarian and personal.

## III. *Wilhelm Löhe and Lutheranism in Germany and America*

Undoubtedly, the most remarkable renovator of Lutheranism in the nineteenth century was a German, the pastor of Neuendettelsau, Wilhelm Löhe.[4] Born in 1808 at Fürth in Bavaria, he was later to recall the first and indelible impressions he received at the morning celebration of the eucharist sung in St. Michael's Church by Pastor Fronsmüller, following the old Lutheran rite. Although subsequently, during his studies at Erlangen, he was decisively influenced by a Reformed pastor (touched by Pietism), Christian Krafft, and was a pupil of Schleiermacher in Berlin, his personal study of Luther, in the light of the great dogmaticians of the school of Gerhard (especially Hollaz), formed him definitively in a renovated Lutheran orthodoxy. As was the case for Arndt and Gerhard in the seventeenth century, Löhe revived the Catholic virtualities in resistance to the reunion with the Reformed churches that was imposed on the Lutherans. The attempt was renewed at this time on the basis of the dogmatic liberalism of Schleiermacher. The reaction with Löhe, more than with anyone else, brought forth a positive renaissance of Catholic tradition, preserved in older Lutheranism, on the dogmatic, liturgical, and spiritual levels.

His principal book, published in 1843, *Drei Bücher von der Kirche,* is like the charter of this renaissance. The catholicity of the "true Church," expressed not only in the living interpretation of the divine word and the celebration of the traditional sacraments but also in the apostolic ministry, is opposed—for the first time in Lutheranism with such clarity—to the Church's subjection to the state.

Löhe completed his ecclesiastical work by a primary endeavor at restoration of monasticism within Protestantism: the foundation of deaconesses, who, as he conceived them, were not only to be something like Protestant Sisters of Charity, but to exercise their charitable function on the basis of a virginity consecrated to Christ, which was taken directly from the fathers of early monasticism.

In the same vein, he introduced the sacramental practice of confession and penance, and even the anointing of the sick. His notion of pastoral ministry is perhaps the most Catholic-tending of his teaching, although for him the simple presbyteral succession sufficed to graft it onto the apostolic ministry.

Supported by the liturgical restoration of the Prussian Kliefoth, this scriptural, sacramental, and patristic neo-Lutheranism had a more remarkable expansion in America than in Germany. The German Lutherans who emigrated there *en masse,* to escape the Union of Prussia and its equivalents, brought with them the principles of these two renovators and were able to develop them freely. They produced the first Lutheran churches that were detached from the state, which were more "Catholic" than those that had allowed themselves to become subject to the state could have remained or become again.

Even in France, Lutheranism (which up to that time was more "Bucerian" than Lutheran) in Alsace and Montbéliard and later, after 1870, in Paris (where it had existed in the first part of the nineteenth century), experienced a lively impetus from this German renaissance, with Frédéric Horning at Saint-Pierre-le-Jeune in Strasbourg and with Louis Meyer, first in Strasbourg and later in Paris. In our own day, the movement of Berneuchen and the Michaelsbruderschaft, which was to emerge from it under the impulse of German pastors such as Asmussen and Stählin, found some of its first and most active adherents in this Alsatian Lutheranism, influenced by the "awakening" of Löhe and Kliefoth.[5]

Generally, it was in this "Evangelical Catholicism" of this renovated Lutheranism, as much as in the Anglo-Catholicism revitalized by the Oxford Movement, that the Protestant ecumenism of the twentieth century had its strongest roots.

## IV. In the Reformed Churches

More slowly and sporadically, the Reformed churches were affected in the nineteenth and twentieth centuries by analogous movements. Not finding the body of traditional factors that had been preserved in Germany by old Lutheranism, they generally began with attempts at liturgical restorations as influenced by Anglicanism. This was the case in France at the end of the nineteenth century, with the liturgy introduced by Eugéne Bersier in his Reformed parish of the Etiole in Paris. An analogous movement developed in the twentieth century in the Presbyterian Church of Scotland, around the "Iona Community." Moreover—exceptional in Presbyterianism—it benefited from ancient local traditions that had been preserved in Knox's *Book of Common Order,* whose eucharistic liturgy had remained more profoundly traditional than that of Cranmer's *Prayer-Book.*[6]

The most interesting of these Reformed groups was formed between the two world wars at Lausanne, around Pastor Pasquier and his periodical *Église et Liturgie.* Here, from the beginning, was an explicit reconstruction of the traditional Church, seeking herself around a liturgical and sacramental renovation. The principal accomplishment of this group was to be the community of Taizé and the essentially ecumenical, spiritual, liturgical, and theological movement of which it was to become the heart.

## V. "Social Christianity"

Nevertheless, the broadest preparation in modern Reformed Protestantism for a renewal of ecclesiological notions has not been in such movements. Again, these churches had too little ancient groundwork, so that "innovations" seemed like foreign imports. Rather, the renewal spread through these churches in the form of the Christian social movement, in connection with the missionary movement.

We have seen, however, that the first attempt at "social Christianity" in the modern sense was that of the Lutheran, Grundtvig; and an analogous movement was taking shape at the same time in England in connection with the Chartist Movement. Its precursor was an Anglican clergyman of the evangelical party, Thomas Spencer (uncle of the philosopher Herbert Spencer), but the organizers were a layman, John Malcolm Ludlow, who was influenced by the "social Catholics" of the Lamennais group (of which we shall speak), and the preacher and popular Anglican writer Charles Kingsley. Ludlow's most profound inspirer was the very original theologian (of whom we shall also speak) Frederick Denison Maurice. Starting with the next generation, in the wake of Steward Duckworth Headham (an Anglo-Catholic priest who also was influenced by Maurice), the heirs of the Oxford Movement took a more and more important part. At the beginnings of the Labor Party, they encountered Nonconformists and, particularly, Methodists from Wales.[7]

In Germany, the Christian socialism of Naumann and the Christian social ethnics of Nathusius were inspired at the end of the nineteenth century by the same concerns.[8] But Christoff Blumhardt, son of the famous Pietist and apocalyptic pastor of Bad Boll, Johann Christoff Blumhardt, was the founder of the most effective movement, relaunched at the beginning of the twentieth century by Hermann Kutter and Leonhard Ragaz, who was to have a strong influence on the young Karl Barth.[9]

All these initiatives were dominated by the tragic religious alienation brought about for the major part of the worker class by its social alienation, a consequence of the savage development of industrial capitalism. Such endeavors attempted to meet the emancipation movements of this class by seeing in the ideal of the Kingdom of God, to be inaugurated on earth, the sole means of reconciling a society that material interests had torn apart, by its effective rechristianization.

We might think, *a priori,* that such movements would have developed more naturally in the Reformed churches, influenced by Calvinism and its strong notion of the independence of the visible church from the state, an independence combined with the right and the duty of inspiring the state with a Christian politics. In contrast, the Lutheran churches and the Anglican Church, having accepted the sovereignty of the state, seemed committed to a kind of political quietism or, at worst, a paralyzing timidity before the social structures accepted by the state. In fact, however, the first "social Christians" of the churches of the Reformation were a Lutheran, like Grundtvig; Anglicans, like the group that formed around Maurice; and, a bit later, the second- and third-generation Anglo-Catholics of the Oxford Movement. The explanation of this apparent paradox is the connection brought out by Max Weber and R. H. Tawney between the origins of modern capitalism and Calvinist Protestantism. Their persistent attachment to the traditional patriarchal-type society made the Anglicans and the Lutherans much freer to criticize modern society, which had issued from the bourgeois ethic that had been christianized by Calvinists. (The same may be said of the "traditionalist Catholics" in France, among whom were the first "social Catholics," who were opposed by the first "Catholic liberals)." It was only in the Reformed milieus, penetrated by Pietism in the nineteenth century, especially in the form found in Methodism, that the same aspirations were able to develop unhampered.

In the introduction to his *Soziallehren,* Troeltsch underlined the ambiguities inherent in all these movements. What did they mean when they spoke of a "social" Christianity? Undoubtedly, Christianity is essentially social, insofar as it supposes a particular society, the Church; but does it follow (and if so, how?) that it can give its norm to the organization of civil society? (In the Gospels, the Kingdom of God, which is at the core of most of these movements, is assuredly not a kingdom of this world, a kingdom that is in men's power—even believing men—to establish. Hence the paradox that these movements, in which the survivals of Constantinian society were roundly criticized, attempted to set up, *de facto,* a neo-Constantinianism—or progressively renounced the specifically Christian character of their "socialism" in order to adhere to forms of purely "humanist" socialism in the modern sense of the word, whether Marxist or not.

Whatever may be said on this point, the Christian social movement in Protestantism in general, as well as in Catholicism, prepared the way for a renaissance of the sense of the Church as a society of charity, and more precisely of the sense of her necessarily visible unity. Indeed, how could Christians, divided among themselves, boast that they would bring reconciliation to conflicting social classes? How could churches, walled up in their particularism, claim to break the barriers of class egotisms?

## VI. *The Missionary Movement*

It is through an analogous bias that the development of Protestant and Anglican missions in Africa and Asia (so considerable in the nineteenth century) contributed to the same awakening, in the very areas where no spontaneous rediscovery of the traditional Church had yet been produced.

Contrary to the spread of Catholic missions, which coincided with the discovery of the new continents, and which never ceased growing throughout the seventeenth and eighteenth centuries, the different Protestant churches practically ignored the missionary problem up to the time of Pietism. Zinzendorf's Moravian Brethren, the Methodists, and then all the milieus affected by Pietism were the first Reformation churches to disseminate the Christian faith throughout the pagan world. In the nineteenth century, the thrust of this movement became as widespread at that of Catholicism.

But little time elapsed before the disastrous effect of rival implantations of different churches in the same mission fields was felt. How could people preach the gospel of reconciliation when they themselves were not reconciled? It is not surprising that the first world conference of Protestant missions (in Edinburgh in 1910) posed to this body of churches of the Reformation the urgent problem of restoring unity.[10]

## VII. The Birth of Modern Ecumenism

The prophetic expression of the necessity for the churches to reunite if they did not wish to confess their failure in the eyes of the world was given at the Edinburgh congress by the secretary of the Christian Young Peoples' Unions, John Mott. And it is equally understandable that the first world assembly of delegates from these churches, which was called with the objective of recovering unity, was a conference for the coordination of Christian social movements. But it is even more significant that the pioneers of this form of modern ecumenism (which arose at the end of the First World War) came from Lutheran or Anglican milieus that were directly influenced by the movements of "ecclesiastical awakening" that we have described above.

The ecumenical movement of the twentieth century took shape in two distinct organizations. One, which came from the Stockholm conference of 1925, was called Life and Work; it sought to promote unity only on the level of common work in Christian social action. The other, which came from the conference at Lausanne in 1927, was called Faith and Order; it sought to rediscover unity on the properly ecclesiastical level: the faith, the sacraments, and the ministry. Of these two movements (which came to fusion only after the Second World War), the inspiration of the first was a Lutheran from Sweden, the archbishop of Uppsala, Nathan Söderblom. The second resulted from the initiative of an American Episcopalian, Bishop Charles Brent. These movements, which came from the churches of the Reformation, sought from the very beginning, as they laid their groundwork, to obtain the participation of Catholics and Eastern Orthodox. After some hesitation, the Holy See did not believe it could accept the invitation. A number of Orthodox churches (most of them outside Russia) agreed from the beginning to take part in the conferences and in the movements that were associated with them. But from the beginning they stated (and maintained throughout these contacts) that, for Orthodoxy, the one Church that was willed by Christ could not be re-created or rediscovered, but already existed in the traditional Orthodox Church.

Despite this fundamental reservation, the participation of the Orthodox in the ecumenical movement was to have considerable impact. Above all, it made it possible for Protestants and Anglicans to rediscover a traditional Church, corresponding in many respects to the ecclesiastical ideal that the Oxford Movement and the analogous movements that we have reviewed had begun to revive in the nineteenth century.

However, this rediscovery would not have been so effective without the ecclesiastical and ecclesiological renewal that Orthodoxy had experienced in the nineteenth century.

## Notes

1. On the Oxford Movement, see P. Thureau-Dangin, *La renaissance catholique en Angleterre au XIXe siècle* (Paris, 1899), which is still an excellent introduction despite its date. This might be completed by the first volume of Meriol Trevor (mentioned above), by Christopher Dawson, *The Spirit of the Oxford Movement* (London, 1933), and by Yngve Brilioth, *The Anglican Revival* (London, 1925), which gives the view of a Lutheran.

2. See Yngve Brilioth, *Evangelicalism and the Oxford Movement* (London, 1934), pp. 18ff.

3. Brilioth, op. cit., pp. 15ff.

4. Cf. Brilioth, op. cit., pp. 12ff., and S. Hebart, *Wilhelm Löhes Lehre von der Kirche, ihren Amt und Regimen* (Neuendettelsau, 1939).

5. On Kliefoth, one may consult the thesis upheld in 1954 by K. Kehnscherfer in *Das Wesen der Kirche nach Th. Kliefoth.*

6. See our *Eucharist*, ch. 12.

7. See A. Vidler, op. cit., pp. 90ff.

8. See Troeltsch, op. cit., the introduction.

9. See H. Bouillard, op. cit. pp. 85ff. See also P. Scherding, *Christophe Blumhardt et son père* (Paris, 1937).

10. See M.-J. Le Guillou, *Mission et Unité* (Paris, 1960), 1:43ff.

11. On all this, see Le Guillou, op. cit., pp. 48ff.

# Chapter 10
# The Renaissance of Russian Ecclesiology

The Orthodox renewal in the nineteenth century is related to what we have adduced in Protestantism (or Anglicanism) and Catholicism. Indeed, since the eighteenth century, Russian Orthodoxy was not averse to opening itself to influences from Protestantism and from what must be called the Catholic Reformation (rather than the Counter Reformation). In his organization of the Holy Synod, with a lay procurator at its head instead of the patriarchal authority, Peter the Great wanted to copy the model of the Lutheran consistories. The theological school of Kiev, on the other hand, was strongly influenced by the seminaries and theological manuals of post-Tridentine Catholicism.

More profoundly and more broadly, in one of the chief educators of Russian piety in the same period, St. Dimitri of Rostov, author of the most popular "lives" of the saints of old Russia, Catholic influence was so evident that the Holy Synod expurgated his work (e.g., developments on the Immaculate Conception of the Virgin). With St. Tikhon of Zadonsk, also in the same period, the influence of post-Tridentine spirituality (in his meditations on the passion of the Savior) is combined with that of J. Arndt's *True Christianity* and the *Meditatiunculae* of Anglican Bishop John Hall, of Puritan tendencies. Something analogous can be observed in the Greek theological school of Eugene Boulgaris, in which the philosophical influences of Kant are pronounced.

But with the patriarch of Constantinople at the beginning of the nineteenth century, St. Nicodemus the Hagiorite, the broadest receptivity to the Catholicism of the Council of Trent was coupled with a rediscovery of the spiritual riches of the properly Orthodox tradition. He adopted both the *Spiritual Combat* of Scupoli and the *Exercises* of St. Ignatius for the use of the modern Orthodox, and propagated among them the desirability of frequent Communion, preached by Catholic spiritual teachers of the sixteenth to the eighteenth century. But in cooperation with his friend, Metropolitan Macarius Notaras (in their *Philokalia*), he reintroduced the great authors of the Byzantine tradition, who had more or less been forgotten.

The Slavic monk, Paissy Velichkovsky of Mt. Athos, brought this traditional treasury as far as Rumania, from where it spread through his disciples, to Russia. This gave rise to a rediscovery of the fathers and the ancient Orthodox tradition.

Near one of the monasteries that had been renewed by these influences (Optina Pustyn), a group of Orthodox laymen, in close connection with the *Startsy,* began the Slavophile Movement, that is, a return to the Russian traditions that had more or less been obliterated by the westernization of Peter the Great.[1]

## *I. A. S. Khomiakov*

The most interesting figure in this group kept the movement from falling into simple and somewhat folkloristic *phyletism* by developing a systematization of Orthodox ecclesiology and sketching a role of ecumenism for Orthodoxy, faced with Protestantism and Latin Catholicism. This man was Aleksei Stepanovich Khomiakov, who wrote two major books, *The Church Is One* and *The Latin Church and Protestantism,* which he published in French to assure them widest readership in the West.[2]

It has been pointed out many times that Protestant influences are diffused in Orthodoxy, and they can be felt in Khomiakov's work. Indeed, the period of Emperor Alexander I was marked by an invasion of Illuministic Pietism. Even some professional theologians, men like Metropolitan Philaret of Moscow, who reacted most strongly against these influences, bore traces of it. It is not surprising, then, that a lay theologian, anxious to revive the pure spirit of Orthodox tradition, was permeated by it. However, if a Western influence is dominant in Khomiakov's thought, it is that of Moehler, for whom he never disguised his admiration. It seems unquestionable that if Moehler's *Unity in the Church* did not furnish his central theme, it provided decisive inspiration. But since Moehler's book was permeated by Greek patristics, it can be said that Khomiakov found his own tradition in it. In fact, familiarity with the same sources is so common to them that they agree on points where Khomiakov could not have known Moehler's thoughts, which had already been formulated but not yet published.

For Khomiakov, what constitutes the historical mission of the Russian people in civilized modern Christendom is the living witness they can bring to the experience of the Church as a unanimity that is lived in love. This is what he never tired of describing as *sobornost*. According to Vladimir Lossky, the most exact translation of this term is "catholicity," since in Slavonic the adjective *sobornaya* translates the Greek word *katholike* in the Creed.[3]

Because Christian truth is the truth of evangelical love, he says it can be preserved and understood only in the community in which this love is seen, the Church. The truth, then, is not preserved by any authority outside and above the Church, any more than it can be attained or retained by individualistic efforts. It is the whole Christian people, through their whole experience of the Christian life, nourished by common participation in the liturgy, who alone are its guardian, just as the people alone, within this living unity, can experience it.

For Khomiakov, "papalism," to which Latin Catholicism tends in its opposition to Protestantism, and like Protestantism itself, is merely a form of religious individualism. On the one hand, it is the individualism of one person, taking the place of the fellowship of all in *sobornost,* and, on the other, the individualism of each, turning his back on it. These two antagonistic individualisms can merely aggravate and harden one another. No other reconciliation is possible for separated Christians in the West than in the common rediscovery of this sole, veritable Catholicity that the East, despite all its weaknesses, has preserved.

It is striking that M. Geiselmann, in an unpublished note of Moehler's, rediscovered curiously analogous notations on the individualism of one person alone in the extreme forms of ultramontanism and the individualism of all in Protestantism, both of which seem equally to misunderstand the true spirit of Catholic tradition.[4]

Like the other Slavophiles, Khomiakov exalted the Russian people as the bearer of a vision of collective life that is opposed to "Occidentalist" individualism. This school saw in the Russian people, adherence, to Orthodox Christianity a basic aspect, not only of its national consciousness but a truly messianic consciousness. But we cannot clearly discern, in more than one of its representatives, whether Orthodoxy provided Russia this experience and message or whether Russian Orthodoxy has become so Russian that it gives it such a value in their eyes.

On the contrary, Khomiakov is explicit on the universal and essentially

Christian value of Orthodoxy. Authentic Russian tradition interests him above all as a striking example of a popular civilization in which Christianity, in all its purity, has been the preeminent formative principle. Also, his vision of the Orthodox Church, as Russian as it may be, is undeniably the vision of a "People of God," created by the common experience of unanimity in love. With him, as with Moehler, the basic intuition is the Christian truth as the truth of the divine love, not only revealed to us by the Gospel but communicated among us in the Church. Conversely, it goes without saying that the only guardian and witness of such a truth can be love, effectively lived and exercised in this human (but supernatural) community. As he emphasized, quoting the letter of the Eastern Orthodox patriarchs in response to the appeal of Pius IX to reunite with the Catholic Church on the occasion of the Vatican Council, it is only this "People of God," this entire people—its most humble members as well as its leaders—which unanimously maintains the true faith by loving with "the divine love poured out into our hearts by the Holy Spirit."[5]

Yet, unlike Moehler, Khomiakov does not seem to see the irreplaceable role of the bishops in the life of this body. Or, rather, he is subject to the criticism that Moehler himself was to make, as we have seen—if not of the thesis of *Unity in the Church,* at least of a divergent view to which it sometimes lays itself open. For him, it seems, the role of the bishops in this domain of the faith is simply to express a "sense of the faithful" that, in some way, is spontaneous. His fear of all authority, as a threat to the freedom of love and therefore of faith, subjects him to a misinterpretation: that the episcopacy does not proceed from the body but from its head, Christ, through the intermediary of the Apostles, and, consequently, that it does not have only the function of conveying the immanent life to the body (i.e. the Spirit of God) but also of seeing that it always proceeds from the historical Christ, who instituted his ministers for this purpose.

One of the best contemporary Orthodox theologians (of whom we shall speak shortly), Fr. George Florovsky, relying on the Eastern tradition, has formulated a double criticism of Khomiakov and his emulators.[6] He says they confuse—in the letter of the patriarchs on which they rely, as on all the other significant documents of Orthodoxy—the function that is proper to bishops, *judging* what the authentic truth is or is not, with the function that is indeed common to the whole People of God, in all its members: *witnessing* to the truth. Behind this primary error, and fully agreeing with Moehler, Florovsky brings out the more profound error of an ecclesiology that wishes to be exclusively pneumatic and not Christological, which would end fatally by misconstruing the essential attachment of the work of the Spirit in us with the historical work of Christ.

## II. V. Soloviev

The same criticism that was leveled at Khomiakov underlies another modern Orthodox ecclesiology of another Russian lay thinker: Vladimir Soloviev.[7] For him, indeed, this unanimity in love—which is certainly, in his eyes, that of traditional Orthodoxy—is condemned to remain a fantasy if it is not realized within the institution of the historical Church, as she has evolved from the work of Christ and the apostles, but this evolution includes the authority of the episcopacy in general and even the Roman primacy. This is the basic theme of his book (which was written in French, as were the key works of Khomiakov): *Russia and the Universal Church.*[8] The opposition between the papal function and the idea of *sobornost* has no meaning for him; as for Moehler, the papal function is, in his eyes, the necessary expression and the providential means, willed by Christ, of the symphony of all the churches in the one Church of Charity. *Roma,* he writes, is but a mirror image, in which all can and must read *Amor.*

Yet, up to this point, Soloviev's views on the papacy caused considerably less impact on Orthodox thought than did another element of his thought (which perhaps is even more unexpected). We mean his speculations on the quasi-personalized "Divine Wisdom," which occupy no less important a place in his book than his views on the desirable reconciliation between the Orthodox East and the Catholic West. People have underlined all that Soloviev's sophiology owes to the "second philosophy" of Schelling and, through this philosophy (but not exclusively), to the rather strange ideas of Jakob Boehme.[9] Behind Boehme is the influence of the hylozoic naturism of Paracelsus, the demiurgic and pantheist-tending neo-Platonism of the Renaissance, and the Gnosticism that survived through the medieval Jewish Kabbalah and especially the Zohar. We see all these sources, for the first time explicitly fusioned, a few years earlier in his own country, by another eccentric who was less ingenious but more erudite, Heinrich Kunrath, the author of *Amphitheatrum divinae Sapientiae,* which was known in Boehme's circle, if not by Boehme himself.

These are, assuredly, very mixed sources, which cannot help but create suspicion. In fact, we need only consider what Soloviev's "wisdom" became with some of his disciples, such as Blok or Biely, in order to verify the ambiguity that the notion gave rise to. However, it would be profoundly unjust to see in Soloviev's use of this notion—and even, to a certain extent, in the use made of it before him by Schelling and first of all Boehme—nothing more than a pantheistic and erotic illusion.

What attracted Soloviev in Boehme's "wisdom" was certainly the fact that the unity of the divine plan, which is precisely the unity realized by "the divine love poured out into our hearts by the Holy Spirit," could not be an abstract unity. It is a living and vital unity. But since it is the unity of persons, it cannot be simply an organic unity; it must be a quasi-personal unity. Hence the interest aroused by the biblical image of this "wisdom," which is God's plan for the world in general and mankind in particular—this design which must come to its historical actualization by and in the People of God, but which appears with God as another self, undoubtedly created but eternally destined to the closest union with him. Could this not express that *sui generis* unity of the Church, which shares in the very unity of the divine life in the Trinity of Persons?

Following Soloviev, this is what other, no-less-powerful thinkers in Russian Orthodoxy thought, even when they were most critical of the "cloudy" elements of his notions.

## III. P. Florensky and S. Boulgakov

Fr. Paul Florensky,[10] as much a scientist (physicist and biologist) as a theologian, wrote an extremely brilliant thesis at the beginning of the century, *The Column and the Support of Truth,* in which he endeavored to construct around an ecclesiology, dominated by this wisdom theme, a complete, Christian system of the world (a striking analogy with the process, being worked out at the same time in the West, of Fr. Teilhard de Chardin). But it is to another theologian (slightly more recent than Florensky), who continued to work until the end of the Second World War, that the major modern Orthodox ecclesiological composition, dominated by the sophiological theme, is due: Fr. Sergei Boulgakov.[11]

After the Russian Revolution, Boulgakov turned from Marxist sociology to Christianity and then to the priesthood. Like Fr. Flovensky, the concerns of this exceptionally powerful thinker go far beyond the ecclesiological problem; but it is characteristic that his theology (which is very personal and prodigiously informative) was synthesized after a first volume on Christ, *The Lamb of God;* a second volume on the Spirit, *The Paraclete;* and a concluding volume on ecclesiology, *The Spouse of the Lamb.*[12] For him, "wisdom" in the created being is characterized by a tendency to personal existence, in relation with the divine Tri-personality. Eminently actualized in the Virgin, as its perfect individual expression, it must find its collective (but in some way suprapersonal) fulfillment in the perfect Church, which assumes and actualizes (in herself) all the virtualities of the cosmos, in a humanity that is "divinized" by the grace of the Holy Spirit, in order perfectly to espouse what he calls the "God-manhood" of the eternal Son.

This vision, grandiose though it may be, was not accepted by all the Orthodox, even among the Russians, and it was condemned by several members of the highest Orthodox hierarchy. They seem to have been disturbed by the massive use of dialectical philosophy from the German Idealism of the nineteenth century (perhaps Hegel's more than Schelling's) and by what can appear to be influence from Protestant spirituality: a clearly kenotic Christology and accentuation of Khomiakov's tendency to depreciate any "authority" in the Church.

## IV. V. Lossky

In direct conflict with Boulgakov and the sophiological theme, we must mention another contemporary Orthodox theological work of equal ecclesiological interest, that of Vladimir Lossky. Again, we are speaking of a layman, who remained a layman throughout his life. However, he is fully familiar with medieval and modern philosophical thought, is supported by an exceptional knowledge of Greek patristics, and is a profound theologian, in the most traditional sense of the term.

Lossky is radically opposed to the sophiological theologies, in which he tended to see only Immanentist-Idealist philosophies that absorbed theological themes. It was not from an assumption of the created, and especially the human, in God—in the figure of Wisdom or otherwise—that he built his theology, and particularly his ecclesiology. On the contrary, he was inspired by the intuitions of a Karsavin, little-known thinker, and took from these intuitions his ideas about the descent of the Holy Spirit upon the world and man in relationship to the Incarnation. And by basing himself on the theology of the Transfiguration, through the light of Tabor, borrowed from the Byzantine theologian Gregory Palamas, he endeavored to account for this "new creation," which is nothing other than the "old creation," recovering within the Church its full, original quality of a divine image.[13]

Two points, which he believed to be closely connected, are essential for understanding his theological thought, and particularly his ecclesiology. The first is the character (in his opinion, unsatisfactory) of Western theology on created grace and Boulgakov's sophiology, seeing in "wisdom" the divine essence itself, insofar as creatures are able to share in it. In his eyes, the "grace" of the Scholastics could not produce genuine participation in the divine life. And Boulgakov's "wisdom," he thinks, makes it possible only by means of pantheism. The only escape from this Scylla and Charybdis is the affirmation, systematized by Gregory Palamas, of a real distinction in God between his unshareable divine essence and the divine "energies" which are its manifestation, but which are no less uncreated. They are communicated by the incarnate Son, as a radiation of his transfigured humanity.

But Lossky thinks this is possible only if we admit his second point: that the Spirit proceeds from the Father alone, and not from the Father *and* the Son, however that may be understood. For only in this way are the divine relations proved as personal relations and not as a simple dialectic of the divine essence, where they would be reabsorbed in its original unity. On the contrary, in the two independent Persons, the Father and the Spirit, of whom the Father is one principle, the dyad is surpassed without returning to the primordial unity: the monarchy of the Father is discovered there as the principle of an infinite diversity.

On the other hand, on the level of the eternal manifestation of the divinity, by its uncreated "energies," which constitute its "glory," the Spirit proceeds from the Father *through* the Son—as it were, after him. This is conveyed on the level of the created, following upon the Incarnation, through the communication (as the work of the Spirit) to all men of the uncreated "energies" that have come into the humanity that has been assumed by the Word.

Only within these perspectives, in regenerated man as in God, Lossky thinks, can the person no longer be a closing in upon itself, in opposition to others, but the common possession of either one divine nature or its uncreated "energies." In the Church, our human persons, like the divine Persons in the Trinity, without being confused or able to separate from one another, are one in the only Son of the eternal Father. At the same time, however, they are consecrated in their diversity by the Spirit of life which proceeds from the same Father.

## V. G. Florovksy

This extremely ingenious (if passably subtle) dialectic has not been accepted by other contemporary Orthodox theologians who are as careful as Lossky to avoid both pantheist-tending confusions and the tradition of the Greek fathers in order to clarify the mystery of the Church. This is singularly the case with Fr. George Florovsky, for whom Lossky is still dependent on the error of the followers of Khomiakov's thought (which is, we repeat, to construct ecclesiology on a penumatology that is relatively independent of Christology). If the Latin error is to do away with pneumatology or, purely and simply, reabsorb it in Christology, the "Orthodox truth" cannot be to substitute for an exclusively Christological ecclesiology an exclusively pneumatological ecclesiology, even if it were juxtaposed to Christology, as in Lossky's thought, but without any organic bond with it. The genuinely traditional (and genuinely ecumenical) ecclesiology is faithful to the economy of salvation and implants a pneumatological development in a Christological ground. The underlying schema in Lossky's thought on the incarnation of the Word, unifying humanity in him, and then the descent of the Spirit, diversifying us anew in this reunited humanity, is artificial. It makes both the primordial *presence of the Spirit in Christ* and our *life in Christ,* resulting from the outpouring of the Spirit in us, unthinkable; and yet they are the basic statements of Scripture and the whole of tradition on the Church and her connection with the Incarnation.[14]

# VI. N. Afanassieff

A final current in contemporary Orthodox ecclesiological thought must be pointed out. It might well open the way for this synthesis, without confusion of the pneumatological and Christological aspects of a balanced ecclesiology whose requirements were so felicitously defined by Fr. Florovsky. We speak of the eucharistic ecclesiology of Fr. N. Afanassieff.[15]

On first sight—even more than the critical remarks of Fr. Florovsky—Afanassieff's reflections, because of their extremely concrete basis, seem totally opposed to the increasingly hardy metaphysical speculations that we have seen from Khomiakov to Lossky. But they furnish perhaps the only solid basis for an ecclesiology whose broadest and deepest visions would find support not on some *a priori* idea but on the most traditional experience of the Church.

Fr. Afanassieff's basic idea is that the concrete actualization of the Church occurs on the local level in the celebration of the Eucharist. Yet all the local churches, in uniting in the Eucharist by participating in the same Christ, are but one Church. This does not mean that the universal Church is composed of all the local churches, added together, any more than the local churches can be considered offshoots of a universal Church which would be supposed to be prior to them. Rather, it must be said that the Catholic Church is present with Christ in all local churches that celebrate the unique Eucharist.

This does not exclude the possibility of a more or less complete representation of all the Church—of a more or less extensive witness to the reality of the Church by the various local communities—for manifold reasons. Nor does this exclude what Fr. Afanassieff prefers to call a "priority" (rather than a "primacy") of a Church "presiding in love of all the Churches." The only thing this ecclesiology renders impossible is acceptance of an external authority over churches (exercised from without) that are supposed to be but fragments of one universal Church. It is of little importance, furthermore, whether this authority be that of a council or a primate.

Although this thesis of Fr. Afanassieff has elements that are excessive or vague, it cannot be denied that he has put his finger on an essential point, which is, as it were, the key to the ecclesiology of the New Testament and the earliest fathers. Yet we cannot fail to be struck by the absolute rejection of any juridical aspect in the life and the concept of the Church, which (for him) seems to be connected with this eucharistic ecclesiology. This characteristic is found again, more or less conspicuously, in all the modern Orthodox theologians, especially the Russians, following in the wake of Khomiakov. It is superfluous to note that the same reflex is found with most Protestants, and even with Catholics, and results in an "organic" view of the Church. It seems that this is a reaction against an aberrant legalism, a confusion between abstract legalism and positive law, in which the latter is only a caricature. The law, which is justice, defined in its concrete application, cannot be opposed to charity—or charity must threaten to dissolve in a dream. What kind of love would wish to ignore justice?

## VII. C. Leontieff

This, then, is what one modern Orthodox thinker understood when he broached the problem of the Church, and it is interesting to note that he seems to attract the attention of Orthodox youth. We are referring to Constantine Leontieff, whose importance Berdiaeff acknowledged, to the point of devoting an astonishingly warm biographical study to him, even though he was intellectually removed from Leontieff in many respects.[16] It is (against Slavophiles in general) an essential claim of Leontieff that Orthodoxy cannot be truly understood if one misunderstands the importance of the nomocanonical work of Byzantium. According to him, it is impossible to discern the authentic notion of the Church if one does not understand its sense of the canon law.

This brief view of personalities who are, at once, extremely original but profoundly enmeshed in a tradition that the West had practically lost sight of for a thousand years, insufficient though it may be, allows us to assess the importance of ecumenism in the rediscovery of Russian Orthodoxy.

Of these authors generally, the least one can say, from the viewpoint of a possible renewal of ecclesiology in our time, is what Vladimir Lossky said about Boulgakov a few days before he died: "Even when the solutions he proposes are most unacceptable, he makes it impossible not to consider the problems he posed."

Therefore, it is easy to understand that the "discovery" of Orthodoxy (and the Russians in particular) revealed to Anglicans, and even to many Protestants, certain aspects of traditional ecclesiastical realities that they had not yet considered. But to Catholics, these Orthodox thinkers can show that these basic, eternal realities of the Catholic Church are rich with possibilities that their current theology is still far from exploiting.

## Notes

1. We have spoken about all this in more detail in our *La Spiritualité orthodoxe et la spiritualité protestante et anglicane*, pp. 59ff. A study by P. Evdokimoff, "L'Ecclésiologie orthodoxe au XIXe siècle," will be found in *L'Ecclésiologie au XIXe siècle*. This can be completed by C. Kern, "L'enseignement thèologique supérieur dans la Russie au XIXe siècle," in *Istina* (1956). pp. 249ff. It is regrettable that the great work of G. Florovsky, "Paths of Russian Theology," published in Russian in Paris in 1937, has not yet been translated.

2. On Khomiakov, see A. Gratieux, *Khomiakov et le mouvement slavophile* (2 vols.; Paris, 1939), as well as his *Le mouvement slavophile à la veille de la révolution. Dmitri A. Khomiakov* (Paris, 1953).

3. V. Lossky, *À l'image et la ressemblance de Dieu* (Paris, 1967), p. 167, n. 1.

4. Geiselmann, op. cit., p. 194.

5. *L'Église latine et le Protestantisme au point de vue de l'Église d'Orient* (Lausanne, 1872), p. 48.

6. Yves-Noël Lelouvier gave an excellent analysis of it in *Perspectives russes sur l'Église. Un théologien contemporain: Georges Florovsky* (Paris, 1968), pp. 58ff., 93ff., 120ff.

7. There are two good studies on Soloviev in French: D. Stremooukhoff, *Vladimir Soloviev et son oeuvre messianique* (Paris, 1935), and M. Herman, "Vladimir Soloviev, sa vie et son oeuvre" (introduction to his translation of

*La Crise de la philosophie occidentale* [Paris, 1947]). To these must be added E. Munzer, *Solovyev, Prophet of Russian Western Unity* (London, 1956).

8. (Paris, 1889). English trans.: *Russia and the Universal Church* (London, 1948).

9. See the articles of A. Kojevnikoff in *Revue d'histoire et de philosophie religieuses* (Nov.–Dec. 1934), pp. 534ff., and (Jan.–Apr. 1935) pp. 110ff.

10. Good notices about him can be found in *Histoire(s) de la Philosophie russe* (published in Paris in 1954), by N. O. Lossky (pp. 179ff.) and B. Zenkovsky (2:437ff.).

11. See again Lossky and Zenkovsky, pp. 196ff. and 456ff. respectively.

12. French translation of *Lamb of God,* under the title *Le Verbe incarné* (Paris, 1943), and *Le Paraclet* (Paris, 1946). The best introduction to his thought is his volume in English, *The Wisdom of God* (London, 1937).

13. In addition to the posthumous work mentioned in n. 3 of this chapter, see his *Théologie spirituelle de l'Église d'Orient* (Paris, 1941) and *La Vision de Dieu* (Paris, 1964).

14. See especially "Le Corps du Christ vivant," in *La Sainte Église universelle* (Paris–Neuchatel, 1948) and "Christ and His Church," in *L'Église et les Églises* (Chevetogne, 1954).

15. See his contribution to the collective work *La Primauté de Pierre dans l'Église orthodoxe* (Paris, 1960): "L'Église qui préside dans l'amour," pp. 9ff.

16. N. Berdiaeff, *Constantin Leontieff* (Paris, 1937). It will be noted that Afanassieff was himself a canonist, but seems to have seen the law only as a necessary evil.

# Chapter 11
# The Present State of Ecclesiology

It would be erroneous to suppose that the recent history of the ecumenical movement or, more generally, the rediscovery of the traditional Church in "non-Roman" milieus, or of Catholic ecclesiology itself, can be described as a harmonious development of seeds that, in the nineteenth century, burst forth almost everywhere at the same time. These seeds have certainly come to flower since and, to a certain point, even borne fruit; but their dispersion has been thwarted, if not precluded, by reactions and, indeed, an inertia that must not be concealed.

In Protestantism, the time of the Second World War was marked by the influence of Karl Barth and his dialectical theology of the word of God. Even though this theology was intended to be equally removed from the old Protestant orthodoxy and the rationalizing liberalism of the nineteenth century, it produced a recrudescence of vitality in confessional opposition. In its first phase, it seemed to go directly against rediscovery of the Church of the traditional Catholic type, which was present (at least sketchily) everywhere—or certainly in both Protestantism and Anglicanism at the end of the nineteenth and the beginning of the twentieth century.

It was soon apparent, on the other hand, that insistence on the sovereignty of the divine word, provided it was freed from the veneer of certain primary or secondary formulations of Barthism, favored an in-depth ecumenism. The point was not to retain the existentialist formulas of the early Barth or his floundering thought in the ready-made Protestant neo-orthodoxy which threatened him, once he sought to systematize his message. Barth, progressively, had to surmount these two temptations, without ever completely escaping from them. But well before this, others, such as the Cambridge exegete Sir Edwyn Hoskyns, were indebted to him for renewal of the ideal that may be called one form of "evangelical Catholicism."[1]

Under Hoskyns' influence, but perhaps even more as a result of meditation on and decantation of the prophetic work of Maurice (of whom we have already spoken), A. M. Ramsey, as early as the 1930s, wrote a short, clear, and informative book which one day may be acknowledged as marking the most decisive turning point in twentieth-century ecumenism. Its title expresses its content: *The Gospel and the Catholic Church.*[2]

Ramsey begins with Maurice's idea that "the Church" is necessarily catholic, that is, visibly and organically one in her faith, her traditional ministry, and her sacramental worship, while her members must be "protestants," if by that term we understand people who are persuaded that they are Christian only through a personal adhesion, a free act of faith in the divine grace that the word of God reveals to us in Jesus Christ. This is the major theme of what is surely Maurice's most remarkable book, *The Kingdom of Christ.*[3] (Unfortunately, it dealt with developments that were often obscure and always diffuse, but these developments were interspersed with insights that were hardly less thought provoking than his central intuition.)

On the other hand, Ramsey, in a condensed but luminous form, developed the idea that the only viable ecumenism cannot be a compromise but must be the effect of maximum (but harmonious) tension between the Church, inherited from Christ and the apostles and fully conscious of the graces which constitute her in existence (which she could not deny without refusing her mission to the world), and the divine, transcendent word, of which the Church is only the instrument. But this word cannot speak effectively to the world except in and through the Church. Thus it is possible for Protestantism to be reconciled as a prophetic movement of permanent significance and import, with the divine institution, outside of which it loses its meaning, since the reformation to which it is directed, if it is not the reformation of the one Church, willed and established by Christ, though composed of sinful men, must see its object, its reason for being, vanish.

Within such perspectives, development of a traditional and, in a word, catholic ecclesiastical renaissance within the churches of the Reformation can no longer seem like the result of an anti-Protestant party but, much more, as the fulfillment (which up to now had merely been sketched out), deferred and finally forgotten, of the first and essential plan of the Reformation. This is not to substitute for the one Church of Christ another church, or, rather, several churches, divided among themselves and cut off from their main body, but rather to restore to this one Church the principle of her permanent vitality: the

Word of the Gospel, the living Word of the living God. This becomes the program of a Church that is truly catholic and, at the same time, truly reformed, and it should be the program of the only ecumenism that can succeed.

It can be said that, in the decades that followed, the most concrete accomplishments of ecumenism verified both the solidity and the fecundity of these views. The best evidence of this is another book, which appeared in the '50s, by a Scots Presbyterian theologian who, meanwhile, had become the bishop of the new United Church of South India: *The Household of God,* by Lesslie Newbegin.[4]

The church in question was the product of a coalescence of four missionary churches: the local dioceses of the Anglican Church, a Presbyterian church of Scottish origin, a Congregationalist church, and a Methodist church. The history of this union has been told with remarkable objectivity by a Swedish missionary, Bishop Bengt Sundkler.[5] It appears that political compromises and doctrinal ambiguities were not lacking, but Newbegin's book attests that a sincere rapprochement among the artisans of this union, in a spirit of clear-headed penance and charity, brought something quite different: a vision of the fact that "Christians in conflict" (to use another expression of Maurice) state complementary truths, while they are divided by little more than their negations (when not, simply, by mutual ignorance). The ecclesiology the new bishop developed in his book is merely "explicitation" of a discovery: insistence on (1) the local church, formed in principle of "confessing" and responsible Christians from the Congregationalists; (2) on the specialized ministries entrusted to certain members for the good of the whole body, from the Presbyterians; (3) on the common effort of Christian co-education and the progressive sanctification of all by their common life and its organization, proper to the Methodists; and (4) insistance by the traditional Anglicans on a ministry, a sacramental liturgy, and a confession of faith inherited from the Apostolic Church. All these "compromises," coming together and cooperating, are found to be not contradictory, but necessarily complementary in the life of the "one Church," faithful to the word of Christ.

At the present time, such intuitions trace a path for innumerable people among the most diverse communities that have a Reformation background. It can be suggested that they represent the future of an ecumenism which, breaking from the circle of academic conversations, may finally emerge into the reality of a recovered Christian unity. A Church that is brought back to the purity of her origins and, at the same time, is ready to face the problems that are posed to her by the world today, strong from having drawn a valuable lesson from the most painful experience of her history, ought to emerge from it.

Alas, we are not yet at this point. Too many obstacles which seem new—but are nothing but old confusions that we thought we had overcome (though we had merely skirted them)—are now appearing on the road that ought to lead to this discovery and renewal. Above all, too much lethargy subsists, so that even the most dire warnings of experience have not been able to dispel it.

First of all, the unilateral transcendentalism of Barthism, like all reactions, has caused the opposite reaction, which had long been predictable: an equally exacerbated immanentism. Belief in God, in his sovereign grandeur, so that the human being and every other created entity is denigrated, which resulted in a notion of salvation whose gratuity people felt could be maintained only by emptying it of any probatory content, caused a contrary belief: the "death of God" and "secular Christianity" theologies.[6] Barth, unconsciously, had prepared men for this, simply by opposing the divine word to all "religion," to all humanly expressible sacrality. If this is the case, man in the concrete, who can neither give up living nor live in a world that is really his own, must sooner or later take the "death of God" as the preliminary condition of his accession to adulthood, and denial of all sacrality as the necessary means for the "humanization" of the cosmos.

This "new Protestantism" is a revival of the old liberalism, pushed to its ultimate consequences. Its apparent "modernity" ignores the nineteenth-century image of the world and man, which it makes its idol. It further dilutes the evangelical phraseology with which Ritschl and his successors camouflaged it; indeed, it died in the meanwhile. But as long as it survived, attracted and fascinated by a world it considered to be "the future" (even though it was yesterday's phantom), "the church," with her unity and living continuity, was no longer a problem. In this post-Bultmannian Protestantism, it is easy to think that "ecumenism has been left behind"—whereas we have simply allowed ourselves to fall away from the Christianity that will survive tomorrow: as well as even better than—what has survived to our own day.

But even more harmful to ecumenism than this passing crisis is the old inertia of the structures, which are all the more immovable since life has deserted them. For too long, ecumenical debates have been pursued in specialized movements and conferences, without much modification in the mentality and behavior of the communities which these meetings (or preliminary organizations) are thought to represent. It was inevitable, under these circumstances, that contentment with the *status quo,* the instinct of self-justification and self-perpetuation of the "churches" that ecumenism, when it was sparkling and creative, questioned, would revert to the manifestations of ecumenism itself. It is a fact that the insidious and unceasingly heightened tendency of the ponderous organizations, which the ecumenical movement provided for itself, has justified and calcified the ecclesiastical state of things that it aimed at making disappear, and, finally, has become installed within it. Consequently, the organs of ecumenism may be blind to their reason for being.

The reactions, particularly of young Christians, to bringing about a union by brushing aside the questions which the ecumenical movement had, as a project, to resolve, and before which it often seemed to capitulate, are explained as much by this undeniable deficiency as by the neo-humanism of theologies (or, rather, non-theologies) which put aside the problem of the Church only by volatilizing Christianity.

In this undeniable crisis, it seems that a new departure could be signaled only by the Catholic Church. It would be necessary, it seems, for her—supporting, broadening, and deepening the effort already made by the Orthodox Church—to witness, with the Orthodox Church—faced with a Protestantism which is more than ever divided between the best and the worst—to the unexhausted power of the authentic Church of reconciling in its truly catholic unity—with so many Christian truths scattered among them—all the dispersed children of God. In thus preparing the reunion of the traditional Christian East and West, and therefore in restoring the beclouded countenance of the original Catholic unity, it would undoubtedly facilitate the decisive choices (even ruptures) and the expected reconciliations, without which the desirable and more-than-ever desired reintegration could not come about.

What is the situation, viewed from this side? From the viewpoint of Christians who are separated from the ancient Church, the hopes that could be thought of as the beginnings of the ecumenical movement, and more generally as the widespread rediscovery of the traditional Church, and their still groping research, have recently been specified. But along the way, they have met apparently mounting obstacles that had not been expected. Nor is the situation without analogy on the Catholic side.

Prophetic works, such as those of Moehler and Newman, have set signposts for the interior rediscovery that is necessary for any hope of reunion with those outside. Particularly for the first of these thinkers, we have pointed out their insufficient but nonetheless promising effects, even in the thought of Roman theologians at the end of the nineteenth century. The second, despite late recognition of his fidelity and greatness by an exceptionally clear-sighted pontiff, is still as misunderstood in the Church be joined (in middle life) as in the one he left.

Yet it is undeniable that their ideas—or rather their rediscoveries—have little by little, directly or indirectly, made headway. In the second half of the nineteenth century, Scheeben (in Germany), who had depended on neo-Thomism for what was most dated and most narrow in his thought, later discovered (after the syllogisms of St. Thomas) his own sources with the Fathers. He then revived, in a first attempt at a "theology of mysteries," the outline, so strongly sketched by Moehler, of this Church-Body and Spouse of Christ, the Mother whose sons we are, the Body whose members we are.[7]

In France, about the same time, a self-taught thinker with aspects of genius, Dom Gréa, made a historical exploration of the liturgy and canon law.[8] This study was touched by Romanticism, but it was in contact with the texts and was vivified by its endeavor to reanimate a spiritual tradition. From this exploration, Gréa reconstructed that Eucharistic Church whose importance for Christian antiquity Fr. Afanassieff has more recently stressed.

But these were isolated cases. Three movements in the twentieth century were to prepare for the extension of these rebirths, as well as an elite from different backgrounds (though they more or less agree with one another).[9]

The first was a movement of spirituality. Propagated at first by popular writers, particularly two Benedictines, Dom Columba Marmion in Belgium and Dom Anscar Vonier in England, it recentered the spiritual life of the "best" Catholics on the theme of our incorporation in Christ by the faith and the sacraments. Nourished by St. Paul and St. Thomas, but especially by the liturgy, rethought and relived, this spirituality represents a first discovery (an existential one, we might say) of the Church as the Mystical Body of Christ.

The Catholic social movement, launched with a painful start in the nineteenth century, after the successive condemnations of Lamennais and the "Sillon," experienced an apparently triumphant revival between the two world wars with the beginnings of Catholic Action and, especially, the Young Christian Workers, created by the future Cardinal Cardijn. It emphasized the "belongingness" of the laity to the Church, as no longer passive but active, and the laity's necessary insertion into the world. Thus Mgr. P. Glorieux and Fr. Henri de Lubac S.J. found a stimulus for theological research, in what de Lubac was to call "the social aspects of dogma" in the felicitous theme of his book *Catholicisme*.[10]

Finally, with Dom Lambert Beauduin, the Malines conversations, the foundation of the monastery of the "monks of union" at Amay-sur-Meuse, and the new periodical *Irénikon*, a Catholic ecumenical movement made its first appearance. The writings of Fr. Beauduin[11]—and those that he inspired—prepared the first theological elaboration of an ecclesiology that could inspire and guide the movement. But it is Fr. Congar S.J., on the eve of the Second World War, who deserves the credit for having attempted the first systematic essay in this field, *Chrétiens désunis, principes d'un oecuménisme catholique*.

Again, though following different courses, these movements frequently crossed paths and, in concert, prepared an ecclesiastical and ecclesiological renewal in the Catholic Church. All three of them were nourished by a threefold renewal, which might be called a "return to sources": a liturgical, biblical, and patristic renewal which was closely interconnected.

Again, it was Dom Lambert Beauduin who initiated the liturgical renewal, when, for the first time, he presented the liturgy not as the source of a vaguely archaic spirituality, reserved to small, elite groups of intellectuals and esthetes, but as the source of practical spirituality for all members of the Church (in his book *The Piety of the Church*). This belief was deepened and powerfully systematized in *Mysterienlehre,* on the basis of patristic research, by the German Benedictines of Maria Laach and especially Dom Odo Casel. In a more popular form, the vital connection between this liturgical renewal and a biblical renewal was strongly upheld and first promulgated by Pius Parsch, a canon regular of Klosterneuburg in Austria, in his review *Bibel und Liturgie.*

All of these influences (and a missionary endeavor) came together, first on the parochial level, in the Centre de Pastorale Liturgique, created in France at the end of the Second World War by Dominican Frs. Roguet and Duployé.[12] Up to the pontificate of John XXIII, however, none of these movements or renewals had penetrated the masses of Catholics, and they seemed to have even less influence (if that were possible) in the governing circles: ecclesiastical authorities and recognized theologians. Yet it was clear to any keen observer that they foretold the future of Catholicism.

Several remarkable encyclicals of Pius XII, *Mystici Corporis, Divino afflante Spiritu,* and *Mediator Dei,* gave evidence of this influence (out of proportion with its spread) by their concern for gaining control of these movements, averting deviations, and making best use of their research. The same must be said of the 1948 *monitum* of the Holy Office on ecumenism. At first, it might have been thought that this warning signaled its demise, whereas it heralded official recognition.

The unexpected accession of Cardinal Roncalli to the responsibilities of the sovereign pontificate precipitated all these movements for a renewal of the notion and reality of the Catholic Church. The council that he convoked would canonize their projects and principles—in a way, indeed, which even now may appear to have gone beyond the scope of even the most earnest hopes. Yet we must also recognize that what followed in the council's wake, and the unexpected but predictable crisis that it let loose, seem to have suspended the realization of these promises—at the precise moment in which they seemed to be in the process of becoming concretized.

Undoubtedly, the idea of such an ecclesiastical and ecclesiological rebirth had penetrated the body of Catholicism insufficiently for ratification by the authorities of this rebirth, and especially a sudden ratification that, from the outset, could assure it more than a superficial acceptance in the masses. What was needed for the most enthusiastic adhesions, so that the rebirth would not be encumbered by misunderstandings, was still too little known.

Well before their official recognition, moreover, the movements we have mentioned were beset by confusions from which the progress of the liturgical, biblical, and patristic renewals (in a word, "the return to the sources") had not had time to free them. But above all—as is true among the churches that have come from the Reformation—the most fecund rediscoveries were to be, and for a long time will remain, restrained and thwarted by various types of inertia and simple reaction, turning around in circles that are becoming more narrow and empty.

Let us say one word about these internal threats and external countercurrents to the Catholic renaissance, which today, paradoxically, is in such danger, at the very moment when it seemed to be winning out. In the first place, let us look more closely at the confusions we have spoken about—more precisely, the perils of confusion within the three movements which were to assure the spread and then the success of the renewal of the Church.

The spiritual movement, by the very fact that it was a movement of spirituality, as well as the first to revive among Catholics the vision of the Church as the Mystical Body of Christ, ran the risk of being so absorbed in the mystical aspect that the corporality to which it is attached might simply evaporate. The ever active example and influence of St. Augustine makes this easy to understand. If the Church, as the Mystical Body, is defined first by the community of life in the grace of Christ, one may be tempted to see in this completely spiritual Church a reality that is, undoubtedly, interior to that of the concrete, visible Church, but the connection, perforce, must be seen as tenuous—on again, off again.

On the other hand, the "social Catholicism" movement tended to restore to the Mystical Body its social corporality—but was tempted, for its part, to look for this reality in human society in general, and to penetrate it with Christian influence, while discarding the *proper* corporality of the Church like a venerable but obsolete relic.

Finally, the Catholic ecumenical movement, because of its effort at being receptive and open, risked seeing the universal Church dispersed (and even dismembered) among the various Christian communities, or conceiving of the Mystical Body (where this reconciliation already obtains) as the simple equivalent of the "invisible Church," in which Protestants have always been tempted to forget their divisions rather than overcome them.

It would be false to deny that these temptations were not very real, here and there, when these movements affected only small elites among Catholics. Yet we could hope that development of the liturgical, biblical, and patristic renewal would overcome them by restoring the whole, original consistency of the idea and the effective reality of the Church as the Body of Christ.

It was necessary that these movements and the renewal mature together. Instead, their abrupt expansion within the Church, following the pontificate of John XXIII and the Second Vatican Council, precipitated them upon the masses without sufficient preparation. This mass of Catholics was poorly enlightened, even the most zealous members, and remained subject to a dialectic of reactions similar to the one we mentioned in the non-Roman Western churches in regard to Barthism and its consequences—bogged down in routines that were no less stultifying than those that had encumbered the Protestant communities.

We have mentioned how the sixteenth-century Reformation gave rise in the Catholic Church to the insufficient and unsatisfactory reaction that has been called the Counter Reformation. To the extent that it deserves this name, this reaction, far from contributing to the restoration of an integral Catholicity, tended to make Catholicism a form of Counter Protestantism, just as the Reformation had degenerated into a counterchurch.

The same reaction was to be reproduced in the Catholic masses and to be aggravated, once after the French Revolution and a second time after the Modernist movement at the beginning of the twentieth century. In the first case, the result has been called "Traditionalism" and in the second "Integralism." But just as the Traditionalism of Joseph de Maistre and Louis de Bonald did not represent a recuperation of the true and authentic Catholic tradition, modern integralism is not the restoration of its integrity. By opposing tradition to freedom and reason, Traditionalism turned tradition into a mechanical and unintelligent routine, passed from hand to hand, so to speak with no attempt either to assimilate it or, for a stronger reason, understand it. Throughout the nineteenth century, traditionalism showed itself to be the worst enemy of the genuine rediscovery of Catholic tradition that would be worthy of the name, as Moehler and Newman had worked to restore it.[13]

In turn, Integralism perfected the false identity between routine and tradition by refusing to admit any development of tradition, which it confused with a dissociating evolution. At the same time, it hardened the opposition between authority and freedom, desiring to raise authority above tradition, as people had earlier been tempted to exalt tradition above Scripture, in order to control—if it were possible—everything that they were afraid to see emerge from one or the other. But like Traditionalism before it, Integralism is evidently incapable of surviving.

With its greatest disciple, Lamennais, the Traditionalism of the nineteenth century provoked the reaction of an exacerbated demagogical futurism: the systematic substitution of *vox populi, vox Dei* for an oracular notion of the patriarchal authority of the pontiffs and kings. Integralism, with which official and popular orthodoxy in Catholicism tended to be confused, has given rise (since Modernism and its suppression, from the instant that authority relaxed its pressure) to a parallel reaction which is still more savage: contemporary Progressivism. An unduly congealed tradition, which was kept intangible by a self-contorted authority, produced—with the first easing of the situation, represented by the reign of John XXIII and the council—not the revival of authentic tradition, for which neither the masses nor most of their guides were ready, but the dissolution of *any* traditional sense. A form of freedom that the authorities were too exclusively concerned with repressing, in order to provide time the possibility of continuing its training, left now to itself, can only float about aimlessly.

It is at this point that the properly Catholic dynamic inertias—I mean the inertias of modern Catholicism—add their force to the dialectical vertigo of the reactions we have just analyzed. In limiting themselves to "conserving," "protecting," and "defending," the controlling agents of modern Catholicism were no longer able to guide, inspire, or elicit the living development of Catholic tradition in the whole body of the faithful. Therefore, despite themselves, they escaped a passive immobility, only to yield without resistance to external impulses. Under these conditions, they can no longer witness to the vitality of a body which still belongs to them, but in which too many of them, and for too long a time, no longer participate.

We must return to a renewed consciousness of this vitality, the vitality of tradition freed from all its spurious imitations, if we are to move beyond the present Catholic crisis and, thus, help Protestants and Anglicans emerge from the crisis of their ecumenism, in order to join us, along with the Orthodox, in the *Una Sancta,* which, more than ever, is needed by a divided Christianity and a ravaged world.

## Notes

1. A. M. Ramsey, *Recent Developments in Anglican Theology* (1967).
2. London, 1936.
3. First ed.; London, 1838.
4. London, 1953.
5. Bengt Sundkler, *Church of South India, The Movement toward Union (1900–1947)* (London, 1954).

6. On the "theology of the death of God," see the collective volume *The Meaning of the Death of God,* ed. Bernard Murchland (New York, 1967), and on "secular Christianity," see the studies of E. Mascall, *The Secularisation of Christianity* (London, 1965), and John Macquarrie, *God and Secularity* (Philadelphia, 1967).

7. See the extract of his *Die Mysterien des Christentums* (1865) in a French translation by Dom A. Kerkvoorde, under the title *Le Mystère de l'Église* (Paris, 1946).

8. *L'Église et sa divine constitution* (1884) was republished in 1907 and again in 1965.

9. On what follows, see our study (1950) in *Revue des sciences religieuses* (Strasbourg): "Où en est la théologie du Corps mystique?"

10. Paris, 1938.

11. We published a first sketch of a biography, *Dom Lambert Beauduin, un homme d'Église* (Paris, 1961).

12. We tried to retrace these different phases of the liturgical movement in *La vie de la Liturgie* (Paris, 1956).

13. We do not yet have a satisfactory study on traditionalism in general. On the stages in Lamennais' thought, see the fine article by Fonck in *Dictionaire de Théologie catholique,* and especially Louis Le Guillou, *L'Évolution de la pensée religieuse de F. Lamennais* (Paris, 1967).

# Part II
# An Essay on Doctrinal Synthesis

# Chapter 1
# The Church in Mystery at the Second Vatican Council

The teaching of the Second Vatican Council on the Church in the constitution *Lumen Gentium* took as its basis the initial affirmation of the mystery of the Church. The perspectives in which this first part of part II is developed are basically biblical, not only because it constitutes an inventory of all the biblical themes relating to the Church but especially because the notion of "mystery," which is implemented from the very first pages, is the same notion that contemporary exegesis has shown to be that of St. Paul, which has its roots in the most constant biblical tradition.

## I. The Pauline Mystery and the People of God

The mystery is basically the secret of God's eternal plan for the salvation of the universe and especially the salvation of mankind, which he created. This mystery, as St. Paul explains in the first chapters of 1 Corinthians, brings out explosively, once it is discovered, the supernatural character of "wisdom," according to which God disposes and guides all things. To the Greek philosophers (if indeed there were such at the time), it appeared as pure folly. Yet to the Jews, directly prepared for its final revelation, its effect was no less that of scandal, for it is in the cross of Christ that its ultimate secret is found. Christ, and especially his cross, accepted by faith, despite these various lacks of comprehension give the only possible key to both the Jewish Scriptures and the whole of human history.[1]

Deden showed this very well: it replaces the Pauline mystery in its literary and historical context—the wisdom and the apocalyptic notions of the Jews—just as we see wisdom extended and surpassed in apocalypse in the beginning of the Book of Daniel. The second chapter of Deden's book contains all the terms revived by St. Paul, in exactly the same relationships.[2]

The Captivity Epistles, beginning with Colossians, emphasize that this mystery, despite the first reaction of misunderstanding by Jews and Greeks, is nonetheless the mystery of their reconciliation. "There is no longer Greek or Jew,"[3] because all have been reconciled, among themselves and with God, in the body of his Son on the cross, where Jews and pagans agreed to put him to death.[4]

In this universal reconciliation, wrought by the cross of Jesus, the Epistle to the Ephesians sees the recapitulation of the whole of history.[5] This undoubtedly signifies that human history succeeds at this point in "summing itself up" in what is a radical new beginning, as well as a definitive fulfillment.

These Captivity Epistles deepen the mystery as the mystery of Christ and ourselves: Christ recapitulating us in himself and fulfilling himself in all of us. "Christ in you, the hope of glory," is the last definition of the mystery in the Epistle to the Colossians.[6]

It is in this view that the Epistle to the Ephesians can say that the wisdom of God, in the mystery which forms its basis, has been revealed by the Church,[7] while it defines the Church as "his body, the fullness of him who fills all in all."[8]

When we take into account all these data (which we have merely summed up), it is evident that it is not enough to speak of the "mystery of the Church" as one of the Christian mysteries, though it would be legitimate to do so. The Synoptic Gospels, St. Paul himself (in different instances), and St. Ignatius of Antioch (the first of the fathers) speak this way of "mysteries" (in the plural), as inscribed in the line of the Jewish apocalypses that designated the body of eschatological realities.[9] But St. Paul, by preference, speaks of one mystery, *the* mystery, that of Christ and his cross. And it is to this mystery that the Church is attached or, rather, belongs: it is properly in her that the mystery is finally revealed.[10]

Yet to say this is to say that the mystery of the Church—or better, the mystery revealed *in* the Church—is in no way a reality that must be invisible. With too many modern thinkers (the tendency can already be seen with St. Augustine), to speak of the mystery of the Church is equivalently to speak of the true Church as invisible. In the same line, the theology of what will be called "the Mystical Body" tends to become the theology of a very "spiritual" Church, which we are tempted to oppose to the visible Church, or do not know quite how to conjoin it. Such an orientation is not biblical; it warps the biblical notions, and especially those of St. Paul, by pouring into their formulas a Platonist-tending content which is profoundly foreign to them. At the same time, it misunderstands the whole sense of this rediscovery, as striking outside Catholicism as within it, for 500 years and more, of the Church as an "organism of truth and love," according to Khomiakov's expression. Nevertheless, it is there, and not elsewhere, that we find the soul of the ecumenical movement. For it is only in accordance with this other line of thought, connecting with that of biblical revelation, that it is stated that Christian unity is not simply (nor can it be) a purely "spiritual" unity that would subsist intact despite all possible divisions. On the contrary, it is necessarily a visible unity, the unity of a common life of concrete humanity, the essential work of the Savior, animated and safeguarded by his Spirit, "pouring out the love of God in our hearts."

The study of the mystery of the Church—rather, of the Church in the mystery of Christ—would lose a foothold if, from the very beginning, it were not constructed as a study of the mystery revealed in the historical society which Christ consecrated by becoming incarnate and dying on the cross. Indeed, it is not some kind of heavenly mystery. It is the mystery of what God has accomplished on earth in history, and does not cease to accomplish in earthly history, in which he has become the chief actor by entering into it in all truth.

This is why the Second Vatican Council, once the mystery of the Church was posited in all its biblical perspectives, set out upon an analysis of the notion—or, rather, the historical reality of the People of God.[11] In the biblical sense, the mystery is above all the secret of the plan of God, who fashioned the history of this People and brought it to its fullness in Christ.

## II. The Fullness and the Body of Christ

With St. Paul, "fullness" is closely connected with the developments of the mystery in relation to the Church. He uses three complementary and accepted meanings of the word.[12] The first is the "fullness of time."[13] The mystery was revealed at *that* time because it was then that the People of God were ready to attain their fullness in Christ. But Christ, as the Epistle to the Colossians says, is himself the "fullness of God."[14] This means that God is fully revealed and communicated in him. And since the Church—that is, the People of God, who have become his Body—is filled with his divine fullness, he finds in her, in return, his own fulfillment; he reaches in her the fullness of his perfect stature.[15] It is here, then, through the transition of this threefold fullness—of time, in which God gives his own fullness to his People in Christ, and finally of Christ in his People—that the changing of the People of God into the Church/Body of Christ takes place through the revelation of the mystery.

Analysis of this notion of the Church/Body of Christ, beginning with the Epistle to the Romans and 1 Corinthians, reveals its fundamentally eucharistic content. If the Church is the Body of Christ in more than a metaphorical sense, she is constructed and built within the celebration of the Eucharist, where the entire People of God participate in the same Body by which they were reconciled on the cross, with God and with themselves, simultaneously.[16]

It is because the Church is thus the People of God, becoming the Body of the dead and risen Christ, that she is the Temple of the Spirit,[17] the earthly society in which the Trinity opens itself to us and gathers us to itself by making us share in its life in charity, in the divine *agape*.

But it is also from the fact that the Church is the Body of Christ, formed and nourished in the Eucharist, that her permanent historical dependence with respect to Christ, as Head, results, that is, as the source and master of this way in her. This dependence, which is also "mystical" (though its "mystique," like the mystery, remains basically historical), is the object of the ecclesiological developments of the Captivity Epistles. The "body" theme unfolds there in discovery of the "head" theme. And this discovery is made from consideration of the "ministries" that Christ established in the Church and that appear there as a permanent representation of his character and function as Head. "And his gifts were that some should be apostles, some prophets, some evangelists, some pastors and teachers, for the equipment of the saints, for the work of the ministry, for building up the body of Christ until . . . speaking the truth in love, we are to grow up in every way into him who is the head, into Christ, from whom the whole body, joined and knit together by every joint with which it is supplied, when each part is working properly, makes bodily growth and upbuilds itself in love."[18]

Here, properly, is consideration of the Church under her hierarchical aspect, with the understanding that "hierarchy" will not be understood as a simple armature, juxtaposed to the Body, but as its vital organization, which assures each member not only his place but his function within the whole. Under this aspect, the Church is evidently at the maximum of her present identification with Christ: as the sacrament of Christ, in which and through which Christ himself is revealed and communicated in those whom he has sent.[19]

But, at the same moment, St. Paul reaffirms, on one hand, Christ's transcendence with respect to the Church in the precise use he makes of "head" in applying it to him,[20] and, on the other hand, the distinction in unity between the Church and Christ by applying to the former the image of "bride."[21]

## III. The Bride of Christ and Mother of the Faithful

The bridegroom and the bride are two *in one flesh,* and they remain *two.* The Church, even sanctified, even washed in the blood of Christ, even united to him in eternity, will never dissolve into him: from him, and from him alone, she will always and unceasingly receive the Spirit, which grants that she may be one Body with him.

Again, we must add to this distinction, which will never be abolished, a historical distinction of the highest importance. In the time in which we find ourselves, and until the Parousia, the Church is not yet fully (and will not be) the Bride of Christ, consummated in unity with him. She is only the Betrothed of the Lamb, whom the Spirit of the Bridegroom is preparing for this wedding, to which it makes her aspire. Holy in her terminus as in her beginning, the Church is nevertheless composed of sinners and bears upon herself, till the end of time, the stigmata of their sins. It is in this sense that St. Paul told the Corinthians: "I feel a divine jealousy for you, for I betrothed you to Christ to present you as a pure bride to her one husband"—at the very moment that he reproached them for the worst infidelities.[22]

Still, in the saints, the Church of the time preceding the Parousia already anticipates it. And this is undoubtedly why the fathers, following chapter 12 of Revelation, did not hesitate to see the Mother of the Elect in the Church. In them the action of the Savior's grace is sovereign, and therefore, in the ministers of the Church, does not use our humanity only as a simple instrument: by the intercession of the saints, by accomplishment in their flesh of "what is lacking in Christ's afflictions for the sake of his body,"[23] the Church has a mysterious part in this last birth of mankind in the "Last Adam"—a mysterious part, certainly, but so real that this Church, which will not be the perfect Bride of Christ until the end of time, gives birth to all her members in time.[24]

This brief outline has allowed us to review all aspects of the Church that the constitution *Lumen Gentium* detailed, one after the other and in the same order. This does not mean that we have traced our study's line of development from this document. Rather, this study, through its elaboration, attests to what may be called a spontaneous order of these various aspects of the Church, imposed by her progressive rediscovery over the course of the last century. Indeed, this order is not artificial. It is the order of germination of the major themes of Christian ecclesiology that results from the development of revelation throughout the Bible and in the ancient tradition of the Church.

## *IV. Elaboration of "Lumen Gentium": The Preparatory Period*

A quick examination of the manner of formation and final composition of the text of *Lumen Gentium* will help us understand it better. For this we shall use data furnished by Mgr. Gérard Philips in his book *L'Église et son mystère au deuxième Concile du Vatican, Histoire, texte et commentaire de la Constitution* Lumen Gentium.[25] No one was better able than he to retrace this history, in which his role was outstanding. We shall clarify or complete what he says with conferences by two other artisans of the text in question; the Chilean theologian, Mgr. Jorge Estévez, and the theologian from the Louvain, Mgr. Charles Moeller, who at this writing is a member of the Congregation of the Doctrine of the Faith.[26] This study will also clarify the council's use of the works of thinkers whose progress we traced in the part 1 of this work.

The preparatory theological commission established a schema on the Church in eleven chapters, following this outline:

1. The nature of the Church militant
2. The members of the Church militant and the necessity of the Church for salvation
3. The episcopacy as the highest form of the sacrament of orders and the priesthood
4. Residential bishops
5. The evangelical states of perfection
6. The laity
7. The magisterium of the Church
8. Authority and obedience in the Church
9. Relations between Church and state
10. Necessity of the Church to proclaim the Gospel to all peoples throughout the earth
11. Ecumenism

To this was added an independent schema, "the Blessed Virgin Mary, Mother of God and Mother of Men."

The bishops on the commission and the theologians who assisted them came from diverse backgrounds. Among the bishops, let us recall, were two Italians, one Frenchman, one German, one Yugoslav, some Americans and Orientals; and among the theologians, with the title "member" and not merely "consultor," six of the twenty were Italians and six were foreigners residing in Rome (the thirty-six consultors included eight Italians). The preparatory document bore the mark of Fr. Sebastian Tromp, S.J., the secretary of the commission, a Dutch theologian who had had a major part in the composition of the encyclical *Mystici Corporis*. From the very first debates, this initial text was so bitterly criticized that it would be easy to miss its positive elements—attested, moreover, by everything that remained of them in the text the council finally canonized!

From the outset, it gave a fundamental place to consideration of the Church as the Mystical Body of Christ. It emphasized the identity between this Mystical Body and the Church as institution, but the developments that followed were dominated by consideration of this other aspect, to the point that practically the only thing that evolved was an ecclesiology of "powers." The reproaches of triumphalism, legalism, and abstraction were one of the first reactions of the council. The discussions underlined the absence of any eschatological consideration (the Church militant was envisaged as if she were self-sufficient), the reduction of the laity to a purely passive role, and, more generally, the unilateral insistence on the aspects of authority (the teaching function of the pope and the other bishops appeared only within this perspective and their liturgical function was passed over in silence), as well as the fact that priests of second rank (to say nothing of deacons) were not even mentioned. On the relations of the episcopacy and the Sovereign Pontiff, the text was criticized for having limited itself to reasserting the doctrine of the First Vatican Council, without bringing forth the necessary and desired complements on the body of the episcopacy (even if it did not tend to absorb its functions within those of the pope).

This project appeared as deficient from the ecumenical point of view (the notion of "member" of the Church was defined too rigidly) as from the missionary viewpoint (the missions appeared merely as a sidelight of the Church). Finally, the paragraph on the Church and the state looked like a relic of a medieval past.

It is only just to acknowledge that many of these criticisms had already been formulated in the preparatory commission and that its president, Cardinal Ottaviani, had pledged that the secretary would take account of this, if he did not want to risk seeing his project discarded.

The most constructive of all these criticisms insisted on the necessity of giving an initial place to the notion of the Church as the People of God. As many bishops immediately emphasized, only in this way could her hierarchical aspect take on its true meaning and its justification: as a service of the whole body, assured by agents so disposed by Christ.

John XXIII was to bring this debate to its conclusion by ordering a profound revision of the schema which would take all these criticisms into account.[27]

## V. Elaboration of "Lumen Gentium": The First Modifications

It would be the task of the theological commission, formed in the council, to do the first work of remodeling. It was guided by a directive from the coordination commission, which at this stage planned a remodeling of the schema in four chapters: (1) the mystery of the Church, (2) the hierarchy of the Church and the bishops in particular, (3) the laity, and (4) the states of evangelical perfection.

The council's theological commission then recognized that this task supposed not only profound reworking of the previous text but composition of a quite different text, even if it were to retain many elements from the old one.

Other projected schemas had already made their appearance, all of which furnished elements and inspiration to the new text that the commission set forth in the second meeting of the council after the death of John XXIII and the election of Paul VI in 1963. A schema of German origin was known from the first debates. The influence of Karl Rahner, S.J., was noticeable, especially in a more supple and broader notion of "belonging" to the Church than by strict definition of its members (given by the original schema). For his part, Mgr. Parente had proposed a partial schema which dealt especially with the relations between the episcopacy in its entirety and the Sovereign Pontiff. The Chilean bishops produced a totally new composition, following the divisions of the first schema but within more biblical and patristic perspectives, which contained a first attempt at inserting the schema on the Virgin within the schema on the Church. Finally, a Franco-Belgian project, in which Fr. Congar, Mgr. Charles Moeller, and Mgr. Philips undoubtedly had the major part, was notable for its developments on the mystery of the Church, the laity, and insistence on the ministerial role of the hierarchy.[28]

This Franco-Belgian text, it seems, constituted the principal basis for the work of revision; it ended in a four-part schema. It complied with the plan suggested by the coordination commission and, therefore, allowed the schema on the Virgin to remain outside the schema on the Church. But it made an innovation by titling the third chapter "Of the People of God and the Laity" and the fourth chapter "The Call to Holiness in the Church."

This explicit appearance of the People-of-God theme was accepted by the coordination commission; also, in a note that was joined to the schema of the special commission, the coordination commission proposed to make this theme a chapter apart: the second chapter, between the initial chapter on the mystery and the chapter on the hierarchy. This latter chapter, however, would still be followed by a special chapter on the laity.

In this decision we may indeed see a major turning point in the history of our text. It had the advantage of giving its proper and fundamental place to consideration of the People of God, but it had the disadvantage (without realizing it) of causing a split in consideration of the laity. Appearing for the first time—at the beginning—as the body of the faithful, the laity was then assigned second rank, after the hierarchy, and was defined negatively: as those who have no special function in the Church. Thus it was difficult to avoid encouraging the tendency of the theology of the laity to define the laity less by its role in the Church than by its role outside the Church. We shall return to the ambiguities inherent in this trend.

## VI. Elaboration of "Lumen Gentium": The Second Period of the Council

Not without very heated discussions, the debates to which this project gave rise at the second session of the council (Sept. 29 to Dec. 4, 1963) led to the final introduction of the original schema on Mary into the schema on the Church. The debates also gave rise to introduction of a special mention of the diaconate, including the necessity of restoring it in the (Latin) Church as a permanent order and not as a simple step on the way to the priesthood.

But the major contribution of these discussions was the vote on the interlocutory questions proposed by the cardinal moderators after the debate on the collegiality of the episcopacy. The aim was to receive orientation on this major point, from the council itself, for the definitive composition. The questions were proposed October 15, withdrawn the next day because of vehement protests, and submitted to a vote on October 30. Here is a literal translation of these questions:

> The Fathers are invited to declare whether they wish that the schema be edited in such a fashion that it will be said:

1. The episcopal consecration constitutes the highest degree of the sacrament of Order;

2. Every bishop, legitimately consecrated, in communion with the other bishops and with the Pope, who is the head and the principle of their unity, is a member of the Body of Bishops;

3. The Body or College of bishops succeeds the College of the Apostles in its task of evangelization, sanctification, and government, and this Body of Bishops, in union with its head, the Roman Pontiff, and never without this head (whose primatial right remains intact and complete over all pastors and faithful), possesses the plenary and supreme power over the universal Church;

4. This authority comes by divine right to the College of Bishops, united with its head.

To these questions a fifth question was joined, on the restoration of the diaconate, which we have mentioned. On all these questions a massive majority was formed: (1) 2,123 *placet* and 34 *non placet;* (2) 2,049 and 104; (3) 1,808 and 336; (4) 1,717 and 408. The fifth obtained 1,588 votes, against 525.

After the new interruption of the council, and on the basis of the 1963 debates, the work of the commission resulted in a project that was amended according to these indications, with six chapters. The schema on the Virgin was added as the last chapter of the five which followed from the new ordering of material, toward which the previous work and the last decision of the coordination commission had been aimed. As a result of other suggestions, which were renewed with particular insistence over the course of the same phase of the council, a seventh chapter was added which fused the consideration of the eschatological aspect of the Church and that of the already glorified saints, responding thereby to various demands.[29]

## VII. Elaboration of "Lumen Gentium": The Final Editing

The council's last session (Sept. 14 to Nov. 21, 1964), before reaching the final vote of November 18 (2,096 *placet* and 23 *non placet*), ratified the agreement on insertion of the refashioned text on the Virgin and, at the request of the religious, split chapter 5 in two: one part on the general vocation to holiness and the other on the religious. This modification may not be totally beneficial. Undoubtedly, the risk would not have been merely illusory, in involuntarily contributing to losing sight of the sense and importance of the religious vocation in the Church, if a special chapter had not been devoted to it. However, the accepted division was not free from obscuring the fact that the vocation to Christian perfection is not a special vocation; hence the last-minute proposition, which could not be followed, for it would have required a new reworking of the whole text. It was suggested that what concerned this general vocation to holiness be placed immediately after the chapter on the People of God. However, in the case where this displacement would have been effectuated, we may wonder whether the text devoted to the religious would not, like the text on the laity, have lost its natural position, rooted within the whole context.

One last point that must be mentioned with respect to the constitution *Lumen Gentium* is the famous *nota praevia* which was added to it at the last moment, even though it specified that it was not part of it. We remember the emotion it caused at the time and the interpretations that were supplied for it with a certain levity, as if one had in this note a pontifical intervention, restricting or wrongly interpreting the text that resulted from the conciliar deliberations! From the distance of time, as Mgr. Philips stresses, all this agitation seems artificial, not to say ridiculous. The aim of the four major points of the note was simply to put aside the baseless objections of some of those who, until then, had been opposed to acceptance of the conciliar text, as if it represented the Church's denial of defined doctrines, especially at the First Vatican Council. It did so in limiting itself to recalling specifications explicitly mentioned in the text or responses that had already been made to the envisaged objections.

The first and perhaps the most important point, though also the most arguable, was that *collegium* in the conciliar text does not correspond to the customary sense of this word (as defined by the jurisconsult Ulpian), which alludes to a body whose members are equal in power and cannot act except as a totality.

The second point declares that since episcopal consecration confers the threefold pastoral function (order, teaching, and jurisdiction), its exercise remains subject to the established rules. Far from reintroducing the idea that the defined jurisdiction, assigned by the pope to the new bishops, would constitute of itself, their pastoral responsibility, it emphasized that this appointment simply defines its area and modalities of application.

The third point specifies that the episcopal college, presided over by the pope, holds plenary and universal power over the whole Church, while the head of the college and its members, in the exercise of this power, must respect their respective missions and mutual relationships. As Mgr. Philips repeats, if the synthetic character of this note confers a precision on it in the expression which the more extended and complex text of the constitution may not have had, "it does not go even an inch further in the matter of doctrine."

Finally, the fourth point is limited to repeating, in the same terms as the constitution itself, that the assent of the pope is required for any strictly collegial act.

The *nota bene* that follows is of direct ecumenical interest, and it is surprising that people were not aware of it from the start. It is aimed at doing away with the supposition that the description in the conciliary text of the normal exercise of episcopal jurisdiction would contrast sharply with the validity (rather, the invalidity) of the jurisdiction exercised by bishops who were validly consecrated but not in communion with the Roman Pontiff. Without this caution, the text of the constitution could easily have been interpreted by some as a condemnation of the Orthodox episcopacy, which obviously was not the council fathers' intention.

On the other hand, it is clear that the four preceding points, without altering or minimizing the content of the constitution, allowed a quasi-unanimous vote, which otherwise would not have been obtained.[30]

## VIII. *Ecclesiological Balance Sheet of Vatican II*

These brief notations suffice, we think, to allow us to measure the point to which the council's work canonized the essential aspect (in many regards) of the rediscovery whose developments we followed in Christian thought of the last century (part I). Obviously, this is not to say that the council was able to say everything in this constitution, and to bring everything into the light, on the subject of the Church. No conciliary text has ever had such pretensions, no matter what subject was under consideration. It is certain, however, that the most salient points of this rediscovery, which we summed up in beginning this chapter, now belong with the great lines of their organic relationship—to the express teaching of the extraordinary magisterium of the Church in its most solemn form.

In passing, we have noted a few points on which obscurities remain, and even ambiguities, to which, for the moment, we shall not return but leave to later discussion. However, we must mention obvious gaps. More than once, as we shall see, the principle of their necessary complements is found in other texts of the same council.

The first insufficiency is a rather poorly developed doctrine of the local Church, and we must also point out the small place the text gives to the eucharistic celebration in relation to the Church. On these points, the constitution on the liturgy supplies elements of the greatest interest, which from now on must be assimilated by every endeavor at ecclesiological synthesis.

In connection with the importance of the local Church, the conciliar text suffered from the reaction caused by the first draft: it was concerned, as we saw, only with residential bishops. On the other hand, the text that was finally canonized has almost nothing on the distinction between their status and that of simple coadjutor or auxiliary bishops and, more generally, the status of bishops who are called "titular," whose number has multiplied in modern times. Nevertheless, considering all the data of tradition is an enormous problem. To imagine, as some people do, that this distinction could have been treated (or rather suppressed *de facto* by this omission) is, we believe, a curious illusion, whose consequences could be disastrous.

We have just used the word "tradition," and perhaps the most surprising lacuna in the constitution *Lumen Gentium* is that the problem of tradition, which is essential for the life of the Church and for understanding it, was not even mentioned in it. Yet it was treated very fruitfully and at length by the constitution on revelation and its sources. Thus one of the major tasks of present-day ecclesiology is to integrate what was said in another context with the authentic understanding of the Church.

A less obvious insufficiency is that scanty material in *Lumen Gentium* on the presbyterate, or the priesthood of second rank, is out of proportion with the importance of the pastoral tasks that over the centuries have come to be entrusted to it. Even the connection between the episcopacy and the presbyterate is hardly touched on. Thus we have a vast zone that is open to work and research. There is no question that an analogical extension of the problem of collegiality should be envisaged here.

This point is just as valid for the relationship between the clergy in general and the laity. The distinction of the ministerial or hierarchical priesthood and the priesthood of the laity, as well as their complementarity, have been stated but not clarified.

On still another point, the first draft proposed a contribution which vanished along the way: the relationship between the Church and the state. This part simply disappeared, without any substitution. Undoubtedly, the pastoral constitution *Gaudium et Spes* states many elements of the relationship of the Church to human society in general, but it is more an account of a series of generous intentions than an elaborated doctrine. And on the problem of the state, the data are particularly sparse.

Yet we are struck above all by two lacunae in the teaching of *Lumen Gentium,* and would search the other conciliar texts in vain to find any compensation for this situation. These two insufficiencies may seem antithetical, but their "simultaneity" is more than striking. The constitution on the Church practically ignores canon law, and, with the exception of a paragraph that is more pious than doctrinal, complely ignores the Holy Spirit!

At the council, many strong statements against "legalism" were heard. It is certain that they were aimed at a very real danger, and that the first draft presented to the fathers gave some basis for these attacks, but it is regrettable that no clear, firm voices in the aula of the council asserted that legalism is not law but a caricature of it. Legalism is sclerosis of law, in abstraction and formalism. To suppose, on the other hand, that the Church should discard law in order to rediscover the Church of Charity would be to enter a path of ruinous illusions. A Church that would stifle law would not become the Church of Charity but a church of capriciousness. For law, correctly understood, is nothing more than justice applied to concrete situations, and the history of the social movement teaches that "charity" that is not concerned with justice, nor with justice applied in the concrete, is merely a mockery of charity.

Here we see the lamentable consequence of teaching canon law in a way that is too often reduced to a horizonless casuistry, based on a merely grammatical commentary on the code and the decisions of the Roman congregations. It is not by throwing law overboard that we extract ourselves from this disastrous situation but only through historical and theological study of canonical tradition. Alas, where in today's Catholic Church will we find such a study? This deficiency is all the more deplorable since, with Protestants themselves (who were the first to balk against ecclesiastical legalism), we are witnessing a renaissance of the study of law in general and canon law in particular, which is of the highest interest. The works of Sohm in Germany, the more modest but provocative studies of Jacques Ellul in France, and the research in the Anglican Church for revision of its canonical legislation are evidence of this revival. To suppose that we could build a satisfactory ecclesiology in the Catholic Church today, and particularly one that has an ecumenical orientation, without engaging in such research, is an idle, catastrophic dream.

It is true that a similar deficiency is found in a great part of the most vibrant Orthodox theology today, proceeding from Khomiakov. There again, reaction against a certain legalism has led to a misappreciation of juridical values, but in this case the reaction has a positive counterpart in a basically pneumatological theology and spirituality. It would be vain to look for anything analogous in the contemporary Catholic Church. In particular, if the ecclesiology of the council is strongly Christological, it gives practically no place to the Spirit, despite a few preliminary statements in the first chapter of *Lumen Gentium*.

It would be hard to reproach the council fathers for this, when we observe that the theologians who ought to have advised them on this lapse seem not to have felt any need for development in this direction. And yet, faced not only with Orthodox theology and the best ecclesiastical ideals of Protestantism, what can the "unknown God" expect (according to the cruel but just remark of the late Fr. Dillard, S. J.), as a Catholic ecumenical approach (if the Holy Spirit abides), from the Pontiffs and doctors of Catholicism? We are obliged to record how much Catholic ecumenism, at the council and elsewhere, is still in the realm of "velleity": the best intentions abound, undoubtedly, but are incapable of being put into effect since there is neither sufficient knowledge of others nor (even less) a sufficient positive grasp of the depth of our own tradition.

This brief, schematic balance sheet of the ecclesiological work of the council has no other purpose than to help us better define the task of the Catholic theologian when he approaches the "problem" of the Church. It allows us to appreciate how many gradually rediscovered major elements on this point are now explicitly and solemnly proclaimed parts of Catholic doctrine. At the same time, it indicates the points which require new research and those on which the door has at least reopened—without forgetting a few others (and not necessarily the least important) which have not yet been grappled with.

The paths have thus been marked for our following chapters, not to find a complete system of Catholic ecclesiology but (at least) to outline the principle lines of coherent Catholic thought on the Church. For this, we shall rely on acquisitions of the council that can be considered definitive, by endeavoring to make an inventory of all the possibilities and, on this basis, attacking a few problems that are still unresolved, or that have not been dealt with, but now, at the end of the twentieth century, no longer seen to be evaded by the Church and by Christians.

## Notes

1. 1 Corinthians 2:6-7 and the whole context.
2. D. Deden, "Le mystère paulinien," in *Ephemerides Theologicae Lovanienses* (1936), pp. 403ff.
3. Cf. Galatians 3:28 and Colossians 3:11.
4. Cf. Colossians 1:22 and Ephesians 2:16.
5. Ephesians 1:10. On the word *anakephalaiosasthai* and its use here, see A. Feuillet, *Le Christ Sagesse de Dieu d'après les épîtres pauliniennes* (Paris, 1966), p. 212.

6. Colossians 1:27.

7. Ephesians 3:10.

8. Ephesians 1:23.

9. Cf. Matthew 13:11 and parallels with 1 Corinthians 4:1, 13:2, 14:2.

10. On all this see the work of M. J. Le Guillou, *Le Christ et l'Eglise, théologie du mystère* (Paris, 1963).

11. See chapters I and II of the constitution *Lumen Gentium*.

12. On the sense of *pleroma* in St. Paul, the best in-depth discussion is undoubtedly that of A. Feuillet, in the work mentioned in note 5.

13. Cf. Ephesians 1:10 and Galatians 4:4.

14. Cf. Colossians 1:19 and 2:9.

15. Cf. Ephesians 1:23 and 4:13.

16. See the whole of the twelfth chapter in both epistles, as well as 1 Corinthians 10:16ff.

17. Cf. Ephesians 2:21, which makes the transition from the image of the body to that of the temple.

18. Ephesians 4:11ff.

19. See chapter III of *Lumen Gentium*.

20. Cf. Colossians 1:18, 2:10 and 19, and Ephesians 1:22 and 4:15.

21. See Ephesians 5:22ff, as well as 2 Corinthians 11:2.

22. Cf. with the text of 2 Corinthians (mentioned in preceding note) Revelation 21:2 and 9 and 22:17. On this aspect of the Church, according to which she is, on one hand, distinct from Christ and on the other called to sanctify herself in order to unite herself to him (and *by* uniting herself to him), see chapters IV to VI of *Lumen Gentium*.

23. Colossians 1:24.

24. The relationship of the pilgrim Church to the heavenly eschatological Church and therefore to the role of the saints in the Church is the object of chapters VII and VIII of *Lumen Gentium*.

25. 2 vols.; Paris, 1967 and 1968.

26. The text will be found in the collective volume *Vatican II, an Interfaith Appraisal,* ed. J. H. Miller (Notre Dame, Ind., 1966), pp. 101ff.

27. On all this see Philips, op. cit., 1:13ff.

28. Ibid., p. 21.

29. Ibid., pp. 22ff.

30. Ibid., pp. 49ff.

# Chapter 2
# The People of God

It is impossible to understand anything about Christ, the Word of God made flesh, if we do not begin by following the progress of the Divine Word in the Old Testament. Similarly, we cannot hope to understand the Church other than by the formation of the People of God in Israel.[1]

Furthermore, the two themes of Christ and the Church, the Word and the People, are constantly and innately associated. Christ is inseparable from the Church, just as the Church is from Christ. The Divine Word never had another interlocutor, properly speaking, than the People of God. If it appeared very early as the preeminent creative Word, it is because this People appeared in history as its creation. Reciprocally, the People of God, from the origins of Israel, can understand themselves only as the People called and constituted by the Word to which they listened. This bursts forth in the deeds of Abraham, the father of the People of believers in the Word.

## I. The Call and Election of Abraham

At this point, we do not have to pose the critical problem of the historicity that must be acknowledged in the Pentateuch accounts concerning Abraham. Yet it must be emphasized that the archeological discoveries of the beginning of this century have shown singular fidelity to the conditions of the time in which these accounts are situated and require us, from a purely historical point of view, to acknowledge in them an objective value that the school of Wellhausen misunderstood. What interests us straight off, moreover, is the representative or germinative value that the biblical writers intended to give the father of the People with respect to the People themselves.[2]

Abraham comes on the scene at the moment when the first civilizations of the Near East (more precisely, the first cities) began to be built. His father, Terah, is shown as taking part in, or associating himself with the setting up of Haran, a city in Canaan. But Abraham's "call" made him break off from this movement: "Leave your country, your family and the house of your father" was the first Divine Word addressed to him, the beginning of the Word of God for Israel. Abraham's call uprooted him from the human city that was built (or in the process of being built) where he was born and cast him into a nomadic state.[3]

Modern scholars tend to argue about the superiority of the city over the country, or vice versa. Harvey Cox claimed to find in the Bible an exaltation of urban life, where the city of man is set in contradistinction to the life of the sedentary farmer, where man remains absorbed (or reabsorbed) in an inhuman nature.[4] This is only a view of the mind, like veneer over the facts, but its opposite would fall under the same criticism. Biblical inspiration, which is eminently concrete, does not know these abstract generalities. It was not with city life as such that Abraham was invited to break. It was with a particular kind of city, which the preceding chapter in Genesis describes, under the figure of the Tower of Babel (i.e., cities men plot to build against God, so that they not only do without him but actually—so to speak—take his place). The rest of the message addressed to Abraham shows he was not called to leave a city of this type, except to prepare for (or prepare himself for) the foundation of another city of a quite opposite type: "Go into the land that I will show you. I will make you a great nation."[5]

The Epistle to the Hebrews finally says it, at the end of a long tradition of encomia of the fathers which goes back to the Wisdom Literature—as we see, for example, in Ecclesiasticus (Sirach)—and which, through the intermediary of the Palestinian Haggadah, extended as far as the *De Abrahamo* of Philo: "By faith Abraham obeyed when he was called to go out to a place which he was to receive as an inheritance; and he went out, not knowing where he was to go. . . . *For he looked forward to the city which has foundations, whose builder and maker is God."* It cannot be better said that Abraham's vocation was neither for nor against city life but, rather, against the city that men build against God in order to dispense with him, to supplant him, and *for* the city that he will build for them.

This is also why—if it is true that the vocation accepted by Abraham, as its immediate result, sent him into nomadic existence—it does not constitute consecration of the nomadic state as such, despite what the Rechabites might have thought.[6] Undoubtedly, God will make use of this phase of nomadism for a purification, a disinvolvement. "The desert is monotheistic" has been written and repeated, with some exaggeration. The desert life—in any case for Abraham and for his People after him, with Moses—broke pernicious bonds and thus allowed for preparation of the reconstructions of which God himself would be the author. Furthermore, the first Christian monks, such as St. Gregory Nazianzus, did not lose themselves in arbitrary allegories in seeing in Abraham's exodus the first example, even the type, of the flight into the desert.[7] Very probably, the Jewish communities of the Qumran type had preceded them in this view and, by doing so, followed an interpretation already suggested by the prophets.

It remains that nomadism here is not a goal but a necessary transition which, at the same time, proved itself to be a providential preparation for the sole end in sight: the new city, which no longer has anything in common with earthly cities, for it is God himself who built it.

A second element to be considered in this calling of Abraham is that he appears as unique, a person consecrated by God's call in the sense of being set aside, of being separated, but in no way alone or isolated. And this must be understood in a twofold way: in connection with the People whose father he will be and in connection with all peoples.

Abraham leaves his family (i.e., the family whose child he was) but not the family of which he is called to be the father. Even before a son was born to him, it was with his wife, his nephew Lot, and a group of servants and household members that he went off. His lot, however individual (or, if you prefer, personal) it may have been, was also their lot, before it was the lot of his descendants. The blessing that was promised him is also theirs. Let us not say that he is merely an eponymous hero or that he is considered simply as the representative of the group. The opposite would be truer; in God's eyes, the group has its existence only in him and through him. But reciprocally, it was he and only he who bore the responsibility for all. The father englobes, so to speak, all his children. And the children, important though the male line is, because it guarantees continuity of fathers and patriarchs after the first one, are not limited solely to blood heirs and heirs who have title to the possessions which are handed down with it.

Consequently, this ambivalent relationship of fathers to the whole family, from whose lot they are not separated—any more than it has a destiny apart from the destiny of its leader—can take on different shades of meaning and be modified, but it remains a constant, basic principle of the People. Whatever the title of the providential individual on whom it is centered, the People will exist as a People only around a king, a priest, a prophet, a "father," in the sense that the latter term can include physical paternity, even though from the outset it surpasses it.[8] For this reason, whether the People pursue their wandering or settle down, or seem to settle down in a temporary or permanent city, they will always remain a family: the children of Abraham.

Yet—and here we enter the most mysterious aspect of the election in the call to Abraham—if it sets them apart (i.e., Abraham and his descendants) from other peoples and other families on earth, and even if it uproots them, it does not make them indifferent to these others. Their special destiny, from the very beginning, is revealed as obscurely connected with the collective destiny of mankind. Let us read to completion that first message to Abraham: "I will make of you a great nation, and I will bless you, and make your name great, so that you will be a blessing. I will bless those who bless you, and him who curses you will I curse; and by you all the families of the earth shall bless themselves."

What is the precise meaning of the last phrase? Equally, we must avoid unduly restricting or extending its import. The most obvious, most immediate meaning is that Abraham and his group will be so blessed in the eyes of all that they will become for all a paradigm of the divine blessings. But it does not seem that the sense can be reduced to only this explanation; the formula implies some kind of reflection of the special blessing extended to Abraham and his race on all races. And it does not seem questionable that those who composed the characteristic episode of Abraham's intercession for Sodom had interpreted the formula in this sense.

This leads to a deeper biblical sense of "election," of which it can be said that Abraham and all Israel, after him and in him, will remain the prototype.[9] Every vocation, every call of God reveals a prior choice, an election, which always remains deeply mysterious. Many times the Bible reveals that those whom men—and men of God first of all—conjectured to be the "chosen ones," the "elect," were not; instead, they are the very last persons one would have thought, or somebody whom one would never have thought of at all. When Samuel was sent to anoint a son of Jesse, he imagined, in seeing Eliab, that Eliab was the future "anointed one" whom the Lord had in mind; but the Lord told him: "Do not look on his appearance or on the height of his stature, because I have rejected him; for the Lord sees not as man sees. Man looks on the outward appearance, but the Lord looks on the heart." All the sons who seemed to have a reasonable chance filed before him, one after the other, but in vain. Then, after the seventh, Samuel states: "The Lord has not chosen these.... Are all your sons here?" Jesse replies: "There remains yet the youngest, but behold, he is keeping the sheep." This son was sent for, and it was before this child, David, that Samuel heard the divine decision: "Arise, anoint him; for this is he."[10]

But this in no way signifies that the chosen one had merely to enjoy an unearned favor in peace. One is never chosen for oneself. The chosen one of the Lord no longer belongs to himself but to the Lord, and if the Lord sets him apart from his brothers, it is for them—for a service that concerns them all. The one whose destiny is apart no longer has a separate destiny, except to contribute to realizing God's plan for others, for all the others, in a way that ultimately will always escape him, and the rest as well.

But there is one more point that directly concerns the vocation whereby the divine plan, the divine election, makes itself known, even though it is first a characteristic of the Word, and it must be specified. Like every divine message in the Bible, this Word of God, which vocation is, is never simply a "revelation." That is to say, it is never limited to uncovering what already existed; quite the contrary, it determines and produces what God had in mind, which had remained hidden in him and now will be impressed in the world, in the course of things, by the sole power of his Word.

It is necessary to insist on this point, for we are all in this respect unconscious disciples of Plato, for whom there was no knowledge, worthy of the name (other than the Immutable), of what existed already and will always exist. From this viewpoint, modern science is Platonic in its notion of the "truth" to be discovered, but biblical revelation is of quite a different nature. The biblical Word never has as its object simply unveiling an eternal truth. It is always a revelation of a divine plan, undoubtedly eternal in God, which, in what concerns the world in which we live, is aimed at introducing and creating what was not there before. The Word of God is not so much the simple communication of this project as the power that had been destined to actualize it—and, we must immediately add, alone capable of doing so. God calls what was not and makes it be by his call. The vocation of Abraham, in other words, like every biblical vocation, did not reveal to him what he already was, without knowing it; it allowed him, and obliged and compelled him, to become it.

This again is a characteristic of biblical revelation, of the plan of salvation of which the people to whom it is addressed will be the bearer, which will be verified at the end as well as at the outset. It is here that the most profound error of Bultmann's "demythologization" must be pointed out. Bultmann wanted to free (to scour, as it were) the Divine Word of all the adventitious "gnostic" elements with which it may have become burdened (according to him) in order to be expressed. But what is the essence of Gnosticism in Jewish or Christian clothes, which is always and substantially deeply pagan and

Hellenistic? It is the noncritical *a priori* certitude that man, in order to be "saved," need only recognize his true nature, his genuine situation in the scale of beings. All the evils from which he suffers or can suffer are, in the last analysis, only illusions. To be "saved," he need only have his eyes opened. The Gnostic "savior" is the bearer of revelation and, to that extent, the "savior" only in this sense.

According to Bultmann, the pure residue of the kerygma after demythologization excludes any idea of divine, transcendent intervention in the heart of our world which would change something essential. Once the supposedly mythical "envelopes" of the object of Bultmannian "faith" have been removed, that "faith" adheres to a vision of an eternal relationship of the believing subject to his God, which does not have to occur but only be discovered. The only "event" which this "faith" knows is its own birth. What, then, is such a "faith," if not precisely the essential feature of the pseudo-Christian "gnosis"?

On the other hand, biblical faith is not a simple subjective discovery of the nontemporal "fact" that one is saved. It is quite the contrary: the discovery that we were not saved but that God intervenes in the world, in our life, so that we become saved. His Word does not bring us the simple possibility of a "decision" that would put us in possession of a ready-made salvation, acquired from the beginning. It is this salvation—not as accomplished but as being accomplished; not as realized, or simply recognized, by our faith but as created by the Word itself—that elicits it. In this regard, faith is nothing by itself. It is valid only as surrender, as handing over oneself, to the Word, bursting into our history. And it is not only in our spirit that the Word creates in this way but in concrete existence in the objective world, outside of which our subjectivity would be but a dream existence.[11]

In short, the Word does not uncover for us some true countenance of ourselves or the world which we did not yet know and which suffices for our happiness and our salvation to discover. It is the divine intervention in the world, and thus in our life, which will create a new life for us here, which we could never have hoped for and which, at the same time, will make a new world. The "blessing" promised to Abraham and his descendants, which must be communicated mysteriously to the entire human world—what the ultimate stages of revelation call "salvation"—is not that the world will learn that it is already saved; it will discover its need to be saved, which it will always have, by accepting the salvation that comes to it in the Divine Word. This salvation is not simply unveiled; the Word brings it about sovereignly, for it and in it.

Election is always prior to vocation, but only in God. In the world of our concrete existence, vocation begins our effective realization of the plan that concerns us. And it is not intuition of our election, the faith, which would have some intrinsic power to bring it about; it is the transcendent Word, the free and gratuitous intervention of the sovereign God, which alone accomplishes it. Man's faith is *in the principle* of this creation, for it is its own beginning. But it is not *its principle,* which is in the divine intervention that the Word envelops and manifests.

Obviously, this does not signify that the Word which calls us has a magic efficacy—though we may wonder whether the object of the apparently incongruous account that immediately follows the calling of Abraham is not to show just that.

Called by God, and accepting this call in obedient faith, Abraham is not thereby transformed into another man—into the man of God, the perfect righteous one. What follows in chapter 12 of Genesis shows him in Egypt, in order to escape the famine, and plotting to have his wife pass for his sister so that he might get in the good graces of Pharaoh by prostituting her to him. This account shocks us, and rabbinical exegeses show that it shocked its first hearers. The account also shows that the procedure, when it was disclosed, shocked this honest pagan, the Pharaoh, just as much.[12]

The sense of this unedifying story seems to be that the chosen man will be tempted to realize the divine promises not solely on faith, surrendering himself to the Divine Word in order to bring them about, but by his wiles. In other words, it is not by a wave of a magic wand that the Divine Word transforms believers; it is by slow and progressive education in faith, in which our first need is to discover our total incapacity to force realization of the divine promises by our own initiatives. If we follow the other path, we thereby deny our faith.

Another account which is central to Abraham's story undoubtedly includes the elementary teaching that underlies this coarse episode, but, by enveloping the first *adumbratio* of what will be the decisive divine intervention for the salvation of the people, it involves much more. This account, of the sacrifice of Isaac,[13] fascinated the Jewish imagination, before it captured—just as strongly—the Christian imagination. And we are not dealing merely with imagination in the flowery setting of the Haggadah, but with profound meditation in the maturation of the faith.[14]

We recall the salient facts. Isaac is the child of the promise, that is, the promised child, but especially the child on whom rests realization of the great and mysterious promise in the call addressed to his father, to the father of the faith. And Abraham, who is asked to offer this child in sacrifice, does not hesitate, but goes immediately to the place designated, Mount Moriah. On the way, as they came nearer, the child, carrying the wood for his own pyre, asked: "Here is the fire and the wood, but where is the lamb for the sacrifice?" Abraham replied, not measuring the "impossible truth" in his answer: "God will provide." But when he had set the wood on the improvised altar, and had bound his son, and made ready to cut his throat, the "Angel of the Lord" intervened: "Do not lay your hand on the lad or do anything to him; for now I know that you obey God, seeing you have not withheld your son, your only son, from me." Then Abraham saw the ram, caught by its horns in the brambles, and understood that he was to sacrifice the ram in place of his son.

There is no question that this text, not as a result of some adventitious exegesis superimposed after the fact, but in accord with its own framework, should be interpreted on two levels. If we balk at such an explanation, which goes against the grain of our Cartesian habits, it is simply that we have difficulty dealing with the fact that intrudes on us: the literary genre of many a biblical account (like many other accounts, religious or not, from the ancient world) corresponds neither to our own habits of mind nor to the habits of mind they reflect.

On the first level, this biblical account envelops an implicit but definitive condemnation of human sacrifice, a prohibition that was renewed by all the prophets. But on another level it supposes a positive sense, in what is asked of Abraham and what he is willing to do.

It could be said that God asks man to do what he knows he cannot do, because it is only God who can do it. Whether by giving what is best in himself or by returning to God his own gifts—and even the preeminent gift of supereminent grace, the gift which is the very promise of God—man cannot supply the sacrifice that will consummate the realization in him, for him, and by him of the divine plan. God himself, and only he, can intervene for that.

And yet this is not the innermost kernel of the account, for it would not be enough to say that man must at least begin, at least grant, what God alone will accomplish. We must go further and say that the man of faith, the man by whom the Word makes itself heard, the man in whom this Word dwells from now on, carries within himself the image, and more than the image, of the action and presence of the Divine Person.

It seems that this is what the Epistle to the Hebrews indicates when it tells us that Abraham will recover his son, "figuratively speaking."[15] This means that the "only son," Abraham's beloved child, was the image of the beloved Child of God himself, whom he alone would offer for our salvation. But it means still more: in Abraham, in his action, in the figure he clothed and that was one with him, God revealed himself as the One who was to complete Abraham's faith.

Thus, if we cannot say of the representative man of the People—king, priest, or prophet, but "father of the faith"—that the Divine Word has been made flesh, we must say, in a mysterious but real sense, that the Word is already in the process of becoming incarnate. In relation to such an account as this does, St. Irenaeus' formula on the Word of God take all its force and meaning: From the first steps taken by the People of God, the Divine Word "accustomed itself to living with the children of men."

This explains the unequaled importance and mysterious significance that Abraham's sacrifice has kept in Jewish tradition, for which this sacrifice is the preeminent *abodah* (i.e., cultic service, liturgy), which God acts to consecrate his People to himself in actions performed by the man of God.

It also brings us back to earlier texts—on conclusion of the covenant between Abraham, and his posterity with him, and the God who spoke to him.[16] The notion of a special covenant with a divinity was common to the Semitic peoples, but the special aspect of this particular covenant is that God takes the initiative and remains sovereign in it. In this case, the covenant is not a kind of contract between equals, in which the conditions are debated back and forth because each has need of the other. The prophets emphasized that the God who made a covenant with Abraham had no need of him or his people. In particular (contrary to the Semitic *baalim*), God has no need that man commit himself to feeding him regularly by sacrifices, and consequently, in contracting the covenant, he did not place himself in any way at the mercy of man; he in no way subjected himself to satisfying his desires and whims. The covenant of the God who spoke to Abraham is pure grace. On the other hand, if it requires obedient and (as the episode of Isaac shows) absolute faith (obedience without reserve), it introduces its partner to a divine friendship that no one had any idea of up to that time. This is what the last texts about Abraham show, and we must examine them.

God's covenant with Abraham is described as formally concluded by a sacrifice in which we can say that God himself is the priest, just as he provided the victim in Isaac's sacrifice.[17] God had ordered Abraham to prepare a covenant sacrifice, typical of the customs of the time, by setting the halves of the slaughtered victims between which face to face, the two allies were to pass. An unusual darkness then came upon him and filled him with religious dread; then a flame of fire appeared from the midst of this darkness and passed between the victims. This is the first divine manifestation in darkness and fire, which multiplies in the Exodus accounts.

The following chapters, after the birth of Ishmael (the child of Hagar, on whom a special blessing rests, though not the hereditary promise), complete this covenant sacrifice with the seal of circumcision.[18] This practice was relatively current among the Semites and was prescribed to Abraham and his descendants, as well as to everyone who would be (or want to be) incorporated into the chosen people. Reciprocally, Abraham's legitimate descendants who would not comply with this requisite would automatically be excluded from the covenant.

It is worth noting that this episode occurs after an explicit promise of fecundity, which is expressed in the change of the original name, Abram, into Abraham (explained as signifying a multitude). It is clear that, in this context, circumcision signifies the consecration of human fecundity to the covenant. The People of God will be the people of the sons of Abraham, but it already appears that sonship in the flesh is but a material means of their propagation. Of itself, it does not suffice. Each generation must be joined to the People in renewed consecration, and, what is more, it is evident that carnal generation is not necessary: consecration brings adoption that is not simply juridical but fully real, to the point of making an outsider a "son of Abraham," that is, a son of the covenant without restriction.[19]

However sovereign and free the personal intervention of God might appear in building the chosen people, the intimacy of the relationship into which they are led with this God, whose People they become, is no less profound. The contrary is true. This God will be "their" God reciprocally, in a much purer and much deeper sense than was the case for the "lords of the covenant" of the other Semites.

This will be shown by the last account concerning Abraham, which we must examine. It is connected with the last and most formal renewal of the promise of a chosen posterity in the person of Isaac, who finally was born, in the wonderful vision of the three "men" under the oak trees at Mamre. The salient characteristics of this narrative, which are practically on a par with the sacrifice of Isaac, condense the significance of the vocation of Abraham and, in him, all his people (Israel). Its popularity will be no less great among Christians. From the mosaics of San Vitale in Ravenna to the famous icon of Andrei Rublev, traditional iconography adduces all its implications.[20]

While his nomadic camp slept, Abraham watched and meditated, and three mysterious travelers suddenly appeared to him. Immediately, he hastened to them and bade them accept his hospitality. (As the response of the Latin liturgy says: *Tres vidit, unum adoravit.*) In them he perceived the veiled revelation of the divine presence, coming to him. He wished not only to retain that presence but to receive it in his home. They consented and, at his table, shared in the meal he prepared. Christian commentary sees this episode as a prefiguration of the Trinity and the Eucharist. This does not necessarily mean that Abraham was clearly aware of this, but even the Jewish commentaries emphasize the textual implications in which Christians legitimately find the nebula (as it were) for condensation of these dogmas.

Once again, God has no need for the covenant with man. He carries within himself his own fecundity and (dare we say) his own society. But in his limitless goodness, he approaches man. As will be said later, the God whom the heavens of heavens could not contain comes, as a traveler, to the home of man and agrees to be received and to take his place there. (This is what the rabbis call *Shekinah*: the special presence of the transcendent God among his own.) By accepting the meal the man offered him, God does not enter human society but, rather, the man is introduced into the divine society. Having taken this meal with the man in his transitory, nomadic dwelling place, as he searched for the eternal city, God felt so friendly to the man that he would no longer hide his plans from him.

We thus enter the second part of the narrative: Abraham's audacious intercession after announcement of the imminent judgment on Sodom. Exegetes argue over the dates of the two parts of the account, and it may be that the conversation with Abraham and his prayer belong to a later development of the vision of faith. But even if this were the case, the attachment of this episode to the first episode is full of meaning. It may show that the apparent partiality of the election of Abraham is not the negation but the principle of a future universalism. To a unique extent, Abraham and his people were introduced into the divine intimacy so that they could become universal intercessors.

The first and fundamental collective realization of the promises made to Abraham and his progeny are accomplished in the exodus and the mission of Moses. But before we reach this point, we must make a few observations on the intermediary phase of Isaac, Jacob, and the twelve patriarchs who descend from Jacob.

On Isaac there is very little more to be said. He appears simply as the bearer and transmitter of the promise to his posterity. His fidelity sets him apart with respect to the fidelity of God's providential guidance on his behalf, which is particularly evident in the circumstances of his marriage with Rebekah.[21]

The same is not true with Jacob. Once again, the freedom of the God of the covenant will be illustrated in the election of those to whom his promises are entrusted. This promise and its fulfillment were to come to Esau, in accord with the principle of primogeniture, but he was put aside, and Jacob, the younger, was chosen. In a dream, Jacob saw the angelic ladder connecting earth with heaven, where he dwells in passing, but it is on earth that the promise (made from the beginning of the People's possession of it) will be concretized. The twelve sons who were born to him would become the eponymous fathers of the twelve tribes.[22]

The story of these sons and Joseph is a psychological novel of keenest interest. Again, with the gratuitousness of the election, it illustrates the mysterious ways in which God works for the salvation of his People. In his hands, the infidelities of men become the occasion of proving his unfailing fidelity. Joseph's brothers, jealous of his tokens of election, want to get rid of him, but, unwittingly, they were preparing for the possibility that Joseph would save them, with their children, from famine. Reciprocally, with the installation in Egypt, which was to follow, the salvation of the People was changed to enslavement. In this way, however, God was given the occasion for the preeminent deliverance which will be the real vocation and collective creation of the chosen people.[23]

Behind all these ups and downs, the singular image of Jacob/Israel, wrestling with God in the darkness of night in order to wrest from him his blessing in the morning, remains the paradigm of the whole history of salvation, whose seed it carried within itself.[24]

## II. Moses and the Exodus

It can be said that the birth of Isaac was the pledge and "down payment" of the divine promise to Abraham. The exodus under Moses' leadership, will be its initial realization, and, will remain the type and the root or seed of later realizations.

The exodus, first of all, is the recapitulation for the whole People of what happened with their ancestor: a voluntary call to separation, to a pilgrimage of faith through the desert to the promised land.[25]

But the exodus from Egypt is more than a freely accepted separation: it is a deliverance. The children of Israel are touched by the new, divine call at a moment when their first situation in Egypt, as privileged guests, had changed to a situation of slaves. So they can follow their vocation, it was necessary that God who called them, intervene in order to make them free. Yet this does not say enough. The divine intervention was necessary, not only so they might follow their vocation but, first of all, so they might hear it. Like their deliverance, the slavery in which they found themselves was merely material. As their first reception of Moses' message showed, they had lost the sense of their destiny. They had forgotten whose sons they were and what promise they had received. Egypt had enslaved not only their bodies but their minds. Therefore the deliverance would be as much spiritual as material. Or better, the two are one, and the spiritual deliverance is rooted in the material deliverance.

In this saving intervention of God, which was manifested in the ten plagues of Egypt but above all by the passage of the Red Sea, in which Pharaoh and his troops were drowned while Israel crossed safely, the election appears to be connected with both salvation and judgment. More precisely, it appears that the chosen one is saved and the one who is not chosen is condemned. This event, we are told, was called Passover, because the exterminating angel "passed over" the houses of the Israelites, which were marked by the redeeming blood of the immolated Lamb, while his deadly sword smote all the other houses.[26]

This is a new aspect of the election of the people, and we must not conceal the paradoxical tension it introduced, along with affirmation in the election of Abraham, which we have underlined. It appeared that the special blessing that, in his election, separated Abraham from the rest of mankind, was finally to rebound on it. It appears, on the other hand, that the blessing of the chosen people is the counterpart of a curse on others. The chosen people now have the appearance of a firebrand, taken from the fire.

In an enigmatic way, the two themes remained associated throughout Israel's history. Only Israel was saved from a condemnation that weighs heavily not only on its hostile neighbors but, finally, on all the rest of the human race. And yet its particular salvation was to be revealed, at the end, as the means of salvation for all peoples.

After the appearance of the two associated themes of salvation and judgment, and always in connection with the election of the People and their historical fulfillment, we must note the function assigned to Moses, which characterizes his vocation within and for the people.

Abraham is the father of the People. He exists prior to them, or rather, the People and their faith preexist in Abraham in some way. On the other hand, Moses appeared only when the People already existed, at least materially. His election places him apart, in the People and from the People. This distinction and separation are concretized in a function. Moses is the first prophet, the preeminent prophet, and is, at the same time, the source of the priesthood in Israel, rather than the "first priest," properly speaking, even though he fulfilled some priestly functions (like other prophets after him). In this respect, his relationship to Aaron is typical of the relationship in Israel between prophecy and priesthood and, more profoundly, between the Word and the rites. The prophet Moses consecrated Aaron the priest. But reciprocally, from the first words concerning him, Aaron appeared as the heir, transmitter, and interpreter of the prophetic revelation.[27]

Before we go further into examination of this original relationship between prophecy and priesthood, the Word and the ritual, we must examine how the Word is presented in Mosaic prophecy. In the deeds of Abraham, the Word appeared as essentially a promise which, of and by itself, tended toward its own realization. In what Moses did, the Word is at once and inseparably the revelation of the Divine Name and the Law, the Torah, through which, we may say, the divine plan is to imprint itself upon the life of the People.

The first revelation, made to Moses alone on Horeb in the burning bush, is the divine decision to fulfill, at this particular moment, the promise made to Abraham and the other "fathers" of the People. But it is condensed into a revelation of the Divine Name, which is expressed by the unpronounceable tetragram, YHWH, which will be "filled in" with the vowels of *Adonai* (the Lord) in an absolutely unique sense, which is stressed by the unusual form (*Adonai*, not *Adoni*).

But what does the tetragram signify? Modern exegesis is familiar with two lines of interpretation whose origins can be traced to the most ancient traditions of Israel and whose duality may underlie the text itself. Either one chooses the explanation "he is," and therefore sees in the Divine Name the affirmation that God is revealed as the preeminent Being, the preeminent Living One, or one considers the enigmatic phrase "I am what I am" or "who I am," draws the conclusion that God reveals himself as the unknowable or, at least, the unexpressable: the *Deus revelatus tamquam absconditus,* the God who reveals himself as the hidden God.[28]

In favor of the first interpretation is the basic fact that the dialogue with Moses will always be understood as implying, and undoubtedly signifying, communication of the Divine Name, with all that this implies, for the Semites, of communication: God's surrendering himself. It is also sure that "the Lord" will appear throughout the prophetic tradition as "the living God," who is life itself, in contradistinction to idols, who are merely dead gods, and especially to the gods of Egypt, who were properly the gods of death. The bush that burns without being consumed does not seem to be interpretable in any other way.

But this fire of divine life, which will appear in the continuation of the accounts as the "fire of heaven," the fire that strikes the top of the mountain, is also the preeminent consuming fire. There is no contradiction between the two from the viewpoint of the whole of prophetic tradition: "our God [i.e., the God who has not only revealed himself but, in some way, given himself to us] is a consuming fire.'' And again: "It is a fearful thing to fall into the hands of the living God.''[29]

We cannot look upon this living God, this God of life, without dying. It was to Israel's astonishment that this God revealed himself to it without Israel's being struck down.[30] In other words, the living God, the God who is life, is so prodigious a life that it seems to threaten every other life with annihilation, even though it is their source. Also, this is why the shimmering light in which he revealed himself is shrouded in darkness, like the light of lightning—or better, it is one with an inaccessible dark cloud.

It is no less true that the inaccessible God, the God of Heaven, who does not and could not have an earthly abode, wanted to come to his own, not to make them die but to make them live. He will summon them himself to meet him. From the same Mount Horeb-Sinai, where he revealed himself to Moses, Moses was to lead the People to a dreadful and marvelous meeting. It was here that this God, having revealed his Name to the people, specified his plan for them in the revelation of the Torah.

The translation of Hebrew *torah* by the Greek *nomos* (law) has many times risked obscuring its primary meaning. The Torah (before settling from without the form that man's life must accept) is an oracle and gift of salvation. The revelation of the Torah is closely connected with the revelation of the Divine Name, and with all this revelation supposes, not only of condescension but communication, of God's handing over of himself, of his supernatural innerness, of his life, of his inaccessible light. The revelation of the Torah, understood this way, is the principle of the "knowledge of God" in the sense developed by the prophets. This is to say, as St. Paul, at the end of their line, will recall, that the People of God are called "to know God as he has been known" from all eternity. "Known" implies not simple and coldly objective knowledge but special concern, a love without equal, that tends toward union. And "to know God," in turn, is first of all to offer him faith that translates into obedience, and in this way to conform oneself to him, and finally to unite oneself, to be united, with him.

The Torah, which defines the concrete realization of the divine plan for the People, impresses the Divine Name on them, on their whole existence, in the very depth of their being. The Torah is like the seal of the possession of God on the People. But this seal stamps a likeness, and what is more a likeness (if we may say so) of what is most divine in God: "Be holy as I am holy" (a leitmotiv of Leviticus). Jesus translated this formula by giving it a further meaning (which was already in some way present): "Be perfect as your heavenly Father is perfect.''[31] For the People who had been delivered from

Egypt, and led to the divine encounter of Sinai, and received the Torah in cloud and fire would no longer be called only children of Abraham, but children of God.[32]

Understood in this way, the revelation of the Torah, the giving of the Torah to the chosen people, is for the rabbis what Jesus would say of giving his own law of love: "an easy yoke, a light burden." It is said that the faithful angels impose man's equivalent of this heavenly yoke on themselves in dedicating themselves to unceasing praise of God, whom they contemplate face to face.[33] Thus for Israel to bear the yoke of the Torah would be to live constantly in the divine presence, in the incomparable, inexpressible joy of those who praise him without ceasing. Indeed, acceptance of the Torah is consecration—praise of the whole of existence.[34]

At this juncture it is fitting to examine the relationship that the Torah, so understood, established between the Word and the ritual and, therefore, between prophecy and priesthood.[35] The first point is that the Divine Word reveals God to his people, not by dispensing with the natural hierophanies, which are at the origin of the sacred, but by making them signs of personal revelation of the transcendent God.

The "mountain," as the abode of the Godhead, the place where the earth meets the sky-heaven, and the "fire of heaven," as the manifestation of the Divine Life, are taken by the religion of Israel, the religion of the Word, from human religions. But God is no longer confused with this fire, or with sky or mountain: from this point on, he makes them simple signs that bear a revelation that surpasses them. And obviously, God surpasses nature, which manifests him, at the moment he enters and intervenes in this world in the midst of human history, where he becomes the principal actor.

This is the same transposition that will be observed in use of the ritual. The Passover meal was a traditional element of the rituals of the seasons: celebrating, in spring, the victory of cosmic life over its winter of death. From now on, the Passover is the memorial of the free intervention of God in the history of his People, in bringing them from slavery and alienation to the freedom of the "sons of God," and therefore a "passover" from death to life. With Passover, the whole ritual that was to be canonized in the Code of Holiness in Exodus and in the sacrificial regulations of Leviticus proceeds in a direct line from the Canaanean rituals, and nothing sets it apart from the Semitic rituals in general, except the prohibition of divine images and human sacrifice. But its meaning is transformed, like that of Passover: worship of the Tabernacle, and later of the Temple, with the whole network of ritual prescriptions which pervaded the life of faithful Israelites, expressed the perpetual consecration of the People to that God who made himself known to them as their Savior, who adopted them as his children in the Abrahamic covenant and its renewal on

Sinai. Their worship involves this consecration of the faith of Israel in the Word of its God because its ritual is no longer in its totality, just as Passover had become: a perpetual memorial of the covenant, sealed upon the exodus from Egypt on the mountain of the encounter.[36]

The Tabernacle, the building of which was enjoined according to a heavenly model revealed to Moses, we are told, will be only the container of a perpetuation of this encounter: the *Oel Mohed*. God, who came down upon Egypt for a judgment, but "passed over" Israel to spare it, came down on Sinai to meet Israel, not to make it die but to make it live. From this point on—in the nomadic state in which he led them for forty years, in order to purify them of traces of their slavery and infidelity, before leading them into the promised land—this God became the traveling companion of his People. Exodus 33 is of unique importance on this point. After the People, at the moment Moses received the Torah from the very hands of God on the mountain, had prostituted themselves to the "golden calf" that Aaron had cast in order to please them—after Moses interceded, so that the blessing would not be withdrawn from them for this reason, and as God listened— Moses said to God: "If thy presence will not go with me, do not carry us up from here. For how shall it be known that I have found favor in thy sight, I and thy people? Is it not in thy going with us, so that we are distinct, I and thy people, from all other people that are upon the face of the earth?"

It can be said that God seems to have heard this prayer in advance, by ordering construction of the Tabernacle, for this is where his presence with the People is manifested—in the mysterious, luminous cloud, which will per- petuate and safeguard the leadership, which had conducted them by the pillar of smoke and fire at the exodus from Egypt, and especially by the encounter in the withering darkness of Sinai, where God had uttered the words of the covenant.

Thus the God of Heaven, who does not live in a house made by the hand of man, consents to approach his People as he has approached no one else, to travel with them to the land where realization of his plans will lead his People. But this special presence, in the Tabernacle and the cloud, is quite different from that which the Canaanean sanctuaries boasted. God cannot be considered to be shut up in the Tabernacle, at the mercy, as it were, of his worshipers, as was the case (it is thought) with the *baalim* of the covenant in their sanctuaries, which constituted the cornerstone of the Canaanean cities. On the contrary, God reveals himself as the master of the movements of his People. The cloud came to rest on a mobile tent, for as long as it pleased him, and when it rose, the whole Israelite encampment had to move and follow it, wherever it led.

The ark within the holy of holies of the Tabernacle marked the precise place of the Presence, the *Shekinah* (the dwelling place under the tent), which is very revealing with regard to this spiritual transfiguration of a whole ritual. Materially, it resembled the coffin where Osiris, the death god (magically immortalized), was kept. But the ark of Israel had no interest apart from its content: it was merely a support, an empty throne, prepared for the appearance of the cloud in the space between the Cherubim, from which resounded the *bath qol,* the voice of the Invisible, who prescribed to Moses and Aaron the divine decisions concerning the People.[37]

Thus we understand how the Aaronic priesthood, inseparably from its ritual office, preserved, transmitted, and even interpreted the Word revealed to Moses. From now on, the ritual entrusted to him was inseparable from this Word. The ritual is merely a permanent memorial of the great deeds the Word has not only proclaimed but accomplished. Of these great deeds, of the Presence of grace from which they emanate, of their perpetual activity and its own permanence, the rites are only the effective sign, given by the God who speaks, before being the sign also of the faith which receives his Word and surrenders totally to it.

This adoption, but also this transformation, of the natural and the sacred by the Divine Word, and more particularly by the work of purification, of liberation, of re-creation of the chosen people, which takes hold of these signs and rites, will have major consequence in the structure of the Torah. Indissolubly, it will be a moral prescription: the Decalogue, and a ritual prescription: the Code of Holiness,[38] that will be extended by Leviticus. Since, from this point, the ritual expresses the encounter with God, his special Presence constituting the People as his own, the permanent dialogue engaged in with this People by his Word, in order to make them a People who bear his mark, a People after his own heart, this ritual can no longer be enough to constitute the *abodah,* the worship service of the People. By the ritual, it is the whole life of the People that the Word consecrates to itself: all their human life, individual and collective, personal and social. Hence, if you will, a radical moralization of the sacred, a personalization of the ritual.

From this intimate fusion of the Word and the rite, or rather from this penetration of the ritual by the Word, and with the original relationship of the Aaronic priesthood with Mosaic prophecy, flows a religious ethic with a ceremonial religion of a very new kind.

All this will be embodied forever in what can be considered the crucial event in what Moses did: the assembly of the people at the foot of Sinai, where the covenant was formally contracted, this time no longer between God and the father of the People but between God and the whole People.

By its constitution and structure, this assembly had a normative import throughout the later history of the People. In it, it can be said, the People will for the first time attain awareness and effective realization of what they are in the plan of their election. Consequently, all major developments of the People, throughout the history of their salvation, will be registered and embodied definitively in their being and their faith through like assemblies. Precisely at the end of this process, we find the Christian Church. And the Sinai assembly gives us a first sketch of what it will be.

The language itself attests to this filiation. The Greek word for Church, *Ekklesia,* was chosen by the Septuagint to translate the Hebrew *Qahal,* which designates the convocation of the assembly of the People by the Divine Word (the verb *qâhâl* signifies "to convoke"). Another synonymous term, *edah,* is applied to the totality of the members of the People, insofar as they are capable of being convoked in this way and brought together in unity (this is what the other Greek word *synagoge* translates, although the translators of the Septuagint are not consistent in their usage and use the two words interchangeably).[39]

As we see in chapter 24 of Exodus, the *Qahal,* the *Ekklesia,* is convoked first to hear the Word—in this case the Decalogue and the Code of Holiness that accompanies it. It was prepared for it by purifications, as for an extension to all (in some way) of the divine encounter on the mountain to which Moses alone had been called. And when the words are transmitted to them, the People give their faith and commit themselves to obeying them: ". . . and the entire people answered with one voice: We will do all that the Lord has said." Then holocausts were offered to God and Moses sprinkled the People with the blood of the victims, while the People repeated this promise. He concluded the ceremony with these words: "Behold the blood of the covenant that the Lord has concluded with you, on the basis of all that has been said" (i.e., the Word of God and the People's response).

In this assembly, as visibly realized, we see the conjunction of the Word and the rite, which we have explained. The ritual seals both the covenant concluded by God and the commitment of his People to accept its exigencies, to believe and act in the received Word.

The *Ekklesia* thus constituted in this defined structure of its development, where the dynamism of the Word is displayed, it can be said that the People arrived at a fully conscious existence. This assembly shows the People united, or rather uniting, in the common act of faith which receives the Word, and surrendering to it in the ritual. Therefore the *Ekklesia* merely nourishes in the People the awareness of their election: the *Ekklesia* accomplishes this election *de facto.* At this point, the Word elicits faith and the Divine Presence grasps it in order (through ritual consecration) to implant the new life in the heart of the People, the life that their whole existence must manifest.

This is underlined in chapter 19 of Exodus, in terms which the rabbis will revive and the first letter of St. Peter will apply to Christians: the whole People are called to be in the world, in the midst of other peoples, a witness of God and his Word. Therefore they are also called to a priestly role of consecration of the entire universe, of the whole life that men are called to lead in it in the presence of God: "Now therefore, if you will obey my voice and keep my covenant, you shall be my own possession among all peoples; for all the earth is mine, and you shall be to me a kingdom of priests and a holy nation." [40]

## *III. Prophets, Kings, and Men of Wisdom*

Moses led the People to the promised land but did not lead them into it. He allowed himself to succumb (if not to the extent Aaron did) to the idolatry of the People, at least by his incredulity. In a general way—with the exception of the faithful Joshua and Caleb—none of those who had left Egypt were to enter the land, but only their children, born in the desert. These were the ones whom Joshua made cross the Jordan and led into the promised land.

This crossing of the Jordan is described in terms and in a manner that deliberately bring to mind the previous account of the crossing of the Red Sea. [41] This important characteristic of the history of salvation developed from unique events that were accomplished once and for all, and remained the basis of the constitution of the People. But because of this permanent import and actuality, they are periodically reactualized in analogous events, without having to begin all over again. They never reproduce precisely the past events but extend and progressively deepen their meaning and reality. The crossing of the Red Sea constituted the basic liberation of the People; but just as they passed from the trial of slavery to the trial of the desert at that time, they must now pass from the trial of the desert to the land of promise. What follows shows that this new deliverance was, in its turn, merely the prelude to other trials which will lead to other deliverances.

Thus the history of salvation does not appear as a linear development. Rather, it is a progressive spiral which causes the People to go back periodically over analogous (but not identical) experiences, which are only a gradual deepening of the content implied in the original experience. Thus its full significance is revealed little by little, insofar as its content is susceptible of assimilation by the progress of lived experience.

This dialectic is essential to the formation of the People and the development of the Word. The Word, through its own creativity, elicits the history of the People as the history of their salvation. But the unfolding of this history is like a divine pedagogy, inscribed in the facts, and furnishes the necessary basis for further revelations.

The Word of God to his People is unique; from beginning to end, it is the revelation of himself, of his Name, associated with the revelation of his plan: that his Name be stamped on the People and give them a countenance, a heart of children of God. But understanding the Divine Name, like fulfillment of the divine plan, is necessarily progressive. Both become involved in an experience of common life between God and his own. The truths are not added to each other, but one unique truth progressively brings out its fullness. Also, the events do not so much succeed themselves from without as engender themselves within, in mysterious continuity through no less mysterious renewals. In fact, settling in the promised land soon revealed itself as much less an end and a fulfillment than a new beginning.

Reading the Book of Judges, one has the same, inevitable impression that if the Pentateuch and what follows it in the Book of Joshua did not, properly speaking, idealize the history of Israel's beginnings, they starkly schematized it. The lapses into idolatry and incredulity in the first accounts could be read as accidental, but when one reads the following narratives, these lapses, give the impression of an endemic state.

Indeed it seems, following Moses and those who more or less heeded him, that a confused and motley horde left Egypt, finally to settle in Canaan. We may even wonder whether, during and after the Mosaic expedition, there was an incoherent series of migrations. In any case, the evidence of Judges is formal: the mass of the People, settled in Canaan, lost little time in becoming almost completely assimilated by the local agricultural peoples. Along with the latter's techniques and culture (in the most general sense), they adopted their idolatrous forms of worship, and soon were reduced by the Philistines to a new subjection, hardly less overwhelming than what they knew in Egypt.

Hence the schema of the earlier times, described and applied by the author of the Book of Judges: in Canaan, Israel forgot its God and consequently fell back into the humiliating condition from which it had been removed. Then Israel cried for help and God sent them a "judge" who was both prophet and warrior-leader, in the line of Moses and his successor Joshua. For good or ill, the "judge" for a time reestablished the former situation, which was as much material as spiritual. Then the People again fell back into their old habits and infidelity, and everything had to begin all over again.[42]

This explains the insistence of prior accounts, particularly the Book of Joshua, on the *herem*.[43] This practice and, even more, its systematic prescription seem barbarous to us, although the God of Israel ordered it as the condition *sine qua non* of his promise to establish the People in freedom and peace in the land of Canaan, whereas the peoples who had been there before them were doomed to radical destruction. On this level, it could be said that the preeminent sin was any weakness in execution of this order.

This apparently ferocious exclusivism cannot be understood before we understand, as the Book of Judges enables us to do, that any compromise of Israel with its neighbors—their way of life, their mentality, their culture—ended fatally in assimilation of the worship of the Lord to what the prophets would call worship of "golden calves," i.e., the *baalim* of vegetation and natural fecundity, in the form of bulls. Beyond this cultic contamination, the spirit of the Torah was at stake: the whole of its ethical ideal in connection with its rigorous ideal of religious fidelity to the one God, who, after speaking to the "fathers," had made a covenant with their children. Worship lapsing into idolatry, infidelity to the living God, and falling back into "unrighteousness" would all be one. Adoration of idols; human sacrifice; the cult of material prosperity, based on oppression of the unfortunate; unbridled rivalry of antagonistic classes, fomented by the lure and pride of riches—all go together.

Consequently, this will become the object of the curse of prophet after prophet, and thus is explained the close connection (almost to complete confusion at the time of the judges) between them and the men of war. Indeed, at this stage of its development Israel cannot subsist spiritually, except on the material basis of unceasing combat in order to assure physical independence, without which it would have lost its spiritual originality.

In turn, this material combat, conceived from the beginning as the necessary support of a spiritual combat, will become (as it were) the mold or crucible in which Israel, in the image of its eponymous ancestor, will become the wrestler with God. This comes from the activity inspired by the first great prophet (whom we saw following Moses), who finally succeeded in freeing the People for good from the repeated floundering described in the Book of Judges. We speak of Samuel,[44] who verifies what we observed of the positions of prophecy and priesthood in Israel with respect to Moses and Aaron.

This first of the prophets, despite the decline of the priesthood with the sons of Eli, is connected by his origins and formation with the sanctuary in which the ark is kept, as the palladium of Israel, for it is the pledge of the perpetuated presence of God with the People. But the narrative tells us that "the Word of God was rare in those days"! Nevertheless, the divine voice was addressed to the young servant of the ark, who was unable to recognize it. It was the priest of Eli, the guardian despite every tradition, who suggested that God was speaking to him, and even went so far as to dictate to him the admirable prayer: "Speak, Lord, thy servant listens." God, then, from the holy ark, made himself heard once more, and, we are told, "from Dan to Beersheba, all Israel acknowledged that Samuel was a prophet of the Lord."[45]

At the beginning, this prophetic activity does not seem to be differentiated from that of the preceding "judges," and this title was given to Samuel. However, he was to play a decisive role in introducing a new institution, because he was called to prepare for an unsuspected development in Israel: kingship. This introduction was important—in the first place, as the seed of messianic hopes, but also by the correlative introduction of "wisdom" in Israel. However, it was no less important because of the effect it was to have on prophecy. It can be said that, in freeing Samuel from the immediate and burdensome material responsibilities of the judges', it gave the prophet the possibility of enlarging and deepening his vision and, consequently, his teaching.[46]

This did not prevent Samuel from refusing to surrender to the king the application of the prophetic oracles in the effective direction of the people, especially in war, except when constrained and forced to do so. This is conveyed by a visible duality of inspiration in the accounts of the institution of the kingship.

The first level, which is probably the most ancient, sees only one infidelity of the people: they want only to be like the other peoples and, like them, to have a king. The first reaction of the prophet is to interpret this request as a denial of the Lord, more grave because it was more fundamental than all the others. What need would the People have of a king, other than God himself? This is what the Lord tells him: "They have not rejected you, but they have rejected me from being king over them."[47] However, another level of tradition, which we see in the following chapter, knows nothing of this. It presents the anointing of the first king, Saul, as suggested to the prophet by the Divine Word: "Tomorrow about this time I will send to you a man from the land of Benjamin, and you shall anoint him to be a prince (*nagid*) [the word "king" is not used here] over my people Israel. He shall save my people from the hand of the Philistines; for I have seen the affliction of my people, because their cry has come to me."[48]

The end of the preceding account operated as a synthesis between the two traditions: one that interprets positively and one that persists in interpreting negatively the institution of the kingship. Finally, God pushes the prophet to give the people the king they are asking for, but warns them of the extortions they will commit, which will constitute a punishment for the People for their infidelity. We may say that from this idea of king, anointed by the prophet and therefore reigning by a delegation of divine authority, and his human reality, foreseen from the beginning, messianism would be born: the conviction that a real king—even the best king of history—is only a sketch and a promise of another king who is hoped for, who would reign "after the heart of God" in such a way as finally to establish the reign of God on earth.

Saul, who soon showed himself incapable of resigning himself to being a docile instrument in God's hands, will be discarded. Once again, against his wishes, Samuel will be sent by God to anoint David in Saul's place—David, whom the account of his fight with Goliath shows us to be weak, and aware of his weakness, but who had absolute trust in God and, consequently, triumphed in unhoped-for fashion, since it was by a strength that was not his own.[49]

David was the unsurpassed ideal of Israelite kings, not because his faults were hidden but because he did not hesitate to confess them, and to do penance for them and accept their just punishment. Thus David remains, in the view of Israel, the typical king: a war leader even more brilliant than Saul before him, but first of all a man of faith and prayer, the preeminent, inspired cantor, and especially a penitent. After his sin with Bathsheba, he accepted the accusation of the prophet Nathan: "You are that man."[50] And when his own son, Absalom, rebelled against him and sent him into exile (which he had already known under Saul), not only did his faith not weaken, he saw in this supreme humiliation the punishment he deserved for his sins and the necessary atonement for them.[51]

Despite all this, David remains for Israel more a sketch and a promise than a fully realized ideal. It is from another and better David—a "son of David," surpassing his "father" to the point of meriting the title "son of God," applied first by the People whom the king represents before God—whom we await the future and definitive realization of the reign of God on earth.

But this earlier David performed a decisive transition in the history of the People, by making them accede—after they passed from a nomadic to a sedentary, agricultural life—to a city life. He made Jerusalem, the ancient stronghold of the Jebusites, into the holy city of Sion, to which he transported the ark from the last of its camps at Shiloh.[52]

This "urbanization" of Israel must be correctly understood; we must avoid assimilating this transformation to what we understand by the same word today. Not only was it a limited portion of the people, and even of the tribe of Judah for which Jerusalem became the center, who experienced this effect, it had very little in common with what we understand today by "urbanization." In the first place, the city–country opposition at that time in no way signified opposition between industrial and agrarian civilization. Until its destruction, Jerusalem sheltered a population that was in great part agricultural. Its various craftsmen and workers were not in a higher proportion to farmers than in any village, and, as a rule, they had a small domestic garden as part of their workspace. To the end, the ideal of the average Israelite was to enjoy his vineyard and fig orchard in peace, even though these plots were within the confines of a city (which remained quite countrylike) or nearby in the surrounding area. Most of all, the merchant class was closely connected with the setting up of the royal city, and grew in power and influence, but the prophets never ceased stigmatizing superfluous luxury and the spirit of profitmaking which resulted from it.

Aside from this, Israel's concentration on the city of David almost uniquely signifies unification and organization of defense in an appropriate citadel and, especially, centralization of worship. It is chiefly this latter point that earned for the work of David and his successors the encouragement of the prophets, for they saw in them the only means of putting an end to decomposition of worship of the one God into varied forms of idolatry. Again, they had few illusions about the threatening negative aspects of this substantial gain.[53]

When David wanted to crown his work by building a stone temple near his palace on top of Mount Sion, the prophet Nathan did not disguise his suspicion. Was not the claim of providing God with a house tantamount to wanting to chain him to the city of men—to capture him there, like the gods of the pagans—and, in fact, to subjugate him to the earthly king? On the contrary, was it not God who, throughout his People's history, took them in hand and guided them providentially, and made a house for the king, in the sense that God guaranteed the kingdom to his posterity? He caused them to enter his saving plan in what was still an obscure fashion, but one which was already proclaimed definitive.[54]

Here, as at the introduction of kingship, the first prophetic impulse was to say "no," but it was succeeded by a conditional acceptance. If God did not consent immediately to David's project, he authorized David's son and successor to bring it to realization. The parallel account in Chronicles specifies that David could not erect a temple to the Lord because he had shed blood, but his successor, Solomon, whose name means "peace," was a wise man, not a warrior. It was he, then, who would build the sanctuary that would complete the city by making its central point the dwelling place of the Divine Name.[55] With Solomon, as a natural and inevitable consequence of the institution of kingship, wisdom was to be established in Israel.[56]

In the whole of the ancient East, wisdom went hand in hand with kingship. If it did not originate from kingship, its origins were also the origins of kingship in nomadic or seminomadic organizations, where patriarchs made the transition from the authority of the head of the family to that of king, which appeared with the first cities of the East. The most ancient wise men, who even at an early date had become mythical figures, were the ancient chiefs of these tribal bands.

But it was the kingship, with the body of the "kings' men," that systematically developed wisdom. In its beginnings, it was a simple treasury of rules for men's behavior and management of their affairs, which was handed down from father to son. Then it developed into an art of living and of guiding the collective life, the result of decanted and reflected-upon experience. It was always threatened by reduction to a simple art of succeeding, but when it resisted this temptation it proposed a practical science of human existence in the process of organization.

For a long time it remained a kind of earthy realism whose tone clashed with that of the prophets (when we happen upon its maxims, only a few pages away from their oracles). Yet everywhere—in Egypt as in Assyria—this wisdom was religious. It was perhaps not least commendable, in the eyes of the prophets, that the spirit of these religions, after the introduction in Israel of a king and his people, could be introduced there under the guise of wisdom. In fact, their consent (more extorted than voluntary) was justified in what followed, though not without certain risks. Transplanted in Israel, wisdom became impregnated with the religion of the Word: "The fear of God is the beginning of wisdom."[57] A statement of this type had equivalents with Ahikar the Assyrian and Amen-em-ope the Egyptian, but in Israel it was soon specified by this idea: "To fear God and observe his commandments is all that man needs."

This idea is so true that this new orientation, stamped on wisdom in Israel, brought it (under the last kings of Judah) to an encounter with the so-called Deuteronomist school, which endeavored to apply the teachings of the last prophets to the daily life of the people by appropriate legislation. Ultimately, the tone of the Deuteronomists, with the realism of their warm spirituality, was no longer differentiated from that of the wise men, for whom the Divine Word became the primary source of wisdom. Probably the two milieus came to be almost identical.

In the biblical account of the young Solomon, the ideal wise man of Israel not only considered wisdom the preeminent gift but a literal gift of God, which he alone can make and which must be asked for in prayer.[58]

We are far from the worldly character (not only eminently practical but very earthbound) of primitive wisdom, before it was grafted onto the prophetic trunk. This does not prevent the world, and its spirit and maxims, from being too much a presence with the wise man for it not to be a permanent temptation. This is seen clearly with Solomon, whose splendor was not without a touch of megalomaniac pride which was absent in the less polished David. After such a good and pious beginning, this lover of wisdom let himself be conquered by foreign women.[59] And what the prophets feared when the Temple was still in the planning stages indeed happened: contamination of the worship of the Lord by idolatrous forms of worship.

More generally, if Solomon represents the apex of Israelite kingship established in Sion, a spiritual and material decadence was set into motion in his prestigious success. At his death there was schism. The ten tribes separated from Judah and, despite the prophets, who did not cease visiting them, worship and all of religious life precipitately became corrupt. Ruin, anticipating the trials that awaited Judah, was the consequence and punishment of this accelerated degeneration.[60] Only Judah survived the catastrophe, even though offenses multiplied there, and divine judgments, waiting for the next generation, were, when their hour came, just as severe. It was almost exclusively from Judah—at least from a small nucleus of faithful, cemented together by the trial that was to "refine" them—that the "remnant" announced by the prophets was made up. After the torment, what remained of Israel was basically (as the name "Jews" indicates) only a remnant of Judah.

Before these events, Israel (i.e., the separated ten tribes under another king at Bethel or Samaria) had a few of the greatest prophets, like Elijah the Tishbite and his successor, Elisha, who were indigenous to this area, and Amos, a prophet from Judah, who was sent to the northern land. The fierce protest of Elijah against the *baalim* had the effect of total failure, despite the divine consolation of the seven thousand, who, he was told, did not bend the knee before their idols. With Elisha, his community of "sons of prophets" appeared to be more and more an isolated group. Soon, we hear nothing more about them.[61]

Amos was the first "nonprofessional" prophet. He was a shepherd of Judah, not a member of a guild connected with a particular shrine, and he appears as an envoy from the other kingdom, sent to contest the irregular priesthood of Bethel and, especially, the contempt for all righteousness with which a showy but perverted form of worship was colored.[62]

Somewhat later, without toning down the exigency of righteousness which Amos recalled was included in the religion of the Torah, Hosea (in Judah) announced the infinite mercy with which God will treat the unfaithful: as if he loved a prostitute so much he was able to give her back her purity. But Hosea, for both Judah and the northern kingdom, was the first to proclaim that, for this to happen, the People had to be uprooted from their city and sent back into the desert for a new purification, without which the new Passover, the announced new exodus, could not take place.

Isaiah, that great nobleman of Jerusalem, in the vision of the God of Holiness, who dwells in the only authentic sanctuary (which Hezekiah would soon purify, undoubtedly under Isaiah's influence), had the intuition that was never so clearly expressed before: this holiness and the divine exigency of righteousness are one. But also, it is only God who gives the purity he imposes; again, it is necessary that the most entire and most exclusive faith be given to his Word, a faith which of itself gives one over to obedience.

Hezekiah's sporadic effort had so little consequence that Jeremiah (again, a priest-prophet) in the following generation proclaimed that the "Temple of the Lord," the supposedly inviolable palladium of Judah, would be destroyed, since the sins of the people, beginning with their leaders, had desacralized it.

At this moment, however, it seems that the call to conversion had touched the heart of King Josiah and also the heart of a large elite (if not the whole People). Hilkiah, the priest, proclaimed the discovery in the Temple of the "book of the law." This book was certainly Deuteronomy, almost exactly as it has come down to us. That is to say, it is a question of a synthesis of reinterpretation of the Mosaic Torah, confronted with the experience of the People since their entrance into the promised land, in the light of the prophetic teachings we have recalled.

The connection between the ethical prescriptions of the Decalogue and the religious implications of the Code of Holiness came to a state of real fusion: what Isaiah wrought between holiness and righteousness. And the warm and anxious exhortation in which this project is addressed to the People is penetrated by this impassioned love of God for his People that Hosea and then Jeremiah expressed so forcefully.

Josiah and his court, on hearing this reading, decided on a rigorous purification of the sanctuary and worship, conceived as the beginning of a renovation of the whole existence of the People before God. To do this, he summoned a new assembly, a new "ekklesia" of the People. It presented exactly the same structure as that of Sinai: first, the solemn public proclamation of the Divine Word, then its acceptance in a collective act of faith and consecration, and hence, finally, renewal of the covenant with God, sealed in a sacrificial celebration.

But this time the reading is that of Deuteronomy. It is the king who, in terms that are directly inspired by it, proclaims his will to be faithful to it, with all the People giving their assent. And the ritual celebration that follows is that of Passover—a Passover, we are told, that had ever been celebrated since the time of the judges.[63]

For all the People who were to give their "amen" to it, the king committed himself to "walk after the Lord and to keep his commandments and his testimonies and his statutes, with all his heart and all his soul, to perform the words of this covenant that were written in this book."

This revival aimed at definitively inscribing in the existence of the People the decisive progress in the intuition of the plan of God that the teaching of the prophets had drawn from the experience of this People, settled in the promised land: that humanization of the Law, so characteristic of Deuteronomy, which seems to meet the humanism of the wise men, which was opening up to the Divine Word. In this interiorization of divine worship, and in the struggle necessary for preservation of its purity, the holiness, righteousness, and love of God uncovers new depths for us, which could be revealed only to a people who had experienced their inherent weakness and the precariousness of their faith with respect to the sovereign divine fidelity.

It is all the more remarkable that this renewal of the covenant would be sealed by the Passover, the preeminent memorial of the Mosaic covenant, of the first and fundamental deliverance. Meanwhile, the People discovered that not only from external enemies did they need God to deliver them, but from the "enemies" they carried within themselves: their tendency to idolatry and injustice; their lack of faith, stigmatized by Isaiah; and their lack of heart, condemned by Jeremiah. But it is from the same "redeemer" who had saved their fathers from the slavery of Egypt that they now expect to be redeemed from their sin. It is the same redemption that progresses in its fulfillment, which interiorizes it in step with the providential experience and the new lights it makes accessible.

## IV. The Babylonian Exile

It is clear, however, that Jeremiah did not believe that what we may call the Deuteronomist conversion of Josiah (in which he had thought he would be able to involve the whole People) was enough for the necessary recasting, or, consequently, that it could ward off the announced punishments. This new covenant, this circumcision of hearts "which it promised,[64] the man of faith had the power to prepare for, but God alone could accomplish it by plunging the People into a new trial, out of all proportion with those they had experienced previously. Everything had to pass through total destruction and recasting for a new People—at last, a People after the heart of God—to emerge from the other.

This trial was the Babylonian Exile, in which not only the monarchy or the city of David, with its Temple and the Presence that had dwelt in it, but even the People's settlement in Palestine (that basic pledge of the promise) would be taken away from the People. Decimated, led into new captivity, or dispersed among the "nations," they could seem practically annihilated, with all their hope forevermore confounded. It is from this ineluctable death that the true resurrection of the People must and could only come, as Ezekiel, taking up from Jeremiah, would soon proclaim.[65]

In this respect, as much as the new Passover of Josiah revives the vision of the past, it also prepares for the future: without the People having or being able to have a clear awareness of it, it portends this new call to go into the desert, to become detached from everything, and to die in order to be born again—a call which Hosea was the first to announce.

Here we are at a turning point in the hope of Israel. Until that time, its history and particularly the history of the kingship and the holy city it established, despite many obstacles, setbacks, and failures, appeared as a progressive building process. Now it is catastrophe, the apparently irreversible ruin, that is announced with the death of Josiah at the battle of Megiddo a short time after the Passover we described.[66] We may see in this a significant symbol, in the fact that another Pharaoh triumphed over the king, who seemed to have consecrated the chosen people and their destinies definitively.

Moral ruin accompanied this material ruin and uncovered the superficiality of Israel's conversion, which came about, or seemed to come about, under Josiah. His immediate successors relapsed into infidelity and unrighteousness, while they put vain hope in a policy of turning over the covenants instead of trusting in God alone. Jeremiah had predicted this: because they preferred the river of Egypt to the waters of Siloah (the symbolic fountain of the presence of the Lord in their midst), the sudden overflowing of the Euphrates would inundate them. In 597 Nebuchadnezzar, king of Babylon, laid siege to the city, dismantled it, and led into captivity its last king and its prominent citizens. A later revolt brought a second expedition in 586, which wiped out what remained and suppressed the Temple worship, along with the Temple itself.[67]

Up to this time, it can be said, Israel's spirituality had been dominated by an optimistic short-term view of its history. The tangible earthly blessings of creation proclaimed the good work of the God of goodness, and seemed to be the normal, quasi-immediate consequence of the covenant with him. This hope, this basic conviction, was never denied. But a new aspect had begun to be revealed by Amos, Hosea, and Isaiah, from whom Jeremiah drew the definitive lesson.

In proclaiming the Lord's exigency of righteousness, Amos expressed its harsh consequence: "You only have I known of all the families of the earth;

therefore I will punish you for all your iniquities.''[68] This says for the first time, in such an explicit way, that far from being reserved for others, for the peoples who are strangers to the covenant, the judgment must fall first on the chosen people, precisely because they are chosen.

Hosea explained this: all God's gifts to his People were indeed his gifts—so many proofs of his love of predilection—but the People were not able to recognize them for what they were. They worshiped the gifts instead of the giver. They made idols of them, which was nothing other than excitation of their lusts, which made them forget the ethical requirements of the Torah, just as they misrepresented its religious exigencies. It was necessary, then, that God withdraw his gifts, so that the People would come back to look for him and for him alone.[69]

Until this time the rich man; the prosperous farmer, under his vine and his fig tree; the father of a family who rejoiced in a full and amply provided-for progeniture; the victorious king, enthroned in a glorious city, appeared as the Lord's blessed. But Isaiah was the first to dare to say: "Woe to the rich.''[70] And Jeremiah, in his own person—in his whole existence, even more than in his explicit message—was the living proclamation of this fact that, up to then, had been unheard in Israel: the poor man is blessed, that is, the one who no longer has anything in which to place his trust and his joy, except God and God alone.

Jeremiah is a figure the like of which Israel had not yet known. He had no wife, no family. His vocation placed him not only aloof from the people but in opposition to them. The God who forcefully placed dreadful words in his mouth made the effect on him of being his enemy. Jeremiah was tempted to revolt, to refuse his mission and its message; but the Word was stronger. Finally, it appears to have crushed him.[71]

The prophecy of Ezekiel (its beginnings are contemporary with the end of Jeremiah) follows directly. It specifies for the People the overwhelming extremity of the trial that awaits them. But it will also enlighten them by showing them the finger of God and, still more, that he has determined everything—that the upheaval, in which his own worship seems to be destroyed, is only the reflection of his previous decision to abandon Jerusalem to punishment for its faults.

In the temple, desecrated by idolatrous and murderous worship before the invader secularized and destroyed it, Ezekiel saw the Divine Presence, which Isaiah had contemplated in the holy of holies, withdraw. On the *merkabah,* the fiery chariot of the Cherubim and the Ophanim, it flew off, toward the Mount of Olives, as if to contemplate fulfillment of its judgments on the unfaithful city and its sullied sanctuary. Then it disappeared.[72]

But here was an unexpected consolation. Invisible but there, the divine

Presence had not deserted its People. Even in Babylon, for the most afflicted Israelite captives it became a secret, inviolable sanctuary, which accompanied them in their tribulation and which nothing could destroy for them.[73] They need only accept the trial in faith, in the crucible of recasting.

The prophet says formally: The People must be reduced to dried and scattered bones for the Divine Word to pass over them, so that they might come together and put on flesh again. Then the Spirit of God will come into them and they will revive with a totally new life.[74]

The hope of a new covenant, of a new and eternal covenant, in which God's law would be inscribed not only on tablets of stone but on the living tablets of renewed hearts, is taken directly by Ezekiel from Jeremiah. He is more specific in saying that, up to that time, Israel had only a heart of stone. The God who crushed that heart in the trial will ultimately substitute for it that heart of flesh, that living heart of his own life, which will make the People of God effectively his own, no longer merely because he acquired them but because he regenerated them.[75]

For Hosea's image (comparing the People to a harlot, whom a love without measure fell upon and, without merit on her part, metamorphosed her, by its own power alone, into a virgin worthy of divine espousals) Ezekiel substituted something that was even more brutal and expressive.[76] Israel was nothing but an abortion, an abandoned fruit of bastardy, when God met it and took a fancy to it. Its infidelities were only a foreseeable consequence of such sullied origins. But the love of God, despite everything, is stronger. God will forgive everything, and the renewed and *new* covenant, the result of his forgiveness, will be an eternal covenant.

Here, suddenly, the perspectives broaden. The effect of these definitive espousals of God with Israel is that Israel will finally realize the plan of adoption, of union, which God had in mind for it from the beginning. But what is more, the Bride will become a Mother, in the sense that the other nations, her sisters, like the younger Samaria or the elder Sodom (who also had been immersed in infidelity but who, until then, never had the light of hope), will become her daughters in the faith.[77]

The other side of this universalist extension of salvation is an interiorization which arrives with Ezekiel as well, at a decisive personalization. There is no longer any collective salvation or judgment, if by that is understood a salvation or judgment which would touch on a collectivity as a whole.[78] The effect of the trial must be to differentiate the faithful individuals from the mass in order to refashion from them the definitive People, that is, the People promised to the eternal covenant, that of the new heart. Starting with this principle, it will be more and more clear, and will begin to be announced formally, that if all Israel is not the true Israel, conversely, many others, who did not seem able to belong to it, will reveal themselves to have been called to become part of it.

A late fragment of prophecy, inserted into the Book of Isaiah (19:16ff.) after his oracles on Egypt, specifies these perspectives by forecasting a reconciliation between Assyria (at this point Babylon) and Egypt. This same Israel, which had found itself absorbed in their conflict, will bring them together by reuniting them in the worship of the only true God.

Such hopes seemed purely idle at the moment Ezekiel encouraged them. Yet in the last quarter of the century, with the victory of the Persian conqueror Cyrus over Babylon, the People were able to think they were on the very eve of becoming reality.

At this point appear the oracles of the unknown prophet that today form the second part of the Book of Isaiah.[79] They announce the liberation, the imminent restoration of Israel, and the cycle of Servant Songs makes a new figure appear. This image of the "servant of the Lord," beaten and humiliated but promised final salvation because of his fidelity, is undoubtedly a projection (on the "remnant" of Judah and Israel) of the figure of Jeremiah and of what can already be called his "passion." Without doubt, the servant is identified with the chosen community, hand picked by the trial, and his glory, earned by his immutable fidelity, will give convincing testimony for all the nations. But his characteristics appear too individualized for us not to see something more: a first presentment, interpreted within this unprecedented experience, of dereliction and then exaltation. The vision is formed of a unique servant, abandoned by all, humiliated by God himself, in whom, finally, the "remnant" will be reduced, in order to prepare in himself, with this resurrection of Israel (announced by Ezekiel), a reconstitution and salvation of all peoples in the One Elect: "It is too light a thing that you should be my servant to raise up the tribes of Jacob and to restore the preserved of Israel; I will give you as a light to the nations, that my salvation may reach to the end of the earth."[80]

In the interim, between the exile and the liberation, some priest-disciples of Ezekiel at Babylon had prepared the reconstruction of the People and their city and Temple, following lines that Ezekiel had traced in the last part of his book.[81] These are the authors of what is called the Priestly Document, that is, the last group of inspired accounts of the history of Israel. They put them together with the "Yahwistic" accounts, undoubtedly from Judah, or the "Elohistic" narratives, probably from the northern kingdom, around chiefly legislative or directly Mosaic or Deuteronomical traditions, in order to form the Pentateuch as it has come down to us, along with what follows in the historical books. These priestly scribes, through their fixing and final interpretation of the ancient tradition of Israel, were the authors of the Bible and that "Judaism" in which the history of the People was continued down to the New Testament.[82]

Ezra the Scribe, who, after the return authorized by the Persian liberator, led the first coherent endeavors at restoration, appears as the heir of their work and the executor of their plans. The Book of Nehemiah shows him in the city, still in ruins, which was scarcely beginning to put itself back together. There he brought together a third great *qahal*: the "assembly" in which the Jewish People were to assume their definitive appearance.[83] The structure and development remain the same as on Sinai and under Josiah. But we see a new transformation of these elements!

This time the reading went on day after day to the seventh month, until the celebration of the Feast of Tents. This underlines the fact that this return is the new exodus, the new creation of the People in the desert, which the prophets since Hosea had predicted. This time the reading is the entire Pentateuch. The once-more-renewed covenant, after a formal act of penance, is its conclusion. It is not sacrifices that can seal it, but a prayer pronounced in the name of the whole People by the Levites, which anticipates and consecrates the restoration in advance, though it beseeches the Lord to make it possible.

Responding to the reading, which summed up (as it were) the history of their initial salvation for the People, and by drawing out all the meaning that had evolved from the experience and the trials that followed, in the light of the last prophecies, this prayer is like the first model of what today we call the Eucharist. Indeed, it is a thanksgiving to God for creation and the history of salvation, and more particularly for the accomplishment of this salvation of his People over a series of providential trials. The prayer concludes with a confident entreaty that God will accomplish in his People the work that has begun, by purifying them from their faults and by making them worthy to live forever in his presence and in his praise.

As has been often observed, this great "ekklesia" of the People is the prototype, as it were, of what all subsequent synagogal assemblies will be: the reading of the Law (and the prophets) and then renewed consecration of Israel to this Torah (by recitation of the Shema: "Hear, O Israel, the Lord your God is the only Lord, and you will love the Lord your God with all your heart, with all your soul and with all your strength")—between the great *berakoth* of Yozer and the Shemoneh-Esreh.[84]

## V. *From the Scribes to the Rabbis, from Wisdom to Revelation*

However, this restoration, despite or even because of the hopes that its expectation had aroused, soon seemed far from realization. The city, the

Temple, could be rebuilt; a cult purified and enlightened by the synagogal teaching could be restored there; and even the beginning of a restoration of the kingship, in the spirit of the final predictions of Ezekiel, could be attempted around the person of Zorubbabel. Yet also it appeared, as Haggai emphasized, that restoration on the material level reestablished only a faint shadow of ancient Sion.[85] Nor do the last prophecies, added to the Book of Isaiah, hide the fact that the spiritual renewal was far from realizing the promises of Ezekiel or Deutero-Isaiah. But these same prophecies will revive, if need be, and magnify even more the hope of a future Jerusalem whose light will shine on the nations. To it will be brought the offerings of the whole world and a new priesthood will be consecrated, in which, it seems, not only the dispersed will have their place but perhaps even those to whom Israel had appeared to be breaking up.[86] This, at least, is the interpretation of this text by early Christian exegesis, and of Malachi 1:11, which the fathers will quote in its favor and which tends to prove that the very last prophets could have accepted it. It is clear that such perspectives go beyond the present world and history as we know it; hence the cry: "Oh that thou wouldst rend the heavens and come down."[87] However, a Judaism that contracted within itself will appear more and more characteristic in the following centuries.

Under the Seleucids, Persian tolerance was succeeded by a frantic attempt at assimilation of the Jews to Hellenism in their own country. The revolt of a priestly family, the Maccabees, put a definitive stop to this evolution. *De facto,* this family reestablished a kind of new, Levitical monarchy; but despite the unquestionably religious zeal of its founders, their dynasty seems to have secularized the priesthood by politicizing it. Up to the time of Christ, the Sadducees (i.e., the members of the great priestly families), despite their ritual and doctrinal conservatism, had the effect on pious Israelites of "ungodly priests." Vacillating between frankly nationalistic politics and a policy of compromise, first with the Greek and then with the Roman conquerors, their involvement in business, joined to their religious practice (which was looked upon as wholly external), made them suspect of materialism.[88]

As a reaction, there appeared the party of the Pharisees (i.e., the "separated ones"), who were recruited especially among the lay notables of the capital. It first rose against all the hellenizing movements, but it soon came to be equally opposed (if not to the priesthood in general) to the priestly caste of Jerusalem. It was from their number that the rabbis came, the doctors of the Law who were to be the genuine spiritual successors of the ancient priestly scribes. Seeing in the details of the ritual and ceremonial prescriptions of the Torah the "hedge" they felt they needed in order to trace and firmly maintain the demarcation between a faithful Judaism and its threatened assimilation to pagan customs, morals, and ideas, they put at the basis of their teaching a punctilious legalistic casuistry. It became the essential object of rabbinical tradition: the *halakah.*

However, it would be a mistake to isolate this element, as important as it may be, in Pharisaism and, more generally, the rabbinic tradition. If one were to see only this element in it, one would misunderstand its significance. It is not true that the *halakah,* properly understood, is limited to accumulating ritual prohibitions, or that it concentrates exclusively on external practice. It attaches to these prohibitions (as the word "hedge" shows) only the value of a safeguard. And if it is deeply concerned with the material details of obedience to the Torah, it is because of a profoundly thought out conviction that one does not reach the interior of man except through the exterior. But this is not in any sense the result of some misunderstanding of interiority—quite the contrary. One of the most constant and particularly Pharisaic traditions is that of *kavanah* (i.e., the attention not only of the understanding but also of the heart, of the whole inner being) to the rites and the formulas of the prayers and the Bible, which were unceasingly repeated. Without *kavanah,* all the rest had no meaning nor, consequently, the least value. Far from the great Pharisaic doctors' being at odds with Jesus on this point, we might say that he merely ratified and consecrated their doctrine.[89]

The religious ideal of these rabbis was an ideal of constant prayer, but we must immediately specify that such prayer was introduced into all existence, becoming one with it; hence its close relationship with *halakah,* which tends to inform all details of existence by obedience to the Torah. And the prayer about which we are speaking is merely perpetual meditation on and assimilation of the Divine Word. It aims to make the whole life of the pious Jew a response in act to that Word.

The prayer of the rabbis, supported by use of the Psalter, diffuses and at the same time condenses the substance of the psalms in this prayer in a relatively new form, which we have described as immediate preparation for the Christian Eucharist and which first appears in the *qahal* of Ezra in the Book of Nehemiah. Actually, it is only a development of a form of prayer that is typically biblical and evident from the earliest layers of Israel's tradition; it is basically a *berakah* (i.e., a blessing of God for the great things he did for his People), reading their history in the light of faith in the divine Word. A typical example is the prayer of Eliezer, Abraham's servant, when he found Rebekah and thus saw fulfilled the mission entrusted to him: "Blessed be the Lord, the God of my master Abraham, who has not forsaken his steadfast love and his faithfulness toward my master. As for me, the Lord has led me in the way to the house of my master's kinsmen.'"[90]

In the same way in every circumstance, the devout Jew will see the finger of God, fulfillment of his Word for his People, and will bless him for it. All things thus appear to him as divine creations, as tangible actualizations of his Word of love to his own. Still more, all the events of his life become so many integral parts of the history of salvation, in which the Word has involved his People. Thus each action of the day, each object or being he meets, becomes an occasion for celebrating the revealed God as the Master and Creator of everything, and the Savior of those who believe in his Word.

Exactly in this perspective will St. Paul say: "For everything created by God is good, and nothing is to be rejected if it is received with thanksgiving [i.e., a *berakah*]; for then it is consecrated by the word of God and prayer."[91]

As the rabbi recalled who conversed with St. Justin in his *Adversus Tryphonem,* it is by constant repetition of these *berakoth* that Jews become aware that they have become in all reality the entirely priestly people spoken of in the nineteenth chapter of Exodus.[92] In pronouncing them, they consecrate themselves, and the universe with them, by the power of the Word. It will be said that the Jew, through these benedictions extended to all things, prepares the whole world for becoming the tabernacle of the *Shekinah.*[93] The synthesis of these manifold benedictions will be made by the great traditional prayers that follow the reading of the Bible in the synagogue, just as in the assembly of Ezra, and in the no less important assemblies that accompany meals, especially on a sabbath or holy day.

At the synagogue service, before recitation of the Shemah, as a constantly renewed consecration of the People to loving observance of the Torah, the first benediction (Yozer) praises God as the creator of light, visible and invisible: his glory, which shines on all things and illuminates the intelligence of spiritual beings, beginning with the angels. Hence the repetition of the Qedushah (the Sanctus), mentioned by Isaiah, which even in the Temple must have been a chant that accompanied the incense sacrifice:

> Holy, holy, holy Lord God of hosts:
> the earth is filled with his glory!

There follows the second benediction (the Ahabah), after the Berakah of the Cherubim and the Ophanim of Ezekiel, which glorifies the special presence of God in the holy of holies:

> Blessed be the glory of the Lord and of his place!

This second benediction celebrates the love of God for his People, which became known especially to them, with saving knowledge, by the revelation of the Torah.

Then comes the common recitation of the Shemah, followed by the Eighteen Benedictions (Shemoneh Esreh), still called the Tefillah (the preeminent prayer). In a benediction of the Divine Name, they house a series of supplications for accomplishment of his plan for his People. The conclusion asks that this People, gathered together and consecrated in definitive unity, in a Jerusalem restored for eternity, may praise God without ceasing.[94]

The benedictions that accompany the meals, and especially those connected with the last cup, follow an exactly parallel development. But it is no longer the theme of light, but life, that predominates.

The first benediction, giving thanks for the food just received, blesses God as the Creator and Preserver of life.

The second, passing from food to the earth, which produced it (i.e., the promised land), blesses him as the Savior who led his People into the land after he delivered them from their enemies.

The third formula, in more compact form than the great, detailed supplication of the Shemoneh Esreh, again asks him to accomplish his work of gathering the scattered and completing the building of Jerusalem, so that God may be praised there forever by his unanimous people.

These prayers, as Louis Finkelstein pointed out, had a decisive effect on forging the religious consciousness of Israel. They inculcate a definitive interpretation of its history, of the Divine Word which elicited and illuminated that history, outside of which the revelation of the New Testament would be incomprehensible.[95]

This spirituality of the *berakoth,* which is the heart of what can be called the theology of Judaism, is in the direct line of interpretation given by the last prophets to the religion of sacrifices. It is the same, systematic accomplishment of this "sacrifice of the lips," expressing the sacrifice of the heart that Hosea spoke of. It gives true meaning to his statement, which will be repeated by Jesus: "I desire mercy [i.e., *hesed,* both piety toward God and merciful piety in his own image toward men] and not sacrifice."[96]

As contemporary Scandinavian exegesis has shown, this phrase must not be understood as the liberal Protestant exegesis of the nineteenth century. It is in no way a substitution of some sort of lay, secularized "prophetic faith" for the "priestly religion," the religion of the sacrifices. The imaginary opposition is a historical misunderstanding, since prophetism originated in the priestly milieus and achieved its major expression only in the work of the two priests, Jeremiah and Ezekiel. Rather, it is a question, in the line expressed by the theme of the *kavanah,* of the last meaning given to sacrificial religion by the religion of the Word. Sacrifice, like all ritual prescriptions of the Torah, is in no way discredited there, but is seen as the expression and acceptance in faith of a consecration of the whole existence of the People to the God who spoke to them.

Certainly, in the interval of the exile, or later in the diaspora, synagogal worship and the piety that nourishes it will be considered an equivalent of the sacrifices that by this time have become impossible. But far from rendering them useless, they will tend to their transfigured restoration.[97]

In the body of the sacrificial rites, illuminated by their reference to the fundamental ritual of Passover, not simply the act of faith of the believer, consecrating himself to the exigencies of the Word, will be seen, but first, and in order to make this consecration possible, the "memorial" given by God of his creative and saving acts, which his Word announces and produces.

"Memorial" (as J. Jeremias showed so well)[98] does not mean a subjective recalling for man of the great deeds of God. The basic significance of the term is applied to permanent pledges given by God of his past interventions and their permanence. And it is *to him* that the "memorial" must be represented, so that he might "remember" his plan of love, of which his past acts are merely the token, in order that he bring its fulfillment to its definitive term.

This is marvelously expressed by the clause introduced by the synagogue liturgy in both the Abodah prayer at the conclusion of the Shemoneh Esreh and in the third benediction, accompanying the final cup of the meal on a holy day:

> Our God, and the God of our fathers, may the remembrance (memorial) of ourselves and of our fathers and the remembrance of Jerusalem, thy city, and the remembrance of the Messiah, the son of David, thy servant, and the remembrance of thy people, the whole house of Israel, arise and come, come to pass, be seen and accepted and heard, be remembered and be mentioned before thee for deliverance, for good, for grace, for loving kindness and for mercy on his [such-and-such] day. Remember us, JHWH, our God, on it for good and visit us on it for blessing and save us on it unto life by a word of salvation and mercy, and spare, favor and show us mercy, for thou art a gracious and merciful God and King.[99]

This leads us to a final consideration, essential for understanding Judaism preceding the beginnings of Christianity: its eschatological hope and, more precisely, its messianic expectation.

It can be said that the ritual of the Temple and the synagogue, and the observation of the whole Torah (which for Judaism becomes only a "memorial" of the actions and revelation of God in the past, in which the People were constituted), far from enclosing the People within the past, sent them into an eschatological future. This movement was characteristic of the prophets who had preceded and prepared the exile. They had described it in advance, at least since Hosea,[100] as a new exodus, a new Passover, destined to accomplish (at last) what the first exodus and the first Passover had merely outlined.

But it was in an unexpected metamorphosis of wisdom, around the exile itself, that this movement was to uncover its full import. However experimental, empirical, and rational (all at once) wisdom was, we have already said how the ideal Israelite wise man, represented by the figure of Solomon, came to see authentic wisdom as a gift of God which one must wait for, as a grace from on high, entreated for in prayer. We have also mentioned the significant convergence, even before the exile, among the Deuteronomists, who wanted to apply systematically the teaching of the prophets and the meditation of the wise men to the life of the People, seeking in the Divine Word the light they need in order to illumine their plan for a better human life. Formulas like those of the author of Ecclesiasticus (Sivak), describing wisdom and concluding with its identification with the Divine Word, are characteristic of this evolution.

But at the time of the exile, one more step was to be taken, and the Book of Job is the most striking indication of this. Just as in the collapse of the Davidic kingship the People had to acknowledge that God is the sole, invincible king, the people came to the conclusion that he is the only true wise man and that his wisdom abides by itself, inaccessible to mortals: the preeminent mystery. The problem of evil, posited with particular sharpness through the apparent collapse of Israel's hopes, and the problem of innocent suffering, not only of sinners but of the righteous, is the problem of Job. His friends hurled the traditional arguments at him: God always rewards his faithful and those whom he smites can only be sinners who are punished for their sins. Without denying this schema, Job protests that he cannot explain his suffering. Yet he does not deny God. On the contrary, he turns to him in order to cry out to him, saying he cannot understand what was happening to him; and he persists in his faith despite everything. And it is Job, at the end of the dialogue, whom God justifies against his friends and their apparently more rational and certainly more pious theology. At the same time, he invites Job to acknowledge that true wisdom, the genuine explanation of human life, belongs only to God, and remains the deepest of mysteries.[101] In this regard, as the Deuteronomists and the pre-exilic wise men come together, it can be said that the authors of the Book of Job and the Servant Songs correspond.[102]

But if wisdom belongs only to God—if, in the last analysis, it is inaccessible to the efforts of human intelligence to dominate its experience of life—that wisdom is nevertheless one with God's plan that guides and fashions, according to an external blueprint, the history of men. If no speculation can resolve the enigma of human life, and especially the life of the chosen people, the only solution can be obtained through divine intervention, which ultimately will lead the history in which God has involved his People and, at the same time, the whole history of mankind, to its final outcome.

Thus wisdom will live on and will surpass itself through expectation of a revelation. Only God will clear up this mystery, inherent in the existence of men, and in his chosen ones above all, by showing them the ways by which he is preparing to give it a *de facto* solution that is inaccessible to the undertakings and estimates of men. From wisdom, then, we will pass to apocalypse (the word means "revelation," the supernatural revelation of the divine plans and, especially, their ultimate, eschatological realization).

However new apocalypse in Israel may be, we must note that it will answer what seems to have been a long, spontaneous hope of the People: a "day" of the Lord in which all wrongs will be corrected by him and judgment established—a progressively refined hope, sublimated by the last prophets. Indeed, it can be said that the transition from wisdom to apocalypse takes place before our eyes, in the last prophetical book of an eminently popular kind: the Book of Daniel.

The second chapter of this book is one of its high points. As Deden showed in a study on the Pauline mystery (which represents a decisive stage in the exegesis of the texts of the Apostle on this theme), this chapter contains all the characteristic terms that St. Paul used to speak of the "mystery," and he shows us its essential connections.[103] The Chaldean king had a vision that no one could explain. In despair, he had recourse to a captive Israelite wise man, Daniel, who, in the vision of his dream, showed him a premonition of the fulfillment toward which God was orienting not only the history of the People over whom he reigned but, first of all, the chosen people themselves, and, by this fact, universal history.

Daniel's prayer is typical. He gives thanks for the divine illumination which allows him to enlighten the king on this subject: "Blessed be the name of God for ever and ever; to whom belong wisdom and might. He changes times and seasons; he removes kings and sets up kings; he gives wisdom to the wise and knowledge to those who have understanding; he reveals deep and mysterious things; he knows what is in the darkness, and the light dwells with him."[104]

Led before the king, Daniel tells him: "No wise men, enchanters, magicians, or astrologers can show the king the mystery which the king has asked, but there is a God in heaven who reveals mysteries, and he has made known to King Nebuchadnezzar what will be in the latter days."[105]

And again "But as for me, not because of any wisdom that I have, more than all the living, has this mystery been revealed to me, but in order that the interpretation may be made known to the king, and that you may know the thoughts of your mind."[106]

We see in all this what wisdom had become for the last wise men of Israel:

the secret plan of God for human history, according to which he will take control of that history in order to lead it to its fulfillment. The mysteries of this wisdom concerning the decisive moments for his intervention, which he prepared from afar, will be revealed in the acts of his inaccessible wisdom. But before that, he freely gives his servants a revelation (*apokalypsis*) of it which will allow them to prepare for it, and to prepare others as well.

Let us note that here we find the first formal expression of the fact that God occasionally makes authentic "revelations" to men who do not belong to the chosen people, as in the case of the Chaldean monarch. But these revelations, despite all the resources of human wisdom, remain obscure, as long as the Word heard in Israel does not shed its light on them. This is not due, it is emphasized, to some superior, intrinsic quality of Jewish wisdom, which would properly belong to its representatives, but to the absolutely gratuitous revelation that God entrusted to them, and not only for them but for others as well.

The rest of the book, and especially the seventh chapter, shows that the "apocalypse," the revelation of the end of history, is concentrated on the appearance of a mysterious personage, coming on the clouds of heaven to meet God himself (who is referred to as "ancient of days"). The judgment has been entrusted to him (i.e., the ultimate and victorious conflict with all the forces of evil). This personage is simply called "son of man," which signifies that he will appear as a man. Still, that he will appear "on the clouds of heaven" signifies supernatural origin.

What, then, is this "son of man"? Again we meet the ambiguity (more precisely the duality) that we observed in regard to the "servant" of the Deutero-Isaiah. What is said by one of the angels who assist Daniel at the moment of his visions allows us to suppose that this "son of man" is identified with "the saints of the Most High"[107] (i.e., the Israel of the latter days), "who will receive the kingdom and possess it for ever." The "son of man" appears no less as an individual who will accomplish for them, and for God, the triumph over all the powers of enmity and who will therefore lead them into this kingdom without end, which is the reign of God, with which they will be associated.

The heavenly "son of man" will be found again in many other apocalypses that will multiply in Israel to Christian times. No one else will be incorporated into the biblical canon by the Jews, and there is no question that their general teaching will have considerable influence on Judaism, especially the Book of Enoch and 4 Esdras.[108] All have in common the more and more imminent announcement of a "reign of God" which must be substituted for earthly empires, whose succession Daniel enumerated in his explanation of the vision of the statue given to the king. Again, this does not say what is essential: throughout these successive kingdoms, which would destroy one another before the only kingdom that would not pass away would come, is the occult domination of God's enemy, Satan, who is more and more clearly denounced. The opposition of kingdoms thus becomes an opposition of two "worlds" or two "ages," two *aiones* (i.e., radically heterogeneous periods in the history of the world: the *aion outos,* the "present age," and the *aion mellon,* the "age to come"). This underlies the world of the New Testament. And as the Jewish apocalypses said, what characterizes the *aion outos* is that God will reign there, while in the *aion mellon* it is not he who reigns but "Belial" (i.e., the Demon).[109]

People have wanted to see in these oppositions a characteristic influence of Persia on pre-Christian Judaism. When we deal with Iranian influences on Israel, we should be very prudent and sensitive to delicate shades of thought. We must first take into account the singular kingship of Hebrew prophetism and the mission of Zoroaster (which was contemporary with Isaiah and Jeremiah). It makes the estimation of possible influences very difficult in both directions. And even if it were proved that there were such influences, it would not be easy to differentiate so-called importations from simple stimulations, brought to the development of themes already present quite independently.

Certainly Zoroaster preached a strict monotheism in a dualistic framework—a dualism which was not metaphysical but ethical. His god, like the God of Israel, is the unique creator of all that exists, and according to him, evil comes only from free disobedience of the most exalted creatures, which this god will condemn and triumph over at the end of time, after having called them by his prophet to repentance and conversion.[110]

In Israel, on the other hand, if the theme of the last judgment and God's final victory over the powers of enmity takes on special relief with the last great prophets, it was known well before them. The same is true for the idea that idols are not pure nothingness but rebel cosmic "powers," eager to divert to themselves the adoration and subjection of men. And it was considerably earlier than its contacts with Persia that Israel represented the divine nature after the image of a fiery light.

If Judaism, at the very moment when it asserted its religious particularism with regard to the "nations" that successively dominated the Jews, or among which they were dispersed, was able to find some value in Iranian religious thought, it was undoubtedly (and especially) to develop the idea of personal immortality, which to that time had played little or no role in Israel. But the interiorization, the personalization of its religion, so strongly stated by Ezekiel, disposed it to this notion.

In a general manner, it may be said that this was the case for Judaism, *a fortiori* with respect to Mazdaean Iran, where it found so many assertions close to its own, as was to be the case later with regard to Hellenic culture. It violently rejected the religious notions of Hellenism that were in conflict with its faith, but it made its own (without hesitation) some intellectual representations, as well as moral acquisitions, since it perceived that they could be of profit without compromise to the faith.

This also explains the findings that are increasingly emphasized in our day: hellenized Judaism in the countries of Greek culture and language, especially Egypt, remained much closer to Palestinian Judaism, even in the case of Philo, "a Hebrew son of Hebrews," than the nineteenth century supposed. Recent research (Goodenough in particular) has shown that Philo, however much influenced by late Platonism and especially Stoicism, was above all a religious jurist, concerned with applying to the situation of the diaspora the rabbinic *halakah*.[111] His cosmological speculations are much less Hellenic than they might appear at first sight. To a very great extent, his theory of the Logos and the powers is limited to clothing, with a mantle of Greek philosophy, speculations on the Word and the wisdom of the angels which the rabbis had developed previously by (possibly) borrowings from Mazdaism, on a basis that was essentially Mosaic and prophetic. All this comes from a vision of an absolute divine transcendence, which is not exclusive of a very real immanence of grace.

What remains true with Philo is that, at first sight at least, and whatever the case with the body of hellenized "Jews," we do not find the eschatological tension so characteristic of latter-day Hebraic Judaism. To the same extent, the sense of a destiny that is proper to the Hebrew people, of a history of salvation of which its own history is the nucleus (as it were), seems to disappear with him, to the gain of an individualistic mysticism. He allegorizes the accounts about Abraham and the patriarchs, and Moses himself, as if he saw in them only paradigms of the "king's way," that is, the spiritual itinerary that every "righteous man" must take on his own to reach union with God.

Yet, even on this point, we must not hurry to a hasty conclusion. Philo's allegories are not simply the sequel to the encomia of the fathers, already familiar with the Books of Wisdom (such as Ecclesiasticus or the Wisdom of Solomon), which attempted to find models in them for every devout Israelite. They seem to be even more directly influenced by the popular *midrash* of the *haggadic* tradition, that is, the devotional interpretation that the rabbis gave to these accounts. This is all the more noticeable since the apocalyptic tradition seems to us more and more a central form of this *haggadah*, in which the vision of the eschatological future is always nourished by a transposition of the past.

Also, we must not simply oppose the allegorizing mysticism of a certain Alexandrian Judaism, whether directly Philonian or not, to the radical eschatologism of the authors of apocalyptic material. For their part, these latter writings thought that the believer could not only have some kind of anticipated vision of the expected "Kingdom of God," but he must prepare himself for it. And the vision of this preparation given to him by grace, was surely the principle.

Platonizing Hellenism had developed the idea that, to know God, it was first necessary to make oneself like him by one's own efforts. The resemblance of Philonian mysticism to this ideal is deceiving. In fact, it proposes its exact opposite: knowledge of God, which God gives freely to those who approach him in the spirit of the faith of the fathers of Israel, will assimilate them to him. Under philosophical, Hellenic externals, we are brought back to the "knowledge of God" of the prophets: knowledge of the One who knew us (and loved us!) first, whose principle is faith in his Word, involving the obedience of one's whole life and leading to conformation to him in the union with him, or rather in his union with us.

Also, we must not be surprised that the most strictly Jewish of the Palestinians contemporary with Philo, in a spirituality in which eschatological tension reaches its maximum, present many characteristics that relate them so closely to the most hellenized Judaism that exegetes wonder today whether the Pharisees—and even communities like those at Qumran—had not undergone Greek influences!

The casuistry of the later Pharisees might well have competed with the casuistry of the Stoics, without deviating from their intransigent fidelity to the Torah. But what is to be said of the asceticism of the priests of Qumran, of the pronounced dualism of their vision of the final condition of the chosen people as a conflict between the "sons of light" and the "sons of darkness"?[112] It is at least questionable that there was any trace of an "underground" diffusion of Hellenism in the most fiercely separate and entrenched Judaism, not only of the other nations but of the mass of Israel itself, which, beginning with the Jerusalem priesthood, was considered to be corrupt. Even if we acknowledge nothing of the sort, it would be difficult to see there, once again and more than ever, anything other than a free use of convenient expressions (which were forged elsewhere) to convey an experience that, in its core, was purely Jewish, in direct line from the latter prophets and the apocalypses: what the Baptist expressed when he said "Even now the ax is laid to the root of the trees."[113] The flight into the desert, before the expected Messiah, is only the inevitable consequence of the conviction that the hour has finally come "for judgment to begin with the household of God,"[114] when the "present age" was to yield before the all-powerful overflowing of the "age to come," that of the

"Kingdom of God," and when the mysterious figure, recalled by the images of "messiah," "son of David," "son of God," and—above all—the "servant," the "son of man," coming on the clouds of heaven, will appear.

For these priests of Qumran in particular, the real *qahal*, the real *ekklesia*, in which the People in their final faithful remnant must prepare for the encounter with their God, is no longer an ordinary synagogal assembly or, still less, the holiday assemblies at the sanctuary in Jerusalem. For them, these are only a vain extension of a routine form of worship, stained with deep infidelity. It is the meetings of these voluntarily poor men, who "seek in the Scriptures for the consolation of Israel,"[115] and their fraternal banquets, whose traditional prayers and with insistent invocation of the Messiah, of the rebuilding of the holy city, which from now on are the only assembly of the latter-day saints and the only sacrifice which forecasts the new covenant of an everlasting passover.

## VI. The Tradition of Israel

The opposition—or in any case the duality, the tension—between Scripture and tradition in modern Christianity has become such a banal schema for us that we find it difficult to realize a significant yet incontestable fact and, for a stronger reason, to appreciate its import. At the moment the Bible was being completed, when Judaism became preeminently the "religion of the book," it also asserted itself as a religion that was essentially traditional.

This, first of all, is to say that Judaism never conceived the possibility of interpreting the Bible authentically, except by the oral tradition of its rabbis. But also, acceptance of the biblical books as inspired by God has never obscured the fact that they were the product and deposit of an original tradition. In this way, the written and the unwritten Torah were never signified a duality for Israel, but two necessarily complementary forms of a unique tradition.[116]

This sentiment has remained very precise and firm in the believing Jewish people of today, and it is fully confirmed in modern critical study of the biblical documents. In their written form, texts that are both legislative and historical undoubtedly represent the progressive deposit of a much earlier oral tradition, which had not ceased to live and grow until its projection into Scripture.

The prophetic work, as far as the ancient prophets are concerned, has come down to us only by the intermediary of the oral tradition, which was later condensed in the writings we call "historical" but which Jews have always called "the first prophets." For the more recent prophets, we pass unwittingly from oral prophecies (collected by disciples) to dictated prophecies, and only at the end to prophecies that were directly written down. But the placement of the latter in the books that bear the names of later prophets not only betrays the intervention of tradition but is combined with glosses, additions, and extensions of all kinds. The different parts of the book attributed to Isaiah are the most striking illustration of this fact, but the work of Ezekiel, the greatest writer-prophet, who best deserves this title, in the sense that he seems to have *written* directly from the outset (and not merely *told* of his prophecies), has not escaped this process either.

Yet we must go further. We find exegetes, even among the most "independent," who persist in describing the prophetical inspiration as an individual phenomenon, a totally isolated creation in each prophet, isolated from what could be said by others. "Prophets never quote one another," we are constantly told, but this remark is absurd. Obviously, the prophets do not fill their texts with precise references to their predecessors, as modern writers would do, but the greatest and most "creative" are filled with the message of their predecessors, and, as the sketches that have just been read demonstrate, they rely on them constantly. With the latter prophets, we even note an analogical style which, without expressly quoting earlier texts (in the manner of more or less modern commentators), incorporates and transposes their typical formulas, even in statements that, because of their substance, are totally new.

But this is still not saying enough. All the teaching of the prophets supposes, as its obvious basis, the nucleus of Mosaic history and preaching, though it is true that these latter elements did not have a definitively composed form until after the prophets and under their influence. This Mosaism, in turn, implied the essential element of what was done by Abraham and the patriarchs. Moses merely fulfilled the ancient promises, and first revived the benumbed memory of the "God of our Fathers." And all the prophetic teachings that follow would be meaningless if their basis were removed: the covenant of Sinai; the story of the exodus, of which it is the conclusion; the *toroth,* which will concretize it perpetually in the life of the People.

This traditional character of Judaism—of the expression, of the bursting forth of the Word which supports and inspires it—holds to the original and constant connection of this Word to an experience common to all the people, developed from generation to generation but in continuity through all successive generations. It is, then, only the reverse side of the close correlation that we mentioned at the outset, between the development of the Word and the history of the People.

It is not enough to say that the Word is addressed to the People, or even that the People are fashioned by the Word. Rather we must say that the Word is so profoundly incorporated in their life that it is not separate from them. Reciprocally, the People are not simply the bearer of the Word: they are its witness and they bear this witness in their existence; they make one body with it. This is also to say that the tradition of the Word in Israel is an essentially living tradition, not only or primarily because it does not stop renewing itself but especially because it is not transmitted as a simple message, but in a lived experience, the experience of a whole life.

This in no way signifies that the Word was conceived by Israel, or appears to the historian, as a simple deposit of experience, nor even as the simple product of rationalized reflection upon it. This is the attribute not of the Word, in the sense it took on for Israel, but of wisdom as Israel received it from outside. Undoubtedly, wisdom came to be received and absorbed in the Word. Nevertheless, Israel is conscious of having met a reality that surpasses it, of having been captured by it, and finally of being totally entranced by it.

The Word is really an interpretation of the history of the People, received consciously from on high, in whatever manifold ways will accommodate it to human modes of expression and human understanding. Indeed, it is more than interpretation (though interpretation is essential to it); it is an integral part of the history of the People, which makes their history "holy," whose antecedent presence enlightens it—a presence that is active, creative, saving. Thus the Word constantly illuminates its own work, from which man proceeded at the beginning, as did the whole universe, and in which man, despite his original infidelity, despite his numberless relapses, and even *through* them, "finds" himself again, in the last analysis.

Thus the history of the People demands the Word in order to be understood, not only because the Word alone explains it but because it constitutes its sole sufficient reason—just as the Word has no meaning nor even concrete existence, manifest in our world, except in a context inseparable from this history.

When matters are uncovered in this light, we see it is not fortuitous but of the very nature of these things if Word and tradition in the terminal consciousness of Israel, the consciousness of Judaism, are presented as conjoined. Their connection is not artificial or secondary, but original and native.

Two questions then arise, and they follow upon one another. How can we describe the development of this living tradition of the Word throughout Israel's history? How can we define the result, the final inheritance of this development, at the term of this history?

On the first point, we can say that the progress of the transmitted Word is read in the progress of the People in which it is transmitted. It is, as it were, the progress of the consciousness it succeeds in taking of itself but which derives from the consciousness of God, which is imposed on it gradually, with the latter developing correlatively to the former.

We recall the correlation we observed in the Mosaic accounts between the revelation of God's plan and that of his Name.[117] In one sense, the Exodus accounts underline the fact that knowledge of the Name is primary, both in time and in the connection of the realities. The divine plan was to stamp the mark of his Name on the People, and therefore the revelation of one follows that of the other and flows from it. Thus a dialectic is introduced here between progress in "knowledge" of God and progress in intelligent faithfulness to his will. Undoubtedly, it is first necessary that he reveal himself in order for us to obey him, but the obedience which forms in accordance with his will is the first condition of all growth in the knowledge of his Name, of what he is. Reciprocally, the better one knows him, the closer one's conformation to his plan, which also is better known. For the prophets, knowledge of God was always vital knowledge, acquired only through obedient faith; but obedient faith does not simply conform the believer to the divine plan: one "becomes like God" by believing in his Word and in committing oneself in faith by obedience. For this reason, obeying God in faith leads to "knowing" him with a knowledge that is eminently sympathetic, which evolves from the lived experience of an acquired or restored likeness.

Nevertheless, because the Word was believed and, therefore, was obeyed, this likeness evolved from or, rather, was restamped on our being. This comes down to saying, once again, that the relationship between "knowing" and "becoming like" is as close in Judaism as in post-Socratic Hellenism, but that it acts inversely. At the start, man does not try to restore in himself, the likeness with God that was lost, which will produce knowledge of God in its term. Quite the opposite: there is an original gift of God, who communicates his knowledge to us freely and gratuitously, in his Word, and thereby makes us like him.

This implies that knowledge of God in Judaism, from the beginning, supposes a union—not some union of man with God to which man could raise himself, but a union with man which God has willed from all eternity and which all his effort to enter into the history of man—all the effort of his Word—is to produce.

This is why fully developed knowledge of God will be consciousness of this fully accomplished union between God and man. Israel—that abortion, that harlot who unceasingly lapses into her former errors—is still the betrothed of the Lord, whom he will marry in the fullness of shared joy on the last day.

Reciprocally, the principle of all the knowledge of God that can ever be known by Israel is (and is only) God's prior, eternal knowledge of it. God has "known" his People; that is, he chose them, set them apart, is concerned with them and loves them, without merit on their part, through pure and unprecedented generosity. He attached himself to them by preference, as to a firstborn son, Even better: it is only they whom he wanted to know, as an only son. He has loved them from all time and will therefore love them forever as a man loves the "bride of his youth," with a love that cannot be matched.[118]

We have said how this progress in knowledge of God, in the "knowledge" we have of him, to the point of discovering that he has known us from all eternity, appears throughout the unfolding of the history of the People as a progress in interiorization of the relationship with God. We have also seen the paradox which is still conspicuous: this interiorization has, as a correlative, universalization.

At the beginning, though warning signs show greater complexity, it seems that it was the mass of the children of Abraham, according to the flesh, who were chosen. For their election to become an actuality, it seems they had to be set apart from the rejected mass of the other nations, beginning with Egypt. But it soon becomes clear that this cutting off, this separation, is not that easy. Not "all Israel" was "the Israel" of the promises: "only a remnant will be saved."[119] It was this "faithful remnant" that the crucible of the trial (chiefly the exile of Babylon) must free from its matrix. In other words, it is not the simple carnal relationship with Abraham that makes the "children of Abraham" beneficiaries of the promise: it is the heritage of his faith, his tested faithfulness.

Once we have reached this point, there is another possibility: those who are not sons of Abraham according to the flesh, if they hear the Word which is addressed to them, if they listen to it—if, like Abraham, they abandon their earthly city, with its customs and its gods—could they not accede to sonship by Abraham, be gathered into the people and be adopted by their God?

This progressive interiorization of the divine plan, whose perspectives are open beyond any assignable limit, goes hand in hand with progression in discovery (still correlatively) of what we may call the immanence and the transcendence of God. And here, as with the first couple, in the plan of God as in the plan of man, growing personalization of progress in the knowledge of God (as in perception of his plan in the process of actualization) will be asserted.

God does not cease to approach Israel. The amazing encounter on Sinai prepares for the "tabernacle of the meeting," which makes this encounter a daily aspect of the life of the People. This fleeting Presence under the tent, which tomorrow might require to be packed up and will precede them and join them again at some unknown place, succeeds the Presence that was established in Sion. Undoubtedly—and this is the preeminent trial—this Presence will depart in the catastrophe in which all hopes seem to be confounded. But it is then revealed that—with the exiles, the dispersed; invisibly but more truly, more intimately than ever; with those who have no longer any earthly sanctuary—the Presence will make for itself an invisible, indestructable sanctuary. The rabbis will say that wherever ten Israelites are gathered together to hear the Torah, the Shekinah is in the midst of them![120]

Throughout his successive approaches, the God who more and more reveals himself is discovered, at the same time, to be more and more exalted and transcendent. He eludes being grasped in any way, just as he escapes any description and reference. He had first appeared as the flame in the burning bush, which did not consume; as the God of the wild mountain and lightning. Then he covered himself with the luminous cloud. When Solomon built the Temple, God flooded it with mysterious darkness. Elijah, on his return to Horeb-Sinai, again saw the storm, the lightning, and the quaking earth. But, this time, at each manifestation, he was told: God is not in the storm nor in the lightning nor in the earthquake. Then he heard an unspeakable whispering and hid his face.[121]

This growing discovery of God as the Ineffable is accompanied—rather, presented—in the form of a more and more marked personalization: the source of the equally growing personification of worship and worshipers. The holiness of the transcendent God, who wishes to be the companion of his People on earth, is revealed as perfect righteousness. It is imposed on its devotees under this form as the test of their belongingness. But it is also, at the same time, loving kindness, the *hesed* (i.e., love whose gratuitousness, freedom, and liberality confound the imagination). This love calls for a similar love: limitless devotion of one's whole being, acceptance in the faith of the totally incomprehensible, surrender of self to sacrifice without argument. Is the One to whose love our love must respond not the One whose love is revealed first in incomprehensible humiliation: the love of the All Powerful, loving sinners even in their sinfulness?

The parallel or interwoven advancements in experimental knowledge of the plan of God, actualized in knowledge of the Name of God, which becomes more and more ineffable and more and more worthy of worship, seem joined in the development of the messianic theme. It has its prehistory in the theme of Abraham, the chosen individual who bears in himself all the People, and in the theme of Moses, another chosen one, separate from the People, whose purpose was to revive them.

Similarly, the Messiah is the bearer of the hope of the People. Saul, by divine acquiescence to the will of the People to be themselves and to recognize themselves in a representative figure, was given as their first "anointed one." But this consent from on high to earthly hope transfigured them by anointing his kingly reign, by the communication of heavenly power. Before he could be the representative of the People before God, he must be the representative of God before the People. Like the prophet and the priest, the king is taken from among men, but God acts through him. For Saul, who in no way lent himself to this mission, David was substituted, who was weaker in appearance, and no less a sinner than Saul, but a believing and penitent sinner. And he will remain the foreshadowing promise of a "son of David" who will be "the messiah," in the fullest sense of the term, because he will reveal himself to be the "son of God," in a sense in which David could not: more than a man of war, and not only a wise man (like Solomon) but the Man, the King, after the heart of God.

Nevertheless, the figure of the servant will be substituted for the figure of the messiah, the earthly king whose kingship is not of the earth. No longer the facile figure of a glorious, divine king, the figure on the contrary, is that of a humiliated and despised man, rejected by men, who seems to be cursed by God himself. This does not prevent the figure of the preeminent servant from being identified with the People, not in their triumphs but in their apparently irremediable failure, and it is this figure who saves the people from all evil by redeeming them from sin. It is the reconciliation of the People—and not "the People" alone, but all men—with God.

At this point a third figure appears, which seems at first to be the exact opposite of the preceding one. This figure is not humiliated at the lowest point of the People's history but is exalted on the clouds of heaven, at the end and high point of the history where it is manifested. The glory of the expected messiah seems very slight, next to the heavenly glory of this Judge and eschatological Conqueror. Having risen from the outset in heaven, he "comes" there to meet God in order to place the kingdom back into his hands. And yet he is described as a "son of man"—heavenly, clothed with God's glory—and is no less mysteriously identical with the "saints of the Most High" (i.e., with the people who have reached their perfection). Never had the "Chosen One" appeared so exalted, so close to God, and never had it been so explicitly declared that he was one with the People of God, that he was man himself, the "last man," as St. Paul will say.

If now we attend to the concrete form of this historical development of the Word and the People (we have just taken stock of its content), we find it striking that it is in no way presented as a linear development. The "progress" is not linear, over and done with, leaving experience behind it like so many outmoded stages. On the contrary, on first sight, as in the schema that the authors of the Book of Judges give themselves of the history they narrate, the "progress" seems like a series of perpetual new beginnings. We could believe that we are dealing with cyclical history, as in the majority of the ancient Mediterranean myths, in which history (whether human or divine) simply traces the cycle of the seasons and the years.

In fact, the development which we have retraced is obvious and gives the lie to this impression; but it is no less true that it is inscribed not in a straight line but in a kind of progressive spiral. Sempiternally, we seem to repeat the same elementary experience, but each time it "tightens" and deepens a bit more. It can be said, as well, that it does not cease to rise and, similarly, to broaden. This is why the marked reinforcement in latter-day Israel's particularism goes hand in hand with the universalism that Alexandrian Judaism seemed to advance, which in early Christianity proceeds much more directly from Palestinian Judaism.

The model of this elementary experience is the first exodus of Abraham from his country toward the country God gave him, but first through the desert, where he was to wander as a nomad. The entire People are called to live this model with the Passover exodus from Egypt. And the yearly celebration of the Passover (originally a simple seasonal feast of yearly renewal) will from this point on be marked by its indelible connection with this unique event that created the People and was the basic actualization of the promise made to Abraham. But Passover, with its twofold aspect of judgment and redemption, of liberation from slavery and involvement in the trial of the desert, will in turn impress its mark and give direction to all the later experiences of rupture and renewal.

A particularly solemn Passover will seal the renewal of the covenant under Josiah, that is, renunciation no more of Egypt and its primarily material servitudes but of idols and their moral slavery. And it is as a new Passover, leading into a new exodus, that the prophets, paradoxically, will interpret the trial of the exile and the captivity. But the return and its disappointments, in projecting on the eschatological future the expectation of the new and eternal covenant, which will replace hearts of stone with hearts of flesh (which finally will be traced by the finger of God), will spur the People to hope for it as the ultimate and definitive Passover.

Thus we see how the Divine Word is one, and even unique, and the People of God are the same in the continuity of an unbreakable tradition from Abraham to the last elect. But again, for the Word to be fully heard it is necessary that it be repeated many times, with growing precision, throughout renewed experiences which gradually penetrate to the very depths of this People whose heart it seeks.

Hence the form of development that the Bible will take: not as a logical consequence of deductive teachings but as the progressive germination of one tirelessly repeated theme, over a history which is not so much repeated as reproduced, like the race itself, by being extended and enriched as well as pruned and concentrated. Hence the justification of the traditional exegesis in Israel, of the *halakah,* which does not cease to transpose to changing circumstances the same Law, given once and for all, or even more of the *haggadah,* which is not content with explaining a teaching for the present in accounts of the past but elaborates the eschatological apocalypse, starting with the memory of the original events.

Hence the special prayer of Israel: its act of thanksgiving for the past, for creation, accomplished once at the beginning and preserved and unceasingly continued, and therefore—even more—for the work of salvation, for which God in person gradually came into this history of man and the world, which had begun by being the history of the fault and the fall. Hence this supplication in which the thanksgiving is spontaneously extended: that God will renew his great deeds of the past—rather, that he will revive them, follow them through, and lead them to their eschatological term. Then, his work, perfect in unity; his Name, revealed to all; and he himself, known by his People as he knows them, will be glorified forever.

The heart of this prayer is the "memorial," which gives its meaning and substance to the worship of Israel: this ritual of the covenant, sacrifice, fellowship meal, in which the People touch, so to speak, the token that God himself left them of his past actions, of their enduring permanence, so that the People can present the token to their God and, with the assurance of obtaining it, invoke the fulfillment in themselves of the divine work to which, at the same time, they once again unceasingly consecrate themselves.

This prayer is already eucharistic, since *eucharistia* will be, first, the translation of *berakah,* by which Hebrew designates it, and because the Christian Eucharist will retain its schema. It is in this prayer that we can best see how the Word that has come down to man fecundates his wisdom and therein gives rise to the apocalyptic hope. For the aim of the Word was finally to penetrate the whole man, the whole conscious and reflected expression in which he gradually discovers himself by actualizing himself. It was to lead man into a total and unique experience, which constitutes the tradition of Israel, in which the People of God were formed, to go beyond itself, to transcend itself, through obedient faith, conformation to the divine plan, and union with God, so that this perfect "knowledge" might come, in which the knower and the known are one.

We see, then, that the final result of this long and sinuous process, according to which the divine plan for the People reached its term—in a word, the heritage of the tradition of Israel—must be the summation, the acceleration, of all this experience, in which the initial communication of the Divine Name will, at the end, free everything it had implied from the beginning, though all this plodding was necessary to prepare for it. But it is also, perhaps even more, the supreme expectation of the divine revelation in which the "new man," who was prepared in the People in gestation, will be born in an ultimate separation: the absolute Passover of radical death to oneself, in which God, who has become more and more mysterious, to the extent that he reveals himself further, will finally disclose the last secret of his ineffable Name by consummating his own immolation.

Here again, if we ask about the concrete mode in which this consummation will be prepared and the manner in which its expectation will take form in the People (by forming it itself), the only possible answer is that we see both of these things becoming concretized in the transition from "the People" to the Church. As we have said, from the first stage of their formation on Sinai the People had taken form in the *qahal* or *ekklesia,* in which they received the Decalogue, which had been sealed by God himself in concluding the covenant by the offering of the first sacrifices. This same *qahal* with Josiah, we discovered, in which Deuteronomy records the renewed understanding of the Divine Word in the light of the experience of Canaan, was illuminated by the prophets, and subsequent celebration of the Passover renews the covenant on this basis.

Finally, in the account of Nehemiah, on the return from exile in Babylon, the reading of the definitive Torah prepares and gives rise to (in a third *qahal*) a final consecration of the People which this time is expressed by the great *berakah* of Ezra: the whole saving action whereby God put forth the actualization of his plan is acknowledged and the definitive accomplishment of this plan was prayed for, so that the Divine Name might at last and forever be known and glorified, as it should be.

According to rabbinical theology, synagogue worship, with its prayers, is only an extension of this last assembly of Ezra, of this latter-day *ekklesia,* in which the People of God succeed in forming themselves by preparing for the eschatological revelation. In the apocalyptic groups, like that of Qumran, the community meals, with their own *berakoth,* will appear (beyond the ancient sacrifices, which were only preparatory) as an anticipation of the messianic banquet in which (according to the liturgical formula already mentioned) the memorial of the Messiah, and of the People as well, "will rise up and come so that he will arrive, be seen, accepted, heard, recalled, mentioned before God, for deliverance, blessing, grace, compassion and mercy'' on this day of days!

Thus Jesus, by celebrating the last *qahal* of ancient Israel at his Last Supper with his disciples, after his last conversation with them, at the same time that he put his Eucharist in the forms of the supreme Jewish *berakah,* substituted the memorial of his death for all the simply preparatory sacrifices, separated his Church, the *ekklesia Theou* of the latter days, from the People of the sons of Abraham.

For the *quahal,* each time it appears in the history of the People, appears as the means for becoming conscious of all that was included for them in the experiences that were fulfilled, and the occasion of a new thrust which will bring them to the experience that awaited them. The Christian Church is this new and, in a sense, eternal assembly of the People of God that the synagogue had prepared for. ''Preserving and turning over in their heart'' the whole prophetic Word, the people accept and confess the Word made flesh as its fulfillment. Then, celebrating forever the memorial of the perfect sacrifice, the *abodah* of the unique, expected Servant, the Church gives thanks to God for his work, accomplished in this Servant, and asks nothing more than consummation of this work in the People themselves, by the consummation of their union with him. In this way, the Church appears to us as the fullness of Israel, of God's plan for it, which is revealed when the fullness of God is revealed in the Messiah.

## Notes

1. On the substance of this chapter and the next, see the constitution *Lumen Gentium* (the first two chapters), as well as chapter IV of the constitution *Dei Verbum*. What we have said about the Christian ''mystery'' and the place the Church has in it (cf. above, pp. 164ff.) will explain that we are not giving a separate place to the study of the ''mystery of the Church,'' which constitutes the portico, as it were, of the constitution *Lumen Gentium*. Since the ''mystery'' is properly the secret of the Divine Wisdom which is revealed in the history of the People of God, ending in Christ and his cross, it is in study of the preparations for Christ's work in the Old Testament, and its fulfillment in the New, that the meaning of the ''mystery'' of the Church—or better, of the Church in the ''mystery''—will gradually be revealed in the next two chapters.

2. See on these accounts, in general, J. Bright, *A History of Israel* (Philadelphia, 1959), pp. 78ff.

3. Genesis 12:1–9.

4. Harvey Cox, *The Secular City* (New York, 1965), the entire first chapter.

5. Hebrews 11:8ff.

6. Cf. Jeremiah 35:1–19.

7. Cf. Gregory of Nazianzus, *De Virtute,* P. G. 37, Cols. 715ff.

8. Here we have a basic characteristic of the whole of biblical history and revelation, in both the New and the Old Testaments: the People of God, we may say, take form not only in being represented but, as it were, "preformed" in an individual (or individuals) for the providential role.

9. On this theme, see H. H. Rowley, *The Biblical Doctrine of Election* (London, 1950).

10. 1 Samuel 16.

11. See particularly O. Cullmann, *Le salut dans l'histoire* (Neuchâtel, 1966), pp. 18ff. and passim.

12. Genesis 12:10ff.

13. Genesis 22:1–24.

14. See A. Ligier, *Péché d'Adam et péché du monde* (Paris, 1961), 2:214ff. and 414ff.

15. Hebrews 11:19.

16. O. Kaiser, "Traditionsgeschichtliche Untersuchung von Genesis 15," in *Zeitschrift für alttestamentliche Wissenschaft* (1958), 70:107ff.

17. Genesis 15:1–20.

18. Genesis 17:1–14.

19. See Exodus 12:43ff.

20. Genesis 18. See H. Cazelles, *Supplément au Dictionnaire de la Bible,* vol. 7, cols. 125ff., for a discussion of the literary problems posed by this text.

21. Genesis 21ff.

22. Genesis 26ff.

23. Genesis 37ff.

24. Genesis 32:23ff. For this episode, see F. van Trigt, "La signification de la lutte de Jacob près du Yabboq, Genèse XXXII, 23–33, in *Old Testament Studies* (1958), 12:280ff.

25. See the narrative part of the Book of Exodus (1–19).

26. Cf. Exodus 12:13.

27. Cf. Exodus 4:14ff. and Exodus 29.

28. The first interpretation of Exodus 3:14 was recently upheld by W. F. Albright in his *From the Stone Age to Christianity* (Garden City, N.Y., 1957), p. 261. The second is developed in the commentary *ad loc.* of the Jerusalem Bible.

29. Cf. Hebrews 1:10 and 10:31.

30. Cf. Exodus 24:9ff. and 33:20.

31. Cf. Leviticus 19:2 and Matthew 5:48.

32. Hosea 11:1; cf. Isaiah 64:7 and Jeremiah 31:9.

33. This is a central theme in the "Yozer berakah" of the synagogue service.

34. See A. Heschel, *God in Search of Man* (1955).

35. The opposition that nineteenth-century liberal Protestant exegesis thought it found between prophet and priest, religion of the rite and faith in the Word, has been completely dispelled, particularly by the research of the Scandinavian school. See A. Haldar, *Associations of Cult Prophets among the Ancient Semites* (Uppsala, 1945), and I. Engnell, *The Call of Isaiah* (Uppsala, 1949), as well as A. R. Johnson, *The Cultic Prophet in Ancient Israel* (Cardiff, 1944).

36. See our work, *Le Rite et l'Homme* (Paris, 1968), esp. chap. X.

37. On the tabernacle and the ark, see our *La Bible et l'Evangile* (Paris, 1952), pp. 95ff.

38. Exodus 20ff. See H. Cazelles, *Etudes sur le Code de l'Alliance* (Paris, 1946).

39. See the article "Ecclesia" of K. L. Schmidt in *Theologisches Wörterbuch zum Neuen Testament*.

40. Exodus 19:6; cf. 1 Peter 2:9 and Revelation 1:6 and 5:10.

41. Cf. Joshua 3 and Exodus 14.

42. A. Desnoyers, *Histoire du Peuple hébreu, I. La Période des Juges* (Paris, 1922).

43. See esp. Joshua 7.

44. See 1 Samuel 1–24.

45. 1 Samuel 2:18ff.

46. On the setting up of kingship, see 1 Samuel 8–10. On kingship in Israel and the neighboring peoples, see S. Mowinckel, *He That Cometh* (Oxford, 1956), pp. 21ff.

47. 1 Samuel 8:7.

48. 1 Samuel 9:16.

49. On David, see 1 Samuel 16ff. and 2 Samuel 1–24.

50. 1 Samuel 12:7.

51. Cf. 1 Samuel 16:9ff.

52. 2 Samuel 5 and 6.

53. Cf. the imprecations in Jeremiah 7.

54. 2 Samuel 7.

55. Cf. 1 Chronicles 22:8.

56. On wisdom in Israel, see Hilaire Duesberg, *Les Scribes inspirés* (Tournai–Paris, 1938–39; new 1-vol. ed., 1966).

57. Proverbs 1:7.

58. 1 Kings 3:3.
59. Cf. 1 Kings 11.
60. Cf. the end of the first book of Kings and the second book to chap. 17, inclusive.
61. Their actions occupy 1 Kings 17:1 to 2 Kings 1:18 for the first, and 2 Kings 2:1 to 8:29 for the second.
62. On Amos and his successors to Ezekiel, see our *La Bible et l'Evangile*, pp. 57ff.
63. 2 Kings 22–23.
64. Cf. Jeremiah 31.
65. Cf. Jeremiah 31:31ff. and Ezekiel 36:26ff.
66. 2 Kings 23:28ff.
67. See the end of the second book of Kings.
68. Amos 3:2.
69. Hosea 2.
70. Cf. Isaiah 5:8ff.
71. Cf. Jeremiah 16:2 and 20:9.
72. Ezekiel 10 and 11.
73. Ezekiel 11:16ff. Cf. 6:8ff.
74. Ezekiel 37.
75. See the texts cited in n. 65.
76. Cf. Hosea 1:2ff. and Ezekiel 16:3ff.
77. Ezekiel 16:53ff.
78. Cf. Ezekiel 18.
79. See C. R. North, *The Suffering Servant in Deutero-Isaiah* (London, 1948), and esp. Mowinckel, op. cit., pp. 187ff.
80. Isaiah 49:6.
81. Cf. Ezekiel 40ff.
82. See H. Cazelles, "La Torah ou Pentateuque," in A. Robert and A. Feuillet, *Introductions à la Bible* (Paris, 1957), 1:270ff.
83. Nehemiah 8 and 9.
84. See our *Eucharist*, chap. 4.
85. Cf. Haggai 2:3.
86. Isaiah 66:21.
87. Isaiah 64:1.
88. On all this history, which is the subject of the two books of Maccabees, H. Cazelles makes the most pertinent remarks in *Naissance de l'Eglise, secte juive rejetée?* (Paris, 1968).
89. On this point, see the study of G. Sholem, "Der Begriff der Kawanna in der alten Kabbala," in *Monatschrift für Geschichte und Wissenschaft des Judentums* (1934), 78:492ff., and A. Heschel, op. cit.
90. Genesis 24:27.
91. 1 Timothy 4:5.

92. *Adversus Tryphonem,* 116–117, P.G. 6, cols. 745–746.

93. Cf. our *Eucharist,* chap. 4.

94. Ibid.

95. Ibid.

96. Cf. Hosea 6:6 and Matthew 9:13 and 12:7.

97. Cf. our *Eucharist,* chap. 4.

98. See J. Jeremias, *Die Abendmahlsworte Jesu* (1st ed.; Göttingen, 1960).

99. *Seder R. Amram Gaon,* ed. D. Hedegard (Lund, 1951), p. 52.

100. Cf. Hosea 2:14ff.

101. Cf. Job 38ff. and 28:12ff.

102. See Mowinckel, op. cit., p. 238.

103. D. Deden, "Le mystère paulinien," in *Ephemerides Theologicae Lovanienses* (1936), pp. 403ff.

104. Daniel 2:20ff.

105. Daniel 2:27ff.

106. Daniel 2:30.

107. Daniel 7:18 (cf. v. 22).

108. Mowinckel, op. cit., pp. 353ff.

109. Testament of Levi, 18; cf. Henoch, 55:4.

110. See R. C. Zaehner, *At Sundry Times* (London, 1962), the chapter on Zoroaster.

111. E. R. Goodenough, *An Introduction to Philo Judaeus* (New Haven, 1940) and *The Politics of Philo Judaeus* (New Haven, 1938).

112. See J. Daniélou, *Les manuscrits de la Mer Morte et les origines du christianisme* (Paris, 1957).

113. Matthew 3:10.

114. 1 Peter 4:17.

115. Cf. Luke 2:25.

116. See B. Gerhardsson, *Memory and Manuscript* (Uppsala, 1961).

117. Cf. above, pp. 188ff.

118. On the knowledge of God in Israel, see André Neher, *L'Essence du Prophétisme* (Paris, 1955), pp. 101ff. and 255–256.

119. Cf. Romans 11:15.

120. See our article on the *Shekinah* in *Bible et vie chrétienne,* no. 20 (1957), pp. 7ff.

121. Exodus 3:2 and 1 Kings 8:10ff. and 19:11ff.

# Chapter 3
# The Fullness of Christ

## *1. People of God, Church, and Fulfillment*

We have retraced the progressive formation of the People of God in the Old Testament and we have seen the consciousness they had of themselves, developing at the same pace as their "knowledge of God" over the course of a history enlightened and instigated by the Word. What, then, is the relationship between the Christian Church and this People of God?

The last lines of the foregoing chapter gave us a glimpse of the fact that the transition from the Old to the New Testament, from Israel to the Church, was characterized by the same kind of discontinous continuity that has been apparent at each stage of Israel's development. Simply, the tension between the two aspects is brought to its maximum. The Church *is* the People of God, promised in Abraham, founded on Isaac, brought together for the first time at the first Passover. The Church, and only the Church, is this People, who have passed through total renewal, which only the image of death and resurrection, introduced by the great vision of Ezekiel, can describe adequately. Because of this, the Church is the fulfillment of Israel, just as the New Testament is the fulfillment of the Old.

The evangelist Matthew, in regard to the work of Christ in general, gives us three formulas, whose most topical application is probably to this problem of the Church and Israel. On one hand, according to Matthew, Jesus criticized the tradition of Israel by opposing the traditions of the scribes and Pharisees (i.e., the terminal forms of this tradition) to what had been said and done at the "beginning."[1] But Matthew goes much further and seems to criticize this tradition of Israel, of the Word which Israel received, at its very basis: "It was said to the men of old . . . but I say to you . . ."[2]

Yet, conversely, Matthew—and Jesus—are also categorical: "Think not that I have come to abolish the law and the prophets; I have come not to abolish them but to fulfill them." And Jesus gives all the specifics in a style that was purposefully, exactly that of the scribes and Pharisees: "For truly, I say to you, till heaven and earth pass away, not an iota, not a jot, will pass from the law until all is accomplished."[3]

How are we to understand and reconcile such statements? Everything, obviously, turns on the meaning that must be given to "fulfill–accomplish." In Greek, we have *pleroun*, meaning "fill" or "accomplish" and corresponding, in the Septuagint, to the Hebrew *mala*, whose primary sense is also to fill but, in biblical usage, has three closely connected meanings that may shed light on our text.[4] The first, which is obviously closest to it, is to fulfill a promise or a prophecy. The second is to fulfill or accomplish a command. The third is temporal, as in the expression "the time is accomplished," which means that the moment has come when promise and prophecy must be fulfilled, when the divine orders must be accomplished.

These three senses are also connected in the New Testament and their conjunction is noticeable in the use of the substantive *pleroma*, which signifies "fullness" or "accomplishment." This is an underlying notion in the Synoptic Gospels and in the Pauline Epistles, that the appearance of Jesus and his work will come about "when the time is accomplished," "in the fullness of time."[5] He came to "fulfill all things"[6]: prophecies and promises, as well as divine exigencies. And this, it seems, is precisely what corresponds in the New Testament to the uses of *pleroma* in reference to Jesus in its primary sense of fullness.

What can best clear this up is perhaps St. Paul's statement: "For all the promises of God find their Yes in him."[7] Hence the result that all the gifts of God are present in his person, to be communicated to us in unsurpassable fullness. As the prologue of the Fourth Gospel says: "And from his fullness have we all received, grace upon grace."[8] In particular, this fullness, in the sense that joins the ultimate fulfillment of the prophecies to the totality of the gifts of grace, is applied conjointly to the realization of God's plan and the communication of his knowledge. As the Fourth Evangelist says further on: "No one has ever seen God; the only Son, who is in the bosom of the Father, he has made him known."[9] And his First Epistle completes this thought: "It does not yet appear what we shall be, but we know that when he appears we shall be like him, for we shall see him as he is."[10]

This "accomplishment" is really the definitive fullness, because it is unsurpassable. Therefore we have arrived with him at the *eschaton*,[11] the terminus of history.

With respect to all that had preceded, forecast, and prefigured him, he must therefore present to the maximum the character of surpassing the past that each *kairos*,[12] each decisive moment, each turning in the history of salvation had already presented. The prophets had not only, already and unceasingly, denounced the ever threatening involvements by which a watered-down tradition could at each stage betray the previous covenant, they had also, unceasingly, exalted the expectation of the future above the memories of the past, even what was most prestigious. To the Jews who thought they had automatic assurance in the divine Presence in their midst, Jeremiah recalls that this Presence, from the very beginning, had deserted the sanctuary of its unfaithful servants.[13] But renewal of the covenant, which he, and Ezekiel after him, led people to expect, is not a simple return to the covenant as established "with your fathers": it is substitution of a law engraved in hearts for the law engraved on stone.[14] It is the same dialectic as "it was not so in the beginning..." and "your fathers were told, but I say to you..." Jesus pushed it to its limit, since now we have come to the term of salvation history.

And if this same dialectic had not, all along, modified the first orientation, but, on the contrary, had repeatedly gone over the characteristics of the original outline—had renewed, though on a higher level, the initial event; had deepened, far beyond any conceivable hope, the original experience—it must be expected that the same thing would happen, and supremely, when this dialectic reached its term.

More precisely, each stage in the history of salvation had brought the People back to an "assembly," a *qahal*, an *ekklesia*, whose original type, far from being abolished or metamorphosed, merely—over the course of time—was marked and enriched. Always summoned by the Divine Word, this *ekklesia* "heard" its new developments, recapitulating everything that had preceded them; then it surrendered in faith to the exigencies and promises of this Word. The new stage in the covenant was sealed by the celebration of the "memorial" ritual, in which God gave his People a permanent token of his grace and consecrated their faith at the same time.

At each stage, the Word that was heard was enriched on the basis of the whole intermediary experience that it itself had fecundated. Also, at each stage, the final celebration of the covenant became interiorized and broadened in accord with the gift of God: his revelation and his growing communication. And from one stage to another, the schema of the assembly not only remained the same, it never ceased to grow in prominence.

Thus it can be said that the *qahal* represented, each time it was held, a passing of the People from potency to act: becoming aware of latent transformations from the fact of the last divine intervention, accession to a new stage, at a higher plane of actualization.

Since the return from Babylon, since the completion of the Bible, and in the final bursting forth of the wisdom tradition as an apocalypse, the establishment of the weekly synagogue worship had tended to make the People live in a kind of permanent *qahal*. This, may we say, was the penultimate *qahal,* the assembly of the eschatological expectation: expectation of the definitive *qahal* in which, according to the terms of the liturgical prayer, the dispersed will be gathered in, Jerusalem will be rebuilt for eternity, and God will forever be glorified by the complete number of his elect, who will have arrived at perfection. Conversely, we must say, this *qahal,* as such, is impossible to complete. The old sacrificial rites were no longer capable of giving it its conclusion in the definitive covenant that was now expected. Only the messianic banquet could bring this about. Hope for it, and a more and more living expectation of it, "flavored" the meals of devout communities that were "awaiting the consolation of Israel."

Indeed, it is the characteristic of this "intertestamentary" period, between completion of the Old and proclamation of the New Testament, to have progressively concentrated on the eschatological expectation of the promised Messiah.[15] In the Hebrew Bible, this was only prepared for; it was in the Judaism of the synagogue that it began to materialize. Therefore, whatever criticisms Jesus made of the contemporary forms of the tradition of Israel (like the prophets before him), it was to immediate contact with the last stage of this tradition that he brought the revelation, the definitive consummation.

Thus we may say that the Christian Church is the only *ekklesia,* whereas the synagogue tended to absorb the life of the People—the ultimate *ekklesia,* by the final proclamation of the Gospel as the accomplishment of "Moses" and the "prophets." Thus, at last, it completes itself in the Eucharist of the Word made flesh, consecrating his People forever in the memorial of his accomplished work: the cross.

The People of God, under the old covenant, were consecrated as such by these "assemblies," where their faith was nourished by the Word and where that Word, so to speak, took flesh, little by little, within them, by the covenant sacrifice, by the Passover memorial, by the great *berakah:* the act of thanksgiving for the great saving deeds of God and the supplication that they be renewed and accomplished forever.

In Judaism, the People tended to be absorbed in this assembly, the synagogue, as in an activity that was not only determining for all its other activities but also exclusive: as if they had nothing else to do on earth but to know God, confess him, and surrender to his service. Therefore these People tended to pass from the ethnic level to the properly religious community.[16] With Christ the transition is effected: the People are now "only" the Church. Since the Word has given itself to them in fullness, the People belong to it entirely, and it exists only in this state of belonging.

This shows how essential the Mass is for the Church; it is not only constitutive of the Church by the expressive actualization of her whole essence.[17] The whole Church is made—and not only instituted but perpetuated—and exclusively concerned by and with the faithful hearing of the Word of God, attaining its evangelical fullness, the confession of the Divine Name revealed in Jesus, the celebration of this Name in the act of thanksgiving for the plan of salvation, brought about on the cross of the Messiah and the consecration of the Church to the consummation in her and by her of this plan, in her union with Christ and his cross.

This has a twofold consequence. The Church is in direct line with the Jewish People, with Israel and its own "accomplishment," its own "fullness," but she is radically differentiated from Israel as it existed to this point. On one hand, the Church has dropped and detached from herself all those activities other than the activity of the *ekklesia,* by which Israel, although it was the People of God, remained a people like all the rest in economic, political, and cultural activities. This is not to say that the Church is not concerned with these things, or that she gives up having any influence on them, but as Church, as the People of God "fulfilling" their original vocation, she has no other function than receiving the Word and giving herself to it.

On the other hand, radical belongingness to the line of Abraham, or what in the Torah was only consecration to the service of God of this belongingness, no longer has an essential role in the Church. Listening to the Word, accepting it in faith, giving herself over to it in the eucharistic celebration of the memorial of the life-giving death of Jesus—this and nothing else is what makes the Church. Whoever hears this Word, whoever believes in it, whoever agrees to give himself to it, with and in Christ, belongs thereby to the Church. There is no longer man or woman, Jew or Greek, circumcized or uncircumcized, barbarian or Scythian, slave or freeman, but only Christ in all.[18]

These two radically new aspects of the Church of the New Testament are perhaps the most obvious marks of the two types of rupture that consummate fulfillment in her of the People of God.

That the Church is no longer a people like other peoples, a carnal people, but the People of the Spirit, according to a terminology we shall try to explain, is the most radical refutation of the deformations of the messianic expectation contemporary with the coming of Christ. This imminent reign of God that the

People were waiting for, this Messiah who was to establish it for the People in its broadest layers, were expected as a new Maccabean victory, as another David who would assure the reign of God over Israel and, by Israel, over the entire universe—the "reign of the saints," according to the apocalyptic expression.

But from the very beginning of his preaching Jesus placed great distance between such a messiah and himself. In condemning him, the leaders of the people knew very well what they were doing: it was for his statement, which in their eyes was blasphemy, that he is not an earthly messiah but the heavenly Son of Man, that they condemned him.[19] Paradoxically, they obtained the accord of the people without difficulty because the people were disappointed that Jesus refused the kingship they were ready to grant him, while they easily wrested the Romans' consent by persuading them, more or less successfully, that Jesus aspired to this very same kingship.[20]

As Jesus said to Pilate: "My kingdom is not of this world."[21] And because the Church must remain in this world, there can be no question of her appearing merely as one kingdom among others. If Jesus, in one sense, accepted and even claimed kingship, his kingship is that of "truth,"[22] that is, in the Johannine sense of the full revelation and communication of God in the acccomplishment of his plan for us. Similarly, the Church will know no other association with his messianic kingship than by faith, the witness given to this same faith.

The earthly kingship that the prophets hesitated to receive in Israel, but finally accepted by giving it a prophetic sense, lasted only so long as the People were in their preparatory phase. Once they reached their eschatological phase, kingship over the People reverted to God, with the Messiah himself, and the earthly kingship, with which the People as the Church of the latter days had nothing more to do, returned to men. We shall have to analyze all that this signifies, its implications for the Church, and the consequences that flow from it for her relationship with the various states—to examine the sense of the decisive evangelical statement: "Render therefore to Caesar the things that are Caesar's and to God the things that are God's."[23]

No less radical is the other break with the past, which is seen in the Church's opening out, without distinction, to "gentiles." Here we find the first application of the phrase "your fathers were told . . . but I say to you . . ." No longer does belonging to Abraham's posterity, according to the flesh, constitute the basis for belonging to the People of God. It is no longer even attachment to this posterity through acceptance of the Mosaic Torah, beginning with circumcision. It is only on the basis of faith in Christ, which is sealed by baptism, that from now on we enter into the People of God. In this faith, the distinction is abolished between Jew and Greek or barbarian. All are called on this basis, and none can be chosen except on this basis and this basis alone. The "gentile" who is uncircumcized but baptized in faith in Christ will have his place in the Church, without any need for either circumcision or the legal observances of which it was the principle. And the circumcized descendant of Abraham, Hebrew son of Hebrews, Pharisee according to the Law, has no place there if he has not passed through faith and the baptism that consecrates it.

Thus is verified Christ's other statement: "I tell you, many will come from east and west and sit at table with Abraham, Isaac, and Jacob in the kingdom of heaven, while the sons of the kingdom will be thrown into the outer darkness."[24] No statement could be more scandalous from the Jewish point of view.

And yet the "accomplishment" of the People of God in the Church has not yet been achieved, just as the reign of God, even though it has come close to us, even though it is in a sense "among us,"[25] is still awaited and hoped for. The ambiguity of "from now on" and "not yet," both of which apply to the present situation of the Church, will be found in the heart of the first questions that its study will pose. It dominates the first question of the relationship between the Church and the Kingdom.[26]

This ambiguity explains the fact that we must acknowledge: if the People of God in the New Testament tend to be absorbed in the Church, in the definitive assembly of those who believe in the Word of Christ, in the incarnate Word that is Christ, their identification, from the beginning to the end of time, is nevertheless not perfect. The subsistence of the People of Israel, beside and outside the Christian Church, poses a most acute problem from the outset, which the schisms and heresies also pose, in a manner which is undoubtedly different though the problem is the same. The Church of the New Testament, the Church of Jesus Christ, is called to garner in itself and fulfill the People of God. But from the beginning, a mysterious fatality seems to prevent it from fully succeeding. "Many are called, but few are chosen."[27] What is more, many seem to have been counted for a while among the chosen, even though we may wonder, finally, whether they even heard the call. Chapters 9–11 of the Epistle to the Romans (to which we shall return at more length) have posed the problem with respect to Israel (i.e., in the most basic fashion), although they are incapable of dispelling the mystery.[28]

If, however, without forgetting this, we want to characterize how the transition from the People to the Church came about, we cannot do better than go back to a schema drawn up by Cullman in his intriguing study on the Church and the Kingdom of God. It seems that, throughout the Bible, the whole history of salvation, the development of the People of God is characterized by what Cullmann calls a successive systole and diastole.[29]

In a primary stage, the human multitude appears evil; it is *massa perditionis,* of St. Augustine, which verifies Origen's formula: *Ubi peccatum, ibi multitudo.* The elect must therefore be set apart, separated from this mass. Hence the succession of Abraham and the exodus of Israel from Egypt.

But from the settlement in Palestine, in the promised land, experience reveals that "all Israel" is not "Israel." The trials that follow will be understood by the prophets as the necessary path of an interior segregation, as the only true path. In the last analysis, it is not the mass of the People but a "faithful remnant" which alone will be saved.

The latter prophets had a vague notion that this remnant could be reduced, finally, to one unique "faithful servant," which we see actualized in Jesus, abandoned on the cross by the very People to whom he was bringing salvation. He and he alone is the true "remnant" of Israel, the only faithful Servant, the unique progeny of Abraham, who contains the promises in himself.

But starting with Jesus, the movement will reverse itself. Systole is succeeded by diastole. And just as the first movement did not stop before it retrenched itself on the unique, the second will progressively know unlimited extension, universal expansion. Yet it is not at all to the same, original multitude, from which the movement toward unity was effected, that the movement toward fullness will tend. There is no question of some ordinary "return," for it is not a question of again fragmenting the unity that had been acquired with so much pain. Quite the reverse: it is a question of reintegrating the whole multitude into this unity. It is a question of "gathering in the scattered children of God," this whole, immense People for whom "one only" died.

Adam begot mankind in sin by a fragmentation and unending division of mankind. On the other hand, the New Adam is to rebeget mankind to life in holiness by gathering it to himself. This is why St. Paul calls him not so much the Second Adam as the "Last Adam," the Ultimate Man, in whom all of saved mankind is to rediscover itself, reconciled, at the same time, with itself and with God.[30] It is the examination of this process that our study of the Church will now pursue.

## II. *The Fullness of Time and the Gospel of the Reign of God*

If we seek to specify in what sense the People of God attain the fullness of time with the coming of Christ and, consequently, the new condition to which this People accede in the Church of the "new and eternal covenant"—or, what comes to the same thing, the sense of this apparently penultimate phase of the history of salvation, which is properly the "time of the Church"—we immediately come up against the problem of the relationship between this Church and the Kingdom of God, whose announcement fills the Gospel.

Especially since the beginning of the Constantinian Era there seemed to be an irresistible tendency to superimpose the two realities and even to confound the two notions. At the time of the *De Laudibus Constantini,* the confusion was manifested naively: the empire of the caesars, once its inhabitants were baptized, seemed to become one with the Church, and this state of things is interpreted as the equivalent of the establishment of the Kingdom of God on earth. If one is tempted (with Eusebius of Caesarea) to chalk this off to court flattery, we must observe that a piece of writing that is totally exempt from this, the commentary on the prophecies of Isaiah by Cyril of Alexandria, a century later, expresses the same sentiment. And this sentiment did not seem to be disturbed when the post-Constantinian empire, in the West at least, crumbled. For Gregory the Great, the equation "Church–Kingdom of God" continued to persist, all the more easily, perhaps, since the Roman Church seemed at this point to be substituting itself for the Roman Empire, after having appeared two centuries earlier to have been identified with it.[31]

But the New Testament not only protests against any identification of the Kingdom with an earthly empire ("My kingdom is not of this world"),[32] it does not even acknowledge the possibility identification between the Church and a worldly kingdom. The eschatological character of the Kingdom seems too pronounced for it even to be conceivable. The Church, the Church of Christ, the Church of the New Testament, is waiting for the Kingdom, is preparing for it, and anticipates its reality by the realism of her hope, based on faith in the resurrection of Christ and in his imminent return in glory. But nowhere are we told that she is herself the Kingdom, and it is impossible to read the New Testament without feeling that any identification of this kind, far from being implicit in it, will be forced onto texts, violently.

The fact expressed by Loisy's famous remark is no less incontestable: "They were expecting the Kingdom, but it was the Church that came." Was the identification which people tended to make not a mere a misapprehension or misrepresentation, like the artificial effect of patching up a disappointed hope? Although a number of historians and modern exegetes, especially since Albert Schweitzer, are tempted to agree, this simplification is as improper as that which preceded it, against which it was reacting. Indeed, the "time of the Church,"[33] with respect to the "time of the Kingdom," is characterized by "already" whole, as well as by "not yet." To substitute for the mirage of a whole "realized eschatology" the reaffirmation of a completely futurist eschatology is again to bring the New Testament back to the Old. A disincarnate hope is no less neglectful of radical "newness" than too carnal an installation in this world.

The correct relationship is not easy to define, and it is doubtful that we shall ever arrive at it as long as we hold to the translation (however hallowed it may be by usage) of *basileia* by "kingdom" in the New Testament texts. The falsely axiomatic acceptance in most modern biblical translations of the equivalence between the biblical *basileia* and "kingdom" is the most striking indication of the difficulty that modern people had (and still have) in getting free of Constantinian confusions. On this point, Protestants seem to be no more grazed by doubt than Catholics: in French translations, *royaume* (kingdom) is found in Olivétan and his successors, as well as in Lemaître de Sacy. And what is true of French translations is equally true of all the others. Like the medieval translations which preceded his (which Denifle was one of the first to rediscover), Luther speaks of *Reich*. Similarly, the Protestant Tyndale, the Catholic Rheims, and the King James bibles are in agreement on "kingdom." But as long as the *basileia* of the New Testament is conceived as "kingdom," *Reich,* or *royaume*—that is, a society dominated by divine sovereignty—we cannot escape the false alternative: either the Church is the "Kingdom" or it is another society than the "Kingdom," which has unduly taken its place in the minds of Christians. Also, the Church can be a more or less accurate outline of the Kingdom, but it is substantially different from it.

Neither term in this alternative corresponds to the relationship in which the Church is established in the New Testament with respect to the *basileia* preached by Jesus. The Church and the *basileia* are in no way comparable realities—whether in identity or opposition—for the Gospel's *basileia* is not a society and, therefore, it cannot be a "kingdom."

In the Old Testament, where the corresponding term *malkut* only rarely appears, it never designates a kingdom which would be that of God, but first of all the divine kingship—what Philo will call his "kingly power." In the latest texts, marked by the perspectives of apocalyptic literature, we observe deterioration of this first sense, "divine kingship," that is, of the right and the power to reign which belong to God alone, in the derived sense of "reign," the object of the eschatological hope. Nothing is more revealing in this respect than the formula of the apocalypses already mentioned; in the present time, it is not God who reigns "over earth" (whatever the case in "heaven," the domain of his immediate presence), it is his enemy Belial. God will reign only in eschatological times.

The *basileia* of the apocalypses, and of the New Testament in their line, is therefore not a society, a kingdom of which God would be king, it is an *age:*

the time in which God will exercise the kingship which belongs to him from all time but which *de facto,* today on earth, seems to be held in check by rebel powers. It is his hoped-for reign.

This opposition, which is found everywhere in the Synoptic Gospels between the "present age" (*aion houtos*) and the "age to come" (*aion mellon*), exactly situates the *basileia ton ouranon* of St. Matthew like the *basileia tou Theou* of St. Mark and St. Luke: not a "kingdom" but a "reign," *the* reign of God. The future reign, whose expectation is the content of the eschatological hope, whose promised coming and the cosmic and supracosmic catastrophe that this coming represents, is the central theme of all the apocalypses.[34]

What distinguishes the Gospel as "good news" is Jesus' announcement from the moment he begins his public ministry: not only is the divine reign close at hand, as John, the last of the prophets, announced, *it is here.*[35] In what sense must we understand this eschatological reign, which constitutes the irreducible originality of his message? (This is also the opinion of even our most critical contemporaries—those most tempted to be skeptics—with respect to any possibility of disengaging the authentic teaching of Jesus from the glosses and developments of the primitive community.)

The reign of God is inaugurated by Jesus' preaching and other activity: forgiving sins and healing the sick—two closely connected signs of the victory of the reign of God over the reign of Satan. In this way, in an absolutely gratuitous reconciliation, the divine "fatherhood," which the devout Israelite boasted about as the privilege of the "elect," the "righteous," is offered to all: to publicans, women of loose living—to anyone from the people who "do not know the law," as well as (still more so) to the scribes and Pharisees. At the same time, the law is "accomplished," by being surpassed as the miracles of mercy deliberately done on the sabbath

Of course, this is not to be interpreted in the line of the Protestant liberalism of Harnack, with its radically humanized Gospel, in which the divine "fatherhood" is only the reverse side of an "infinite value" inherent in the "human soul" and which needed only to be discovered. Contrary to the naive exegesis of Jülicher, the parables of the reign, far from being simple apologues of a truth of good sense, are the paradoxical proclamation of the most unprecedented grace: the most dispossessed sinners see, through a pure, unhoped-for, inconceivable divine generosity, the divine reign approach them, not to reduce them to slavery (like condemned men) but to associate them with God's "heavenly" kingship as sons of the King and sons of God.

This authority that Jesus claims for himself, implicitly and more than implicitly, in relation to the reign of God and its coming, is strikingly expressed in a statement of singular boldness, whose authenticity seems incontestable even to Bultmann and his disciples. It is that God himself will judge, from this point on, those who hear the word of Jesus in accordance with their reaction to it. Those who give it their faith are reconciled and have gone beyond any possibility of a judgment of condemnation: the reign of God is no longer for them, however sinful they may have been, an object of fear, but of joyful hope. The "Son of Man" on the day of the eschatological judgment will "confess" them as they now "confess" Jesus. In other words, if the reign is announced by Jesus, as present, it is with him, in his Person, that this reign has made its entry into this world. The reign is "in the midst of you (*entos hymon*) because Jesus himself has appeared among us.[36]

How is the reign already here in Jesus? This is the "mystery" of the reign that all the parables proclaim yet leave partially hidden. The reign comes—or better, is already here—"without being observed."[37] It is present in Jesus, but not visibly—only to faith. His word of grace alone attests to its actuality and his activity is its sign: an ambiguous sign which arouses the hostility of those who hold to appearances, supported by their strengths, their knowledge, their traditions; but the faithful humble, the "poor"[38] cannot rely on any of this, but only on the pure "mercy" of God, which in announcing the reign he proclaims as one and the same thing. For "these little ones who believe,"[39] the reign becomes tangible in the healing that accompanies the proclamation of forgiveness and attests the substitution, in Jesus himself, of the Divine Spirit for the evil spirit.

Yet everywhere else this spirit of enmity is present, and remains the apparent and, in a sense, the real master. As St. Paul will say, the latter always appears as the king—and what is more, the god!—of "this age": *ho theos tou aionos toutou.*[40] It seems that even the presence, manifested in this world, of the One who announces another reign merely excites and brings to fullness, in all who do not yield to the call of faith, the demoniacal reign. As an eminently mysterious statement says: the "reign" of God "undergoes violence."[41] It is announced as an ultimate conflict and it can be accepted only by those who accept heartbreak, like Jesus—by those who, in the humility of their faith, do violence not only to the world but to those who are close to them, to their intimates, and (what is more) to themselves.

Progressively, but with sufficient clarity for the eyes of faith, Jesus' announcement of the reign signifies conflict with all authorities, all the powers of this world, whose outcome will soon reveal it to be deadly. The most convinced disciples tried for the longest time—to the last minute and even beyond—to reject what was increasingly obvious, even though Jesus does not cease to urge its compelling necessity. "For whoever would save his life will lose it, and whoever loses his life for my sake will find it."[42]

Paradoxically, his rejection by the chosen people and, still worse, by the uncomprehending or indifferent pagans will put the seal on his proclamation of the divine reign by pushing to the limit its opposition to the demoniacal reign, by his unprecedented claim to bring the divine reign into the midst of a hostile world. The resurrection will justify from on high, "from heaven," this supreme affirmation of the humiliated presence of the divine reign in the One who brought it to earth. Retrospectively, the cross will be transfigured: it will become, as in the hymn of the Epistle to the Colossians, the chariot of triumph over the enemy powers, forever deprived by Christ of their usurped power over creation.[43]

The primitive Christian Church, becoming conscious of having seen *from this point* the divine reign come in glory in the person of the risen Christ, and able to recognize by faith its anticipated presence in the cross and in all of earthly existence that led up to it, will also become conscious of accomplishing in herself the destiny of the People of God.

For with the birth of this Church in faith in the resurrection begins what St. Matthew calls "the reign of the Son of Man"[44] and St. Paul "the reign of Christ, of the Son of God."[45] This reign of Christ is essentially an intermediary phase in the establishment of the divine reign. It coincides with the "time of the Church," because in the Church today, as yesterday in Jesus, we rediscover the same paradoxical juxtaposition of the divine reign, visible only to faith, but already there, despite this invisibility, to the eyes of flesh, and of the demoniacal reign; still and more than ever present, and even triumphant, but for the faith, from now on, struck down and dead.

This transfer to the Church of the situation that was Jesus' during his earthly life holds entirely to the presence with the Church, subjacent to its whole existence, of this risen Jesus in whom the divine reign has definitively triumphed over the satanic reign. And this is why time of the Church" and "reign of Christ" are one. But just as the reign of God, already present in Christ over the course of his earthly life, pressed him, so to speak, toward the consummation of his life on the cross, which would permit the revelation of the hidden reign in the glory of his resurrection, so now the Church aspires to the Parousia in which the reign of the Son, already fully real for her, but for her faith alone, and therefore "in hope,"[46] will be revealed to the eyes of the world itself.

Then this reign of the finally manifested Son will be accomplished in the transfiguration of everything, the "judgment," the eschatological crisis in which the new heaven and the new earth will appear, where righteousness will dwell and the Son will be able to restore the reign to the Father, with all this power that he will have finally submitted to him, so that God may be forever all in all.[47]

It can be said that the primordial manifestation of the divine reign, triumphing over the demoniacal reign in the resurrection of Christ, in the eyes of faith (i.e., in the eyes of the Church), consists in the transformation of the "flesh" (i.e., mortal humanity, which he received from us) into a "life-giving Spirit."[48] It is this glorification, obtained by his death and become fully actual in his resurrection and ascension to the Father, which makes him both the Lord of the Church and the Second Adam, whose glorious image we must put on, just as earlier we had inherited the degraded image of the earthly Adam. It is in this way that Christ is "the Lord," the actual Lord of the Church promised to the future reign over every creature, insofar as he is now the "Spirit," that is, the new humanity, given life by God's own life and capable of regenerating the whole of old mankind.[49]

From now on the Church is introduced into the reign of Christ, even though she remains in the midst of this world, subject to the last vicissitudes of a demoniacal reign which from now on is condemned and struck dead, but not annihilated, because in her the Spirit of Christ is at work—this Spirit who, in the dead and risen Christ, has triumphed over the spirit of enmity. It is thus that the Church herself is the proper fullness of Christ, because in her the Second and Last Adam, the Heavenly Man, is extended (so to speak) to all of fallen mankind, by penetrating it progressively with this Spirit of God, which from now on is his own Spirit in all truth. In this way, Christ is fulfilled in her as the only Son, adopting in himself for the Father the multitude of the "scattered children of God," bringing them together in his own Body, in order to lead them all with him, finally, into the eternal reign of the Father.

## III. Christ, the Fullness of God: " The Lord Is the Spirit"

To understand how the reign of Christ (the immediate preparation, the anticipated if still obscure reign of God in this world, in the midst of the "present age") is inaugurated in the Church, we must first understand how the reign of God was anticipated in the earthly life of Jesus and how the term to which it tended, the cross, was able to make this reign totally actual in the risen Christ.

What anticipates the divine reign in the earthly life of Christ and what impels it toward its consummation and prepares the fully actual manifestation of this reign which will follow is the presence in Christ of the Spirit. Similarly, the Church will anticipate the final reign of Christ over every creature in this divine Spirit, which the risen Christ, who has himself become the "life-giving Spirit," can pour "on all flesh."

The Spirit had penetrated the prophets, the providential men of the history of Israel in general, the anointed of the Lord, priests and kings. It was a preeminent eschatological promise of the day in which the Spirit would no longer be the evanescent privilege of a few exceptional personalities but would be spread over "all flesh." It was not by chance that St. Peter on Pentecost quoted Joel's prophecy: "And in the last days it shall be . . . that I will pour out my Spirit upon all flesh, and your sons and your daughters shall prophesy, and your young men shall see visions, and your old men shall dream dreams; yea, and on my men servants and my maid servants in those days I will pour out my Spirit."[50]

Indeed, this promise would give the unique key to the actualization of all the other promises. It included the actualization of this new and eternal covenant that Jeremiah had promised, which would be differentiated from the old, which had so often been violated by the infidelity of the People and their leaders, because then the divine law would be engraved no longer only on stone tablets but on the living tablets of the heart. It would then be the effect of this circumcision, not of the flesh but of the heart itself, that the prophet had promised. Or, according to the still more radical expression of Ezekiel, this would come down to substituting for the stone heart of old Israel, of old mankind, this true heart of flesh which would distinguish the not only washed and purified but literally resurrected humanity of the future Israel. On the dry bones of ancient Israel will the Divine Word not only put new flesh, but God's own Spirit will pass into it and that flesh will stay in his presence as finally and definitively re-created in his image.[51]

The evangelist Luke, who shows in Acts the nascent Church spreading through the communication and expansion of the Spirit, will write his gospel as the proclamation of the initial presence of this Spirit, established in Jesus from the beginning of his earthly life, manifesting itself progressively and, finally, shining with its glorious conclusion.

Jesus was born of the Virgin once the Spirit "overshadowed her."[52] This is why the Child that will be born of her will, from its birth, deserve to be called "holy" and "the Son of God."[53] At his baptism by John, the same Spirit appeared, and the heavens opened up, descending upon him as a dove, while the Father himself attests it by what the Jews called a *bat qol,* a heavenly voice: "Thou art my beloved [i.e., only-begotten] Son; with thee I am well pleased."[54]

Filled with the Spirit, Jesus returned from the Jordan to confront the Spirit of enmity in the desert, and he conquered him on all the points on which he tempted him, as he had tempted Adam and Eve: concupiscence of the flesh—concupiscence of the eyes and pride of life.[55]

Then the same Spirit brought him back in Galilee to begin his ministry of preaching, forgiveness, and healing. In the synagogue of Nazareth he read chapter 61 of Isaiah: "The Spirit of the Lord is upon me, because he has anointed me to preach good news to the poor. He has sent me to proclaim release to the captives and recovering of sight to the blind, to set at liberty those who are oppressed, to proclaim the acceptable year of the Lord."[56] And in characteristic fashion in this same gospel, his last words on the Cross will be: "Father, into thy hands I commit my spirit!"[57]

A formula from the Epistle to the Hebrews can summarize the sense of his death and his life, and of his death as the fulfillment of his life: "Christ . . . through the eternal Spirit offered himself without blemish to God."[58]

It can be said in these perspectives that the history of salvation and the whole of human history arrived thus at its consummation, in the consummation of the earthly history of Jesus himself. He did not appear only *in the fullness of time:* his appearance, the manifestation of the reign of God in him, in his life, and above all in his death *is and actualizes the fullness of time.* For in Jesus, living and dying, the very "fullness of God," we might say, fills, fulfills, and consummates this human history.

This is in effect the sense of this presence on the Spirit in Jesus, not proportionately but in fullness, a fullness from which all can receive, and grace upon grace: in him the God who wishes to reign in us and over the whole universe, by being finally "all in all," from now on is perfectly manifested. Now his reign has come, for the dead and resurrected Jesus appears, according to the expression of St. Paul to the Colossians, as the one in whom "all the fullness of God was pleased to dwell, and through (whom) to reconcile to himself all things."[59] Even though the Apostle will say again, somewhat later, that "in him the whole fullness of deity dwells bodily, and you have come to fullness of life in him."[60]

The presence of the Spirit in fullness in Jesus during his earthly life—the fulfillment of this life by the Spirit in his death; the fullness of God, of his divinity, dwelling and manifesting itself as bodily present in the risen Christ—so that we may find in him our own fulfillment, since we are brought by Christ into the universal reconciliation that has been brought about "in his own body," as Paul will say elsewhere: all of this holds true.[61] It is in this that we see how these fullnesses are united and controlled: the fullness of time in which Christ appears—rather, which he consummates—the fullness of God embodied in him, this fullness of the Spirit which consequently we find in him and which becomes ours, so that we finally appear as we are, our real selves, and the Church appears as the "fullness of Christ."[62] The center, the unity of this constellation of fullnesses, is evidently the totalizing fullness of the Spirit, that is, the presence of God in Jesus Christ. Revealed throughout his life—bursting forth, so to speak, in his cross, in his resurrected and glorified body—it gathers all of mankind in the Church, in itself.

The reign of God "comes" in Jesus Christ because in him the fullness of the Spirit, i.e., the fullness of God himself, dwells bodily in the humanity received from us. And Christ reigns in us, "in our mortal bodies,"[63] as St. Paul will say, at present in the Church, insofar as the Church is the humanity in which this fullness of the Spirit of God , proper to the humanity of Jesus, is poured out—a fullness which is and remains completely his, completely "Christic" in us as in him.

But how does the fullness of God in Christ reveal its presence in his earthly life? More precisely, how does his death on the cross convey it perfectly?

It can be said that the reign of God is manifested as present in the life of Jesus, the Spirit dwelling in him, the fullness of God incarnate in him, because Jesus reveals to us, inseparably in his words and acts, the love, the *agape* of the Father. The Sermon on the Mount is preeminently the gospel of the reign, the "good news" of his coming, not as the judgment of the condemnation of sinners but as the salvation of believers. It announces the coming of the reign, *and this coming in grace,* precisely because it is the proclamation of the divine Fatherhood. This means primarily that it announces the possibility of becoming children of God and describes what it consists of. This means again, more profoundly but inseparably, that the description of this sonship which is given to us opens to us the ultimate mystery of the heavenly fatherhood from which it emanates. It is here that we find in the accomplishment of God's plan for his People the revelation in fullness of his own Name. It is no longer simply said to the chosen people: "Be holy as I am holy." This holiness now is concretized in a perfection of the divine sonship, offered to men, which supposes and exposes the proper perfection of the Father: "Be perfect as your heavenly Father is perfect."[64]

This perfection is described as that of the unique, incomparable love of the Creator, the Savior—in one word, the Father who gives life, who gives his own life, who gives it with limitless generosity, beyond any prior merit that might justify the gift, beyond any self-interest on the part of the donor: a love which is grace, which is a gift, which is the gift without reservation and without the possibility of return, the gift of all we have, of all that we are, of the very being of all being, to what is not. To love in this way is the life of God; it is his life as Father. To be the object of such a love, to be promised the possibility of loving in such a way, to live in this way, to be the children of the Father in all truth, however unworthy we may be, is what is meant by admission into the reign of the Father, not as slaves but as heirs of this reign.[65]

Jesus can reveal this mystery of the Fatherhood of God and of our possible sonship, and offer access to this reign, only because the reign is perfect in him by the power of the Spirit, because he is *the Son,* the eternal Son, the Only Begotten, who will communicate to us the power of being made children of God. Thus we shall not only be *called* children of God, we shall *become* children of God[66]: sons in the Son, in the Only Begotten, who has become the Firstborn from among the dead by his resurrection, as he was the Firstborn of all the Father's creation, from before the fall and the sin which exiled us from the reign.[67]

This presence in Jesus of the announced reign, the forgiveness he brings, the healings that seal it, attest to this presence which annihilates the demoniacal reign.[68] But the fully effective revelation, the supreme and decisive attestation of this victorious confrontation, will be the cross of Jesus. For as St. Paul says in the fifth chapter of the Epistle to the Romans, it is ultimately the cross which is *the* revelation of the *agape* of the Father to mankind and, at the same time, its communication: the principle of the outpouring into our hearts, by the Spirit, of this love which is the love of God, the love with which God loves, which is the very life of the Father. It is in this, we are told, that God has demonstrated his love for us, in that Christ died for us even though we were sinners.[69] He has said that one righteous man might consent to die for another; but what kind of love—what unexpected, unknown, unhoped-for love—is that of God who consents to the death of his Son for sinners? Such is the love of the Father; such is its unique revelation to us in the human life of his Son by his cross. Not only does it reveal this love to us, it incarnates it, so to speak, in his humanity. Thus, beginning with this humanity, triumphing over sin and death and Satan by this love and resurrected "by the Spirit," who had animated humanity with it,[70] the Spirit will be poured out in us without measure, pouring the same love into our hearts. The Spirit of Christ in us, the love of the Father whose gift of the Spirit will fill our hearts: this is what the Sonship of Jesus will communicate to us, what will make us enter into the reign of the risen Jesus and, in the Church, anticipate the final reign of the Father.

## IV. The Church: The Fullness of Christ and Temple of the Spirit

It is because she is the Church of the Spirit, the Church whose ingathering, convoked by the Word of the Son, is consummated by the communication of the Spirit of the Son, of the Spirit of the Father's love, that the Church leads us into the reign of Christ. Therefore the reign of God in her is anticipated, as it were, in the very heart of this world, as it was in Jesus himself. In the whole New Testament, following the line of the prophet Joel, the Spirit appears as the anticipation of the eschatological reign. The gift made to us, according to St. Paul, is the guarantee of our future heritage; the Apostle places it in relationship with the seal with which we are already marked by Christ, that is, the seal of our belonging to God. "But it is God who establishes us with you in Christ, and has commissioned us; he had put his seal upon us and given us his Spirit in our hearts as a guarantee (*arrabona*)," the Second Epistle to the Corinthians states.[71] In the same way, with the same comparison of the image of the seal stamped on us and the guarantee which accompanies it, the Epistle to the Ephesians says: "[You] were sealed with the promised Holy Spirit, which is the guarantee of our inheritance until we acquire possession of it, to the praise of his glory."[72]

Again, it is necessary to see that it is not only a question in this guarantee and accompanying seal of a guarantee for the future: the guarantee is itself a foretaste, a beginning of the effective possession of the inheritance. What indisputably marks it is the fact that, parallel to the expression of a guarantee applied to the Spirit, St. Paul uses the still stronger expression in its immediate realism: "first fruits" (*aparche*). Arriving at the high point of the great development of the eighth chapter of his Epistle to the Romans, which proposes a genuine realism of the Spirit, he said that we have "the first fruits of the Spirit" from now on—that is, assuredly in the gift of the Spirit, the first fruits of what remains the object of our hope: the inheritance of the heavenly reign.[73]

This eschatological reality of the gift of the Spirit, of an eschatology that is not yet realized but outdistanced (so to speak), causes us from now on to be sons, just as Jesus was in his earthly existence, even though he had to await his resurrection in order to be established in his divine Sonship (*horisthentos hyiou theou en dynamei*),[74] according to the Spirit of holiness by the resurrection of the dead. This is why St. Paul says, again to the Romans, "For all who are led by the Spirit of God are sons of God. For you did not receive the spirit of slavery to fall back into fear, but you have received the spirit of sonship. When we cry, 'Abba! Father!' it is the Spirit himself bearing witness with our spirit that we are children of God";[75] or again to the Galatians: "And because you are sons, God has sent the Spirit of his Son into our hearts, crying, 'Abba! Father!' So through God you are no longer a slave but a son."[76] In other words, it can also be said that we are sons because the Father has sent into us the Spirit which makes sons, or that He sent the Spirit of his Son into us because he has made us his sons.

But this actuality of the gift of the Spirit, with the reality of the communicated sonship, is the presence in us of the Father's *agape* which manifests it—the presence of this unique love that is so properly divine and which he manifested preeminently in the death of his Son. It is through this communication of God's love, brought about by the Spirit, that Christ reigns at present over the Church and in her, and that the Church now makes the reign of God present in the midst of the world, just as Christ did during the days of his earthly life. Participatory sonship, the Spirit which is not only its guarantee and seal but the already effective first fruits, the love which anticipates the reign of God over all things—all these things make the Church today, with respect to this reign, like Jesus before her, exist in the "already," even though the world in which she is immersed remains, and keeps her, in the "not yet." This "already" is possible for her only through faith, and faith possesses its object only in hope, but hope already touches on its realization in love, to the extent that the love from which the Church lives is the "*agape* of God poured out in our hearts by the Spirit of God who has been given to us."[77]

This makes the Church Christ's own fullness, according to the formula of the Epistle to the Ephesians: *to pleroma tou ta panta en pasin pleroumenou*,[78] since she is already the Temple of the Spirit which is built again—as long as history lasts and in which the Spirit already resides. The exact translation of the verb *pleroumai* (depending upon whether it is a middle voice with a purely active or a reflexive sense) must determine the meaning of the phrase and, especially, the word *pleroma* (fullness), when applied to the Church with respect to Christ.[79]

Does it merely state that Christ, by filling all things (*ta panta*) with himself, is thereby fulfilling the Church—even that he not only fills her completely with respect to our human capacity but that he fills her with all the gifts that were deposited in him by God for mankind (*ta panta en pasin*)? Or does it go so far as to say that, in doing this in the Church, he finds his own completion, his own fullness, so that the Church is not only filled with Christ and the fullness of his gifts but is herself the fullness, the completion, the complement of Christ?

The first interpretation is preferred by a number of exegetes who rely both on a philological reason (the generally passive and not active sense of Greek nouns ending in *ma*) and on a theological reason: the impossibility (as they believe) of admitting that Christ would need any completion and, even less, any external complement.[80]

It goes without saying that there can be no question of considering the Church (any more than any other created or creatable reality) as capable of bringing to Christ a perfection from without that would not belong to him properly. Christ is assuredly the active subject of the participle *pleroumenou:* there is no question here of taking this term for a passive, but only for a reflexive middle. We are talking, therefore, only about a perfection, a fullness, of which Christ remains the sole first author, although he finds it, rather actualizes it, only by coming out of himself, by "completing himself." In this case, evidently, the rather simplistic philological objection that *pleroma* has only a passive sense, "that which is filled," and not "what fills or fulfills," falls of its own weight. There is no question that the Church, once again as a distinct subject, fulfills or completes Christ, but even that Christ is fulfilled and completed in her, so that she is that in which he brings about his own perfection.

The biblical image of the creation of man and woman that the same Epistle to the Ephesians applies to the union of Christ and the Church seems to orient us in this direction.[81] According to the biblical narrative in Genesis, the woman is not precisely a complement of man, added to him from without. The failure of his endeavor to find such a complement in one of the other living creatures was emphasized. Then one part of him was taken by the Creator and from this "rib" he made for man another self, which is just as much *himself* as it is *another.* Only then, in this autonomous development which still proceeds totally from him, does man sees himself complete: with the one whom he can call bone of his bone and flesh of his flesh, it is possible for him to be "two in one flesh."

This interpretation is in no way opposed to the idea that the Church would be entirely filled with the gifts of Christ and with all these gifts; on the contrary, it extends this idea. Far fom implying an ordinary independence or self-sufficiency of the Church in regard to Christ, it denies her any separate, distinct existence.

This sense, attributed to the phrase from the first chapter of Ephesians, seems to be in line with Pauline thought. That it is indispensable is made obvious by the parallelism with a no less characteristic (and no less enigmatic at first sight) phrase from the Epistle to the Colossians. In verse 24 of chapter 1, St. Paul, immediately after a passage on the Church and Christ, parallel to that of Ephesians writes:, *antanaplero ta hysteremata ton thlipseon tou Christou en te sarki mou hyper tou somatos autou, ho estin he ekklesia.* What precedes this text shows that he wants to speak of the sufferings that accompany the apostolic ministry, and in what follows in this "ministry," St. Paul considers himself not only the simple servant of Christ but also the servant of the Church. It is no less unquestionable that he is the subject of an active verb, formed on the same root as *pleroma,* whose sole meaning is "to complete," with a double prefix in which *ana* underlines that the complement in question supposes an effective lack (which will be underlined again by the object, *ta hysteremata*), and *anti* emphasizes that the complement is brought by the subject in place of another subject—obviously, Christ.

This text therefore cannot be translated any other way than "I complete myself in my flesh what remains to be suffered of the sufferings of Christ for the Church which is his body"; and it requires us to take all these expressions in the strongest sense. This comes down to saying that St. Paul in the Epistle to the Colossians does not hesitate to affirm about the Church with respect to Christ, but about a simple "member" of this Church, much more than what we hesitate to read in Ephesians. He is ready to say not only that Christ completes himself in the Church but that the Church, and even one simple member of the Church, may have to complete for Him what he has left unfinished, even in what is, according to Pauline doctrine, the preeminent redemptive act: his cross. Without in any way being annulled, this is immediately rectified by the fact, on the one hand, that the Church is expressly described in this text not as an addition exterior to Christ but as preceding from him, as belonging to him, in the strongest sense, since she is called his own Body. On the other hand, it is as an entirely dependent minister of Christ and, by Christ's will, of the Church, that the Apostle can attribute to himself the role in question.

In other words, the parallelism with the Epistle to the Colossians and its *antanaplero* confirms and reenforces the orientation sketched in the Epistle to the Ephesians by what St. Paul calls there the "mystery" of Christ and the Church; and we cannot doubt that we must understand the *pleroma* of the same epistle in such a way that we must translate the phrase in question by: "the Church, the fullness of the one who completes himself perfectly in all."

Nothing is more normal than this. In the whole perspective of the New Testament, Christ does not find his reason for being—nor his completion, for that matter—in himself. This is opposed to the tendency of many earlier christologies, which wrongly thought they could exalt him further by separating him from the rest of mankind. Following a felicitous formula of Fr. Serge Bulgakov, this tendency does not belong to authentic Christianity; rather, it characterizes a "Jesuanity" which is merely its caricature. In St. Paul's view in particular, Jesus is the Second Adam. This is to say that he does not exist for himself, apart from the rest of mankind and in opposition to it, but for it and inseparably of it. He therefore is entirely himself only when he has made mankind what he was destined by his own election to make it.

On the other hand, it is true that he is differentiated from the First Adam because mankind, which must proceed from him, does not originate from him by differentiating and separating itself from him. It is reborn in him—and this is quite different—by being reunited and reintegrated in him—without, however, losing its distinct existence but by expanding it to the fullest. This is why St. Paul does not call Jesus simply the "Second Man", in contradistinction to Adam, but the "Last Adam" (*ho eschatos Adam*)—that is, the Ultimate Man, in whom all mankind, following another characteristic expression of the Epistle to the Ephesians, must finally be "recapitulated."[82]

It is that the divine love, the *agape* of the Father, which, we can say, is incarnate in the Son made flesh, is incarnate in him only so it may extend itself and be communicated to all flesh by the power of the Spirit. And the Church, the Church of God of the new and eternal covenant, this "assembly" of the People of God who have reached the latter days of their history, this Church which is preparing, with the final Parousia of her king, Christ, for the definitive establishment of the reign of God, is precisely this community among men of the "*agape* of God poured out in our hearts by the Spirit which has been given to us." It is as such that the Church is reassembling herself today for the Word of Christ, and in this reassembling, which is the completion not only of his work but of himself, his Body, she is building herself as the Temple of the Spirit.[83] Indeed, the Spirit can have no other temple than a temple of "living stones," in which Christ is the cornerstone and in which all are called to form, with Christ, one society in the *agape* of the Father. Jesus has revealed this *agape* to us in his life and death, and his death, by the resurrection which made him not only "the Lord" but the "Life-giving Spirit," has given it to us. The Spirit in us, the Spirit of the Son, the Spirit of Sonship[84] who proceeds from the Father himself,[85] is its permanent source, and the Church of the New and Eternal Covenant is its realization, which is still progressive though already fully actual.

## V. The Church as a Unanimity in Love: Unity, Truth, Charity

The Church, the Church of God in Jesus Christ, is therefore the human community of the divine *agape*, of the love of the Father communicated to men by his Son in the Spirit. This is what radically distinguishes the People of God in the New Covenant from what they were in the Old, the definitive Church of God "of the Churches," the successive and progressive *quehilim* which had preceded and outlined it. And this is what identifies it, from now on, with the heavenly "festal assembly,"[86] with the Church of Eternity, in which all the elect will finally be gathered together to be led forever into the reign of God, which will have no end. It can be said that here we have reached (and drawn out) the very essence of the Church: what she is from now on and what she will always be in the reign of God, consummated in this reign of Christ, which his glorification and the communication of his Spirit on Pentecost inaugurated.

This allows St. Thomas to describe the Church as associating us with the Trinity, with the society of the divine Persons, starting with that Person who was incarnate, the Son, in the fellowship of his Spirit, which is the very Spirit of the Father.[87]

This is what the Pseudo-Dionysius expressed even more strongly when he said that the heavenly hierarchy, after the angelic hierarchy and in continuity with it, is only a descent into the humanity of the divine thearcy.[88] We must be very careful not to see in his "hierarchy," any more than in the divine thearcy, a static fixation of successive levels of being which are ordered but separate. Quite the contrary. Just as the thearcy of the divine Persons is only an outpouring, an incessant circulation, a *perichoresis* of the flow of divine life, of the divine love from the Father, the unique and universal principle, the Dionysian hierarchies only convey this fact, that the gifts of God to creatures are the gifts of his love, and the gift of this love can be possessed only by being communicated.[89] Thus even in creatures, from the most exalted to the most humble, this gift, which is the divine life itself, is reflected and extended authentically, and the Church is only the supreme irradiation in mankind of this very love which is the life of God. By this, by the uncreated Spirit in the eternal Son, every created spirit is made the child of the Father, and all beings, created or uncreated, become one choir of the unique love.

Undoubtedly, the Pseudo-Dionysius was the first to underline what the most exalted speculations of the neo-Platonists had been able to anticipate of such a vision, by presenting the gods as *aphthonoi* (without envy), so that the benefits they enjoy freely will be poured out by them at the same time without measure.[90] But there is a radical difference between this necessary emanation (which is also involuntary, and even unconscious) of a "Good" that is naturally diffusive of itself, as Plato said, and this universal communication of the *agape,* so essential to the Dionysian hierarchies and so revealing of the life and nature proper to the Church. In the latter case, on the contrary, it is a question of a fully conscious and fully free love, whose essential generosity is directly opposed to the basic acquisitiveness of the Greek *eros,* and the *eros ouranios* as well as the *eros pandemos,* as Nygren correctly showed.[91] In the Church it is a question for all those who are conscious of being loved in this way by God of discovering that the very gift of this love is to love as we have been loved, and in such a way as not to be able to love God in return without loving with him all that he loves, without loving as he loves, in his inimitable way. It follows, as Dionysius saw and said, that the more exalted the gift received (i.e., participation in the divine love), the more generous must be the intention to communicate this gift to those who are still without it.

A second point, equally emphasized by Dionysius, is no less important for differentiating from the Platonic or neo-Platonist city of the "spirits" the society of divine charity constituted by the Church. And in the Church the transmission of the divine gift does not imply any degradation of it.[92] The love of God is inseparable from God himself. We cannot have it in ourselves except by having God in ourselves as a person: the preeminent indivisible Person. Consequently, we do not transmit this love except by transmitting God, or better: each time this love passes from one creature to another, God himself is communicated. Thus even if it is by another creature, more exalted than we, that we receive the gift of God, we always receive it immediately and, therefore, integrally. The mediators, whoever they may be, in the perspective of the Gospel, beginning with Christ himself, and because all mediation is only an extension of his own, are never intermediaries who persist in separating as much as they join. In principle, the only Christian mediation is that of Christ and those whom he makes his instruments. Their "transparency" is total. God gives them the grace, as his supreme grace, of associating with his gift, but he is in no way thereby set in a kind of dependence on them, nor are those to whom the gift is transmitted. Whoever transmits it to them, it is the Spirit in them who is transmitted; it is Christ who is the transmittor; and it is from the Father himself that the gift is received, as that of his own life in his own love.

There flows from this a last consequence, which again is underlined by Dionysius and shows better the basically Christian character by which his "hierarchical" vision is radically distinguished from the neo-Platonist *taxis*, from which he was not afraid to borrow his images and part of his vocabulary. The initial "hierarchy" of the original transmissions of the gift of grace, although it cannot be transgressed on its own level (for it is God himself who sovereignly established it), is only provisional. It in no way corresponds to the final order of proximity, that is, assimilation to the paternal and divine principle. This order results uniquely from the unfathomable union of the divine freedom in the communication of his graces and of the human freedom in receptiveness to it. Undoubtedly, the bishop or the priest, by the eminence of the responsibilities conferred on them, are called to a proportionately intense fidelity to the grace; but here, preeminently, vocation and election no longer necessarily cross-check, any more than the free response coincides with the free divine initiative. The lowliest among the faithful need the hierarchs of the Church to receive the gifts of the Father, and he cannot "keep" them except by remaining respectful of the distinction of vocations and corresponding gifts, but it is nevertheless *the* gift of God that the former receive, in which God himself is given or rather *gives himself* in an ultimately immediate way. In these circumstances, if this is the divine pleasure and if the one who is its object corresponds to it, he can rise as high—even higher—than those who were the ministers of this gift for him. Still better, in this case, the most exalted saints of the earth, if God wills it and if they are faithful to him, can rise to equality with the angels, and even surpass them, in their intimacy with the Father.[93]

When we have properly understood this very specifically and very profoundly Christian sense of the Dionysian hierarchies and the fashion whereby their dynamism of grace and charity, as Dionysius himself said, is only an extension to mankind of the divine "thearchy" (i.e., of the ineffable communications that constitute the life of the Trinity), we also understand that his view was universally imposed, in the East by St. Maximus and in the West by St. Gregory, Scotus Erigena, and finally St. Thomas. This view of the *Ecclesia de Trinitate* also allows us to understand how the most penetrating and strict analysis that could be of the basic opposition between the Platonic *eros* and the Christian *agape,* as between the most sublimated desire and the most unlimited creative generosity, finally recognized that the divine *agape* also is desire but not a selfish or egocentric desire: *a desire of communion.*[94] To him could be applied the words of the soul to the angel in *The Dream of Gerontius:*

> I wish to speak with thee, only for speaking's sake:
> I wish to hold with thee conscious communion[95]

In a fashion that was perhaps more poetic than scientific, but assuredly quite thought provoking, the members of the Saint Victor group, particularly Achard,[96] followed and popularized by Richard,[97] showed how the Trinitarian society is the eternal, absolute realization of this *desire of communion* which is the basis, the *Urgrund* of what Meister Eckhart will call the *deity* in what is most ineffable about it.[98] The Church, we can say, is the refraction, as it were, on the level of the created, but drawing the created into the Uncreated, without reabsorbing it, of this divine desire beyond all conceivable desire, which is what is most divine, so to speak, in God—the transcendent perfection of the deity in itself and, at the same time, the source of creation, and of a creation destined to wed perfectly the divine image of its Creator. By this the Church is the definitive projection on the level of humanity of the Divine Wisdom, of this other self, on which God has placed the image on nothingness from the beginning and has not ceased since to seek out, recall, and bring back across the chaos of our sins to him. In the incarnation of his Son in our mortal flesh, in the communication of the Spirit which unites all flesh to the flesh of the Son of Man, who has himself become the "Life-giving Spirit" as, eternally, he unites the Son to the Father, this plan is consummated in effect, which was to bring mankind to "know" God as from all eternity mankind was known, with that knowledge that is fidelity, conformation, and union.[99]

This spurs us to specify (if possible) the character assumed by the primordial love of the Father by being reflected in this ultimate face of mankind which is discovered in the Church, as the humanized Divine Wisdom, which the Son, the Divine Logos, calls forth from earth by coming down from heaven and adopting the earth in himself.

Received by mankind in the Church, the divine *agape* is necessarily diffracted there under a double and inseparable aspect. As a gift that has sprung forth from God and in God, transported in us, the *agape,* to remain itself, to remain the *agape* of God, the love with which God loves, must first of all be recognized as received. The supreme gift that the source gives us, as St. Gregory of Nyssa says, is to make us the source in turn.[100] Again, this is possible only by awareness and in the strongest sense, recognition of the fact that it is in the primordial source, the only *arche,* that we are the gift and only by receiving it from the source that we can be that gift.

This is why for St. Paul, as has been often (and correctly) pointed out, love for God cannot be the direct response to his love for us, but faith; nor can his love flow "symmetrically" from it, but rather a love that simply extends it.[101]

Finally, this does not mean that the divine love for us, according to the New Testament, must not create in us a love in which God himself, and God alone, is the final object. St. John, after St. Paul, confirms the teaching which was already the summary of the Law: God, who loves us with unique love, must thus be loved in return, and no other love that we can conceive is legitimate except within and for this supreme love.[102] But the pure desire of communion, the love which responds to his, can never be in us except under the specific form of a response. The initiative belongs to God alone, and even fraternal charity, which imitates or reproduces this initiative, must finally be consummated in the unanimous response of a faith which is fulfilled and surpassed in pure glorification.

It is not another kind of love in man, consequently, that can directly respond to God's love for us, but rather "the faith." For the divine love, the love of the Father, of the Creator, the Savior, which gives everything, which gives itself without reserve, is properly and (in a sense) incommunicably divine. We can possess it only by "knowing" God, that is, by "recognizing" him in this gift as *the* Gift. Faith thereby is certainly knowledge, and not only essentially supernatural, essentially given knowledge, but knowledge and recognition of the gift, of grace, and of God in his grace.

Yet, according to Isaiah, to which the Gospel's revelation of the cross gives supreme clarity, this gift can be known only in the obedience it implies, only in acceptance of the new habit, the new orientation of service of God which it supposes and requires.[103] This is not simple conformity to a law that remains obscure because it is heteronomous; it is conformation to the fully interiorized law of God, who had made us in his image and who becomes more "deep seated" in us than we are ourselves. Therefore, finally, the union of this God with us, and us in him—the most perfect and satisfying union it is possible to conceive—is consummated in the total dedication of self to the service of his creative and saving love.

Thus realized, in the very perfection of its consummation the union reveals its dissymmetry to the fullest. A perfect friendship—a perfect equality of love, if you wish—is certainly its goal. But this equality and harmony is in no way identity or unison. Indeed, on one hand is infinity and on the other our finiteness, which conjunction with the inifinite can only return to its nothingness. On one hand, then, is the gift, properly speaking—the most substantial gift there is. On the other hand, what other symmetrical gift could there be? In return the divine gift, in the perfect "recognition" (*epignosis*)[104] of consummated faith, can give rise to only an unreserved *surrender,* a disappropriation of self: recognition of our poverty in the superessential richness which becomes infinitely poor to enrich us with itself—complete and total surrender to the love with which we are loved, in the pure joy of no longer belonging to ourselves but of being his, his alone and without reserve. Thus, just as faith in the divine love—that is, faith which accepts it in us, which yields fully to it—is immediately conveyed in the most humble as well as the most exalting act of thanksgiving to the One who has given us everything, by abandoning oneself to the thrust of this love which commits us, correlatively, to his service: to the service of its essential, and essentially universal, expansion to all other creatures, in the service of its communication in a charity in which we are totally consummated in order to transmit perfectly the received gift, the gift of giving oneself.

Thanksgiving and fraternal charity are then the double and inseparable response of love to the divine love which characterizes (in the Church) this love of the Trinity, of the Father himself, insofar as it is "poured out into our hearts by the Holy Spirit who has been given to us" by his Son. The two aspects can never be separated. If we do not give ourselves to our brothers as the Father gives himself to us, we cannot say that we received his gift: the gift of his love, the gift of himself. And we cannot hope to give ourselves in this way, except by receiving by faith, by "recognizing" in faith, by praising, by glorifying—with our whole heart opened by faith to the invasion of the Divine Other—the divine gift, this gift of God in which God himself is given, in which he gives himself.

Thus the conjunction is indivisible between this double orientation to the Father and to our brothers, where we cannot turn (as we should) to our brothers if we have not first turned to the Father, by the "faith of Christ." And we are not truly open to the Father if we have not, at the same time, turned to our brothers—so indivisible is the eternal love of God in himself and his love for the world, which fills the history of creation and salvation. Thus only God's *agape*, communicated to men, from now on constitutes the eternal life and the eternal structure of this definitive Church of God, which is the proper fullness of Christ and, therefore, the indestructible Temple of the Spirit.

We can now grasp the sense of the equation between truth and love and therefore between Church and truth and, finally, the sense of the unity and unicity of the Church so strongly stated by Moehler or Khomiakov, which is assuredly the deepest and most basic teaching on the Church that can be drawn from the New Testament and the fathers. The Christian truth, according to the perspectives we have just explored, is not a sum of particular truths. It can and must be expressed, defined, and applied in a multitude of statements of inexhaustible richness, which, however, are always capable of proliferating again, *ad infinitum*. But behind all this—before it and in it—it remains and must be perceived. Otherwise all the rest loses its sense as a unique truth, the truth of the love of God revealed in Jesus Christ and communicated by his Spirit.

This also is why the Christian truth can be received, understood, and have meaning only in the lived experience of this communicated love. "To know the truth," in the biblical, Johannine sense,[105] is this and this alone. But this experience is properly the experience of the Church. To participate in it, to participate in the Church, to enter into it, to live in it and from it—all these things are one. The connection between the authentic truth of the Gospel (its preservation, expansion, and propagation) and the Church is not, then, an accidental or arbitrary connection. It is essential to the nature of things.

Obviously, however, this supposes that the Church be acknowledged as unanimity in love, the common life of the truth *of* the divine life (not only *about* the divine life) in all who by faith, following the channels we have endeavored to follow, are introduced into this common life, immersed in it, consent to it, work within it, and are lost in it more and more totally. This is the sense of tradition and its necessity: transmission, communication, sharing, and expansion without limit of a love (of a life) which is the life of God, which has become fully human, for the whole of mankind.

Hence the no less necessary unity and unicity of the Church, for the Church is (and is only) the "recapitulation"[106] of the whole of mankind in this life of the Father, this love of the Father, which can be discovered only by our being and becoming brothers to one another and to all together. There can then be only one authentic Church, just as there is but one Father, whom it pleases to gather all into the Body of his only-begotten Son in order to animate us with his one Spirit by and for a unique love, the unique love.

For an even stronger reason, she must be one. Her unity cannot be artificial, produced or manufactured externally; it must be essential, flowing from the Source, from the unique Source of living unity: Love, which is the only Source of all things and in which all beings can and must come together.

The continuation of our study will be limited to drawing out (insofar as possible) these implications in the concrete actualization of the divine plan, in the way that the work of his Word made flesh imposes these implications on our recognition and our assent. But it is by starting out from this basic vision, and always (if we may say so) as so many necessary elements of its historical concretization, that they should be grasped. Here we have a center, a nucleus of references, or better, the living heart, without which the versatile and complex structure that we must retrace would not only remain incomprehensible but would be done away with, if ever we yielded to the temptation to separate one from the other.

## VI. Toward the Fullness of Christ's Adulthood: The Church Tending toward the Reign of God

It is important that we understand that all we have just developed is not a utopia—expression of a simple, unrealized, and perhaps unrealizable ideal nor an anticipated description of a future Church, after the judgment, after the Parousia, of which the present Church would only be a preparation or, at most, a sketch and a promise. The whole of Catholic tradition, for the fathers in particular and, we believe we have shown, in the very line of the most exacting fidelity to the New Testament, is true of the present Church, founded by Christ on the apostles—the Catholic Church.

And it seems, even if they reject this last identification, the Protestants who are most faithful to the intuitions of the reformers of the sixteenth century—whatever hesitancy they may have about endorsing the witness of the fathers or the medieval theologians we have mentioned—would have no more difficulty than the Orthodox in recognizing that such a Church corresponds to the image in the New Testament, even if they maintain that it does not correspond to any "concrete church" of the present and that its actuality, though real, remains invisible. Yet, stating this in no way means ignoring that the Church remains unfinished and imperfect. Consequently, however present the reign of Christ is for her, the ultimate accomplishment of this reign in the reign of God is still only the object of Christian hope.

This Church, which we have described, already exists and has since Pentecost, and is capable of bringing us together in herself, as in the Church which has not only the promises of life eternal but its "first fruits"[107] by the Spirit. On one hand, she must still spread "to the ends of the earth"[108] and, on the other hand, each of her members—those at least who are on earth—is still in the process of perfection. Hence a final fullness that the Church is still waiting for, which she will not be given before the coming of the divine reign, with the definitive Parousia of the Savior. This is what St. Paul, in a text from the Epistle to the Ephesians, calls the "stature of the fullness of Christ" in us.[109] This text, if we take what it says seriously, is a supplementary confirmation of what Christ completes and finishes in us, in the Church.

The Apostle has underlined and explained most forcefully this unity and this unicity, which are inseparable from the notion and the reality of the authentic Church. But what is proper to this text, and what distinguishes it from the more or less analogous texts of the Epistle to the Romans and the First Epistle to the Corinthians, is that it presents the unity of the unique Church as an essentially dynamic reality. It is the unity of one Body and one Spirit, actualizing the vocation to one hope, beginning with one Lord, one faith, one baptism, one God; it must be conveyed in the concurrent, coordinated, and a finally convergent development of a multitude of members. All of them, in their manifold complementary activities, which are necessarily associated, must tend to their final encounter in the unity of faith, and the *epignosis* of the Son of God, in such a way as to constitute "a perfect man, attaining the stature [or adulthood] of the fullness of Christ (*eis metron helikias tou pleromaios tou Christou*)."

What follows shows that the Apostle includes in this growth the maturation of the faith and of the life in the faith of each Christian. But as the body of the text also shows, this individual preoccupation cannot be isolated from what he calls "the growth of the body (*ten auxesin tou somatos*)" in its entirety. And although this is not said explicitly, every time the Apostle applies to the Church (as he does in this text) the combined images of the growth of the Body of Christ and the building of the Temple (or House) of God, he applies them basically to expansion of the Church throughout the world through apostolic preaching, which he never separates from the individual and collective witness of the life of all Christians.

It can be said, then, that the Church already exists, and from its earliest beginnings, in this unity we described; but she must grow until the Parousia, in each of her members as in her totality. She is already, and has been since the first moment of her existence, "the fullness of Christ": that in which he is accomplished and completed. But this complement, this accomplishment in us (i.e., in the Church) of the "total Christ" (according to an expression dear to St. Augustine),[110] must be pursued until the total Christ, which we are forming, has reached the fullness of his age or adult stature in each of us and in all of us. This later fullness, as the Pauline texts when brought together make clear, requires that all the elect shall have entered into the Church and that each has arrived there, at the perfection of his conformity to Christ, by living faith and perfect charity. It seems undeniable, according to the text of Ephesians 4 in particular, that the moment of this supreme maturation will coincide with the moment of the Parousia and, therefore, with the coming of the reign. Thus development is situated exactly between two decisive moments: the first creation of the Church, at Pentecost, in faith in the resurrection, sealed by the gift of the Spirit of the risen Christ, and the return of Christ and the definitive establishment of the reign of God, in which this same Church will attain her fullness in her complete totality, as in the perfection of each of her members.

We shall have to return to the associated images by which St. Paul describes this development: growth of a body, building of a temple. The text we are commenting upon is typical of the way he brings them together, almost to the point of confusing them. Does he not speak here (twice) of "building up" the "body"?[111] Let us simply note that these two metaphors were much less surprising to the ancients than to us, for it was a familiar idea that a temple, constituted for the divinity that consented to dwell in it, was the equivalent of a body. Egyptian temples, in particular, were conceived in a very pronounced symbolico-realist application of this idea (as were medieval Christian churches, which tried to give an image of Christ on the cross).

Whatever may be said of this point, we must specify the exact relationship established by St. Paul with all the ancient traditions, between the final coming of the reign and the progressive development of the Church, where the confusion is between the Church and the "kingdom," as if the development of the Church brought with it a parallel and concomitantly progressive realization of the kingdom. Any confusion of this kind is dispelled the moment it is pointed out that *basileia* is not a "kingdom" but a "reign," which, as such, is not capable of development. But now it is perhaps possible for us to substitute for this fallacious identification a completely adequate vision of the true relationship.

On one hand, the development of the Church prepares the reign by gathering together and preparing the way for all who are destined to reign with the King, adopted by him in his only-begotten Son, to enter into the reign together. On the one hand, it is not this immanent development, even if we understand it as the fruit of the Spirit in us, that, of and by itself, can determine through its completion the coming, the establishment, of the reign. Quite the contrary; only the transcendent coming of the reign can complete and definitively consecrate the growth of the Church. The totality of the Church can enter into the reign of God, and each of her members can be found individually perfect for this collective entrance, only if, and when, God's judgment intervenes. The whole of mankind, believing or not, remains interdependent and is bound to a cosmos in which the powers of enmity still reign, even though in principle their reign has been condemned.

No human individual, then, can be perfect for the reign, if he is not finally liberated from this double interdependence; and the whole society of the elect, even when it has reached its definitive totality, cannot reign with God over the cosmos if it is not separated from the body of still thoroughly rebellious wills, and if these wills are not excluded from this cosmos for its restoration. But neither can this separation, this necessary sorting out, be effectuated—nor can its favorable moment, its decisive *kairos,* be observed—except by the divine power and wisdom. It is therefore only God who can determine, with the Parousia of Christ, the moment in which the Church must reach her perfection and the divine reign will begin.

Yet, and this teaching is no less clear, if nothing can determine the "day" that God alone knows,[112] the Church, and each Christian in her, can contribute to hastening its coming.[113] They do so by tending toward the perfection of the Church, a perfection both of inner, essentially personal holiness and essentially collective missionary dissemination. As St. Paul shows in the text from Colossians, on the completion in our flesh of what remains to be suffered of the sufferings of Christ for his Body the Church, both endeavors go hand in hand. It can even be said that in depth they are one: personal "sanctification" and the incentive of the collective "apostolate." This is eminently true of the "apostle," the one who has the responsibility (the "service") of missionary preaching. But we shall see that just as this preaching, entrusted to a few in a special but not exclusive fashion, relies on the "witness" of all, this is equally valid for all members of the Church.

In other words, this maturation of Christ in the Church, this progression toward a definitive adulthood of the fullness of Christ in us, which both implores (for it depends on it) and causes or hastens the coming of the kingdom, is therefore a progress, a consummation of our assimilation to Christ, above all in our assimilation to the mystery of his cross. This is normal, for, as we have seen, this mystery of his cross is the very mystery of the communication, the realization of the *agape* of the Father in our fallen humanity, which alone can save it, restore it, and adopt and adapt it for the reign.

In preparing himself for the cross, Christ said to the Father: "Sanctify them in the truth; . . . And for their sake I consecrate myself, that they also may be consecrated in truth."[114] This sacrificial "consecration" is properly the knowledge, the "recognition," of the divine "truth," communicated by the faith, unreservedly giving us over to the divine love which determines it in us. It is accomplished for each one in his consummated association with the cross of Christ. And it blossoms in the communication to others, to all others, of the saving love of the risen Christ in the Spirit—is poured out on all his "members"—and, through this very communication, extends his "body" to the ends of the earth. In this way, and only in this way, the Temple of the Spirit is built and perfected in history.

This gives us the sense of the Our Father, of the prayer for the coming of the reign, announced in the Sermon on the Mount.[115]

So that we may ask with good conscience that the reign of God come on earth as in heaven, we must first ask that his Name be sanctified. The Divine Name is "hallowed" in us, when we know it, by acknowledging the sense of Christ's cross; that is, by accepting it and following him in obedient faith, by being perfectly conformed to the revelation that is given us of the heart of God, and by being consummated in the union with this heart by the surrender of our whole being to the consuming power of the Spirit.

At the same time, this requires that we also ask that God's will be done: that is, that we become the servants, the instruments, of this will of re-creative and saving love in this world: that we surrender to the incarnation of the divine love, humiliated and scoffed at in this world, completing in this *exinanitio,* this emptying of self, the forgiving of sinners, the healing of the sick, and the resurrection of the dead.

All of this, let us note, is nourished and renewed unceasingly and constantly tends toward its fulfillment as toward the highest grace in the eucharistic assembly of the Church of Christ in which this Church comes together, becomes aware of herself, and tends toward her eschatological actualization. Echoing the definitive Word of the Gospel, the proclamation of the Father's love, manifested for us by the Son, poured into our hearts by the Spirit given to us, the Church responds in the eucharistic prayer by acknowledging by faith this descent to her of the paternal *agape,* in the first work of creation, in the whole history of salvation, and in its final culmination in the cross and the resurrection of the Savior. She then entreats that this mystery have its accomplishment in her and, through her, in the entire world. She asks that the Spirit associate her with the cross of Christ. At the same time, she asks that each of her members attain in her the perfection of faith and love, and that she, spreading throughout the universe, may gather into herself, as in one Temple of the Spirit and the only Body of the eternal Son, all the scattered children of God.[116]

By this, the Church develops the human response in faith to the love of the Father pouring into our own hearts under the inseparably twofold aspect which we have described. But let us point out: since it is from an exultant contemplation of the mystery, from the knowledge and "recognition" of the divine love *for us,* from the surrender in faith to the gift of this love that the prayer proceeds, the universal supplication that gives evidence of the fact that this divine love has indeed been poured out *in us,* so that it may be extended *by us* to all men, to the whole universe—this communicated prayer of love, by its own development, ends at the conclusion of the Eucharist with a universal doxology. This is to say that the prayer of brotherly charity, communicating the love of the Father, the gift of the Father, the gift of giving oneself to others as he gives himself to us, means ultimately being absorbed and tends to absorb everything in the initial response, in "recognizant" contemplation, in the simple, exultant surrender to the revelation of the divine love.

This completion of the prayer of the Church, proceeding to her perfection, toward the fullness of Christ's adulthood in her—this completion in unity and in the sole glorification of God is preeminently the anticipation of the reign of God in the time of the Church.

Precisely when the reign comes, the twofold aspect inherent in our response to the *agape* of the Father will be reabsorbed. Just as the descent to us of the paternal *agape* (which eternally finds its perfect fulfillment in the bosom of the Trinity) is only a temporal refraction of this eternal perfection upon nothingness, similarly, the extension in ourselves, in fraternal and missionary charity, of this descent of the creative and saving love will find its accomplishment in the final, total unanimity of love. Then all will rediscover themselves and turn about, having arrived at the perfection of their unity, toward the Father from whom all fatherhood proceeds, on earth as in heaven, in order to glorify forever his unity in his Son by the Holy Spirit.

## Notes

1. Cf. Matthew 19:8.
2. Matthew 5:21 and 33.
3. Matthew 5:17–18.
4. See the article from *Theologisches Wörterbuch* by Delling, as well as A. Feuillet, *Le Christ, Sagesse de Dieu,* pp. 117ff.
5. Cf. Mark 1:15, John 7:8, Galatians 4:4, Ephesians 1:10.
6. Cf. Matthew 3:15 and passim.
7. 2 Corinthians 1:20.
8. John 1:16.
9. John 1:18.
10. 1 John 3:2.
11. See Kittel's article on this word in his *Wörterbuch.*
12. See Delling's article on this word in *Wörterbuch.*
13. Jeremiah 7:12.
14. Cf. Jeremiah 31:31 and Ezekiel 37:26.
15. S. Mowinckel, *He That Cometh,* pp. 261ff.
16. Antonin Causse, *Du groupe ethnique à la communauté religieuse* (Paris, 1937).
17. Cf. what the constitution *Sacrosanctum* says on this (second paragraph of the preamble).
18. Cf. Galatians 3:28 and Colossians 3:11.
19. On this point, see J. Héring, *Le Royaume de Dieu et sa venue* (Neuchâtel–Paris [new ed.], 1959), pp. 101ff.
20. Cf. John 6:15 and 19:12.
21. John 18:36.
22. John 18:37.
23. Matthew 22:21 and parallels. See also chap. 6ff.
24. Matthew 8:11. Cf. Luke 13:18.
25. Cf. Luke 17:21.
26. On this situation, see O. Cullmann, *Le salut dans l'histoire,* pp. 167ff.
27. Matthew 22:14.
28. See chap. 8 below.
29. O. Cullmann, *La Royauté du Christ et l'Eglise dans le Nouveau Testament,* Cahier biblique de Foi et Vie (Paris, 1941).

30. Cf. 1 Corinthians 15:45.
31. Cf. *Homilia 38 in Matth.*
32. John 18:36.
33. See the work of H. Schlier, *Le Temps de l'Eglise*, and the study of P. I. Dalmais, with the same title, in *L'Eglise et les Eglises* (Chevetogne, 1956), 2:87ff.
34. See the article of K. L. Schmidt on *basileia* in *Theologisches Wörterbuch.* A good bibliography on the debate, particularly in German exegesis, is H. Küng, *The Church* (New York, 1968).
35. Cf. Matthew 12:18 and Luke 11:20.
36. Cf. Luke 17:21. On all this among contemporary exegetes, see particularly E. Kaesemann, "Das Problem des historischen Jesu," in *Zeitschrift für Theologie und Kirche* (1954), pp. 125ff., which insists on the presence of God and his reign, manifested by *the teaching of Jesus*, and E. Fuchs, *Das urchristliche Sakramentsverständnis* (Bad–Cannstadt, 1958), which underlines the implications of God's "behavior."
37. Cf. Luke 17:20.
38. Cf. Matthew 11:5.
39. Cf. Matthew 11:5.
40. 2 Corinthians 4:4.
41. Matthew 11:12. Cf. Luke 16:16.
42. Matthew 16:25 and parallels.
43. Colossians 2:15. On the theme of the cross illumined by the resurrection, see the second paragraph of chapter 7 in Wolfhart Pannenberg, *Grundzige der Christologie* (Gütersloh, 1964).
44. Matthew 13:41, 16:28; cf. 20:21.
45. Colossians 1:13; cf. 1 Corinthians 15:24–25.
46. Cf. Romans 8:24.
47. Cf. 1 Corinthians 15:52 and Revelation 21:5; 1 Corinthians 15:24 25 und 2 Peter 3:13; Revelation 21:1.
48. Cf. 1 Corinthians 15:45–55.
49. Cf. 2 Corinthians 3:17.
50. Joel 3:1–5, quoted by Acts 2:17ff.
51. Cf. Ezekiel 37. On the Spirit in the Old Testament, see Daniel Lys, "Ruach," *le souffle dans l'Ancien Testament* (Paris, 1962).
52. Luke 1:35.
53. Ibid.
54. Luke 3:21ff.
55. Luke 4:1ff.
56. Luke 4:16ff.
57. Luke 23:46.
58. Hebrews 9:14.
59. Colossians 1:19.

60. Colossians 2:9.
61. Colossians 1:22.
62. Ephesians 1:23.
63. Cf. Romans 6:12.
64. Matthew 5:48 and the entire context.
65. Cf. what St. Paul says about the love of God (i.e., love that is proper to him) in Romans 5:5ff. with the love that the Sermon on the Mount invites us to exercise.
66. 1 John 3:1.
67. Cf. Colossians 1:15 and 1:18.
68. Cf. Matthew 12:25ff.
69. Cf. esp. Romans 5:8.
70. Cf. Romans 1:4 and 8:11.
71. 2 Corinthians 1:22. Cf. 5:5.
72. Ephesians 1:14.
73. Romans 8:29.
74. Romans 1:4.
75. Romans 8:14–16.
76. Galatians 4:6–7.
77. Romans 5:5.
78. Ephesians 1:23.
79. Again, the most complete discussion of this text is undoubtedly that of A. Feuillet, op. cit., pp. 277ff.
80. This is the view finally taken by Feuillet. We cannot follow it unreservedly, though we are in agreement with him on the essential point, as what follows will show.
81. Cf. Ephesians 5:22ff., commenting on the narrative of Genesis 2.
82. Cf. 1 Corinthians 15:45ff. and Ephesians 1:10.
83. Cf. 1 Corinthians 6:19 and Ephesians 2:21, also 1 Corinthians 3:16 and 17; 2 Corinthians 6:16.
84. Cf. Romans 8:15.
85. John 15:26 On the object of this section, see the two volumes of H. Mühlen, *L'Esprit dans l'Eglise* (Fr. tr.; Paris, 1969).
86. Cf. Hebrews 12:22.
87. See the study of Fr. Congar, *Esquisses du Mystère de l'Eglise* (Paris, 1941), pp. 59ff.
88. See our *The Spirituality of the New Testament and the Fathers* (London, 1960), chap. XVI.
89. Ibid.
90. Cf. R. Roques, *L'univers dionysien* (Paris, 1954), p. 316, n. 1.
91. A. Nygren, *Eros et Agapè* (Fr. tr.), 1:235.
92. Cf. E. von Ivanka, "La signification du corpus areopagiticum," in *Recherches de science religieuse* (Paris, 1949), 36:18.

93. See *Hier. cael.*, 12, 3 (P. G. 3, col. 293B), and *Hier. eccl.*, 1, 3 (col. 376AO in particular).

94. See A. Nygren, *Reconciliation as an Act of God* (1934).

95. J. H. Newman, *The Dream of Gerontius,* p. 339 (from *Verses on Various Occasions* [Longmans ed.]).

96. J. Chatillon, *Théologie, spiritualité et métaphysique dans l'oeuvre oratoire d'Achard de Saint-Victor* (Paris, 1969).

97. Cf. his *De Trinitate,* ed. J. Ribailler, (Paris, 1968).

98. See Louis Cognet, *Introduction aux mystiques rhénoflamands* (Paris, 1967).

99. See the conclusion of the present work.

100. Gregory of Nyssa, *Ninth Homily on the Canticle,* P.G. 44, col. 977.

101. Note all that the preceding pages owe to A. Nygren's *Eros et Agapè* (Paris, 1944). However, it will also be observed that we do not think we can follow him when he excludes, even in Scripture (the Johannine writings in particular), all that would be implied by a redirection of the *agape* toward the Father, from whom it proceeds.

102. Cf. Matthew 23:37ff. and parallels with 1 John 5:1 and 2

103. Cf., in our volume *La Bible et l'Evangile,* the pages on Isaiah.

104. Cf. the frequent use of this term by St. Paul: Romans 10:2, Ephesians 1:17, 4:13, Philippians 1:9, and especially Colossians 1:9 and 10, 2:2, and 3:10.

105. Cf. 1 John 8:32 and 2 John 1.

106. We know the importance of this notion, borrowed from Ephesians 1:10, in the view of Christianity developed by Irenaeus.

107. Cf. Romans 8:23.

108. Cf. Acts 1:8.

109. Ephesians 4:13. Cf. the whole context, on which we will comment in what follows.

110. See in particular the texts assembled by E. Mersch in *Le Corps mystique du Christ,* 2:80ff.

111. Ephesians 4:12 and 16.

112. Matthew 24:36 and 25:13.

113. Matthew 24:22 and its parallel, Mark 13:20. See also Revelation 6:10 and 22:17 and 20.

114. John 17:17–19.

115. Cf. Matthew 6:9ff. and Luke 11:2ff.

116. Cf. John 11:52.

# Chapter 4
# The Church: The Body of Christ

## *I. The Corporality of the Church:*
## *The Local Church and the Eucharistic Celebration*

What precedes is certainly a vision of faith: it is the Church as seen by the Christian faith, when this faith becomes fully conscious of itself; but it is also the Church as she is. For faith is not "a beautiful dream with which to charm oneself" nor even the simple vision of an ideal to be realized. It is the vision of what God does or will do. This vision can certainly bear on the future, as is eminently the case when we are speaking of the divine reign. But the Church, which from now on is preparing herself and us for the reign of God, is not a future work of God. Since Pentecost, she exists, and has not ceased to exist to our own day. And whatever her past or future development, the same Church will subsist to the eternal reign. For in her the reign of Christ is already a present reality, and it is not over "another Church," another society, that this reign is to extend in order, finally, to be absorbed in the reign of God, it is only over the present Church, having reached the terminus of her development: the Church that has gathered all those who are destined to belong to her forever and ready to be consummated forever with them in the perfection of the eternal reign.

This means that if the profound reality of the Church, to the last day, is accessible only to faith, the Church is in no way therefore an invisible community. To maintain that the true Church is invisible because the divine grace that creates and sustains it is an object of faith is no less arbitrary than maintaining that humanity is invisible because men are basically "spiritual" beings. Just as the human soul manifests itself in the body and even subsists only in a body, the grace of the Spirit, with which the Church is animated, is manifested in a corporality and, we may say, subsists only in it.

Since the Church is made up of men and not angels, it is not only by verifiable aspects of human behavior that her most spiritual reality is conveyed, but in concrete human institutions that she is constituted and sustained.

To say that the Church is "incarnate," like the Son of God himself, would be to say too much. The Son of God possesses eternal existence, independent of the "flesh of humanity" which he put on. The Church, on the contrary (unless we agree to turn to the most aberrant Gnostic speculations and make her into preexisting "eon"), exists, has always existed, and can exist only in this "flesh" which is ours. Before existing there,—she did not exist, properly speaking, except as a project in the divine thought: his unrealized plan, his unexpressed wisdom.

Like the Jewish *qahal* before her, the Christian Church is a completely and naturally concrete reality: it is an "assembly," an assembly of concrete men, which could not have existence outside the means of communication, which are no less concrete, which allow men to come together and to unite. It is in grasping these means of natural communication that the Divine Word, faithful to its nature, reaches these men and joins them in a unity which, in order finally to be as supernatural as the Word itself, is not supernatural in another fashion.

To be precise, what creates the Church is the Word of faith in the resurrection of Christ. But as St. Paul says, faith comes from what one hears—and how can they hear if there isn't an envoy to speak to them?[1] Like the Jewish *qahal* before her, the Christian Church, in all stages of her development, is brought together by proclamation of the Word by those whom God has sent for that purpose. And this Word brings them together, first of all, in the collective response of a prayer of faith: expression of the common faith created in their hearts united by this Word.

But just as the Divine Word is creative of what it proclaims, the response it elicits brings the men who utter it not into a simple declaration of pious intentions but into an effective covenant with God. In turn, this covenant is not only expressed but actualized in a covenant rite, a sacrificial rite: a banquet of communion in which God becomes the table companion of man and becomes his very life. In receiving this communication, man is committed to living in the same communication, the same vital communion, between him and God and, similarly, among all those whom God unites among themselves definitively, at the same time that he unites them all with him.

This was already true, to some extent, of each successive *qahal* in which God deepened the sense and the reality of the covenant with Israel, which was already his People. But now it is the definitive and total Word that is proclaimed: the Word of Christ, the Word of his cross, in which the mystery of paternal love is discovered and the divine reign announced as being the final reign of this love. And the response of the People is the definitive *berakah*, the Eucharist of Christ, in which the definitive Church, as she contemplates in faith the whole plan of fatherly love, surrenders herself without reserve, with her heavenly Leader, to the sanctification of the Divine Name, the Name of the Father revealed in his Son, so that the divine will, the will of the crucified *agape*, the will to reconcile all the scattered children of God in the Body of his only Son, be done—so that the reign of God might finally come on earth as in heaven.

This eucharistic prayer, which is adhesion to the Word made Flesh, in its total sense, consecrates the messianic banquet in which God's gift is completed, which is made to us in Christ, so that all may become one Body and one Spirit: *his* Body animated by *his* Spirit.[2]

It is in this way that the Church is made and unceasingly maintained through the Mass, for the Mass is the assembly in which the evangelical Word is proclaimed, the Christian faith confessed, the Bread broken, the Cup shared, which this Word and the prayer that receives it have consecrated—where the Parousia is therefore hoped for, the coming of the reign is besought and accelerated. This is to say that the Mass is, and is only, the Church in act, the Church becoming, sustaining, and developing herself without ceasing. This does not mean, as the Second Vatican Council specified, that the Mass, the eucharistic liturgy, exhausts in itself (in some way) the life of the Church. It is the center, source, and summit of that life: the summit toward which all evangelization tends, the witness given to the Word, and first of all the faith which receives it—the source in which are nourished prayer and fraternal charity, which must fill individual and collective Christian existence and prepare the world by preparing us for salvation, for judgment, and for the reign of God.[3]

The Church of the present time is therefore essentially the "festal gathering,"[4] the festive assembly in which the reign of Christ is celebrated as the inauguration (from now on) for those who believe in this reign of God that the presence of the Spirit (which has been given to us) and the *agape* (which he pours into our hearts) effectively anticipates. This is to say that she is both inseparably what is most "heavenly," most "spiritual," most eschatological, and the most present, the most concrete, the most visibly definite reality that can be for human existence, which she from now on transfigures: the "heaven on earth," as the Eastern Orthodox tradition says, both of the liturgy and the Church, the first being only the exercise by the second of her preeminent activity, that which makes her exist and be what she is.

If it is thus that the heavenly vision of the preceding chapter comes down on earth, so to speak, the result is that the first manifestation, the basic realization of the Church, is what is called the "local Church."

On this point there must be no hesitation in justifying the Congregationalist theologians who deny to the Church any existence apart from the concrete "congregations" in which believers come together to hear the Word, to pray, to celebrate the Supper of the Lord, and thus to be involved in a life, indissolubly common and personal, of faith and charity.[5] No less correct, basically, is the claim of Fr. Afanassieff[6] that the Church exists from the outset not as a world organization of worship, evangelization, and Christian charity but, first of all, in the necessarily local gathering of communities of believers who have come together to celebrate the Eucharist.

Certainly such considerations can still become the pretext of aberrant developments which ignore the unity and unicity of the Church, and we have seen how essential these two qualities are for the Church. But all the aberrations that can be attached to poorly understood truths could not excuse us from misunderstanding the obvious. And this is that the Church does not exist from the outset as a kind of enormous universal extension device: a *Gesellschaft* destined to set up branches everywhere, which would display, for this purpose, a centripetal network of systematic evangelization so as to install, little by little, a chain of worship or charity "stations." On the contrary, she proceeds from essentially local communities and has never, truly speaking, any real existence except in these communities: in the *Gemeinschaften* in which concrete men concretely live a common life of shared faith, unanimous prayer, and fellowship in praise and charity. Everything else in the Church is only in the service of these communities and has no real spiritual existence, except in their actual life.

Saying this is not to ignore that the Church was established by Christ, first of all on the foundation of the Apostles,[7] etc. It simply states that St. Peter did not found the Church by running off at the beginning to Rome, as to the center of the ancient world, in order to set up a mass of committees which would then methodically implant their subsidiaries throughout the universe. He founded the Church on Pentecost[8] by announcing the risen Christ to those around him, by baptizing, by having "those who had believed" baptized by his apostolic coworkers, by having them share in the first celebrations of the eucharistic banquet and by thus involving them in a common life of thanksgiving and charity. The Church of all times and all places was founded, then, in the first local Church, that of Jerusalem, and she was propagated from this Church in similar local Churches by planting cuttings, as it were from the main shoot.

If the primitive Church of Jerusalem disappeared in the calamities of A.D. 70 and the Roman Church succeeded her in the function of "Mother and Head of all the Churches of the earth," it was never with the Vatican bureaus that this appellation was coupled by the Roman tradition but with the Lateran cathedral, where the popes throughout the centuries preached the Gospel to a faithful assembly, baptized, and presided over common prayer and the eucharistic banquet. This view of things, forgotten as it may have been by recent theology, is drawn from the New Testament with such obviousness that to ignore it, one needs all the invincible force acquired by the least justifiable prejudices.

For St. Paul as for the early Church herself, as the Acts of the Apostles describes her for us, the Church is always the *qahal adonai*, that is, a physical assembly—in this case that of the first believers in Jerusalem on Pentecost or some other analogue in which it is in some way repeated.[9] In it, the People of God become aware of its existence, or to put it better, awaken to existence by being gathered together, first materially by an "apostolic" word, then spiritually united by the common faith it engenders. And the same People are sustained and progress in their distinct being by "persevering in the teaching of the apostles, fellowship, the breaking of the bread and prayers."[10] The *koinonia*, which is their central characteristic, and which we have translated by "fellowship," must be understood in a sense that is both broader and more precise. It is much more than merely a vague "fellowship of the spirit" or "communion of minds," as we would say today. For the early community, this took shape in the "breaking of the bread," that is, the eucharistic banquet, which seals the common faith engendered by the apostolic preaching and aims at a community of material good. This shows the instinctive realism of this "fellowship" or "communion." Certainly "community of charity" covers the term, on the condition that by it we understand not a simple community of sentiments but an effective common life, in which innermost sharing is brought about through the realism of the community of life.

This is why it seems so essential to the most "spiritual" Church, that of Pentecost, to come together in one place, as Acts emphasizes from the outset: "When the day of Pentecost had come, they were all together in one place. And suddenly a sound came from heaven like the rush of a mighty wind, and it filled all the house where they were sitting. And there appeared to them tongues as of fire, distributed and resting on each of them. And they were all filled with the Holy Spirit."[11]

Whoever says "communion in charity," in the powerfully realistic vision of the New Testament, says *a fortiori* "community of life," and to be capable of having a common life we must begin by living it together. Charity or communion in charity is not an abstract convergence of completely interior sentiments: it is a sharing of the whole of human life, in and by which are united, not by desire or intention but *in fact,* hearts into which the same Spirit has been poured from on high. Again, if the Spirit has been poured on *all together,* it is because they *were all together.*

This realism, essential to New Testament spirituality and therefore to the Church, which we see being formed in it, finds its touchstone in the Gospel notion of "neighbor." What is meant by "neighbor"[12] in the sense that Jesus constantly uses when he describes the charity by which men will become "perfect" as their heavenly Father is perfect? When Jesus invites us to the love of men, of all men, he does not intend an interior sentiment vis-à-vis mankind in general. Certainly, charity must be radically interiorized, in the sense that it must penetrate not only our actions but our "felt" reactions, our most intimate thoughts, and it must be universal in principle. However, it is as love "of neighbor" that it is always defined and through a series of concrete behavior with regard to "the neighbor" that it takes form. But as the well-intentioned scribe said, "Who then is my neighbor?" Christ's answer is that the neighbor, the one toward whom we must evidence the same love which the Father evidences toward us, is the man (whoever he may be) whom we must encounter in existence and, therefore, the one with whom we are called to live. Just as we could not seriously love God, whom we do not see, if we do not love our brother, whom we *do* see, according to the Johannine formula, we can say that we will never love "men" if we do not concretely love this or that man with whom Providence has put us in contact.

The "communion" of charity, which preeminently defines the Church in depth, is therefore a communion which must exist first, which *can* exist first only among people who live together. The "Church of the Spirit," in the Church of Pentecost, appears to us from the outset not as some invisible *civitas platonica* of pure souls but as a group of men "meeting in one place," in which each person receives the Spirit, for his part, but in which all receive it together. When they receive this Spirit, their first reflex is no longer even to think of living separately.

When the mission extended the faith beyond Jerusalem and all Christians could no longer assemble in one place, the "Church of God," in the customary language of St. Paul, and in the first and supereminent sense, is still this first "assembly." All groups of Christians are considered as having received the faith, and all that this implies, of the Jerusalem Church, which is not only the source but the archetype. This does not preclude each new group, from the moment common faith in the apostolic preaching founded them, from local celebration of the "Lord's Supper," exercise of the broadest practical charity (if not the holding in common of all goods), and the right to be called "the Church of God at Corinth," the "Church of God at Colossae," or the "Church of God at Philippi." But it is remarkable that, even for St. Paul, "the Church of God" never became a global designation which would bring all Christians together in the abstract. In that sense, the Apostle and the Christian writers of the first generation always said "the *Churches* of God," in the plural, so obvious was the concrete designation of the word "Church."[13] For Paul and everyone else, "the Church" remained *an assembly* where the faith is sustained in common, where men pray in common, where men "communicate" preeminently in the eucharistic meal, which everywhere is the most "spiritual" participation in "the mystery of the faith" and the most tangible actualization of brotherly charity. When he uses "Church of God" (in the singular), without a qualifier, it either signifies the "Church" where the people whom he is addressing regularly meet or it designates the Church of Jerusalem as the source and model of all other Churches. It never designates a totality of the body of Christians, setting aside their common life in a local assembly.

No one, however, has a more vivid sense than St. Paul of the unity of all the "Churches" in one unique People of God, reaching their final "fullness" in Christ. For him, as for his Christian contemporaries, this never had the result that they envisioned the "Church" as a generalized abstraction, detached (or detachable) from a concrete assembly of worship and charity, nor as an organization of these "Churches," envisioned independently and separately. When he designates "all Christians" by "the Church," he nevertheless sees the "Church of Jerusalem" in the oldest texts: the seed from which the whole, new, and definitive People of God must spring, in which he contemplates them to be in some sense precontained. Or more and more in his later Epistles, he sees in each local Church the sketch of and the preparation for the unique eschatological assembly, in which all the faithful of all time will be finally accepted by Christ in his Parousia, to celebrate God forever in his eternal reign.[14] He sees the Church, the unique Church, founded in the first Church, that of Jerusalem, as fulfilled in the ultimate Church of the Parousia, or being prepared for in each local Church. His notion of "Church" is never detached from a concrete assembly. It is never an abstraction nor, still less, some sort of organization which, while capping all these assemblies, could be conceived as having existence outside them. In this, once again, he conveys the spontaneous reaction of all the first Christians.

This evidently had been long prepared for by the Jewish notion of the *qahal*. It was in the *qahal*, particularly since the synagogue assemblies made it a quasi-permanent institution, that the one and unique People of God became concious of themselves and developed, preserved, and sustained this consciousness of their unique existence. According to the rabbis, there was a valid meeting of the People of God when ten adult Israelites were assembled. Then the ceremonial reading of the Torah could take place and the great *berakot* could be recited, as an equivalent of the sacrificial offerings. All these *qehilim* made but one *qahal*, not through evaporation into some abstract general notion or fusion into an uprooted cosmopolitan organization, but because all were thought to radiate from the unique Temple of Jerusalem. This was shown in the material arrangement in the synagogues, where the liturgical *qahal* was assembled in every place in the diaspora. Listening to the reading of the Torah and responding to it in the *berakot*, the assembled turned toward Jerusalem, on whose axes the buildings were built. Thus, everywhere, the synagogues met as one *qahal*, centered on the unique Presence in the unique holy place: the location of the *heikhal*, the Holy of Holies. The Temple was destroyed, but, according to Ezekiel's vision, the Shekinah, visibly established there at the time of its consecration, had away from the desecrated sanctuary and, invisibly, joined its People (wherever they were) in their exile. And the hope lasted that it would gather all the People together in the restored Temple in the days of the messiah.[15]

Similarly, the first Christians began by looking upon their local "Churches" as an extension of the "Church of God" of Pentecost, the Church of Jerusalem. But this first Church could be dispersed and scattered, with the destruction of the holy city, without their being disturbed. This is undoubtedly the historical origin of the definitive Church of God in Jesus Christ. But this was no longer the object of her faith nor the center of her hope. It was no longer in Jerusalem, the earthly Jerusalem, that the new "assemblies," spread throughout the world, expected to see themselves reunited forever in one Church, but in the heavenly Jerusalem. It would come down from heaven to earth at the Parousia with the Son of Man. Nor would it be on the old Jerusalem that the Christian Churches would converge, but on the East, which had become symbolic of the Parousia: "The day shall dawn upon us from on high to give light to those who sit in darkness and in the shadow of death."[16]

It was here, toward this heavenly horizon, where the Parousia would appear, that the many local Churches saw themselves by faith as already gathered into the one Church of the latter days: "Mount Sion, . . . The city of the living God, the heavenly Jerusalem, . . . innumerable angels in festal gathering, . . . the assembly [i.e., Church] of the firstborn who are enrolled in heaven."[17]

In this sense, the first Christians believed that Jesus, calling upon the famous rabbinical dictum: "Where ten Israelites are assembled to meditate the Torah, the Shekinah is in the midst of them,"[18] had said that where two or three would be gathered together in his name, he would be in the midst of them.[19] For them, as we shall see, the Parousia was anticipated at each eucharistic celebration, as the risen Christ descended invisibly to reunite them in his Body. The unique eternal Church, gathered in herself, in advance, each local Church.

## II. The Multiple Members of the One Body

The concrete realism of Christian charity, of "the love of God poured into our hearts by the Holy Spirit who has been given to us," obliges us to see the actualization of the Church in the local Churches. The Church exists only in these assemblies in which men meet one another as "neighbors," who together hear the Divine Word in order to unite in a common faith by celebration of the "Lord's Supper," in which their love, of the Father and the brethren, is exercised inseparably in unanimous praise and charity.

But this necessary localization of the Church, inseparable from the visibility and tangibility that are essential to human realization of the communion of the divine love among men, in no way signifies (as we have seen) that the Church can be limited to a particular, isolated group nor, still less, to what is visible and tangible in her. The simple deepening on this local plane of what this common life in love, in the Spirit, signifies for those who experience it suffices to bring it to light. And it is from this deepening of the life and nature of the Church, first as a local Church, that perhaps the most convincing demonstration will result, from the fact that, however necessary for her local existence, no place (or particular epoch) could enclose her within its limits. Again, it is the case for the Church *a fortiori,* as it is for every man: however spiritual he may be, he has no human spirituality except in a localized body, living at a determined moment in history. Conversely, his body is bound every moment to the extremities of the universe, and not a second of his existence can be isolated from his whole past, from which his present springs, nor from the unlimited future whose perfection is essential for the creative freedom of the present. Fully understood, this inevitable broadening of his corporal existence reveals his spirituality. For St. Paul in his Epistle to the Romans and First Epistle to the Corinthians, consideration of the materiality of the common life of Christians in the local Church must lead to recognizing the transcendent and spiritual (in the strongest sense) character of their community. It is the first thing he intends when he tells them that they form but one Body, of which they are the members, each in his own part, which is the Body of Christ, animated by his Spirit.

As Mgr. Cerfaux has shown in these parallel texts, "body" is applied to the Church in an obviously metaphorical fashion.[20] We have here an equivalent of the famous apologue of Menenius Agrippa, aimed at explaining to the Roman *plebs* and aristocracy their incapability of existing without the other. In both authors the origin of the image and its application is probably in a *topos* familiar to the Stoic school. In the case of the Apostle, it is also the necessary solidarity between the different activities proper to Christians, and the different situations resulting from them, which calls for use of the metaphor.

In the Epistle to the Romans, where its development is not as full or thorough as in the First Epistle to the Corinthians, it will be noticed that the Church is not even mentioned. The Apostle starts from the inner circle of the Christian community and expands, without apparent difficulty, to Christians in the whole human community. That he could revive in the Second Epistle a closely analogous development is very revealing, even though, in this instance, he makes a formal application of it to the Church. Nothing could better illustrate how essential it is to the Apostle's notion (however definite this notion may be for him) that the Church be open to all mankind and at least tend to penetrate it or envelop it entirely.

However, the text of Romans 12 takes its departure from the statement of the sacrificial character of Christian life: it is the offering of our whole being to God, who must conform us to his plan for us and not to "this world." The result must be the humility which proceeds from the fact that, having received the gifts of God as the gift of his *agape,* we cannot exercise them, we can no longer live, except by placing ourselves at the service of one another. This mutual service must characterize the life of Christians in the community they form among themselves, as well as their life in human society in general. Finally, both have only one law: *agape.*

The Apostle begins by explaining this sacrificial character of the whole of Christian life: "I appeal to you therefore, brethren, by the mercies of God, to present your bodies [i.e., your existence, your very being] as a living sacrifice, holy and acceptable to God, which is your spiritual worship (*logikèn* [i.e., in conformity with both the Divine Word and with reason]). Do not be conformed to this world, but be transformed by the renewal of your mind (*nóos*), that you may prove what is the will of God, what is good and acceptable and perfect."[21]

Of this living and holy offering, this spiritual worship, the immediate translation into practice will be that humility that comes from the fact that we know that all we have, we have received from God: "For by the grace given to me I bid every one among you not to think of himself more highly than he ought to think, but to think with sober judgment (*me hyperphronein par' ho dei phronein, alla phronein eis to sophronein*), each according to the measure of faith which God has assigned him."

It is at this point that the "body" metaphor intervenes: "For as in one body we have many members, and all the members do not have the same function, so we, though many, are one body in Christ (*hoi polloi hen soma esmen en Christo*), and individually members of one another."[22]

This mutual belongingness will regulate our exercise of these gifts as gifts which belong to all, in the generosity of a humility which recognizes that everything comes to us from God for others.

"Having gifts that differ according to the grace given to us, let us use them: if prophecy, in proportion to our faith; if service, in our serving; he who teaches, in his teaching; he who exhorts, in his exhortation; he who contributes, in liberality; he who gives aid, with zeal; he who does acts of mercy, with cheerfulness. Let love (*agape*) be genuine; hate what is evil, hold fast to what is good; love one another with brotherly affection; outdo one another in showing honor."[23]

Therefore, it goes without saying that this mutual charity will be extended to those who do not yet respond to it, as to those who already repeat it: "Bless those who persecute you; bless and do not curse them. Rejoice with those who rejoice, weep with those who weep. Live in harmony with one another; do not be haughty, but associate with the lowly; never be conceited."[24]

Hence after concrete applications to the most delicate aspects of life in the world, as well as relationships with its different authorities, the final conclusion brings this program together by clarifying its principle: "Owe no one anything, except to love one another; for he who loves his neighbor has fulfilled the law. The commandments, 'You shall not commit adultery, You shall not kill, You shall not steal, You shall not covet,' and any other commandment, are summed up in this sentence, 'You shall love your neighbor as yourself.' Love does no wrong to a neighbor; therefore love is the fulfilling of the law (*pleroma oun nomou he agape*)."[25]

Therefore the life of a Christian is a sacrificial life, fulfilled in the devoted humility of charity. Regulating the exercise of all the gifts received "in Christ" according to the principle that all belong to each and each to all, as in one body, we Christians, in exercizing the gifts which belong properly to the Christian community, as well as all our activities in the human community, are invariably moved by this charity of God, which is poured out similarly on the good and the bad.

The First Epistle to the Corinthians does not have this sacrificial interpretation of the Christian life or this generalized application of the law of love for all mankind. It concentrates, on the Church herself, this central view of the gifts made to each for all, which leads to the comparison with the body. Thus it applies the image systematically to the relations in the Church which should characterize the exercise of the functions that correspond to the different gifts of the Spirit.

Addressing the Corinthians, the Apostle did not propose to give them a simple program of Christian life for outside and within the community of Christians. He combated the factions and rivalries that were disorganizing and disrupting this community because of the naive egotism with which each person was absorbed in the particular gift of the Spirit which he believed he had received. Hence the preamble on the unity (and unicity) of the Spirit, which led him to speak of the unity of the body in order to apply it to the different functions in the life of the local Church.

"Now there are varieties of gifts (*charismaton*), but the same Spirit (*to de auto pneuma*); and there are varieties of service (*diakonion*), but the same Lord; and there are varieties of working, but it is the same God who inspires them all in every one. To each is given the manifestation (*phanerosis*) of the Spirit for the common good (*pros to sympheron*). To one is given through the Spirit the utterance of wisdom, and to another the utterance of knowledge according to the same Spirit, to another faith by the same Spirit, to another the working of miracles, to another prophecy, to another the ability to distinguish between spirits, to another various kinds of tongues, to another the interpretation of tongues. All these are inspired by one and the same Spirit, who apportions to each one individually as he wills."[26]

From this unity of the Spirit, which exercises all these activities of grace, we make the transition to the unity of the body. "For just as the body is one and has many members, and all the members of the body, though many, are one body, so it is with Christ. For by one Spirit we were all baptized into one body—Jews or Greeks, slaves or free—and all were made to drink of one Spirit."[27]

What follows revives the very terms of the apologue of Menenius Agrippa: the body remains *one* body, despite the multitude of members, and each member needs all the others; and the weaker one is, the more the others must show their concern for him. The conclusion is that "God has so adjusted the body, giving the greater honor to the inferior part, that there may be no discord in the body, but that the members may have the same care for one another. If one member suffers, all suffer together; if one member is honored, all rejoice together."[28]

And this is the final application: "Now you are the body of Christ and individually members of it. And God has appointed in the church first apostles, second prophets, third teachers, then workers of miracles, then healers, helpers, administrators, speakers in various kinds of tongues. Are all apostles? Are all prophets? Are all teachers? Do all work miracles? Do all possess gifts of healing? Do all speak with tongues? Do all interpret? But earnestly desire the higher gifts."[29]

What, precisely, is the highest gift? What immediately follows states unequivocally: charity.[30] It alone, when it is pure and perfect, surpasses all the other gifts, all of which remain in its service. Only charity, therefore, must be the object of rivalry of Christians.

In this new development of the theme of community in charity, this time given explicitly as the community of the Spirit living in us, it is applied to the Church and, more precisely, to cooperation in her of the gifts and ministries (*charismata* and *diakoniai*). This cooperation must be like that of the members of a body, for it is to make one Body (Christ) that all have been baptized in one Spirit and all have drunk of this Spirit.

As we have observed,[31] moderns tend to oppose the gratuitous "charisms" to the "ministries," the regular, official public functions. St. Paul is not only ignorant of this distinction but seems particularly interested in showing in all these gifts of the Spirit, and their corresponding functions, the equally authentic "charisms" of the Spirit and the "ministries" which are necessary to the totality of the Body. No "charism" is given except for some "ministry" and there is no "ministry" that does not suppose a particular "charism." The only "charism" which embraces and goes beyond all others is the one which brings the most devoted, most humiliated "ministry" on earth, as the only glory that remains: charity.

Furthermore, this in no way excludes an order of ministries and corresponding charisms: the Apostle, discreetly but firmly, underlines it at the end of his development. And it is clear that, for him, it is not the gifts or the most brilliant ministries that hold first place, but what is basic: the apostolate (we shall specify the sense of this word further on), then the inspired teaching, then the ordinary teaching of the faith, and only then the different gifts of a more or less miraculous appearance. Of course, this order remains subject to the principle that those who receive the most must be all the more concerned with those who receive less, and not only serve them but honor them. And all gifts, the most exalted and the most lowly, pale before the supreme gift of charity, in whose service all must equally cooperate.

This vision of the Church and her life, however strictly applied it may be in a local Church (the Church at Corinth), is transposable to any Church. Every

Church must therefore be seen as a community of charity and, therefore, of the Spirit. In this community and different functions and gifts, among which we must differentiate an order or, if you prefer, an organization, a structure. But everyone and each one is exercised together, in harmony—for the good of all, as the property of everyone.

Some of these gifts appear to be given in complete freedom, to arise spontaneously in a given person, but they must be exercised for the service of all, like the most regular functions. On the other hand, the most impressive gifts are not necessarily the first in order of importance. And functions which may seem to be more routine in their exercise than inspired are no less gifts of the Spirit, and perhaps more precious than the extraordinary gifts. In the long run, furthermore, these distinctions are of little importance, and all relevant discussions (and *a fortiori* all rivalries) are vain: all the gifts to each individual belong to all, are in the service of all, just as each person no matter what his gifts, needs all the others. The most lowly, *because* they are lowly, must be objects of concern by the loftiest, because they are so actually, not only in appearance. The only admissible rivalry, the only superiority that remains, is that of charity, which thinks only of humbling itself, which claims nothing for itself but gives all it has, and which, finally, forgets itself. It is enough that God "knows" it, and it aspires only to "know" him one day, and him alone, as it has been "known," that is, chosen and loved without measure.

It is interesting to follow, through later tradition, the development and deepening of this view of the Church, of the "corporality" of the life of the Spirit in her, as the life of charity lived among men.

The Church of Corinth, particularly exuberant but also particularly susceptible to confusing "the Spirit" with any kind of enthusiasm and of forgetting that Spirit and charity go together, will cause, before the end of the first century, the first revival of the Pauline theme. This deserves very special study because it fills out the first document that emanates from another Church: the Roman Church, whose special position among the other Churches Ignatius of Antioch would soon express in saying it "presides in charity."

We want to speak of the Epistle of Clement of Rome to the Corinthians, which seems to be motivated by the fact that the faithful of Corinth, still boasting of gifts of the Spirit that appeared obvious to them, thought they could discharge from their functions those who exercised the ministries which we see, at the end of the apostolic age, taking a more and more prominent place alongside the apostles (before succeeding them): bishops and "presbyters." Under these circumstances, Clement, and the entire Church of Rome with him, reminded the Corinthians of the teaching they received from the

Apostle. His application to the new conditions of the life of the Church has lost nothing of its immediacy and, remaining strictly faithful to the teaching of St. Paul to the Corinthians, develops in remarkable fashion his theme of the life of Christians as sacrificial or sacral life (from which the Epistle to the Romans, as we have seen, took its treatment of the image of the "body," applied to the common life "in Christ"). Clement underlines the importance, clearly though discreetly indicated by St. Paul to the same Corinthians, of the order that God set up in the Church, as in the world. Far from being opposed to the spontaneity of the Spirit, this order is essential to the harmony of charity which the Church inspires.

To describe it as it should exist in the Church, Clement refers to the Old Testament, where the order observed in sacrificial worship holds his attention. He sees there the outline of a principle which, according to him, must become even more obvious in the Church, that is, the worship and charity assembly of the New Covenant. With the Church acting as one Body which is moved by one Spirit, her activity is essentially communitarian. But he immediately specifies, this in no way means that everybody does the same thing, nor that just anyone can fulfill any function whatsoever. On the contrary, this community of worship and charity, of the whole life of the Church moved by one Spirit, is manifested by what he calls particular "liturgies," proper to each individual, though none can be exercised separately, for each of these liturgies is but a part of a whole and loses all its meaning outside this totality and in the totality itself if it mislocates its place there, whether it deserts it or infringes on the place of another.[32]

The choice of the term "liturgy" (*leitourgia*) is significant; we see there the origin of the application of the term to the worship functions in the Church. But it is also important to note that Clement uses it in a sense that is very close to the classical Greek, that is, as *a sacred function filled for the community by an individual*. For him, it is in this sense that everyone in the Church—bishop, presbyter, deacon, lay person—must perform a particular "liturgy." Each individual has a function that is proper to him; no one else can exercise it in his place, and he cannot exercise anyone else's. Each has need of the "liturgies" of all the others to exercise his own, and only from the faithful and concordant exercise of all can worship result and the whole life of the Church, harmonized in the multiform charity of one and the same Spirit.

According to Clement, this was outlined by the order of divine worship in the Old Covenant, which differentiated among and seemingly coadapted the respective "liturgies" of the high priest from the priests of second rank, the Levites, and the people, the *laos*. To this order the order of the Church corresponds.

But perhaps most interesting is the way in which he conceives this correspondence. The bishop corresponds to the high priest and his liturgy; the Levites of the Old Covenant have their replica in the deacons; but what corresponds to the ancient priests (*hiereis*) and their function? There is no doubt that, for all of Christian antiquity, it is with the Christian *laos* that the function equivalent to the priestly function of the Old Covenant corresponds. Before the end of the patristic period, we never see *hiereus* (or its equivalent, *sacerdos*) applied to the "presbyters," our "priests of the second rank." At that time the word *archiereus* was always applied to the bishop as president over the eucharistic synaxis, as was *hiereus* to *all the faithful*. The ancient *laos,* excluded from priestly functions in the Old Covenant, no longer have a corresponding term in the New. In the Church of the New Testament, all the laity are priests and exercise all the functions of priests.

How must this be understood? For Clement and all the ancient fathers, as for the First Epistle of St. Peter, which explicitly mentions the formulas of Exodus 19 on the destiny of the People of God to become a "royal priesthood" (rather, a "kingdom of priests"), what differentiates the Church of the New Covenant from that of the Old is that the Church has become a People who are entirely priestly.[33]

But again, this does not mean that each individual in the Church may fulfill any function whatsoever. It means that the Church—above all, by and in the eucharistic celebration—is associated with, entirely in unity with, the priesthood of her Head, Christ. The Eucharist is at once essentially collective and essentially priestly. All celebrate it together, but each individual exercises his proper function, which cannot otherwise be exercised, in accord, in "symphony" with the functions of all the others. To the bishop alone belongs the presidency over the assembly, in which he is assisted by the body of presbyters. To deacons alone belongs the service that is intermediary between this presidency and the totality of the assembly: they gather the gifts of all and transmit to all the directives that will order and unify their "liturgies" into one service. But all have to pray, to offer, to communicate, and these are the preeminent priestly actions, although they can be exercised only with the concurrence of all the Church in one concord, of which the bishop, assisted by his presbyters, is rector and guardian.

This vision of the unity necessary for the very existence of the Church, of which the common eucharistic celebration must be the preeminent manifestation, which can neither be nor subsist without the union of all with the bishop and his *presbyterium,* is a major constant of the correspondence of Ignatius of Antioch a generation later.[34] The importance of the bishop, his unicity corresponding to the unity of each local Church, will be developed by him in a very special way, to which we shall return. These views will find an echo in all the Church in the second century, and with Irenaeus in particular, before they are systematized by St. Cyprian in the following century.

This development over the patristic age of a theology of the episcopate, still in an embryonic stage with St. Clement, will leave intact for a long time the correlative statement of Clement: If the bishop is like the high priest of the Church, all Christians are priests there, and especially in the Eucharist. All exercise together, under the presidency of the bishop, one priesthood by the common offering of one unique sacrifice.

Particularly worthy of our attention in this regard are certain statements of St. Justin in his dialogue *Adversus Tryphonem*. With Rabbi Trypho, the author discusses the interpretation of the prophecy of Malachi: "For from the rising of the sun to its setting my name is great among the nations, and in every place incense is offered to my name, and a pure offering."[35] The rabbi explains this by saying it refers to the *berakot* that devout Jews repeat unceasingly in the diaspora, thereby actualizing the priestly vocation the People had been promised in Exodus 19. Justin protests that the sacrifice offered in every place must be understood (according to the context) not only of a sacrifice offered *in the midst* of once pagan nations but *by* these nations themselves. Therefore, only the offering of the Eucharist by Christians brings about the prophecy of Malachi, and even that of Exodus, in a truer sense than the Jewish *berakot* have ever done.[36]

This is doubly interesting. On one hand it is the strongest second-century text we have on the sacrificial sense of the Christian Eucharist. On the other hand, it is no less strong in attributing to the whole Christian People the priestly power.

It would serve no purpose to weaken this text by maintaining that the priesthood in question can only be a metaphorical priesthood. If that were true, we should have to admit, *pari passu*, that the Eucharist as well is only a metaphorical sacrifice for Justin. To the contrary, the whole of the text shows that the Eucharist is *the true sacrifice* for him, if any is worthy of this title. The same then is true of the priesthood which offers it.

Again, no more for Justin than for Clement, this in no way means that each Christian can offer the Eucharist individually. For him as for Irenaeus, his contemporary, it is the sacrifice not of an individual but of the whole Church, assembled.[37] And this can validly be an assembly, and therefore capable of offering the definitive sacrifice, only under the presidency of the bishop, whose role is to utter the eucharistic prayer over the common offering.

We shall return to what in its very principle differentiates the ministerial participation of the bishop in the unique priesthood of Christ from the universal participation of the faithful. For now, we repeat that, to the end of the patristic era, the distinction of the roles of the different ministers and the whole Christian People is maintained—no less than their necessary conjunction in the eucharistic offering. And no less clearly and strongly, they maintained the full reality of the participation of all and its properly priestly character. St. Gregory the Great will state that the ministers of the Church cannot legitimately consecrate the Eucharist without a People who offer it with them.[38]

In line with Clement's explanation and in the light of the ancient liturgies and the fathers' commentaries on them, it can be said that the celebration includes five actions, two of which belong solely to the president of the synaxis and the other three to all its members; but all these actions overlap and cannot exist independently from one another. To the ministry of the celebrant are reserved the proclamation of the Divine Word, with apostolic authority, and consecration of the eucharistic banquet. But this Word is announced only to be received in the prayer of all, and the consecration can have no other matter than the offering of all, nor can it prepare any other end than the communion of all in the unbloody sacrifice. To pray, to offer, and to communicate—these are always the three essential actions in the eucharistic celebration and they belong to the faithful. And in the Roman liturgy of this time, three moments of silence were observed, which supposed the successive accomplishment by each individual of these three functions (which the three "collects" of the president are limited to "collecting"): the oration, the secret, and the postcommunion.

On this sacrifice, which is preeminently the action proper to the whole Church "as a body," the teaching of the fathers, from the first apologists well into the Middle Ages, is constant. On one hand, they say that Christians have no sacrifices in the sense of the pagan ones; that is, they do not immolate bloody victims on earthly altars. But, in a direct line from St. Paul, they say (on the other hand), reviving and transfiguring an expression common to the philosophers, that they consummate, throughout their life, a "spiritual" or "logical" sacrifice which is the conformation of their entire existence to the divine will. However, when pressed to specify what they understand by this, they declare that, in this sacrifice, all vow and consecrate themselves in the Eucharist, where, in a mysterious, real, but unbloody manner, Christ, "the Lamb immolated from before the creation of the world," does not cease to present to the Father the offering of his life, consummated forever on the cross.

This doctrine may be called unanimous from St. Irenaeus to St. Augustine, and from it results a view of the function and "charism" of the laity in the

Church that must be drawn out, with all its consequences. The first point is that in the Church—and first of all in this eucharistic assembly, where she becomes conscious of her nature by actualizing it in an action that is collective, "corporative," and basic—the laity are not differentiated from the ministers by a role that is in some way passive.[39] The action of all, to be accomplished, has need of actions that are peculiar to the ministers, but the former is no less active. On the contrary, this action of the Body, this sacrifice of the whole Body, is the term of the action proper to the ministers. Their "ministry," their *diakonia,* is precisely in the service of this action of the whole Body. The sacrifice of the Church in the final, ultimate sense of the term, Augustine will say, is the sacrifice in which the whole Church offers and is offered with Christ and in Christ.[40]

Consequently, not only are all active there together but they take part in what is most sacred in this "action." Even in the Church, when we single out the "lay person" as someone who does not exercise a particular ministry, the lay man is not therefore—in patristic theology, in any case—a "secular outsider" but, in his own way, a "consecrated person" like the bishop and, in a fully real sense, even a "sacrifier" as well. On the other hand, he is this only with the Body, inserted in the Body's common action, but no less personally. In the view St. Clement so clearly stated, the common action in the Church is in no way a "mass" action in which everybody participates in everything, confusedly and indistinctly. Quite the contrary: the common action is made up of the necessary composition of actions proper to each individual, which each has to accomplish as an integrating part of the corporative action. Everyone, then, has the obligation to pray, to offer, and to communicate in the eucharistic synaxis, and no one can take the place of anyone else.

Furthermore, the ritual action within the Christian perspective on the "body of Christ," on the "sacrifice" consummated there, is not an end in itself. It ineluctably brings all Christians together, and each in particular, in an action in the heart of the world, as we have seen from the Epistle to the Romans. This action of each individual, who fulfills or must fulfill his whole existence, makes the "royal sacrifice" more evident in a total consecration of human and cosmic existence. Having celebrated the Eucharist with his brothers, the Christian must preserve in everything he will do afterward his eucharistic attitude: thanksgiving to God for all things known and "acknowledged" as so many gifts, or rather one continuous gift of his love. As the Eucharist of the Church consecrates the banquet of charity, of the common life in "the love of God poured out in our hearts by the Holy Spirit given to us,"[41] this permanent Eucharist, which must stamp its form on all Christian existence in the world, is in fact, at the same time, a permanent exercise of charity. In this way the whole Church, by the "witness" of each member, as well as by that of their common life, opens and extends to all men (whoever they may be) and proclaims to the whole world Christ crucified, Christ reconciling the world with the Father in his own Body. Also, it is in this way that each member, introduced into Jesus' sacrifice through the Eucharist of the Church, "completes in his flesh what is lacking in Christ's afflictions for the sake of the body, that is, the church."[42]

If this is the case, we must at the end of this explanation, as at its start, acknowledge the correct principle in the Congregationalist positions and particularly in various statements in contemporary theology of the Orthodox East.[43] On one hand, Congregationalists have the whole sense of the patristic Church, as well as the formal statements of the New Testament, when they maintain that *all the faithful* in each local church, without exception, must be actively interested in all the life of the church, and that nothing essential in this life can have any place there without their consent—or better, without their cooperation.[44] On the other hand, contemporary Orthodox, when they maintain that the faith is safeguarded by the whole Body of the church (her lay members as well as her most exalted hierarchs), are also right,[45] for the realities of the faith, far from being taken away from the laity or being offered to them only for their passive acceptance, are present in their activity in such a way that it can be said they would disappear from earth if this common action of all (in which all are involved together and each is committed personally) came to a halt. All the laity, therefore, not only *have* the faith but all *live* in it, and it is in their life that it remains a living reality.

The following part of this study will show other ineluctable aspects of the common life of the Church, and especially her life of faith, as they relate to the New Testament and tradition. Far from these fundamental aspects being toned down or diminished, we shall see that they always suppose the New Testament and tradition, to the extent of deteriorating if the latter are slighted.

## III. The Body of the Risen Christ and the Body of Christ Which Is the Church

All that we have seen up to now does not necessarily imply St. Paul's use of "body" for the Church in other than a metaphorical sense. But as St. Paul begins with this usage (made familiar to his contemporaries by the Stoics), it is uncontestable that the Captivity Epistles suppose more than this.[46] In fact, the Epistles to the Colossians and the Ephesians speak of the Church as the "body" of Christ and, reciprocally, of Christ as the "head" of the Church in a sense that is narrower and more realistic. Only this sense, which corresponds to what we have said about the Church as the "fullness" of Christ, can give final justification to the explanation we have proposed. While the word "body," applied to the Church in relation to Christ, is in the order of analogical meanings, the analogy in Paul's last Epistles is undoubtedly restricted. The term "body of Christ" becomes a designation of the Church and supposes a conjunction with Christ that must be called organic.

The passage from simple apologue to privileged analogy, by a very special *sui generis* bond, is outlined in the First Epistle to the Corinthians. It is enough to read its twelfth chapter side by side with the twelfth chapter of Romans to observe the undeniable tightening of thought, whose explanation is found in the context: in what St. Paul said of the Eucharist in the preceding chapters.

Discussion of a problem of Christian ethics, raised by the eating of meats consecrated to idols (in chapter 10), led the Apostle to insist on the very special and very exclusive bond that the Eucharist establishes between Christians and Christ. Hence his account in chapter 11, on the institution of the Eucharist by Christ himself: its permanent sense (until the Parousia), its necessary implications for the life of the whole Church and each Christian in her. The most significant words for our present study are from chapter 10, verse 16 and following: "The cup of blessing which we bless, is it not a participation in the blood of Christ? The bread which we break, is it not a participation (*koinonia*) in the *body* of Christ? Because there is one bread, we who are many are one *body,* for we all partake of the one bread."

The interpretation of this text hangs on the sense (or senses) that must be given to "body," twice repeated a few words apart. The first time, as the parallelism with "blood" shows, it cannot be anything other than the real body of Christ, who died on the cross and is today risen. Can the second instance, then, be a use of "body" that would be simply metaphorical? Since the distance between the two words is so small, this seems quite unlikely, and appears to be absolutely excluded by the parallel use of "participation in the body" and "partake of the one bread."

It seems that the Apostle has in mind a mysterious participation of the whole Church in the Eucharist, in the true body of Christ, but a participation so real that it makes this whole Church one "body" in a sense that is no less mysterious or real. It may be said, with Mgr. Cerfaux, that common participation in the body of the dead and risen Christ makes the union of Christians, in one "body" in the Church, one with their union with Christ and, by doing so, tends to make one reality of these two bodies.[47] In other words, this "body of Christ which is the Church," as will be expressed in the Epistle to the Ephesians, draws its reality and unity from the effective union of all in the body of Christ, in which, as the Epistle to the Colossians will say, we have been reconciled with God.

If we want to carry the matter further and ask what kind of union we are dealing with and, consequently, to what extent the two "bodies" are one, we must limit ourselves to observing (with the encyclical *Mystici Corporis*) that we are dealing with an absolutely *sui generis* reality: the expression "moral union" would be insufficient, while the expression "physical union," which such fathers as St. Cyril of Alexandria did not hesitate to use in this regard, cannot be applied here in the technical sense of Aristotle (as if the united terms simply melted into one another).[48]

What is certain is that in this mysterious reality of the faith—no less real for being and remaining so mysterious—we find the last explanation of the fact of the great salvation event, implied in the Gospel preaching of the reign: the sonship of the Son, of the Son preeminently, of the "well beloved," the Only Begotten, becomes ours, and the love of God that he revealed to us in his life, and especially in his death, is "poured out in our hearts" so that we become "perfect" as "the heavenly Father" himself is perfect, and the Spirit of God, the Spirit with whom the Son was filled from birth, and who, since the resurrection, has transfigured our mortal nature in him and is given to us in turn—and, therefore, that in the reign of God we will be called to be the coheirs of Christ, to inherit with him the divine kingship. As St. Augustine will say: "Where then is the Spirit of Christ if not in the body of Christ? We must then enter into his body in order to share in his Spirit."[49]

If Christ must and can be completed in us—can find or rather develop his "fullness" in the Church—it is, as the fathers say so often, that he embraces all in potency from his earthly existence and that, since the resurrection made him the "life-giving Spirit," this New Man, the Last Adam, gathers all within him.

This is the sense and the content of the eucharistic celebration; and this is the supreme revelation, as it were, of the unity of the Church: the "communion" of the Church.[50] The Unity, the communion of the *agape*—of the very love that makes the eternal life of the Father—is the communication of the Spirit of the Father, who is also the Spirit of the Son, because it is the communion in the Body (i.e., in the concrete, total human existence, definitively glorified through the cross, the Son of God made man), the communion in his Blood (i.e., in his life, which from now on is transfigured, "divinized"). Simultaneously, this vision of faith gives inexhaustible realism and depth to the affirmation that the Church is "the body of Christ." It signifies that the life of the Church, her concrete life, when she is gathered together especially for celebrating the Eucharist—but also all the activities, collective and individual, which flow from it, within the Christian community itself or in the midst of the hostile world—it signifies and certifies that all this is the life "with Christ" and "in Christ" about which the Apostle constantly speaks; indeed, still more directly, what he says in the Epistle to the Colossians is the most profound definition of the "mystery": "Christ in us, the hope of glory."[51] It is because of this that the Church not only is understood solely in this ineffable union, which the Epistle to the Ephesians calls the "mystery" of Christ and the Church, but she constitutes in herself "the revelation of the mystery" of Christ, to angels as well as to men.[52] In all truth, she is the proper "fullness" in which he finishes revealing himself, since it is he who, in some way, is extended in her, and communicated, and tends toward his final perfection.

We have in this properly eucharistic nature of the Church (i.e., what results from what she becomes in "making" the Eucharist,[53] in consecrating the Bread as the Body of the dead and risen Christ, and in consecrating herself, by the power alone of the Spirit of Christ, as his Body blossoming forth in many members) the justification of the excellent developments that Augustine devotes to his idea of the "total Christ, head and members."[54]

This is quite certain for St. Paul: to be a member of Christ (which is the Church) and to be a member of Christ in the strongest sense is one and the same thing. In taking Communion and in living together in the Church, we become, as he says again, "one in him" (not hen, as "one single thing," but heis, "one single being"; we are tempted to say "one single person," the person of Christ).[55] It is therefore true of us all together, a fortiori, what St. Paul says of each of us, that "it is no longer I who live, but Christ lives in me"; and the Church, more than any of her members taken separately, can say: "For to me to live is Christ: emoi gar to zen Christos."[56]

But this has a capital consequence. Since the Church is herself only in her union with Christ, the union of all with one another "in Christ" becomes most real in her through the Eucharist, but each time the Church comes together to celebrate it, it is necessarily a local Church which is assembled. But it is also the entire People of God, invisibly but really, who assembled. Christ's union with us, the union of all in the Church through the Eucharist, is so real (as we have just seen) that Christ, by becoming present to the local Church, makes all his members present with him as well.[57]

We have pointed out that the synagogue assemblies, all turned toward

Jerusalem, heard the same Word from the unique Presence of the one God and were conscious of making but one *qahal* of the living God. Similarly, all Christian Churches assemble each "Lord's Day" and, turned toward the east as symbolic of the Savior, anticipate their reunion and final consummation in the heavenly Jerusalem, which will come down from heaven with him at the moment of his Parousia; but they do not anticipate this reunion and final consummation only in hope. The Parousia is anticipated in act by all, in the eyes of faith, in each celebration of the eucharistic banquet. The same Christ, present in all the local Churches, communicating himself to all indivisibly, already unites them in him. We must look at this more closely to complete and deepen our knowledge of the meaning of the Pauline statement that the Church "is the body of Christ."

## IV. The Body of Christ and the Eucharistic Concelebration

St. Augustine said to his catechumens: "When you take Communion, you will be told: 'The Body of Christ,' and you will answer: 'Amen.' But you yourselves must form the Body of Christ. It is therefore the mystery of yourselves that you are going to receive."[58]

We would not know how better to say that to receive Christ in the Eucharist, to become one with him in all truth, is equivalent to being united to all to whom he unites himself or has already been united, as really and inseparably as he is now united with us. Consequently, to "communicate" in these holy realities, these *sancta* whose substance for the faith is the very Body of Christ, is also to "communicate" with all the "saints," those *sancti* who are members of the Church and members of Christ, here and everywhere. The communion among the sanctified becomes a reality in the Communion in the same sanctifying gifts—in the gift made to all, indissolubly, of the One who has "sanctified himself in Truth": "I believe in the Holy Catholic Church, in the communion of the *sancta,* for the forgiveness of sins."[59]

The result is that the local Church where the Eucharist is celebrated, where the common eucharistic life in charity finds its basic actualization, is much more than the visible assembly of those who are materially present. It is an epiphany of a universal Church which is one and unique—neither a lifeless abstraction nor an impersonal organization but a fully real and effective communion (though accessible only to the faith) among all those, here and everywhere, who live "in Christ Jesus." It is with all, in him, that we communicate. It is they who invisibly but really are brought together by the

Sacrament in each celebration. And it is not only all those who celebrate it with us, everywhere at the same moment, whom we are called to meet. It is all those whom this Sacrament has ever united in him and who, faithful to the gift of his love, following the Johannine formula, abide in him as he abides in them: "abiding in his love."[60]

Each local Church supposes all the others. Better: the local Church does not "gather herself together"; she cannot maintain herself in being the "body of Christ" without coming together, invisibly but really, with *all* the Church—without renewing herself in being common to all, so that this "body of Christ" constitutes all together.[61]

The result and, at the same time, the most direct evidence of this certitude is that whoever becomes a member of an authentic local Church thereby becomes a member of all the others. If he should move away, wherever other faithful Christians assemble to celebrate the Eucharist he finds himself at home in such an assembly. He is received as a partaker in their banquet, not as a guest but as a child of the house.[62]

Nevertheless, laborious arguments have arisen, particularly in the third century (after persecutions caused numerous infidelities), about the conditions in which lapses in fidelity can or cannot be forgiven. Although variable circumstances or considerations incline toward different solutions in various places, we are persuaded that no one can legitimately be excluded or reintegrated in a particular Church without the same thing happening in the whole Church, or to state it better, in the Catholic Church, which is one and the same in all the Churches. Indeed, the members neither constitute it by their addition nor divide it by their differentiation; rather, each Church and all the Churches mysteriously, but really, contain all the others and are not and cannot be anything but concordant manifestations of the unique Church, entirely present where the "body" of Christ is "discerned" by faith in the Eucharist. This feeling of the unity and unicity of the Church of Christ, present in all the local Churches, is expressed in the most solemn form of the eucharistic concelebration.

For Christian antiquity, concelebration was not simply or basically an ingenious means for permitting several Christian bishops (or "presbyters"), united in one place, to exercise their ministry together, thereby "consolidating" otherwise multiple celebrations. It was (and is) an affirmation that all the Churches are but one—that all the eucharistic celebrations, which the Churches themselves seem to multiply, are but one concelebration.[63]

When a bishop visits the Church of one of his colleagues, the fact that both bishops join in a common eucharistic celebration means that their respective Churches are one, in two different places. More broadly, every encounter of a

large number of bishops gives the opportunity, in a still more extended concelebration, for recognition *in actu* of the communion among their Churches
and, therefore, of the unicity of the Church, which is gathered together in
them all. It may be said that in such an episcopal concelebration the catholicity of the unique Church in some way becomes a palpable fact. In concelebration the Churches are, and appear as, one eucharistic assembly and, therefore,
one Church.

This is why there remains in the tradition that has come down to us, as the
basic given of every council, of every meeting of bishops and Churches, in
and by their bishops (constituted not as a deliberately ordinary assembly but as
a liturgical assembly of Church heads), the concelebration of the Eucharist, in
which the respective Churches discover themselves, mutually and conjointly
in their assembly, as one Church. In conformity with this principle, the
deliberations they subsequently enter into and the decisions that result, to be
considered valid, must never appear as the mere result of either a political
compromise or the victory of a majority over a minority, but rather as the fruit
of their unanimity, based in eucharistic faith and charity. Indeed, the authority
of a council is only that of the Church, one and inseparable and recognizing
herself as such among all the Churches gathered together in their responsible
representatives. If such recognition is not the fruit of a meeting, it is because
the meeting failed: people were incapable of drawing the consequences of the
"concelebration." Therefore, such an assembly cannot have any authority,
even when materially it brings together an imposing number of participants. It
is not a real council.

Reciprocally, a conciliar meeting that is relatively small, if it reaches such a
unanimity (i.e., conscious expression of what, in the life of all the Churches
represented, goes beyond their local particularism and, therefore, their simply
human reality), will be recognized, even by the Churches which were not
actually represented at the meeting in question, as representative of the
Catholic Church and therefore endowed with authority that is universally
binding. Thus relatively small councils receive the title "ecumenical" while
others, of a much more impressive quantitative generality, are denied it; for
example, the famous "robber" Council of Ephesus was denied any legitimacy whatsoever. What is more, certain purely local councils, such as the
Council of Orange for the West in the fifth century or the Constantinople
council that settled the Palamite controversy in the East in the fourteenth
century, are acknowledged an authority practically equivalent with that of the
ecumenical councils.

We shall return to all these points. We mention them here only in the
perspective (of primordial importance) of the catholic unity of the Church in

the different Churches, attested by this major form of eucharistic concelebration that a council is. This catholic unity and unicity, we would say, are qualitative rather than quantitative realities. Two or three Churches, gathered together for such a concelebration of their respective pastors, if they become aware of what is common to them *on the plane of the Eucharist,* by this fact become aware of what is common to the universal Church. Conversely, if an important mass of prelates is not unified in the reality of what can be called a common eucharistic consciousness, it does not constitute a council worthy of the name. One Church, grouped around her bishop, if she is truly united in the Body of Christ, would (if need be) attest to the catholicity of the Church much better than a sorry collection of Churchmen—provided that, instead of turning back on herself, she opened to all the complements that the other faithful Churches could bring to her witness to the unique Church that subsists in all of them.

As Moehler underlines, the fidelity of each Church to the consciousness of what in her goes beyond her limitations must open her up to all the others. Knowing that in being united in Christ she is united to all his members, she will seize all opportunities at fruitful contact that closeness with her neighbor Churches offers her, to receive from them in humility and to communicate to them in charity the gifts peculiar to one or another. On the collective level, we have the equivalent of what is true on the individual level. We have emphasized that, according to the Gospel, just as there cannot be true charity that is not realistic, it is toward his neighbor that each Christian must exercise charity first: toward the one whom he must meet every day, with whom he must live. Hence the primordial existence of the Church as a community of charity on the local level. Similarly, each local Church must first manifest her solidarity—her awareness of the unity and unicity of communion in the divine love—in a concrete opening to the needs and the riches of her neighbor Churches, with whom she is immediately and necessarily in contact.

Nevertheless, she cannot be limited to these relations, imposed on her by force of circumstance. The spontaneous movement of charity in each Christian, in each Christian community, overflows the limits of the local community of Christians to reach out to those who are not Christians, or at least not yet (we saw this from our reflections on the Epistle to the Romans). For a stronger reason, it must go beyond the narrow circle of unavoidable contacts with neighboring Christian communities. If it is authentic, it must—starting with the circle of those ineluctable relationships where the authenticity of this charity finds its first and necessary touchstone—be concerned with all the others, open to them, and go before them, to the greatest possible extent, in order to give to them without counting and to receive from them tirelessly.

Hence these exchanges of all kinds: material aid, reciprocal information, letters and messengers, adaptations of experiences, multiform collaborations in the common work of the upbuilding and expansion of the Church that are so striking in the ancient Church, despite the precariousness of the means of communication.

But this still does not say enough. Each Church, as she came together, was aware of having come together in principle with all the other Churches and, with all of them, extending the Church to the ends of the earth. Again, it was with those who were united with Christ—by whom the faith and its sacred signs had to reach the present Churches, who not had rejoined the "apostle and completer" of their faith—that each Church came together: the "saints"—prophets, apostles, martyrs, witnesses to the faith, known or unknown. Together in Christ at each eucharistic celebration, they came to meet the Churches.

Still better, the Head of the Body came—the Second and Last Adam, the Heavenly Man, in whom all mankind, dismembered by sin, must recover its reconciled fullness at the Parousia. He came with the Mother of the God made Man, already reunited with him in glory and thus promised to a universal motherhood, of both the Body and the Head. He came with the angels, those "firstborn whose names are written in heaven," who await, proclaim, and foment the indestructible reconstitution of the original choir of creation, where the sons of the dawn sang to God the eternal canticle, which had become dissonant by the fall but resonant again in the eucharistic symphony. It is already the heavenly "festal gathering," the assembly of the eternal feast, that each Church is conscious of inaugurating at each celebration.

This is what its Sanctus and Benedictus express: association with the angelic liturgy and anticipation of the eschatological liturgy. Pictorially, the phalanxes of the blessed progress along the walls of a church of stone; the "divine liturgy" of the angels exhibits the instruments of the passion above the altar; the praying Virgin, among the apostles, rises from the earth with the Oriental conch, toward the celestial dome where the Pantocrator appears, among the Seraphim. Everything is attested in the traditional liturgical iconography. And on the threshold of the modern age, the same vision of the total Church, the total Christ, Head and members, starting in the Eucharist, is again conveyed with unimpaired vigor and renewed freshness—even, perhaps, by the most gripping of Luther's eucharistic sermons.

In each eucharistic celebration the rite of the *fractio* and the distribution of the Host attest this properly catholic vision that the Church has herself, as affirmed by extension into space of this limitless "concelebration" that every Eucharist is in principle, through the mixing in the chalice of the *fermentum,* received from the celebration of the bishop, metropolitan, patriarch, or pope "presiding in charity"—its extension through time itself by the *sancta*, reserved from preceding celebrations.

This, then, is the catholicity, in the unity of the unique Church, that each Church manifests, above all in the eucharistic celebration where it is actualized—in the most concrete exercise of charity that can exist for beings of flesh, for us and our neighbors. We also, of course, acknowledge the Spirit in "the body of Christ," the same wherever two or three are gathered in his Name—the same yesterday, today, and tomorrow, in time and in eternity.

## Notes

1. Romans 10:17. On the matter of this chapter, see pars. 7 and 8 in chapter 1 of the constitution *Lumen Gentium* and par. 10 in chapter 2.
2. See our *Eucharist,* pp. 429ff.
3. See the conciliar constitution on the liturgy, chap. 2 par. 9.
4. Cf. Hebrews 12:22.
5. Cf. above, pp. 133ff.
6. Cf. above, pp. 141ff.
7. Cf. Ephesians 2:20.
8. Cf. Acts 2ff.
9. L. Cerfaux, *La théologie de l'Eglise suivant saint Paul* (2d ed.; Paris, 1965), pp. 85ff. On the Church in the New Testament according to contemporary exegetes in general, see R. Schnackenburg, *L'Eglise et le Nouveau Testament* (Fr. tr.) (Paris, 1964).
10. Cf. Acts 2:42.
11. Acts 2:1ff.
12. Cf., above all, the parable of the Good Samaritan: Luke 10:25ff.
13. Cf. Cerfaux; op. cit., pp. 163ff.
14. Ibid., pp. 253ff.
15. For more details, see our *Architecture et Liturgie* (Paris, 1967).
16. Luke 1, 78–79.
17. Hebrews 12:22–23.
18. See our article "La *Schekinah*" in *Bible et vie chrétienne*, no. 20 (1957), pp. 7ff.
19. Matthew 18:20.
20. See Cerfaux, op. cit., pp. 226ff.
21. Romans 12:1–2.
22. Romans 12:3–5.
23. Romans 12:6–10.

24. Romans 12:14–16.
25. Romans 13:8–10.
26. 1 Corinthians 12:4–11.
27. 1 Corinthians 12:12–13.
28. 1 Corinthians 12:14–26.
29. 1 Corinthians 12:27–31. On all this, see Cerfaux, op. cit., pp. 227ff.
30. Cf. 1 Corinthians 13.
31. Cf. above, pp. 7ff.
32. Clement of Rome, Epistle to the Corinthians, 40ff.
33. Cf. 1 Peter 2:9 (also Revelation 1:6, 5:10, 20:6) and the epistle of Clement, 41, which prescribes "that each of us, brothers, in his own rank, 'eucharist' God by remaining in a good conscience, because he does not transgress the fixed rule of his own liturgy in dignity." The whole context shows that, for him, common eucharistic celebration is the equivalent in the New Covenant of the sacrifices of the Old.
34. Cf. J. Quasten, *Initiation aux Péres de l'Eglise* (Paris, 1955), pp. 78ff.
35. Malachi 1:11.
36. *Adversus Tryphonem,* 116–117, P.G. 6, cols. 745–746.
37. Cf. Justin, *First Apology,* 65–67, and Irenaeus, *Adversus Haereses,* 4, 17, 5.
38. Cf. *Moralium lib.,* 25, cap. 15, P.L. 76, col. 328, and *Dialogorum lib.,* 4, cap. 58 and 59, P.L. 77, cols. 425ff.
39. Cf. in Justin, with the text of the *Adversus Tryphonem* (mentioned in n. 36), First *Apology,* 13, P.G. 6, col. 345.
40. Cf. book 10 of *The City of God,* chaps. 5 and 6, P.L. 41, cols. 261ff. It can be connected with a text of St. Cyril of Alexandria in *De adoratione et cultu in Spiritu et veritate,* book XVI, P.G. 68, cols. 1012ff.
41. Romans 5:5.
42. Colossians 1:24.
43. From a rather different perspective, but with the same conclusion, see J. Hamer, *l'Eglise est une communion* (Paris, 1962), pp. 208ff.
44. See Leslie Newbigin, *L'Eglise,* the whole second chapter and especially its second section.
45. See, for example, Jean Meyendorff, *Orthodoxie et Catholicité* (Paris, 1965), p. 136.
46. See Cerfaux, op. cit., pp. 248ff. and 250ff.
47. See ibid., p. 236.
48. This point is underlined by the encyclical *Mystici Corporis* of Pius XII. Fr. S. Tromp, who had a great part in the composition of this document, brought together in his *Corpus Christi quod est Ecclesia* (Rome, 1946; pp. 87ff.) the richest anthology of patristic texts on the notion of the Church Body of Christ. On the origins in medieval eucharistic theology of the expression "mystical body," see H. de Lubac, *Corpus Mysticum* (Paris, 1944).

49. Augustine, *Tractatus 27 in Joannem*, P.L. 35, col. 1618.
50. Cf. the book of Fr. Hamer mentioned in n. 43. See also J. M. R. Tillard, *L'Eucharistie, Pâque de l'Eglise* (Paris, 1964).
51. Colossians 1:27. See the whole of chapter V of Newbigin (op. cit.), which has this Pauline expression as a title.
52. Ephesians 3:5 and 10.
53. See on this point Tillard, op.cit., pp. 227ff.
54. See the texts mentioned in E. Mersch, *Le Corps mystique du Christ* (Louvain, 1933), 2:34ff. See also *Le Visage de l'Eglise*, texts of St. Augustine, brought together by H. Urs von Balthasar (Paris, 1958), pp. 95ff.
55. Cf. Galatians 3:29.
56. Philippians 1:21.
57. See, on this point, the very fine sermon from Luther's Augustinian youth, "Von dem hochwürdigen Sakrament der heiliger wahren Leichnams Christi, und von der Bruderschaften," of 1519. A broad florilegium of patristic texts on this subject will be found in Gasque, *L'Eucharistie et le Corps mystique* (Paris, 1925).
58. Cf. Augustine, *Sermon 272*, P.L. 38, col. 1246.
59. See again Hamer, op.cit., pp. 173ff.
60. Cf. John 15:9 and 17:20ff.
61. On this point see Afanassieff, op. cit.
62. Cf. above, pp. 22 and 129.
63. See the issue of *La Maison-Dieu* devoted to concelebration.

# Chapter 5
# Christ, the One Head of the Church, and the Apostolate

## I. *Pneumatological Ecclesiology and Christological Ecclesiology*

The New Testament Church, as she appears when the People of God, born of Abraham and heir to Abraham's faith, arrive in Christ at the fullness of time, is revealed as the community of the divine *agape* communicated to men. But this love belongs to God "from whom all fatherhood gets its name." It is the Father and the Father alone who has "poured it into our hearts through the Holy Spirit which has been given to us." This is to say that the Church is the community of the Spirit, the "communion" created among men, among the "saints," through their communion in the possession or, rather, inheritance of the "holy things": of the Holy Spirit who is the superabundant and sole source of all holiness.

But we inherit from the Spirit only by becoming coheirs with Christ, and to do this we must be incorporated in him. The Temple of the Spirit can be built in living stones only if we become "members of Christ."[1] For the presence of the Spirit in mankind (as in a sanctuary) is not or, rather, is *no longer* "natural," whatever meaning one gives the word.

For medieval Scholasticism, this presence was never natural, for it is the preeminent "gift of God." It is not only the most exalted of the gifts God can give us but the gift in which God gives himself to us, so that his life becomes ours. Nevertheless, since in the beginning God created man only to associate him to his own life, the presence of the Spirit in man, without the fall, would have been natural in the sense used by St. Augustine and the Greek fathers: it would have been "native" although purely gratuitous. By alienating us from this original grace, sin has taken from us our share in God's life, which would have been correlative with our coming into existence.

Therefore the Spirit returns to dwell in mankind, to consecrate it anew as his Temple, only in the Second Adam and mankind that is reborn from or, rather, in him. This is to say that mankind must therefore be reborn from on high, by water and the Spirit—in other words, through baptism—to be associated with the death and the resurrection of Jesus Christ: with his death to mortal life, inherited from Adam along with sin, and with his resurrection to divine life.[2] This life is returned to us only in the "New Man," the "eschatological Adam," who through his resurrection became "life-giving Spirit," whereas the old Adam was born only as "living soul."[3]

Consequently, the new mankind, the Church of the Spirit, the community of the *agape,* can emerge in human history only following and dependent on the birth in our flesh of the Son of God and the redemptive work accomplished by him, once and for all, in this flesh which has become his own.

It is true that the Spirit was at work in mankind in the Old Covenant. And still today, in areas where Christ has not yet been proclaimed, he produces a more or less obscure yearning for his revelation. But in both cases this anticipated presence of the Spirit is like the *shadow* of the descent or the *approach* of the Divine Word, "becoming accustomed [to use St. Irenaeus' words] to living with the children of men."[4] It is only in Jesus Christ, the Son of God made flesh, that our flesh, our whole humanity, is snatched from the domination of sin and death, is freed from obsession by Satan, to be brought back to the presence of the Spirit, which is not by chance or foreign, but permanent, because mankind has again become connatural. Only in Christ and in those who are his, whom he has made his own, is the Spirit at home.[5] It is only in Christ that the Spirit returns to mankind as the Spirit of genuine adoption whereby we are not merely *called* children of God but *become* so,[6] and it is only through Christ that revelation operates—revelation as well as communication of this Sonship which is one in us with the life of the Spirit.

Indeed, there can be no intimate, life-giving, and sanctifying presence of the Spirit in us which is not conscious: recognized by faith for what it is. The knowledge of faith comes to us by the Word of God, and the knowledge of perfect faith, by which its ultimate eschatological object is revealed, comes by the Word made flesh in Jesus Christ.

In this regard (as St. Irenaeus put it so well), the Son and the Spirit are like the two hands of the Father, by which he forms us and remakes us for eternal life. One hand is the Son, who reaches and touches us as if from the outside, coming to meet us in the world, in the history in which our lives unfold; and the other is the Spirit, rising from our depths, from the deepest part of ourselves.[7] It is not enough to say that the work of one of these "hands" would be incomplete without the collaboration of the other; one hand cannot operate, no matter how minimally, without the other. We have no natural knowledge, other than through the senses, nor can we have knowledge of the cosmos, in which we are immersed, except by an intimate sense which is most personal and incommunicable. By the same token, the "sense of the Spirit" is necessary for us to arrive at "the understanding of Christ,"[8] and the Spirit is awakened in us only in contact with the Christ of history.

Indeed, we cannot interpret what St. Paul calls the "ineffable groanings" of the Spirit unless we accept by faith Jesus' teaching about life in the "reign of God," which we have seen to be the life of the Spirit in us. And the Spirit can communicate it to us, in being poured out in our hearts, only because the risen Christ associates us with his death and resurrection, so that we are transformed in his image from glory to glory "by the Lord who is the Spirit," which is to say by the Lord whom the risen Jesus has become for us, that is, the "life-giving Spirit."[9]

The formation of the Church, whose unity and unicity, as we have seen, are those of the risen "body of Christ," communicated and extended to us in the Eucharist, cannot be the result of "spontaneous generation," scattered over the cosmos, with no connection with history. This is not the way that the Spirit is communicated, since this communication is one with the extension of the Sonship of the Only Beloved. Christ and Christ alone communicates the Spirit, so that he can be called (as in so many pages of the New Testament) "the Spirit of the Son," "the Spirit of Christ," "the Spirit of Jesus." It may even be said that Christ is (in himself) the "life-giving Spirit" and that "the Lord is the Spirit."[10] And the Christ we mean is of course no "ideal Christ," nor a merely "invisible Christ," as if his ascent into heaven had made him a foreigner on earth, nor even less a Christ who is so "interiorized" that he would be merely another name for our own best self. We are dealing with the historical Christ, the incarnate Son of God, forever incorporated in a history he did not abolish or transcend in ascending into heaven, but completed and thereby eternally consecrated. And this Christ, through the Spirit, comes to dwell in our hearts only by fulfilling this plan of God, which he accomplished once and for all by living a man's life among us, which was not only forevermore exemplary for our individual lives but a life in which (and only in which) resides the permanent seed of our lives, renewal by the Spirit. This is why the

Spirit in the Church always remains his Spirit, whom the Father gives us only at his request. And the Spirit, who has nothing else to announce to us, belongs to Jesus himself.[11]

The life of the Church, from her beginning, is therefore in perpetual tension, as has been said, between the always radically new and immediately actual "event" and the "institution," established once and for all on earth, in permanent and unbreakable continuity with the *ephapax,* the "once and for all" of a history that cannot be erased or begun again.[12] But it would be better to say that what here is called the "institution" is in reality the unique, decisive, definitive "event" of Christ, of the redemptive incarnation, which is extended to us, which embraces all in him in that other event: the coming to us (and in us) of the Spirit.

What distinguishes the presence of the Spirit in the Church (the communication of the Spirit which makes the Church) from his manifold entreaties that preceded Christ's coming, or that precede the proclamation of the Messiah in the Gospel Word and his acceptance in faith, is the adhesion to Christ by which this presence is received. Of those who receive this presence, this adhesion makes not an ephemeral and indefinite assemblage (nor a group without continuity) but the Church of God which remains in permanent contact with Christ himself, for it is the "body of Christ."

But as the Pauline Captivity Epistles demonstrate so forcefully, the Church, in a sense that is as strong and true as the one we have just explained, is the "body of Christ" only to the extent that Christ is its effective Head, its leader.[13] This emphasis means that the Church is not constituted by the "determination" of man or men (following the Bultmannian notion of faith, which in going back to the old Lutheran formulas completely reverses their meaning). We are not the ones who, through our act of faith, are able to give faith its content, to constitute this "body of Christ" which the Church must be. Our faith can only adhere to the reality that is given to us, a reality that is brought to us by the historical Christ and by him alone. It is to him, not to us, that the existential "determination" belongs in that sense. Our faith, insofar as it is ours, is not substituted for some uncertain or empty history, nor can it in any way create on its own the history of salvation. It arises only from the fact that the Christ of history and he alone, on his own initiative, has reached us.

In this sense, Wolfhart Pannenberg is quite right in turning Bultmann's argument around, saying that our faith in the resurrection of the Savior does not of itself constitute or at each instant reconstitute the existence of the Church; it exists only as a consequence of the historical fact of Jesus' resurrection, which in some way reaches us through its own reality.[14] Nor does the

Church exist solely through the permanent impact on human history in general of the historical fact of Christ and his resurrection, but, in a still more precise fashion, through the divine will, historically affirmed, manifested and actualized in the Christ of history. It is not an extension of the incarnation in the sense that it would be a homogeneous prolongation of it. It exists only by virtue of and in its historical continuity with what Christ was, willed, and did once and for all.[15]

Even if we suppose that Calvin was right in his interpretation of the New Testament, which draws from it a fixed model of the Church, we should not have "the Church of Christ," because men, independently from Christ, at different times and in different places would undertake to actualize this model on their own. And no hypothetical infusion of the Spirit could authenticate such an autonomous process of assembling or reassembling the Church.

As Hooker objected to the Calvinists of his time, it is an illusion to want to deduce the Church from the New Testament by such an artificial process, however many invocations of the Spirit one would want to make.[16] For the Spirit does not come at our beckoning to infuse life in our works, even though they may be accomplished (hypothetically) in strictest conformity with a plan in Scripture. To believe this, following Pauline terms, would be to reduce the Gospel to the Law and to have the Spirit intervene only to consecrate "the works of faith."[17] But the Spirit does not consecrate such a church nor, in general, any work of which man would be the author, even if it were done on a model furnished by God. Or if he did it temporarily, he does it no longer, which precisely characterizes the preparatory Church of the Old Testament.

The case with the New Testament is quite the contrary. The Spirit does not consecrate as his definitive Temple any mere work of man, even that of a man instructed by God, but only the work *of Christ,* and a work that is so incorporated with him that it can be called *his body,* just as he is and forever remains *its Head.* Therefore there is no authentic New Testament Church, nor could there be, other than the one Christ founded and which is continued historically, beginning with his history through our own history, at every age. The "members" of the Church do not preexist his "body" and cannot, even with the aid of the Spirit, gather it together, undo it, or reassemble it when they wish. It is only the Head who in this sense preexists the Body which is his and who, from his own substance and by his own will, constituted it as it pleased him, provided it with organs he deemed indispensable, and infused in them with his own life not the written, external Law but the internal, vital law of their development and that of the whole. This "law of the Head" is obviously that of the Spirit,[18] but since the Spirit in us is the work of the Head, accomplished once and for all in our flesh, this law also results from the disposition he gave to his Body once and for all, so that it is always Christ, "the same yesterday, today, and tomorrow,"[19] who governs his Church.

Man, even if endowed with the Spirit, would be incapable of making "the body of Christ" without this unique "New Man," Christ himself, who appeared in the history of mankind in order to renew it and reconstitute it forever. It is only in this "body of Christ," which proceeds historically from him, that the Spirit is given, and in such a way that he makes of us all his everlasting Temple "in Christ."[20]

Suppose that (*per impossibile*) this historical Body of Christ reached the point of withering away, breaking apart or dissolving, and that this would be the lot of the Church for all time. To reconstitute it authentically would presuppose a new incarnation, for only he who founded the Church, in his own history among us, could refound it.

But the hypothesis is obviously fantastic, since the unique act of redemptive incarnation is incapable of failing. The unity of the Church, "the body of Christ," throughout history must be as unbreakable as the unicity of the incarnation. This is the teaching of the New Testament, particularly St. Paul: The Church was founded, once and for all, on the Apostles by Christ himself, and no one could assign to it any other foundation.[21] As Matthew's gospel says as well (rather, as Christ himself tells the first of the Apostles, according to Matthew's testimony): "You are Peter and upon this rock I shall build my Church and the gates of death's realm shall not prevail against it."[22] But it is in the Epistle to the Ephesians (which we have mentioned), in which the theme "the Body of Christ which is the Church" reaches its final development, that says best and most completely what is essential here:

> I therefore, a prisoner for the Lord, beg you to lead a life worthy of the calling to which you have been called, with all lowliness and meekness, with patience, forbearing one another in love, eager to maintain the unity of the Spirit in the bond of peace. There is one body and one Spirit, just as you were called to the one hope that belongs to your call, one Lord, one faith, one baptism, one God and Father of us all, who is above all and through all and in all. But grace was given to each of us according to the measure of Christ's gift. Therefore it is said, "When he ascended on high he led a host of captives, and he gave gifts to men." [What does "he ascended," mean, but that he had also descended into the lower parts of the earth? He who descended is he who also ascended far above all the heavens, that he might fill all things.] And his gifts were that some should be apostles, some prophets, some evangelists, some pastors and teachers, for the equipment of the saints, for the work of the ministry, for building

up the body of Christ, until we all attain to the unity of the faith and of the knowledge of the Son of God, to mature manhood, to the measure of the stature of the fullness of Christ; so that we may no longer be children, tossed to and fro and carried about with every wind of doctrine, by the cunning of men, by their craftiness in deceitful wiles. Rather, speaking the truth in love, we are to grow up in every way into him who is the head, into Christ, from whom the whole body, joined and knit together by every joint with which it is supplied, when each part is working properly, makes bodily growth and upbuilds itself in love.[23]

In a word, the growth of the Church in unity is the work of the Spirit in us, but this unity is not actualized only in Christ—"the whole Christ," to use St. Augustine's term—even though he is the final object on which it is focused, toward which it tends. Christ, the historical Christ, is its prime mover, but he remains its subject through those "ministries" he gave the Church, beginning with the apostles and established once and for all, and through the living bond they constitute with him, which results in the fact that it is always he, at all times, who nourishes, sustains, and develops the same Church as his Body through the Spirit.[24]

This unique historical initiative of Christ remains as the beginning, as the sole possible origin of the one Church, and it is the historical continuity that flows from it, and through which it never ceases to develop in the same unity, that we must examine more closely. Thus it will appear to us that it is in the "apostolate," in the strongest and most precise sense, that the initial and permanent dependence of the Church of the Spirit with respect to Christ has been established for all time and is unceasingly asserted from age to age.

## II. Christ, "Envoy of the Father," and the Apostles

To understand how the structure of the Church Christ "established" on the foundation of the apostles, at the beginning and once and for all, allows him, over the centuries, to continue to govern the Church through the Spirit, who is also his, we must first understand how it pertains to Christ alone to accomplish God's plan, to reveal and fulfill his will, by "sanctifying" us in the Spirit so that the reign of the Father will come "on earth as it is in heaven."

Indeed, the parallelism between the "mission" (or sending) of the Son by the Father and the "mission" (sending) of the apostles by the Son is constant throughout the New Testament. It is not only that in both cases this "mission" is indeed a "sending" (= Latin *missio,* as *apostolos* in Greek signifies the "one sent," deriving from *apostello,* "I send," which the New Testament seems to use indiscriminately with *pempo,* which has the same meaning).[25] It is also that Christ emphasizes and specifies the parallel both in the Synoptics and in the Johannine Gospel. The conclusion of the discourse that follows the designation of the apostles ("the Twelve," to whom the Evangelist first gives this title) in St. Matthew is: "He who receives you receives me, and he who receives me receives him who sent me."[26] Similarly, in the Fourth Gospel he says to the Father: "As thou hast sent me into the world, I also send them into the world," before his passion, and to the apostles after the resurrection: "As the Father has sent me, I also send you."[27]

This last phrase corresponds to what Matthew again attributes to him in the same circumstances: "Go and teach [literally, "make disciples of"] all nations, baptizing them in the name of the Father and of the Son and of the Holy Spirit, teaching them to keep (*terein*) all that I have taught you. And behold: I am with you all days even unto the consummation of the world."[28] This promise of a presence of Christ, accompanying those he "sends," has its parallel in St. John in the gesture and the declaration that follow the last words we have quoted: "And having said this, he breathed on them and said to them: 'Receive the Holy Spirit. Whose sins you shall forgive they are forgiven, whose sins you shall retain they are retained.'"[29] And this last statement has its equivalent in a phrase in Matthew, twice repeated and first addressed to Peter alone: "I shall give you the keys of the Kingdom of Heaven and what you will bind on earth will be bound in heaven, what you loose on earth will be loosed in heaven,"[30] and then to the whole group: "Amen I say to you, everything you will bind on earth will be bound in heaven, and everything you loose on earth will be loosed in heaven."[31]

But to the assertion of Christ's presence with his apostles in St. Matthew and of his Spirit's being with them and in them in St. John correspond Jesus' repeated statements in St. John: "He who sent me is with me" and "I am not alone for the Father is with me."[32] (Let us point out that in St. John, Jesus customarily refers to God as "the Father who sent me" and to himself as "the one whom the Father has sent."[33]

We may say, then, that the "apostolate" of the "apostles" has its model and source in the "mission" of the Son by the Father and that, in both cases, the one who sends is present in the one sent in such a way that his work is accomplished by the one sent—or better, that the sender accomplishes it in the one sent. This is true in both cases: of Jesus with respect to the Father and of the apostles with respect to Jesus, especially in relationship to the "Word" of which they are the bearers. This is so true that the sense in which Jesus ultimately will be called the "Word" of the Father is derived from the certainty that not only does he authentically communicate, in his own words, the Word of the Father but the Father speaks in him, through him, by what he does and what he is as much as by what he says.[34]

The "Word" of God, which is in the One sent by God, so strongly presupposes God's personal presence in the One he sends that this "Word" retains the creative and saving effect it has in the mouth of God himself. According to St. John in the First Epistle, not only to speak to us has God "sent his only-begotten Son" but that "we might live through him," for, as he immediately adds, "he sent him to be the atonement of our sins."[35] In this context, the apostles are not sent only to preach but to forgive sins, even though, as the gospel states, only God can forgive sins, and he does so on earth only through his Son though when the apostles forgive them they are indeed forgiven.

The work of reconciling man with God is accomplished in Christ, and in Christ alone—"in the body of his flesh,"[36] as St. Paul emphasizes—because God himself (St. Paul again) "was in Christ, reconciling us with him" on the cross.[37] This is the meaning of Christ's "apostolate," of the "mission" of the Son in our flesh. And the "ministry of reconciliation"[38] was given to the Apostles, we may add, because in them, whom Christ chose, instituted, and gave to us, it is he who continues to speak and act, through his Spirit.

Again, we must have a proper understanding of this parallelism. It does not mean that the apostles would be free to act as they pleased in a sovereign way, any more than it would imply an autonomy in Christ of the same kind. Quite the contrary. Just as the "sending" of Christ—the presence with him and in him of the One who sent him—guarantees his fidelity in accomplishment of the divine plan, the parallel relationship in which Christ instituted his apostles (with respect to him) involves them in a similar fidelity. They have power, according to the Word mentioned by Matthew, only to teach us to "keep" what he taught them, just as, according to John, he exhorted them "to keep his commandments" in order to remain in his love, as he himself "kept the commandments of his Father and abides in his live." Provided they imitate this fidelity to the Word made Flesh and received from the Father, to communicate him to us and the "power to become children of God," they will be able, in transmitting Jesus' word to us to transmit him to us. Or again, it is he in them who will give himself to us.[39]

Again, we must underline the essential difference between Christ and the apostles, between his work and theirs. It is he and he alone who accomplishes the *opus redemptionis,* the work of our reconciliation, in the flesh he received from us. All the apostles can do is apply that redemption, that reconciliation, to us. Or just as the Father effected our redemption in him, it is Jesus who, through the ministry of the apostles, announces reconciliation to us and makes it effective for us. The effects of the redemption are inseparable from the Redeemer: it is *in him,* "in the body of his flesh," that we have been reconciled. Therefore, reconciliation will not be given to us without his being somehow, mysteriously but in a very real way, extended to us through apostolic activity. In proclaiming to us *his* redemption of our faults, in baptizing us into *his* death and *his* resurrection, in celebrating among us the eucharistic banquet, the banquet of reconciliation effected in *his body,* it is he himself— the "mystery" of what he did, once and for all; of what he remains forever— that they bring to us. Rather, it is he who through them—in the words of their mouth, in the signs given by him and reproduced in his Name by those he sent for that purpose—will come to us, who will insert us in himself and nourish our life with his own.

This "mystery" of Christ, as transmitted to us by the ecclesiastical apostolate, is somewhat elucidated if we connect it with the traditional Jewish notion of the *shaliach,* the "one sent," which served as a stepping stone for the Christian apostolate.[40] One of the most commonplace maxims of the rabbis, frequently reproduced in the Mishnah, is that "a man's *shaliach* is another self." So much is the sender deemed present in the one sent that what the latter institutes in the formers name is considered no less irrevocable than as if the sender had done so himself. It is certain that this idea is not a product of later rabbinism; the tradition of the rabbis merely took it from the oldest biblical tradition. This was the case in the time of Abraham and Isaac with Eliezer, the "one sent" by Abraham to conclude the marriage of his son. Once Eliezer found Rebekah, chose her, and she agreed—even though Isaac and she had not met—the marriage was considered definitively concluded.[41]

Nevertheless, if this juridical institution, which had always been familiar to all Jews, supplied the basis for the New Testament "apostolate"—Jesus' apostolate with respect to the Father and the apostles' in relation to Jesus—the latter aspect is subject to two radical modifications. In the Christian apostolate, we are not dealing with a juridical fiction. In the special gift Jesus made of the Spirit to the apostles in "sending" them, we have, so to speak— following the *shaliach* analogy—the nominal presence of the sender in the one sent, which is elevated by a mystical *reality* that is inaccessible to the senses yet unquestionably real for faith—as real, in its own way, as the presence of the Father in the Son. This comes about not "as if" the Father were in Jesus, nor "as if" the Son was and acted in his apostles through the Spirit. "God was in Christ, reconciling the world to himself,"[42] and Christ is forever with the apostles through his Spirit, acting through them to extend "his body" to the whole universe until the final Parousia: "all days, even unto the end of the world."

On the other hand, it was essential that the purely juridical mission of the Jewish *shaliach*, limited (as it always was) to a strictly defined object, be untransferable. In implicit but conscious opposition to this customary situation is the Christian apostolate, where it is essential that the apostles be sent by Christ *just as* he himself was sent by the Father. And since this transmission is aimed at a state of affairs characteristic of the Church, which is to last "until the end of time" (even if the function of founding the Church, which is proper to the Apostles, is no more transferable than the initial function of its salvation, which is proper to Christ), we can see that transmission of the presence of Christ, of his mystery, must pass from the apostles to their "successors" until this very same end of time.

But just as Jesus, in sending them out required them to "keep" his commandments, as he had kept the Father's, we see in the final pages of the New Testament the apostle enjoining those whom he was preparing to succeed him to "keep" the deposit he had handed on to them.

What is therefore the *paratheke,* the constant object of the transmission essential to the apostolate (which passes from the Father into the Son, from the Son to the apostles), is once again, and is only, the mystery of "Christ in us, the hope of glory." The mystery of the reconciliation is but one with him in whom we have been reconciled, who always reconciles us with the Father only "in his own body." Yet the transmission of the mystery which was once entrusted to chosen men, Christ's apostles, will of necessity present a twofold aspect, which is evident from the beginning in those Gospel texts where we have seen it described. Again, what the apostles must first transmit to us through the special gift of the Spirit, given to them for us, is the very presence of the Head and his mystery, passing into us, operating in us, reaching out to us. In other words, it is in his Word and the sacramental signs of the permanent efficacy of that Word, for us and in us: something that goes beyond these men, who are merely its instruments, its passive transmitters. In this sense, as St. Augustine said, "It is of little importance whether it is Peter or Judas who baptizes, since it is always Jesus himself who baptizes."[43]

But insofar as it is impossible to transmit this gift effectively, this "gift of God," without applying it concretely to changing circumstances—without, also, explaining it in the face of incessantly renewed difficulties—the apostolic "charisma" will also imply a special grace, adapted to the capacity (but always in the name of Christ) and through the lights and abilities of personally limited and fallible man, to make the necessary decisions in the concrete. In the particulars of the teaching they must give every day, even more in the consequence of the pastoral applications they must draw from it, this grace in the apostolic "ministers," contrary to the preceding case, must yield to needs that are essentially renewable and limited in each case by a definite human situation.

Hence we have what is called the twofold "power" or rather, the twofold "function" of the apostolic ministry. On one hand, it is the sacramental *order,* where the phrase "who hears you hears me, who receives you receives me, and who rejects you rejects me" is literally true, for here the gift is transmitted independently from the personal qualities of the minister, whether qualities of nature or grace. On the other hand, it will be called *jurisdiction,* where, though the function is always exercised in the name of Christ and always definitively by him, it is not exercised so directly or purely that the human instrument, through his imperfections, could become a serious obstacle to the working of grace. Hence only in special cases, where the permanence and continuity of the covenant of grace would be hindered, the indefectibility promised to the Church by her Head assures us that he will preserve his representatives from erring.[44]

We have pointed out the radical difference between two inseparable aspects of the apostolic ministry, as we have just defined it, and in doing so we have brought out a problem, posed from the very beginning by its second aspect, that touches on the adaptations that must unceasingly be made of the "mystery" of Christ, "always the same—yesterday, today, and tomorrow," in view of mankind in a perpetual state of transformation. Continuation of our study will lead us to specify the relationship between the two aspects and the concrete conditions in which the problem that the second ineluctably brings with it must incessantly be posed and newly resolved.[45] Let us add that this problem will not have a definitive solution, until Christ takes his Kingdom into his hands at the Parousia before returning it to his Father. At that time, since his mystery will have found its ultimate accomplishment in us, the sacraments and the sacramental order will vanish into the reality they were preparing for. "Christ in us, the hope of glory," will become forever "God, all in all."[46]

## *III. Apostolic Succession and the Episcopacy*

This presence of Jesus in the "apostles," in those he "sent" to speak and act in his name (so that their words and actions would remain his), is so characteristic of the Church of the New Testament as to be constitutive of it. Through these vital "bonds,"[47] which he established in "his body," he remains forever its "Head." It is in this way that the resurrection, in establishing him as the Second Adam, as the "life-giving Spirit," permits him, despite the ascension in which it is completed, to exercise this function of "Head" in the Body. Although he is visibly absent, he remains present to the Church in his "apostles." Or, since it is present "in heaven" through its "Head," the "body," which remains on earth, receives his "Spirit" because of the permanent communication the Head established between him and us through the apostolate.

If Christ's return in his final Parousia had come about (as people were more than tempted to hope) before the end of the apostolic generation, the survival of the Church in the condition in which Christ established it would not have posed other problems. But the reality is that the apostles died, one after the other, without Christ's return, as did St. Paul, who had been added to their number. Had the primitive organization of the Church then ceased to be? In other words, had Christ ceased to be the Head of the Church? Or would he exercise his "capital" role, outside history, through an outpouring of the Spirit on new "ministers," with no historical connection with the redemptive incarnation in which the history of salvation was consummated?

Unanimously, the second-century Church, and the Catholic Church down to our own day, responded in the negative to these questions, which are closely interrelated. We cannot observe the slightest disaggreement, the least uncertainty, in the beginning or in what followed. Christ's presence and the presence of his mystery in us are so essential to the Gospel of salvation that it is inconceivable that this could change without the Church's ceasing to be herself. If the primitive Church, as close as she was to Christ, had need of a "ministry" that would represent him in his role as Head in relation to the Body, this must be all the more true for the Church of the following centuries. And since this "ministry" was exercised in the beginning by those whom he sent, as the Father sent him, the Church of the subapostolic generation had the spontaneous, general, and unrefuted conviction that other "envoys" exercise it, now and forever, in continuity with the first ones, just as they were in continuity with Jesus. It would soon be said that the bishops "succeeded" the apostles, but it might be more precise to say that the apostles "survive" in the bishops, to whom they transmitted the very core of their function: guaranteeing the active presence of Christ as Head among us, just as the presence of the Son introduced the presence, the reign, of the Father on earth.

The first use of the idea or formula of the "succession" of the bishops from the apostles is found in St. Irenaeus.[48] With him, its application was defined by a precise concern: guaranteeing that the doctrine preached by the Church of the second century was the same as that of the first. This constancy in the faith, proclaimed with the authority of Christ himself, is verified, according to Irenaeus, in the fact that everywhere there were lists of local bishops succeeded the apostles and that the first on each list had always been established by an apostle.[49] Lists of this type multiplied everywhere, down to a time when their composition became too late to rely on. Pertinacity in trying to form these lists, far beyond a time when one could do so with certainty, shows the unanimous conviction (as well as the importance attached to them): no bishop in the Church is legitimate if his episcopacy, through that of his predecessors, is not in continuity with the "apostolate" in the strict sense.

An interesting divergence has been noted in the lists in question when they attempted to enumerate the successions. Some consider the original apostle "the first" in the episcopal list while others reserve this title for the first bishop to succeed him.[50] This reveals the sense of a problem: if bishops succeed the apostles, they do not succeed them in their entire function. Again we find the analogue of what we have already pointed out with respect to Christ and the apostles: Christ sent the Apostles *just as* he was sent by the Father. We emphasize "just as" to point up what the two "sendings" have in common: just as the Father was with or in the Son, the Son is with or in his apostles. Yet the difference is no less striking. Christ was sent to us to be the author of our salvation; the Apostles were sent to us only to transmit to us the salvation brought about by Christ.

Similarly, the bishops, after the apostles and like them, transmit salvation to us in the Word and the sacramental signs accompanying it, in which the active presence of the proclaimed mystery is affirmed. But only the apostles have the function of being the "foundations" of the Church, which is no more transmittable than the function of bringing about salvation.[51]

Indeed, it was essential for the apostles to have been the witnesses of the resurrection, to have been chosen, and, above all, to have been sent by Christ himself to bear witness with authority and, on this basis, found the Church.[52] And once the Church of Christ was founded by the apostles whom Christ sent for that purpose, no one had the right to build on any foundation other than the one established by them. We may even say that they themselves constitute this foundation—first by their very existence and then by the exercise of their proper function.

Unlike the apostles, bishops exist only in an already existing Church, which is the very one founded by the apostles and is exactly as they established it. Their function, then, is not to set up another Church nor, even less, to modify the fundamental creation. Their function is to preserve and "keep" it as it has been established and, of course, to extend it, but always on this basis and never on any other.

It is precisely this incumbent need, to "keep" what has been transmitted to them by the apostles, that defines the essential aspect of their ministry in the line of the apostles: to represent, in turn, the person of the Head in the midst of his Body. Consequently, in all subsequent generations, as in the first, it will always be Christ who speaks with authority, who acts and decides in the Church (through the men he chose), so that his "mystery" may be communicated and his Body extended to all men (at least to all who believe in their word).

We thus arrive at a second meaning of the expression "apostolic succession," where we no longer consider only the local succession of the bishops of a particular Church, one from the other, and all of them from an apostle who was a founder. We are now concerned with succession in the act of "sending," that is, in what what will be called the "consecration" that each bishop receives from the episcopal college of his time and which the college, in its entirety, received at the beginning from the apostolic college. But it is important to point out that if the technical use of "apostolic succession," to designate this continuity of the acts of "sending" the chief ministers over the centuries, is secondary or later in date, the idea appears at the end of the apostolic age. The epistle of Clement of Rome, however "archaic" it may be (it is generally considered to be contemporary with the New Testament Pastoral Epistles), was already categorical: the apostles themselves established the first responsible men of the *episkope* and it was by their command that this function is to subsist as a matter of course.[53]

The conviction of the second-century Church, that it had handed down all essentials for all other centuries to the Catholic Church, causes no problem: the bishops are everywhere established and everywhere they are considered to have succeeded the Apostles, in the limited but very strong sense that we have just defined. What causes a problem and what explains (to a certain extent) the difficulty that many Protestants have in accepting this notion of the apostolic succession, passed on to the bishops, as essential to a legitimate ministry in the Church is that, lacking sufficient documents, we have no clear view of the modalities whereby passage of the properly apostolic function to the episcopal function was carried out—an episcopal function, as we know it, from the second century. As has been said, in the first century we see the apostles established and establishing the Church: in the second century, we discover that the bishops occupied, without question or hesitation, the place that the apostles left free. But in between is a kind of tunnel in which we are unable to discern the details of a transmission which may have been conducted in rather complex forms.[54]

The Pastoral Epistles and, to a certain extent, the epistle of Clement, confirmed by fragmentary recollections or apparent local anomalies which seem to be in disaccord with a modified situation, allow us to grasp some of the conditions that must have prepared the transition and facilitated the transmission. It is certain that in an age when the apostles still controlled the Churches they founded, and the question of their succession had not yet been posed or had barely been mentioned, they were encouraging, if not causing—in any case "consecrating," in one way or another—ministries other than their own.

After the great Pauline epistles, which speak only of "prophets" and *didaskaloi* within each Church (although they also give a glimpse of the work of the "apostles" of second rank whom the "preeminent" apostles joined to themselves—as well as the deacons, whose ministry, however important, is and will always remain essentially subordinate), the Pastoral Epistles speak of "bishops" and "presbyters."[55] Clearly, we are dealing here with stable functions into which one enters through the laying on of hands.[56] But we are scarcely informed about the possible distinction between the two functions or, furthermore, the precise obligations and capacities that both might carry with them.

At least by the middle of the second century, when there had been no "original" Apostles for several generations, there was *a* bishop, everywhere, who claimed apostolic inheritance and was assisted by a council of "presbyters." We are assured by the epistles of Ignatius of Antioch that from the beginning of the century, in Asia Minor at least, not only did this situation exist, it could pass as strictly normative.[57]

One or two generations later (judging by the epistle of Clement) it seems at first sight that in Rome itself the situation was not so clear. Reading certain passages from this text, we should say that *episkopos* and *presbyteros* are terms that may still be applied undiscriminatingly to the same persons, and the *episkope* in a given Church is not the function of one person alone but of a college.[58] We must admit, however, that elsewhere in the same epistle the function of the *episkopos*, at least at the liturgical assembly, already seems to be the function of one person alone.[59]

On the basis of these apparent divergences, to state that the "monarchical" episcopate was everywhere established from the outset, following the apostles and at their command, would seem to go beyond what reasonable proof can support. And there is no better reason for asserting that a plural presbyterateespiscopate was the general rule, succeeding the apostles locally, which was progressively concentrated and differentiated, within one *episkopos*, assisted by a council of *presbyteroi*. Starting with such hypothesis, we cannot satisfactorily account for the essential fact: this latter system, and it alone triumphed practically everywhere in 150 years, at the most, and no one can point to hesitancy or resistance anywhere. Everywhere, at this date, the bishop has the conviction of being—in a sense that pertains only to him, a "successor" of the apostles, at the head of Christ's flock.

Whatever the case and by whatever simple or complex devolution the transition was made from the apostles to the episcopate, it is—once again—a conviction essential to the Church of the second century (as to that of the first) that Christ, invisibly but really, through a special ministry remains present in the Body of his Church as its Head. The institution of this ministry goes back to him, in historical continuity with his activity prior to his cross and resurrection. In the first century, this ministry is that of the apostles, whom he himself sent, as he had been sent by the Father. In the second century, this ministry is that of the bishops, and everyone acknowledges that they, similarly, were "sent" by the apostles with the function of "keeping" their work, in the sense we have defined.[60]

To reject this succession is to reject not only a particular ministry—that of the episcopate as it appears fully constituted in the second century—it is also to reject any possibility for the Church of the postapostolic generations to continue being the same Church established by Christ on the foundation of the apostles, that is, a Church in which Christ, in his representatives, remains actually the "Head," the "Head of the Body," through a ministry in historical continuity with his own activity on earth before and after his resurrection. If this were the case, Christ's promise could no longer be applied to any ministry in the Church: "Who hears you hears me, who rejects you rejects me, and he who rejects me rejects him who sent me." The Church would have forever lost the historical relationship with Christ in his redemptive incarnation, which alone makes it possible to attribute to him and to him alone, in a realistic sense, the title "Head of the Church."

What, then, is to be thought of the supposition that is sometimes upheld in the churches of the Reformation, where the continuity of the apostolic succession has been lost but a ministry has been reconstituted, that they be acknowledged as the ministry of Christ himself: the whole Church, as a totality, succeeded the apostles? Would it pertain to her, in her entirety, at each age, under a form most appropriate to the circumstances, to transmit this succession to her pastors?[61]

Like most of the errors that, sooner or later, vitiated the development of the Protestant Reformation, this theory is not an invention of the sixteenth-century reformers or their disciples. We see it appear at the close of the Middle Ages, with civil jurists like Marsilius of Padua and with theologians like William of Ockham.[62] But it is completely unknown to the whole of ancient Christian tradition, and for good reason, for its origins have nothing either

Christian or religious about them. They are a simple tracing onto Christian theology of a juridical fiction of late Roman law, according to which authority in the state belongs originally to the mass of people, which delegates it to the sovereign. Under more or less nominally democratic externals, we are dealing with a demagogic justification of dictatorial powers, concentrated in one individual, which is the lot of all democracies that degenerate: the tyrannical rule of the last Roman emperors or, most precisely, the so-called absolute monarchies at the end of the Middle Ages, which Marsilius of Padua and his successors wished to justify. Even with William of Ockham the introduction into ecclesiology of theories of this kind, while claiming to bring the Church back to her evangelical origins, tended to turn authority in the Church over to the princes. With the Gallicans, who tried to revive these theories—Marca, Marcantonio de Dominis, Ellies Dupin[63]—when they did not hand the Church over to the political sovereign, these theories put her under the power of any kind of ruling caste which was deemed to express "the people" but was more capable of exploiting them than concerned with representing them.

Even when this was no longer the case, this "democratism" was completely opposed to the constitution of the Church, willed by Christ, on the basis of responsible persons chosen and instituted by him. And, let us add, it completely misunderstood the meaning of the gospel at the end of the Bible, where salvation, far from being able to proceed from the masses, can come to them only from an exceptional individual, prepared and produced by a completely gratuitous divine intervention.

Moreover, to say this is quite different from excluding any association of the whole Body of the Church from the designation of her members who may be called to lead.[64] That such an association would be fully natural and, as such, highly desirable is again the unanimous feeling of Christian antiquity, and we shall see the reasons for it. The fathers and the sacred writers never confused this association of the whole Body with its management, particularly in the choice of its representative heads (who, according to the divine plan, must represent first and above all the only real Head, Christ) with the source of the pastoral function in general or the capacity to exercise it. This source, according to all the fathers and the whole of the New Testament, can be found only in the institution by Christ of the essential pastoral function and the "sending" of his successive appointees, always going back to him alone, by those whom he alone chose and sent at the beginning and by those whom they in turn chose and sent in his Name.[65] The apostolic succession concerns the whole Church, as we shall see, but at her beginning and at each period of her history it was not from the Church as a totality that it proceeded but from Christ to the apostles, from the apostles to the first bishops, and from them to their successors. Whatever the intermediary stages of transition from the apostolate to the fully formed episcopate, there is no hint of the masses' hold on the primitive apostolic authority, from which it would have been extracted to the advantage of the bishops. Individually or otherwise, it was to the men they instituted that the apostles transmitted, on their responsibility, everything that was transmittable; it was from these latter that the bishops received it in turn; and it is only the bishops who continue the succession.[66]

One final consideration must be added. The notions of the ministry and its authority in the Church that claim to be democratic are based on an illusion. Even if the theories we have just discarded had not been products of a legalism that invoked democracy, the better to stifle it by transposing to the Church notions which belong solely to the city politic, we should not disregard the radical difference between the two. Undoubtedly (we have stressed this sufficiently to dispense us from returning to it at length) the Church exists only in concrete communities, localized in space and time, but (as we have also said) the local Church, each time she comes together, invisibly but really calls together and assembles with her the Church of everywhere and every age: the one and total Body of Christ. Consequently, a ministry which must be representative of the Church, the whole Church, will never be such if it represents only those who are visibly assembled, not even if it represents an organization of churches on a worldwide scale. Even in the name of "democracy," properly understood and applied to the *demos* under consideration, the People of God, we must take exception to the representativeness of any ministry that would represent merely the *present* members of the Church. Such a ministry could never represent the Church in her true reality, the true People of God in their catholic unity, transcending time and space, unless it can represent this Church not only in its strictly limited actuality but also in its historical totality: the whole "communion of saints," in which those who have transmitted the faith to us remain inseparable from this life in love, in the Spirit, which they have transmitted to us with their own human experience of reality.

This historical reality of the Church—a reality, we must add, which is also eschatological, including the future "saints" as well as all those of the past in the Christ of the Parousia—exists only as rooted in the historical Christ from whom she proceeds, in her common subsistence and in the concrete form which he impressed on her once and for all. Therefore there cannot be an ecclesiastical ministry that represents the whole Body of the Church if, first of all, it does not represent her Head: if it does not emanate from the Head himself in the way he chose and instituted—that is, the way of his apostles and those to whom the apostles, in turn, gave the task of perpetuating this responsibility with regard to Christ's flock, entrusted to them by Christ—to them and to no one else.[67]

## Notes

1. Cf. 1 Peter 2:4 and 5 and Ephesians 2:16-21. On the object of this chapter, see par. 7 in chap. 1 of the constitution *Lumen Gentium* and pars. 18 to 20 in chap. 3.
2. Cf. John 3:3-6 and Romans 6:3-11.
3. 1 Corinthians 15:45 and Ephesians 2:15 and 4:24.
4. Cf. *Adversus haereses,* lib. 4, cap. 10, and esp. cap. 12:4.
5. Romans 8:15
6. 1 John 3:1.
7. *Adversus haereses,* 4, praef., 4; 4, 20, 1; 5, 6, 1, and 5, 28, 3. Cf. J. Lebreton, *Histoire du Dogme de la Trinite* (Paris, 1928), 3. 2:579ff.
8. Cf. Romans 8:6 and 27 and 1 Corinthians 2:16.
9. Cf. 2 Corinthians 3:17 and 1 Corinthians 15:45.
10. Cf., with the two texts cited in the preceding note, Acts 10:38, 13:7, Romans 1:4, 8:9, Galatians 4:6, Philippians 1:19, 1 Peter 1:11.
11. Cf. John 14:16ff. and 16:7ff.
12. Cf. J. L. Leuba, *L'Institution et l'Evènement* (Paris, 1950), and O. Cullmann, *Christ et le Temps* (Paris, 1947), pp. 86ff.
13. Cf. A. Feuillet, *Le Christ Sagesse de Dieu,* pp. 225ff.
14. See W. Pannenberg, *Offenbarung als Geschichte* (1961).
15. The idea of the Church as an extension of the incarnation is undoubtedly found for the first time in J. A. Moehler, *Symbolik,* pars. 34 and 36. It is obvious that this idea cannot be taken literally, but it aims at expressing a twofold, incontestable truth: (1) the conjoint instrumentality of Christ's humanity, whereby—according to St. Thomas—his divinity saves us in the redemptive incarnation, is extended to us in order to apply grace to us in the sacramentality of the Church; (2) the Church therefore has existence only in her historical attachment to the unique incarnation of the Son of the Saving God. Cf. Geiselmann, "La definition de l'Eglise chez J. A. Moehler," in *L'Ecclésiologie au XIXe siècle,* p. 162.
16. Cf. above, p. 248.
17. See Galatians 3.
18. Romans 8:2.
19. Hebrews 13:8.
20. Cf. Ephesians 2:14-22, 1 Corinthians 3-17, 6:19, and 2 Corinthians 6:16.
21. Cf. Ephesians 2:20, 1 Corinthians 3:10-12, and Revelation 21:14.

22. Matthew 16:18.
23. Ephesians 4:1–16.
24. Cf. Ephesians 5:29–30.
25. In *Theologisches Wörterbuch*, see the articles by Rengstorf.
26. Matthew 10:40.
27. Cf. John 17:18 and 20, 21.
28. Matthew 28:19–20.
29. John 20:22–23.
30. Matthew 16:19.
31. Matthew 18:18.
32. John 8:19 (cf. v. 16) and 16:32.
33. John 4:34, 5:24 and 30, 6:38, 9:4, and 3:34, 5:38, 6,29, 10:36, 17:3.
34. See G. Kittel's article, in his *Theologisches Wörterbuch*, on the term *logos*.
35. 1 John 4:9, 10, and 14.
36. Colossians 1:22.
37. 2 Corinthians 5:19. Cf. Colossians 1:20 and 22 and Ephesians 2:16.
38. 2 Corinthians 5:18.
39. Cf. Matthew 28:20 and John 14:15 and 15:10; 1:12.
40. Rengstorf (in the article mentioned) and after him Dom Gregory Dix ("The Ministry in the Early Church," in Kirk, *The Apostolic Ministry*, pp. 228ff.) were among the first to underline the connection. Yet it must not be exaggerated. What is merely a juridical fiction in the Jewish *shaliach* becomes a mystical reality in the Gospel. This is why the Christian apostles, contrary to the *sheliim*, could furnish themselves with associates or successors.
41. Cf. Genesis 24.
42. 2 Corinthians 5:19.
43. *Tractatus VI in Joannem* and *XV*, P. L. 35, cols. 1428ff. and 1511.
44. See the study of Fr. Congar, "Ordre et juridiction dans l'Eglise, "in *Sainte Eglise* (Paris, 1963), pp. 203ff.
45. See below, chap. 11.
46. Colossians 1:27 and 1 Corinthians 15:28.
47. Colossians 2:19 and Ephesians 4:16.
48. *Adversus haereses*, 3, 3, 1.
49. Cf. *Adversus haereses*, 3, 3, 3.
50. On the ancient episcopal lists given by Eusebius in his *Ecclesiastical History* and his *Chronicle*, see the article "Evêques" by F. Prat in *Dictionnaire de Théologie catholique*.
51. As we shall see, most difficulties of Protestant theologians with the idea of apostolic succession arose from untoward expressions of this doctrine: as far back as the Middle Ages we see theologians or canonists expressing themselves as if the bishops were other apostles, succeeding the first in all

their functions and powers. On this subject, see Y. M.-J. Congar, "Composantes et idée de la succession apostolique," in *Oecumenica, Jahrbuch für ökumenische Forschung* (Minneapolis–Neuchâtel, 1966), pp. 61ff. This position, if taken literally, is as indefensible on the basis of patristics as on the New Testament. That it could have been upheld is explained by the fact that the New Testament itself uses the word "apostle" sometimes in a strict sense and sometimes in a broader sense, including the associates of the Twelve or of St. Paul, or even, quite simply, retains the word in its ancient Jewish acceptation (as seems to be the case when it mentions the "apostles" of the Churches).

52. On the exact nature of the apostolate in the strictest sense and the problems posed by the different uses of the word in St. Paul, cf. Rengstorf, op. cit., n. 25, and H. von Campenhausen, Kirchliches Amt und geistliche Vollmacht (Tübingen, 1953), the whole of chaps. 2 and 3.

53. Cf. Clement de Rome, *Spirit of Corinthians* 42.

54. This question has been especially studied in recent years by Anglican theologians for their discussions with other Protestants in connection with the development of ecumenism. See in particular (in K. E. Kirk, *The Apostolic Ministry* [London, 1947], the studies of A. M. Farrer and Dom G. Dix (pp. 113ff. and 183ff.). We must also mention J. Colson, *Les fonctions ecclésiales aux deux premiers siècles* (Paris, 1956); P. Benoit, "Les origines apostoliques de l'épiscopat dans le Nouveau Testament, "in *L'Evêque dans l'Eglise du Christ* (Paris, 1960), pp. 13ff.; M. M. Bourke, "Reflections on Church Order in the New Testament," in *Catholic Biblical Quarterly* (1968), 30:493ff,; J. Ratzinger, *Das neue Volk Gottes* (Düsseldorf, 1969), pp. 75ff.

55. On the prophets and the *didaskaloi,* see 1 Corinthians 12:28–29, 14:29 and 32, and Ephesians 2:20, 3:4, 4:11. These texts connect them with the Apostles. 2 Corinthians 8:3 and Philippians 2:25 (at least) use this latter term to designate people other than the Twelve or Paul. *Episkopos* is already found in Philippians 1:1 (as well as *diakonos*), then in 1 Timothy 3:2 and Titus 1:7. *Presbyteros* has the certain sense of a minister of the Church in 1 Timothy 5:17 and Titus 1:5 (also James 5:14).

56. 1 Timothy 4:14 and 2 Timothy 1:6.

57. See in particular his epistles to the Philippians (4), the Smyrniots (8, 1 and 2), the Magnesians (6, 1), and the Ephesians (4).

58. This is the case particularly in chap. 44.

59. Cf. 40:5.

60. This is well explained by J. Langmead Casserley in his *Christian Community* (New York, 1960), pp. 37ff.

61. There is a good discussion of this point by T. G. Jalland in K. E. Kirk, op. cit., pp. 305ff.

62. Cf. V. Martin, *Les origines du Gallicanisme* (Paris, 1939), 1:33ff., and B. Tierney, *Foundations of the Conciliar Theory* (2d ed.; Cambridge, 1968), pp. 7ff., 44ff., 177ff.

63. Cf. above, p. 49.

64. Cf. below, chap. 8.

65. Besides the texts of Irenaeus mentioned in n. 48 and 49 and the lists of Eusebius mentioned in n. 50, cf. Tertullian, *De Praescriptione,* 32, P.L. 2, col, 52, and Jerome, *In Tit.,* 1, 5, P.L. 26, cols, 595ff.

66. It is surprising that H. Küng's book *The Church* does not even seem to suspect the existence of the texts and facts we have just examined.

67. This is the meaning of the famous definition of the Church by St. Cyprian: *"Ecclesia plebs sacerdoti unita et pastori suo grex adhaerens. Unde scire debes episcopum in Ecclesia esse et Ecclesiam in episcopo"* (Epist. 69, ad Pupian., 8, P.L. 4, col. 406). In other words, in the Church established by Christ upon the apostles, the People of God can no more exist separately from the bishops than the bishops can exist outside this People. See the excellent reflections of J. Mouroux in *Vers l'Unité* (March 1970), pp. 21ff.

# Chapter 6
# Apostolic Succession and Tradition

## I. *The Apostolic Mission and the Service of the Incarnate Word*

The apostolic ministry and its succession (to which our previous chapter was dedicated) are undoubtedly essential factors of the Church as willed by Christ—the Church that, immediately after the resurrection, was the result of his teaching and action, the apostolic Church that has been perpetuated to us through the Catholic Church. This point is perhaps most commonly lost sight of today among Protestants, and it is essential, for full ecumenism and for authentic Christianity, that its importance be stressed. Since the First World War, in Protestantism itself, the New Testament studies of Karl Ludwig Schmidt and, especially, the school of Uppsala, under the instigation of Anton Friedrichsen and his followers, and Olof Linton in particular, have greatly contributed to a new emphasis on this point.[1]

Yet this problem of the ministry and the apostolic succession cannot be reduced to its formal aspect, which we have just examined. Precisely this temptation (or rather this more or less conscious and radical attempt) to so reduce it gave rise to the most negative reactions from Protestants. It is a fallacious exaltation of the ministry in question if we would separate it, in fact or intention, from what may be called its matter, its content, or its object (the term is unimportant).

We have already brought this out, and it is not without profound significance. The first formulations of the apostolic succession in the second century did not so envision it, but never considered it apart from its primary reason for being, which is continuity in a teaching that remains substantially the same from Christ down to us. For if Christ instituted the Apostles, "the Twelve" it was so they might be his "witnesses": first the witnesses of his teaching and then of his works, which are inseparable from it, and finally of his divine incarnate Person, recognized and received as such in accordance with the two ways of doctrine and holy action, which are basically one.[2]

In other words, the phrase "he who hears you hears me, he who receives you receives me," addressed to the apostles by their Master, is not for them, even less for their successors, a kind of blank check that bestowed on them an authority that would not only be unlimited but undetermined. Quite the contrary: the authority that devolved upon them—participation in his authority— is so considerable only because it is (and can only be) a simple instrument of the perpetuation (a progressive and unceasing extension of) *his own* authority.

The apostles and *a fortiori* their successors are only "ministers" or "servants" of Christ, for his Body everywhere and at every stage of its development. The essential aspect of their ministry, and its very basis, is handing on the truth of Christ, that very truth he taught, the truth of what he did, of what he is and forever remains. As responsible and authentic "witnesses" (because they were instituted and commissioned by Christ himself and are unceasingly assisted by his Spirit), the apostles are witnesses of a truth that surpasses them, to which they were the first to submit.

As was the case with the prophets, the truth the apostles hand on, the Word they proclaim, is not a truth over which they would be masters, however this may be understood. It is not even a truth that would properly belong to them as an individual communication. All together, they are witnesses of a unique public truth, which is public insofar as it is the truth that belongs *to all the People of God:* the last and final development of the revelation that began with Abraham and unfolded with Christ.

Again, each prophet had his own words to say in this progressive unfolding, his new note to bring to it, even though no revelation, or rather no progress in revelation, can be isolated from its totality. But with the apostles and even more with the Church after them, this is no longer the case. The whole truth, all *the* truth that was to be revealed to us with the coming of Jesus, the Christ, the living Word Made Flesh, exists now that he has appeared, spoken, and manifested himself in his life, death, and resurrection. There could no longer be a question of an apostle's complementing this revelation, which is ultimately, and can only be, the direct revelation of God in Jesus Christ. Undoubtedly, one or another apostle, or some of their companions, whom they chose as "evangelists" (whom, in this context, the Church placed on the same level as the apostles), through a providential disposition could have been capable of shedding more light on a particular aspect of this inexhaustible revelation which is made to us in Christ. But for all of them as a whole and for each one individually, as later for their disciples and successors, the revelation was *something received,* and *received from without.* The fact that they received it will not distinguish them from the rest forever—only the fact that they were the first to receive it and that only through them, as intermediaries, others receive it forever.

If this is true of the apostles, it is all the more true of their successors. Undoubtedly, they too, like the apostles, must develop the received truth (in a way that will never be so "fundamental") in order to communicate it—a truth that is always the same under indefinitely varied circumstances. If, with the apostles, there were different and complementary points of view on the unique and total truth that allow us to grasp its various dimensions, it is not on this level that diversity and development come into play with their successors and their collaborators. It is simply in concrete, progressive application of the basic evangelical truth, starting from its first formulation by the apostles, and, in building the Church over the ages, its extension from one place to another and from one civilization to another.

In the first stage, no less strictly than in the following, the truth—whether transmitted to the apostles or by their successors—is received and handed on, a "deposit" faithfully preserved and communicated, a *paratheke:* a tradition in the sense of something that is handed on, which from the outset transcends those who transmit it and remains transcendent in later ages. This is reflected, as it were, in the ministry of the apostles and in that of their successors: it is only a *paradosis,* a tradition indeed, but this time in the sense of handing on the deposit, the *paratheke.*[3]

Contemporary studies of the New Testament, particularly those of C. H. Dodd, make a clear distinction between two correlative elements from the beginning of this tradition, *kerygma* and *didache,*[4] and one can follow their development throughout the patristic age. *Kerygma* is the objective announcement and proclamation of the great deeds of God, accomplished once and for all in Jesus Christ. It is the object of the missionary teaching of the Church: the proclamation of Christ to all peoples. Its preeminent formulation is in the symbols of faith, whose composition and development have received special study by Kattenbusch and Kelly. The great dogmatic "definitions" of the later councils had no other aim than to specify their exact meaning when confronted by distorted interpretations.

From the very beginning, the *didache* has been much more complex. Following Dodd's studies, it can be said that if the *kerygma* specifies what God has done for us, the *didache* endeavors to determine what must result for us and, especially, what our response to the divine initiative must be. Its matter is everything that can be called spirituality and Christian ethics, as well as the *praxis* of the Church on the canonical and, particularly, the liturgical plane: the whole content of the Church's preaching to her members. "Catechesis" is the passage from *kerygma* to the details of the *didache*.

Yet this difference must not be overstressed. In a sense, the *didache* is contained in the *kerygma,* properly understood, for the *kerygma* inspires it, gives it its meaning, and (above all) its form. On the other hand, the *kerygma,* cut off from the *didache,* might lapse into abstraction or (at the very least) a fallacious "objectivism" which would conceal the extent it touches, takes possession of, and reforms our very lives.

An even more profound error would be to consider the *kerygma* or the *didache* collections of formulas, whether their interrelationship be perceived or not. Undoubtedly, neither can have a definite reality outside carefully set formulas, and it is the letter of these formulas and their relative fixedness (particularly as regards the *kerygma*) to which the Church seems to have been most attentive from the beginning; and there is no doubt that she took this concern from the systematic teaching of Christ himself. This does not obscure the fact that there has been from the beginning, and constantly throughout the tradition of the fathers and again with the great Scholastics, a keen sense of the *kerygma's* unity, and that this unity of a group of formulas could not be reduced to a supreme formula that would engulf all the others or from which the others could be deduced.

This unity of the *kerygma,* from which are derived its extension in the much more multiform richness of the *didache* and the same unity which is no less subjacent to it, can indeed be called vital. Still more precisely, it is the unity of a living person: the divine person of the Word Made Flesh. The common schema of all varieties of the symbol of faith attests to it. This personal unity of the Christian truth is asserted within the unity of a history, the history of salvation, extending to the whole world at the very moment it was concentrated on the personal history of Jesus Christ.[5]

This corresponds exactly to what St. Paul, at the beginning of the First Epistle to the Corinthians, calls "the mystery." And it can be said, reciprocally, that the object of the whole of Christian tradition, the content of the *paratheke,* radiating throughout the *didache* and concentrated within the *kerygma,* is also (and only) "the mystery." Correlatively, St. Paul defined the apostolic ministry as one of "servants [*hyperetas,* the term applied to the *hazan* in the synagogue] of Christ and dispensers of the mysteries of God."[6]

This explanation of what he understands by "the mystery" (we have already mentioned this but now is the time to show its consequences) appears in a context of "wisdom" and "apocalypse." We find this context precisely defined in the Old Testament, in the second chapter of the Book of Daniel, whose terminology is taken up word for word in the First Epistle to the Corinthians, where divine "wisdom" is God's plan for the history of the whole of mankind, which tends toward its resolution through the special history of the People of God. The unfolding of this plan not only surpasses the conjectures of human wisdom but eludes the calculations of the Jewish wise men who endeavored to decipher the Divine Word by relying on their own lights. For this reason it is wisdom *en mysterio:* a scandal for the Jews and folly for the Greeks. The key to the Scriptures, like the key to the history of the whole of mankind, can be found only in a final "revelation" of the Spirit. This revelation coincides with the supreme divine act that completes the history of salvation, which the Old Covenant made ready for and sketched out in advance. This key is "the mystery," the last secret of the divine plan which is discovered only in its realization. Again, in order to be grasped it demands the final communication of this Spirit of God, who alone can plumb the divine depths. This communication results from the accomplished "mystery" and, in turn, illuminates it.

The mystery, then, is Christ and, even more precisely, the unity of all he said and did, which is discovered in his cross when illuminated by faith in his resurrection. It is from this mystery that sacred history acquires its definitive meaning, while human history in general and each man in particular ultimately finds in it not only its own explanation but its own resolution.

As the Captivity Epistles emphasize, in this mystery of Christ on the cross, in his Body reconciling all men among themselves as well as with God, the separation between Jews and pagans is removed: all discover that they are "one" in the unique Body of Christ—so that the Apostle summed up everything in this statement: "the mystery, Christ in you, the hope of glory."[7]

This, then, is the tradition of which the apostles are the first transmitters, and the bishops following them: a once-and-for-all revealed truth, a communicated truth of which they are the authorized witnesses, the *economes* who are to dispense it to mankind. And this, at the same time, is their "service" to this "lord," who, despite the fact that he is "Lord and Master," willed to appear among us in the condition of a servant.[8]

## II. The Word of the Mystery and Its Life Content

If the tradition of evangelical truth, which is the reason for the apostolic ministry and its perpetual succession in the Church until the parousia, is the handing on of the "mystery" (a transmission we have just explained), there are fundamental consequences for this tradition and for the ministry which, properly speaking, is its service.

In the first place, if it is the tradition of a truth, revealed once and for all in the Person of the Incarnate Word, in the personal history of Jesus of Nazareth, Son of God made man, it is the tradition of a *truth of life,* which is inseparable in its transmission from the transmission of this life. The *kerygma* announces how the entry of the divine life into human history, progressively prepared throughout Israel's history, burst forth in the personal history of Christ. The *didache* teaches, as a consequence immediately flowing from it, how this divine life, lived in our humanity by the Son of God, signifies renewal of the life of all mankind and, above all, our own life, since we receive this teaching in faith.

To receive the tradition of evangelical truth in the Church and to enter into the communication of this life which constitutes the Church of the New Testament is therefore one and the same thing. By the very nature of this truth, "believing" the evangelical truth is inseparable from "doing" what is true, according to a typically Johannine expression,[9] for "believing," in the Gospel sense, is believing that this life of God, manifested in his Son made man, tends to take possession of our life as men to make it a life of "the children of God." This is the experience to which a man who enters the Church is called: the experience of the Church becoming his own.

This life communication, supposed by the communication of evangelical truth, is affirmed in the sacraments. Indeed, they appear as the tokens of the reality proclaimed to us by the Word of God, by which they are proposed as actions that we reproduce in faith but in which we are "actuated" by God. Still more definitely, they are the symbolic (but essentially realistic) encounters in which, if we approach them in the faith, their saving action, accomplished once and for all in Jesus Christ, takes over our activity, assimilates us to Christ in his mystery of salvation, and makes this salvation present in us.[10]

As we have said, even the Old Testament saw the acceptance in faith of God's Word by the People of God and, at the same time, the consecration of this same People through the power of this Word—to the accomplishment in them of the plan it revealed as they came together and the plan was fulfilled in the covenant ritual. The liturgy of the Israelites, and particularly their sacrificial liturgy, thus became a perpetual "memorial" of God's actions, given by God himself so that their permanent efficacy might be extended into the history of the People and thereby lead them to ultimate fulfillment of the re-creative plan. In the successive assemblies of the *qahal,* of the *ecclesia* of the People throughout the stages of their history, the re-presentation to God of the memorial of his great deeds called for realization of his promises with certainty that they would come about. The supplication accompanying the memorial was a flowering of faith in God's fidelity, since it was based entirely on this pledge, given by him to continue, renew, and complete the work that had begun.

In the last cultic assemblies of the synagogue, more than ever—after the reading of the Word of God and at the end of the community meals—the act of thanksgiving for the history of salvation sketched out at the time of the "fathers" and now tending toward its eschatological term, was extended in an invocation of this kind. Based on this presentation of the "memorial" as a pledge of the promised future (outlined in the past, though still imminent), it called for its last fulfillment. Within this context, Christ, after he announced and promulgated the definitive fulfillment in himself of all the prophecies at the Last Supper, made bread and wine the immediate objects of his "eucharist," the memorial of his saving death. In representing them to the Father in future acts of thanksgiving for his resurrection, his followers will invoke his ultimate Parousia with assurance, anticipated in their communion in his body and blood—one broken, the other poured out "for the forgiveness of sins."[11]

Within this perspective, the eucharistic celebration is unceasingly renewed for the Church. An event in which the "mystery" which is fundamentally Christ and his cross and has been accomplished, once and for all, becomes in all reality, for the faith that accepts the divine signs, "Christ in us, the hope of glory." For the Church, therefore, the Eucharist is an actualization of the mystery of the cross, revealed in the resurrection, illuminated for us at the same time that it was appropriated by us in the gift of the Spirit; and the Parousia is anticipated, at the same time, as the definitive accomplishment of the mystery of the Head in his members.

The first part of the eucharistic celebration, dominated by the reading of Scripture, in which the proclamation of the Word culminates, is directed toward the preeminent proclamation of the "mystery" in the Church. The eucharistic banquet is its natural consequence: the "mystery" celebrated in the praise of faith finds in us, in the Church, its sacramental fulfillment; that is, it is mystically real. Only because of this is its "proclamation" effective, as the proclamation of a fact which concerns us and reaches its fulfillment only "in us."

We said above that the tradition of Christian truth, entrusted to the apostolic ministry, is properly the tradition of the "mystery." Since it is in the eucharistic celebration that the mystery is not only proclaimed but communicated, or rather proclaimed as communicated, we can say that the tradition of the New and Eternal Covenant is more concretely the tradition of the Eucharist. Since the evangelical truth is a truth of life, it is especially in what the Church does, which is most essential to her life, that she transmits this truth.

This comes down to saying that in the heart of Christian tradition is a certain cultic model, a dynamic schema of the eucharistic celebration which is not merely a particularly enlightening consequence of the truth transmitted to the Church by Christ and entrusted to the apostles, but the radical expression of this truth. At the heart of the tradition is the tradition of the eucharistic prayer, the canon or *anaphora,* on which the whole celebration is centered and in which all its "force lines" are revealed in harmonious conjunction.[12]

From this comes the analogy that has long been observed between the structure of the confessions of faith, in which the *kerygma* finds its fundamental expressions, and that of the eucharistic prayer. But it would be wrong to imagine that this prayer was modeled on a previous symbol of faith. Undoubtedly, at a late date the more elaborate confessions often took the form of "remodeled eucharists;" however, the systematic formulation of the *kerygma* did not give rise to the primitive "eucharist," but the opposite. The adage *Legem credendi statuat lex supplicandi*[13] must *not* be understood as if the prayer of the Church, the most immediate response to the Divine Word, had been traced from a previously explicitated credo and reflected it. The opposite happened; and beginning with the Church's adherence to the evangelical Word in the prayer of her faith, the definite formulation of this faith evolved and was poured out.

Jesus did not teach a theory of his sacrifice, so that it could be incorporated in the eucharistic institution. On the contrary, in the definitive transfiguration of the Jewish communal banquets, brought about by him at the Last Supper and, preeminently, in the new sense he gave to their traditional *berakoth* over the bread and wine, he gave the Church the revelation of the meaning of his whole life and especially his cross. By making the two acts of thanksgiving into one unique Eucharist of his saving death, centered on the memorial of the consecrated bread and wine as communion in his Body and Blood, he forever fixed the meaning of the redemptive work he accomplished in his flesh.

On Maundy Thursday evening, Jesus completed the revelation of his Person and his work, and, in doing so, his teaching as well, by projecting on the first Christian "eucharist" the whole content of his preaching and his prior actions. Here, somewhat later, in light of the resurrection, in discovering the meaning of his cross, the disciples finally saw the meaning of his life and his message. With this supreme revelation, they formulated their *kerygma* and developed their *didache.* Consequently, in the Church's eucharistic celebration the *whole* proclamation of the mystery, and its realization in us, continues to be concentrated in the *actio eucharistica* and the prayer that consecrates it by defining it. The proclamation of the "mystery" of all the Scriptures, of the whole apostolic teaching, of the teaching of the Savior himself, handed down in the Gospel, and at the same time the numberless echoes in the totality of the Church's prayer as she attests her faith, and concentrated on this privileged and heart-felt expression constituted by the eucharistic prayer. Praise, celebration, and confession of the mystery consecrate its realization in us—communication in the Church of the Head to the members—just as this prayer expresses the mystery with unequaled fulness at its very source.

Beyond the Mass itself, the whole of the Church's worship (of which the Mass is the "hearth") contributes to detailing and thereby to illuminating and developing this same mystery, which abides in her living heart: in the eucharistic prayer and its sacramental actualization of the mystery. Above all, this is true of the divine office, which in its psalmody and hymnody extends the praise of the mystery to all the hours of the day, nurtured by unceasing meditation on the Divine Word, within the yearly unfolding of the unique mystery in the particular mysteries that make it up: from the creation, recalled before Lent, to the Parousia, anticipated at Epiphany.

This is even more valid for the sacraments and the sacramentals, whereby the sacraments are extended to the whole of human existence. The sacraments of initiation, baptism and chrismation, along with penance, which restores the virtue that is altered by infidelities, adapt us to the eucharistic celebration of the mystery in the Church. By conforming us individually to the death and resurrection of her Head, they consecrate us as living temples of his Spirit and priests of the mystery

By perpetuating the succession of the apostolic ministry in the Church and by perpetuating, at the same time, the sacramental presence of the Head as the principle of the action of the members within the Body, the sacrament of orders is the root, as it were, of this celebration, this essentially eucharistic communication of the mystery. On the other hand, the sacrament of the sick completes the fulfillment of Christ's sufferings in our flesh and consecrates us definitively for participation in his resurrection. Symmetrically, the sacrament of marriage (to which we must connect, as its complement, the consecration of solemn monastic profession), by giving to the natural fecundity of created life the seal of the cross, prepares the supernatural transfiguration of the cosmos which will follow the Parousia.

This shows that the apostolic ministry and its succession, in addition to being a ministry of teaching the evangelical "truth," is a liturgical ministry so it can be the efficacious ministry of the propagation of *this* truth. If the apostles and their successors, the bishops, are basically doctors, they can teach the truth entrusted to them, can truly transmit it, and can communicate its life content only by presiding at the liturgical and, principally, the eucharistic celebration. For it is in this way, and only in this way, that the proclaimed mystery is communicated. The very realism of the Word of salvation makes the ministry to which it is entrusted a sacramental ministry.[14]

However, throughout all this—throughout the building up in the very heart of the world of this cultic, sacral world that is the liturgical and (more precisely) sacramental world—we must not imagine that this simply opens some sort of escape from the real world into an ideal world. The sacramental world, in which proclamation of the mystery is completed in its effective communication, is not a world removed from the real world, in which we live and are called to live by the essential vocation of our being, which is one with our creation by the same God who saves us in Jesus Christ. In fact, the Christian sacramental world does not exist distinct from the real world; it is simply an intermediary between two realities. Or would it be better to say it is only the effective possibility, continually offered us, of direct communication between this surreal world, which is the Body of the Second Adam, of the Heavenly Man (in whom even "flesh" has become "life-giving Spirit"), the risen Christ, and the everyday world in which we live and in which mankind will live until the Parousia, the world to which belongs "the body of our lowliness," as St. Paul says (i.e, the whole concrete reality of our fallen humanity and its universe)?[15]

Important as the place of worship is (the Christian worship of the Word received by faith and acting through the Spirit in the sacraments) in the center of the Church's life, at the heart of that tradition of life in which truth itself is transmitted (this place is precisely central), it is in no way final nor can it be isolated from our individual and collective existence in this entire world.[16] Quite the contrary. Through the Sacrament, the reconciliatory power of the Word is introduced into our whole life and, through our life, tends to penetrate the world from top to bottom.

The world of the liturgy, of the Word and the sacraments; the world of prayer and sacrifice; the world of faith, in short, has no substance other than the world pure and simple: the substance of our day-to-day existence. It is *only* this existence—this world opening out through the Word of salvation, through the redemptive incarnation, through the outpouring of the Spirit, to the Presence of God revealed and given to mankind in Jesus Christ, to become "God all in all." Better, it is this Incarnate Word, with the explosion of the Spirit, who since the resurrection and Pentecost has spread to all flesh, paving the way throughout the world in the whole existence of Christians.

In one word, the expression, the transmission of evangelical truth which constitutes tradition, is not complete or real except in communication of its content. This communication works by the sacraments, in which the Word, as the Word of Life, expresses itself. But this communication, in turn, is fully present, is not only in process but is working effectively (though imperfectly), only in the total reality of Christian life in this world, the life of each Christian and of the entire Church. Again, the sacrament which brings it about has no consistency of its own: it is only a transition, a way, a coincidence that leads toward fulfillment between Christ and us, between the Creator who is also the Savior, and the whole of saved creation. The sacrament is the mystery of Christ, who has fundamental existence in the Resurrected One. But it is a mystery that is in the process of taking possession of our existence. Our faith receives the Incarnate Word in the signs of its communication, and therefore this Word comes hither to renew all flesh by the power of the Spirit.

It is therefore not in the liturgy—not even in the totality of its celebration—that the tradition of the "mystery," the "eucharistic" tradition which establishes it "in us [as] the hope of glory," is completed. It is in the whole of Christian life, individual and collective, and the Word is the source of inspiration for this life. The eucharistic celebration brings its effective fecundity, but its concrete existence, in every detail, is the sole ultimate realization. Here and only here does the mystery definitively find its complete expression, awaiting the perfect realization and, therefore, the supreme expression of "glory."

The object, the content, the matter of tradition, of the basically "eucharistic" tradition of the "mystery" of Christ, when all is said and done, is Christian existence itself, with all that that denotes and implies. In other words, the "mystery" is fully expressed, insofar as that is possible at present, and is fully communicated only on the level of the existence "in this world" of those who, like their Master, are "no longer of the world": no longer of the present world, the *aion outos* in which Satan still reigns, but of the world to come, the *aion mellon,* the "eternal kingdom." Ultimately, it is only through all that we might call "Christian behavior," in which the Christian "spirit" succeeds in being expressed (the *nous Christou* which the Spirit of Christ, the divine *pneuma,* creates in us and must be adequately conveyed), that the tradition of Christian truth is transmitted as a truth of life, of that life which is God's own love, poured out in our hearts by his Spirit.

This leads to a third aspect of the apostolic ministry and the ministry of the apostles' successors as well—an aspect which not only flows from the two preceding ones but includes them. As a teaching ministry, of the truth of life of the "mystery" and, consequently, a liturgical, sacramental ministry, this ministry is preeminently a pastoral ministry. This does not mean (as was the tendency during the Middle Ages) that the episcopal ministry is above all *potestas* and, therefore, only teaching and celebration. Far from it. It means that it is a service, a service of truth, a service of the life it begets, and therefore a service of Christ in his members. We shall return to this point, but let us first examine the system that results, for expression of Christian truth, from the fact that it is a truth of life, communicated in the sacraments and enclosing the entire existence of Christian people.

## III. Doctrinal Development and Christian Existence

Not only the preaching but the liturgical life, and not only the liturgical life but the whole, holy life of the Church, which does not exist apart from the faithful existence of the whole of her members in the midst of the world—all of this is the one and complete "witness" that is bound to its duty to give witness to the truth. Therefore, it is in the total context of this witness that the *kerygma*, "reverberated" by the *didache*, takes on its full meaning, so that we can say that both elements, if artificially separated from this witness, would be nothing more than formal repetitions of words emptied of meaning. This is why, even though tradition is (and must forever remain) the tradition of a truth given once and for all, both in its totality and impervious unity—a truth that was transmitted to the apostles in order that it be propagated to the ends of the earth and to the end of time—this tradition must continually, unceasingly, be developed. Once, therefore, the "mystery" is understood as the gift to man of God's own life, it is only in the life of man that it can be completely expressed. It is in this essentially changing, moving, and progressive life that everlasting life must be inscribed.

The Word in which such a union of the Creator with a creature is revealed could be conveyed, it can be said, only within this union that is in process of being realized: the Word was listened to only at the moment man began to respond to it. This is why the Church's first confession of faith was response to the Word's mystery—the only response that truly assimilates it, the response that is the eucharistic prayer. What St. Luke says about the Savior and the disciples at Emmaus can be said about the Church herself: "They recognized him in the breaking of the bread," for the point of this episode was surely to give us such a teaching. Under its most ancient form, as discerned by exegetes in the New Testament texts (and which may indeed go back to the apostles), the *kerygma* would be merely the witness to this radical experience, given by the early community and to the world at large: the experience of the Eucharist, of the Lord who has become "life-giving Spirit," who renews us through the eating of his resurrected "flesh." Therefore, under a foreshortening of the history of salvation, which we are invited to penetrate, the *kerygma* conveys the Church's experience after the resurrection and Pentecost, in which, finally, she was embraced by this history which was achieving its term in Christ.

For those who let themselves be convinced by the preaching they hear (with the Father drawing them from within toward the Son whom the preaching proclaims, through the ineffable aspirations of the Spirit), catechesis will prepare them for entry into the Church as entry into its eucharistic life, which is one and the same with what St. Paul calls "understanding of the mystery." Yet for Paul, this understanding must be deepened in the *didache* with the eucharistic meeting with Christ the Savior: total renewal of our human experience in the world. The Church's liturgical experience, in which she associates those to whom her missionary preaching reveals the mystery, is nothing else than the principle and the jumping-off point, as it were, of this total experience, totally renewed.

Thus just as the formulation of the *kerygma* sprang from the apostolic Church's first living acceptance of the Word of Life, the *didache* gives rise to, and accompanies, development of the whole of Christian experience as an integral experience that is totally regenerated and grows in turn. The history of Christian doctrine, from the earliest days, has placed it in an irrefragable light: a teaching that adapts a truth of life (such as that of the Gospel) to our whole life cannot be completely given *a priori*. It is only very gradually that the *didache* develops, as it is applied—as a slowly established balance sheet, set down with many hesitations and corrections and much experimentation at the beginning.

The *kerygma* dominates the *didache* and cannot be detached from a vital source of "magnetic" understanding of the data of faith, which it is incapable of exhausting in its formulas. In turn, it cannot exist without receiving many later specifications of all this experience of the Christian life, in which the *didache* is extended and ramified. For the problems posed by concrete human life with regard to the truth in the Church, in the midst of the world, will often question the interpretation of the *kerygma*. The exact meaning of the original, unchanging expressions must almost constantly be reinterpreted and specified in light of the inseparably practical and speculative questions posed by life.

Thus we see how this often debated problem of doctrinal development in the Church, associated with the certitude of a once-given truth—a certitude the Church could not endanger without undermining her foundation—depends on our notion of Christian truth, the truth of the Gospel. Neither the truth of a series of juxtaposed formulas nor the truth of a succession of formulas can be deduced from a primordial truth. Ours is the truth of the "mystery," the truth of a person: the Son of God made man—in his personal history, directed toward the cross and climaxing in the resurrection. This history must be understood as the "accomplishment" of the history of salvation, "accomplishing itself," in the same way, in the Church.

In one sense, in Christ, who is supreme, "everything is already accomplished," for Christ "recapitulates" in himself the whole of sacred history which led to him, and as the Second Adam he not only carries the seed of the eschatological fulfillment of the whole of human and cosmic history but—as the Last Adam as well—incorporates himself into that history. Thus we must maintain that everything—absolutely everything—of what was to be revealed to us was done, once for all, in Christ—in what he said, what he did, and what he remains in the glory of his resurrection.

Yet, in another sense that is no less traditional, revelation was complete only at the completion of the apostolic period. It was completed not so much, as the manuals say, with the death of the last apostle, but at the moment in which the Church Body of the risen Christ was fully constituted in what will be, from now on, until the Parousia, the essential aspect of her being, structure, and vital dynamism. A "revelation" of life cannot be conceived in its pure objectivity, but such a gift can be effectively received by one to whom it is destined. Now as always, the Word of God is directed at the People of God, and only this Word is able to call the People into existence, by bringing them out of the chaos of sinful mankind.

In this sense, Karl Rahner is perfectly right in saying that since revelation includes the Church in her relationship with Christ as its ultimate element, it can be completed only with the Church.[17] However, does it follow that, even today, revelation is in the process of completion, since the Church is not to reach fulfillment until the Parousia? It seems that this deduction cannot be accepted, for it is based on an ambiguity inherent in the term "fulfillment." If by "fulfillment of the Church" we mean her coming to being in her constitutive elements and their present existence, the reasoning holds up—but not if by this phrase we mean to denote the full growth of an organism which, from this point on, remains always the same, even though it is extended to the limits assigned for its growth and, to this extent, never ceases to manifest its potentialities. Here, properly speaking, we no longer are dealing with a growth that is correlative to revelation but only with an extension in depth and breadth of its application.

It is perfectly correct that revelation and its effect are so closely bound together that it may be difficult, even impossible, to determine with perfect precision where one ends and the other begins. Nor do we hesitate to say that the application of revelation began well before its completion. It is no less true that these are not merely two notions but two realities that cannot be confused without, in practice, confusing the Creator with his creation, the Redeemer and the salvation he brought to the world. How, then, are we to differentiate what we call the "development" of revelation from its application? Both contain a progressive transition from the implicit (or the imperfectly explicated) to the explicit. And in both cases there are simple deductions and *more* than simple deductions, at the same time.

In the teaching of St. Paul, for example, we find formulas that are not found with Jesus, and this novelty cannot be reduced to a process of deduction, though this form of dialectic is not more prevalent in Pauline thought than in the Jewish and Hellenistic systems in which the Apostle was trained. And the same thing may be said of the patristic age and of all "creative" ages in the later history of the Church. The two developments, nonetheless, remain profoundly different from one another, just as they differ from the development in the Old Testament.

It is precisely in relation to the Old Testament that light is shed on the difference (let us again recall the excellent formula of Oscar Cullmann in his remarkable exegetical essay on the Church and the Kingdom of God).[18] In the Old Testament, we see the wicked multitude of fallen mankind (*ubi peccatum, ibi multitudo*) progressively appearing, then becoming refined and unified by reducing itself. From the mass of the first civilizations, based on the undertakings of human pride and associated with idolatry and magic, the branch of Abraham and his son detached itself. The chosen people were freed from Egypt with the Passover and the Sinai covenant. Their history, up to the decisive trial of ruin and the Babylonian captivity, was the progressive extrication of the "faithful remnant," which alone is the true Israel or at least its promise, its "seed" in the bosom of carnal Israel. After this, even the "remnant" had to be sorted out, and was ultimately reduced to the one "faithful servant": Jesus in the solitude of his cross.

Yet starting with the cross and through the sequel to the resurrection, inaugurated at Pentecost, the movement seems to be reversed. Systole is succeeded by diastole, which will end only with the Parousia. From the One we return to the many in the Church, the Body of Christ, Christ's fullness. But this is not the same multitude as at the beginning. It is no longer a multitude whose mass congeals an irremediable division of men among themselves and from their Creator. Pentecost is not the equivalent of Babel and the dispersion of tongues; on the contrary, it is its definitive opposite. Whereas the first unity of the race burst into a dissociated multitude, the multitude must now be reintegrated into the living unity of the Second Adam, the Last Man, in whom all the scattered children of God must be reconciled in his own Body with his Father and, consequently, reconcilied with one another.

Hence we have not two but three quite different kinds of developments. The first—with the necessary death of the "old man," the death of mankind descended from the sinful Adam, born and evolved in his sin—is the emergence of the New Adam, the Heavenly Man, the Son of God. Throughout this period of the Old Covenant, according to St. Irenaeus, the Divine Word accustomed himself to living with the children of men. His approach projected a kind of shadow, growing over the history of mankind; but this shadow, the shadow of faith, was finally revealed as the shining that foreshadows the dawn that is to come, that was already coming.

In the second phase the light has come, as the Life from above became incarnate in the Son of Man. In turn, this Son of Man progressed toward death and the darkness of the cross, but at this nadir the movement was reversed: the cross is transfigured in the resurrection and the resurrection is completed in the ascension of the Son to the Father (clothed in our glorified flesh) and in the correlative descent of the Spirit on all flesh. From those whom he must associate with the triumph of the Lamb, by giving them the power to complete in their flesh what still must be suffered for his Body, the Church, the Spirit set up the Church. Here we enter into "understanding of the mystery," which was promised and outlined, then revealed and communicated, and now is assimilated, propagated, and accomplished. Now we are at the third phase.

Just as "the time [or development] of Israel" does not cease abruptly with the appearance of Christ but persists until his death (and even beyond), the "time of the Church"—of assimilation, propagation, and accomplishment in us of the "gift of God"—begins not only at Pentecost but even before the resurrection, since the call of the first disciples is prior to it. It is no less true that even though these three *kairoi* seem to engender one another and be continued in one another, they are radically distinct in the relationship they suppose between God and man, as are the corresponding developments.

Seeking to define these differences leads to what is customarily called the "problem" of Scripture and tradition, in which is contained the "problem" of the preparatory, then definitive, Word of God to his People and the response of this People, which will be complete only at the Parousia.

## IV. The Tradition of the Word in Life: Scripture and Tradition

Since the time of the Reformation, the Catholic position vis-à-vis the Protestant *sola Scriptura* has been defined in the formula "Scripture *and* tradition.''[19] But three remarks are necessary for anyone who wants to know how these antagonistic positions came to be stated in such a way. The first is that the stress on *sola Scriptura* (Scripture alone) was not original in the Protestant movement, nor does it express the fundamental position of the greatest reformers. The second is that the formula "Scripture and tradition," in Catholicism. The third is that in medieval theology we can find support for either formula, and usually in the same authors.

In the first and most important of Luther's writings, something quite different than "Holy Scripture" is stressed as the sole source of revelation: "the Word of God." That the Word of God has unequaled expression of purity and fullness in Scripture was obvious to Luther, who merely returned to a constant theme in theology, commonplace since St. Augustine and the patristics of the fourth century, and even since Origen. For Luther, moreover, this did not exclude the value of the testimony to the Word by the fathers and the great theologians. On the other hand, this does not signify absolutization of the sense of a word, page, or even book of Scripture if it is isolated from the whole of the biblical text or from Christian witness in general—as is evident in the cavalier fashion with which Luther treated biblical texts that might embarrass him (such as the epistle of James).

With Calvin, and even with Luther in his later writings, we see a stricter and therefore more exclusive identification between "Word of God" and "Scripture." But it is only with the Lutheran or Calvinist scholastics of the end of the sixteenth century (and not with all of them or at all times) that we see the transition from "sovereignty of the Word of God" to the unique, absolute, and uniform authority of "Holy Scripture." Like Luther, Calvin gave great importance to the doctrinal testimony of the fathers and certain medieval authors, such as St. Bernard, and the great Lutheran—and even Calvinist—theologians did the same for a long time afterward. All declared that they called upon the fathers solely as interpreters of Scripture, but this is what the men of the Middle Ages had said long before, and it is not so easy as we might think (according to the manuals) to fix precisely when and how these expressions came to be taken by the classical Protestant authors in a sense that is decidedly no longer that of their predecessors.

On the other hand, it is certain (which justifies our third consideration) that with the medieval authors in a general way and especially with the great thirteenty-century Scholastics (particularly St. Thomas) there is not only constant recourse to tradition, side by side with recourse to Scripture, but, what may seem surprising, though it is no less incontrovertible, statements of the necessity of recourse to tradition that go hand in hand with statements that are identical to those that appeared later as exclusively Protestant: Holy Scripture contains *all* revealed truth; the *sole* source of this truth is the Word of God;

the Word of God is found in its pure state *only* in Scripture, where it is everywhere present; etc.[20]

Yet this does not obscure another fact, which verifies our second observation: in medieval theology we find few texts that systematize the contrasting elements by saying (as will be repeated later, to the point of satiety) that the source of revelation (still less its source*s*) is (or are) in Scripture *and* tradition. Even after the Reformation, it was not immediately or easily that this formula came to be dominant in Catholic theology. It is enough to recall, in this regard, the difficulty the fathers of the Council of Trent experienced in canonizing a formula of this kind. They reached agreement on it only after dropping the "*partim . . . partim . . .*" that the *copula* underlined, even though the manuals, in their process of simplification, hastened to reintroduce it!

To understand and in some way reconcile these facts, we must go beyond not only formulations posterior to the sixteenth century but beyond the Middle Ages, and even to the end of the patristic period. We must return to the first three centuries of our era, where a surprise awaits us that may be greater than any of those occasioned by our preceding findings. As Damien van dem Eynde established in what might be called a definitive way, for the fathers of the first three centuries there was only *one* source of revelation—if "source" is taken in the modern sense of the word (i.e., the document or documents that communicate revelation to us)—and that was *the* tradition.[21] Therefore it was never a question of Scripture alone—it was never a question of Scripture *and* tradition either. It is from tradition, and tradition alone, that the Church receives the revealed truth. On this point (which cannot be overemphasized) the evidence of the early Church—once again, the Church of the first three centuries—is so unanimous and categorical that it may seem surprising to us.

The matter is clarified when we specify what the earliest fathers understood by "tradition" (*paratheke* and *paradosis* together, as explained above). For the apostolic fathers—that is, the first of the fathers, of whom the earliest (such as Clement of Rome) may have been contemporaries of the last authors of the New Testament—it was obvious that tradition comprises the Old Testament writings; in other words, the Jewish Bible. But obviously, it was no less essential to this tradition to refuse to accept the Bible received from the Jews separately from its interpretation by Christians. The epistle of Barnabas presents an extreme but meaningful form of this position: for the author of this epistle, the Christological and ecclesiological sense that Christians gave the Old Testament is its only true sense, and the Jews, by understanding it in a different way, attest to the fact that they never understood it at all![22]

In the following period, when the different writings that make up our New Testament were collected, recognized in the Church, and looked upon as so many parts of one totality of sacred Scripture, which was added as a second volume to the Bible received from Judaism, the position remained the same. *The* tradition communicates revelation to us, but *within this tradition* the complete Bible, the Old and New Testaments, came to occupy the central place that was accorded the ancient Bible from the very beginning. Even at the end of this stage (and for a long time afterward) it cannot be said that the Scripture-and-tradition problem was ever posed, for the simple reason that Scripture was always looked upon as *part* of tradition, an integral and capital part but a part nonetheless. We hasten to add that a tradition which did not include Scripture or did not assign it a central place would not be "Christian tradition" in the eyes of the fathers.

The common position is best expressed by St. Irenaeus in his controversy with the heretical Gnostics, who boasted of an esoteric tradition that supposedly went back to the apostles. On the other hand, they knew and used the Scriptures, often with material knowledge and extraordinary virtuosity, but they showed the vanity of their possession of the Scriptures and the inauthenticity of their tradition by the fact that, in themselves, they did not possess what Irenaeus called *hypothesis tes pisteos,* which is explained by an enlightening comparison. Without this *hypothesis,* which only the Church, established on the succession of the apostles, can transmit, when faced with the Scriptures, they were like ingenious but ignorant mosaic makers who can assemble the colored cubes in many ways but are incapable of forming the king's portrait, for which the cubes were assembled; the only ones who can do this are those who know the king.[23] Authentic tradition transmits, along with the Bible, the "hypothesis of faith" that corresponds to it, that derives from it the complete, living, and single vision of Christ and his work. And this brings us back (in other terms) to the Pauline idea of "the mystery" as the essential object of tradition.

In the view of the early Church, we cannot set Scripture and tradition in opposition to one another. Among the many written and unwritten forms of tradition, we have a body of written documents of exceptional importance, which, even so, cannot be separated from the totality of traditional factors without becoming incomprehensible. For their part, these factors would be eviscerated of everything that constitutes the heart (rather the brain) of their fundamental union.

We must emphasize that the problem is not even one of differentiating written from oral tradition. The Bible is far from being the totality of written tradition; it is but a part of it. And the unwritten tradition is not the totality of oral tradition either. A quantity of elements essential to tradition, properly speaking, are neither written nor oral: customary patterns of behavior, individual or collective common reactions—everything that the Latin *mores* can signify.[24]

A great part of written or oral tradition is limited to reflecting all this, but expresses it only indirectly or implicitly. For example (as we have indicated), the tradition of the eucharistic prayer throughout Christian antiquity shows remarkable consistency and continuity with the great Jewish *berakoth* and, also, with the new aspects that completely transfigured their sense. But this is never expressed didactically in however unsystematic a fashion. It cannot be reduced to either a sequence of once-determined ideas or a consistent plan, or even to a series of ideas that had become fixed and orderly arranged. We can observe a bit of all this, within a perpetual development that has never materialized into one unique formula nor even into one unique and definitive schema. Even when all of this is noted, catalogued, and classified, it does not exhaust the expressed content or, even less, the latent virtualities in the eucharistic prayer. Again, it is no less true that its formularies included from the beginning a fullness of living truth whose characteristic unity survives all later developments, provided they are authentic, without any special one, or all taken together, being able to express all its inconceivable richness.

Although this example is the most revealing, we could multiply other examples which, however bound up with written or oral traditions, are merely reflected in them. They go beyond them and may even escape them, more or less completely. For example, in the realm of worship, archeology yields a similar disconcerting mixture of constants and variants in the arrangement in Christian places of worship: the buildings, whether they were simply made use of or built *ad hoc,* bear the solid marks of practices that were never the object of either a prescriptive definition or a completed theory, but whose traces in the silent stone seem to retain the warmth of the life that was harbored in them. We have to grasp all this—the profound yet intimate unity, with its apparently unlimited tractability, that the life of the Church, the life of Christ in the Church (which is precisely the "mystery"), unquestionably possessed throughout all this, though it eludes simplistic expression—in order to account for this tradition from which the early Church drew the evangelical truth, as constantly and inexhaustibly fecund as it is immutably the same.

Yet it is quite true, in a general way, that the oral and the written forms of tradition in the Church are not merely united: they proceed from one another, and in a general way we may say that the written tradition proceeded almost completely from the oral tradition, including that especially important portion of the written tradition which we shall call in the strongest sense, and in a sense that was felt very early on to be very special, "Holy Scripture."

Still, this point ought not be forced. Even in the Old Testament, we have "writing prophets" in the strictest sense, prophets like Ezekiel (who was undoubtedly the first) who were not limited to fixing in writing at a later date prophecies they had first uttered orally but who immediately wrote them down. Similarly, a characteristic of the epistles of the New Testament is that they were composed and written down from the start. This does not mean, however, that many of these writings do not incorporate elements whose primary and immediate source was oral, although they were able, in turn, to enrich the oral tradition by new elements which were not present in it before.

The oral tradition came first, both in the New and the Old Testaments, and the importance of this is pointed up by the fact that here we are no longer dealing with a revelation that began in a milieu that, for all intents and purposes, did not yet have writing. Although Christ and the apostles were not scholars, they were not illiterate. As Origen pointed out, in a remark whose humor was emphasized by Berulle, the Gospel shows Jesus writing only on one occasion—and that was on sand and we don't know what he wrote![25] Christ's teaching and its first transmission by the apostles were purely oral. We had to await missionary needs and, more precisely, the need of keeping contact with the communities that were founded during the course of an itinerant ministry, for the first writings of Christian tradition to make their appearance, with St. Paul.

This was certainly not a chance happening. Jesus' resolution of keeping to oral preaching and providing, by the institution of the apostles, only an oral transmission of his teaching was certainly deliberate. Unquestionably, it reflects a fundamental and essential character of the Gospel message: neither a formula nor a system but the "mystery" of a person, of a personal destiny in which our history and the whole of sacred history are brought to their end. As Moehler emphasized, it is not by accident that the Gospel is first an "interior Gospel," passing by a living word from the heart of the Master into the hearts of the disciples; orally transmitted as a "Gospel in the hearts," it was passed directly from the heart to the mouth, long before there was a "written Gospel." This is due to the nature of the Gospel message: its content commands its initial form, to the extent that the second form it will take, writing, cannot supplant it. It can merely, at the most, help its transmission as a living message. This transmission, the "oral Gospel," is not only first historically; it will *always* be first, primordial, in personal witness, missionary preaching, and liturgical proclamation.

It may be said that the source of Gospel revelation (its initial and unique source) is the ineffable vision of God, man, and the world that was formed in Christ's human soul. This source burst forth for us—for the Church, properly speaking—in Christ's expression of this interior experience by his words and acts, mutually clarifying one another, just as in the Old Covenant the Divine Word was expressed inseparably in events and in their inspired interpretation.

Revelation was completed by being fully received from Christ in the Church and, for the first time, transmitted by her. In the preaching of the apostles, the light of the resurrection illuminates their own testimony—for the witnesses themselves, under the special influence of the Spirit of the risen Christ. Thus the faith of the Church will ever be a living echo, called forth by the faith of the apostles. This is why the written testimony of the direct teaching of the apostles and their disciples, under their authority, has such great importance. Because of the providential preservation of an expression of faith which is not only first in time but unique in the union it represents between direct contact with the Master and exceptional participation in the Spirit received from him, we recognize the privileged idiom of the New Testament. This is and will always be the only directly inspired expression of the "mystery," to which all other expressions must be referred to test their authenticity and conformity to the supreme norm. Yet this communication of the Word, of exceptional immediacy and a fullness of equivalent inspiration, does not mean that the New Testament was dictated (as it were) to passive minds and that nothing had to pave the way. Nor is the book it constitutes assured (or even capable) of being understood exactly by those who would read it but ignore all other testimonies left by the Gospel truth about itself in the Church.

Indeed, the inspiration of the apostles, like that of the prophets before them, did not suppress or put aside any of their natural capacities, or what they had received from prior tradition in the whole of the Old Testament (already written and oral), or their experience or their personal reactions to it.[26] Quite the contrary. They made use of all this and simply refined and deepened it, starting with the shock to their understanding and their whole being caused by their encounter with Christ—with the fact of Christ in all his human dimensions, which constitutes the definitive expression to mankind of the saving plan of God. Starting with this fact of Christ and its impact on the consciousness of the apostles, inspiration elicited, guided, and authenticated their testimony. Their human reaction to this primordial fact of Christ, transmitted to us in the Church, passes through the New Testament in particular but also, now and always, through the whole life of the Church—in her preaching, liturgy, and Christian existence. And the same Spirit, at work in us today, as with the apostles, sustains and unceasingly renews the faithful interpretation of their testimony.

The New Testament thus proceeds from oral tradition and, more generally, from the whole, living tradition of the early Church. It is the providential deposit, in an especially inspired idiom, of a central part of what, in this apostolic tradition, could be expressed in the words of the apostles and their Master. Once it was written down, put together, and canonized by the Church, it did not suspend the complementary ways whereby this tradition clears the way to him. Quite the contrary: it cannot be received, understood, and assimilated except where these paths extend to us. Thus the New Testament is only one way of access to what is most central in the apostolic testimony; but if it is taken "literally," and removed from everything that gave it meaning in the life of the early Church (which extends down to us in the Catholic Church), it could no longer give access to the Spirit of Christ.

Again, the New Testament's teaching about Christ cannot be received authentically except where a celebration of this Eucharist, in which the first disciples recognized their Master "in the breaking of the bread," has remained constant and habitual, thanks to a faithfully preserved living tradition. This celebration in turn, to be understood, requires a whole experience of Christian life, of a life in faith and charity. In one word, the New Testament is "in place" only in the community in which and for which it was written: a community gathered around the successors of those who wrote it or had it written.

This situating of the Scripture in tradition, from which it proceeds and which it does not abolish but reenforce, constituted no problem for the early Church. It denoted the renewal and the survival of relationships that united the Holy Book to an oral tradition which was similarly deposited in the Bible of the Old Covenant, without becoming frozen there. The continuity of the situation of the People of Israel and the Church was further proof, and perhaps the most gripping attestation, of the continuity of one People of God to the other.[27]

On first sight, we could say that the parallels between the position of the Bible in the tradition of Israel and that of the New Testament in its wake, in the Church, are almost identical. In both cases a long oral tradition is deposited at a later stage, at least in what is essential, in a series of books that were written more or less independently of one another, though in strict correlation with the common tradition from which they emerge. And once their composition ceased and their canonization was closed, the same tradition, within which they had taken form, continues to be extended and developed, while it claims the privilege or, quite simply, capacity to interpret them faithfully.

Although the parallelism goes so far or, if you prefer, is so close in both cases, and even though we assert that "all Scripture is inspired,"[28] we set aside two sections of particular importance—in one case the Torah and in the other the Gospels. What is more, these sections present the paradoxical peculiarity of encompassing the most ancient and basic elements of the whole tradition, both oral and written, while, at the same time, being composed after the greater part (at least) of the other texts and bearing visible signs of their influence.

Beneath their very striking similarities, therefore, reality is quite different. In the Old Testament, the writings were accumulated over several centuries, having been preceded by centuries of a more or less purely oral tradition. On the other hand, the writings of the New Testament were composed during the course of only one generation.

But especially the later stages of tradition in the Old Testament, whether we are dealing with its last written monuments or manifestations (which are either unwritten or written but not canonized as "inspired"), are not limited to projecting the light of a completed experience with regard to the essential attainments over its earlier phases. In the Old Testament, whatever the fundamental and normative importance of the first strata of tradition, those that follow convey constant progress in revelation, and not only in assimilation by the People to whom they were applied. Rather, the assimilation of ancient truths led this People to the discovery of new truths, and these, in turn, renewed the ancient truths. Thus the final result is a promise whose expectation is carried to its maximum, while the outline of its future realization has never ceased to be clarified, though this did not prevent it from becoming less mysterious. Thus when the Bible of the Old Testament was completed, it was in expectation of a new revelation, another covenant, to which alone eternity is promised.

Undoubtedly, we can say that the New Testament ends on the last words of Revelation: "The Spirit and the Bride say, 'Come.'" And he who witnessed these things says: "Behold, I am coming soon."[29] But the explanation is quite different, for the supreme revelation, which is still awaited, is now the last revelation of the One who has already been manifested, and the Spirit and the Bride, at the moment that he says to them again, "Come," with increased ardor can call to him, "Amen. Come *Lord Jesus.*" This is the conclusion of the book and the whole of this new compendium.

Even in the heart of the New Testament—contrary to the Old Testament— there is not so much progress in revelation—once Jesus lived and manifested himself it was total—as progress in its expression, which is bound up with the formation of the Church. Once the Church is fully constituted and has developed, progress is no longer a correlative development of the application of revelation, now complete, to the whole of human experience.

Certainly this might include development of the formulas of the *kerygma,* for, as we have said, the *didache,* which applies it to the whole of existence, cannot do so without positing questions that touch upon the understanding of the *kerygma* itself. Yet, even if in the Church these questions receive a fitting answer, we can no longer say that they enrich the knowledge of Christ and his mystery which the *kerygma,* and before the *kerygma* the basic "confession" of the apostolic Church, throughout the witness of her existence has transmitted to us. The new formulas merely draw new consequences for new human situations of this original knowledge of Christ. Far from adding to the content of the oldest and first formulas, they can never exhaust it. In the Gospel as Jesus proclaimed it and in the apostolic testimony that received and initially transmitted this Gospel, there is much more truth than in all the formulas assembled in Denzinger-Bannwart.

At this point it is fitting to specify that after the apostles—at least on the doctrinal level, though not only on this level—if one speaks of development, one does not for that reason necessarily speak of progress. Even dogmatic or legitimate doctrinal developments (i.e., those that were necessary) do not represent progress uniformly or, even less, every point of view.

As Newman emphasized in his *History of the Arians,* the distinction was clear for the fathers of the fourth century with regard to the first dogmatic definition: the *homoousios* of Nicaea. Athanasius and/or the Cappadocians, from the moment they justified it and declared it inevitable, because of the necessity of guarding against the subtleties by which the Arians adulterated the sense of the scriptural formulas, deplored the fact that the Church had been driven to a definition of this kind. They saw in it an indispensable safeguard against a threatening deformation of the apostolic faith; but the simplicity and purity of the Church was the unsurpassable model for them, the unique exemplar to which one must always return. Far from adding these formulas to those that this primitive faith spontaneously chose (much less replacing them), the act of definition could only return to them. It preserved them against fallacious interpretations, but not without incurring the risk of splitting the original unity and of narrowing, even altering, their perspectives. Whoever calls Christ "Son" and "Logos" in the biblical context, and only that, Athanasius repeated, says not less but more—does not recall less fully but more totally what Christ is than the person who calls him *homoousios.* This new term, of itself, teaches us nothing about Christ that we did not already know. In a new intellectual context, created by subtleties foreign to the perspectives of the Divine Word, it merely saves us from radical misinterpretation of the inspired expressions.[30]

No idea was more foreign to the ancients than the modern idea that the multiplication of definitions constitutes progress. This proliferation corresponds (in their view) to scars on the Body of truth, inflicted by the errors over which it triumphs. The only genuine progress in the knowledge of God, beyond what has been transmitted from the beginning by Christ and the apostles, results, according to the fathers, from the transition from faith to vision on the last day. The only anticipation that we can have of it is not in doctrinal develop-

ment, either in scientific theology or even in dogmatic definitions that constitute it, but in what they call the "science of the saints": the *gnosis* of Irenaeus
and Clement, the "mystical theology" of the Pseudo-Areopagite—the ineffable glimpse of the eternity of the blessed, which can be gratuitously communicated by God to those whose hearts and minds are sufficiently purified,
whom the divine *agape* has sufficiently enflamed that they may have some
foretaste of the beatific vision. Short of this, this mystical experience is
essentially impossible to convey for it is inseparable from the only qualitative
progress, which is progress in personal holiness through assimilation to
Christ, in "faith working through love."[31]

The accumulation of new formulas has no positive value but an indirect
one, insofar as it corresponds to successive penetration of different cultures by
the Gospel and, more directly, to attraction to and fuller saturation with the
different possibilities of human experience by the Spirit of Christ. Outside this
gradually universalized accession of everything human to the reign of Christ,
logical development of the propositions in the primitive *kerygma* is absolutely
sterile. If it does not veer from orthodoxy, it is merely tautological. But its
invincible tendency with minds that misunderstand the necessarily analogical
character of any formulation of revealed truth will be to draw consequences
that are absurd or meaningless. The *Contra Arianos* of St. Athanasius and,
especially, the *Contra Eunomium* of the Cappadocians demonstrate this,
which was too soon forgotten, even though it is unimpeachable.

Only to the extent that "faith working through love" extends the Christian
affirmation throughout human life does valid induction, faithful to the analogy
of faith, substantially nourish deductions that are not simply verbal but real. It
is for this reason, and this reason alone, that fruitful development in doctrine
is capable of being authenticated by the Church.

Again, this kind of development always clarifies human experience in the
light of the Divine Word. The supplementary notions that it may seem to
project on this Word are never more than a reflection. They specify superficial
details of the divine truth at the risk of destroying its depth and altering its
unity.

## V. Episcopal Tradition and Prophetic Tradition: Tradition and the Magisterium

Therefore in life, and only in the life of the Church—in all her members and
in their society, in her slow advance within the heart of mankind—does the

development of Christian doctrine proceed. As Newman demonstrated so well, this development is that of a truth that is always the same, but is more vast in its mystery than the greatest amplitude that can ever be attained by the evolution of human reality. If the expression of immutable truth must unceasingly be modified, it is so it may remain effectively the same in its constantly renewed application to a context that is in a perpetual state of becoming.[32]

The possibility of this development, which is therefore not an end in itself but an ineluctable consequence of the tradition of the truth of life, of the living transmission of the Gospel truth in the very life of the Church, which gives it her faith and bears witness to that faith by living it, is a characteristic of the entire Body. For the position in the world of the Body, in all its members, is characterized by the development in question. It reaches as far as directly doctrinal expressions, through a necessary reverberation of total experience on the thought which, at the same time, guides this experience and is nourished by it.

Let us repeat: the liturgical life is like the original place in which the Divine Word, in all its mystical realism, encounters human life and takes possession of it. Starting from this point, the whole ascetical, moral, and spiritual life of each Christian is involved, remodeling, from within, his intellectual and sensate life as well as his material existence and his professional, family, social, and political life. And this in turn, intensely personal as it is, is inseparable from the life of the Church, which is the organization and concrete realization of the life of charity among Christians, for its deepening in each of them and its extension to the universe. In all of this is the tradition of the Gospel truth transmitted and from all this does its development proceed. Thus the Church exists in her members, though she always transcends them. Or the Church exists only through the truth of Christ, but the truth of Christ is revealed only to men and is communicated only by entering into their existence. It is transmitted only by the association of men with this supernatural experience of the life of the Holy Spirit in them, which gradually becomes their own and properly is the experience of the Church—of the common life of the Divine Trinity extending to mankind. This life extends to all men and exists for them only in their common society with God in the Holy Spirit. It is communicated to them in a common history which the community owes to their historical attachment to Christ, who lived, died, and rose among us once and for all. Because they are members of this historical body, which Christ bestowed upon himself, and which he organized so that it might be progressively built throughout history on the foundation of the apostles, the Spirit lives in them and they live together in the only Son from the love of the Father.

As Newman described exactly, a twofold aspect results in tradition: what he called "episcopal tradition" and "prophetic tradition."[33] But, he emphasized, since there are not two lives or two bodies, there are not two different traditions in the Church. There is only one tradition, which is differentiated in the Church according to the functions of members who complete one another so exactly and necessarily that they could not survive if separated.

The prophetic tradition, as the tradition of truth in the life of the whole Body, in all its members, is primary. And it is also last. This means that one cannot envisage a tradition which would not be the tradition of the whole Church, which would cease to belong to the whole Church and cease being effectively transmitted in and by all her members. If the tradition continues to be transmitted, it is only to penetrate and vivify other members and thereby awaken in them the spontaneous desire and radical capacity to transmit the truth in turn, the life and the love they have received, which, according to the observation of Dionysius, can be possessed only by being transmitted.

Thus the whole Church is the witness of the truth. The whole Church is missionary and, to be so, prophetic in each and all of her members. In this regard, Khomiakov and his school are certainly right when they maintain that the truth in the Church belongs to all, or is entrusted to all in such a way that the entire Christian people are the guardian of this truth. For it is certain that all must live from grace, that the Spirit pours out the *agape* of the Father into the hearts of all men, and that the unity of all is not a constraint imposed upon them from without but the fruit of this intimate presence of the love it awakens and maintains in them. Christian truth is the truth of this life, this love, this unity in the Holy Spirit. It is not, then, the privilege of a sacerdotal or doctoral caste but the treasure of all the faithful. This treasure is kept in their hearts, in the biblical sense of the term, fusing the intellect with free will in order to seize life and make it one's own by the same movement whereby the intellect adheres to truth.

It is equally the case, here as everywhere, that in the life of the Church the participation of all in one life of truth in love does not suppress the diversity of gifts or the functions that correspond to them. All are called to witness to the truth, but the witness of all does not operate in a uniform way but in accordance with harmonious and complementary modalities that also are diverse and even contrasting. We may even say, as Khomiakov does, in a profound sense, that final authority in the Church belongs only to the *sensus fidelium,* to that *nous Christou*[34] that the Holy Spirit communicates to the whole Body of the faithful and to each person in particular, to the extent of his place within the Body and his effective participation in the Spirit which gives him life in the unity of charity. But the *sensus fidelium,* the life in the Spirit with the "insight into the mystery"[35] that accompanies it, does not flourish in an isolated way in individuals, as a diffuse phosphorescence in the whole of the Body. In accord with the participation of all, each with his part and in his place, in the organic life of the whole, the *sensus fidelium* is awakened in spontaneous harmony in which this living unanimity, which is that of the Spirit, is conveyed.

It is in this context that the episcopal tradition and its irreplaceable role appear, not outside or above the prophetic tradition but in it, as its directing and coordinating organ.

The function of the successors of the apostles consists in watching over and safeguarding the authentic transmission of the truth entrusted to the apostles, by which the Church, founded on them, must build herself, until the end of time in the world and out of its human substance. For bishops as for all Christians, it is from the common life of the prophetic tradition, as we have just described it, that this truth evolves, for there is no other means whereby it is transmitted. They participate in its transmission and its possession (if such a word may be used) precisely like all other Christians. The means of access to this truth, like those of spreading it, are the same for all, and each person, whether clerical or lay, shares in them equally, to the measure allowed by the capacities of nature or grace accorded by God and to the extent that he responds to these gifts.

But the episcopal charism in the line of the apostolic charism is to preside over this life of truth in love and, therefore, to assume the final responsibility of its preservation and communication in unity.

This proliferating life of truth in the Church, which we have just described, is the fruit of the Spirit, but it is a "mixed fruit" in which man's ignorance and sin are mingled unceasingly with the light and life from on high. For the Church herself and for her mission in the world, it is important that there be a continual sorting out, which is the first function of bishops—not to do this on their own but constantly to guide it throughout the whole Body. Since it was the apostles' function to bring the authentic message of Christ to the Church and the world with his authority, it is the permanent role of bishops, as successors of the apostolic mission, to authorize its ever renewed expressions by publically authenticating their fidelity. This defines their authority in the most basic and precise sense, which does not mean that they are the only witnesses of the faith nor even that they are always its most faithful or clearest witnesses. When difficulty in interpretation of the Divine Word arises, bishops may not always be the ones to bring the solution to controversies nor those who show most courage in upholding their resolution toward and against all adversaries. It is certainly incumbent upon them, with very special urgency, to acquire the necessary competence and to be the first, when necessary, to show the heroism of martyrs. They have often but not always done so, and there is nothing that automatically impels them to do so. A special grace is guaranteed them because of their special responsibility, but no more for them than for other Christians is this grace irresistible or independent in its efficaciousness on personal cooperation.

This is why, if there are many doctors of the Church (in the most eminent sense) among the bishops, there are as many eminent persons (even more eminent than doctors at times) among simple priests of second rank. Nor are similar doctors among the religious and the laity precluded, provided they have sought to acquire, through ways open to everyone, the necessary competence—such as St. Teresa of Avila (who was also a woman). *A fortiori,* many martyrs, and laymen among them, have defended the acknowledged truth at the price of their blood when there were no bishops to do so. We need only mention, in this regard, such a person as St. Thomas More.

What belongs definitively to bishops alone in this area, what they alone can do, is authorize, before the whole Church and the world, new definitions of the immutable truth as called for by changing circumstances. This is true even if others have produced and authenticated them by martyrdom at a level of holiness to which bishops are personally incapable of rising. It belongs to everyone in the Church, according to his light and graces, to be a witness of the faith. But only the bishops have the right to be the judges of the faith.[36]

Again, this does not mean that bishops have other, private means for discerning the authentic faith than the means that are available to everyone. For bishops as for everyone else, it is by probing the Scriptures in the light of the whole of tradition, in full participation in the life of the whole Body, with what prayer and crucifying asceticism it demands—even though, once again they have special responsibilities in this regard—that they can expect special graces. For these graces to be efficacious, they must be disposed, in the humility of faith and the fervor of living charity, to surrender to them! Consequently, like all other Christians, they must be ready, and more ready than the rest, to allow themselves to be taught first by those who may be wiser or holier than they and then by the lowliest, for God is the sole dispenser of his gifts. Even a scholar can learn much from one who, in St. Francis' phrase, is "a simpleton and an idiot." A saint can learn from a sinner!

In the last analysis, it is the bishops' function, and theirs alone, to decide and to promulgate what may or may not be taught in the Church as the teaching that is faithful to that of Christ and his apostles. Through the apostles, Christ has sent the bishops for this reason, and no one can arrogate this function to himself in their place. Whether they perform well or badly, and even if they "just perform," their decisions are not always guaranteed to be irrevocable, but even if they are, they do not always supply the complete and therefore definitive solution of the questions posed. But deference to their authority by other Christians, even where it is sure that it is not infallible, is a basic element of preservation of the fructification of the truth in the whole Body of the Church. For if Christ, through his apostles, established the bishops' function and, in accord with his promise, does not cease to assist this function by his Holy Spirit (as long as a bishop has not lost his position as a result of some indignity, recognized by the whole Church), whatever his ignorance and moral faults and the judgment God reserves for him, something will always be derived from his directives (however little it may be). And if we live in the Church, as we should, in a spirit of faith, this "something" can be decisive in leading us toward the fulness of truth. For Christian truth is found only in unity, and the bishop, above all, is its spokesman and guardian, however unworthy he may be of his responsibility, as long as it has not been taken from him.

If this is true of each bishop individually, it is even truer (*a fortiori*) of bishops meeting in council or, quite simply, agreeing on a positive point of doctrine, firmly and after full reflection. Finally, when the body of bishops seems to be unanimous, either in a council that is representative of the whole Christian world or in an ordinary, common teaching, it would be extremely rash to reject its teaching. If this teaching takes the form of a solemn definition, it should be considered infallible—not in the sense that it exhausts all that can be said on the point, nor even that it gives the best possible formulation of it, but in the sense that it cannot contradict the truth of Christ. The definition in question must be understood, of course, in the context of the whole of Christian tradition. Since this is the case for the *words* of the Gospel, how could it be different for their most authoritative human commentaries? To reject the infallibility of such definitions, understood within the limits and with all the reservations just mentioned, would be to reject the promises Christ made to his Church through his apostles. If their successors, whatever their individual or collective faults, have received the apostolic mission of speaking in the name of Christ (as we see this mission in the New Testament), how could we believe in Christ's promises and suppose that he would allow the totality of pastors deliberately to teach error to his People?[37]

A detrimental result of the controversies of the last centuries—and a fine example of the harmful counterfeits we spoke of, of even the most necessary and, *in se,* most justified definitions—is that examination of the episcopal function in tradition has concentrated on the distinction of cases where it is exercised fallibly or infallibly. Infallible definitions have been the rare exception, and moreover, the negative character of infallibility cannot account for such preoccupation. As we have just recalled, this function must be exercised in the name and to the benefit of the characteristic unity of the Church—a unity of the life of truth in the supernatural love poured into our hearts by the Holy Spirit. For this, it is necessary that the episcopal function be acknowledged and function as a living bond between the local Church and the universal Church—and especially, perhaps, between the Church of today and the Church of the Apostles. The magisterium is not fully faithful to its role, nor does it fulfill it best, unless it is fully united to the life of the Church of its time—that is, is sensitive to the needs peculiar to the world in which it exercises its mission, attentive to the gifts bestowed for this reason by the Spirit on the whole Body—and unless it remains faithful to the tradition once and for all entrusted by Christ to his apostles: *Quod semper, quod ubique, quod ab omnibus creditum est.* Its proper task is to promote unity in the Church of today by observing its continuity with the Church of all times, beginning with the time of the apostles.

If what we have described as the life of truth in the Church, the life of tradition, is kept in mind, it goes without saying that these two aspects of the episcopal task will not appear contradictory but will be conceived and understood as complementary, to the point of being inseparable. The renewals that are constantly necessary in the Church are not possible, or even thinkable, except in a perpetual return to the sources that spring from the Gospel. But this cannot be authentic if it makes use of abstract, bookish, or other means and tries to get back to Christ "above the head of" the apostles or their successors. Contemporary psychology has taught us that in general, no illusion is more harmful than wishing to forget or suppress something in one's past in order better to confront the future. Only with the resources of the present is the future built, and the present is made up of all the past, both conscious and unconscious. What is not assumed is not therefore abolished, but escapes our grasp and may paralyze us before we can build our future. A total experience, on the contrary, totally accepted and therefore susceptible to criticism, in accord with its fidelity (or lack thereof) to the deepest origins and impulses of our being, is the only basis for completing and spreading a truly creative freedom.[38]

For a much stronger reason, this is the case with Christian freedom, which is rooted not only in the "first creation" of our being and the world but in the new and eternal creation—in the New Man, the Ultimate Adam, the risen Christ. In the Body of the Church, the episcopal function assures, above everything else, full play of this liberating fidelity to history and its origins, without which the freedom of Christians could not be exercised concertedly in the charity of Christ.

It is an egregious error to believe that the bishops do this only in council or when they legislate individually. They do so, first of all, by being—or striving to be—*facti forma gregis ex animo*[39] (examples to their flocks by the authenticity of their faith and the fervor of their charity); by their habitual "ordinary" teaching and competent and faithful *didaskaloi* (including that of priests and laymen) and especially by liturgical worship, which it is their duty to perpetuate authentically, to organize, and to reform when there is need. Finally, they do so by the vitality and, even more, the coordination they must bring to the life of truth in the Church, which cannot develop fruitfully unless it is communicated efficaciously to the whole world. In short, they do so to the extent that, in each Church, they "preside in charity," as the universal Church, the Church of Rome, above all in the person of her earthly head, must do.[40]

This comes down to saying that the magisterium is not outside tradition but in it. Its duty is to guide tradition in its development, from within. Again, *tradition remains one,* and episcopal tradition does not exist apart from the prophetic tradition that is common to the whole Church. It is ordained by Christ so that the Church will persevere in unity. When the magisterium defines the faith of the Church (as it alone can do, with the authority inherited from the apostles, which they transmitted on behalf of Christ), it defines the faith that is *implicit* in the Church—not a *new* faith that it would instill into the Church, as from without, but the faith that the Church already possesses (if, up to then, in an imperfectly explicit way), that she has always possessed. A new definition adds only awareness that a particular point is or is not decidedly essential to this faith. A new formula is an elaboration of the truth revealed in the life of the whole Body, and its canonization by the episcopal authority, which merely authenticates this elaboration, finds not only passive acquiescence but positive corroboration in the adhesion of the People.

Yet how must we understand, in the last analysis, the relationship between episcopal decisions, especially in dogmatic matters, and their confirmation by the *consensus fidelium*? A purely "passive infallibility" of the *Ecclesia discens,* blindly accepting the "active infallibility" of the *Ecclesia docens,* according to the formulas proposed by the extreme forms of Ultramontanism, is an inadequate description. It would split the Church into two Churches, without any organic connection, for it substitutes for the Body of the Church a cadaver, manipulated from without by "teachers" who can no longer be called her "leaders," since they are separated from the other members of the Body. Equally unacceptable is the ultra-Gallican idea (taken up by some disciples of Khomiakov) according to which the *consensus Ecclesiae* is understood as agreement of the faithful among themselves, which alone would possess infallibility and, in receiving episcopal decisions (which would not be infallible), would communicate infallibility to them. Indeed, it identifies the Church with the faithful laity and reduces pastors to passive proxies of the community. But according to the New Testament and tradition, the apostles and the bishops were put at the head of the Church not by the faithful but by Christ, and it is from him, and not from the faithful, that they have authority and responsibility over his flock.[42]

In fact, the bishops define the living faith in the whole Church, attested by the whole Church, and they do so in virtue of a function which is an essential object—rather, an essential part of the object—of this faith. For this reason the adhesion by the faithful to their definitions and, more generally, to all their pastoral governing of the Church is a confirmation of this essential point, for it is a positive act of faith through free understanding and will, illuminated and fortified by grace. This does not mean that the decisions of the episcopacy would not be valid without the subsequent consent of the people, which would deny any proper role or consistency to episcopal authority. Rather, this means that the bishops, in the exercise of their function, are preceded and accompanied by the indispensable cooperation of all the faithful, first in undivided possession of the living faith in the whole Body and then in the *consensus* concomitant to this exercise of their episcopal function. Under these conditions, they produce decisions which, if they are regularly obtained, are guaranteed to be the final consensus of the entire Body, for under these conditions they correspond to the instinct of the Spirit, which vivifies the Body.[43]

If this is the case, the magisterium is inside tradition and, far from dominating, can only recognize and authenticate it and thereby bring the Body of the Church to specify the awareness it already had in itself, even though it may have been in an imperfectly explicit way. For an even stronger reason, neither the magisterium nor tradition can rise above the Word of God, as Scripture has formulated it for all time.[44]

The whole of tradition, despite its necessary developments (which, when the magisterium authenticates them, are legitimate), merely preserves and transmits the Word of God, given once and for all to the Church. This Word is sovereign for the Church and its expression in Scripture (of divine authority) is of a fullness that is forever unsurpassable. The entire Church, beginning with her bishops, is ever at the service of the Word and subject to the incomparable formula that the inspired Word itself gave in the Scriptures.

The Church alone can validly interpret all expressions of the Word, and this is the duty of the episcopal magisterium: finally to decide, within the Church, authentic interpretations. This does not mean that the Church in general or the bishops in particular can impose, as if from without, an artificial meaning on

Scripture or produce a dictum which adds to what has been given to us definitively in Christ. The Church is susceptible of recognizing the true sense of Scripture, of understanding the Word of God as it should be understood, and it is to the bishops alone that this pertains by virtue of the authority transmitted to them by the apostles of Christ, in and with the Church: to declare for the whole Church, through the Spirit, the sense that the Holy Spirit willed to give this Word.

## Notes

1. This was demonstrated by F. M. Braun in his *Aspects nouveaux du problème de l'Eglise* (Fribourg-Lyon, 1942). See K. L. Schmidt's "Ecclesia" in *Theologisches Wörterbuch* and "Le ministère et les ministères dans le Nouveau Testament in *Revue d'histoire et de philosophie religieuses* (1937), 17:320ff.; A. Fridrichsen, *Eglise et sacrement dans le Nouveau Testament*, in ibid., pp. 345ff.; O. Linton, *Das Problem der Urkirche in der neueren Forschung* (Uppsala, 1932).
2. See above, pp. 10ff.
3. Cf. 1 Corinthians 11:2, 2 Thessalonians 2:15 and 3:6, and 1 Timothy 6:20, as well as 2 Timothy 1:12 and 14. We have observed that both words tend to blend their meanings (particularly *paradosis,* which will often be taken in the sense of *paratheke*). On all that follows, see the constitution *Dei Verbum,* chap. 2, pars. 7ff.
4. C. H. Dodd, *The Apostolic Preaching and Its Developments* (London, 1936).
5. See J. N. D. Kelly, *Early Christian Creeds* (London, 1950), esp. pp. 23ff.
6. 1 Corinthians 4:5. On the Pauline mystery, see above, pp. 159ff.
7. Colossians 1:27.
8. John 13:13ff. On the nature of Christian tradition, Catholic theology since the *De divina traditione et scripture* of Franzelin (4th ed.; Rome, 1896) has remained singularly fecund. In 1960, with a penetrating essay by Fr. H. Holstein ("La Tradition dans l'Eglise"), the two volumes of Y. M.-J. Congar, *La Tradition et les Traditions* (Paris), appeared. Since then, the conciliar constitution *Dei Verbum* has given the magisterium's text, which is undoubtedly the most complete and delicately shaded statement on the question. It has been pointed out to what extent the discussions of the ecumenical conference of Toronto approached the subject with a similar explanation. H. von Campenhausen wrote one of the most constructive Protestant works on the question, *Tradition und Leben, Kräfte der Kirchengeschichte* (Tübingen, 1960).

9. John 3:2 and 1 John 1:6.

10. In this perspective, see E. H. Schillebeeckx, *Le Christ sacrement de la rencontre de Dieu* (Fr. tr., 1960), pp. 70ff.

11. See above, pp. 275.

12. On all this, see our *Eucharist,* especially the conclusion.

13. Indiculus of Celestine I, *De Gratia Dei,* cap. 11 (Denzinger-Bannwart, 139).

14. See our book *La Vie de la Liturgie* (Paris, 1956), pp. 95ff. On the fact that the life and the work of Christ are objects of tradition, with the doctrinal faith, see Tertullian, *De praescr. her.,* 32 (cf. 20), and *Adv. Marcionem,* IV, 5, P.L. 2, cols. 53, 37, 395. More generally, on the tradition of all the gifts of grace, see Ambrose, *De poenitentia,* II, 2, P. L. 16, col. 520C.; Pacianus, *Ep. 1,* 6, P.L. 13, col. 1057; *Qu. vet. et n. test.,* XCIII, 2, and CX, 7; Epiphanius, *Adv. haer.,* LXXV, 4, P.G. 42, col. 507D.

15. Cf. with the book of Schillebeeckx (mentioned in n. 10) our volume, *La Vie de la Liturgie,* esp. p. 325.

16. See the conciliar constitution on the liturgy, chap. 2, par. 9.

17. See *Ecrits théologiques,* vol. 4 of the Fr. tr. (Paris, 1966), pp. 89ff., and vol. 8 (Paris, 1967), pp. 9ff., as well as his article in *Concilium* on pluralism in theology (June 1969), pp. 56ff. On the recent discussions on this question, see (with the article of N. Lash, mentioned earlier) H. Hammans, *Recent Catholic Views on the Development of Dogma,* in ibid. January 1967), pp. 60ff.

18. See above, p. 264. On what follows, cf. Congar, *La Tradition et les Traditions,* 2: 28ff

19. On all that follows we shall refer especially to Congar, op. cit.: all of vol. 1 and pp. 137ff. in vol. 2*m* as well as G. Tavard, *Ecriture ou Eglise?* (Paris, 1963), completed by *La Tradition au XVIIe siecle* (1969).

20. This was well viewed by A. Humbert in *Les Origines de la Théologie moderne* (Paris, 1911).

21. See D. van den Eynde, *Les Normes de l'enseignement chrétien dans la littérature patristique des trois premiers siècles* (Gembloux-Paris, 1933).

22. See esp. chaps. 13 et seqq.

23. *Adversus haereses,* 3, 4 (the whole chap.). Cf. our study "Holy Scripture and Tradition as Seen by the Fathers," in *Eastern Churches Quarterly* (1947), pp. 1ff.

24. See Congar, op. cit., 1:64ff.

25. *Com in Joannem,* 8, 8.

26. Cf. P. Grelot, *Bible et Théologie* (Paris, 1965), pp. 105ff., and the two studies of P. Benoit, "L'Inspiration scripturaire," in the volume *Somme théologique* in *La Prophétie* (Paris, 1947), pp. 293ff., and "L'Inspiration" in *Initiation biblique* (3d ed.; Paris-Tournai, 1954), pp. 6ff.

27. On all this, see B. Gerhardson, *Memory and Manuscript.*

28. 2 Timothy 3:16.
29. Revelation 22:17 and 12.
30. Cf. *Contra Arianos,* bk. I, par. 28, and *De decretis Nicaenae Synodi,* par. 19; P.G. 26, col. 69, and P.G. 25, cols. 448D ff.
31. Galatians 5:6.
32. Cf. above, pp. 145ff.
33. Cf. above, pp. 111ff.
34. 1 Corinthians 2:16.
35. Ephesians 3:4.
36. See Congar, op. cit., 2:88ff.
37. On the exact sense of this notion of infallibility, applied to the most solemn doctrinal decisions of the Church, see B. C. Butler, *The Church and Infallibility* (London, 1954), as well as the ecumenical discussion on this subject: *Infallibility in the Church,* by A. M. Farrer, R. Murray, J. C. Dickinson, and C. S. Dessain (London, 1968). Also see *Colloque sur l'Infaillibilité* (Rome: Ed. E. Castelli, 1970).
38. See, in the same sense, the criticisms of L. Dewart's *L'Avenir de la Foi* (Fr. tr.) (Paris, 1968) by E. Mascall in *Downside Review* (October 1968).
39. 1 Peter 5:3.
40. Ignatius of Antioch, prologue of his letter to the Romans.
41. Cf. Congar, op. cit., 2:81ff.
42. On the fact that the Gallican errors or others in the same vein did not justify rejection of active participation by all, in accord with different modalities, in the definition of revealed truth in the Church, see the remarks of Fr. Congar in the conclusion of the collective volume *Le Concile et les Conciles* (Chevetogne–Paris, 1960), pp. 301ff.
43. On all this, see Congar, *Jalons pour une théologie du laïcat* (Paris, 1953), pp. 394ff.
44. See the decisive formulation of this point in the conciliar constitution *Dei Verbum,* chap. 2, par. 10.

# Chapter 7
# Collegiality and Catholicity

## I. The Episcopal College and the Pope in the Universal Church

Our last chapter began by concretizing the way in which the life of truth organically developed in the Church, as the life of a body with manifold and diverse, but coordinated, organs. Much deeper study of this point will be the central object of this new chapter, but before we see how clergy and lay people have to harmonize the complementary modalities of their "symphonic" activities for the Church to live and grow in charity, we must circumscribe the problem within the clergy. This problem is found on the highest level, among the successors of the apostles, the bishops, just as it was a problem for the apostles themselves. This was a subject of heated debates at Vatican Council II, in the name of episcopal collegiality.[1]

The major difficulty was undoubtedly due to the possible ambiguity of the term "collegiality," as was shown by the *nota praevia* that attempted to dispel it. Indeed, in traditional juridical language, *collegium* designates a group of persons who act together and who therefore form a kind of moral person. Ulpian, the great third-century jurisconsult, defined "college" with more precision: a grouping of equals, all of whom possess the same authority in an undivided way.

Taken strictly, this definition obviously cannot be applied to what is called the "episcopal college." On one hand, the totality of bishops always acts as members of a community, a "body," we might say: the episcopal "body," which, in its totality, forms the most eminent member of the "body" of the

Church, insofar as it represents the invisible Head in the midst of other, invisible members. On the other hand, each bishop has his own responsibilities over a particular flock within the one flock of Christ, as pastor of a local church, and he exercises them in relative independence from his fellows, but in such a way that the unity of his local church is assured with the others in the one Church, thanks to his union with the other bishops. It must be added that, in accordance with Catholic tradition, one bishop, among the other bishops, has special responsibility for the unity of all the bishops and, consequently, of the whole Church. This is of course the pope, the Bishop of Rome.

Episcopal collegiality is therefore a kind apart, and, we now add, this is true to a great extent of the collegiality in the Church—of all collegiality which is essential to the Church's structure. In all cases, as we shall see, collegiality or, properly, "ecclesiastical collegialities" have this in common, despite the differences we shall point out among them: they presuppose a certain autonomy in the collectivity of *all* individuals of which it is composed. This autonomy is essential to the living character of the unity of the whole. But this unity, for its part, is the object of a special function of *one* individual, in accordance with different modalities in each college.

However, in the case of the episcopate we shall observe (and this is the characteristic of episcopal collegiality) that this twofold difference must be understood within a fundamental equality. Whatever their individual responsibilities, all bishops have a function which is naturally the same, and, in principle, all possess it in its fullness. It is no less true that each habitually exercises it within a defined area which is his exclusively, though always in cooperation with his colleagues, and that one of them, the pope, in addition to his particular area, has the equally peculiar responsibility for the unity of the whole, a unity in which all must cooperate.[2]

Both Vatican councils made an effort at particularizing and connecting the contrasting elements of this complex situation, which proceeds in a direct line from an analogous situation that characterized the apostolic college before the episcopal college. To define it more precisely, it is fitting that we examine the apostolic college more closely by returning to the problem we have touched upon in order to bring to it new specifications: In what sense is the episcopate in the Church the successor of the apostolic body, in the strongest sense of this concept?[3]

We have said that the situation of the apostles differed from that of their successors—first, from the fact that they received Christ's revelation directly and were the first to transmit it as a revelation of life, a living revelation which was also a revelation given to the apostles alone. From the point of view that has now become our own with regard to the constitution of the Church and her permanence in the model of life in which she was established in the beginning, we can add that in the time of the apostles the Church was still in the process of her creation. What by distinction we may call the "age of the bishops" is still a development process, but development of a being that is now definitively constituted in its essential structure. Again, the bishops are successors of the apostles, not in the sense (which Protestants still suspect lies beneath the Catholic formulas) that they could change anything essential in the Church (established on and, to a great extent, by the apostles), but, following them, they have received the gifts necessary for forever preserving and developing this church in fidelity to her original institution.

Obviously, the distinction must not be exaggerated. As in the time of the apostles, it can be said today, and until the parousia, both that the Church exists and that she is still in a state of becoming. She was at the time of the apostles, and will be until the end of time, both *in esse* and *in fieri*. In consideration of this fact, as is said in the Epistle to the Ephesians of Christ himself, that he reaches the full stature of his adulthood in us only at the parousia, it can be said that the Church will reach *her* adulthood only at this moment. But this metaphor ought not sidetrack us from the subject of the Church or from the subject of the risen Christ living in us: from the resurrection, Christ, both in his humanity and his divinity, is essentially what he always will be. The same is true of the Church at the close of the apostolic age.

In that sense, the Church has left the hands of the apostles as an adult, endowed with all the organs necessary for her life until the parousia, even though she has still to be immeasurably extended. And this is why (as we have stressed) it does not seem possible to follow Karl Rahner when he asserts, with regard to future development, that the Church, in order to hold that revelation, must still experience the process of being completed. Certainly the Church is an element so essential to the mystery of Christ that he, as St. Paul says, is fully revealed only by the Church (i.e., by what she is). But in essence, the Church was transmitted by the apostles to the bishops as she must subsist to the end, and this is why revelation was completed with them.

If we scrutinize the difference between these two successive situations of the same Church, we shall say that the Church of the Bishops is more *in esse* than *in fieri*, while the Church of the Apostles—especially at the beginning, but also up to the conclusion of their incommunicable task—remained more *in fieri* than *in esse*. In the beginning, at the calling of the apostles by Christ, it can be said that the Church did not exist at all, except in them. As we have said (and clarified), she preexisted in the People of God in the Old

Covenant—but at that time the definitive People of God, of the New and Everlasting Covenant, had not yet sprung from them. The choice and the mission of the apostles only foreshadowed the Church and prepared for its appearance, after the resurrection at Pentecost.

The apostles, then, were the foundation stones of the Church, and no other foundation stone can be added to her—nor, even less, substituted. This makes their function unique, at least in certain aspects which are properly basic.

As eyewitnesses of the resurrection and as Christ's immediate cooperators, chosen by the Lord of the Church to be his coworkers, the apostles had to provide the Church her basic teaching and establish her in life, including the vital structure which was to remain her own. Both these functions are really one, since life and truth in the Church are one and the same thing. The word of God, transmitted to the Church by the apostles, is not, then, merely a word entrusted to her but a word which gives her being, to the point of forever determining the essentials of her structure and her mode of life.

This comes down to saying that the word of God, to which the apostles gave its definitive and, in the strongest sense, inspired form, included what we call the sacraments, and "orders" in particular, in a radical way. As we cannot repeat too often, the Gospel is not an abstract teaching but a doctrine of life which is, by nature, the common life of men with God in Christ, by the power of the Spirit.

With this in mind, both the difference and the continuity between the apostolic college and the episcopal college stand out, and the close relationship between the two is clarified. The apostles had once and for all to proclaim a Gospel which the bishops would have to transmit after them, a Gospel that was always the same and could not be added to, deducted from, or substituted for in any way. And with that—or rather included in that—they had to found a Church which would live from that Gospel and bear witness to it through her life, which, consequently, should also remain substantially the same, provided with the same means of grace in the Word and the sacraments of the Word, with the same basic structure established at the beginning by Christ and the apostles. Having taken form through Christ's institution of the apostles and their activity, the Church will remain substantially the same until the end of time, while, at the same time, extending to the ends of the earth. Of course, this presupposes all kinds of developments, which, however, can only be developments of what the apostles alone established and were able to establish only by following Christ.

Consequently, the basic difference between the apostles and the bishops, their successors, is that the institution of the apostles preceded the existence of the Church of Christ, while that of the bishops supposes that she was already established by the apostles. The latter took place within this establishment as the organ which guarantees her subsistence once the apostles were no longer there. The apostles were associated by Christ with his earthly work before he sent them, as if in his place, to complete that work in the foundation of the Church. Similarly, the bishops seem to have been first associated by the apostles with their pastoral task within the churches they founded (before they were established) to nourish these churches in their stead.[4]

This was essential for the apostles and for their function of founding the first churches. And it is essential that the bishops rose out of the existing churches to preside over their development, once the apostles were no longer there. This explains the confusion, observed in apostolic times, between the functions of *presbyteros* and *episkopos*. (Their differentiation was settled after the death of the apostles, although, at least to the fourth century, a bishop did not hesitate to call his presbyters *sympresbyteroi*.)

Indeed, by its origin, the apostolic ministry comes from above, from Christ, and radically preexists the Church, since its aim was to create and organize her. In primitive Christianity, as in Judaism, the presbyteral ministry comes from below, from the existing churches, which it represented to the apostles before they progressively associated it with their pastoral task, and especially with the *episkope* (i.e., the responsibility with regard to the development of these churches). But according to the unanimous tradition of the ancient Church, at the moment when the apostles completed their task and their lives, the ultimate responsibility, the *episkope* in fullness, was transmitted by them in each church to one of the *presbyteroi-episkopoi*, who thus became, of all the local *presbyteroi*, the preeminent *episkopos*, the successor to the responsibility and, therefore, the authority of the apostles in all that was transmittable.

It may be that at first, in certain places, the transmission was not made to one individual alone in the local presbyteral college but to several, or even to the whole college. Yet, at a very early stage—at least from the middle of the second century in all the churches—it was to one presbyter alone that the episcopate of the apostles was given, and this situation is everywhere acknowledged to be in conformity with their intentions and, even, as the direct result of their initiative. In fact, Jerusalem is a typical case, for there, in the lifetime of the apostles (while some, like Peter and John, still resided there), the entire governing of the Church seems to have been in the hands of James, the "brother" of the Lord, even though he was not one of the Twelve. This not only influenced further evolution, as has been said, it attests that it was done with the express accord of the apostles; and this is the *least* that can be said.

Thus we see that what we can call the episcopal college was not substituted for the apostolic college (nothing can be substituted for it), but was prepared by the apostolic college to succeed it in the function of nourishing the Church, which only the apostles had the power to found and to organize radically. But at the same time we see what differentiates them: the first churches proceeded from the apostles, while, on the other hand, it is from the existing churches that the episcopate proceeds, and within them, but through an association of their representatives with the pastoral task of the apostles, and, finally, through the commission from them to guarantee their succession.

It is therefore essential that the bishops were *presbyteroi*, eminently representative of the local churches from which they were recruited, and that they received from the apostles, on the other hand, participation in their mission, coming from Christ alone, so that, having been associated in the pastoral function with regard to the churches the apostles founded, they could succeed them in their responsibility. Hence the principle which (to our knowledge) was not formulated in all its clarity until St. Cyprian, though it certainly corresponds to primitive practice and to a manner of conceiving it that goes back to the beginnings: "There is no Church without a bishop and no bishop without a Church"[5] ("Church" meaning the local church). The bishop, then, is not an "apostle" in the strict sense (i.e., someone whose existence and function preexist the Church for her foundation), but a successor of the apostles, coming from the Church herself—her representative, her most eminent "presbyter"—and consecrated by the apostles in order to succeed them in the pastorate of this Church, of which the apostles remain forever the founders.

What is more, as St. Ignatius of Antioch stated at the beginning of the second century, the local unicity of possessors of the episcopal function (which in a very few years would become generalized) both expresses and foments the unity of the Church: this internal unity of the local church in truth and charity, in the truth *of* charity, which at the same time makes the unity of all the local churches among themselves at a given moment, and of the Catholic Church everywhere and always, across time and space.[6]

This is the episcopal function, and this is its original situation in the Church—so bound up with the very essence of the considered function that it does not seem capable of being separated from it. In distinction to the apostles, the bishop exists only in the already existing Church as established by the apostles, and, more precisely, in a concrete and therefore local church. His proper function is to perpetuate in this church whatever can be perpetuated in the apostolic function of proclaiming the Word by the authority of Christ and, consequently, of celebrating the sacraments, and above all the Eucharist. Thereby, in the unity of the life of the Spirit, he must guide this local church, in which the bishop first appears, within the catholic community of all the churches, in which all the bishops are associated, as their responsibility and their task, just as the apostles were before them.

As different as they may be, the apostolic and the episcopal functions present convergences that guarantee continuity. On one hand, the apostles' function, universal in its principle, has nevertheless, by dint of circumstances, progressively contracted local bonds for each of them. On the other hand, the bishops' function, local in principle, remains no less bound up—like the local church where it is exercised—with the life of the universal Church, to the extent of being always associated (if not with the original foundation of the Church) with her progressive extension through the foundation of new churches. The apostles were missionaries who became pastors, after the success of their mission. The bishops are pastors whose pastorate is inseparable from pursuit of the apostles' mission.

The function of the apostles, as Christ himself seems to have defined it, is chiefly an itinerant function: "Go therefore and make disciples of nations, baptizing them in the name of the Father and of the Son and of the Holy Spirit, teaching them to observe all that I have commanded you."[7] They must everywhere bear witness to Christ—to his resurrection, to his inseparable teaching and work—in order to elicit faith, seal it through baptism, and thus found the Church in every place. In this Church, in each place in which she is founded, they instituted "presbyters" (i.e., "elders") as representatives of the community. When the apostles left for other places, to pursue their "proclamation" of the Gospel and the foundation of the Church (which is its result), these "presbyters" continued the preaching and baptism begun by the apostles, and presided (in their place) over the eucharistic assemblies and over the whole life of the Church which unfolded around these assemblies. When the apostles were on the verge of leaving this life, the "presbyters" (at least some of them), who had first exercised the *episkope* (the pastoral responsibility) with regard to churches founded in a delegated manner by the apostles, were called upon by them to assume, in their place, the ultimate responsibility.[8] Thus the episcopal function, in distinction to that of the apostles, seems in principle to be a sedentary function, bound up with the existence and subsistence of the local churches.

However, the apostles themselves—by the lasting bonds established among them and the churches they founded, or in whose foundation they played a dominant role, without ceasing to be acknowledged as collectively responsible for the worldwide spread of the Gospel and the Church—became especially responsible for a local church or a group of local churches. Even in the New Testament, we see this with St. Peter in Antioch and later in Rome, according to the most ancient tradition; and it seems that the same thing is attested to John at Ephesus and throughout Asia Minor. With a lesser guarantee, but not without foundation, is the tradition that puts the ministry of Mark the evangelist (associated with the apostolate of Peter) in Alexandria. Subsequently, people assigned each apostle a special area of missionary work, and the correlative foundation of local churches.[9]

However late and therefore questionable these traditions may be, they attest to an ancient conviction which, on the whole, seems justified: the universality of the apostles' mission, as we see in Acts, was unable to prevent one or another of them from being connected with the spread of the Gospel in one region rather than another and, therefore, with the foundation of the churches of this region. Even Paul, the preeminent missionary to the Gentiles, contracted special bonds with the churches of Macedonia, then with those of Corinth and its surrounding area, and finally with those of Asia Minor, before the circumstances of his captivity probably brought him to Rome, where he had long wanted to go and where he suffered martyrdom.

Thus however universal and itinerant each apostle was in principle, the apostolate contracted local bonds. Reciprocally, originating from the contact of the apostles with the local communities they founded, the "presbyteral" ministry, from which the properly "episcopal" ministry evolved, preserved from the beginning (and always will preserve) a universal outlook.

Among their converts, the apostles selected not only people responsible for local ministries but associates in their missionary function—"apostolic men," like Silas or Barnabas.[10] It could even be that the local "episcopate" (in many places, at least) came to be entrusted not simply to one of the local "presbyters," judged more worthy of this superior responsibility than the others, but to a "presbyter" who had already been put to the test in his association with the itinerant mission of the apostle (this seems to be the case with Titus and Timothy).[11] Whatever it was, the first bishops, individually and collectively, considered themselves, after the death of the apostles, charged not only with preserving and developing their work where they were but with spreading it. On the local plane, they continued the evangelization in the urban centers where they were established and, starting from there, throughout the neighboring countryside. Either personally or through envoys, they were concerned with increasing their areas of influence and implanting the Church in every place they were able to reach. The initiative, however, did not always proceed from them; it could be the doing of lay people, profiting in moving from one place to another by bearing witness to their faith, or of "presbyters" or deacons with more or less spontaneous zeal. However, each time new Christians gathered in a place where there had not been any previously, the bishops, like the apostles before them, concerned themselves with setting up a new church by instituting a supplementary bishop, either recruited on the spot or (with the agreement of the local people) procured from the more or less organized mission at the origin of such expansions.

Individually and collectively, however local the attachments of the different bishops and the origins of the episcopates, they remained, like the local churches over which they presided, not only "open" but spontaneously oriented to the universal Church, which is both actual and in a state of perpetual becoming.

This explains why, from the outset, the bishops, no matter how locally fixed they seem, consciously strove to form a college, as the apostles did before them. For each of the churches, congenitally bound up with each episcopal see, never looked upon itself (as we have seen) as other than a cutting or slip of the primitive Church in Jerusalem—as a locally anticipated manifestation of the definitive Church of God, "the assembly of the firstborn who are enrolled in heaven,"[12] the one, unique Church which is the Body of the risen Christ, who has ascended into heaven and gathered to himself all the scattered children of God through the power of the Spirit.

This is why, after the apostolic generation, when the first bishops were instituted by the apostles so that they might succeed them, one came to the episcopacy by being joined to the episcopal body through the rite of the laying on of hands. Traditionally, the consecration of a bishop cannot be done regularly by one bishop alone but always by at least three, representing the whole college.[13]

This unity and unicity of the Church in all the churches, whether existing or still to come, was not merely prepared for by and rooted in the basic unity of the apostolic college which gave rise to them. Within this college of the apostles, by its very constitution, as Christ created it, one apostle was set aside from the very beginning to preside over the universal expansion of the Church and to make sure that this was done and was continued in unity. Obviously, this apostle was Peter.

We cannot understand the united functioning of the apostolic college unless we examine the special position occupied by Peter in the New Testament. Consequently the functioning in unity of the episcopal college will be articulated in parallel fashion on the special function of one bishop, to whom will be acknowledged not so much the "privilege" as the formidable responsibility of succeeding Peter in a special way, just as the totality of the bishops succeeds the totality of the apostles.

Even in a simple reading of the New Testament, it is difficult not to be struck by the special role played by Peter at the beginning of the Church. Moreover, according to the testimony of this Church, this role was not due to personal qualities, as was Paul's, but to a disposition explicitly willed by Christ.[14]

As for the singular place that Peter came to have, one need only open the Acts of the Apostles to realize this. In every regard, it is he who speaks to unbelievers, whether to the crowd at Pentecost or to the judges of the Sanhedrin, in order to explain the attitude of the whole Church or to give an account of her faith. And within the Church, it is he who presides over all deliberations of the apostles, and even, as in the conversion of the centurion Cornelius (so pregnant with consequences for the future of the Church and her missionary policy), goes beyond any deliberation of this type and sets out on paths that seem to have no return.

This foreground activity is prepared for in the Gospel by the fact that Peter is not always the one first named among the Twelve but is frequently "taken aside" from the group, either alone or in the company of James and John. Yet there is much more. St. Matthew, in the famous passage on "Peter/Rock," on which Jesus declared he would build his Church,[15] and St. John, in the astonishing additional chapter, in which Jesus gives Peter the charge of feeding the lambs and the sheep,[16] attribute to him—within the apostolic college itself—a very special responsibility. And they are so categorical that it is possible that Jesus willed it, and said it in the clearest, most solemn form.

That Peter, even so, was not made sinless, or even incapable of mistakes, is emphasized by the same evangelists. Shortly after Peter heard himself given the "keys of the kingdom of heaven" (according to St. Matthew), he showed such inaptitude in understanding the divine plan that Jesus said to him: "Get behind me, Satan!" In St. John, the pastoral commission of the lambs and the sheep (i.e., probably the whole flock, including its other leaders) is closely connected with Peter's pardon for his denial of Christ, which is recorded by all the evangelists. This, moreover, seems to be a direct echo of Jesus' words, mentioned by Luke:[17] "When you have turned again, strengthen your brethren," which follows the announcement of the iminent denial.

For the evangelists, these personal weaknesses were far from annulling or diminishing the authority conferred upon Peter by Christ. The plan seems more or less systematic with all of them, stressing the contrast between the weakness of the man and the dignity of the function, particularly in chapter 21 of the Fourth Gospel—so that a Protestant exegete (Maurice Goguel) has questioned the historical authenticity of Peter's denial.[18] But chapter 21 is simply an imaginative illustration of the contrast, asserted by Christ himself, between the frailty of the one he chose to be his preeminent minister and the loftiness of his charge, which could not be fulfilled without an exceptional gift of grace. Such a doubt is certainly exaggerated, but it is the exaggeration of an unquestionable remark: the evangelists John and Luke, in addition to Matthew, were persuaded that Peter's role in the primitive Church was not the result of a special personality but a formal disposition by Christ, and therefore of an assured, unequaled, and corresponding charism.

Yet how, according to the New Testament, can this conferral on Peter of responsibility for the whole Church and, it seems, over the other apostles be defined with respect to the responsibilities entrusted to the Twelve collectively? According to St. Matthew, it is not so much that Peter was raised up by some distinctive power over the rest of the Twelve; rather, he received, personally, the same power that will be given jointly to the Twelve (including Peter). The statement in Matthew 18:18 (which is found again in Jn 20:23), according to which the sins forgiven or retained by the apostles on earth will also be forgiven or retained in heaven, is an exact equivalent of the statement in Matthew 16:19, which gives Peter the keys of the kingdom of heaven, so that what he will bind or loose on earth will, similarly, be bound or loosed in heaven. The power to grant forgiveness appears in the Gospel as the very power of Christ in its most "heavenly" manifestation. That it was communicated to Peter or the Twelve comes down to saying that the fullness of his authority is communicated to them because the special presence of Christ himself (cf. Mt 28:20), or his Spirit (cf. Jn 20:22), is promised to them in the exercise of their apostolic function. In this regard, Peter does not appear as a "super apostle" but as the apostle in whom is found, personally reunited, everything that is shared or possessed in common by the whole apostolic college. Through this, it seems, Peter will be constituted as the foundation of the whole Church, not only as he appears from the narrative of Matthew (because he was the first to receive what the Twelve were to receive together later on) but because he expressed, and realized in himself from the beginning, the unity of the apostolic work and, therefore, of the work of the Church which is its result.

Indeed, this characterizes Peter's activity at the beginning of the Church, as we find from the Epistle to the Galatians and the Acts of the Apostles. On Pentecost, and in the early days when the primitive Church was being organized in Jerusalem, while the other apostles (and particularly John) were closely associated with him, Peter unquestionably had the role of head. Cullmann showed that Peter was recognized as the one to whom the risen Christ first showed himself. And it is at least very probable, according to the converging testimony of the discourses of Acts and the First Epistle of Peter, that Peter was also the first to interpret the cross of Christ in accordance with the biblical teaching on the "Servant of the Lord," to which Jesus, until then, had vainly tried to attract the attention of the disciples.

In a second phase of his activity, after leaving to James, "the brother of the Lord," the leadership of the primitive Church, now established in Jerusalem (which can be considered the foundation of the episcopate in the full sense of the word), Peter took the mission outside Jerusalem in hand, at first to the Jews of the diaspora. Then, after the conversion of the Roman centurion Cornelius, Peter took it upon himself to extend this mission to the pagans, and he brought the Judeo-Christian Church, despite manifest repugnances, to admit this development; and Peter was the first to foresee it and to accept all its consequences. This is to say that Peter saw, since pagans were to be admitted into the Church on an equal footing with Jews, that there was no place (contrary to a persistent tendency, of which James was presented as guarantor) for making pagans Jewish proselytes, subject to the requirements of the Law, before making them Christians. Even better, he drew a still graver consequence, in that the letter of the Jewish Law, as St. Paul said, no longer obliges Jews in an absolute fashion. In effect, Paul gives testimony that Peter, on his own, though he was a Jew, in the midst of non-Jewish Christians began to live with them as they lived. The new solidarity created in the Church by common faith in Christ, precedes the old racial and ceremonial solidarity.

In the Epistle to the Galatians, St. Paul is the irrefragable witness of all this. Again, as Cullmann shows, the undeniably heated altercation that opposed Paul to Peter did not mean that he misunderstood Peter's special authority, or that there was opposition in principle on the point at issue between them. It signified quite the opposite.

In the first place, if Peter had been "just an apostle," like the others, it is clear that Paul would not have been so moved to see him favor (if only apparently) a policy different from the one on which the whole of Paul's mission was organized. The opposition of James (whatever his authority, whether real or imaginary) and his group does not seem to have given rise in Paul to anything but sarcasm. On the contrary, the very fact that Peter *seemed to change his mind* and condemn (if only implicitly) the form of his mission to the Gentiles was so serious that it seemed, in his eyes to be a question of life or death that his work obtain Peter's permission to return to his previous practice, as well as an unambiguous declaration. This shows that the relations of one apostle with his colleagues (i.e., of one apostle with the chief of the apostles) were not burdened with modern ecclesiastical protocol. If also shows that Peter's authority, in what he said and in what he would allow to be believed, was of capital importance for Paul.

As for the heart of the problem, the Epistle to the Galatians is absolutely explicit: Peter, on his own, thought like Paul and, spontaneously, acted like Paul. The divergence between them (exploited against Paul by James's people) came about from what we might call a "diplomatic" attitude. Paul, under the circumstances, thought it was cowardly, and without too much trouble, apparently, convinced Peter.

This gives us a good opportunity to settle two questions, insofar as we can. The first was raised by Cullmann in his study (so excellent in many ways), according to which, in leaving Jerusalem to pursue the Christian mission, Peter would have left James not only the government of the Church of Jerusalem but the government of the *whole* Church. In some way, he would have resigned his function as first head of the Church, which he received from Christ, and given it to James.[19]

This might well have been the view of a more or less important group of Judeo-Christians, but it is hard to know what James himself thought about it, or even if he considered it at all. Nothing in the New Testament texts is capable of establishing that Peter saw things in this light, or that this opinion was generally admitted in the primitive Church. Moreover, though Cullmann sees insurmountable difficulties in the idea that Peter could have transmitted to his Roman successors the primacy that, he acknowledges Christ entrusted to him, it is surprising that Cullmann seems unaware of the unlikelihood of such a resignation and disposal of his function to a person who did not even belong to the Twelve, at a moment when Peter was fully active and entering what may be his most decisive phase of "building up" the Church of Christ. This "passing on" to James of pastoral charge of the first church, the Church of Jerusalem, coinciding with Peter's systematic undertaking of a mission that was first to the diaspora, but had already gone beyond these bounds, seems to have the exactly opposite significance.

Undoubtedly, the mission over which Peter assumed leadership was in principle, as Paul recalls, first of all a mission to the Jews. But even then— and it was Peter himself who took the initiative—it was open to the Gentiles; what is more, what we may call the Church's "center of gravity" in her future development was *already* projected beyond the restricted area of Judaism, and included her proselytes. Under these circumstances, Peter's transfer to James of pastoral charge over the primitive Church of Jerusalem, far from signifying the handing over of leadership of the whole Church, implied the fact that the People of God no longer had, and could no longer have, their center in Jerusalem. Jerusalem and Judaism, nonetheless, remained a bond, not only with the former People of God but with Christ—and the importance of this bond cannot be minimized. Hence Peter's concern not to break the bridges between the old community, in a state of renewing itself and the new communities that had already come forth from the old community through the irresistible pressure of the Spirit. Must we add that Peter's concern, corresponding to his mission of unity, at a moment when the problem of this unity would suddenly take on the most pointed form, was combined with very real anxiety? Indeed, at this moment, the human and other resources of the mission still came, almost completely, from the Jewish church. In these circumstances, it is not surprising that Peter's peasant prudence again turned toward timidity, from which only sudden and forceful awareness of the gravity of the situation could again rescue him.[20]

But perhaps more interesting than Peter's relationship with James and the other Judeo-Christians is the light this episode casts on the relationship between Peter and Paul. It is significant that the mission, now addressed directly to pagans and no longer necessarily (depending on circumstances) through the medium of the diaspora, was entrusted by an extraordinary intervention of the risen Christ to a supernumerary apostle outside the Twelve (whose number signified the renewal of Israel), whose call was marked by the same, unprecedented gratuitousness that was expressed in the calling of the Gentiles. It is no less remarkable that this "Apostle of the Gentiles," in distinction to the Twelve (Peter included), was not a simple, pious Jew but a rabbi, and a particularly eminent one. James's rabbinism, which had become deeply Christian, had remained very conservative—and even, perhaps, became increasingly so.[21]

By comparison, the rabbinism of the Apostle of the Gentiles seems to guarantee the fact that the mission to the pagans, while avoiding the iron collar of retarded Judaism, retained the imperishable legacy of a Judaism that was not only messianic but eschatological as well, open to the coming of the Universal King and the universal kingdom. Without this, the teaching and presence of Christ would not have converted the Gentiles; nascent Christianity would have melted into paganism (as we saw with the heretical *gnosis*). To be possible, the transposition had to keep the connection (for some time, at least) with a Christianity that was still deeply and entirely Jewish, like that of James and Jerusalem. Between the two, it is likely that the unity could not be better maintained than by a Jew like Peter, who was sincerely and profoundly Jewish but, also, totally Christ's from the beginning. No specialized training, either in Palestine or the diaspora, predisposed Peter to narrow partisanship—unlike Paul, who was a "product" of both, and James, who seemed more and more enclosed within the Palestinian "school."

Torn between the two tendencies, Peter seems to have had the very clear sense that the future was with the mission to the pagans, and that it was important, above all, that it *have* a future but *not* be cut off from its biblical and Jewish sources. In this regard, his final installation in Rome, attested to by a tradition that Cullmann shows is not assailable, is most significant.[22] For Peter, it did not signify that the future framework of the Church had become exclusively Roman. What caused him to go to Rome and to settle there must have been the very thing that, early on, motivated Paul's interest in the Roman church and his explicit desire to visit it and to associate it with his work (even though the foundation of this church was independent of him). Rome was one of the most important Jewish communities of the diaspora, and its relations with Jerusalem were possibly closer than with Alexandria, for the Jews had adapted themselves (with comparable success) to life in a pagan milieu, and Roman proselytes were scarcely less numerous. Consequently, at Rome—as much as or more than at Alexandria—the transition could be made from Judeo-Christianity to a Christianity that would bring Jews and pagans together by preparing an essentially "Gentile" Christianity which, nonetheless, would not lose its necessary roots in the Judaism of Christ.[23]

The later tradition of the Roman church, corroborated by many non-Roman witnesses of the early Church, according to which it was to this church and her bishops that Peter transmitted (among the future churches and their bishops) the role and the responsibility that was his, among the apostles and in the primitive Church, is not at all surprising.[24]

The objections that Cullmann opposed to this transmission—despite everything he acknowledged (better perhaps, than any other modern historian), such as the historical conditions that prepared for it—come up against one difficulty: the confusion he supposes to be essential to Catholic tradition between the role of the apostles and that of the bishops. Peter's function in the New Testament, he rightly stresses, is preeminently the apostolic function: of foundations and founders. Now because this function, by its very nature, cannot be present *except* at the beginnings of the Church, it therefore appears to be untransmittable.[25]

But it is quite different when we are aware that the function of the popes, like that of the other bishops, as successors of the apostles in general or of Peter in particular, is not understood in authentic Catholic tradition as a function of redoing in each generation what the apostles did, and could only do, in the first generation. When we understand that the bishops' apostolic succession, according to this tradition, signifies that they received from the apostles the gifts necessary to carry on the work that they alone could do, and developed it along the lines in which they alone could involve it, the problem changes. It is no longer a question of seeing other "Peters" in the successive popes, any more than we see successive bishops as other "apostles." It is simply a matter of acknowledging that the concern for unity, which from the beginning of the Church led Christ to give to one apostle (among the others) a special function and capacities, makes it likely that an analogous responsibility would be given to one bishop among the rest, *mutatis mutandis.* The envisioned need is obviously no less urgent when the development continues, but is more and more manifest as this development brings growing dispersion and complexity with it.

In fact, as we see, from the time of the subapostolic Church the bishops were everywhere in place and were everywhere acknowledged as successors of the apostles in the sense we specified; and we also see that the bishops of Rome claimed to be depositaries (among the other bishops) of the function of unity which had been Peter's among the other apostles, with analogous consequences. From this time on, evidence is not lacking that nowhere in the Church did this statement give rise to opposition in principle. What is more, even if it is from Rome (as is natural) that the first systematic justifications of this function came, Rome's interventions, throughout the first centuries, seem much more often called for by local demands than resulting by its own initiative.[26] Still better, we need think only of St. Basil or St. Cyprian to see numerous. churchmen grumble about the Roman way of doing things— Rome's lack of understanding or inconsistencies—while, at the same time, they were concerned with obtaining, at any price, Rome's concurrence and sanction for what seemed essential to them in the life of the Church. In this regard, what is verified between Paul and Peter in the incident at Antioch seems to be verified over and over again over the course of the first centuries: incidents of maximum tension between the Roman bishop and the other bishops (when they are examined a bit more closely) show that this tension would never have come about, or would never have been so intense, if a singular authority had not been acknowledged, *nolens volens,* to the Roman see.

Certainly the transmission, or to be more exact the transposition, at the end of the apostolic age, from Peter to the Roman bishop of the primacy in the Church, and first of all within the episcopal college, is surrounded with obscurities that the modern historian does not have (or no longer has) the means to dissipate. However, this obscurity is no different from that which surrounds the transmission, or transposition, of the function of the apostles to the bishops, and which permits the bishops to call themselves their successors. We must even say: However few and late may be the attested facts or the explicit documents relative to the succession from Peter to the bishops of Rome, the assured facts and explicit documents on the succession from the apostles to the bishops are perhaps even rarer.[27] With the exception of Ignatius of Antioch, Irenaeus, and Cyprian, the historical foundations between the doctrine of the apostolate, formulated in the New Testament, and that of the episcopate, which the Church of the Fathers transmitted to the later Catholic Church, are few and far between, but they allow us to conjecture a *de facto* continuity, postulated unanimously by the faith of the Catholic Church. They alone would not suffice to establish it. With St. Leo the Great, on the other hand, we find a doctrine that is fully conscious of the Roman primacy, which modern Catholic theology and the First Vatican Council were able to state in more technical terms, though they neither surpassed nor exhausted it.[28] In essentials, this doctrine attributes nothing more to the pope, among the bishops, than the New Testament does to Peter among the apostles. (These statements, that the popes were like Peter in this, are more numerous and more certain than those that allow us to maintain that the bishops, in general, succeeded the apostles in general.) To maintain—as has been and still is done—that the notion of the papacy and its function, as defined in the First Vatican Council, is a product of medieval developments, and flows from either the Donation of Constantine or the False Decretals, supposes that one has never read St. Leo, or that one is unaware that his doctrine, at the time he formulated it, caused no opposition, even from those who, had no direct role in its development. In essentials, Leo's doctrine merely systematizes the transposition to the Bishop of Rome, among the bishops, of the primacy of Peter among the apostles, and its legitimacy is attested to, from subapostolic times, at least as copiously and forcefully as the succession of the bishops from the apostles.

It is evident, then, that the difficulties brought against the Roman primacy, like those brought against the apostolic succession (*a fortiori*), are due much less to the primacy and the defined doctrine that takes account of it than to deformed notions of that doctrine, connected with accidental circumstances that accompanied the exercise of the primacy but are in no way essential to it. This is more or less true of all objections that are brought up by every kind of ecclesiastical function. However, there is no reason for surprise if such an important and singular function gave rise to particularly regrettable abuses or, especially, caricatural interpretations. More than detailed historical arguments—however important they may be for clarifying the problem—an exact notion of what is or is not essential to this primacy ought to dissipate the objections to which it still gives rise.

Catholic doctrine teaches, according to the texts of the First Vatican Council,[29] corroborated and clarified by those of the Second,[30] that the pope is no more an "Apostle" than the other bishops are. On the contrary, he is a bishop *like* the rest—a *successor* of the apostles in the very precise and defined sense that the others are. But as *the* bishop of the Roman Church, and like all the other bishops of Rome before him, the pope is a *particular* successor of Peter, who before he died had settled in Rome in the task to which he had been assigned from among the other apostles. This task was (and remains) keeping the Church and her development in unity by personally exercising (always within the college to which he belonged and in conjunction with it) the responsibilities which were (and are) those of the whole college. To be understood, this requires that we no more look at the pope as a "superbishop" than at Peter as a "super apostle." Indeed, as we have seen, Peter's unique role and function were not different from the duties of the apostolic college of which he was a part. His primacy was due to the fact that what was entrusted to all (including him) was first entrusted to him; even more, it was due to the fact that he received personally what all were to receive collectively. He was thereby called not to supplant, nor even to govern from above and without, the other apostles, but to express, guide, and foment their unity of action from within.

N·B·

Among the bishops, the same is true for the pope. No more than they is he a "modern" apostle taking the place of the "old" apostles. Like all bishops, he is a successor of the apostles only insofar as he is established (like all of them) to keep the Church alive and to develop her in the same life: the Church which was founded on or by the apostles, while Christ forever remains the cornerstone. Among the other bishops, the pope is particularly the successor of Peter in that he succeeds him, among the bishops, with the duties and capacities proper to the episcopate, and with a task of unity analogous to Peter's among the apostles. The pope is entrusted with the same responsibilities, and the same capacity to exercise them, that all bishops possess together with him.[31]

This supposes, therefore, that the pope is not a "superbishop," just as Peter was in no way a "super apostle," but a bishop among the others—just as Peter was an apostle among the others, even though he was the "first" of all of them and the preeminent apostle.[32] Since this is essential to the episcopate (as we have established, though we shall return to this point), it is essential that the pope be the bishop of a particular church, the church of Rome, where Peter ended his career and where he deposited what was transmittable in his function, so that the bishops of this church might exercise it after him, *mutatis mutandis*.

Let us note that it is also essential to the episcopate (otherwise, he would not truly succeed to the apostolic college) that each bishop, beyond and inseparably from his responsibility to his local church, have a share with all his brothers in the episcopate in the "care of all the Churches" and, more precisely, in the concern that, in them, *the* Church of Christ develop and develop in unity. This, in turn, is connected with the very nature of the local churches, which, accumulatively, do not so much constitute the one and Catholic Church as manifest her locally—everywhere the same, in her indivisible unity with Christ in the Spirit.

What, therefore, definitively differentiates the pope from the other bishops is not what is added to his direct and immediate responsibility over his church, that is, a general responsibility over the universal Church. Again, this is common to him with all the other bishops. In his case, this general responsibility takes the form of a particular responsibility for the unity of the episcopal work, for the unity of the whole Church, about which all the bishops are also concerned, as are all the churches. For this function over all churches other than his own, and over all the bishops, and the authority (and responsibility) proper to the first of the bishops, instead of being indirect or mediate in its ordinary exercise (contrary to the function and authority of his colleagues), or direct and immediate only in its individual exercise in the extraordinary case of a council, is ordinarily direct and immediate.[33] If this were not the case, the *sollicitudo omnium ecclesiarum* of the Bishop of Rome would not differentiate it from that of all the bishops.

Does this mean that the pope must, or at least *can,* in every instance intervene in the place of each bishop in the affairs of his local church, or, at the very least, in a general way substitute himself for the totality of bishops in the governing and harmonious development of the whole Church? In no way. A pope who would so act, or try to act, would prove that he understands nothing about his function. And, let us add, ultramontane theologians, who may have lost a sense of balance, to the point of inciting the popes to act in such a way by proposing anticipated justifications of this behavior, did at least as much harm to the radiance of the papacy as the occasional weaknesses of its incumbents. Such notions in no way correspond to the authentic Catholic *and Roman* tradition. Their best refutation is the explanations furnished the First Vatican Council by Mgr. Gasser on the modifiers "episcopal," "immediate," and "ordinary," applied to the papal function, or the authorized exegesis of the council texts by the German and Swiss episcopates with the explicit approval of Pius IX. However, the best explanation is the one that Gregory the Great gave long before for the effective exercise of the pontifical primacy and the authority necessary for its mission of unity:

> I do not consider it an honor that I know how to make my brothers lose their honor. My honor is the honor of the whole Church. My honor is the firm support of my brothers. I am truly honored when the honor proper to each of them is accorded.[34]

This comes down to saying that interventions (whatever they might be) of the pope in the life of the universal Church ought never be aimed at diminishing or thwarting the activity of the totality of bishops, or each or any bishop, but ought to uphold and develop their activity in this unity of the Body of Christ, which it is essential that this activity promote. To do so, the pope can, and when necessary must, intervene with an authority that no one can question, which is why the pope (as was the case with Peter and the apostles) can do everything that each bishop or all the bishops together can do, always and everywhere.

This is precisely the meaning of the formula of the First Vatican Council, according to which the pope's universal authority is "episcopal, ordinary and immediate." That it is "episcopal" does not mean that the pope is a "bishop of bishops," which would suppress the bishops' episcopal authority or reduce it to a simple delegation of his own. Rather, the pope possesses the same authority they do when they are united with him to contribute to the fruitful exercise in unity of their authority (the authority of each alone and all together). That it is "immediate" does not mean that the pope must be introduced as a perpetual third party between each bishop and his local church, or between all the bishops and the universal Church, but that he can intervene each time his responsibility is required—with everyone, whether a layman or other bishops—without an intermediary being necessary. That it is "ordinary" does not mean that it must be exercised, in every instance, everywhere and all the time, but that it can be exercised every time the pope deems it necessary.

In the concrete, this supposes that the pope can evoke and judge (in appeal) every decision made in the Church by an authority other than his, while his authority cannot be appealed before any other.[35] In particular, an appeal from the pope to an ecumenical council seems deprived of any meaning, since an ecumenical council, on one hand, cannot exist without the pope and conversely, the pope alone can exercise the authority that is that of all the bishops (including himself in a council of this type.[36]

Obviously, it is not only in a judiciary matter, nor *a fortiori* in an appeal, that the pope's function must be exercised; this is not his most habitual or most important function. His most important function is to stimulate, guide, and sustain in unity the totality of episcopal activities. As we shall see, these activities are a service of the Church, and his function makes him, according to the formula of St. Gregory (which is found in the abovementioned letter), the "servant of the servants of God."

This is why the "question" of the pope's superiority over the council, or over the totality of the episcopate—or the opposite—is a badly put question. It is relevant only from the moment the papal or episcopal (papal *and* episcopal) authority is seen in the Church as an exclusive *dominatio* in itself. If, on the contrary, it is conceived essentially as a service, diverse but organically coordinated authorities no longer appear as naturally in conflict or opposition, but as called to cooperation, to mutual aid, which is in the very nature of things. In particular, an authority such as that of the pope, which tends only to unity in the exercise of all the other authorities (since these others have meaning only if they are exercised in and for unity), has no meaning, according to the teaching of St. Gregory, except insofar as it fortifies the others. Conversely, the latter, if they believe they develop by developing *against* papal authority, do nothing more than undermine their own support.

To be understood, this requires that we constantly return to what we have said about Christian unity in the spirit of Moehler and the fathers, whose doctrine he so well summarized. It is not just any unity: it is the unity of truth preserved in love, of the truth that is the "love of God poured out in our hearts by the Holy Spirit." This explains that the pope, among the bishops, like Peter among the apostles, cannot have special responsibility for everything that touches upon the unity of the Church without having authority that extends to the whole proclamation of the truth and to the whole manifestation of divine life in the Church. These things are not separate in Christianity—they are but complementary aspects of one reality, which is the communication to men of the love which makes up the life and the truth of the Divine Being.[37]

This means, of course, that for the pope, as for every bishop, and for the pope more than for any other, there is no legitimate activity other than one that is completely in the service of this supernatural, divine love. In the person of her bishop, the successor of Peter, the Roman Church must always (following the formula of St. Ignatius of Antioch) appear as the one "presiding in charity." But "service" in the Church—here more than ever—must be properly understood. If all possessors of authority—all the bishops and the Bishop of Rome, as the first of all the rest—are only servants, and servants of all, they are not servants in a sense that could signify, or justify, abdication of their responsibility and, therefore, of their final power of decision. Indeed, they are the servants of all because they are chosen, consecrated, and sent by the One who wanted to be the preeminent "Servant," but is no less "Lord and Master." Therefore, each according to his rank, they must exercise in their special place, in *his* name, *his* authority for the good of all, as he himself had done, that is, for the development and full growth of his love in all and among all. It is precisely this love, and its authenticity, that pope and bishops would betray by rejecting the requirements of the truth of the inseparable Christian life, which is theirs (and theirs alone) to maintain.

## II. Presbyteral Collegiality and the Bishop: The Local Church

The preceding cannot reach full clarity except in a concrete theology of the life of the local church. Again—and we cannot say this too frequently—the universal Church appears, and even exists, only in the local churches. This is why we have studied the essentially eucharistic life of the Church in these communities before we explain the apostolic mission which presides over their foundation, and then the succession of bishops, which must sustain and develop the Church (i.e., these communities). Only by seeing how the episcopate plays its fundamental role in each church does the collegiality of the episcopate take on all its meaning, and, at the same time, the pontifical primacy.[38]

From this point of view, the first thing that ought to strike us in the local church is that, since the bishop is consecrated only in being introduced into a universal college, he exercises his function only by becoming, in turn, the consecrator of a local college, that of the "presbyters," the "priests of second rank," as we say today.

We have shown that the presbyterate, in one sense, is older than the episcopate, for before there were bishops there were the apostles. And one of the first things the apostles apparently did when they founded a church was to install "presbyters." What were these presbyters in the beginning? The fact that their title is taken directly from an office of the synagogue inclines us to think that, in the primitive Christian Church, they must have been an equivalent of what they were in the synagogue, where presbyters (the title means "elders") formed a representative council of the faithful, called to direct the local community. What an archaic document like the third-century *Apostolic tradition* of Hippolytus tells us about the Christian presbyters does not allow doubt that such was their recruitment and their function in the beginning. They were, particularly, representative members of the faithful, to whom the general responsibility of community life was entrusted.[39]

In what sense were they representative? It does not seem that they were objects of a democratic election that was already familiar in the Greek city-states. It seems, rather, that their choice was the result of consultation among the apostles who were founders of the local church and community, or, in any case, the most active portion of it. The Pastoral Epistles, corroborated by the unanimous testimony of the documents of the immediately subapostolic Church, stress the decisive role of the apostles in providing their authority. Chosen in agreement with the faithful, it was through the apostles that the first presbyters were "established."[40] This is why, even though they were taken from the mass of the faithful and were first conceived of as their representatives, from the beginning they had a share in the *episkope,* the pastoral responsibility that belongs to the apostles, which the apostles received not from the Church but from Christ.

As long as the apostles were there, this was especially manifested, it seems, by deliberation with the presbyters, which at the same time associated them, though indirectly, with the whole community from which they came and with the final decisions. Yet the apostles alone, in the last resort, assumed the responsibility of governing the Church, by the fact that they communicated to her acts the authority that they alone were able to exercise in Christ's name. But it seems that when the apostles, momentarily or definitively, left the Church, thus constituted, either the totality of the presbyters, or some among them, or just one among them was led to exercise the *episkope,* no longer simply by association with the apostles but by delegation of their proper powers. As long as the apostles lived, they kept, or rather could keep, control over the exercise of this delegation, whether by intervening or by people's recourse to them in serious cases. But when they were no longer present and *could* no longer be present, we admit, the *episkope* (with the reservations we have made) passed entirely from the apostles to the local *presbyteroi-episkopoi.*

The first, intermediate case of a *presbyteros-episkopos* (or several) acting in an ordinary fashion, as delegated, with the apostolic *episkope,* corresponds to the curial function at a later date: as rectors of nonepiscopal parishes, under the higher authority of a bishop who is absent and only occasionally intervenes. The last case, by contrast, is that of the bishops, as they became after the final departure of the apostles.

Yet from the instant that an apostle was no longer part of a fully established church, the *episkope* of the *presbyteroi,* by the force of things, made a transition from a consultative to a decision-making function. What we have said about the apostolic function shows that the pastoral function it implies is not, first of all, a governing function. The naturally eucharistic nature of the Church manifests it, and the manner of Christ's institution of the apostles implied it: it is first a function of proclaiming the evangelical Word as ambassadors of Christ, with whom and in whom Christ makes himself present. Consequently, it is also the function of presiding over the Eucharist, in which the mystery of the life of Christ, having been announced, becomes sacramentally present, so that we may be united by being incorporated into Christ himself. It is only as a consequence of this basic ministry of the Word and the sacraments that the apostolic ministry implies a governing power, that is, a power of applying the Word to the whole existence of the community, in such a way that this community draws the consequences, in the total life of its members, of its faith in the Word and its participation in the Sacrament. The pastoral function in the Church, far from being reduced to a governing function, involves governing only in this sense, from this perspective. This is why the governing it must exercise, in assimilation of the Word of life in the whole thought and existence of the faithful, brought a close association between the faithful and this governing function, through the intermediary of such representatives as the presbyters.

Once the apostles were no longer there, even the simply delegated exercise of the *episkope* that the apostles entrusted to them therefore supposed, *before anything else,* the responsibility of preaching the Word and the sacramental celebration. There is every reason to think that the apostles, when they were in the communities, had prepared the presbyters for the full exercise of that *episkope* by associating them with their preaching and their presiding over the Eucharist.

It may be, nevertheless (as certain documents of the early Church lead us to think, particularly the *Didache,* which could shed light on certain allusions in the New Testament), that the presbyters did not immediately deduce that they were to preach the Word in the absence of the apostles or to preside at the Eucharist. It seems that the "prophets" and the *didaskaloi* often exercised the first responsibility under the direction or simply with the agreement of the presbyters; and it even seems that they were allowed, at least for some time and in a few places, to be called to celebrate the Eucharist, since there was such keen sentiment about the close connection between Word and Sacrament. On the first point, in any case, the apostles seemed to be the first, even when they were present, to encourage the prophets to sustain their preaching with their witness and the *didaskaloi* to extend and "mint" it (so to speak) into a systematic teaching. That the second practice, attested to by the *Didache,* of allowing the prophets (particularly) to preside at the Eucharist, was also encouraged by the apostles is much more questionable. However, the New Testament does not allow positive inference in this sense, and the feeling of the primitive Church on the Eucharist, as a union between the Head and his members, seems to have supposed from the first (as with the celebration of the Jewish ritual meals) the celebration of the common Eucharist by one person alone and, more precisely, its being presided over by one who exercised the apostolic *episkope* and represented, like the apostle himself, the Head among his members.[41]

Whatever the case, it is undeniable that the first or major duty of episcopate (improperly called "monarchical" from the second century on) was not the governing of the Church, under the ultimate responsibility of one person alone, but the eucharistic celebration, flowing from the proclamation of the Gospel, with apostolic authority, by one local successor of the apostles. At the same time, the bishop never appeared except in the midst of the *presbyterium,* which was associated with him in each eucharistic celebration, as in the whole of his pastoral task. In fact, if the bishops were prevented from doing so, it very soon became the function of the presbyters exclusively, with the assent of the bishop, to preside at the Eucharist, and normally it devolved upon the presbyters to preach in the framework of the Eucharist, when the bishop did not do so himself.

Thus the presbyters—not only or because of their call to participate in the governing role of the apostles or the bishops, but because of their association with the apostolic responsibility of proclaiming the Word with the authority of Christ and of presiding at the sacramental celebration of his mystery—are found, from the beginning, associated with the apostolate (in the strongest sense of the term) in its source. Even when the fullness of the apostolic *episkope,* insofar as it is transmittable, was conferred on one of them, and only on one of them, it appears always to the Church that he exercised it in a way that was faithful to the apostolic institution, in cooperation with a group of other presbyters. The bishop, even though he is the only depositary of succession to the apostolic *episkope* in its fullness, in order to exercise it, appoint the presbyters to assist him, just as the apostles had done before.[42]

Habitually in the early Church, presbyters were associated by their presence with the bishop's presidence at the Eucharist, and consequently, more or less effectively, with his proclamation—with the authority of apostolic origin—of the evangelical word, as well as with his pastoral responsibility and, in particular, all his major decisions concerning the life of his flock. On occasion, when a bishop was absent or indisposed, one of their number, with his assent, could replace him, both for preaching and for the celebration. Temporarily, in such a case, the *presbyterium,* as a body, could manage the affairs of the local church.[43]

Later, the extension of primitive episcopal "parishes," similar to our modern dioceses, brought the further breakdown into secondary parishes. At the head of each parish, a presbyter came to exercise—always under the control of the bishop and in dependence from him, but in ordinary fashion (i.e., stable and constant)—a quasi-episcopal pastorate.[44] That is, the presbyter, habitually presiding at the local Eucharist, assumed the responsibility for preaching and the "cure of souls."

Without doubt, this is the extreme form of participation by the presbyterate in the episcopate. That of a vicar general is undoubtedly greater, on the level of jurisdiction; but it was on the pastoral level, where jurisdiction is secondary, the function of pastor of a parish (as just defined), however locally or numerically limited its exercise, that the presbyterate was most closely assimilated to the episcopate in an individual. Again, the bishop is not primarily an ecclesiastical administrator, but a pastor. And the pastorate, derived from the apostles, is first of all proclamation, with the authority of Christ himself, of his Word; presiding at the eucharistic celebration, at which are assembled in Christ those who believe in this Word; and, finally, governing the whole life of the community which results from it—and, only for this reason, the exercise of jurisdiction. It is in the pastor that all this is communicated by the bishop to a member of his *presbyterium,* insofar as it is permissible for him to communicate his function and responsibility.

Whether in the immediate exercise of his responsibility or in its exercise by intermediary pastors, it is always in cooperation with a *presbyterium,* of which he is the most eminent member, that the bishop exercises his *episkope.* To this extent, the episcopate is not collegial only in the sense that it is always exercised by the bishop as a member of a college of bishops, in union with him; it is collegial in a second sense, because it is always exercised in the center of a college of presbyters, and in communicating to them everything that constitutes the episcopate—radically from the fact of their ordination, which establishes them in the presbyterate, and effectively from the fact of their constant (if multiform) association with the exercise of the *episkope.* A ministry of the Word; a ministry of the sacraments, including the Eucharist, a primordial sacrament; and finally a pastoral responsibility; and for a bishop to exercise it in the Church, the presbyterate must participate in all this with him, even though the ultimate responsibility, as well as the primary source on the local level, resides in the bishop alone, the only local successor of the apostles.[45]

This suffices to show that the collegiality of the episcopate around the pope, the Bishop of Rome, and therefore the successor to St. Peter, and the presbyteral collegiality around the local bishop, the local successor of the apostles, though analogous, are not identical.

Just as Peter was an apostle *among* the Twelve, even though he was the *first* of the Twelve and, personally, had received everything the Twelve received collectively, the pope is a bishop *among* the other bishops, even though he is the *first* of the bishops and realizes in himself the unity of the whole episcopate, all of whose powers he alone (in certain circumstances) can exercise. In the midst of "priests of second rank" (as we now call successors of the *presbyteroi* of antiquity), the bishop is the sole successor of the apostles. Taken like him, moreover, from the midst of the Church, and in principle representatives of the life of this Church, engendered by the apostolic ministry, priests are the necessary means of associating the whole Church to the pursuit of the apostolic work by the successors of the apostles. Did not the apostles reckon that they could not carry out this work without communicating the broadest participation of their responsibility and their gifts to such representatives of the churches, "established" by them in all the churches? Through ordination, the bishops therefore bestow on priests the power to do practically everything that they themselves have to do: preach the Word; sacramental celebration, beginning with the Eucharist; and, finally, exercise of the *cura animarum*, with all the authority received from Christ that all this presupposes. As in the case of pastors, priests, when there is need, can exercise all this with very broad autonomy. However, they never exercise it except through a communication of responsibilities and the corresponding gifts of grace which come to the bishop from the apostolic succession. Whatever their proper extent of special responsibility and relative correspondent autonomy, they must exercise it in harmony with one another. Still more, they must exercise it in union with their bishop and in dependence from him, since it is from him alone (or, more exactly, from the episcopal order of which the bishop is the local representative) that their own order flows, as a derivation.[46]

But just as the bishop can exercise his proper function only by sustaining the life of charity in the Church, which the apostolic ministry has elicited, he needs to receive, even cause, the most effective collaboration of the entire Church in his task. He therefore, *a fortiori*, needs to associate his supreme responsibility in a very special way with the representatives of this Church, the priests, to whom he must communicate his apostolic gifts. Incumbent on him is the final responsibility of the apostolic work, just as it is from him that communication of the gifts flows, which makes it possible. But since he cannot exercise his functions without communicating the gifts which are attached to them, he cannot fruitfully exercise his responsibility without uniting those who are associated with his function to the decisions it entails in a very special way, to the extent of their association with his tasks.

The canonists will say that, in an ecumenical council, each and all of the bishops who are called to it are legislators by right, while their totality with the pope does not make two distinct subjects of authority, but only one. In a diocesan synod, they maintain, the bishop is the sole legislator, properly so called.

This does not obviate many decisions that a bishop cannot make validly without at least consulting the episcopal chapter which is like a permanent delegation of the synod, nor certain decisions, such as suppression or erection of parishes, without the agreement of these chapters.[47] Specification reveals the constant direction in the Catholic Church of the necessity of the presbyterate's association with the responsibilities of the episcopate, and the reality that such participation entails, not only in *de facto* exercise of episcopal responsibilities but, ultimately, in the very right to exercise them.

In other words, it is only by a call from the bishop to participate in his responsibility that the presbyterate acquires its own, while the pope, because of the divine institution of the primacy, has a responsibility that presupposes the college to which he belongs, of which neither he nor Peter was the institutor, but only Christ. But that this appeal be made, and be fully effective, does not belong fully to the *bene esse* of the local church but simply to her *esse,* resulting from what the apostles established.

Yet this does not say enough. It is not simply in the local church that the presbyterate is necessarily associated with the bishop. Indeed, we have said—and could not say it too often, because the one and universal Church does not manifest herself, nor has she any concrete existence, properly speaking, except in the local churches—that it is true also that every local church is nothing other than the local manifestation of this Body of Christ which is also present (the same everywhere) in all the other churches. This is why the local church can exist only by having a bishop as her head, who is a bishop only because he was introduced into the universal college of bishops, the successor of the college of the apostles, by episcopal consecration. But since he cannot be a bishop locally except by remaining in communion with his brother bishops and, thereby, maintaining and developing the communion of his church with the other churches, the bishop cannot associate the presbyterate of his Church with his function without associating it with this work of Catholic unity. Through the intermediary of the bishops, and always in conjunction with them, there is a real communion of all the presbyterates, as well as all the local churches. This is why a priest of a particular church, even though he is attached to the bishop by a very special bond, does not need a new ordination to exercise, with the assent of the respective bishops, his functions in other dioceses—any more than a baptized person needs to be rebaptized to be admitted to communion.[48]

Many consequences result from this, but one of the most interesting has been admitted with regard to the pope and the exercise of his proper function as guardian of Catholic unity. Just as every bishop can and must associate his presbyterate as broadly as possible with all his functions, including that of binding his church to the other churches, the popes did not fail to associate their own presbyterate (or, at the very least, its chief elements) not only with their function as local bishop but with their personal function with regard to the universal Church. This is only a normal consequence of the reciprocal connection of the bishop with his church and, in particular, of the relationship of the bishop's ministry of apostolic origin to the ministry of the whole presbyterate of this church.

Of course, on the basis of this communion of all the churches, and all their presbyterates, not only the faithful of every church but also the priest of every Church can be received, in his rank and proper functions, in any other church. The association of the Roman church with the proper responsibility of her bishop, in order to be exercised as best as possible, demands a movement of exchange and intense communication between it and all the other churches. In particular, the greater extension of the papal function (over the course of history) with the universal Church, the more desirable that the presbyterate of the Roman church attract to itself eminent priests from all the churches. What is called the "internationalization" of the Curia, and more especially of the Sacred College (i.e., of the central section of the Roman presbyterate especially associated with the universal responsibilities of the Roman bishop), assuredly belongs to the *bene esse* of the Roman church and of the whole Catholic Church.[49] However, if the preceding (regarding the general relationship of every bishop with his presbyterate) is correct, it must be said that it is to the very *esse* of the Roman church, and every church, that the pope find cooperators for his function—dependent, certainly, but indispensable and associated with all his responsibilities in his own church. For if the pope, as we have established, is not some superbishop but a bishop like the others—though he is first among them and is charged with a special responsibility with regard to all and to their unity—he must, like every bishop, belong to two distinct colleges that cannot be confused, without the whole apostolic institution of the Church being utterly ruined.[50]

Again, as a bishop, he himself is a member, and, in his case, the "first" member of the episcopal college; and it is in conjunction with this college, as the one preeminently responsible for this conjunction, that he must exercise both his local function and his universal function. But as Bishop *of Rome,* he is the source of another college, the presbyteral college of the bishop of Rome, and again, like every bishop, it is only by calling this representative college of his church to the broadest cooperation with him that he can exercise his episcopal functions, both in what touches on his "solicitude for all the Churches" and for the *cura animarum* of his own church. Hesitating to admit this comes down to breaking the connection of the first bishops of Christendom between the episcopal function and the local church on the only level in which the life of the pope can be a life of concrete community in the faith and the sacraments. But this connection was established by the apostles in establishing the first churches, and is certainly of the very being of the Church.

The depth of the bond between the episcopate and the local church and, especially, the presbyterate that represents her to the bishop, and to which, in turn, the bishop cannot avoid communicating his responsibilities as broadly as possible, and the proper gifts which relate to them, is manifested in a very special way when the episcopal see of a church becomes vacant. In this case, in this interim, the episcopal function does not normally revert to the neighboring bishops, nor even to all the bishops together, nor even to the Bishop of Rome, but to the totality of the local presbyterate, represented by the local chapter, which will delegate one of its members as vicar capitular for as long as the see remains vacant.[51] (Of course, this is merely an interim state, which could not be prolonged without creating an ambiguous situation.) During the interim, the power of the presbyterate, of the chapter, and finally of the vicar capitular cannot go beyond maintaining the life of the diocese *in statu quo.* No permanent new law could be promulgated by the presbyterate or its emanations (the chapter or vicar capitular); no parish could be established or suppressed. On the other hand, even though they may have received it from the deceased bishop, all the pastors of parishes retain their jurisdiction; all the priests retain their power of forgiving sins in the sacrament of penance. It is through *effective* participation in the episcopal authority, received from the apostles themselves, that all priests proclaim the Word of God with authority and validly celebrate the Eucharist and the other sacraments. Still better: where the needs of the diocese require, the vicar capitular can institute new pastors and give them the powers necessary for execution of their responsibility, even though, as we have said, this is the most complete·participation in a bishop's pastorate. And if the diocese lacks priests, and though the vicar capitular cannot validly ordain candidates to the priesthood, he can give them, as a bishop does, dimissorial letters which oblige, *sub gravi,* a neighboring bishop to ordain them (as long as the latter has no reasonable objection).[52]

In the same way, *mutatis mutandis,* without being able to innovate or substantially modify the situation of the universal Church in which a deceased pope left it, the apostolic see, during vacancy, belongs to the Roman presbyterate and (particularly today) the cardinals who constitute the part habitually associated by the pope to his function, to maintain the unity of the universal Church, of which the pope is its major expression and preeminent guardian and originator.[53]

In the same way, in the early Church, election of the local bishops belonged in principle to the local church, but in fact was given to the presbyterate which represented it, under the presidency and the approval of the neighboring bishops, who provided consecration of the one elected. Very early, Rome maintained that, since the regularity of episcopal elections was essential to the life of the local church in the unity of the universal Church, no election could be valid without Rome's approval, at least *per conniventiam* (i.e., by tacit acceptance). When irregularities multiplied, due to local intrigues or especially to the interference of temporal powers, Rome refused to recognize as valid an episcopal election which did not have its explicit confirmation. It maintained this requirement all the more after the end of the Middle Ages, when it had to accept (in many places) that, in fact, election was reduced to a simple formality—ratifying choices dictated by princes. Later, the modern concordats between states and the Holy See, having tacitly accepted (in most cases) the disappearance of elections, tried to compensate for the loss by prior conversations between Rome and the temporal powers. Lastly, in the "secularized states," since there was more or less no interest in these matters, the choice of bishops redounded (in principle) to the pope himself—in practice, to a Roman congregation, obliged by the force of things to rely more or less completely on the opinions of nuncios.[54]

This situation, explainable by history, is certainly not the ideal—and it would be a singular mistake to infer that the election of the pope, which almost alone continued in his church in accordance with the traditional procedure, ought not escape it. Quite the contrary. It is desirable that, from providential persistence, there flow a renovation of the ancient elections in every place which is inspired by the authentic improvements to pontifical election in the past.

People, early on, began to associate with the college of cardinals, particularly for election of the Roman bishop, the neighboring bishops (so-called "suburban bishops," of whom the first, the "dean," was the bishop of Ostia, who had the traditional role of presiding at the consecration of the pope, if the latter were not already a bishop at the time of his election). Then, among the cardinal-priests (to say nothing of the deacons who were joined to them and about whom we shall speak later), ecclesiastics were introduced who were particularly representative of the Church of the West, beginning with the titularies of the most influential episcopal sees.[55] Finally (quite recently), the patriarchs of the East, in communion with Rome, were added. Thus the College of Cardinals (i.e., the kernel of the Roman presbyterate), without ceasing to be the organ of participation in the pope's church, and in his election, has become representative of the universal Church.

Similarly, it would be desirable that all episcopal elections rely essentially on an eminently representative presbyterate of the church in question (what the cathedral chapters ought to be), to which would be joined the bishops of nearby sees. This group would act in close connection with all the local clergy and laity, with the proviso of final ratification, which the Holy See could give (or refuse, for that matter), either directly or through a legate in rapport with the church in question.

## Notes

1. See above, pp. 164ff. The decisive text on episcopal collegiality is in the constitution *Lumen Gentium*, chap. 3, par. 22.

2. See the collective volume published by Y. Congar and B. Dupuy, *L'Episcopat et l'Eglise universelle* (Paris, 1962), as well as *Le Concile et les Conciles* (Chevetogne–Paris, 1960), and especially, *La collégialité episcopale, histoire et théologie* (Paris, 1965). See also J. Ratzinger, op. cit., pp. 171ff.

3. On collegiality in the New Testament, see Dom B. Botte's study, "La collégialité dans le Nouveau Testament et les Pères apostoliques," in *Le Concile et les Conciles*, pp. 1ff. See also "Le ministère apostolique dans la littérature chrétienne primitive. Apôtres et épiscopes, 'sanctificateurs' des nations," by J. Colson, in *L'Episcopat et l'Eglise universelle*, pp. 135ff., as well as his *L'Episcopat catholique: Collégialité et primauté dans les trois premiers siècles* (Paris, 1964).

4. On the relationship of the episcopal college to the apostolic college (in addition to the works mentioned above, see A. M. Javierre, "Le thème de la succession des apôtres dans la littérature chrétienne primitive," in *L'Episcopat et l'Eglise universelle*, pp. 171ff., as well as J. Colson's *L'Evêque dans les communautés primitives* (Paris, 1951).

5. cf. note 67, Chapter 5.

6. Cf. the texts of Ignace of Antioche and Cyprien.

7. Mt 28:19–20.

8. Clement of Rome, *Epistle to the Corinthians*, 42.

9. See the episcopal lists given by Eusebius and mentioned above (pp. 21ff.).

10. On the first, see Acts 15–18 and 2 Cor 1:19, 1 Thes 1:1, 2 Thes 1:1, 1 Pt 5:12. On the second, see Acts 4:36, 9:27, 11–15 passim, and 1 Cor 9:6, Gal 2:1, 9, 13, Col 4:10.

11. In addition to the pastoral epistles addressed to them, see, on Timothy, Acts 16–20, Rom 16:21, 1 Cor 4:17, 16:10, 2 Cor 1:1, 19, Phil 1:1, 2:19, Col 1:1, and Phlm 1. On Titus, see 2 Cor 2:13, 7:6, 13, 14, 8:6, 16, 23, 12:18, Gal 2:1, 3.

12. Heb 12:23.

13. Chapter 2 of Hippolytus' *Apostolic Tradition* gives the earliest descrip-

tion of this consecration. The Council of Chalcedon specified that three *residential* bishops, who were active, should at least participate in it.
14. On Peter in the New Testament, see especially O. Cullmann, *Saint Pierre, disciple, apôtre, martyr* (Neuchâtel–Paris, 1952), as well as Dom J. Dupont, "Saint Paul, témoin de la collégialité apostolique et de la primauté de saint Pierre," pp. 11ff. of the collective work, *La collégialité épiscopale* (Paris, 1965).
15. Mt 16:13ff.
16. Jn 21.
17. Lk 22:32.
18. See Maurice Goguel, *L'Eglise primitive* (Paris, 1947), pp. 191ff.
19. Cullmann, op. cit., pp. 28ff.
20. On the altercation at Antioch, cf. Cullmann, op cit., pp. 42ff., as well as the study of J. Dupont. As what preceded showed, we do not think that, at this moment, Peter's authority was only that of head of the primitive mission, emanating from Jerusalem, but visible head of the whole Church.
21. We can generally follow his activity in Maurice Goguel, *La Naissance du Christianisme* (Paris, 1946), pp. 128ff. and esp. 141ff.
22. Cullmann, op. cit., pp. 62ff.
23. See our *Eucharist*, pp. 215ff.
24. The whole of the texts will be found in Mirbt, *Quellen zur Geschichte des Papstums un des römischen Katholizismus* (5th ed.; Tübingen, 1934), or Rauschen, *Textus antinicaeni ad primatum romanum pertinentes* (Bonn, 1914).
25. Cullmann, op. cit., pp. 192ff. See above (pp. 331ff.) for the general discussion of this problem: In what sense does the episcopate succeed the apostolate?
26. T. S. Jalland (Anglican), in *The Church and the Papacy* (London, 1944), seems to have effectuated the interpretation closest to objectivity in regard to the totality of witnesses of Christian antiquity on the function of the papacy in the Church and its relationship with Peter's function in the beginning. The very fact that he undoubtedly minimizes the value of certain facts (such as the role of Victor in the paschal controversy) merely gives more weight to his final judgment (p. 542). Such a historical conclusion is more than sufficient to support the explanation of the Catholic doctrine which we endeavored to give, in complete fidelity, to the texts of the two Vatican councils, examined (as they should be) in the light of Scripture and the whole of Catholic tradition.

Let us simply point out that, after the *"Tu es Petrus"* itself, the two texts whose establishment and interpretation gave rise to the most recent controversies are Irenaeus, in the *Adversus haereses* (3,3.2), especially the words: *"Ad hanc enim ecclesiam propter potentiorem principalitatem necesse est omnem convenire ecclesiam, hoc est eos qui sunt undique fideles, in qua semper, ab his qui sunt undique, conservata est ea quae est ab apostolis traditio,"* and

Cyprian, in par. 4 of his *De catholicae Ecclesiae unitate* (see Labriolle, op. cit., pp. 8ff.). On the first, it is characteristic that a commentator as anti-Roman as F. W. Puller, who nevertheless has an unquestionable fund of knowledge, had to forgo much of the minimizing interpretation he gave of it in the first edition of his *Primitive Saints and the See of Rome* (London, 1893), beginning with the third edition (1900). Cf. pp. 19ff. of the latter with the corresponding texts of the preceding editions.

As for the text of Cyprian, Dom J. Chapman and then Fr. M. Bévenot seem definitively to have established the authenticity of the long version, which is the most categorical on the Roman primacy and its relationship with the primacy of Peter. See, on these two texts, Jalland, op. cit., pp. 109ff. and 161ff. See also, on the whole question, the studies of P. Batiffol, collected in the volume *Cathedra Petri* (Paris, 1938).

27. Such authors as Langmead Casserley seems not to be aware of this fact, even though he perceived and expressed the solidity of the tradition on the episcopate in general. That he seems not to have been aware of this points up the difficulty with which, even today, authors of the most ecumenical tendencies treat the problem of the papacy without *a priori* judgments.

28. On St. Leo, see again T. S. Jalland's *The Life and Times of Saint Leo the Great* (London, 1941), esp. pp. 303ff.

29. Denzinger Bannwart, pp. 1821ff. (the constitution *Pastor Aeternus* of the First Vatican Council).

30. The constitution *Lumen Gentium*, pars. 22ff. of chap. 3.

31. See, in particular, Karl Rahner, "Quelques réflexions sur les principes constitutionnels de l'Eglise," in *L'Episcopat et l'Eglise universelle*, pp. 541ff.; G. Dejaifve, "Primauté et Collégialité au premier Concile du Vatican," in ibid., pp. 639ff; R. Aubert, "L'Ecclésiologie au (Ier) Concile du Vatican," in *Le Concile et les Conciles*, pp. 245ff.

32. The recently upheld theory, according to which the papacy would constitute a degree of the sacrament of orders, superior to the episcopate, seems fantastic to us, with no possible support in tradition other than the court formulas that were never accepted literally in the Church, which are sadly typical of certain curialist tracts from the end of the Middle Ages.

33. See G. Dewan, "Potestas vere episcopalis' au premier Concile du Vatican," in *L'Episcopat et l'Eglise universelle,* pp. 661, and G. Thils, "Potestas ordinaria," in ibid., pp. 689ff.

34. See above (p. 318) concerning this text. On explanations of the true import of the Vatican I definition, which were furnished immediately after the council and which we have already mentioned, see O. Rousseau, "La vraie valeur de l'épiscopat dans l'Eglise d'après d'importants documents de 1875," in *L'Episcopat et l'Eglise universelle,* pp. 709ff. The chief texts in question will be found in the new *Enchiridion* of Denzinger-Schönmetzer, pp. 603ff.

35. On the first point, see the canons of the Council of Sardica (342) and a discussion of them in Jalland, *The Church and the Papacy,* pp. 219ff. On the second point, even though the famous formula *Prima sedes non judicabitur a*

*quoquam* appeared (as a quotation from an apocryphal council!) only in a letter of Nicholas I to Emperor Michael in the year 865 (cf. Denzinger-Bannwart, p. 330), the statement that all judiciary causes found their final conclusion in Rome, and there alone, is very clear in the letter of Innocent I to the African bishops in 417 (ibid., 100), given in P.L. 20, col. 651, under the name "Zosimus." Cf. the text that is even closer to the famous formula, by Gelasius I in his letter 13 to the bishops of Dardania (P.L. 59, col. 66).

36. On the texts of the councils of Constance and Basel, affirming the superiority of the council over the pope and their approval, respectively by Martin V and Eugenius IV, see the analysis of Dom P. de Vooght, "Le conciliarisme aux Conciles de Constance et de Bâle," in *Le Concile et les Conciles*, pp. 143ff. Cf. the commentary on the text of Constance, in particular, in H. Küng, *Structures de l'Eglise* (Paris, 1963), pp. 313ff. (cf. *L'Eglise*, vol. 2, pp. 621ff.). Küng is certainly right when he maintains that one cannot dispense with these texts as easily as so many modern Catholic authors do. The reasoning of Fr. de Vooght (in the article cited), according to whom the papal confirmation would not make these texts authentic documents of the magisterium because this confirmation was not given under the conditions required by the First Vatican Council for an infallible papal definition, it seems to us, is pure sophistry. Nothing obliges us to transfer what is said in the constitution *Pastor Aeternus*, of a definition pronounced by the pope alone, to the simple confirmation by the pope of a conciliary definition.

On the other hand, it is our opinion—contrary to Küng, if we understand him properly—that the opposition between the pope and the council is artificial, once, as a norm, the ecumenical council is not conceived of without the presence of the pope with the other bishops. The opposition makes sense only from the moment when, as at Constance, there is no reigning pope whose legitimacy is without question. In these circumstances, and as long as they are not corrected, the council's authority becomes supreme in the absence of a valid pope, even those who may have only an apparent title to the papacy. See P. de Vooght, *Les pouvoirs du Concile et l'autorité du Pape au Concile de Constance* (Paris, 1965), which arrives at a position very close to what we have just maintained.

Deliberately, we shall not enter the argument that was bitterly debated after (as well as before) Vatican II: Are one or two subjects distinct (adequately or not) from the supreme authority in the Church? Indeed, it seems to us that this is a badly stated problem which makes no sense, unless we confuse, or tend to confuse, "authority" (episcopal, in general, or papal) and *dominium*. In these perspectives of authority as *ministerium*—as a common service, under complementary forms, of the unity preserved in the truth of love—the problem loses all its sharpness—and we may wonder if it still has any significance.

37. See the last pages of the study of J. R. Geiselmann, "La définition de l'Eglise chez J. A. Moehler," in *L'Ecclésiologie au XIXe siècle*, pp. 190ff. Cf. J. Ratzinger, op. cit., pp. 121ff.

38. K. Rahner himself, who we think may not admit certain notions on the

nature of the episcopal function and, consequently, of the Church, has nevertheless described the importance of the local church very well: "The Church, when she becomes truly an 'event' in the fullest sense of the word, is necessarily the local Church: the total Church becomes understandable in the local Church" ("Principes constitutionnels de l'Eglise," in *L'Episcopat et l'Eglise universelle*, p. 551). The following pages show the connection of such statements with the sense of the eucharistic celebration.

39. See, in particular, *Apostolic Tradition*, par. 7.

40. Cf. above, pp. 394ff. In particular, for the origin and the evolution of the terms *episkopos* and *presbyteros*, see Maurice Goguel, *L'Eglise primitive* (pp. 119ff.), even if many of his interpretations of the facts are more or less arguable. On the relationship of the episcopate and the presbyterate in the Church of the ante-Nicene fathers, see G. Dix, "The Ministry in the Early Church," in Kirk, *The Apostolic Ministry*, esp. pp. 216ff. The constitution *Lumen Gentium* has only one paragraph on priests (no. 28, chap. 3).

41. Ignatius of Antioch (*Smyrniots*, 8,1) tells us that the Eucharist may not be celebrated without the assent of the bishop. But the most ancient text that tells us that a *presbyter* alone can replace him in presiding at the Eucharist is the fourth epistle of Cyprian (par. 2, P.L. 4, col. 236), even though it considers. ers the matter to be self-evident.

42. It has not been sufficiently noted that Ignatius of Antioch seems to hold equally to the necessity that the bishop have a *presbyterion* around him and the necessity that the "presbyters," and the whole Church, never to do anything without the bishop.

42. In antiquity, the eucharistic concelebration of presbyters with the bishop seems to have consisted in their presence at his side, attesting to their moral union with him in this celebration, as in everything. On this subject, see the studies collected in the special number of *Maison-Dieu* on concelebration.

On the other hand, we know, through St. Jerome, that in certain churches at least—in Jerusalem, in any case—each priest had his share in preaching.

44. The first explicit text on such a delegation to a presbyter seems to be a letter from Pope Innocent I to Decentius (P.L. 20, col. 557).

45. On the presbyterate in its association with the ministerial or hierarchical priesthood of the bishop, see J. Lécuyer, *Le sacerdoce dans le mystère du Christ* (Paris, 1957), in particular pp. 393ff., and the collective volume that appeared the same year, *Études sur le sacrement de l'ordre*, in particular the two contributions of Dom B. Botte, "L'ordre d'après les prières d'ordination" and "Caractère collégial du presbytérat et de l'épiscopat," pp. 13ff. and 97ff.

46. This explains the resistance that long was manifested by theologians, from St. Jerome to St. Thomas Aquinas and beyond, to the idea that the episcopate constitutes a superior degree of the sacrament of orders. The idea was finally stated by the Second Vatican Council (constitution *Lumen Gentium*, chap. 3, par. 21). But certainly we must not understand it in the sense

that the bishops would possess, on the level of orders, whatever priests of second rank do not have (as is the case with them with regard to deacons); rather, they constitute the root, as it were, directly derived from the apostolic seed, of a ministry communicated to other priests as simply shared, and whose exercise with them always remains dependent on the bishops.

47. Can. 1428, 1532, 1541, 2292.

48. In *Dictionnaire du Droit canonique,* see the article "Incardination" by R. Naz.

49. See Victor Martin, *Les cardinaux et la curie* (Paris, 1930), as well as the article "Cardinal" in *D.D.C.* by A. Molien and G. Alberigo, *Cardinalato e collegialità* (Florence, 1969).

50. This is where the suggestions of K. Rahner went wrong: whether to have the pope elected by the totality of the episcopate or (which would be the same thing) to reduce the College of Cardinals to constituting a permanent representation of the world episcopate. Cf. the conclusion of his study, "L'épiscopat et la primauté" (in *Quaestiones disputatae,* 4), and the paragraph on cardinals in *Das Amt der Einheit: Grundlegendes zur Theologie des Bischofsamtes* (Stuttgart, 1964). See below, pp. 551ff.

51. Can. 391, 431, 432, 435, 437, 444.

52. Can. 113, 282 (par. 1), 286 (par. 1), 455 (par. 2), 958, 959.

53. Can. 241, which refers back to the apostolic constitution *Vacante Sede Apostolica* of St. Pius X (Dec. 25, 1904).

54. On the election of bishops in antiquity, see L. Mortari, *Consecrazione episcopale e collegialità* (Florence, 1969), as well as A. Dumas, *Les élections épiscopales* (pp. 190ff.), from vol. 7 of Fliche and Martin, *Histoire de l'Eglise* (Paris, 1940).

55. On all this, see the work of V. Martin cited in note 49.

# Chapter 8
# Catholicity and Apostolicity in the Parochial Community: Laity and Hierarchy

As revealing as the election of the pope may be from the way the episcopal function sets the life of the Church in her entirety in motion, first on the local and then on the universal level, still more important in this respect is a final question that we must now study: the problem of the relationship between the ministry, inherited from the apostles, either in their successors, the bishops, or in their coworkers, the "priests of second rank," and the whole of the members of the People of God, the *laos theou*, or laity.

The role of the pope is conceivable only within the episcopal collegiality and in rapport with it. The role of the bishop (including the pope) supposes, and requires, presbyteral collegiality. But it is still truer that the apostolic ministry in the broadest sense, that is, either the ministry of the apostles themselves or that of their successors, the bishops, or finally of their coworkers, the priests of second rank, the "presbyters," has no meaning or primary reality except within the community of the faithful. Here, if you wish, is a third form of collegiality in the Church, which is properly her catholicity, in the most profound sense. The great Orthodox thinkers of the nineteenth century powerfully contributed to clarifying this under the term *sobornost,* which is the Russian translation of "catholicity": unanimity in love or the unity of truth—unity and truth that cannot be preserved except in love, the love of God poured into our hearts by the Holy Spirit.

## *I. The Problem of the Laity*

In the first part of this book, we pointed out the dangerous tendency of medieval ecclesiology which progressively caused it to see in the Church only the hierarchy, or what we have come to call by this word, that is, the "clerics," or the bishops alone. All the rest—the faithful laity in particular—appeared in the body of the Church only as a kind of conjunctive tissue, though blest, as long as they did not create "foreign" bodies! Hence the natural reaction which, outside the Church, causes people to consider as essential to the lay state, to the state of the laity, alienation vis-à-vis the Church and a sort of counterchurch. Hence, also, the reactions which were manifested in the Church herself at the time of the Protestant Reformation, and of which we see so many analogues today: substitution for an extrinsic Church, where the laity could not feel at home, a completely lay Church, divested of this clericalism, which by monopolizing her seemed to have emptied her of her proper content.

The only positive reaction, however, would be to rediscover the Church as a "body" in the primary sense St. Paul gives the expression: a complex but single organism, constituted of different members who, each and every one, have their own function, but where each member needs all the others, and the most worthy members are at the service of the lowliest.

This, obviously, supposes—above all—rediscovery of the laity in its relationship with the hierarchy, or, rather, rediscovery of the fact that the hierarchy, in the original meaning of the word are not the Church's ministers, considered statically, but the Divine Life's means of communication and circulation in the whole body. Indeed, far from being an end in themselves, the ministers have no meaning except in and for the body and, therefore, in conjunction with it. Again, this is not to bring it, as from without, a life which would be alien to it, but to maintain in it the life that comes from a place higher than they but which belongs to all equally.[1]

This cannot be studied fruitfully in the abstract. What prevents the "theology of the laity" from developing in a fully positive and spontaneously balanced way, it seems, is the tendency to develop it in the abstract, just as (for too long) people developed a similar "theology of the Church" which, in effect, was nothing but a "theology of the clergy." To rediscover the true significance, the true role of the laity, it must be studied in the concrete life of the Church, where the laity are articulated with the apostolic ministry. The place where they meet, in the word's fundamental sense, is the "parish," the local church. Indeed, it is here that the faithful gather together, *all* together, around their pastors, in order to receive from them the evangelical Word, to make it theirs in prayer, to offer themselves in response to the presence of Christ, and, finally, to communicate in his mystery. Presence and mystery are consecrated for them so that they may be consecrated by the same ministry that brings them the authentic Word of Christ.

Again, the Church not only finds her essential manifestation there but, basically, becomes a reality only where men—all men, in principle and in fact—are called to meet one another. They are called there by the divine Word, which will make them one in the faith, and will consecrate them, all together, in unity, so that they will form one body in Christ, and his Spirit will accomplish in their flesh the mystery of his cross and his resurrection for the salvation of the world.

In the beginning, in this sense, the parish was simply the local church, gathered around her bishop. But from the moment evangelization was extended to the countryside, instead of exaggeratedly multiplying and frittering away the episcopate it became inevitable that the original, episcopal parish be broken down into secondary parishes. They were entrusted to as many priests of the second rank, the pastors, who (as we have seen) by force of circumstances became real quasi bishops.[2]

This evolution posed a problem for the Church, and we must admit that it has never been resolved in a completely satisfactory fashion. As the Anglican liturgist, Gregory Dix, pointed out, it resulted from the unexpected fact that the original relationship of the episcopate with the presbyterate became reversed in practice.[3] St. Hippolytus' liturgy of presbyteral ordination (in the middle of the third century) evokes a situation which was not completely contemporary and presents the institution of the presbyters as a means, both for the bishops and for the apostles before them, of giving others a share in their task of governing, so that they might more freely dedicate themselves to their primordial task of proclaiming the Word and celebrating the sacraments. But more and more it was the priests of second rank who appeared to the faithful as the ministers of the Word and sacraments, while the bishops played the role of distant administrators, as a sociological evolution accentuated this reversal. Since the bishop had become a *grand siegneur* in the Middle Ages, he became more and more a "prefect of clerical affairs" after the Napoleonic concordat. With the exception of a few solemn public celebrations in his cathedral (or elsewhere) on rare feast days, or for equally exceptional occasions, he no longer appeared to be a sacramental minister, except in conferring ordinations or giving confirmation. He no longer preached, except for special circumstances, and it was hard to look upon these talks as real homilies.

Today the tendency is far from reversing itself—and seems, rather to be accentuating. Even according to eminent theologians, the "bishop of the future" seems to be looked upon as a kind of ecclesial technocrat. His connection with his local church seems, in fact, to have become so lacking in intimacy that not only are we accustomed to frequent episcopal transfers but we have come to consider as something from the dead past the axiom "No Church without a bishop, no bishop without a Church." People recommend, along with accentuated relaxation of the bonds between the bishop and his flock, the multiplication of bishops without their own churches, as directors of movements or activities attributed to the Church but without local roots. Bishops who remain in principle ordinaries of a definite place tend to ask either for the possibility of delegating confirmation to simple priests or of being given auxiliary bishops, who would more or less "free" them from their pastoral cares of this type, in order to allow them to devote all their time to the work of commissions, on a national or even world scale.[4]

While the evolution of the episcopate outside the specific, pastoral sphere is accentuated as a result of the fragmentation of the original episcopal parish into many secondary parishes, entrusted to priest-pastors, these parishes seem threatened from two sides at once. On one hand, the evolution of modern life, with the depopulation of rural areas and the separation in cities of workplace from residence, seem either to prevent or to make precarious any community determined by a particular place, especially the place of residence.[5]

Here again, we see flourishing theories which, far from hindering this tendency to evaporation of the parish, reenforce it in the name of "arguments of principle." We are told that, in the modern world, it is one's occupation, and still more one's belonging to a given social class, rather than the place where one lives, that must supply a basis for every human community, and that the Church cannot escape this. Consequently, far from deploring the "inevitable" withering away of parishes, we should rejoice. It is fitting even to accelerate this process by hastening the building of new community structures, modeled on the "natural" communities of modern mankind, and prepare for the necessary insertion of the Church in the "mankind of tomorrow."

Others follow a different path, and do not propose substituting communities that have another sociological basis for the parish community. They seem no longer to see a particular incarnation of the Church possible in a world dominated by the mobility of individuals and the fluidity of all transient groups, where they may gather in passing. They expect nothing more from the Church than the always provisional installation of spiritual "recharge points" where individuals in transit could, on occasion, receive the Word and the sacraments. Even so, they would not have to contract particular relationships, either with others of the faithful or even with the priestly teams that they would occasionally meet, but whom they probably would not meet again in everyday life.

Still others recommend an empirical combination of the two methods: chaplaincies for modern sociological groups and temporary churches, which would serve as intermittent "service stations" for more individualistic members of the faithful, whom the specialized movements could not "canalize" or could do so only imperfectly.

It must be admitted that as long as we try to create a theology of the laity in such a context, where the bishop is no longer looked upon as a pastor, or only if we agree to reduce his pastoral function to administration, while priests are restricted to a role as anonymous distributors of the Word and the sacraments to an equally anonymous faithful, or as animators of groups of men determined not by their common life in Christ, members but by the sociological conditioning they share with a profession or a social class, this theology would not be satisfactory. The Church in which the theology of the laity ought to introduce the layman seems to have dissolved into pure abstraction, since it has been split into groups of people who no longer bring Christians together as Christians but as members of a class or as agents of a particular function in society. Or else it is fixed more than ever into an organization that, theoretically, has spiritual goals but in fact is essentially administrative, and the idea that the laity could "belong" to it no longer has any meaning.

Under these circumstances, as we see generally today, the theology of the laity will tend to split into two antithetical parts which will never succeed in meeting, for everything incites them toward mutual rejection. On one hand, as a reaction against the clerical theories of the Church from the past, there will be a healthy insistence that laymen, like the clergy, are consecrated by the Word they hear with faith, by the sacraments they receive, and particularly by the Eucharist, in which they take part. On the other hand (and this is no less healthy), it will be stressed that, in distinction to the clergy, it is the laity's role to penetrate the mass of mankind, making use of the fact that they, unlike the clergy, have never stopped belonging to it through their everyday occupations.

Today, we are induced to set these two aspects of the lay vocation in opposition to one another. Since the Church has ceased to be looked upon in such a way that the clergy propose to the laity, not only in fact but even in theory, a view of her as a genuine human community, capable of being open to mankind in general and becoming part of it, we are told that if the laity are consecrated by the same sacrality that differentiates the clergy, by the fact of their reception of the Word and the sacraments they cannot (we are also told) and, furthermore, must not aspire in turn to consecrate the world in any other way than as secular, in its very secularity. Since the Church's sacrality apparently has lost all humanness, the only "consecration" the laity can bring to, or rediscover in, the world in which they are immersed is necessarily a "consecration" that has nothing to do, nor could at any price have anything to do, with that of the Church and the clergy, with the sacrality of the Word and the sacraments. Irremediably, the position of the layman in the Church, in this case, would be destined to ambiguity. As a layman, he could not refashion the unity of his life, except by renouncing the Church, nor could the Church do so, except by renouncing its sacrality.[6]

We can see that it is not by taking up the analysis on the sole level of the laity that we shall be able to make the episcopacy and the parish more satisfactory. As an indispensable preliminary, there must be a renewal both of the episcopacy and the parish, which will prepare, in a return to sources that is more necessary than ever, the inevitable adaptation to the data of the human situation in general, which today are in an accelerated state of change.

## II. *The Bishop, the Apostolic Ministry, and the Laity*

The connection of the local church and the whole Church to the bishop is so close and so profound that there is no hope of rediscovering (in a positive way) the meaning of the Church's laity as long as the bishop's role is obscured by a radically unsatisfactory exercise of his function and, *a fortiori,* if we justify the unjustifiable by *ad hoc* theories.

In France, the Civil Constitution of the Clergy (1790) among many unacceptable (not to say unreasonable) suggestions, formulated a few that deserve examination. Perhaps the most interesting proposed to make the bishop the pastor of the "first" parish of the diocese, that of his cathedral, and to make him personally fulfill all its functions. The suggestion can be easily understood if we are aware that, today, the bishop ordains priests in order to make them able to participate in apostolic functions that he no longer fulfills himself. Hence (let us say in passing) the extravagant idea of certain modern theologians that the distinctive function of the bishop is (and is only) to ordain other ministers. If this were the case, we should be falling back into pure and simple magic with the sacrament of orders. On the contrary, however, one of the most traditional notions of St. Thomas explains the power of ordaining as the simple power of communicating what one possesses oneself. In particular, ordination to the priesthood is communication of all that the bishop possessed in fullness, but a communication with priests of second rank that remains dependent both in its exercise and its principle on that fullness which remains with the bishop alone. The words no longer have meaning, however, and this communication and fullness appear to vanish into the unreal if the communicator of the fullness that he is supposed to possess does not in fact exercise any of it himself, or exercises merely a formal appearance which is in the process of disappearing.

How can the bishop be "recognized" by the faithful (according to the phrase of Clement of Rome, and repeated by all the ancient consecration liturgies) as the high priest of this priesthood received from Christ, shared in by the priests of second rank, with which the laity are associated through their baptism and confirmation, if he not only no longer baptizes them but wishes to "free" himself even from confirming them (a role which is still his), and especially if he never celebrates the Eucharist for them and with them? In such circumstances, the bishop does not exercise an effective pastorate in a truly human relationship with them, and understands, by the word "pastoral," merely administrative decisions, perhaps concerning them but made in their absence and extraneously of them.

It is extraordinary that certain theologians merely wave such considerations away, claiming to see in them only some sort of sentimentality. In their eyes, would not that charity which makes up the life of the Church also be mere sentimentality? Or if this is not their thought, toward whom, then, can charity be exercised in accordance with Christ's teaching, if not toward one's neighbor? But what does the bishop, whose role is to "preside in charity," become if his existence is so ordered that he no longer has any neighbors or, which comes down to the same thing, in the exercise of his ministry he no longer has an opportunity to meet his neighbors? Again, if the local church is so important, to the point that the Church exists only in her, in a sense which is primary and basic, it is because there—and there alone—people come together as neighbors to hear the divine Word together, to respond to it together, and to be seized by and brought together in its mystery, so that this mystery may thus "be completed" in everyday life. But if the bishop no longer has a real part in all this, if he absents himself from it (which is the same thing), either he has ceased being what he is in principle (Christ's preeminent minister for his Church) or the Church has ceased being herself (the community of charity). For if this community of charity is not first of all a human community, its charity is merely wind, and if its ministers are not ministers in the most human possible relationship (which is also divine), they are no longer ministers of Christ. They are either phrasemongers with nothing serious to say—mechanized performers of rites and forms emptied of their content—or administrators of a machine whose purpose and workings no one knows.

It will be said: "If our bishops wanted to exercise these functions of the ministry, where would they find the time to fulfill their governing function?'' Again, it is precisely that bishops be sufficiently free of these governing functions to continue to fulfill, *themselves,* the functions of doctor, liturgist, pastor, *which are essentially theirs,* that the priests of second rank were instituted. And we must add: the governing functions which bishops ought to share as widely as possible with the presbyterate are the functions of *spiritual* governing, directly connected with teaching the faith, the celebration of worship, and the religious and moral life of their flock. Those functions of *material* governing, which so often occupy three quarters of the bishops' time (and too much of their priests' time)—financial cares, construction and maintenance of buildings and such, and even authentically, charitable concerns when they extend to material details—do not belong to the proper domain of bishops *or priests.* Properly they are tasks of the deacons (as we shall see in a moment). It was only after the practical disappearance of the diaconate that bishops and priests found themselves more and more immersed in these matters, often to the point of drowning in them. As long as there are no deacons to fulfill these tasks, this lack is one of the first things to which bishops and priests should turn, to free themselves, and give them (as much as possible) to laymen of good will.

Moreover, let us note, without effective, personal exercise by the bishop of the curial function in a central parish (which is still a practice in some countries, such as Great Britain and the United States), entrusting to auxiliary bishops the principal pastorates of the diocese. In dioceses that are particularly extensive or populous, auxiliary bishops are given to residential bishops especially to alleviate their administrative responsibilities, and this practice (whose results are generally acknowledged to be excellent) shows that effective exercise of the pastoral task—the task—the Word, the sacraments, the *cura animarum*—is not made impossible by the exercise of administrative responsibilities in the Church—except when people *want* this to happen!

However, attribution to the bishop in his own diocese of a particular parish is assuredly not necessary, and could be merely a palliative. What must be remembered, and what he must be reminded of, is that he is the first pastor of *all the parishes* of his diocese. Undoubtedly, the stable handing over of immediate responsibility over each parish to a particular priest, to be effective, requires that the bishop not intervene in every instance in the work of the pastor whom he himself placed there. But it also requires that the bishop, first of all, make himself the pastor of his pastors.

We must hasten to add that this does not mean he must aspire to or become their ''spiritual director,'' in the modern sense of the term. It is, on the contrary, a beneficent evolution of the canonical rite that ends with differentiation, even relative separation, of the *external forum* from the *internal forum,* that is, a rite whose jurisdiction is generally exercised in the Church (on the social plane) by a different person than the one who takes direct responsibility for her members' affairs of personal conscience. Nothing would be more opposed to the spirit of the Church and, we might add, to the spirit of the Gospel; nothing could constitute a graver fault for the bishop (if only from the psychological point of view) than wishing to control the direction of the consciences of his priests (or the most "involved" laymen) under the pretext of better governing them on the social plane. The only thing that this would accomplish would be degradation of the community of love into an absolutely intolerable pseudo-spiritual despotism or totalitarianism.

On the other hand, the bishop should be the spiritual guide of the other pastors by associating himself with their particular concerns, just as he associates them (to the extent possible) with *his* general concerns; accepting requests for opinions or advice and the information they contain; communicating, in response, the necessary knowledge to his collaborators of the total context of their special problems; accepting, even asking for, their counsel, without any semblance of force; and reserving final decisions to himself on major cases but leaving them to others in other cases—but always, if possible, so that no decision, is made in an important matter without prior communication in both directions. (This latter ought to be his first concern in a modern diocese.)[7]

To reach this point, in cooperation with secondary pastors—as closely as possible, without "going over their heads"—the bishop must have direct contact (if not with all the faithful) at least with those who are most representative of the totality of his flock, and also with all those who, rightly or wrongly, want direct contact with him, whether for a personal motive or for a more general interest.

Again, we must specify that the representativeness in question could never be reduced to belonging or not belonging to some "privileged" movement. Every layman who sacrifices himself to bear witness to the Gospel and its exigencies (in his whole life) is representative, and must be considered as such. In more general fashion, every layman is also representative who represents a form of life or position in the life of the Church or the world which poses, in regard to the Gospel, a particular problem to which neither a priest nor a bishop can say the right word, if the Christian had not first supplied the bishop with the report of his own, irreplaceable experience.

This attitude of openness, which is so necessary for the bishop, first with respect to priests of second rank and especially pastors and then, in cooperation with them, with respect to the laity, would be vain if the bishop did not make it serve the efficacy and, especially the applicability of mature doctrinal teaching. This teaching must be given as directly as possible and must be extended in the celebration of the sacraments, and above all the Eucharist, with which, in order to attain full realism, both supernatural and natural, every teaching of the Divine Word must be united.[8]

One of the first or major objects of cooperation between bishops and pastors, whom he has associated with himself for particular parishes, should be that he preside effectively, throughout the year, at local eucharistic assemblies where he can proclaim the Divine Word in a maturely prepared fashion, and that his visit constutute the departure point or kernel of the teaching which will be given in the area during the year. Such *pastoral visits,* which would take on their real meaning in this way, could be combined with the celebration of confirmation and the ordination of ministers, originating in the parish in question, and adult baptisms. But these visits, of course, could also be made apart from such occasions. In any case, they ought to be dissociated or carefully differentiated from simply formal or official objectives of special but generally superficial import that today motivate or constitute the major part of episcopal visitations: inaugurations, fairs, awards presentations, meetings of groups that are of concern only to their members, etc.

In the interval before this effective exercise of his ministry of the Word and the sacraments begins in the parishes, the bishop, even if he is not the pastor of his cathedral, ought to celebrate and preach there publicly. And this should not be reduced to the solemnization of a few great feasts but should be performed every Sunday or holy day of obligation when his presence elsewhere is not required. Again (lest we are told we are looking for the impossible), why would it be an "intolerable burden" for Catholic bishops, unless because they start with a false idea of their real obligations, to resume what all Orthodox bishops continue to do as something perfectly natural and expected?

Habitual celebration and preaching by the bishop, in his cathedral, ought to go hand in hand with reestablishment of its normal function as spiritual center of the diocese. This would suppose, above all, restoration of the daily office, in a form adapted to effective participation by the faithful, as is the case in all Anglican cathedrals. More generally, it is necessary that the cathedral, through a combination of model worship, a life of unceasing prayer, rich doctrinal teaching (of which the bishop is the animator), special possibilities for confession and spiritual counseling by experienced priests, and the regular presence of delegations in perpetual renewal of the faithful and priests from the parishes and the various movements, again become the heart, as it were, of the spiritual life of the diocese. Thus the bishop could appear there (above all) as "the man of collective prayer" and, at the same time, as the doctor and presider of the Eucharist, as the preeminent initiator of new, adult Christians.

Reconstitution in each cathedral of such a center of prayer, teaching, worship, and evangelical mission goes hand in hand with resurrection of the episcopal office as a pastoral office, in the true sense of the word, and not simply or fundamentally as an administrative office.

## III. The Parish as a Place for Inserting Laity within the Church

This restoration of the cathedrals, as necessary as it may be for restoration of the episcopal ministry as an essential ecclesiastical ministry, to which the laity must orient themselves, could not resolve all the problems that arise today in particular parishes. The cathedral can and must become a model and guide for the other parishes, at the same time that family homes are recentered and revitalized. But just as the bishop, alone, cannot accomplish the whole task, which has also become the task of pastors, the cathedral cannot be a substitute for the totality of parishes.

The local base of parochial life is threatened in present-day circumstances, so that we cannot ignore it. If we have to "fit out" a parish of a traditional type, adapt it to new individual- and collective-life situations, and even contemplate its being replaced by organisms that have another material basis than the residential community, it must be done by understanding the basic needs to which the parish has responded until now and by endeavoring to continue to satisfy them in other conditions.

In this respect, neither replacement of the local parish with professional or class basis communities nor, even less, disappearance of every stable Christian community and replacement by worship and pastoral centers, adapted to the transient needs of individuals on the move, could offer satisfactory solutions. The local parish, like the local episcopal church before it, presented durable values that must subsist, throughout all possible mutations, in "leading men" who live as Christians by living in the Church, leading *those who are "neighbors" to one another* to hear the Word of God together, from a successor of the apostles or his responsible delegate in their group—to pray together with him and, with him presiding, celebrate the Eucharist together.

From this point of view, a reconstruction of the Church which would try to build on the basis of professional or (for a stronger reason) class communities would not only be gravely insufficient, it would run the risk, from the start, of orienting itself against the very spirit of the Gospel: "You have one teacher and you are *all* brothers," and "There is neither Jew nor Greek, there is neither slave nor free, there is neither male nor female; for you are all one in

Christ Jesus.''[9] In other words, the Christian community must not cement, that are by absolutizing them, the natural, essentially restricted communities that are founded on race, nationality, or social milieu (occupation or class). Quite the contrary. Despite natural tendencies toward self-enclosure and exclusiveness by all communities of this type, the Christian imperative must force them to be open by forcing their members to enter into a wider community that does not know these barriers, that transcends and can effectively combat all forms of opposition that it will inevitably cause.

Therefore the basis of the Christian community of the Church can be only the human community, in all its universality, which it restores by gathering it around Christ and in him. It is also essential that it not be an abstract community of people who do not meet; on the contrary, it must be the most concrete community there is: people who live in almost constant relationships, both in the world and in the church—a community of ''neighbors'' in the Gospel sense.

This is why, in the ''former society,'' which is not perhaps as dead or dying as some would like us to believe, the local, residential community furnished so natural and felicitous a basis for the community of the Church, if it was open as widely as possible (first, for the practice of hospitality) to all other communities of the same type. Indeed, there and there alone, in a habitual way, the rich rub elbows with the poor and may effectively meet them, and those in different occupations offer their hands to one another and, of themselves, tend to similar encounters. And to the extent that nationalities can meet and races can tend to come together and melt, Christian hospitality has everywhere made people feel at home, even though everything else appears to separate them or set them against one another.

To attempt to consecrate social strata (the ''classes,'' as people say today) by supplying them with exclusive religious communities (or, similarly, occupations, nationalities, races, cultures, tastes, etc.) is to ''resacralize''— contrary to the basic orientation of Christianity—these separations, these rivalries, these oppositions which the Gospel has taught us to relativize, surpass, and if necessary destroy, so that all may be one in Christ Jesus and that we may recognize one another as brothers because we are sons of the same Father.

Setting up Christian professional, political, and cultural groups is admissible only if it helps the evangelization of the corresponding milieus and their human and Christian openness, and especially those who are most naturally alien or most spontaneously hostile. But how would this be possible if, for Christians who entering such groups, the Christian community disappeared, which brings them together *as Christians,* that is, as men who, quite simply, were won by Christ and thus won for brotherly charity, even when everything else seemed to make them strangers, even enemies, to one another? Let us say again, repeatedly, that this universally human community to which men are called, in being called by Christ, cannot be abstract without being meaningless. This is why "service station" churches, where members of the faithful could listen to the Word and receive the sacraments as they please, without binding themselves to other members or entering under the pastoral responsibility of particular priests, would *not* be churches. When we say "church," we say common life under the pastoral responsibility of the successors of the apostles or their representatives—and a common life which cannot be limited to hearing the Word or receiving the sacraments. This common life is *Christian* only if it becomes the common exercise of charity, a mutual, reciprocal exercise of charity, first among those whom it has touched and who live in it together, and, as a consequence, the common exercise of this charity in the world in which they are inserted.

The "old world," both by the stability and the complexity of its communities and its facility of communications (which did not tend to drown communities in an anonymous mass), offered, in the organization of a parish in the area of residence, such facilities for the establishment and development of the communities of the Church. This is an indication of a human value which ought to incite Christians of today—not, certainly, to unrealistic conservatism with regard to such a world but (at least) to a certain prudence—when we see this world dissolving or in a fair way to dissolving. Instead of rejoicing or taking heart at this dissolution, we should take care, on the human and Christian plane, to substitute equivalents of the old parish, which had a human and therefore Christian value. From the preceding analyses, we see that this is not the case with the replacements that are proposed today. Some go contrary to the spirit of universalism in Christian charity and, let us add, the best tendencies of modern mankind, to go beyond particularisms and the limitations of the past, others too easily and uncritically adopt the most dangerous tendencies of the modern world, which confuse unlimited generosity with abstract generalization and, under the pretext of universal life, would destroy all life by uprooting it.

Under these conditions, how are we to conceive this revitalization, adapted to the present necessities of the "parish"? (Let us understand by this the concrete realization of the local church, outside of which the Christian individual, the lay person, could have no real existence, nor could the People of God, the *laos theou,* to which he is supposed to belong and which gives him his name.) The first observation is that a very important distinction must be made between the fact that the local, "traditional" parish (based on place of residence) can no longer be sufficient of itself and the rash supposition that it is no longer necessary for the Church and must be suppressed.

Without doubt, for its own vitality, the parish is in need of various "movements," and not professional or social ones (in the sense of class movements). These needed movements must develop on an inter- or paraparochial plane within the diocese, and even in close relationship with analogous movements in other dioceses. But these movements cannot play their whole role if they isolate their militants and uproot them from the parish. If they do so, if they *tend* to do so, the movements will unfailingly end in a pseudo Christianity of class, clan, race, nationality, or some other absolutized specialization, which would be a negation of the Christianity of Jesus Christ, of common life in the unity of his Spirit, which is the only life possible for the Church and the Christian. The real solution could be facilitated if the life of the cathedral were restored on the lines we have sketched—for the moment, at least, around a central parish. Then the movements could have not only their "global" but also their general meetings, movement after movement, in this central location. Far from hampering meetings on a parochial level, this centrality would encourage them.

To this, three remarks must be added. The first is that the importance of the place of residence as a basis for the local parish is still so closely connected with family life, as the essential cell in the body of the local church, that in the present stage of human evolution we must continue to envisage it as a basis of parochial organization.[10]

Secondly, to suppose that mankind of the future ought to center its activities on the place of work, rather than on the place of residence, corresponds to a view of evolution that is no longer current. What is proving to be true, rather, is that tomorrow's mankind will be centered not in the place of work but in the place of leisure, by which we understand the place of one's cultural occupations. It is certainly an open question whether the place of leisure will coincide with the place of residence, but it is even less probable that the place of leisure will coincide with the place of specialized work. It is therefore in the place of cultural leisure, as the meeting place of the most diverse sociological milieus (professional or otherwise) that the reconstitution of parishes must come about—if, because they are locally rooted, in the place of residence, the traditional parish is condemned to decline and disappear.

In reality (our third and last remark on this point), the human problem vis-à-vis the modern parish is much more complex, even in its purely sociological aspect, and is not foreseen by certain hasty generalizations on the inevitable "urbanization" and "mobilization" of mankind. Urbanization, accelerated by the concentration of industry, as we see more and more clearly in the most sociologically developed countries (e.g., the United States), is accompanied by reflux phenomena whose importance we can no longer ignore. Men who are attracted to the city because of its lucrative opportunities are more and more concerned (as we see in France) with securing a "second home" in the country, at least for their leisure time, or (as is the case in the United States) they endeavor to live and spend their leisure time not at their workplace or, even less, in their homes, which they use primarily for sleeping, but in "base communities" that are essentially rural, at a sufficient but not too great distance from urban centers, and preferably outside them: the "weekend home."

In both cases the problem is much less the disappearance of the residential parish, and especially the rural parish, than opening the latter to a new kind of hospitality. In other words, we have to develop, during part of the year (as is still the case in France in "vacation parishes") or throughout the year (as is the case elsewhere), a receptivity of the urban element of the population in basically local and rural communities, although this element must accept a profound transformation of its past way of life. In both cases, regeneration of the cathedrals and the collegial churches (which are more or less monastic) ought to offer, as a necessary complement, not the undesirable pseudo-spiritual "service stations" (whose inanity we have pointed out) but real "encounter centers," which are more necessary than ever. Only stable communities that are particularly rooted and, at the same time, particularly open can be proposed as such, either to individuals on the move or to the movements, so that far from "escaping" the community of charity, they may be reimmersed in it and enrich it with what they bring to it.

## IV. The Christian Layman in the Church and in the World

It is in connection with the apostolic ministry, thus understood, and realizing its profound nature in deeds in the bosom of the "parish," whether old or evolved (i.e., the most concrete realization of the Church), that the layman must define himself and that this definition can escape contradictions without vanishing into the unreal.

The layman is introduced into the Church, that is, into the habitual eucharistic celebration of a group of his Christian "neighbors," by his baptism and confirmation. He is therefore a man who has died and risen in Christ and is consecrated by and for the radiant presence of the Spirit of Christ. Through this gift of baptism and confirmation, he is made capable, above all, of participating in the Eucharist, in the priestly act in which the whole People of God see themselves united, by Christ himself, to his own priestly action, and by which this people, all together, assemble in the body of the Son. Again, their participation in the eucharistic celebration is accomplished by three acts: prayer, offering, communion.[11]

In the specifically Christian prayer, in which the Mass begins by forming him, the layman learns to listen with his brothers to the divine Word, which is addressed to them all together, and in their community he becomes able to grasp its meaning and, therefore, give it the response of faith. This response, animated by the same realism of the Word which elicits it, is extended under the species of the basic food of our life, bread and wine, which are offered at the table of the Lord, giving back to Christ our very being in its very source. Our life is acknowledged as coming from God, and is returned to its original ownership. Hence, being gathered into the reconciliatory sacrifice that Christ offered on the cross in our humanity—an "assumption" which is completed in our communion in the gifts we bring—we become, through his consecration, Christ's own body. His life, offered to the Father in the death that makes reparation for our sins, then risen—transfigured forever in the resurrection by the sanctifying and life-giving presence of the Spirit—is thus made ours.

It is here that we understand the connection of the laity with the apostolic ministry as it appears in the fullness of its extension to us in the bishop and, in dependence on him, in the priests of second rank, especially in their exercise of the curial function. The prayer of response to the Divine Word supposes its communication, not only authentic in its content but as an act of Christ himself in his legates, which is the radical function of the apostolic ministry. The consecration of our offering in that of Christ, which will make possible our final communion in Christ—in his body and his life, dead and resurrected, in the divine Spirit—supposes the same ministry. The sacramental celebration of the whole body makes the Son's own Eucharist ours, by which he has forever given himself to his Father on the cross in giving himself to us in the Last Supper, which remains his "memorial."

The layman is thereby unceasingly renewed in belonging to the local community of Christ and, along with it, he inserts himself in the one Church of always and everywhere. At the same time, the layman grows unceasingly in his new reality, in his new humanity as a member of the apostolic flock, led by Christ, the Sovereign Shepherd, by means of those whom Christ sent for that purpose, and he is animated by the same Spirit which is both theirs and his, because it is the Spirit of Christ, the Spirit of God, the Spirit of charity.

His initial consecration, his baptism and confirmation, unceasingly exercised, maintained, and developed for effective sanctification of his whole being, his whole life, by participation in the Eucharist, must be extended to the whole of existence. After each grave fault, penance reconciles him with the heavenly Father by reconciling him with the community of his brothers in Christ. The sacrament of marriage consecrates his natural fecundity, unless religious profession sacrifices it for an even more immediate consecration to the supernatural fecundity of the cross. At the end of the Christian's existence (or each time it is threatened), the sacrament of the sick consecrates completion in his flesh of Christ's sufferings for his body, the Church, and prepares this member for the final resurrection, in union with all the others, by introducing in him, in his hardest and innermost trials, the pledge and the seed of the ultimate victory over death.[12]

However, these complementary consecrations—rather, this total consecration of all aspects of human existence—does not introduce the layman into a sacral existence in all aspects of daily reality. What we have said implies exactly the opposite. Everyday reality is consecrated, in its beginning, so that it can be consecrated consequently in all its concrete aspects; and this becomes effective only through *development* of the living faith, which alone gives the faithful person completely to Christ and to the power of his Spirit.[13]

Practically, this signifies that the layman's whole life becomes eucharistic on the basis of his unceasingly renewed participation in the Eucharist. Everything that his activity encounters in this world—all human beings with whom it associates him, in any way; everything he does, on the personal, familial, professional, social, political, and cultural planes; and everything he becomes—must be made an occasion of giving thanks to God in the faith. This "eucharist" of the faith becomes real only by being exercised in charity toward our brothers on all occasions, in all these paths. In this way the Christian extends in the world, in the life of every day, the royal priesthood whose fundamental exercise is his participation in the Eucharist, but which takes on its fullest meaning and reality only if his participation brings him consecration of his whole existence, preparing (insofar as he is in it) for the consecration of the universe.

Thus the Christian (every Christian) layman, in an irreplaceable way, becomes a "witness" of Christ, of the truth of the Gospel, not only to the world but *in* the world. His witness is a beginning of the transfiguration of the life of the world. His consecration in the Church by no means takes him out of the world, but sends him back into it. This universal consecration must be rooted in the most internal consecration of every person but must extend to everything and everyone. The Christian's consecration in the life of faith, in the liturgical and sacramental life, becomes effective only to the extent to which he transmits it to the world in all his activities in which existence makes him share.

With such a vision, there is no possibility of conflict between the consecration of the faithful layman in the Church and his vocation to life in the world; the two obviously are one. For within the perspectives we have traced, the actual Church, the concrete "parish," is the core of human society of the society of men who have discovered in Christ their total human and, therefore, divine vocation of being children of God in all that they are. Thereby they have been recovered by Christ, and by the "apostolate" he extends to them, in his personal action, the gift of the Spirit of love, that is, real and integral life, and the world is called to recover it through them.

It is to produce this "witness" in life, which alone can extend the faith and spread charity, that the "hierarchy" is destined. It is in the service of this witness that the apostolic ministry was instituted by Christ. In this way, and only in this way, can human society be progressively consecrated by the consecration of its members in the Church, and the world, in turn, can be consecrated by the consecration of their re-newed activities. The apostolic "preaching" and the sacramental consecration which seals its whole, divine reality have no other meaning, no other finality, than to make possible this "witness" and this "royal priesthood" of the whole of lay existence, restored by Christ.

The People of God, therefore, could not, without absurdity, be designated "passive," whether in faith, love, or the life of Christ, vis-à-vis the hierarchy, which alone is sometimes alleged to be "active" in the Church. Quite the contrary. The hierarchy, understood as it should be, is only the communication network through the body, which, by appropriate organs, binds it to its Head, the historical Christ, who died and rose in the heart of history and offers life that belongs to all its people. This life, though not properly theirs by the nature of things, is their life in the Spirit of Christ, of God, in truth and love, which are inseparable.

Again, this must not be understood as if the Spirit descended first on the apostolic ministers and belonged to them in some way proper to them, and then, in a second stage, was poured from them onto others. The Spirit, on the contrary, belongs to all, and is communicated solely in conjunction with particular "liturgies" (according to the expression of St. Clement) during the celebration of the Eucharist, which is the most striking manifestation because it is the most radical. Everyone possesses the Spirit directly, or rather is possessed, grasped, and penetrated by it directly, to the extent of God's unforeseeable and gratuitous generosity and one's free response to his gifts.

But since this Spirit is the Spirit of love, the Spirit of Christ, it is communicated to each in connection with all the others in whom Christ established it. Each member has it in himself in communion with all the others, and in accord with the order willed by Christ, which attaches to his action, accomplished in this world once and for all, all the later developments of his Church, all flowering in her of the gifts of the Spirit. This is why, conversely, the

People of God are not a "laity," isolated or isolatable from the hierarchical (i.e., apostolic) ministry.[14] The People of God exist *only* in the laity, united with one another by being united in Christ through the Word he proclaimed and the sacraments that those whom he sent for that purpose celebrate and to whom he gave the responsibility of his flock.

Nevertheless, the continuity between the apostolic preaching and the witness of the whole body in all its members, between the eucharistic celebration, at which only those preside who are legates of the Head, so that his "body" may be consecrated and the one sacrifice in the flesh of all its members accomplished, is such that both aspects of the Christian reality, the reality of the Church, are inseparable. It is in the faith, the living faith of all, that the apostolic preaching finds justification, and it is in the holy life of all members of Christ that the liturgical celebration of his mystery discovers the efficacy of the ministry established on the foundation of the Apostles.

The ecclesiastical ministry, apostolic in general and episcopal in particular, unable to abdicate the responsibility entrusted to it—the mission which rests, first of all, on its shoulders—therefore cannot be exercised except in cooperation with the laity. The laity are the ones who, to the extent of their faith and their charity, must effectuate in the world the gifts of God which pertain to the apostolic hierarchy, who must announce them. They alone preside over their effective communication, which, in the last analysis, is a gift which God alone gives to each, according to his pleasure. As ministers, they are most closely associated with the world; they are and must be, we repeat, the representatives, the "presbyters" of the Church—members of the apostolate that comes from Christ alone. Thus they cannot exercise their function except in close union with the Church, with all her members: by accepting their experiences, their initiatives, and by eliciting, harmonizing, and guiding them as long as necessary, and always ready to recognize and authenticate them as the prophetic voice of the Spirit, of whom they are the "first" servants, even though he communicates himself to all according to his will.

The final portion of this chapter will examine some essential modalities of this cooperation.

## V. The Diaconate and Other "Ministries" or "Charisms" Associated with the Apostolic Ministry

The participation of the layman, every baptized and confirmed Christian, in the life of the Church is exercised in this life of faith by charity, by the divine love which the Spirit pours into our hearts, which we have defined and described as eucharistic life. The layman (in distinction to those who are consecrated to the apostolic ministry), by this life of faith and charity, is enabled to penetrate and transfigure, to impregnate with eucharistic reality, the whole of ordinary existence, in the concrete details of family, professional, social, and political life, and cultural life in general. But the layman also can be called—and is always called, in one way or another—by the obligation (an internal necessity) of bearing explicit witness to his faith before nonbelievers, being concerned actively with the interior life of the Church, and exercising a special ministry in the Church and in the world, corresponding to the "individual gifts," the particular "charisms," which the divine Spirit may have given them.

In the wake of Protestantism and the anti-institutional tendencies that followed, many people in the modern era, even in Catholicism, have opposed these charisms, these very personal and free gifts of the Spirit, which are sources of freedom in one who is their object—and of a very special gratuitousness by God, who confers them (according to his will) among the naturally social, institutional "ministries," which are regulated by the discipline of the organized community. Indeed, we must never stop repeating it: the New Testament, like the early Church, not only does not know such opposition but does not pay particular attention to the distinction it supposes. From the texts of St. Paul on charisms (especially chapter 12 of Epistle to the Romans and chapter 12 of the First Epistle to the Corinthians, as well as chapter 3 of Ephesians—to say nothing of the Pastoral Epistles), it is obvious that, in the Apostle's eyes, the most institutional ministry he knows (i.e., the ministry of the apostles, like that of the *presbyteroi-episkopoi* somewhat later) is a "gift" of the Spirit, a "charism," as much as (or more than) the most miraculous gifts, such as healing of the sick or speaking in tongues. All "gifts," all "charisms," are the principle of corresponding "ministries" which place them at the service not of the individual who benefits from them but of the whole Christian and human community. As chapter 13 of the First Epistle to the Corinthians establishes, the preeminent "gift," in whose service are all the others, ultimately and solely, is charity.

It is interesting to observe how these ministerial charisms are defined and progressively arranged by the Apostle. In the Epistle to the Romans we see, successively mentioned, prophecy, *diakonia* (literally "service," but early in the Church, the word seems to refer especially to "practical" charity, in distinction to "spiritual" charity), and *didaskalia*. Finally, Paul extends the list with a series of activities that usually pass unnoticed, from the exercise of specified functions (such as the foregoing) to what we should call "Christian virtues": exhorting (or consoling), sharing, presiding, mercifulness.[15]

In chapter 12 of the First Epistle to the Corinthians, which in many respects is parallel to the foregoing but has a marked tendency to greater systematization, St. Paul does not limit himself to the problems raised by the relationship among the functions that can be exercised by those to whom he is writing, but takes the "problem" of the life of the Church in general. Hence the prominent mention of the apostles, who are followed by prophets and the *didaskaloi*. Again, he mentions gifts which are functional but less specialized than the preceding ones: miracles (*dynameis*) of healing, assistance (*antilepseis*), governing, of speaking in tongues or interpreting tongues.[16] In the Epistle to the Ephesians, the enumeration is even clearer: apostles, prophets, pastors, and *didaskaloi*.[17]

It is certain that none of these lists is exhaustive or, even less, limited in the thought of their author, and that all are aimed at particular problems that were raised by those to whom each epistle was addressed. Keeping in mind the total absence of opposition or clear distinction between the "ministries"—what we would call the "clergy," "gifts" or "charisms," and the "laity" (the terms were interchangeable in the early Church)—we shall note a few points that are especially worthy of attention with respect to these lists and their evolution.

The first is that St. Paul always puts the gifts of prophecy and *didaskalia* in greatest prominence among the gifts to the faithful in general, immediately after the gift to the apostles (when they are mentioned). Both are teaching gifts; but while prophecy appears to be a faculty of inspiration that is in some way spontaneous, *didaskalia,* on the contrary, seems to be an ability to instruct, founded on a meditated study of tradition. It is all the more remarkable, perhaps, that *didaskalia,* like prophecy (though after it), is considered by the Apostle as no less a gift of the Spirit. We have here, in two complementary forms, the most primitive statement of this conjunction with the apostolic function, by the simple witness of the faith of the faithful—whether of witness in extraordinary form, recalling the inspiration of the ancient prophets, or witness which seems to have more to do with knowledge than inspiration, like that of the Wisdom writers or their successors, the rabbis. Yet we must emphasize: with the first Christians, as in the most creative periods or milieus of Judaism, the more ordinary form of witness is acknowledged to be "inspired," if not equally, at least similarly.

The evangelists and pastors whom the Epistle to the Ephesians puts between prophets and *didaskaloi* (or "doctors," as we would say) seem to be, in the case of the first, the associates of the itinerant apostolate and, in the latter, the local presbyters, who were associated with the *episkope,* the pastoral responsibility of the apostles with respect to the churches that were already founded.

Among them are distributed the common capacities mentioned in the Epistle to the Romans: exhortation or consolation, sharing (of material gifts, obviously), presiding (which may be understood of any form of leadership, as well as the exercise of stable pastoral responsibilities), and mercy. In the case of the Corinthians, whose concern was whetted by ecstatic *gnosis,* the Apostle paid particular attention to the extraordinary gifts, such as miracles in general or, more definitely, healing, speaking in tongues, or interpreting these tongues, as well as—once again, and right in the middle—the gifts of governing or assistance. In other words, not only are the most institutional ministries systematically mingled with the freest, most gratuitous gifts, but among the former, if their supernaturalness is not immediately manifest, are the more extraordinary gifts. Finally, the *diakonia* of the Epistle to the Romans seems so important that it is inserted, as are the functions of "evangelists" or "pastors" in the Epistle to the Ephesians, between prophecy and *didaskalia.*[18]

Without pushing these remarks too far, we can find many teachings in them whose import is not limited to the primitive Church, to the first stages of her organization. We shall limit ourselves, for the moment, to three principal points, and the first is that the most important "ministry" that can come to the faithful laity, the most primitive and most basic in the life of the Church, results from "gifts," from special "charisms."

We have already said it but we must always go back to it: the first function of the apostolic ministry is to announce and proclaim, with authority and, when necessary, the supernatural power of the incarnate Word, the Gospel, the definitive fullness of the Divine Word. The first gift of the faithful, the People of God, is receiving this Word in themselves and making it come to fruition in the gift of spiritual understanding, which is inseparable from the communication it announces and realizes of God's own love and life. Consequently, the concurrence that the faithful, as simple faithful, bring to the apostolic ministry is to attest to this truth they proclaim in Christ's name. The "gifts," the "ministries" of "prophecy" and *didaskalia,* are therefore, in a certain sense, the first and most important that the faithful can be called to exercise. And, may we say, everyone must exercise them, more or less. No one can be disinterested in the apostolic proclamation of the Gospel truth, and all—each on his own part—must corroborate this proclamation with the witness of their living faith.

The second point is that on the basis of this spontaneous "gift" and this radical "ministry" that flows directly from it, the apostles, it seems, began choosing men among their disciples, who were representative of their communities, to associate them with the apostolate, as itinerant evangelists or as local pastors. Hence the origin of the *presbyteroi-episkopoi,* whom we see first associated with the apostolate by the apostles themselves, then the bishops, who will succeed the apostles in their pastoral responsibilities, and then the priests, who will be similarly associated with them. Here, in other words, on a "gift" directly granted by God, the immediate source of a personal witness, is superimposed an association with the gift and the apostolic ministry, which introduces the representative layman, the faithful one whom God himself seems to call, by the gifts he has given him, into participation in the responsibilities and, consequently, the capacities to represent the Head to his body, which Christ entrusted to the apostles alone.

Yet (this is our third point), alongside this association of the laity to the very substance of the apostolate, in the episcopate and the presbyterate, on the basis of the association of "witness" to authoritative "proclamation" of the evangelical truth, another possibility subsists, of associating the lay "ministries" with the apostolic ministry: the *diakonia*. The functions of the *diakonia* are all functions, all ministries, which the gift of charity, diversified into indefinitely multiform gifts of service, can accomplish in the Church and which sustain and corroborate the apostolic preaching through the witness of life. It is first the material services, rendered to the Christian community for the celebration of worship, in which its faith is maintained and developed. But since fraternal charity is inseparable from this celebration, it is also all the charitable services which will be naturally connected with the eucharistic assembly.

It was in this way that the "seven" who surround Stephen in Acts appear to have been chosen to help the apostles, by applying themselves "to the service of the tables," that is, inseparably, to the material details of the eucharistic meal and to the entire activity of charity, or "mutual aid," of which they were the core. Still, as the continuation of this account shows, to this principally material aid, which they brought to the properly apostolic task, will be added (particularly in Stephen) such vivid "witness" that it will constitute an extension of the apostolic preaching. Whether the institution of deacons was inaugurated in this narrative or was inspired by it later, it presents the character of a calling, emanating from the apostles or their successors, to support them in their task by assuming the material responsibilities it entailed, which were consecrated by their relationship either to the Eucharist or to the charitable works of the Christian community. In connection with this, deacons will be called to a particularly elaborate witness, which, associated with the apostolic teaching, can go so far as to exercise it in an at least subordinate and delegated fashion.[19]

In substance, there is nothing that the deacon is called to do in the Church, on either the plane of worship or charity, that every Christian cannot be called to do, solely on the basis of his baptismal consecration, at least occasionally. The deacon will be differentiated from the ordinary layman by the fact that he is called not in an extraordinary but in an ordinary way. Just as the apostolic function of the apostles and their successors became a proper function, judged to be so absorbing that it was substituted for ordinary, workaday professions (indeed, in their service to the *familia Dei* they assumed a natural place, as a member of a natural family), the same attitude will redound to the deacon as a result of his functions, even though a nondeacon occasionally fulfills them. In distinction to episcopal or presbyteral ordination, the ordination of a deacon does not bestow a capacity of doing what could not otherwise be done, for it does not make him a minister who represents Christ before his Church but, rather, a minister of the Church, representing—quite the contrary—the association of the entire Church to the work of her Head. It consecrates the deacon in the most direct and most constant form of this association: on the level of the celebration of worship and charitable activities, exercised in the name of the entire Christian community.[20]

Consequently, under the designation "minor orders" a series of secondary, specialized ministries was introduced as subdivisions of the diaconal ministry: porters, lectors, exorcists, acolytes, and subdeacons. *A fortiori,* what we said about deacons is also true of them: everything they can do, every layman can do. In principle, what differentiates them from others is that they are consecrated to perform such actions habitually and, so to speak, professionally.

This diversification of minor orders is a secondary matter of ecclesiastical organization. Traditions other than the Latin were familiar with the practice under more or less different forms. In the Latin Church, such functions as cantor or sacristan, though not a specific ordination, often became the equivalent—indeed, a superior equivalent—of the official minor orders (which too often today are only a formalistic survival for those on whom they are conferred, simply as steps on the way to major orders). More generally, every Church function a layman is called to perform, whether accompanied by a ritual of consecration or not, from the instant that it becomes habitual—and therefore carries a responsibility expressly recognized by the apostolic ministry—is *de facto* a minor order.

This brings us to a final specification on the relationship between layman and "cleric" in the Church, which is not a distinction between consecrated persons and others who are not. The baptismal consecration, completed by confirmation, is no less consecratory than the episcopal consecration. On the contrary, it is the foundation of every Christian consecration, to the extent that any ordination, even episcopal consecration, must, by the constant practice of the Church, be considered invalid if given to someone who had not received baptism previously. What is more, inability to celebrate the Eucharist and the other sacraments supposes Christ's leadership as head of his Church, who gave this power only to those who were consecrated for exercise of the apostolic ministry. Therefore every layman who is called to this ministry by the Church can, even before his consecration, validly fulfill its simple doctrinal or jurisdictional functions.

If we consider what constitutes the "layman" (not the simple fact that, as a rule, he is not called to the apostolic ministry, either in the fullness of its episcopal succession or in direct association with the consecrated presbyterate's responsibilities and capacities), we see that his consecration to the apostolic ministry, or (for a stronger reason) to the diaconal ministry (or to ministries that we can call "subdiaconal") does not make him lose what he had already received from Christ. The ministerial priesthood of the apostles; of their successors, the bishops; or of their cooperators, the priests of second rank, presupposes—with laymen—the royal priesthood of all the baptized. Indeed it would not be possible to proclaim the Word without having previously received it in the prayer of faith, or to consecrate the offerings of others without having first offered all that one has, all that one is, to Christ, or to distribute Communion in his Body and Blood without having first taken part in that communion.

People will perhaps object that bishops and priests, unless they are given the possibility of exercising a so-called "secular profession" and founding a family through marriage, lose the faculty of consecrating the secular world to Christ, which is the proper function of laymen. But the objection rests on an ambiguity from which only sophist consequences can be drawn. Indeed, people forget that the consecration in question is the *Christian* consecration, which restores everything to its original nature by restoring everything to its normal relationship with the Creator. It follows that one cannot participate in such a consecration, even at its source of bursting into the world, *except* by participating in that world as much as anyone else, though in another way.

Christian consecration, by faith or by the preaching that awakens it, and by the sacraments, given or received, does not alienate anyone from the world but returns everything it touches to its most profound authenticity, by bringing the world back to God. And this consecration is wrought by human and cosmic acts that are not diminished by the fact that they act in the service of grace, but are thereby intensified and restored. To proclaim the Word, the minister of Christ must submit himself to an operation of his intellect and to all compatible means of insertion in the world—a task more exigent than any other intellectual task. Similarly, the liturgical, sacramental celebration entails use of all the media of culture, which, for the minister to be what he must be, calls not only for a synthesis of his sensitivity and mind but for art in the most exalted sense of the word: integral humanity and cosmicness. There is no work more human in the psychology and sociology it supposes, in the total realism of its wisdom, than the pastoral task, considered as a whole.

Whatever presence mankind's richest occupations and professions (those most inserted in the world) can have with respect to everything created is, at most, equivalent to what is required in the task of the apostolic ministry, in order to be accomplished in a truly satisfactory fashion. As St. Paul said so well, the more supernatural the faith that moves vocation to this ministry, the greater obligation it imposes "to become all things to all men," so that Christ, and God himself, may come to be "all in all." Adaptation to the purely transcendent gift of God, far from hindering an "apostle" (in the most general sense of the word) from adaptation to men in the world, postulates and brings it forth. If Terence's phrase, *"Homo sum et nil humanum a me alienum puto,"* is not taken only in the negative sense he gives it ("Human only insofar as one has all human weaknesses") but in the richest and purest sense, "Human such as God willed man to be," with the tendency both in oneself and in others to develop all human virtualities, it is (or ought to be) the motto of the "man of God," who is called and consecrated to proclaim God and bring Him to his brothers.

Once we understand this, the supposition that the priest, Christ's minister, to be fully human must add to his ministry another profession, must seem to be naive. For a stronger reason, even more naive should the supposition that, for the same purpose, he should have a human family of which he would be the father in the flesh. The spiritual fatherhood which his special vocation entails is so absorbing that it is uneasily reconciled with natural fatherhood and its responsibilities. Once this kind of fatherhood is sacrificed, it causes the person to discover, on a more elevated or more profound level (as do all authentic sacrifices), a wider appreciation of precious human reality.

We must therefore say without hesitation: If his vocation is precisely understood and faithfully followed (i.e., in accordance with all the exigencies of being rooted in mankind and in the universe), the priest, the bishop—the minister of Christ in general—is—must be—as true a representative of mankind as possible. To represent Christ before men, before the world, supposes as a necessary or prior adjunct that one is representative of mankind, of the cosmos, before God. This is why it is to the *presbyteroi,* the representatives of the lay community of believers, that the apostles entrusted the succession of the apostolic ministry, after they had searched among their closest collaborators.

# Notes

1. Even if we may argue with one or another of his orientations or conclusions, the monumental work of Fr. Yves M.-J. Congar, *Jalons pour une théologie du laïcat* (Paris, 1953), not only by the richness of his documentation but for the depth of reflection that accompanies it will long remain the preeminent source work on this subject. On the question of the laity, see the whole of chapter 4 in the constitution *Lumen Gentium*.

2. On the history of the term and notion of "parish," see P. Imbart de la Tour, "Les paroisses rurales du $V^e$ au $XI^e$ siècle," and A. Dumas in vol. 7 of Fliche and Martin, op. cit., pp. 265ff.

3. Cf. *The Shape of the Liturgy* (London, 1945), p. 270.

4. See in Kirk, *The Apostolic Ministry*, the remarkable study of T. M. Parker, "Feudal Episcopacy," pp. 351ff. On the modern episcopate, see P. Andrieu-Guitrancourt, *De la théocratie à la collégialité* (Paris, 1967).

Among the numerous studies on the parish and its present problems, the best collection is perhaps the volume edited by K. Rahner, *La Paroisse* (Fr. tr.; Paris, 1961). There is a bibliography in a chronicle of Fr. Rouquette in *Etudes* (Nov. 1966).

6. In our opinion, the most serious criticism that can be made of the work (remarkable though it is) by Fr. Congar (mentioned at the beginning of this chapter) is that he does not entirely escape the dichotomy just pointed out.

7. We are sorry to say that all the foregoing seems more or less misunderstood by Fr. Rahner in his most recent studies on the episcopate. Despite what he has said so well elsewhere about the local church (cf. above, p. 390), a view of the role of the bishop as associated with governing the universal Church, as interesting as it is in itself, beclouds the sense of his functions that are not administrative, beginning, it seems, with omission of his fundamental role as pastor of a particular church and, especially, as a preacher of the faith and a guide in prayer.

8. Interesting notations on several themes in what precedes will be found in the second volume of *L'Episcopat et l'Eglise universelle*, on the ministry of the bishop in the midst of the particular church, and especially in the work of B. Bazatole, *L'Evêque et la vie chrétienne au sein de l'Eglise locale*, pp. 329ff. See also the work of Fr. P. B. Legrand, in the volume of commentary on the decree on the pastoral responsibility of bishops (*La charge pastorale des évêques* [Paris, 1969]).

9. Mt 223:9 and Gal 3:28 (cf. Col. 3:11).

10. The Anglican theologian, J. Macquarrie, has some very correct reflections in this regard in his *Principles of Christian Theology* (New York, 1966); and it would be difficult to accuse him of conservatism.

11. Cf. above, pp. 366ff.

12. On the participation of the layman in the priesthood of Christ in the Church, see P. Dabin, *Le sacerdoce royal des fidèles dans la tradition* (Brussels–Paris, 1950), and Congar, *Jalons pour une théologie du laïcat* (pp. 158ff.). A brief synthesis, which is also very much up to date with regard to both tradition and contemporary problems, by an Anglican theologian, H. Balmforth, *The Christian Priesthood* (London, 1963), should be pointed out because of his sound balance on all elements of the question. See the constitution *Lumen Gentium,* chap. 2, pars. 10ff.

13. On what follows, Congar, op. cit. (pp. 488ff.), is especially full of insights. We only regret, once again, that the connection between this latter part of his book and what precedes is not closer; hence the appearance, which is becoming hard to avoid, of opposition between the layman in the Church and the layman in the world. It seems to us that beneath this remains an insufficiently critical notion of properly Christian sacrality. Despite quite justified nuances that the author brings to the current definitions of Catholic Action (at least in France), it seems to us that the place he gives to this movement is out of proportion with both doctrinal and practical reality. On lay activity in the world in general, see the constitution *Gaudium et Spes,* esp. chap. 3, and the decree *Apostolicam Actuositatem.*

14. Cf. the definition given by St. Cyprian, which we mentioned above (p. 270, note 67).

15. Rom 12:6ff.

16. 1 Cor 12:28ff.

17. Eph 4:11ff.

18. On this whole question of charisms, see the article "Charismes" (of Fr. Lemonnyer) in *Supplément du Dictionnaire de la Bible,* and especially the book (already mentioned) by H. von Campenhausen, *Kirchliches Amt und geistliche Vollmacht.*

19. On the problems posed by the diaconate in the New Testament, see the article "Diakonia" in *Theologisches Wörterbuch* and J. Colson, *La fonction diaconale aux origines de l'Eglise* (Paris, 1960).

20. The possible restoration of a permanent diaconate in the Latin Church seems to have been first suggested by the essay of J. Hornef, "Wiederbelebung des Diakonats," in *Die Besinnung* (Dec. 1949). In an excursus of his *Jalons pour une théologie du laïcat* (pp. 308ff.), Fr. Congar gives a first outline of the developments of this idea. It had great success at the Second Vatican Council, where it was admitted in principle (end of chap. III of the constitution *Lumen Gentium*). Since then, attempts at application, despite an abundant but rather superficial production of articles on the subject, have been rather disappointing. See again W. Schamoni, *Familienväter als geweihte Diakone* (Paderborn, 1953), Congar, in *Sainte Eglise* (Paris, 1963), and the study of Karl Rahner, "Théologie de la rénovation du diaconat," in *Ecrits théologiques* (Fr. tr.; Paris, 1966), 6:67ff.

# Chapter 9
# Ecclesiolae in Ecclesia

The fundamental constitutive assembly of the Church is the eucharistic assembly, in which all the faithful, called to live together, meet in the faith in the divine Word, prayer, and the sacramental and sacrificial memorial of the Lord. This always local assembly is limited, since it is defined by time and space, but it evokes and anticipates the eschatological assembly of all the elect in Christ at the Parousia. Nevertheless, for the life of the Church between Pentecost and the Parousia, all sorts of intermediary assemblies are necessary, what we might call *"Ecclesiolae in Ecclesia."* They are of varied types that respond to diverse needs. Faithful to their function, they contribute to the development of local churches in catholic communion, tending all together, in each member and in each assembly, toward the fullness of the eschatological community. If they should *ignore* this function, they risk (either locally or universally) introducing themselves in the place of the Church they are to serve and arresting the development they are supposed to promote.

To avoid this deformation, we must unceasingly be reminded that none of these assemblies is *the* Church nor even *a* church properly speaking. They are never, nor should they ever aspire to be, anything but organs of *the Church* whereby she will be developed in the local *churches,* by causing them, all together, to tend toward the fullness of the body of Christ. They must therefore always be conceived in this complex relationship, without forgetting any of its terms. This is the only way they avoid degenerating into an end in themselves.

We can differentiate three categories among the *ecclesiolae.* The first includes all councils by which contacts among the different members of the

Church are maintained, particularly the hierarchy and the faithful. These councils must allow for decisions by those who are responsible for the apostolic succession and must permit them to be representative of the "capital" impulse of the historical Christ and the life of the Spirit, which remains his in all his "members."

The second category is constituted by intermediate realizations of the catholic communion of the churches, between the planes of their local life and the life of the universal Church. After and above the episcopal dioceses, so to speak, are the metropolitan groupings, which are called (improperly) the "national churches," the "patriarchates," etc.

Finally, the third category brings together all groupings of Christians who are particularly sensitive to a special need for development of the Church in the churches. These Christians meet together to combine their efforts in religious orders, congregations, confraternities, secular institutes, and modern "movements" of every kind. Just as groups of the second category must facilitate the life of communion of the local churches in the universal Church, the latter elicit the growth of the Church in all her members, in all her special applications, as well as in catholic unity toward the ultimate Church, the perfect Church of the Parousia. (The councils, which form the first category, are essentially organs of coordination which must perpetually promote the concerted "symphony" in this progression.)

# I. Church Councils: Councils, Synods, Chapters, and Other Representative Assemblies

Of all the *ecclesiolae in Ecclesia,* the most important—and the only one to which this designation is applied in strictest terms—is the "council," and especially the "ecumenical council."[1] In the council, and preeminently in the council where, in principle, all the bishops are assembled, we have a representation, indeed a genuine sacramental presence of the whole Church, in what constitutes the organ of her unity: the totality of the episcopate meeting around the bishop who is the successor of St. Peter. Let us repeat: the celebration of Mass at the beginning of each conciliar session is not merely a pious formality. The council is a concelebration in which, in the common Eucharist of the heads of the churches, the fellowship of these churches in the one Church is affirmed—the evolution of common awareness, the *nous Christou,* in those who are now a body in Christ, *his* body.

The council does not create the reality that is expressed in it, which becomes conscious within it. The catholic fellowship of all the churches, rooted in the episcopal fellowship, is perpetually maintained by the celebration of the Eucharist, in every place, by all the bishops and priests with their flock, with all that this implies. In the conciliary meeting and concelebration, however, we see a means, the eminent means, for the Church to become more acutely aware of these implications of the Eucharist, of the catholic unity which it manifests and maintains.

The council is therefore a coming together of bishops who are in charge of individual churches, by means of which these churches are called to renew their common consciousness and form one universal Church in Christ.

This is why the only bishops who by right are called to take part in the councils are "residential" bishops, who are at the head of an actual church.[2] Granting the connection we have established and underlined between the bishop and his church, we may even say that only residential bishops are bishops in the fullness of the term. Indeed, they alone, through the ministry they exercise in their churches, are bishops not only in potency but in act. For a bishop is unthinkable without a church, and it is the quality of a bishop, in distinction to a priest of second rank, to have in and for his church the source and fullness of the apostolic *episkope*, which are inseparable.

This is why titular bishops (by themselves) are but priests who have received the episcopal character but not the actual exercise of the episcopal function. The church (*in partibus infidelium* or elsewhere) attributed to them, with its fictitious existence, recalls the inseparability of the bishop and the local church and the fact that their episcopacy cannot find adequate realization anywhere but in a local church, which at the moment they lack. Inadequate realization also attends the functions of an auxiliary, who, as a rule, cannot exercise them, just as priests of second rank cannot exercise their functions, except by delegation from genuine bishops, the residential bishops, and in association with them.

But once they receive such a delegation, they still (even imperfectly) do not become bishops of the dioceses where they are to exercise their ministry. According to the formula of the canonists, they remain simple "episcopal laborers," employed by the effective bishops of these dioceses or by the Sovereign Pontiff himself, to fullfil momentarily a possible deficiency or lack. Their power of episcopal orders is secondary and dependent vis-à-vis the pastoral function and the power of authoritatively proclaiming the divine Word, which remain in the hands of the residential bishops alone. Also, it can be said without paradox that a simple priest of second rank, if he performs either a cruial function or that of an episcopal vicar (whether vicar general or not), participates more fully in the *episkope* of the one bishop than a titular bishop who performs neither function.[3] This has been understood and affirmed with the greatest vigor throughout the whole of tradition since the Council of Chalcedon, which required that every episcopal consecration be conferred by at least three *residential* bishops who were functioning at the time.

These truths seem to have been momentarily obliterated (in the eyes of some people) by the fact that Pope John XXIII graciously invited titular bishops to take part in the last council by granting them a deliberative voice. The same thing was done at the First Vatican Council, and precedents can be found back to very ancient councils; but these precedents must be understood precisely. We must emphasize that this was not and is not the exercise of a right but a condescension on the part of the Sovereign Pontiff or, more generally, of all residential bishops together. We must add that this favor was never restricted to only titular bishops, and it is not because they were titular bishops that it was granted to them. From all time, it has been admitted that, in addition to residential bishops, others may be invited to take part in councils: those to whom the exercise of pastoral responsibilities is communicated in an "ordinary" fashion, in a fashion that is stable and permanent. It was in this way that abbots of monasteries were called and, later, all heads of religious orders (exempt from episcopal jurisdiction), representatives of universities, and many others who were not bishops but who, in teaching the truth, exercised a quasi-episcopal responsibility on the pastoral plane, which could not be communicated to them except by the totality of the episcopate or the pope himself—all those who have long been associated with the episcopate have been called by the pope to be united in his deliberations, as they are united with him *de facto* in the ordinary exercise of his responsibilities. This invitation may be extended even to members of the laity who are directly (or indirectly) charged with considerable pastoral responsibilities, as was the case with emperors and kings in ancient Christendom, where a number of matters, because of the overlapping of Church and state, became "mixed matters."[4]

Let us point out that, as modern canonists underline, obvious abuses have been connected with this way of acting: a *de facto* intrusion of the temporal power into settling matters which go beyond it and are out of its hands. Conversely, we must not see abuses in all cases of this type. From the moment it is admitted that the apostolic responsibility can and, to a certain extent, must be shared by the apostles with other men in different degrees (everything we have said about development of the apostolic and the other ministries shows to what extent this is both original and in conformity with the deepest nature of the Church), it appears normal and highly desirable, if not necessary, that all who are associated with such responsibilities also, to the extent of this association, be associated with the deliberations that these responsibilities entail. It is within this perspective that, in modern councils, the closest possible association of titular bishops with residential bishops is understood. Titular bishops, following upon the responsibilities of simple episcopal character that are customarily entrusted to them by bishops in the fullness of the term, today become their auxiliaries or coadjutors, in so effective a sense that it has certainly been fitting to grant them a privilege that has long been granted abbots and heads of orders.

Yet the canonists' question on the extent of participation in councils, not only of nonresidential bishops (when they are called to them) but of all the others—bishops or not, or even simple laymen who may be called as well—is whether they must be given a deliberative or simply consultative voice. Unanimity is far from being reached on this subject. Without claiming to give a definitive answer, we can make two remarks in this regard which may clarify and, especially, temper the debate.

The first is that no episcopal council can function without all sorts of experts and investigators who enable it to work on the most solid data, with the best instruments. Professional theologians and canonists, on one hand, thus play the role of the old *didaskaloi*. On the other hand, the representatives (whether priests or not) of all the functions in the Church—of all situations of the faithful in the world, of all the secondary communities, and of all the movements—have a role as witnesses *in* the Church, symmetrical to their fundamental role as witnesses *of* the Church in the world, which can be likened to the prophetical function. In principle, with respect to the roles of the council fathers (in whose hands, along with the responsibility inherited from the apostles, the final decisions rest), there roles, however important they may be, are essentially consultative. But even on this level (unless we suspect the fathers of a singular lack of sense pertaining to their responsibility), it is certain that the more competent or inspired these experts or witnesses, the more weighty their opinions or advice, even if they are not given a deliberative voice. Let us repeat what we said above about the episcopal tradition and the prophetic tradition: The proper task of the former is not to be taken as the sole source of truth, but as authenticating the truth which evolves from the totality of the prophetic tradition, in which, certainly, the episcopal tradition fully shares, but cannot limit to itself.

Our second remark is that, in the foregoing perspectives, it pertains to bishops alone, who are actually (not simply in potency) the successors of the apostles, to decide whether to associate others (titular bishops, priests, other ministers, and even laymen) with their decisions by conferring on them a deliberative voice in a council. However, it would be singularly illogical for them to refuse to do so when, in fact, they have previously associated the auxiliaries in question with the ordinary exercise of their pastorate in an equivalent fashion.

In this regard, it may again be pointed out that the question would be posed differently if the councils were political assemblies, such as the legislative bodies of parliamentary democracies, where decisions are made by majority vote. Again, it is not the majority that must decide in a council, but unanimity, for it is not a matter of deciding on the basis of a simply legal representation of the citizenry, identified through a juridical fiction with majority votes. In the perspective of the council, as a conscious reunion of the entire Church in the eucharistic concelebration, decision is a matter of a *real,* not fictitious, unanimity. And unanimity not simply of those who are actually assembled but, in the last analysis, of all believers. (It is, still less, a matter of simple human accord.) Conciliar unanimity is the result of the action of the Holy Spirit on minds and hearts: "It has seemed good to the Holy Spirit and to us . . . ,"[5] according to the spontaneous formula of the "first council" of Jerusalem.

Consequently, the purpose of the voting—when there is voting—is to acknowledge the fact of this unanimity in love, when it occurs and becomes apparent. If the vote is not practically unanimous, it has no value. And even if it were unanimous, or seemed to be, if it were the fruit not of this "awakening," of this *awareness of all in one,* which is the awareness of the whole Church and which the bishops merely acknowledge and authenticate, but of external pressures, internal intrigues, factions, or some kind of maneuvering within or around the assembly, even a small minority would be enough to prevent the apparent, pseudo unanimity from winning. The totality of the faithful would not acknowledge an irregularly obtained vote; and approving or anticipating this reaction, the pope would have the duty to refuse to give confirmation to such a vote.

Under these conditions, since the decisive votes are not a purely material question of voters in conflict, it is perfectly natural that all whom an effective share of pastoral responsibilities closely associates with the bishops' task be called by the bishops to judge, with them, what does or does not represent this *mens Ecclesiae* in which, through the Holy Spirit, the *nous Christou* is extended from the Head to the consciousness of his whole body.

These remarks lead us directly to a question that is perhaps the spiniest of any that can be raised with regard not only to an ecumenical council but to the whole body of "councils," which, we have said, are neither *the Church* nor particular *churches,* but are called to *represent* either the Church herself or the churches in her. The question is the nature and modalities of the "representation."

Two equally simplistic and fallacious notions tend to set minds at odds on this point. Some want the "authorities" in the Church to limit themselves to evolving and expressing a supposed consensus of the masses, or the opinion of a simple numerical majority. This view describes itself as a "democratic"notion of the Church. Others, in the opposite camp, defend the idea that decisions in the Church derive their authority from the fact that they are not made by representatives of the mass of the faithful but by Christ alone— not by the body but by its Head. This view, opposed to the first, calls itself, or allows itself to be called, "authoritarian."

Formulated this way, both notions represent the forcible introduction in the Church of ideas and practices foreign to her tradition, spirit, and nature. They must be rejected as attempts at adulterating the Church in her deepest reality. Any compromise between them could merely add to the defects of both, while undoubtedly, through reciprocal neutralization, losing even their superficial advantages. Indeed, in themselves, these notions have nothing Christian about them, nothing biblical. And when one tries to convey them in biblical language, the resultant incongruities reveal the violence done to this language in forcing it to express something for which it was not made.

For example the "democratic" theory of the exercise of decision making in the Church will be described as a "pneumatological" notion, in which the "Divine Spirit," who is the sole final authority, is present in all Christians. In a parallel way, the "authoritarian" theory takes refuge behind a notion of the Church that is claimed to be "Christological," in which authority can come only from Christ or from those on whom he bestowed it. But we cannot set one theory against the other without absurdly and sacrilegiously opposing the Spirit to Christ or Christ to the Spirit. The opposition between a supposed authority, emanating solely from the Head of the Church, and a supposed authority, emanating from the body alone, ends up as pure nonsense. What could the body be without the Head, but a cadaver? Where, then, does the divine Head of the Church manifest his presence and authority on earth *except* in the body of this Church, the body she herself constitutes? And the Spirit is not given in confusion to all members of the Church, prescinding from her organization willed by Christ, but reattaches the body to him, as to its Head, within this organization.

The option between "authoritarian" authority or "democratic" decision-making power in the Church is unreal, and well-intentioned efforts to "reconcile" such a pair of freaks and it is futile; they cannot live together, anymore than they can live separately. Neither a "democracy" nor a "monarchical" or "oligarchical dictatorship" can have real existence in the Church. The Church is not a state, in which such a choice could make sense.

What is sought, in a confused way, in such notions: effective participation by all in decisions that concern them, effective exercise of responsibilities by those to whom they are given, who cannot dispense with them by passing them on to others—the real "representativeness" of decisions made in the Church with regard to Christ and to Christians, the essential harmony between Christ's influence over us and the life of his Spirit in us—all this, of course, must be found (not statically but dynamically) in the symphony of the life of the Church, properly understood.

All this depends on the *matter* of decisions in the Church in development, over the course of the life of the Church. They touch on the truths of life which concern the life of God, communicated to men in Christ by the Spirit, which is essentially the life of the love of God poured out in our hearts by his Spirit. This truth is known to us only by Christ's revelation of it in what he said, in what he did, and in what he is and remains forever. Knowledge of it, a precisely vital knowledge—the only knowledge that corresponds to this truth of life, which is first of all living truth—is communicated to us by the apostolic ministry which Christ himself instituted for that reason, assuring his perpetual presence and assistance until the Parousia. Therefore it is to the apostles and their successors, the bishops, that this ultimate responsibility is given.

The truth of the life of the Gospel is entrusted to them so that they may spread it; and its expansion into hearts, into human lives, and into the life of the Church in the midst of the world goes hand in hand with the expansion of the Spirit of Christ himself. Thus for the apostles, and *a fortiori* for the bishops after them, everything signified and implied by the truth of which they are the bearers is spread only in the life of Christians, in the life of the Church that this truth must animate, through the Holy Spirit. If the apostolic preaching, the first fruit of the Spirit, engenders the faith and witness of all Christians in the same Spirit, the apostolic preaching, both in its expression and its progressive awareness, by bishops as well as others, of its whole content, is in turn nourished by this life and this witness. Life and its witness can no more develop, except on the basis of preaching, than preaching can remain living and true without relying precisely on what it elicits.

This is why pastors, and bishops first of all, in order to be authentic representatives *of Christ in the Church,* must first be authentic representatives *of the Church,* of the work of the Spirit of Christ in her: *presbyteroi* in the original sense. The *episkope* inherited from the apostles is participation in the Sovereign Pastor's pastorate of the sheep. By making bishops, through consecration to service of the Head, the representatives of the Head, as head to all the body, the *episkope* prepares and adapts bishops to an understanding of the body—of its needs, capacities, and weaknesses, as well as its gifts—which, far from diminishing their representativeness vis-à-vis the body, makes that understanding more intimate. Again, it is necessary that this principle be applied through a vitally logical manner of behaving.

In other words, the original and conjoined twofold representativeness of the episcopate with respect to the Head and his members, far from being given all at once, is bestowed with regard to the Head, at the same time that it is acknowledged with respect to members in the episcopal consecration. However, this responsibility is consecrated in order to be maintained and developed throughout the concrete ministry, that is, effective exercise of the pastoral *episkope*. An essential part of this maintenance and development is that the bishop, since he must continually scrutinize the sources of revelation in Scripture and the whole of tradition, in living faith and in prayer, continually listen to the needs and the gifts that the Spirit stimulates or lavishes on all his brothers: his cooperators, the priests; their secondary ministers; and all the faithful. The means can vary infinitely; but all of them include, in one form or another, contact and dialogue—and more: *de facto* cooperation among bishops and everything that is representative (not juridically but really) of the life of the Church, of the life of the Spirit in all her members.

It is the fruit of all this effort that a council must bring to maturity and garner. And it is to prepare for such garnering and assembling that all other "councils" in the Church must contribute in their own way, even though this task surpasses all "committees" of whatever type, just as the work of the episcopate far surpasses that of the councils, which are extraordinary and not habitual events of the life and function of the Church.[6]

This "insertion," this ever renewed immersion of the episcopate in the whole Church, with its closest collaborators, which is necessary for the exercise of its function, has (or ought to have) the meeting of the diocesan synod as the principal occasion for thorough examination.[7]

In a *council,* and especially in an ecumenical council, the collegiality to which every bishop belongs finds its most tangible expression. United around the bishop-successor to Peter, all the bishops constitute, together with him, one legislative body in which all are legislators with him. In a *diocesan synod,* the residential bishop (whether there are coadjutor or auxiliary bishops or not) is in principle the sole legislator. But collegiality, of which the bishop is the source in the presbyterate of his own church, has its most remarkable manifestation in the synod, where the bishop's law-making power draws upon all its fecundity, acquires all its reality, and expresses its rootedness in the experience associated with that of his cooperators, the priests of second rank. (Let us add that there is nothing to prevent—and everything to recommend— the diocesan synod's being open to a broad representation, not only of lesser ministers but of laity as well. In this way the bishop and his *presbyterium* will be assisted by the whole experience, individual and communal, of the local church.)

Like the council the synod is essentially a eucharistic concelebration, with all its implications—a process of self-awareness which the local church, within the universal Church, could not reach by any path other than the Eucharist. It is a concelebration in which the fullness of the episcopal pastorate—communicated, poured out, and divided among priests of second rank—is assembled around the one who is its source and, consequently, capable of imparting to all who share in it the fullness of its unity in a fecund diversity. If to the presence of priests is added an effective representation of all other ministers and the body of the laity, the bishop, assisted by his *presbyterium* and supported by the concurrence of his flock, will be able to make decisions that are most adequate for the total experience of that flock.

The local church cannot achieve true awareness of herself in the faith *except* by materializing epiphany of the universal Church, which is the body of Christ. Also, it will always be an essential task of every synod to open its members to the current experience of the universal Church, while renewing them, with respect to all problems, even the most special ones, in their acute awareness of the uninterrupted tradition of the Church of Christ. Participation by representatives from other churches, as well as informed theologians and canonists, will make it easier to respond to the twofold necessity.

Although the source of a synod's legislative power is assuredly in the bishop, it goes without saying that he should associate it with those whom he has summoned, in proportion to the motives that bring residential bishops to do the same in a council vis-à-vis their "consultors."

Conceived and regularly held in this manner, synods ought to make fertile the work of councils by preparing bishops for them and by imparting the digested experience of their churches. They would thereby permit them to draw all practical consequences by applying conciliar decisions and orientations to everything concrete in the life of the Church.

Councils and synods are plenary assemblies, of the episcopate or the presbyterate, and are consequently "extraordinary." Regularly, they have to reanimate the collective catholic consciousness, in which the entire work of pastors must be constantly carried on as a work of unity, as *the* work of unity, of unanimity in love. This not only unites them among themselves but makes them instruments of the unity of life in charity for this redeemed and renewed humanity, which is assembled in the Church of Christ by the power of his Spirit.

In the intervals between councils and synods, ordinary pursuit of this life is assisted by less weighty instruments. These instruments do not have the representativeness of councils or synods, but they maintain constant exchange between the center and the periphery. Consequently, they contribute to guaranteeing continuity of the collegial exercise of the pastorate in the catholic unity of the life of the Church.

The first to be mentioned are obviously the permanent episcopal conferences,[8] in the process of being organized everywhere in the Western Catholic Churches at the present time, but which have been long established in the Eastern Catholic and Orthodox churches in permanent synods (*synodoi endymousai*). These synods, around the patriarch or other heads of autocephalous churches, are permanent delegations of representatives of the episcopate, most of whom are ordinarily (and frequently) renewed by rotation.[9] The result is that all bishops of a region will, in turn, have their say about common problems, and there is no danger that the assembly, representative in principle of the whole body, will cease to be so, because those who make it up will *ipso facto,* at the end of a certain period, no longer be in the same condition as those whom they represent.

And here we have a problem that attends all parliaments. Even when they are composed on the basis of an election which, at the moment, assures effective representation of the totality of electors, the inevitable "professionalization" of the elected, after they have been in office some time, risks destroying their representative character. In this regard, even though it has the defect of introducing a lack of continuity in government (which can be extenuated by frequent but partial renewals), the rapid rotation of representatives, especially if it is combined with unceasing contact among them and their colleagues, whom they must represent, is much more efficacious than the most scientifically apportioned modes of election.

Here, for the first time, we touch on a general problem that it may be well to treat now, once and for all. We have already said that the successors and cooperators of the apostolic ministry, bishops and priests, according to the institution of their function by the apostles, must be *presbyteroi,* that is, representatives of the community of the faithful, in which they recognize the best of their Christian experience and aspirations. We have stressed that their consecration to this ministry ought not diminish this human and Christian "representativeness," but enrich it. Even the obligation of celibacy, to which, since the patristic age in both East and West, bishops and priests in the West are bound (to foster the exercise of spiritual fatherhood by their freedom from natural fatherhood), ought not destroy or diminish this representativeness.

In fact, however, two factors threaten this dedication and representativeness. The first (which is not always the most grievous) is that habitual exercise of authority or, more generally, responsibility tends to weaken the executants' humility, individually and collectively. This factor leads to the second, which is a danger for every specialist, and all the more when his specialty is exalted: to forget or neglect, in himself and others, the common humanity of the children of God. These two psychological difficulties are at the origin of all deformations of ecclesiastical authority, and the ministry in general, that are included and rightly stigmatized under the term "clericalism."

As experience shows (it was easy to foresee), it is not sufficient to counterbalance the power of bishops and priests by representative assemblies of the laity, even when they are elected in the most democratic forms, to obviate these deformations. From the instant a lay person is invested with a share of responsibility or authority, he becomes a "cleric" *de facto,* just like a bishop or priest, and is therefore separated from the *vulgum pecus,* which is the People of God in their richest and most manifold reality. But even before this, since he was undoubtedly chosen because, one way or another, he is a "militant," a member of a group of a particularly active movement, the price to be paid for this superior or (at least) eminent quality of person and activity is to make him a specialist before he has a share in directive responsibilities. Thus with the danger of deformation from the exercise of authority comes the danger of specialization, of "professional deformation," whose varieties are numberless. And thus a possible clericalism (which is often too real) of "committed" lay persons, which can be just as harmful—and often worse, because it is less conscious—as the clericalism of other clerics. (These considerations apply directly to "assemblies" [still in nascent stages], whose creation was decided by the council, and to "episcopal conferences": priests' councils and pastoral councils, which to their responsibility for pastoral care add the broadest variety of lay representatives.)[10]

The usefulness of such organisms and their foreseeable importance in the evolution of the Church toward fuller realization of the one and catholic communion in the Holy Spirit (which it could not fail to be in substance) do not need to be underlined. In the Catholic Church, their functioning ought to favor assimilation—in the most authentic tradition—of all values of ecclesiastical life that Presbyterianism (of Calvinist origin) endeavored to recuperate and safeguard—even when it compromised these values by associating them with questionable or insufficient views on the ministry and its relationship to the body of the Church. That ministers must be the first to be representatives of the Head of the Church, proceeding from the apostolic succession, and representatives of the whole body, and that they need the constant cooperation of its most diversified representatives, corresponding to the different activities of the Spirit in the community, in every age and in every place, is one of the most fertile intuitions of Calvin. It corresponds to a deep understanding of the life of the Church from apostolic times. Even if the Church is frozen in an organization of debatable authenticity in certain details, supported only by theory of the origins of the ministry and the partly chimerical constitution of the primitive churches, the observations of secondary weaknesses do not discredit the correct intuitions of Presbyterianism.

Still, it is a just criticism, addressed by Congregationalism to Presbyterianism, that it is not enough to add other *presbyteroi* to the ministers of the Word and the sacraments or, more generally, other representatives of the laity so as to avoid the dangers of clericalism. On the contrary, giving the "care of the churches" to a supposed elite would alienate the mass of the faithful and, in fact, deprive them of intervening directly, and by themselves, in the discussion and solution of problems. Far from monopolizing the life of the Church, restricted "councils" or "commissions" must, on one hand, take care to foment it, as must the apostolic ministry. On the other hand, authentic representatives of the faithful (whoever they are) must accept, with the bishops and priests, all suggestions and reactions of the faithful, if they deserve attention (even outside the "clerical" or "presbyteral" context). Manipulated "surveys," showing that the "masses" automatically approve, or seem to approve, what their acknowledged representatives once and for all decide, are not enough. It is necessary that concern for associating *all people* to the life of the Church and to decisions concerning it, and therefore concern for listening to what the Spirit can suggest to *all,* be not only sincere but practical, and lucid as well. No organizational arrangement can provide a once-and-for-all, desirable solution. The Church can unceasingly rediscover itself only through constantly renewed efforts of openness and contact. Again, for this to happen it is necessary that all permanent "councils" or "commissions," far from considering the more general councils or synods superfluous, once they are there to assure the interim, be limited to *assuring* that interim. Especially, they must recall that no matter how directly representative they are, councils and synods are only extraordinary efforts to reanimate a spirit of catholic unity which must be pursued in the Church, always and on every occasion.

To these observations must be added another, which, though it is the last that we shall formulate, is no less important. In the Catholic Church of the

West at present, episcopal conferences, in distinction to councils, have no proper authority. Unless their suggestions are confirmed by the Sovereign Pontiff or personally by each bishop on his own incentive, they do not have the force of law. This is especially true of presbyteral or pastoral councils in their present form; they cannot (at present, in any case) replace the chapters or be substituted for them. These chapters, whose decline in the majority of Catholic countries of the West is lamentable, are differentiated from pastoral councils on this capital point, which canon law makes necessary for the validity of many episcopal decisions: not only prior consultation but, in certain cases of particular importance, prior agreement is required. To develop purely consultative bodies (though undoubtedly they are destined to persist for some time to come) while stifling the only representative bodies of the clergy which, at present, have a deliberative voice in a diocese, under the vain appearance of "modernity" and "liberalism," would be the most reactionary undertaking possible and the most cynical *de facto* negation of the "conciliar spirit" they claim to promote.

Consideration of "councils" in the Church must evoke a form which, in the West, over the last centuries, has had particular importance: the congregation of cardinals, and another form which, in the near future, might play as prominent a role: the episcopal synod, instituted by Paul VI.

Undoubtedly, the Roman congregations constitute the most remarkable example of what we have called "presbyteral collegiality"—as well as the most striking case of participation in exercise of the *episkope,* inherited from the apostles.[11] Indeed, the cardinals who make them up—even if they are priests (or only deacons)—receive from the pope a share in his decision-making power on matters that touch more or less closely on the unity of the Catholic Church, though their decisions are submitted to later confirmation. Moreover, their decisions are taken only after examination of the matter at hand by consultors, who are, for the most part, priests, called in limited or plenary sessions to state, motivate, and discuss their opinions, by writing or orally. Of itself, such a system obviously will not function infallibly; what is necessary, in addition, with a judicious choice of cardinals who decide and consultors who prepare their decisions (with all those involved), is sufficient diligence, joined to the catholic spirit, whose characterization is one of the aims of the present work. But it is quite permissible to point out that jurists, and specialists in running large, modern businesses, who have examined the organization of the Roman congregations (and could hardly be suspected of clericalism), have recognized that this conciliar interaction is capable of bringing the most open and most efficacious cooperation to the person who has supreme responsibility.

To this association of the Roman presbyterate (which is open to qualified representatives of the universal Church—*in partem sollicitudinis* of the successor of Peter, to use the old formula) the episcopal synod ought to bring a complement that gives it balance. Periodically, if not permanently, representing the whole episcopate before the "first bishop," the synod ought to permit him to benefit from the experience and counsel of his colleagues in making his decisions. Also, it could help him clarify and therefore augment their concern for catholic unity, so that his function in their midst and their common function around and with him (but diversified in each) may be harmonized.[12]

In developing, the synod will probably give rise to commissions of bishops and experts that will be more or less similar to those that were charged with the implementation of the last council. It is also to be expected that at least part of these commissions' personnel will confer with the personnel of the Roman congregations. But far from confusing these two kinds of bodies—any more than we would confuse the College of Cardinals and that of the bishops—we affirm a conjunction, a synergy, between them that can produce fertile tensions, provided they are resolved in symphonic development. Harmony would reign—or, rather, be unceasingly reestablished—between the catholicity of the episcopal function, exercised collegially, and the unity of this same function for which the pope has the ultimate responsibility. To meld these two bodies together would mean to sacrifice (almost fatally) unity to catholicity or catholicity to unity, by reducing the pope to an "authorized agent" of the bishops or by reducing the universal episcopate to a dependency of the Roman curia. On the contrary, to maintain constant exchanges can be a particularly appropriate way in the modern age, with its incessant contacts from one end of the world to the other, to make the Gregorian formula more and more a reality: *"In necessariis unitas, in dubiis libertas, in omnibus caritas."*

## II. Associations of Local Churches: Ecclesiastical Provinces, Partriarchates, and "National Churches"

The councils that we have examined have this in common: they tend to represent the *whole* of a church, of the churches or the Church, in an easy grouping of a few individuals, to discuss and prepare decisions (and even make them) in a collegial fashion. Other groupings, which we shall now mention, procede differently, but tend to the same symphonic process in the life of the Church: the more or less *limited* associations of local churches. Outlined in the apostolic period, they took their first (though flexible) form in

the patristic era (on the two levels of metropolitan and patriarchal organization) and tended to decline in the Middle Ages and in modern times, first in
the West but also in the East, to the advantage of what have been called
"national churches" or, in the East, "autocephalous churches."[13]

All these groups, their fluctuations allow us to say, are not common products of the same factors. We can discern, throughout their development, a
tension, even a conflict, between motives which seem to oppose one another
irreducibly. Under one aspect, these church groups—as Moehler saw and
demonstrated—correspond to a need for catholic unity, grafted, so to speak,
onto mankind's natural tendency to cooperate and unite. But under another
aspect, they are the result of another tendency, which is also human (and
perhaps *too* human): to find unity not in universality but in splitting into
classes, nationalities, cultures, or races.

From apostolic times, we see such groups in the process of forming. To say
nothing of the distinction between the Judeo-Christian and the Helleno-
Christian churches (to which we shall soon return), it is obvious that geo-
graphical circumstances, connected with the individual work of an apostle or a
helper of the apostles, determined the "spontaneous" growth of groups of
churches. Even if legend tended to specify and generalize this process, we
very soon see the Church of Palestine forming around James, of Syria (around
Peter), of Achaia, Macedonia, and the Lycus Valley (around Paul), of Asia
Minor (around John), etc. The four or five great patriarchates at the time of
the fatners claim to correspond, with more or less justification, to these
primitive or quasi-primitive divisions of the apostles' areas of activity: Rome
to Peter and Paul, Alexandria to Mark (a disciple of Peter), Antioch to the
beginnings of Peter's activity, Jerusalem to James, and Byzantium to Andrew.

More generally, the Roman metropolises (centers of local government,
commerce, communications, etc.) naturally became centers of the spread of
Christianity, then the centers of regrouping Christians and their churches. The
bishops met there periodically to confer on common affairs of the Church, on
the basis of their associated experiences. The bishop of a metropolis, at the
time of these meetings, continued to exercise the presidency under a more or
less centralized and authoritarian form, which customarily would have been
given him each time they took place. Was he not the natural intermediary
between the local churches of the province and between the province and the
rest of the universal Church?

As Moehler insists, Christians understood the necessity for encounters
among neighboring bishops and churches (beyond the merely local level but
in a very concrete form) to exercise the supernatural charity to which they

were urged by the Holy Spirit. But as Moehler also emphasizes, and rightly, the power and the exigency of this charity went beyond natural realizations, and not content with Christianizing the inevitable neighborly relations, they urged Christians—the churches—to enter into reciprocal communication with their most distant brothers, even when no material necessity impelled them to do so. Just as, consequently, bishops are by nature the organs of unity within their churches and of their communion with other churches, the metropolitans favored the communication of local groupings of churches among themselves, as well as assuring the union of immediately neighboring churches. It is here that their activity connects with the pope, who, by his institution, is ordered to promote catholic unity in the Church.

In this regard, a word must be said about the opposition between the theories of Eastern Orthodox and Western Catholic canonists on the source of metropolitan and patriarchal jurisdiction. Easterners have always tended to see in it an ordinary concession of the authority of local bishops, all equal in principle, to one among them for what pertains to the common affairs of their eparchies (or "dioceses," as we would say). The others look upon it as a delegation of properly papal authority, which alone is directly qualified, by Christ's institution, to impose itself on local bishops for the sake of unity. These views have nothing that is mutually exclusive *in se*. On the contrary, the most normal form of elaboration of intermediary authorities in the Church is to connect the bishops' freely given renunciation of part of the exercise of their power with a corresponding delegation of *his* power by the "first bishop," the guardian of catholic unity. Under these conditions, it may be said that there is a *rapprochement* between the concern for unity, which must be common to all bishops, and the responsibility of guaranteeing it, insofar as he can, which belongs to the pope.[14]

The foregoing is the normal functioning in the Church of the communication and active fellowship that are essential for the development of her life in the unity of charity. But can the same thing be said of the formation under a synod, a partiarch, or even "episcopal conferences" of the modern kind, of "national" or "autocephalous" churches, which everywhere in the Orthodox Church (as in the Catholic Church) have tended and perhaps still tend, more than ever, to substitute themselves for the metropolitan organization?

To answer this question, we must begin by introducing very important distinctions, and the mere observation of the beginning and the development (including the decline) of the great patriarchates suggests them. To repeat more specifically what we have more than hinted at: they correspond to certain "natural" divisions of the world of antiquity where Christianity was spread and the activity of the apostles, though universal in principle, was "divided." Of course, in the five traditional patriarchates the correspondence with apostolic sees or territories is not, and has never been perfect—nor can the concept be taken strictly. What justifies these partriachables is a distribution of churches and the authority that unites them in correspondence with geographic groupings, or at least a type of geographic groupings, in which the activity of the apostles was modeled. As long as we view things in this spirit, with the various patriarchs in a special union with the pope, considered the "first" among them (since he is the "first" of bishops), and associated with him in a special way as the most eminent representatives of the episcopate in promoting catholic unity and the unity of the Church, everything is fine. But this is not the case if we consider each patriarchate as constituting "a church" complete in herself and capable of living apart from the others or of imposing her particular forms of life on them.

The first deviation was "autocephalous" Orthodox churches, when they tended to identify Orthodoxy with the particular forms of religious culture of their peoples (Greeks, Russians, Serbs, Romanians, etc.)—which the Orthodox themselves stigmatize under the term *phyletism* (i.e., "tribal" or "nationalist" Christianity)—and so-called "national" Catholic churches when they fell into one or another form of Gallicanism. The second, opposite temptation proceeds from the first: intransigent, narrow Byzantinism and, in the strictest sense, Roman "ultramontanism."

Having identified the Catholic (or Orthodox) faith with its expression in a local idiosyncracy, it was inevitable that this idiosyncracy would be identified with the faith and that powerful leaders would wish to impose it everywhere. Thus the Byzantine liturgy came to be propagated authoritatively throughout the East, to the detriment of other liturgies which were even more venerable because of their richness and age, and the Greek language and Greek theology came to repress the remarkable modes of expression and thought of Christian Syrians and Copts. Similarly, at a later date in the West, the Roman liturgy supplanted the Gallican, Mozarabic, and Celtic liturgies, and Scholastic philosophy practically annihilated every other form of religious reflection, while Church Latin preempted any possibility of another Christian language, at the risk of making traditional worship unpopular and esoteric.

These "imperialisms"—which are only provincialisms tending to a false universalism by stamping out legitimate particularisms—gave rise to catastrophic reactions against genuine Christian unity. The ruptures caused by Monophysitism and Nestorianism in the East and Protestantism in the West, if they did not find full rationalization in reaction against these uniformities, imposed from without, assumed more and more gravity, and spread and perdured, in great part for this reason.

Disintegration of the ancient patriarchates in the East and abnormal development of the Roman patriarchate in the West, which (in the eyes of the East as well) compromised the papacy by confusing it with freakish turgidity, were equally harmful consequences of the same process. The patriarchate of Constantinople in particular was dismantled by the "autocephalies," which claimed for their own nationalities their own Christianized cultures—if not the universal dominion dreamed of by Byzantinism, at least an independence and local sovereignty equal to that of Constantinople, and often (as with Moscow, the "Third Rome") much more. And the papacy, too often substituting the activity of its curia for that of the local episcopates, either reduced the latter to insignificance, thus paralyzing the proper development of their churches, or by various forms of Gallicanism, provoked a growing misunderstanding of its basic mission or, with Protestantism, impassioned rejection.

Other sides to these historical truths are too often lost sight of. Certainly all cultures, all natural peculiarities which are not the result of sin but of the diversity inherent in creation, have an equal right to develop in the Church. Undoubtedly, all have a providential role to play there, so that when one is unduly oppressed by others it does not suffer alone, but the entire Christian and human community.

This does not mean, however, that all cultures can play the same role or even an equal role in the Church. It is questionable, for example, that the Greek culture, under its Byzantine form in the East, and the Latin culture, in its Roman form in the West, could have imposed themselves by the brute strength of authority. As is shown by abundant translations from Greek into Coptic and Syriac (even long after the divisions in the East) and the spontaneous rally to the Roman liturgy in the West (well before Rome thought of imposing it), the problem is not so simple. The supernatural unity of the Church—like everything supernatural in Christianity—has a natural foundation in the unity of human nature, created in the image of the Creator and redeemed in the personal "image" of his taking on our flesh. Consequently it relies, legitimately and necessarily, on natural means for fulfillment.

Universal or largely international cultures, such as the Greek and the Latin, which were deeply united in their origins and modes of communication, as attested by humanism (in the most exalted sense of the word), contributed a very precious vehicle of unity and authentic Christian fellowship. No unity, no communication, is possible among men except by means of a common language and a common culture, which are quasi-indispensable means. Again, so that this benefit would, not be too costly, it was necessary that the means never be confused with the end and in order to do this, that the means never be considered exclusive of itself. This consideration is extensive in import, and if we start with it we may be able to differentiate the effectively Christian consecration of every legitimate characteristic and the inadmissible apotheosis of other characteristics.

In a general way, what is improperly called a "national" or "autocephalous" church (each local church, the church of each bishop, *is* autocephalous in a sense, but they do not form *"one* Church," uniting all local churches, or present in all, except on the universal level), corresponds to a necessity—or at least unquestionable usefulness—when the grouping of churches, thus constituted, permits them to respond as one to a number of common problems and to develop, as one, common characteristics that are of themselves good and beneficial. Yet these benefits change, for the churches under consideration as well as for the universal Church, into positive dangers if the grouping is seen as terminal rather than as a stage on the road to the universality of fellowship, which cannot rely on uniformity but only on the harmonization of differences.

On the other hand, the development of differences (linguistic, cultural, national, social, etc.) will be Christian and humanly sound only if this development is conceived as a service of all in humility, rather than a self-affirmation. Thus it is necessary that it be accompanied by recognition of the complementarity of analogous characteristics. Accordingly, it is fitting to recall that the great cultures, and the most original ones, remained alive and vital only as long as they remained open to others, not closed off from them. Far from losing their sense of originality, they asserted it, and not so much by falling back on the past as by continuous creativity, based on the past. For a stronger reason, this must be the case of cultures that are fecundated by grace and, in turn, put to the service of the Gospel.

One point especially ought to command our attention today—as in all ages that are marked by numerous and rapid transformations. Consecration by the Church of specific human characteristics, legitimate peculiarities, which she can and sometimes must preserve in cultures that are threatened from without—which, even so, have in no way exhausted their possibilities—must never bind the Christian faith to forms of life that are either out of date or incapable of evolving further (especially if this consecration was made in such a way that it contributed to such a standstill).

All these considerations seem to urge a flexible constitution of federations of local churches, surpassing (as far as possible) purely national limits and cultural (such as Latin America or black Africa) and political blocs (such as the "Atlantic states" or those behind the Iron Curtain), except by maintaining the broadest, most constant, and cordial relations with like groups from other blocs. In preserving flexibility amid the fluidity of such groups, "episcopal conferences," with temporary and frequently changing "presidents," can often be preferable to new patriarchates, which would run the risk of immobilizing and disagreeably identifying a mobile situation with developments that are still unforeseeable. On the other hand, a particular problem, if posed by "national churches" (in the broadest sense of the term), can lead to a mundane problem that is quite general and current.

Over the last centuries, the survival of a few small churches of the East or their reintegration in communion with the Catholic Church, which has become narrowly Western, has posed a special problem which is analogous with the one we have encountered with regard to the base, territorial or not, that is fittingly part of a renewed parochial life. Surrounded and hemmed in on every side by the Latin Church, these communities of the East were able to save something of their legitimate characteristics, which are of inestimable value for preserving in the church, which is Catholic in principle, her *de facto* catholicity, but only at the price of radical measures of conservation. The most notable measure determines membership in one of these communities on the basis of baptism and rite, not residence, so that several bishops in one place (one Latin and one Eastern or, as in Syria and Lebanon, several Eastern bishops: Maronite, Melkite, Syrian, etc.) "share" the resident Christians, according to these differences. An analogue was the ancient Celtic churches, where belonging to an ecclesiastical unit was based on clan, rather than residence, and especially the churches of nomadic Germans and their *Volksbischoff*, who was not the bishop of all Christians who lived together in one place but of Christians of a distinct people, intermingled with other peoples.

Historically, in the Eastern churches united to Rome, this situation is partially justified. Nonetheless, it is radically unsatisfactory, for the reasons we pointed out: any church of a clan, race, nationality, or class is unsatisfactory. Where there should be a common life of Christians, it is a scandal that the Church, instead of lowering the human barriers that tend to separate, serves to raise them and therefore to solidify opposition. This, quite rightly, is resented by many Catholic Christians of Eastern origin.

What then can be done, in the present situation of the dispersion and intermingling of allogenic populations, to assert Catholic unity without falling into a uniformity that is either imposed from without (by an imperialistic particularism) or results from a fusion in which traditions would lose some of their most estimable riches by being reduced to a least common denominator?

Certainly, where diverse communities tend to melt together, the Church should not prevent it; rather, it should help them work out a harmonious synthesis of their respective traditions, either by encouraging exchanges or, on the basis of these traditions, preparing new common cultural creations. But in the intermediary phase of a cohabitation that is tending toward genuine integration, which alternative would be least oppressive or, for a stronger reason, least destructive for the original communities?

It seems that the best alternative (between premature unification of an episcopate and a pure and simple juxtaposition of episcopates from different obediences, more or less ignorant of one another) would be restoration and rearrangement of the archiepiscopal or metropolitan function. The situation of these "churches" would be transformed if, in every place where they were juxtaposed, the bishops of the different rites or nationalities were combined under the authority of a local archbishop, in such a way as to take under his presidency all decisions involving the common life of Christians of different origins (i.e., synodally) and, individually, decisions of special application, but always within the context of the situation.

Such a renewal of metropolitans and their role in the modern world could have many other applications. The most interesting, perhaps, would be adaptation to the situation created for the Church by the development of large urban centers, counting several million inhabitants in a restricted space. In this case, the breaking up of large dioceses into small dioceses "on a human scale" and the governing of *one* diocese by *one* bishop seems impracticable. The solution could be a series of associated dioceses, each with its own bishop. All these bishops, every time that circumstances require, would take decisions that were either common or coordinated, under the presidency and the responsibility of the archbishop, who has the special responsibility of a central diocese around which the others can be articulated. The experiment in the Paris area in recent years seems to have demonstrated the realism and fecundity of such coordination.

### III. "Pilot" Communities in the Church: Monasticism, Religious Orders and Congregations, Secular Institutes, and Various Lay Groups and Movements

The different groupings in the Church (or groupings of churches) that we have examined have tended to make individual Christians and local churches live in the catholic unity of the entire community of Christians of a given time; but we have emphasized that the inseparable unity and catholicity of the Church is not reduced to the total actuality of contemporary local churches nor to their grouping that is actualized in her eucharistic celebration. If it is the Eucharist which makes the Church, out of those who celebrate it together, it is first of all because it makes them one in the body of the risen Christ. It follows that their catholic unity embraces not only all Christians who participate at the same moment in the same Eucharist in every place, but all the saints who have consummated there, from the beginning of Christianity, their union with Christ. Moreover, this unity anticipates the universal ingathering, in this same eucharistic conjunction of his body, of the whole of redeemed mankind on the last day: the eschatological fullness of the "One who completes himself totally in all men."

If this is the case, it is not enough that catholicity in the unity of the Church tends to reunite all Christians today. It is still essential that the Church orient them, all together, toward the fulfillment, the fullness of the body of Christ, which constitutes Christian eschatology: "that we all encounter one another in the unity of the faith and of the knowledge of the Son of God [so as to form] one perfect man [reaching] the adult growth of the fullness of Christ."

The vocation of the last *ecclesiolae in Ecclesia,* of which we have still to speak, is unceasingly to urge the whole body of Christ, which is the Church, to this growth, toward this final term. These "churches" are groups of Christians who are differentiated from the others by their particular endeavor toward this eschatological plenitude, toward which the whole Church must tend in order to be one and catholic in the fullness of love. They are therefore "pilot" communities which must guide and lead the whole Christian community, the whole Church, toward the sole end, where she can be perfectly fulfilled: her ultimate encounter with Christ at the Parousia.

Strictly speaking, the only community which fully matches this definition, at least in principle, is the monastic community. In the Church, it is (or should be) only the community of those who have resolved to take Christ's precept literally: "If someone wants to be my disciple, let him renounce himself, take up his cross and follow me." For here the opposition between the letter and the Spirit is not relevant: the Spirit becomes truly incarnate only to the extent of the literalism, or realism, with which the exigencies of his incarnation are accepted. The radicalism of these Christians, in their acceptance of the cross and their following Christ, brings them to meet him in the glory of the final resurrection. Monasticism, faithful to its vocation, is therefore a vanguard community which should lead, or tend to lead, the whole body of the Church toward its final destiny, resolutely taking the only path that can bring it there.

From this viewpoint, the apparently paradoxical theory of Dom Germain Morin contains a large share of truth: it is not monasticism, as a particular community, that represents something new in the Church of the fourth century, but life accommodated to the world of the Christian masses, which accompanies and follows the official reconciliation of the world and the Church in the Age of Constantine. The first community of Jerusalem, with its communism broadened to include material as well as spiritual things, and directed toward the Parousia (though it undoubtedly included a number of married people), was certainly much closer to original monasticism than to what the average Christian's life became. And the same must be said of Christian life in the first centuries, the centuries of the martyrs.

Before organized monasticism, more-than-implicit acceptance of the possibility of martydom (included in baptism) and preparation for facing it (to which the world's hostility drove the Christian) turned the everyday life of Christians to asceticism at every moment and caused Christian life at the time of the persecutions to appear to be "premonastic." If celibates and virgins were not yet separated from the body of the community, they constituted an elite that showed the way to all and contributed to involving them in it.

Freely and consciously, monasticism developed these beneficent constraints for an authentic Christianity which existence in the world, so precarious up to then, had long imposed on Christians as expected. But it soon incurred the risk of being stabilized as a kind of "superior Christianity," separated from the masses and static. With its organization and observances catalogued and codified, it ceased to represent (as it did at the beginning) an essentially spiritual movement, constantly maintaining its members on the alert on the ever-ascending path of unlimited perfection and thereby making them guides and trainers of all their brothers—were they to follow them, though only at a distance, in this relentless march. All successive teachers and all "renewals" of monasticism are characterized by an endeavor to return to its original condition, not as a separate state, which is entered once and for all and one need only maintain oneself, but as a renewed thrust which must always correct itself, which is nothing more than the original thrust of Christian faith, hope, and charity that all the baptized have equal need to revivify constantly in themselves.

Thus if monasticism remains what it should be, what it began by being, and what all genuine renewals make it become again, it appears to be the sole solution to the old question: a multitudinist Church or a Church of the professing? This solution is certainly not a Church of two levels, which accepts but abandons to their wretched lot incipient Christians who will never go much further, while consoling herself with the culture of an elite which is turned in on its own "perfection," supposedly acquired once and for all. Nor is this Church a unification of all on the most mediocre plane—nor from the outset, the illusory raising of all by "conversion" to the level that is supposedly highest. It subsists, and can only be, in the call to all, unceasingly renewed, to constant progress in detachment from this world and in adhesion to Christ crucified. But this call cannot be heard, cannot be effective, without the vocation of a few to a radical generosity or, better, a more immediately radical generosity, which, by its internal witness to the Church, urges all Christians (even if they cannot follow them in their special form of detachment) to recognize its urgency for themselves at the same time that they appreciate its fecundity.[15]

This interpretation of monasticism and its role in the Church, in terms and realizations that are quite different in appearance, coincides with Wesley's dynamic notion of the Church and, following him, the best of the Methodist movement and all the "Awakening" movements in the modern churches following from the Protestant Reformation. Here the Church is considered, in her concrete members, not as a social reality, simply constituted and established once and for all, but as a community, we would say, of permanent, mutual education where all must contribute to "building one another up," and where this work is never ended. The first and the most deeply touched by the evangelical call are not separated in this Church from their brothers who did not reject it absolutely but have become more or less insensitive toward it. On the contrary, the former progress in their development *by helping* the latter, their insensitive or lapsed brothers, to respond to the call, and it is perhaps by contributing to this "awakening" of others that they "awaken" themselves.

This is an exact correspondent of the dynamic schema of monastic development, conceived by antiquity. The monk does not separate himself from the mass of middle-class Christians, as a sectarian would, to flee definitively from them and set up another spiritual society cut off from theirs. He goes into the desert only to confront the devil, completely possessed by the Spirit of Christ in his solitude. And this solitary struggle, of itself, sends him back into the world so that he might exercise spiritual fatherhood toward others. Only in this way does the monk become a true monk, and only then can he affirm that he has become a monk—not only by his habit or vesture but according to the Spirit.

From the monastic institution, consequently, the different "religious orders," the modern "congregations," arose, and finally the contemporary secular institutes. Monasticism is of lay origin, even though it soon attracted priests and more and more recruited them, especially in the East. Bishops, from the fifth century on, tended to create an essentially clerical monasticism or, more precisely, to "monasticize" the clergy in the West. Instead, it made them accept consecrated celibacy (in a general way) and a life ideal that was frugal in principle, but laity and clergy alike were confused, it seems fearing that a monasticized clergy risked double separation from the mass of the laity and that the clergy would reject the idea. On the other hand, as in primitive monasticism among the laity, the "religious" clergy (among the other clergy), at the same time that they obtained highly specialized strength—the

Franciscans in popular evangelization, Dominicans and their "intellectuals," Jesuits in the struggle against heresies in Europe and their missions elsewhere, etc.—were able to help them (to the extent that they did not engage in rivalry with "seculars") to aim for that holiness whose means the priests must bring to the laity; but they were unable to persuade them to do so if they themselves had not done so.

If we follow the development from ancient monasticism to the post–Tridentine congregations, we see that it is characterized more and more by a fundamental insistence on rendering service to the Christian (and human) community, yet never forgetting the original aim of monasticism: personal progress in Christian life. At the beginning, monasticism especially, but not exclusively, was very conscious that one cannot sanctify oneself without contributing to the sanctification others, and the modern institutions tended to sanctify their members by their work for their Christian (and human) brothers. This became explicit in the missionary and charitable societies of the nineteenth century, and even more explicit perhaps in the contemporary "movements"—in distinction to the medieval "guilds," which, even when they brought Christians of the same profession or social background together, while professed the primordial intention to contribute to the sanctification of their members being very interested in their concrete problems.

We must ask whether there may not be a dangerous ambiguity in this. Today, many secular institutes are more immersed in the world, in order to serve better in it, than any "order" or "congregation" in the past, concerned with the sanctification of their members not only *through* their activities but *because* of them. The same reservation applies to the latent crisis in movements of specialized Catholic actions, conceived with the goals of activity and witness and supposing their "militants" to be already formed in the essentials of Christian life—and not needing other supplements to this formation than what results from their activity among or for others. They seem to elicit, among their own members as well as outside them, an analogous reaction. There is a desire and a search for doctrinal and spiritual formation, for the quality of "apostolic" action itself, which is not reduced to the simple exercise of such action.

Finally, beyond monasticism and the traditional orders or congregations, the "third orders" (which extended their influence), the institutes, and the more recent movements, we must consider the need described by Jacques Maritain: for very free and spontaneous groupings of laymen who want to help themselves in deepening their Christian life and in exercising effective witness.[16] Conscious of the necessary distinction between these two endeavors, as well as their profound unity, these groups unite men from similar backgrounds (as in the specialized Catholic Action of yesterday) or, perhaps preferably, men from different backgrounds, first for enrichment of their Christian life and then its natural consequence: greater capacity to serve their brothers in the whole of existence and, closely connected with such service, to bear witness to Christ and the Church. Such groups, assisted by priests and guided by authority, ought to exert their spontaneity to the maximum, no less to be true with their members than with other men. And perhaps the most traditional form of monasticism (in the best sense of "traditional"), which is most attentive to the essentials of its vocation, could, by reviving itself, best furnish the centers of intense and free ecclesiastical life that such groups need to nourish and maintain themselves.

All these groups—whether institutionalized or not, whether specialized or not in a particular Christian work—insofar as they aim, among their members and among all men, at a purer and more intense development of faith, hope, and charity, appear as so many providential means of mutual and permanent education of Christians by one another. The great merit of Wesleyan tradition is that it explicated and systematized the importance of such a concern in the Church. Wesley would have been the first to say that he did not invent it—that it is one of the most traditional elements of the life of the Church and that it must be acknowledged as such. Did not St. Benedict, many years before, define the cenobitic monastery as a "school of the service of God"?

In conclusion, it may be well to point out the importance of Catholic schools, and especially universities—provided they do not limit themselves (as they too often have in the recent past) to giving a simple imitation of contemporary non-Christian teaching in a segregationist framework. If, on the contrary, they aim at complete education of *homo christianus* on the basis of a wisdom in constant renewal, assimilating, positively criticizing, and thereby Christianizing contemporary culture—which presupposes a deepening of the divine Word that must always be renewed and pursued in the light of the whole of tradition—these schools, and especially the universities, ought to be (or become again) one of the most important forms of pilot communities in the Church.

## Notes

1. Fr. Congar has brought the councils in the life of the Church together in "Sainte Eglise" (pp. 303ff.), a study published in the *Informations catholiques internationales* of 1959, immediately after announcement of the

convocation of the last council. Cf. J. Ratzinger, op. cit., pp. 147ff. In general, see *Le Concile et les Conciles,* as well as *L'Episcopat et l'Eglise universelle, L'Ecclesiologie au XIX<sup>e</sup> siècle,* and *La Collégialité épiscopale.*

2. Canon 8 of the Council of Nicaea excludes the possibility of more than one bishop of one place. Canon 223, following the usage created by the First Vatican Council, admits a simply possible convocation of titular bishops, even with a deliberative voice, by allowing it to be understood that neither of these two points constitutes a strict right of those involved, contrary to the case of abbot-presidents or general superiors of exempt orders.

3. All this is completely misunderstood by K. Rahner in his most recent studies on the episcopate, where he tends to separate it unduly from the local church, to the point of wanting it to be given to all major superiors (at least) of religious orders. The Franciscans must have been equally surprised, as they may have been touched by the solicitude one could believe he gave them—if we are to keep to the prudent choice of his examples. See especially his study, p. 490, n. 50.

4. See the article "Concile" in *Dictionnaire de Droit canonique,* by N. Jung.

5. Acts 15:28.

6. Although in different ways, it will be observed that we are arriving at positions concerning this problem of the cooperation of the laity in the exercise of authority, especially of the magisterium, that are very close in practice to those developed by Congar in *Jalons pour une théologie du laïcat* (pp. 327ff.). See the whole conciliar decree, *Apostolicam actuositatem.*

7. The very interesting treatise of Benedict XIV on the diocesan synod has not been surpassed.

8. Actually, episcopal conferences, like particular councils, are connected with these intermediary communities between the local church and the universal Church, and we shall study them in the following paragraph. We thought we must introduce the problem of their composition and their functioning without further delay, for it commands the composition and functioning of other permanent bodies of the same kind (e.g., the presbyteral and pastoral councils and the Episcopal Synod created by Paul VI), which were created from the developed experience of episcopal conferences. On everything that follows, see the conciliar decree on the pastoral responsibility of the bishops, *Christus Dominus.* See also P. Duprey, *"La structure synodale de l'Eglise," Proche-Orient chrétien* (1970), pp. 123ff.

9. On the episcopal synods of the East, see the manual of Byzantine law by St. Nicodemus the Hagiorite, *The Rudder* (Chicago, 1957), pp. 56 and 659. Cf. J. Hajjar, "Synode permanent et collégialité épiscopale dans l'Eglise byzantine au premier millénaire," pp. 151ff. in the collective volume *La Collégialité épiscopale.* See also M. Clément, "La collégialité de l'épiscopat dans l'Eglise maronite," pp. 481ff. in *L'Episcopat et l'Eglise universelle.*

10. On these organisms and their role, see the volume (already cited) of Fr. Legrand, *La charge pastorale des évêques.*

11. In addition to V. Martin's volume (already mentioned), *Les Cardinaux et la curie,* see his other work, *Les Congrégations romaines* (Paris, 1930).

12. These are the arguments developed by Paul VI himself in the different discourses he gave in regard to creation and the two convocations of the synod.

13. In *L'Episcopate et l'Eglise universelle,* see the studies of O. Kéramé, "Les chaires apostoliques et le rôle des patriarcats dans l'Eglise," pp. 161ff.; Dom H. Marot, "Unité de l'Eglise et diversité géographique aux premiers siècles," pp. 565ff.; and C. Vogel, "Unité de l'Eglise et pluralité des formes historiques d'organisation ecclésiastique, du IIIᵉ au Vᵉ siècle," pp. 591ff.

14. See the article "Patriarche" by C. de Clercq in *Dictionnaire du droit canonique.*

15. See our *Spiritualité du Nouveau Testament et des Pères,* pp. 368ff. On the religious in the Church, see the constitution *Lumen Gentium,* chaps. 5 and 6.

16. J. Maritain, *Carnet de Notes* (Paris, 1965), pp. 235ff.

# Chapter 10
# The Church and the World

Behind the problems raised in our preceding chapter is a deeper problem, which underlay the previous chapters: the relationship between the Church and the world.

"World" may be taken in different senses, depending upon whether we mean the whole of created reality or, more strictly, human reality alone. In the Bible (almost exclusively the New Testament), we understand it as the human world, but always considered as rooted in the material world and on the fringe of a spiritual world, far vaster than we know.

A second distinction has to be made in modern usage: when we say "world" we are thinking ordinarily of the totality of created beings and things or, more simply, human beings and things. But in the New Testament the word we translate as "world," that is, *kosmos,* designates above all the organization, the order that reigns in the elements. From this viewpoint (as we have said), the apostolic writers differentiated two epochs, the *aion houtos,* the present world or age, characterized by the fall of man (and, before him, the fall of the angelic powers) and therefore sin, which is set against the divine will, and the *aion mellon,* the "world to come," where sin will be no more, where the divine will be accomplished without hindrance, where God will reign.[1]

When we have these distinctions before us, the complex declarations of the divine Word about the "world" are clarified and become explainable—the "extreme" passages of St. John and the Gospel's apparently contradictory formulas. "God so loved the world that he gave his only Son, that whoever believes in him should not perish but have eternal life,"[2] and "I am not praying for the world . . . ,"[3] which is emphasized in the first epistle by such statements as "Do not love the world or the things in the world," and finally (which gives the key to these seemingly harsh statements), "The whole world is in the power of the evil one."[4]

It is clear that this world for which Christ refuses to pray, in which his disciples are dissuaded from loving anything, is the "world in the power of the evil one," insofar as everything is ordered in accordance with the diabolical will and not the divine will. But the same world is no less the object of the Father's love, to the point that he sacrificed his Son for it—that is, the world insofar as God is its author and as he wills to return it, since it left his hands, to the perfection to which he destined it. Hence the other apparent contradictions between equally traditional formulas, such as "Flee the world," "Become detached from the world," and "Save the world."

In fact—as all great Catholic spiritual writers have emphasized—they are not at all contradictory. Since the world where we find ourselves has become what it has, we must begin by escaping from it, freeing ourselves from it, in order to be able to contribute to saving it, that is, liberating it from the demoniacal domination which oppresses it and makes it an instrument of oppression. It is in this sense, to return to another Johannine expression, that "our victory over the world is our faith." Without being unfaithful to him— indeed, by developing the thought in John 3:16—it is only this victory over the world that can allow us to reconsecrate the world to God and thereby give it back to him—to return it to all the initial possibilities that God's creation bestowed upon it.

It is precisely here that the Church and her mission in the world are inserted.

## I. The Church and Her Mission in the World

We may "define" the Church's mission in the world (or the Church's mission *to* the world) by saying that it is not destined to serve the world, as it is at present, but *to serve men in it,* so that they may be saved not from their *created* condition, willed and brought about by God, but from their condition *at present,* alienated by sin, which comes down to wresting the physical cosmos itself, in them and by them, from the domination of the evil one. This is exactly what is envisioned by St. Paul when he says that

> the creation waits with eager longing for the revealing of the sons
> of God; for the creation was subjected to futility, not of its own

will but by the will of him who subjected it in hope; because the creation itself will be set free from its bondage to decay and obtain the glorious liberty of the children of God. We know that the whole creation has been groaning in travail together until now; and not only the creation, but we ourselves, who have the first fruits of the Spirit, groan inwardly as we wait for adoption as sons, the redemption of our body.[5]

This passage, sufficiently self-explanatory, is reenforced when it is connected with the text of 1 Corinthians 15 on the ressurection:

I tell you this, brethren: flesh and blood cannot inherit the kingdom of God, nor does the perishable inherit the imperishable. Lo! I tell you a mystery. We shall not all sleep, but we shall all be changed, in a moment, in the twinkling of an eye, at the last trumpet. For the trumpet will sound, and the dead will be raised imperishable, and we shall be changed. For this perishable nature must put on the imperishable, and this mortal nature must put on immortality. When the perishable puts on the imperishable, and the mortal puts on immortality, then shall come to pass the saying that is written:
"Death is swallowed up in victory."

"O death, where is thy victory?
O death, where is thy sting?"
The sting of death is sin and the power of sin is the law. But thanks be to God, who gave us the victory through our Lord Jesus Christ. Therefore, my beloved brethren, be steadfast, immovable, always abounding in the work of the Lord, knowing that in the Lord your labor is not in vain.[6]

The last specifications are supplied, perhaps, by the parallel and complementary text of the second epistle to the same Corinthians:

For we know that if the earthly tent we live in is destroyed, we have a building from God, a house not made with hands, eternal in the heavens. Here indeed we groan, and long to put on our heavenly dwelling, so that by putting it on we may not be found naked. For while we are still in this tent, we sigh with anxiety; not that we would be unclothed, but that we would be further clothed, so that what is mortal may be swallowed up by life. He who has prepared us for this very thing is God, who has given us the Spirit as a guarantee.[7]

In a word, what we expect in this world is not that the world, with our body, which is part of it, vanish or be annihilated, but that they, together, be transfigured—transformed from top to bottom by the resurrection, wherein they are clothed by the glory of God. And we prepare ourselves for it, we prepare the world for it, by struggling against the power of sin, first in ourselves, by living faith in Jesus Christ, "our victory over the world."[8] But faith cannot be living unless it "works through love"[9] and, thereby, tends to be spread to others. In other words, the mission of the Church in the world is to proclaim Christ, to make him live in people's hearts by the power of the Spirit, and thereby to prepare the transformation, the transfiguration, of the entire world. Again, this transfiguration cannot be brought about with the resurrection of our body, except with and through the return of Christ in glory. All together in the Church, in meeting him, we "complete what is lacking in Christ's afflictions for the sake of his body, that is, the church."[10]

The transfiguration of the world, like that of man's body, is therefore the goal; but it is a goal that the Church "in the present age" cannot attain, any more than she can force the coming of the reign. In other words, she cannot make the present world into the reign of God. But by proclaiming the coming of this reign, as Christ did, and its coming *in Christ,* who is dead and has risen, she can prepare men for it in this world. Therefore she prepares the world itself for it, a world with which and in which people form one body, since in it they have their bodies through which they communicate. And let us repeat: this preparation, by the gift of the Spirit in the Church, which is extended with the extension of the Church, is not only a guaranteed pledge (*arrabon*) of the future reign but, already, the first fruits (*aparche*), the beginning. [11] Even more precisely, it is to the extent of the expansion of the divine *agape* in this world that the power of the Spirit, that the Christ of the Parousia, is already present there and reigns in his people. But for them as for him, the *agape,* proclaimed and manifested in this world, as it is today, ultimately signifies the cross. Yet Christ's cross, in us as in him, signifies the progressive "completion" of his body in all its members and thereby directly prepares for the resurrection of the whole "body of Christ" and, therefore, the transfiguration of the world.

All this cannot be deduced from mere generalities unless we envisage the relationship of the Church with other groups which, through their mutual imbrication, constitute the world in the sense we are using the word. In these groups, the relationship of the Church with human individuals is concretized in their whole, real situation. In effect, by being inserted in the world that is common to them they lead a common life, on both the spiritual and physical levels.

## II. The Church and Temporal Communities

We shall defer to a later paragraph the relations between the Church and the state, for this poses special and complex questions. We shall begin by studying the proper relations of the Church with collectivities that are more particular than the state and whose aims are limited to the organization of present life. We reserve for the following chapter her relations with other religious societies.[12]

Among the societies that bring men together, and often the same men on different planes, it may be well to differentiate those which Tönnies refers to as *Gemeinschaft* and those for which he uses the term *Gesellschaft*. The first, which we might call "communities," are societies that are in some sense natural, such as the family, the tribe, the collectivity, formed by a small rural agglomeration. The others, which we might call "associations," seem, on the contrary, to be artificial products. People are not born in them nor are they involved in them by life itself. They are formed or made by a kind of "social contract," more or less analogous to what Rousseau imagined at the origin of every society, and have real existence only in societies of this kind. These are the industrial or financial companies, mutual aid societies, etc.—in general, all groupings that are constituted by a kind of contract for pursuit of a common good, conceived in advance.[13]

Evidently, there are many intermediary types. For example, a club that arises from spontaneous friendships participates in both types. Furthermore, one type is capable of evolving into the other, and it is not always easy to say when one is substituted for another. At what moment, for example, does a rural village that develops into a city cease being a *Gemeinschaft* and become a *Gesellschaft?* The answer is not easy yet the distinction is well founded, and Tönnies' annalyses have shown how fertile it can be.

One could be tempted to think, *a priori,* that since the *Gemeinschaft* is a "natural" reality, it would be in spontaneous harmony with the Church, herself the work of the author of nature, even though she is "supernatural," whereas she would by nature be in a relationship of opposition (or at least tension) with every *Gesellschaft,* an "artificial" product of man's activity and, for this reason, certainly marked with original sin.

But to a great extent, such a supposition is only a result of the ambiguity of "natural." It can be thought, on one hand, that it is in the nature of man, sinner or not, to establish groups other than those to which he belongs naturally. Does not the family, founded by a man's getting married, seem to be a

*Gesellschaft,* substituted for the original *Gemeinschaft?* On the other hand, because original sin consists essentially of the rejection of supernatural life, it goes against the orientations essential to human nature (by its creation), and therefore vitiates them, and we must expect that the natural societies to which man belongs be vitiated also. So perhaps—without going so far as the untenable excesses of Harvey Cox—we may maintain that many artificial societies reflect at least an effort of man to provide against the consequences of his original fall and try, though unsuccessfully, to escape them.

This distinction between natural and artificial societies, between *communities* and *associations,* must not be overlooked in the problem which concerns us. It is certain that the Church, whose end is restoration and fulfillment of human nature, must see that man be not unduly deprived of societies that are bound up with his development, which could no longer continue if man were uprooted from them or if they were attacked. Above all, this is the case with the family. Furthermore, the Church must be attentive to the special danger that threatens these societies, not from without but from within, because of our fallen nature, namely, the danger of taking themselves as ends and *exclusive* ends.

For example, the Church must bless and encourage the family, but she must be careful not to make it, or help it make itself, into an idol. The natural family, with the help of the Church, must introduce its members to the family of God, which makes them brothers of all men. But since human nature is at present what it has become through sin, it is only "too natural" that the family may not care about this wider brotherhood, and even oppose it. Hence inevitable conflicts with the Church: "Whoever loves his father, his mother, more than me is not worthy of me."

The same is true, *a fortiori,* for all other natural societies. Cox exaggerates when he describes rural society as essentially pagan, and is completely wrong when he tries to demonstrate that urban society, by its very "secularization," anticipates the exigencies of the Bible. It is perfectly correct, nevertheless, that societies that have been most burdened with ancestral traditions, prior to their encounter with the Gospel, have a considerable remodeling task, so that their members may accept Christ without entering into conflict with their non-Christian traditions. It is also true that many elements of this heritage, once they have passed through this process of death and rebirth, know a new vitality which is authentically Christian.

The problems are different in the encounter of the Church and a *Gesellschaft,* an association deliberately set up by men. As the Bible shows in the Tower of Babel narrative (as well as the life of primitive man, in what is called, through oversimplification, "the state of nature"), to the extent that every civilization (from its origins) aggrandizes prideful and selfish power, which is basically rebellious against its Creator, the Church must be on guard against this undesirable tendency that contributes to the formation and development of such societies. More particularly, she must react against the frequently manifested tendency, which is always more or less subjacent, of providing man with a substitute "super nature" in the absence of lost grace: of making him into a "super man"—in fact however, a "subhuman" man, fatally crushed by the effects of his pride, who completes the degradation of his nature by pretending to raise it above itself, without and against God. It is certainly not because modern civilization is an urban civilization that the Church must criticize it, but for what is Promethean about the cities that men have created: their excess. In wanting man to vie with God, cities have often reduced man to an interchangeable cog in the monstrous machine that man has produced. The Faustian ambition at the basis of capitalism, which presided over the first developments of industrial society, is undeniable. The inhumanity of the city it built, whose first victims were the very ones it made its craftsmen, revealed that it is, to this extent, an accursed city. Only too clearly, we see that the same thing is true of the collectivist city, as long as it does not criticize these premises in depth but limits itself to extending or transposing, for the benefit of another "class," the same self-indulgent and self-assured materialism which dazzled the founders of capitalism.

There is, then, an incurable naiveté behind the "concordisms" of such people as Teilhard de Chardin and those who followed him (with even less critical Christian spirit), who claim to discover a preestablished harmony between modern industrial society and Christianity. What can be said when they salute an "implicit Church" in this society which is "purer" than the explicit Church, or profess to see an "anonymous Christianity" which, to be satisfactory, would need only to recognize itself or be recognized by "aware Christians" as being what it is already? Of course, an important kernel of truth may be extracted from these errors and purified, saving it from the counterfeit. We are certain that these aspirations of our age and the societies that characterize it—better knowledge of man and the universe and, on the basis of this knowledge, better organization of man's life in this world, which completes the humanization of the world in which man is immersed, and even the Promethean instinct to raise man not only above the world but above himself (though this instinct is deformed by diabolical error)—correspond (more or less obscurely) to mankind's human and divine vocation, to become sons of God.

The Church must discern and recognize this. But for this very reason, in the name of the Word she proclaims, she must oppose inadequate views of human nature, spoiled by materialism, and illusory view of its vocation, perverted by demoniacal pride from the true, enlightened wisdom from above, which alone can enlighten man about himself and the unique, mysterious ways of his authentic fulfillment, which are those of Jesus Christ—and Jesus Christ crucified.

This prophetic criticism is essentially constructive, and even sympathetic, but it is also inexorably lucid (with the lucidity of the very love of God the Creator and Savior), and it is the first duty of the Church with regard to temporal societies and, especially, those that are most characteristic of our time. But this criticism does not exhaust the problem of her relationship with them. Indeed, if the societies of which we speak should accept this criticism (in all their members), this judgment (but also this redemption that the Gospel, announced by the Church, offers them), what would be their lot? Should they dissolve into the Church, or at least subordinate themselves to her? If not, what kind of cooperation could or should there be?

Even if this hypothesis could be considered achieved or achievable, it would not follow that the Church should absorb the other societies, even though granting them relative autonomy or submitting them to her, properly speaking. Again, the Church is not the reign of God: she merely prepares us for it. And even in the reign of God, which will follow the Parousia, the Church will not absorb the other human societies within herself. She will subsist alone, in a sense, as a society of divine praise. But the transitory activities that characterize her today: proclamation of the divine Word, celebration of the sacraments, pastoral function (which are the pilgrimage of the People of God toward this reign), will have ceased, as will the temporal activities of societies that are only temporal. It makes no sense to say that these latter activities would melt into the former: they will be surpassed and replaced by ever-lasting activities, which even today, the Church could assist, but not by substituting itself for them or by absorbing them, nor even by directly subordinating them.

We do not see that the Church, even if we suppose that a state of ideal Christianity is achieved or achievable, can take the place of temporal societies absorb them in herself, nor even subordinate them to her. Responding to limited ends, which are anterior to the existence of the Church and subsist alongside her, these societies should not disappear when the Church is accepted by their members. The church could never aspire to absorb them, for their tasks are not hers, neither in time nor eternity. They can never be subordinated to her, even though pursuit of their limited goals, by their members who have become Christians, be subordinated to the unlimited and eternal ends of the Gospel. In fact, the Church authority is directly aimed at the ultimate ends of man: to know God as he has known man, to love God in return, to inspire man's whole life with this love. She has no special authority nor do her organisms have any power that can be applied (as such) to pursuit of secondary ends, which are those of the societies about which we are speaking.

As long as all members of temporal societies are not Christian, the Church obviously, would act in an ill-considered manner were she to impose on non-Christians the realization of her own ends, and she would only compromise that realization. But even if all men became Christians, they could hope to have societies concur with the ultimate end of the reign of God only by the freely consented orientation of their activities in the proper organs of these societies, and by respecting their immanent laws. In other words, only by making their temporal activities more human in the light of faith and the warmth of charity, in the measure of a humanity that not only acknowledges itself made in the image of God but, in this context, accepts adoption by God, could these Christians ''Christianize'' all temporal societies in which they act. This supposes that they purify, but also respect, the nature or deepest aim of these societies insofar as it is simply human, as well as the activities in question. For never does grace more deeply respect the nature of everything that is human than when it requires the purifications necessary to fulfill itself by surpassing itself in God.

It must be added that the hypothesis of an integral Christian society at the present time, far from being the Christian ideal of society today, is in formal contradiction with this ideal. The Christian ideal of the reign of God, which the Church must unceasingly propose to man and for which she must allow him to prepare himself and the world, is not, according to the Gospel, an ideal that even Christian man can actualize in the ''present age,'' though he must never cease tending toward it. It is the prerogative of God alone to bring it about in ''the world to come'' by the Parousia of Christ, returning in glory. Even if, under special circumstances, men count among their members a majority of Christians (by which we understand societies that are capable of emulating the Christian ideal), this state of being would not be tantamount to the reign of God), nor even societies that are capable of directly preparing men and the world for its fulfillment (which is true only of the Church).

Indeed, societies are Christian, or in the process of being Christianized, in proportion to the individual and collective efforts of their Christian members, insofar as they are faithful to their vocation of impregnating all their activities with faith and charity. But insofar as these activities are pursued in the present world, both because of them who remain sinners (on the road to being saved, though not yet saved in fact) and because of the world itself, "in the power of the evil one," however much human societies may anticipate the reign to come, they will never *be* the reign. They will never be more than a promise of it and an outline of its realization. Consequently, like those who comprise them, such societies are imperfect and fallible as regards their own ends and, *a fortiori*, the reign of God.

This does not mean that we must fall back on the opposite extreme and conclude that temporal societies, even when they contain Christians, must remain "secular," not only in the sense of being immersed in "the world" but as belonging to it unreservedly. The foregoing position bears an inadmissible confusion between the "present world" and "the world to come," which some people wish to substitute for the former—the fallen organization of divine creation, centered on sinful man, in the sense in which this creation must be reorganized around men recentered in God. Even when Christians are in the majority, or even the totality, in a human society, they cannot make it into a divine society. Nor can they accept a society that deliberately ignores God and wishes to take his place, even if they are only the smallest minority. With gentleness, with total respect for the freedom of others and the proper nature or purpose of the structures to which as mere men they belong, at the same time that they belong to the Church, they can and must bear witness by their activity to all that the Gospel requires of every human activity. They must also bear witness to the fact that, far from these exigencies subduing or restraining mankind, they are the only way it can be fully what it is and become everything it is called to become.

Neither clerical imperialism nor atheistic secularism can enhance such behavior. Only this sense of the charity of Christ and the inalienable responsibility of each Christian in his place in the world and in the Church—only life in the Church, faithful to what it must be—can inspire lay Christians.

## III. The Church and the State

The problems posed by relations between Church and state are more complex than those between the Church and every temporal society, because the former are posed on a much grander scale. But what makes them particularly critical is not simply a matter of dimension; rather, the state is a society that covers and embraces *all* temporal societies. Responsible for their harmonious cohabitation, the state invincibly tends to make them concur in its own ends and, in doing this, to impose itself as the ultimate end (at least in this world) of every human activity, both individual and collective. Through all of these characteristics, the state tends to enter into conflict, or at least tension, with the Church. Hence a reaction that is hard to resolve on the part of churchmen, and especially those who are most responsible in the Church: they tend to preempt the state, and even the authority of the state.[14]

We should not be surprised or scandalized by these impulses, since the origins of the state are undeniably religious and its residual tendency is to remain so, or become so again. This tendency, moreover, is not always weakest in states that claim to be "secular," that is, independent from the Church. Hence the tendency to be like the state, on the part of churchmen, and the tendency to be like the Church, on the part of men of the state.

Indeed, the state evolved from the old kingdoms and especially those which had more or less successfully sought universal domination: Assyria, Egypt, Persia, and later the empire of Alexander and its heir, Rome. The king or emperor, the *paterfamilias,* ennobled in accordance with his power, more or less literally represented this "fatherhood," which has always been recognized as the preeminent expression of the divinity in its relationship to the world. Even in modern states that are most desacralized, by intention or in appearance, the fact that the state constitutes or tends to constitute the framework in which the lives of its subjects or citizens will be realized as "all in one" connects with what Jung called "the most religious archetype" and Mircea Eliade "the fundamental hierophany." The state, therefore, inevitably orients itself toward pretensions that are religious, if not quasi-divine. In the fallen world, the tendency to identify the divine representations with the divinity is spontaneous. Human sin flows from angelic sin, by which the spiritual in the created universe wants to be taken for God himself. Throughout our self-indulgent egotisms, it tends to connect with the diabolic pride that inspired it by making the cosmos its idol. And every state, by its claims to the universal, tends to become the most satisfying idol for man, for man, by adoring a humanized cosmos, can have the impression of adoring himself.

The "biblical" reaction against this fact is shown on two levels. The beginning of both the People of God and the still obscure and implicit revelation of the divine reign was Abraham's break with the first civilizations (e.g., the Tower of Babel), which was repeated in the whole people in the break with Egypt. From this viewpoint, the later demand of the Israelites to have a king like the other nations was first interpreted by Samuel (and prophecy in general) as a denial of the God who revealed himself to their fathers, a fallback into idolatry. But God, at a second stage, not only accepted the monarchy in Israel but consecrated it, and the king, the anointed of the Lord, was not only the representative but, especially, the "first servant" of the heavenly King. And these formulas, though they were known to the neighboring peoples, conveyed a still-unknown reality, because the earthly king depended *ad nutum* on the divine Word. This was conveyed by Saul's replacement by David, who was king "according to the heart of the Lord," and by the later development of messianism—that is, expectation of an ideal king, throughout whose reign the divine kingship would be manifested in perfect transparency.[15]

In one sense, this tension is surpassed in the New Testament. The divine kingship appears as already manifested, even though the divine reign over the world is deferred until the Parousia. In this reign of Christ, which his cross makes possible and which his resurrection and ascension inaugurate, the divine kingship shows through. But does it follow that earthly kingships disappear, or should disappear, in Christian eyes? The position of the early Church and, notably, St. Paul is not so simplistic: it is the development of Jesus' teaching and attitude, as also revealed by the Synoptic and Johannine traditions.

In John's gospel, Jesus declares before Pilate: "My kingdom is not of this world," and this must be taken—as the context proves—in the same sense as his declaration reported by the three synoptics: "Render therefore to Caesar the things that are Caesar's and to God the things that are God's."[16] However enigmatic these sentences may be at first hearing, in the context of the Gospel they can support no explanation other than that of St. Paul, as Oscar Cullmann explained (perhaps more lucidly than any other exegete). The authority of the state, of the *polis*—as the New Testament would say, its *exousia*—is not the authority of God himself but it is an authority which proceeds from his, like that of the angels over the cosmos (to which, furthermore, it is closely related). Like theirs, an authority that has rebelled, it tends to be exercised not as a service, a *ministerium,* but as a *dominium,* to make "Caesar" a *kyrios,* master and possessor of all things, in a sense that belongs only to God. This is why today, in principle, the *exousia* of the state, like that of the fallen angels, has been taken from it and restored to God by Christ. Even though it is no longer only "for a time," its exercise subsists until the Parousia in every interregnum. When this authority is exercised against God and his will, it must be repelled at any price—not by armed revolt (like the Zealots) but by nonviolent resistance, ready even for martyrdom. On the other hand, as long as it is exercised with justice, its original legitimacy, resulting from the first order of creation, must be recognized and its prescriptions obeyed.[17]

What happens, however, if Caesar is converted and the mass of his servants passes with him to Christ's service? Must he refuse to acknowledge his conversion, or may he continue to exercise his office?

Undeniably, there was hesitation among the fathers in dealing with the problems associated with a sovereign's conversion and, therefore, the "conversion" of a state's machinery—with the possibility, that is, of a Christian as a functionary or magistrate, and especially a Christian who wielded the "sword" about which the Apostle taught explicitly, which had been given to the *exousia* by God himself. But it does not seem that there was any hesitation in the Church about recognizing the conversion of the prince or his continuing to exercise his office. From all that we can observe, the initial problems and efforts—undeniably, there were some—pertained to *how* he should exercise it: what he would have to abandon in his previous exercise, as well as preserve and tranform, and how.

Until Galerius, Christian emperors retained the title Pontifex Maximus; then they abandoned it *de facto*. It does not seem that they caused any outrage or that people in Christian antiquity were shocked by their exercise of the right of life and death in penal matters or armed force in time of war. The evolution of law under Christian emperors tended toward humanization of punishments, and the distinction between just and unjust wars was a more and more acute problem for moralists. The most difficult problem for the fathers, for some time, was whether intervention of the "secular arm" against heretics or schismatics could be tolerated, accepted, or required. St. Martin stands out by his radical opposition, and St. Augustine, because of the "Donatist affair," reversed this negative attitude, which brought the practically universal adhesion of the Church.

Slower, more limited, and fraught with difficulties was the transition of the Church from a dubitative attitude with respect to military service to a simply reserved attitude. Only in the Middle Ages was there a consecration of the warrior (in chivalry), just as the Middle Ages passed from admission of purely defensive wars to the Crusades. ("Admission," perhaps, is too feeble a word; as with chivalry, which is closely connected with it, we might better use "consecration," despite isolated resistance or recrimination, such as that of Isaac of the Star.)

Perhaps more interesting is the evolution of legislation pertaining to slavery. Never officially suppressed, it withered away in Christian relations between master and slave—to reappear almost immediately, though in mitigated form, with serfdom.

But again, the basic problem is not so much the influence of the Church on the state, whose origins are independent of the Church and which remains external to her, as the assimilation—possible or not, willed or not—of the state by the church or conversely, the problem which was never posed to the same degree with other temporal societies: assimilation of the Church by the state. It is here that the religious character of the state becomes fully prominent, whether actually and explicitly or in a residual and more or less implicit fashion.

As we have pointed out, the practical and the theoretical "solution" of both patristic and medieval theology was to resurrect the ancient notion of kingship and apply it first to the empire and then to the Christian kingdoms which claimed to be its heirs—the same "solution" to which, over stifled protests, the prophets had ultimately rallied in the Old Testament. Not content with accepting the king and his state, the people had consecrated him. But he, in turn, was obliged to consider himself a simple servant of God, as well as his representative, and where people had endeavored to make this authority and its exercise dependent upon the divine Word, they now turned to the Gospel.[18]

Let us recapitulate the undeniable regression: whereas the kingship in Israel was progressively sublimated in the messianic ideal, to be radically transposed in the person and transcendent work of Christ, an "anointed of the Lord" arose in Christian times (a mere man) and a "kingdom" which claimed to be an anticipation (if not an inauguration) of the reign of God on earth. Yet we must also repeat that, despite deliberate imitations and the more or less forced assimilations of the empire and Christian kingdoms to the Israelite kingship, certain transpositions are of unquestionable reality. In the first place, though consecrated by the Church and recognized by her as a sacred person, exercising a sacred function, the emperor or the king, in the East and in the West, even when people consented to call him or allow him to call himself "the bishop from outside," was much more clearly dissociated from the priesthood of the successors of the apostles, including the power of teaching with authority, than the kings of Judah or the Northern Kingdom from the Jewish priesthood (except for prophetism). On this point, at least in theory, the teaching of the *Epanagoge* in the East was no less categorical than that of Pope Gelasius in the West.

In the second place, the Christian empire was not considered a particular kingdom, where God exclusively reigned over a people set apart, but a necessarily universal kingdom, corresponding to Christian universalism and bound in fact (as was thought) to its realization in expansion of the Church throughout the *oikoumene*. Even the renaissance of nationalities, corresponding to the breaking down of the empire among the French, Spanish, English, German, and other monarchs, did not destroy the juridical fiction, according to which *four* emperors did not divide the empire but administered it in concert. The kings of Christendom always claimed to be "brothers," exercising in harmony, as it were, the kingship which is Christ's.

Finally and especially, the imperial or royal "ministry" was not only conceived as exercised in dependence on Christ, but as an intermediary reign, to be ultimately placed in his hands, so that he might return every reign to his Father for eternity.

All this, however, did not present an undeniable corrective of regression from the New Testament to the Old, except by incurring the risk of evaporating the eschatological expectation into a supposed but realized eschatology. Nevertheless, we must admit that if the risk was shown to be too real, it was not perhaps unavoidable. Under these conditions, it is permissible to wonder whether the apparent regression could not represent a legitimate survival—a suggestion made by F. D. Maurice and later used independently by Charles Gillouin. It deserves examination.[19]

The Old Testament was characterized by a particular reign, proclaiming and prefiguring the reign of God (by the law of God) in the midst of kingdoms that were ignorant of the divine law and the divine reign. Therefore, would not the ideal situation of the New Testament be the pure and simple surpassing of the law, and every human kingdom, in the reign of God, that is, the perfect *agape* (an illusory but realized eschatology)? And would not the proclamation and immediate prefigurement of this reign in the Church, superseding the old law and its more imperfect prefigurement—that is, its more mediate preparation of the eternal reign—be extended to all nations? From now on, in other words, would not all individuals in the Church escape all earthly reigns, though still subject to them temporarily in their bodies, in belonging (internally) only to the reign of God, because of the Gospel? All simply human collectivities would lend themselves to this transition by submitting to the divine law, instead of the reign of idols, and by waiting (as the kingship of Israel had done before them) to be absorbed on the last day in the reign of Christ and God.

This theory is attractive, but it is important to emphasize that it represents only one possibility, which must not be rejected *a priori* when it is presented in the historical circumstances (e.g., the conversion of Constantine). But it must not be held to be necessary for the final coming of the divine reign, and therefore it cannot become the aim—nor even one of the aims—of evangelization.

This is the case, in effect, with "Judeo-Christianity," with which Christianity is closely related. Without doubt, Jewish observances lent themselves to Christian interpretation and transposition, and better and more directly than any other form of pre-Christian civilization, because they had been worked out providentially. Judeo-Christianity, the first form of Christianity that was possible, and an eminently legitimate form, was momentarily necessary for the later birth of other forms. But when Christ came, Judeo-Christianity could not—nor could *any* cultural form—be presented as the only possible and therefore the definitive expression of his mystery. On the contrary, it is necessary that *all* human cultures—all peoples, all men—lend themselves to expressing it, either together or in turn.

Undoubtedly, they could not do so without borrowing a great deal from Jewish culture—through the Bible, primitive Christian liturgy (which proceeded directly from Jewish liturgy), and the whole inheritance of supernaturalized "wisdom." Was this transfiguring wisdom not already developed by the nations in contact with the Word, received in and through Israel, which displayed the proper and unique experience of Judaism through the experience and reflection of pagans? Christianity, nevertheless, cannot be enclosed in forms that have become exclusive to Judeo-Christianity, nor in the forms of any Christianized cultures that succeeded it. For if Christianity can use all cultures and all civilizations by fashioning them to its purpose, its orientation to the reign of God, its anticipated realization of his reign in the reign of Christ, surpasses and transcends them all, even more radically than it transcends those of Israel, in which Christ (*whence* Christ, we may even say) was born.

When we refuse to acknowledge this truth, what happened in Judeo-Christianity in the first century happens again in an intensified form. Confusing an expression of the Gospel with its substance, we cease to Christianize a culture in order to "naturalize" (i.e., distort) the Gospel. By identifying the reign of Christ with a reign that, in principle, is in his service but remains of this world, the Church does not assimilate the state (an impossibility); rather, the newly repaganized state assimilates the Church.

St. Paul saw this in a Judeo-Christianity closed in on itself: not a preparation of the reign of Christ by the genuine consecration of an earthly kingdom but a new form of idolatry, an insidious repossession, under the guise of divine kingship, by the "powers," the *exousiai* in revolt, of the usurped domination over men and the world.

In effect, "Christian unanimity," which makes a Christian state, is always misleading because it is always uncertain and precarious. If, at a given moment, adhesion to the Gospel of the mass of a population is unanimous and sincere, it is never assured of its fidelity nor, for a stronger reason, the fidelity of its descendants. Thus, as we saw when we retraced the evolution of Christian institutions (including directly ecclesiastical institutions) in the Christendom of the past, a "Christianized state" can one day wake up pagan and misuse its Christian title to paganize the Church. Moreover, the efforts the Church will make to re-christianize the state, or simply maintain its Christian character by imposing herself on it, will bring the Church to usurp the temporal functions of the state, which are not hers to exercise—any more than those of any temporal society. By this fact, she will incur the risk of being paganized as much as, and more scandalously than, the state, which is Christian in theory but already secularized. She would secularize herself no less than the state.

Yet the Church cannot fail to proclaim the Gospel to all men, including the governing or responsible "princes" of the city (whether actually in power or in readiness) as well as the "humble and the little ones." And if they convert, she cannot refuse to accept them or, even less, to help them Christianize their governing, since every Christian must be helped by the Church to Christianize his function. But the Church must never set up, or allow to be set up, a new idol of some apparently or momentarily "Christian" state. Painfully, experience has taught her she must, in the person of her leaders, resist the temptation to use the constraint which a supposedly Christian state will offer her: the facile possibility of winning over, or keeping within her, some specially significant individual or group.

Between a "Christendom" and a "secular" situation, even theoretical choice is impossible. The Church does not have the right to refuse the possibilities of concrete application of the Gospel to the whole of human life and, therefore, to culture and civilization if, say, a Christian state (at least one that is Christian by intention) offers her such a possibility, as long as the intention of the leaders is sincere and is shared by the great majority. But at this stage she ought to be even more vigilant, particularly in her leaders, to refuse to condone any oppression of conscience, which would destroy the authenticity of her evangelizing task at the roots.

When this vigilance is insufficient, as is the case in the modern age, the Church must accept as a divine judgment, both just and merciful, the providential opportunity to correct past errors by purifying herself. Voluntary separation and disengagement of the state and the Church—whether in hostility and rivalry, or persecution, or even in a so-called "Christendom" or "ideal" situation, must be accepted as a possibly crucifying trial, but also as inevitable, necessary, and finally beneficent, to which God will put an end in his good time. We may hope that, in this way, new, freer, and thereby truer forms of Christendom will be prepared, but no more than those of the past will they be assured of lasting forever. In any case, they can escape degeneration only as long as they do not set themselves up as idols and confuse their very imperfect preparations or prefigurations of the reign of God with the eschatological reality.[20]

# IV. The Church and the Person

The paramount conclusion of the foregoing discussions is that the relationship of the Church with the world, the mission of the Church in the world, is not directly or primarily with the various societies that make it up (we are still speaking of the mundane world) nor the society which aspires to embrace and cap them all: the state. In these societies—and outside and beyond them—the Church's mission is directed toward *men*—toward human persons as such. For the Church has only one thing to bring to the world: "the love of God poured into our hearts by the Holy Spirit." And this love, of course, this supernatural charity, exists only between person and person, and the possibility of receiving it, of making it theirs, distinguishes personal beings from other kinds of being. For her part, the Church is the only essentially interpersonal society; all others receive this character only incidentally and share in it only secondarily and imperfectly. Again, this is why all societies, other than the Church, will disappear in the reign of God, in which the Church will lose all the transitory sociological characteristics which relate her to temporal societies.

Basically, in this regard, the Church escapes Tönnies' distinction between *Gemeinschaft* and *Gesellschaft*. Every *Gemeinschaft* is anterior to the persons who make it up, and if it is true that they are born *in* it (rather than *from* it, as is eminently the case with the family), it is also true, in our fallen world, that the *Gemeinschaft* finds it difficult to see the person as distinct from itself and thus it tends (underhandedly, as it were) to reabsorb the person in itself. On this point we acknowledge a certain accuracy in Cox's analyses, however harmful they may be to the so-called "natural" societies. On the other hand, every *Gesellschaft* is posterior to the persons who create it, and under the conditions of today the individual tends to be forgotten and to lose himself in it. It is true that, at first, he seems to be ennobled, but he is soon dissolved in it

The Church, on the contrary, awaits the nascent personality, and it is in her encounter with it that success depends: the only blossoming that can be authentic, rooting the person in his native being without absorbing it, unlimited in its development. The Church is not the only society in which the person can flourish, but she alone is truly the Mother (the family is only its matrix), and it is because of the existence of the pilgrim Church, the historical Church, that—throughout all other societies, and well beyond—interpersonal relations are able to flourish in order to fructify, finally, in the eternal Church of the reign of God.

The relations of the Church with temporal societies are always aimed at safeguarding and fostering her relationship with the persons who compose them. On the other hand, through this relationship—fecundating, we may say, all persons by developing them in interpersonal relationships, in *the* preeminent interpersonal relationship, which is charity—the Church, indirectly, vivifies all other societies, provided they aim at developing authentic human values. She thereby gives them the ability to exercise their influence in what is best in human life. And in line with human life, but crossing the line that separates fidelity to the divine image from man's completing himself and his adoption into the life of God by grace, she permits these societies to prepare for their part in harmony with the pilgrim Church, the Church of eternity in the divine reign.

The first point is verified particularly in the concordats and more generally in the relations the Church maintains with the states, when these relations are what they should be. Always and uniquely, these relations aim at assuring the Church the possibility of evangelizing men, of freely organizing their worship, which unites them, in her, with their charitable activity (which results directly from it), and, in all this, exercising her leaders' pastoral responsibilities toward her members.

It is the proper, free, and responsible activity of Christian laymen in temporal societies, and not of the Church as such, to confer on these societies the human fullness which must be the first fruit of charity, informing all their acts, as well as opening out to the eternal perspectives of the divine reign which will bring this fruit to maturity.

If the activity of the Church as such—that is, of her leaders—endeavors to bypass the lay intermediary or, practically, to annihilate it by suppressing by undue authoritarianism the exercise of its natural responsibilities in its proper domain, the leaders of the Church commit a capital fault. The infallible result, under the guise of "sacralizing" lay life, is to "secularize" ecclesiastical life. If such were the case, the Church would not be consecrating the profane; she would profane herself.

People may object that there are circumstances, such as those in which the West found itself at the death of the Roman Empire, where Church authority, for want of a secular authority that is capable of fulfilling its task, is pushed into its place (following a principle admitted by all jurists: in the absence or nonexistence of rightful authority, a *de facto* authority which is exercised instead, if it is exercised for the public good, *becomes* the rightful authority). This is perfectly correct, but again it is fitting to analyze what happens in such a case, and not draw undue consequences.

It may have been legitimate, even required by charity, for bishops in troubled times—again, in the absence or nonexistence of legitimate leaders—

to make themselves defenders of, say, cities—even to the point (at times) of taking the reins of government themselves. Again, we specify that this was not and could not be a result of their properly episcopal ministry as successors of the apostles, but only as *presbyteroi:* eminent representatives of a Christian community which, if not the *major pars* numerically, was at least the *sanior pars* of the city in question. And again, it is necessary that this be only an interim situation and that the ecclesiastical authorities, far from wanting to retain this extrinsic task (which came to them through exceptional circumstances), endeavor to elicit conditions for return to the norm.

More generally, not only does it *not belong* to the Church to dictate the practico-practical application of Christian principles to the states or to other temporal societies, it is not *fitting* that Church authorities pretend to inculcate details of this application in Christian individuals, in lay people, whom these societies count among their members. To these and to all men, whatever their situation, to individuals as well as collectivities, she must preach charity and specify its concrete exigencies, but details of application belong, and can only belong, to the *"vir bonus experientia praeditus,"* following Aristotle's expression—that is, in the present case, to the layman involved in the concrete tasks of the communities or associations in question.

It will be said that exact limits are not always easy to set, which is true. Nevertheless, the authority must take utmost care not to transgress the limits and thereby be discredited. To accumulations of prescriptions, it must always prefer the formulation of mature personalities who are capable of making sound use of their freedom, even if the details of this use must be sought gropingly. Proceeding by minute regulations (even if irreproachable on the grounds of doctrinal correctness and practical realism) would risk paralyzing conscience with burdensome precepts, rather than forming the superior understanding of life that comes only through authentic faith and charity, impregnating experience. If the authorities in the Church act in any other way, they would succumb to the temptation of the "Grand Inquisitor" in Dostoyevsky's *Brothers Karamazov*. Not only would the consequences be ruinous for the Church in general, as well as for the world (and for the ecclesiastical authority in particular), but this authority, in yielding to this temptation, would have already ruined itself.[21]

## V. The Church and Law

The questions discussed in the present chapter lead us to posit the inevitable problem of the Church and the law. This problem is so vast (and so little studied today in the Catholic Church!) that it could require an entire volume. It is such a great task that we cannot even outline it here. Let it be enough, then, to pose it correctly.

The first problem is knowing whether the Church of Christ, as such, recognizes—or can and must recognize—subsistent validity of the law in general: unwritten divine law, natural law, or positive (divine or human) laws. After this come problems of the Church's attitude toward the laws of the state, her own laws, and (should such be the case) all "nomocanonical" legislation (i.e., the law of the state *and* the law of the Church, or vice versa).

On the first point, which dominates all others, reaction against a recent "legalism" (from which the Church has too much suffered) risks, and more than risks, confusing *a* law, *the* law, and *legalism* in a common censure.[22] The Pauline themes on grace, which liberates us from the law, on the love that transcends all law, are manipulated by many modern Christians, and even Catholics, with disconcerting facility, as if they imply that grace and love suppress and abolish law.[23] Nevertheless, the gospel of Matthew preserves a decisive saying of Christ on this very subject, of substantial and undeniable textual authority, for (on one hand) it is the only key to the Sermon on the Mount and (on the other hand) it is expressed in the unique language of a Palestinian Jew, as Christ was. Besides asserting that Jesus came to fulfill, not abolish, the law, this phrase specifies that one cannot with impunity eliminate the slightest bit of the law.[24] If we examine the teaching of St. Paul and compare it with St. Mark, we see that they come down to precisely the same thing. For Mark as for Paul, and no less expressly, love is the fulfillment of the law; and far from suppressing or diminishing the law's authority, when we say we are "liberated" from the law by grace, or that love in itself is above all law, we actually exalt it.

It is true for St. Paul, as it is for Christ, that no written law, even if it is divine in origin, can express what love (i.e., supernatural charity) requires, and it is in this sense that love is above all law. Our "emancipation" from the law does not mean that we are dispensed from fulfilling it or that we no longer need it to know what love requires from us concretely. Only when our incapacity to fulfill the law on our own condemns and reduces us to slavery, under the power of sin and death, does grace raise us up, forgiving past faults and making us able to satisfy (and even more) the exigencies of ever-present law by charity. As the community of grace and charity, the Church is not an enemy of the laws that exist outside her—nor, even less, a community which, on its own account, would be ignorant or would have to be ignorant of law. Quite the contrary—and we could not repeat it too often: a lawless community, far from being (or ever being) able to be the community of charity in this world, has never been, and will never be, anything other than a community of the arbitrary.

We have just said what the first part of this chapter led us up to: the Church, as a community of charity is preeminently—even in the sense which belongs exclusively to her—a community of persons as persons. But the law—the true and just law in this world—is like a shelter in which the person can be born and develop, and this shelter cannot be dismantled without disrupting or crushing personal life. The law, as we have come to understand it, the very idea of law, originates with the conviction that the personality has value superior to an atom in a collectivity. Properly speaking, the notion of law evolves in transition from the arbitrariness of the strongest member of a gang to the justice of a leader or head who attributes to each what belongs to him, *cuique suum*. The imperishable value of Greek humanism (in the criticism of Socrates, the protestation of Antigone) is to have recognized and proclaimed that all human laws depend from divine, unwritten laws, which are the sole basis for the freedom of the individual—not mere negative and destructive license. Accordingly, the law must resist any constraint of the masses against obeying God, our moral obligation, and, if necessary, human injunctions. The transcendental value of what can be called "Jewish humanism" is that it accepted a divine law which, by penetrating human knowledge, prepared for and made possible the divine humanism of charity.

The last revelation of charity, it is true, uncovers the relativity of all law, whether human or divine, but when we speak of relativity we do not necessarily speak of uselessness or, *a fortiori,* invalidity. Consequently, in human laws—provided they are legitimate (i.e., open to the divine plans), conform to what the divine nature communicated to us of itself, and are receptive to its project of raising us to itself—the Church acknowledges an authority that comes from God. For the same reason, she grants similar authority to those who are announcers and guardians of such laws. But she must escape, and help everyone escape, the idealist illusion of Plato, for whom human laws must coincide with immutable divine laws, including (for example) the empirical law of Savigny, according to whom everything prescribed by the "social conscience," in its incessant evolution, would be law. Since she is the chief instrument of the divine plan of communicating with man through his history, the Church will always insist on the paramount legitimacy of the laws which correspond to this plan of the Creator vis-à-vis the creatures he prepared in his nature, as well as the provisional character of every human realization of this plan. For every realization of this type must be pursued in time, or be allowed to be pursued, though it will never reach the perfect, supernatural, supratemporal realization of charity which belongs only to the reign of God, to the eternity we are waiting for.

What is more, the Church in her canons imposes laws on herself which regulate her pastoral activities, around her teaching and her celebrations of worship. She always acknowledges the provisional and perfectible character of these laws, corresponding to these preparations and sketches of the divine reign which she is to project in history in always changeable circumstances, depending on the cultures and civilizations she encounters. But this changeability of the laws of the Church does not proceed from capriciousness in her leaders or license among the masses. On the contrary, it must correspond to an ever-renewed approximation of a realizable, indispensable minimum, without which the charity in which the Church must live could never have effective realization in the individual and collective behavior of her members.[25]

To the extent to which human societies (with the reservations we have formulated above) are Christianized, their legislation will be penetrated by Christian influences and, therefore, be connected with canonical legislation, just as the latter, will legitimately lend itself (at least to a certain point) in turn, to influencing societal legislation.

A properly nomocanonical legislation (as in the Byzantine Empire or that of Charlemagne) will regularly emerge—to the extent that, formally or tacitly, the Church judges that her consecration of the temporal state is compatible with its authorities' formulations in "mixed" matters (e.g., marriage Law) or even in matters that are more intrinsic to the life of the Church (such as the legislation she accepted on episcopal elections, e.g., the Pragmatic Sanction). There will be symmetrical equivalency when the Church, through her influence, imposes certain laws inspired by her own policy (or the policy of her leaders) on the state. Theoretically ideal cases of such encounters are concordats, where in principle, freely and spontaneously on both sides, the two authorities, civil and religious, together produced a common arrangement. (Such cases, however, as experience shows, whatever their legitimacy in principle, are not immune to dangerous ambiguities or unforeseen and even unforseeable consequences.) Finally, of course, no historical situation in which the Church finds herself can be absolutely ideal, even those which, in the abstract, seem so—where a perfect balance of elements seems to have been obtained.

In the Church and outside, as indispensable and precious as the law is, it must always be seen—and never in any other way—in the perspectives of charity, necessarily relying on justice though always surpassing it. Thus the Church must be the first to say that the primary exigency of justice is to respect persons, who alone can become subjects of charity, but not if they are oppressed, even with the "best intentions."

A modern tendency which seems habitual in both canonical and civil legislation (given the growing complexity of problems and the correlative multiplication in society of individuals capable of exercising more extensive responsibilities) is enactment—on the level of the universal Church, first of all—of "nuclear" laws rather than detailed codes of minute prescriptions. Also, on the civil level—in the broadest possible way, with the greatest representativeness—the whole body of the faithful is associated with the civil authorities, and application of these latter laws must be specified according to the necessities of the moment and the needs of particular communities which, in turn, must encourage positive initiatives (even though eventual mistakes might have to be corrected) rather than anticipate or substitute for them. Today therefore—once again—Church law, refusing to impose false or inadmissible constraints on the personal and gratuitous inspirations of the Spirit, will continue to guarantee civil law a firm basis in historical reality and protection against both the license of individuals and the capriciousness of leaders, the two caricatures of truly creative initiative.

## Notes

1. We have developed this question at length in "Les deux économies du gouvernement divin," pp. 503ff. from vol. 2 of *Initiation théologique* (Paris, 1952). On the matter of this chapter, see the constitution *Gaudium et Spes* and the decree on the missions, *Ad Gentes*.
2. Jn 3:16.
3. Jn 17:9.
4. 1 Jn 2:15 and 5:19.
5. Rom 8:19–23.
6. 1 Cor 15:50–58.
7. 2 Cor 5:1–5.
8. 1 Jn 5:4.
9. Gal 5:6.
10. Col 1:24.
11. Cf. above, p. 264.
12. Everything that follows owes much to J. H. Walgrave, *Cosmos, personne et société* (Paris, 1968). Cf. chaps. 2ff. of *Gaudium et Spes*.
13. F. Tönnies, *Gemeinschaft und Gesellschaft*, published in Germany in 1887.
14. On the historical vicissitudes in the relations of Church and state, the best overall study seems to be that of T. M. Parker (mentioned above, p. 474, n. 7).
15. See above, pp. 241ff.
16. Jn 18:36 and Mt 22:21.

17. O. Cullmann, *Dieu et César* (Neuchâtel, 1956).

18. See above, pp. 47ff.

19. F. D. Maurice, *The Kingdom of Christ*, 2:171ff. (in the Everyman's Library edition). Charles Gillouin's writings were published after his death by his brother René: *Charles Gillouin, un chrétien philosophe* (Paris, 1931).

20. On recent fluctuations in Catholic theology touching on a subject we have been able only to skim over, read A. Latreille, "La pensée catholique sur l'Eglise et l'Etat depuis les dernières années du XIX$^c$ siècle," pp. 281ff. of *L'Ecclésiologie au XIX$_e$ siècle*.

21. For this whole paragraph we are very indebted to the book of Fr. Walgrave, mentioned in note 12. See *Gaudium et Spes*, chap. 1.

22. See the excellent reply of Newman's friend, the jurist James Hope-Scott, to F. D. Maurice on this point, in *Memoirs of James Hope-Scott*, ed. by R. Ornsby (London, 1884).

23. See Gal 2:16 and 5:16-24, connecting with Rom 4:16-25 and the entire 7th and 8th chapters. See our commentary in *La Spiritualité du Nouveau Testament et des Pères*, pp. 112ff.

24. Mt 5:18.

25. For a Christian doctrine of law in general and a justification of canon law in particular, see the work of P. Andrieu-Guitrancourt, *Introduction l'étude du droit en général et du droit canonique contemporain* (Paris, 1963). Let us recall that Quaest. 90 to 108 in the Prima Secundae of the *Summa Theologica* form a treatise of laws, which is a summit in the work of St. Thomas Aquinas and perhaps one of the most durable parts of his work.

# Chapter 11
# The Spouse and the Betrothed of Christ

## I. *Duo in carne una: sponsus et sponsa*

Our last developments, by specifying that the Church is the preeminent interpersonal society, aims directly at the personal being in man, and develops only by developing his being to its perfection, prepare us to take a further step: to assert that the Church—however dependent upon Christ, however united in principle may be her activity with his, however *one* her being with his, to the point of forming one body with him, of being *his* body—remains, in another aspect, radically distinct from him, as one person is from another.

And this, let us point out, is true not only of the Church *in via,* of the Church *in fieri,* of the Church still imperfectly one with Christ; it is just as true, and in one sense truer of the Church of eternity, of the perfect Church, consumed in her union with him.

It is here that we must pass from the analogy of the Church with a body, of the Church described as the body of Christ, to an apparently opposite analogy, yet one that is intimately bound to the preceding: the Church as the Bride of Christ.[1]

Opposed as this image is to the preceding one, which stressed the unity of being (since it stresses the radical and untransmittable distinction of two persons united but forever inconfusible and, more particularly, of a dependent person attaining its full maturity through this very dependence), this new image is nevertheless related to the preceding one. In the Bible, in effect, the Church is presented first as the body of Christ and then appears as his bride;

every bride and bridegroom are described as "two in one flesh." The Apostle returned to this formula to apply it to Christ and the Church, but he said of human spouses that the bridegroom must love his bride as "his own flesh."[2]

It is here that pneumatological ecclesiology is finally articulated on basically Christological ecclesiology, for although the work of the Spirit proceeds in us entirely from the work of Christ and consummates our union with Christ and our unity in Christ, it also consummates our personal existence in this union. This is the merit of the Russian Orthodox school of theology, illustrated especially by Vladimir Lossky: to have emphasized with incomparable force that the work of the Spirit is certainly a work of unity, but of *essentially interpersonal unity,* in which—far from doing away with their distinctness—persons succeed only in being themselves.

And it is here, we add, that the necessary juxtaposition of juridical and organic categories, in regard to the Church, finds its ultimate justification. Again, it is the property of law to guarantee personal existence as such and to keep it from foundering or becoming reabsorbed in the pre-personal unity of organisms that are only organisms. Shall we have to say, therefore, that the Church herself is a personal being, developed over against Christ himself, and completing his humanity, which, in him, is personalized only in the divine person of the Son, in a supreme human personality? Could one not say then that in this personality the divinity, reciprocally, became not only man, but by grace someone personally human? The final chapter of this book will endeavor to show that, in a certain sense and with certain reservations, it seems that we must indeed go to that point. But at present, we must underline that this personality, so often attributed by Scripture to the Church, exists only in human persons that have arrived at their perfection, just as the personality of God himself does not exist except in the three divine persons. What we are told about that personality of the Church helps us to understand that in entering into the Church—far from melting into one another, all together in Christ—our persons prepare to find in their union with him and their unity in him, brought about by the Holy Spirit, a supernatural superexistence which, as such, is eternal, not only in the sense of perpetual duration but of participation in the very life of the divine persons.

This, in turn, brings that reciprocity that we will not be truly ourselves, completely ourselves, as God foresaw and wills us from all eternity, except in the eschatological Church. In her alone will be revealed that ultimate human personality of the divine-human being of Christ, the Head and the body—of the Head completing himself in the fullness of the consummated union with his body, the total Christ, Christ everything in all.

The Book of Revelation shows us the Bride of the Lamb, descending with him at the end of time from the side of God.[3] Yet under another aspect, in another perspective which is nevertheless implied in the preceding one, the Church in her transcendent personality is presented to us as preexisting the whole of creation, as its very principle, as St. Epiphanius will say.[4] And yet, historically, it is from the passion of Christ that she is born and, therefore, at the moment when this passion was consummated in death—as Eve is described in Genesis, being born from the slumbering Adam.[5]

Thus, for the Church and for Christ, according to tradition, we arrive at the vision of a threefold birth. Strictly speaking, Christ was born from all eternity, before all things, as the Firstborn of all creation. But in time, he will be born of the Virgin, in the midst of time. And beyond time, he is born in each of us through baptism, through the emergence in us of the "mystical" life, that is, of the life in his mystery which anticipates for us the Parousia itself.

Symmetrically and properly speaking, the birth of the Church, in which her personal being in our persons' acceding to their supernatural perfection, is not only unveiled but actually came about in our world, and is preeminently the consummation of her unity with Christ and in him, in the wedding of the Lamb at the time of the Parousia.

But this birth is anticipated in Christ's death, whereby his mystery was able to pass into us: the mystery of the life of God in human beings.

Already, it was present in the plan that God bore within himself from all eternity and which he uttered outside himself, from the first instant of creation: for creation tended to nothing other than God, as everything in all things; to the life of God communicated to others in fullness; to the divine *agape*, living in us as it lives in him. From creation, the thearchy of love, the eternal life of the divine persons, began to be extended and communicated in the divine hierarchy of the Church.

There is, then, a twofold aspect to the Church in relation to Christ, depending upon whether she is considered as an extension of Christ to us or as his present and eternal partner. The two aspects are inseparable, for it is insofar as Christ and the Church are *duo in carne una* that the Church is the Bride of Christ, and vice versa. But under the first aspect, shown by the apostolic ministry, Christ is not only present *to the Church* but present to the world *in the Church* by the Word entrusted to her, where it is always Christ who speaks, by the sacraments she celebrates and, above all by the Eucharist, where Christ fulfills his proclaimed mystery in us. Under the second aspect, which is like the constant reverse of the first, the Church has come together and assembles saved mankind in herself in order to be united to Christ (without ever being confused with him) by freely corresponding to the divine initiatives which are brought to her by the apostolic ministry: in listening to the Word of Christ, the Word which is Christ, and in responding to it by eucharistic praise—by making the sacrifice of Christ her own, in such a way as to be the offerer and the one offered "in him," adopted in him, the only Son, as the only daughter of her Father.

The first aspect is only instrumental and transitory; it belongs essentially to the present time. It constitutes what we have defined as the reign of Christ, that is, his work in us which prepares us for the reign of God. When Christ reappears for his last Parousia, at the same time that, by the judgment he completes, the resurrection and the glorification of his people, the work of his reign, he will bring her to her term. Then he will return the kingship to the Father alone. From then on, only the final aspect of the Church will subsist, which is also her eternal aspect. She will then be for all time, as we see in the Book of Revelation, the Church of divine praise, the Church of the accomplished sacrifice described in book 10 of *The City of God,* where, perfectly united forever to her Bridegroom, she will be led by him forever into the immediate presence of the Father.

Then the apostolic functions and all other ministries will come to an end, since they had no other ultimate purpose, and for a stronger reason all the social functions in mankind, which responded only to temporal purposes, will also cease. Then the Word will yield to vision. The sacraments will vanish in what, from now on, is their substance: "Christ in us, the hope of glory." God will be completely in all; that is, the love that makes his life in the eternal Trinity will be ours in the perfect Church.

The fact that in the Church at present, the means which is the communication of Christ to us and also the end, the already realized communion in his mystery (at least inchoatively), are thus so closely connected, is, if we dare say so, quite natural. Since the end is the realization in us of the love which gives, and gives itself, the means to arriving there can only be to participate already in the end: to give God by giving oneself with him. It is only by being united to Christ in all that he does, in all that he is, that the Church can be fully herself.

## II. *The Earthly Church, Christ's Betrothed*

To this irreducible difference between Christ and the Church, which eternity, far from doing away with (even though it must consummate their union), will consummate, is added another difference, which is destined to vanish at the last coming of the Lord. The Church of the present time is not only distinct from Christ, she bears within her an invincible tendency to separate herself from him. She is, and will remain till the end of time, a Church of sinners.

It is not that she does not count true saints among her members, even on earth. It is that these saints are converted sinners, whose conversion is never perfect nor, above all, definitive until the end of their earthly lives. Around them, the Church counts an undoubtedly greater number of sinners who want to give up their sin but, more or less gravely and unceasingly, fall back into it. They keep the faith (though all do not persevere in it), but they are inconsistent with this faith, and even if it cannot be called "dead" absolutely, it is far from "being exercised by charity."

This present situation of the Church, which will last until the Parousia, makes her, in relation to her members who are still on earth, not yet the Bride of Christ but only his Betrothed. It is in this sense that the Book of Revelation presents the wedding of the Lamb as the terminus of history,[6] while St. Paul, in speaking to the Corinthians (whom he has sternly reminded of their wicked deeds), still says to them: "I betrothed you to Christ to present you as a pure [i.e., holy] bride to her one husband."[7]

The Church is undoubtedly "pure" (holy) already, insofar as she is the body of Christ; and Christ is present in her, acts in her, through the apostolic ministry, the sacraments it administers, the Spirit whom Christ thus communicates to his whole body. She is also pure to the extent that this Spirit takes hold of our being and makes us "holy," as he is the "Holy" Spirit. But to the extent of our faults, our infidelities, our defects, the Church remains a Church of sinners, undoubtedly on the way to sanctification but far from having attained it.[8]

Does it follow that we must say that the Church is sinful as she is holy, *simul peccatrix et justa*—to apply to her the formula Luther applied to every Christian, *simul peccator et justus?*

In reaction to an overly idealistic view of the Church as appropriating the holiness of Christ, many today are tempted (and more than tempted) to admit the truth of Luther's axiom, rather than examine the complexity of the problem, which prohibits a simplistic answer. First, we must discuss the application of Luther's formula to the individual Christian. In one sense, it is obvious that his formula is true, but this was obvious well before the sixteenth century, in any number of equivalents. They teem in St. Augustine, with whom all the fathers were in agreement (even if they did not use such gloomy colors). Yet, following Diadochus of Photice, the situation of the Christian, though still a sinner, was thought to be totally different from that of the non-Christian sinner, even when he is attracted by the grace of Christ.[9] With the latter, the spirit of evil remains the master, present in him as if in its home since the fall, even though its domination is threatened and attacked on all sides by the reign of Christ. With the baptized Christian, on the contrary, as long as the faith is not definitively dead in him (who could ever say it is?), Christ is set up as master in the deepest part of his being—at the source, as Newman said, of all his thoughts and all his affections. However violent the provocations of evil against the Christian—whatever complicities they find, not only in "the world" but even in his "flesh" (which continues to be of one body with it)—they are, from now on, external. For his true being is already the new being of Christ in him, despite all the inconsistencies of which his "outer nature" (St. Paul) still feels capable.[10] Sanctification, however progressive it may be, is shackled with many obstacles, within and without, and results from the conversion supposed by baptism and the faith that accepts it. If there is still some distance (even seemingly enormous) between our justification in Christ and the sanctification worked in us by his Spirit, the former would be deprived of all reality if it were not the principle of the latter: Christ effectively died for us only at the moment he begins to live in us.

All that has just been said, which is valid for every Christian, is of course valid also for the whole of the Church. But added to it is this major element: although each Christian individual, as long as the trial of his earthly life is not over, can ultimately be lost, the Church is assured of arriving at eternal life. She is indefectible. The word of Christ about the gates of hell not prevailing against her are enough to assure us of this.

Not only the human element but even our fallen humanity, though in the process of being raised up in Christ's incorruptible humanity, already shares (in a certain way), if not in his impeccability, at least in his victory over sin.

Certainly each local church, each group of local churches, can fall, and can fall and not get up again. But, despite everything, an unshakeable element of the Christian faith is that the *whole* Church, at whatever age in her development, could never fall in this way. If only in a few faithful members, united around a handful of bishops, the Church—*one* Church—will always remain faithful to Christ until the last days. Though only a very small flock, whose existence and survival appear insignificant, she will never lose the faith.

Certain Protestant authors, especially in line with the early Barth, thought they could question, or even reject, this certitude as contrary to pure faith, which can be only faith in God alone, in his Word alone. Today, certain Catholics seem tempted to follow in their footsteps, and Christ's painful phrase, "When the Son of Man comes, will he find faith on earth?"[11] could seem to support them. In any case, this phrase obliges us to be much more prudent than certain Catholic (and Orthodox) theologians have been in modern times, in our endeavor to concretize and define the survival of the Church until the end of time, which is (we persist in believing), with all of tradition, an essential object of our faith. No particular church, even the local Church of Rome, can be assured of never failing—and for a stronger reason, no hierarch. It is very true, as the canonists maintain, that every pope who would cease to have the faith would cease being pope, *ipso facto,* and consequently that the infallibility acknowledged in the exercise (in certain cases, at least) of the papal function would not be put into question by such a defection. (Something analogous is true with regard to every bishop, and every Christian.) But if the sacramental character of the apostolic ministry, or baptism, is indelible, this means that God has committed himself forever to those whom he has consecrated. This never means that they cannot become even totally faithless to their vocation, and even to their effective consecration, and therefore lose the power of exercising it. *Corruptio optimi pessima*—the Middle Ages recalled this more willingly than we (''princes'' of the Church, unfaithful to the One they represent, are the worst of the damned). Wishing and hoping that this will not be the case, we cannot say more (or less) of any church, of any hierarch, than we can say of any Christian: they are not indefectible.

Could the Church of Rome herself fall, and her head, and the charism of ''presiding in charity,'' pass to another church? We may hesitate to think so, and suppose that if her head should personally falter, the presbyterium of the Church (in fact, the Sacred College) would maintain itself in the faith and would provide a faithful successor—or, if the Church in her totality or the presbyterium should falter, the lawful successor of Peter would transfer his see to another place.[12] But it does not seem that this can be asserted dogmatically. All that can be said is that if such a default came about, the bishops of the remaining, faithful churches would undoubtedly depose what had been, to that time, the Apostolic See and at the same time, in acknowledging Peter's function, in one of the deposing bishops, they would acknowledge the power—as Peter was the first to do—of transferring the see to where he would think it wise.

In the extreme, it could happen that the Church would one day subsist in only one faithful bishop, surrounded by a few believers. Then, *de facto,* this bishop would be the successor of Peter, and it would fall upon him to reconstitute the episcopal college around himself. All of this, however, is hypothetical; we cannot materialize our faith and our hope in the indefectibility of the Church. God alone definitively knows how the church will subsist until the last day, but the word of Christ on the insecurity of faith *a parte nostra* cannot be opposed to his words on the subsistence of the ''little flock'' until the coming of the reign.[13] In the last analysis, God alone will reconcile what happens.

These reservations do not prevent Christ's work, accomplished in history from now on, from dominating history: history will be interrupted by the coming of the reign at the very moment when human incredulity *seems* to have triumphed over faith, or the Church, however diminished, will pass more visibly from the cross to glory. In any case, she will subsist until the end of history, one and the same, as he founded her, in order to be brought together in glory, even through tribulations and obscurities about which we have no idea.

What is called the "infallibility" of the Church is a necessary condition for this indefectibility of her faith, for the subjective faith of a concrete group of men, however reduced it may be. *Fides ex auditu,* indeed—which comes down to saying that subjective faith cannot subsist if the supernatural means which Christ brought into play do not first subsist, in order to create and maintain this faith: the apostolic ministry, its faithful preaching, and the sacraments that communicate its content. But witness by the faithful to their faith and the means of grace from on high which maintain this faith are so necessarily united, or rather one in their root, that infallibility belongs to the testimony of the faithful as much as to the apostolic ministry. Or better, there is not, on one side, an "active" infallibility of the ministry and, on the other, a "passive" infallibility, belonging to the faithful. The infallibility of the faithful is as active in its way as that of the ministries, though not in the same way: the infallibility of testimony to a received truth, insofar as this truth has been assimilated. It may even be said that, since there are no successors to the apostles who are not first "presbyters" (representatives of the community of believers), and the infallibility of the Church proceeds from the infallibility of Christ, the infallibility of the ministers depends equally on the infallibility of the faithful in their testimony, because it is its source in the exercise of their teaching ministry.[14]

This, however, cannot legitimize the false consequence of believing that the act of defining the faith by those who exercise the apostolic responsibility (and therefore authority) would not be infallible except by virtue of the subsequent consensus of the faithful. In this supreme act of their function (exercised by all the bishops collegially or by the pope alone, in union with the entire college), definition of the faith is imposed as infallible *ex sese,* for it is by virtue of the apostolic mission, going back to Christ himself (and not otherwise), that they proceed.

Definitively, then, the infallibility of the totality of the faithful is not expressed solely in definitions of the hierarchy acknowledged by all, nor is infallibility proper to the hierarchy which would be transmitted to the faithful by their passive adhesion; there is but one infallibility, of the whole Church, manifested in the accord of all, as the infallibility of the testimony in the act proper to apostolic ministers, which is no more divisible than preaching and testimony are divisible from one another.

Yet this infallibility, in neither one nor the other, is no guarantee of perfect expression of truth in and by the Church. It is an intrinsic guarantee of the divine truth of Christ, namely that all accumulated faults and infidelities of ministers and laymen in the Church will never separate her from the active presence of Christ, who will make use of the Church, until the end of time, to guide the body of the elect toward him and to gather them together in him.

Therefore the church in general, in her uni-totality, cannot cease being holy, in the twofold sense that she cannot cease having the presence of Christ, acting through the means which he himself established in her (the apostolic ministry, the preaching of the faith, the sacraments of the faith), and in sovereignly using these means (rather, the grace of Christ) she cannot cease having some efficacy of holiness, if only in a few souls. But she is stained, and will be until the last day, by the numberless sins of her ministers and members, and even betrayed by the always possible defection not only of all her individual members but all the churches, outside of which she has no existence. Hence the unceasing necessity that is incumbent on the Church, of struggling against sin, not only as an evil foreign to her, though only of and in the world, but first of all as an evil she carries within herself: the evil of her own "flesh," not yet transfigured by the Spirit of the resurrection.

## III. *Ecclesia semper reformanda*

The ineluctable consequence of the situation that we have just described is that the holiness essential to the Church, which she could not lose without complete contradiction, be opposed to the possible necessity of reforms within the Church. We must say more, according to a formula which appeared at an early date with Protestant Christians, who were persuaded they had brought about a decisive reform: The Church needs to reform herself at every moment. She cannot work for the salvation of the world without working unceasingly, first of all, for her own reformation: *Ecclesia semper reformanda.*[15] Eschewing generalities to see precisely where the evil she must unceasingly combat is introduced (and continually reintroduced) into the Church, we must examine more closely the articulation of divine and human elements in the pilgrim Church.

In ecclesiology as in Christology, we must avoid the twofold error which Christology produced and threatens to reproduce, Monophysitism and Nestorianism: absorbing the human in the divine, to the point of doing away with the former, or differentiating but artificially separating them. Indeed, it is easy to say that the Church is immutably holy in her means of grace (apostolic ministry, preaching the faith, sacramental celebration) while she remains sinful in the lives of her members. But the objection is immediate: on one hand, what would this objective holiness of the Church be if it were not translated into some subjective sanctification of the men who are part of her? On the other hand, since ministry, preaching, and the sacraments present the gift of grace (the life of the Spirit), derived from the Source through essentially human channels, how, in their operation, could the means of grace not be influenced by the sins of men?

To deepen this problem, we must begin by pointing out that neither in the same manner nor (if we may say so) in the same proportion are the divine and the human elements combined in exercise of the pastoral function in general: preaching the faith and celebrating the mysteries.

In the sacraments, undoubtedly, the divine element is at its maximum with the so-called *ex opere operato* efficacy (i.e., which comes from what is— though visibly done by men, an essentially divine act that has no proper substance, we might say, except in Christ's decision to make it the efficacious sign of his presence and his action). On the other hand, only by pure faith can it be recognized. To empirical arguments, nothing is offered but sensory objects: water poured on a person, bread to eat or wine to drink, a human hand which is laid on or blesses, etc.

In preaching, the human element is obviously much more important, even in the most solemn definitions of the Church and the inspired words of Scripture, including the Gospel. Under one aspect at least, the communicated grace is proportionate to the capacities proper to human instruments, that is, the preacher's intelligence and skill in the cultivation of words and phrases. On the other hand, it is by the maturation of their own intelligence that believers receive the divine Word in the preaching of the Church and thereby develop their faith. This essential aspect of faith arises *ex auditu,* by the communication of human words, the renewed content of human meaning, though its import goes beyond its limited means of expression.

In the exercise of the pastoral function—in particular, in the control and authoritarian direction it impresses on the life of the Church as a whole and each believer—the importance of the human element is even greater. Here, though the assistance of the Spirit is as certain as in the sacraments and preaching, the Spirit does not allow itself to be grasped in any *ex opere operato* action about which we cannot be certain—in any *inspiration,* in the strongest sense, nor even infallibly, in the simple negative sense which guarantees that communicated revelation of the outpouring Word will not be positively betrayed. Certainly the special assurance of infallible Providence, which will lead the Church to the end through the activity of her human pastors, is given to us; but there are no errors of judgment, at any level of leadership; there are no sins, individual or collective, in the exercise of authority or pastoral responsibility, that pastors cannot commit. Our only certitude is that the faults of the human instruments of Christ's reign, however serious or numerous, can never destroy the Church. There is no treason that not only Judas, but even Peter, could not occasionaly commit or consent to. All that we are assured of is that no act of treason, by the watchful grace of Christ, the conquering power of his Spirit, can ruin the building that the incarnate Son of God founded, nor ever estrange it from the presence of the Spirit of life.

On the other hand, it is through the human nature of pastors, which, as such, is fallible, that Christ governs his Church. Also, it is through their love of Christ that Christ feeds his Church. Thus they not only nourish the faith of the Church, they lead her in exercising her faith in charity and, therefore, making the gift of grace pass not only into our understanding but into the whole human nature of believers, which is tantamount to creating a genuine (though anticipated) experience of the eschatological reign.

Following our line of reflection, it is only in the sacraments that the action of God meets ours in the pure state, in the "darkness" of faith. In the Church's preaching, this faith becomes conscious of itself, it takes possession of our understanding, but, by the force of things, through a human intermediary. Even in original inspiration, this intermediary is never perfectly transparent, and in the habitual case of the assistance assured by the Spirit to the teaching which transmits the truth originally formulated by the prophets, the apostles, or Christ in person, this teaching is assured, when it comes down to decisive definition, only of never falling explicitly in error.

Finally, in the case of governing and, more generally, the pastoral leadership of the flock, divine action is very much present, but it works through human actions, individually and collectively, imperfect and fallible, but their final result cannot ruin the edifice which is Christ's own body and, therefore, the definitive temple of his Spirit. It is on this level that love, in the form of pastoral charity, awakens, maintains, and unceasingly regenerates the charity of all the faithful. Indeed, although the preaching of the apostles and their successors did not benefit from the testimony of the faith of all, their charity was often energized by the faith of the lowliest of their flock.

This, however, does not exhaust the problem. As Newman saw, the kernel of the difficulty is in the necessary connection between these three offices of the Church, however constantly threatened. In fact, the three offices can be isolated only in thought; better, they can only be differentiated never separated.

The sacrament of the Eucharist cannot exist apart from the teaching of the faith, without which it would be reduced to either pure magic or a contentless mechanism. And it is not enough that this teaching be juxtaposed to the faith, as from outside. In the liturgy, the truth of faith must find concrete and vital expression for real faith to grasp the sacramental reality, which of itself is invisible and ineffable.

But the teaching of the faith in its most systematic form, in the totality of its authentic expressions (of which the liturgy is most weighted with suggestions), is not separable from the witness of the entire life of Christians nor from the pastoral action which leads this life and regulates and organizes it.

From this, as Newman also knew, results the permanent need for reform in the Church, precisely corresponding to the permanent temptation to separate and therefore adulterate what must subsist and live in unity.[16] Again, all Christian truth is a life of truth, the truth of this life, which is life in the Holy Spirit, the life of supernatural love. The truth of preaching therefore develops the reality of sacramental communication, which of itself is nothing if it does not display and spread the life of love in unity, the life of the Holy Spirit in us.

Conversely, human sin in the Church—in all her members, and in her ministers in particular—will always be a defect of love and, therefore, an extensive incapacity of no longer seeing and, consequently, no longer realizing the essential unity of the truth of faith. Thus the various activities of the Church would lose their meaning by becoming isolated from one another, even opposed to one another, and at the same time would be adulterated. No longer loving in God, people would no longer know the meaning of what they do, and by thinking they exalt the activity on which they concentrate, they would deprive it of its meaning, adulterate it more and more, and render it more and more incapable of blossoming by making it incapable of harmonizing with those who constitute not only its complement but also its necessary development.

Apart from the truth of the mystery to be taught and from the life of the mystery to be celebrated, pastoral governing would cease to be pastoral. The actions of the leaders would no longer be able to fecundate the members' and be vivified in return.

Proclamation of the truth would degenerate into deadly intellectualism, because its reception in the faith would be divorced by individualism from common life in the body of charity, by being opposed to the necessary organizing apostolic function of this body or by neglecting the sacramental experience in which the truth of the Word is revealed as the truth of life.

Finally, celebration of the mysteries would become a ritualism, divorced from both subjective faith and the collective life and its organization willed by Christ, and would nourish nothing more than a mystique of evasion.

In all cases, loss of unity would obscure the truth of the Church as Christ willed her; and this loss would be the result of sin, a defect in love. The resulting error would become a new source of innumerable sins which, in turn, would more and more stifle the living testimony, without which truth cannot survive.

Reciprocally, all true reforms will be conjoint rediscoveries of truth in its catholic unity and charity—rather, of the truth in charity which makes its unity. All permanent efforts of reform can only be this always-renewed effort of charity, which vivifies the faith, the faith which enlightens charity by renewing the circulation of life throughout the body, in the harmony (always to be re-created) of its complementary organs—the symphony, always pursued and renewed, of its inseparable functions.

## IV. Current Problems of the Ecclesia peccatorum

The considerations we have just developed would remain too abstract if we do not try at least to sketch their application to circumstances in which the Catholic Church presents herself to us today, after twenty centuries of history whose meaning the beginning of our study endeavored to clarify. We could not develop here a complete program of reforms, but in the light of our last remarks, which shed light on the general reforming orientation of the Second Vatican Council and find in it their best confirmation, it seems impossible not to attempt to specify what this orientation is, or better, reorientation, which seems to be obligatory at the present time. In doing this, we are aware not only of the inadequacy of what we are going to say but of the much more conjectural and therefore disputable nature of what we are going to advance— more than everything that precedes. Indeed, up to now, we have tried to develop from the Word of God, seen in the whole of Catholic tradition, what the Church is in her beginning and what she must tend to be, more and more, in all her phenomenal reality. By the force of things, even though the council remains our guide, we are left with solely human resources to try to determine where realization of the essence of the Church is defective in the present situation and, therefore, where we must work to try to better things. Here, we must involve ourselves in prudential judgments, on complex realities of which God alone, in the last analysis, can be the judge, and about which he will make his judgment known only on the last day.

Yet, if we want our vision of revealed truth to contribute (in whatever small way) to helping the reality of the Church—her present, changing reality—lend itself to this revelation which animates it (though unable to dominate it completely), we must take this path. Therefore, conscious of the partial and therefore uncertain nature of the remarks we are going to make but conscious, also, of the duty imposed on every Christian, every priest, and especially every theologian to try to see clearly and to help his brothers see clearly—not only in the Christian ideal, in accordance with its ultimate perfection, but in the duty of the present moment—we propose (with all these reservations) the following remarks.

In the light of twenty centuries of Christian life and ecclesiology and all the reflection to which this gives rise, as we try to bring judgment to past history and its present materializations, one point seems obvious, and is, in fact, found beneath most reform suggestions of Vatican II: what most encumbers the evolution of the Catholic Church is a deformation of pastoral authority. Especially over the last centuries, pastoral authority has tended to be isolated from both the preaching of the faith and the celebration of the mysteries. It is not that these two elements disappeared from the Catholic Church, but to too great an extent, instead of acting in symbiosis with them, the exercise of authority has tended to be its own end, causing the proclamation of evangelical truth and the liturgical life to suffer harmful distortion, and has altered itself at the same time. Hence a threat of strangulation for Catholic charity, which ought to be, and cannot cease being, the soul of the Church, the common life in the Holy Spirit. Instead of being subordinate to the truth to be proclaimed to the world, as the service, the "ministry of truth" about the life of Christ in its mystery, communicated by the sacraments and unfolding in common and mutual love, authority having made itself its own goal, has oppressed this, common life by exaggerated justification of itself, thereby reducing (or at least threatening to reduce) the sacramental liturgy to an ornament of its power.

But the crisis in which today the Catholic Church is plunged seems to attest, first of all, that it is not enough to be aware of the evil to be capable of healing its effects, nor even to extirpate its roots. The *proton pseudos,* the primary error, has so seriously altered, or tended to alter, everything around it that even when it is denounced, it does not stop, nor do its consequences. The primary error has lasted so long and sunk its roots so deep that the most energetic efforts must be made to uproot it.

The way in which this primordial evil was born and developed was the central part of our historical study. In the West, faced with absorption by a state that had supposedly become Christian, authority in the Church—the legitimate authority of the Church: the pope and the other bishops—

endeavored throughout the Middle Ages to recover its necessary independence. But unfortunately—and here was the fault and the mistake—it too
often tended to do so by taking possession (on the rebound) of the temporal
authority or, what could be still more serious, by allowing itself to become
fascinated by the ideal of this authority before Christianity touched it:
*dominium*, or possession of its subjects, and not *ministerium*, the service of
Christ in our brothers. Hence, by immediate consequence, the conflict that so
long divided ecclesiastical authority itself in the West. While the "service"
proper to the pope, as St. Gregory so clearly stated, could sustain only the
"service" of other bishops, *dominium* caused the relationship among them to
be an endless conflict: the mutual *potestas* of the bishops, fatally excluding
the powers of others, and vice versa.

At the First Vatican Council, the claim of Gallicanism to reabsorb the papal
function into the body of the episcopate was condemned, but, in principle, the
general episcopal function was not diminished. The Second Vatican Council
developed what was implied by the formulas of the First, when properly
understood: Ultramontanism was in no sense the victor, since papal primacy,
far from denying episcopal collegiality, presupposes it.

But between Vatican I and Vatican II—and it is hard not to recognize
it—Rome feared (the popes or their curia) that Gallicanism might rise again,
and, unfortunately, it used the prestige it had acquired or regained in 1870 to
extenuate the exercise and the reality of the episcopate. First, there was an
endeavor to admit to this function only men who were little capable of exercising it in a responsible fashion; then there was the business of restraining their
action, peremptorily directing it, and even (quite simply) binding it hand and
foot. The Modernism crisis, which arose between the two councils, served as
a pretext or justification for completing what had begun.

Vatican II, without destroying or minimizing the doctrinal work of Vatican
I—quite on the contrary, confirming it—proclaimed its desirable complements. But during the course of this council, and even more in what followed,
it became apparent to what extent misunderstanding of the real sense of
Christian authority was inviscerated in the consciousness of its possessors.
Even though the doctrinal texts had formally acknowledged that conflict between primacy and collegiality can arise only in an ecclesiology of power, not
in one of service, the episcopate again, in tending to its regeneration, too
often thought of itself in terms of ecclesiological power. Even after the council, under the false cover of a restoration of collegiality, there were attempts to
resurrect Gallicanism. In the council itself, it was shown to what extent the
restoration of the power of a number of bishops signified capacity to act with
regard to their subordinates exactly as they had reproached the "curia" for

doing in the past. Neglect of the presbyterate and the priests of second rank in the conciliar deliberations and, even worse (when one thinks of it), the almost exclusive concern to bully them (though with honeyed words) constituted scandal for anyone who, desirous of reform, was exasperated by the long-latent crisis in the Church.

The "contestation of priests," which closely followed the council, deplorable as it was, not only in certain aspects but basically, is the inevitable consequence of such a reaction in the episcopate, of such misunderstanding among those in authority, who were responsible for the problem. But this contestation, in turn, showed how the deformation of authority (in its conception of itself) spread to the point that even those who rebelled against it remained imbued with it, to a degree they did not even suspect. What else is signified by claims that a priest be able to do secular work, marry, and especially, get involved in politics, if not a persistent, cruder, more brutal involvement than ever of the priesthood of second rank in the confusions which since the Middle Ages have adulterated, or tended to adulterate, the consciousness the priesthood of the first rank, forged of its own function? It was thought that an adult presbyterate had been attained because conciliar priests had overturned everything that had been painfully asserted since the seventeenth century in order to return (at least to priests of second rank) the Christian and spiritual sense of their vocation. They now claim for themselves, as their right, in this confusion between service and a function of the Church, a function that is secular, an autonomous affirmation of self, which for so long, and not only in appearance, had been the major temptation of the episcopate. With priests today, as with bishops of yesterday, this goes hand in hand with a quasi-total neglect (even ignorance) of their primary function of proclaiming the Word of God and an avowed contempt for their derived function of celebrating the sacramental liturgy (disdainfully called "cultic function").

Even among the laity, at the moment the bishops thought they had associated them with their own emancipation, the same confusions, obtain, and occupy, it seems, the whole terrain.

Mingled with great missionary generosity at the beginning of Catholic Action, strange, hyperclerical confusions sullied the will to re-Christianize the "milieus." The curious "liturgy," fabricated for the Feast of Christ the King at that time and in this atmosphere, was described with disarming candor: "to make Christ reign," as people used to say. Essentially, however, this seemed to mean that mayors would again follow processions at the head of their municipal councils, all children would go to Church schools, and legislation would convey the "social teaching of the Church" in terms of public law;

apologetic literature, edifying art, etc., would be disseminated. This was so true that, in Italy, Catholic Action was soon reduced to little more than a militia of the Christian Democratic party, while in France, the little influence it had on the re-Christianization of society, on which its hopes had been based, was translated into the creation (and prompt demise) of the Mouvement Républicain Populaire (a "Catholic" political party).

Lay militants and clerical theoreticians of the movement ought to have promptly recorded, or at least admitted to themselves, the total unreality of this hope of a new Christendom, lay in theory but superclerical in fact. At the same moment, the vision of their rivals, the militant Marxists, then in their first fervor, fascinated them, so that they passed without transition—without realizing it—from the childish claim of reforging a new "Catholic order" to conviction that the only realistic alternative was to yield to the materialists' "sense of history." With renewed candor, they promised themselves that, having become collaborators in building the New Babylon, they would Christianize it from within—without, however, the slightest idea how they would do it. But this velleity was so vague that we must pass to the next phase of an equally ingenuous earthly messianism: "consecrating the secular as secular" and, in an "integral secularization" of society, saluting the coming of an anonymous reign of God, thought to bring about the evangelical salvation of mankind. Then, the humor of the world having seemingly changed, they changed again: from unreserved adoration of the modern world, such as it is in the "world of contestation," to contestation itself!

A tragic and pitiful evolution this, which reproduces, before our eyes, in the Catholic laity, that evolution which in past centuries led bishops and clergy from claiming spiritual authority and independence from temporal authority to domination over it, in principle and fact, which ended by secularizing the spiritual authority itself, in fact if not in principle!

It seems that there is only one remedy for all this: reestablish the authority and every exercise of the pastoral function in the acts that should never have been adulterated—preaching the evangelical truth and the testimony it must awaken in all members of the Church, sacramental celebration, and life in supernatural charity (which must be the result) for the whole body of Christ.

The deterioration of authority, incurring on itself, has brought deterioration of the ecclesiastical ministry in the ferment of secular activities, and consequently the "Catholic action" of the faithful through immersion in politics that is entirely of this world and, more generally, in the uncritical mentality of a "humanism" closed in on itself. Correlatively, preaching the faith is dangerously concentrated on the self-justification of authority. Not only is the whole of eschatology constructed in an ecclesiology of power, but Christology is made to deviate into "divine defense" of the present authority of the Church and soteriology into a "consecration" of clerical mastery over the world. In the following stages, it is inevitable that ecclesiology will become an apotheosis of the "sociological evolution" immanent in fallen mankind; Christology a "mythology" of the modern *homo economicus,* tending (or supposed to tend) toward "socialist man" through successive versions; and soteriology an "eschatology of revolution."

In a parallel way, sacramental liturgy, having hardened into a "court ceremony" to heighten the prestige of authority, while serving passive obedience through a body of rubrics bereft of meaning, is inevitably—once people pretend to bring it back to life—turned into a "mass meeting." Under the pretext of "opening" it to the aspirations of the "man of today," people will substitute, for the worship given his Father by the God-Man (associating with it his "brother men"), the worship of man by man—celebration of all the modern slogans for "communication" of the mystery of Jesus, manipulation of crowds in behalf of collectivist ideologies, rather than consecration of persons for the life of charity in the Holy Spirit.

This diabolical circle cannot be broken at one or a few points, it has to be exploded. In its place, harmony must be reestablished in evangelical truth, proclaimed and received in the heart of ever-living tradition, between the authentic authority of the apostolic ministry and the holy freedom of Christian testimony. For this, the proclamation and anticipated revelation of the reign of divine love must be diffused throughout the world, beginning with the sacred banquet of the *agape,* the eucharistic celebration that has again become itself. This celebration must again become the nucleus of the sacramental life and the heart of life in the Holy Spirit in the heart of the world.

This essential reform requires at its base—rather, at its source—an inseparable effort of truth and holiness, since evil has come from sinful error—or, if you prefer, from a sin that consists in closing oneself to the Catholic view of truth, which is the truth of the communicated divine charity, which people have become incapable of even conceiving.

It would be necessary that, beginning with bishops, all ministers of the Church be persuaded that what is most necessary for her—today more than ever—is that they immerse themselves in the Word of God. That they study it, with all accrued means, to arrive at an exact understanding as supplied by modern methods of exegesis. Let them be nurtured in it by truly theological meditation, that is, contemplation of the divine mystery "informing" a culture in them that is not only superficially up to date but, integrally and profoundly, as human as possible. Let them be persuaded, above all, that proclaiming the divine truth, thus received and unceasingly rediscovered, is their basic public function, and only for this reason do they have any authority whatsoever.

It is also necessary that the bishops, and their priests after them, understand what an authentic liturgical life is. Despite adaptations which are only mimicry, It does not have to become a method of propaganda and mind conditioning, copied after political assemblies. It must be implanted in the living tradition of the Church, in what this tradition forever preserves as most alive, that is, its tradition of prayer and worship. The vital, necessary milieu will be found only where the Gospel truth can be received and communicated as a truth of life.

Then the bishops, and the priests with them, will understand how their function as pastors, before being a function of administrators, is a function of preachers of the truth, a function of men of prayer and guides of prayer.

After that, they need no longer be reminded—much less, have it laboriously explained to them—that, as bishops or priests, they are not called to be organizers of socio-political activities but fishers and shepherds of men, animators of a society of persons which cannot be built except in charity, which bursts forth even were only two or three gathered together in Christ's name, assured of his presence in their midst.

Quite obviously, this requires of pastors, as well as flocks (pastors first, so that their flocks may understand it after them), not only renewed understanding of their apostolic ministry and Christian witness in general, but renewed appeal to the holiness of Christ, which is recognized, accepted, and followed.

Unfortunately, it is at this point that the shoe pinches most. The Counter Reformation, inaugurated at Trent, became (though insufficiently) a real Catholic reform from the moment it was taken in hand by such holy bishops as St. Charles Borromeo and Blessed Bartholomew of the Martyrs, surrounded by a *turba magna* of holy priests and religious and innumerable laymen, attracted by and toward their holiness. What particularly characterizes the clergy in our postconciliar period—and, one would say, "religious" more than others—is the desire for a freer, easier life, without the constraints of celibacy, without the asceticism of a life separated from common life, to the extent that it wants to be specially consecrated. Whatever we think or say, as long as we do not shed this state of mind, whose unhappy developments we see all about us, and overturn such "fashionable" trends, *nothing* will come of the reform that the present state of the Church requires, and what are offered as reforms will do little more than complete our decadence.

Revivification of the Church's consciousness as a community of true charity cannot happen without renewed acceptance of the cross of Christ. But how can this happen in a Church where everybody seems to be running away?

## *V. The One Church and the Divided People of God*

We have not yet come to the most serious stigma in the body of Christ: the sin of its members, including (perhaps above all) the sin of her visible leaders. Accordingly, we want to speak about the present division of the People of God.

It is important to differentiate carefully between "schisms" and "heresies," inevitable accompaniments of the development of the Church, which essentially are not sins of Church members, who remain with her, but of unfaithful members who separate themselves from her and from the majority of divisions that afflict the People of God at present. These divisions are the result of sins, and *persistent sins,* of supposedly faithful members, and particularly of responsible leaders in the Church.[17]

Certainly, the distinction is not always easy to make in practice. It can even be supposed that no or scarcely any schisms or heresies could have developed without the presumed or actual existence of culpable inadequacies in faithful (or supposedly faithful) Christians, and especially in their leaders. For example, deeper Christian reflection in the early Church might have prevented, or at least considerably limited, the Gnostic and, later, the Arian crises. Yet these crises lasted for one or two generations because churchmen did not more forcefully reassert the truths misunderstood by the Gnostics and the Arians, although they were able to understand the gravity of the problems the latter had posed and poorly resolved, and to give them satisfactory solutions. The misunderstandings were soon clarified, and all that remained of these ancient heresies was their errors, and all men of good faith rapidly abandoned them, so that they were extinguished "automatically."

Nothing like this followed the schism between the Church of the East and the Church of the West, nor even the proliferation of undeniable heresies in which, later, the Protestant movement became involved, dividing itself against itself as well as from the Church. Of course, the problems in these latter cases were not so simple as the problems in the former; but are we right in thinking that, in such a situation, the initial faults must have been widely shared on both sides for there to have been no reconciliation, after so many centuries? In the Church herself, did the faithful and their pastors not know how, or not want, to correct their faults? This suspicion becomes a certainty when we observe that those who separated from us, and remain separated, have produced results of undeniable holiness. They are quite capable of positive missionary endeavor. In fact, they continue to develop essential elements of the Catholic tradition which today, with Catholics themselves, have only a dwarfish existence or a barely visible survival. In such cases, it is clear that comparison of the schismatic or the heretic with a detached branch of the trunk, condemned to swift death if its connection with the stock is not quickly restored (as verified in the schisms and heresies of antiquity, and many others since), has no or hardly any application. It must be acknowledged that even the possibility of such a situation poses a problem that menaces the faith.

Could it be possible, then, that the Church that Christ established in unity, as his own body, in which his Spirit lives and to which he assured survival until his return, might be fallen from this unity? But this unity is so constitutive that to say that the Church has ceased to be one, to be *the* one Church of Jesus Christ, would come down to saying there is no longer *any* Church in the New Testament sense and that Jesus' work in history has therefore failed. If this were the case, not only would there no longer be a Christian Church, a Catholic Church that is worthy of the name; we would have to say that there *never will be* any. For if the Church founded by Christ fails, if her very existence ceases, no one other than Jesus Christ, returning into our history before his time (which seems unthinkable), could resurrect her.

Consequently, we must believe that, despite all contestations, the Church still subsists, is still one and unique. That she could subsist in a series of social bodies, independent and different from one another, and even in endemic conflict, is absolutely contrary to the vision of the New Testament and the ancient Church. The contrary idea, that, whatever her vicissitudes, there is not and will never be but one Church of Jesus Christ, is therefore essential (and rightly so) to Catholic tradition. It is no less essential to Orthodox tradition. Neither, without denying themselves, could abandon it.

## A. Orthodox and Catholics

It is precisely here that the first major difficulty arises—the first and perhaps the greatest scandal for the faith. On first sight, there are two Churches: the Catholic Church, whose distinctive sign is communion with the successor of Peter, and the Orthodox Church, which no longer has (or seems to have) this communion. But each claims for itself, in equally exclusive fashion, this identification with the *una, sancta, catholica*, which both confess in the same Credo. It would seem that one or the other might be right, but not both at the same time. After so many centuries, their apparent incapacity to reconcile themselves may suggest that one or the other is in error and that the *una, sancta, catholica* has simply disappeared from earth. This is the greatest scandal given by members of the Church, by "men of the Church," charged with the highest responsibilities, so that it becomes very difficult for the faith itself not to see this scandal of the Church, her preeminent scandal: the Church teaching her unity as the greatest gift of God but, in fact, seeming to be divided (against God's will).

There seems to be only one answer: the Orthodox Church and the Catholic Church, though dreadfully tempted by the spirit of division, remain one Church, in fact and by right, despite contrary appearances.[18] This is verified by the most thorough historical investigation of this problem, however painful it may be. In fact, neither the conflict and reciprocal excommunications of the patriarch Michael Cerularius and Cardinal Humbert, nor the scandalous Crusade, redirected toward Constantinople, and its consequences, nor even the fruitless attempts at reconciliation at Lyon and Florence, which merely embittered the oppositions, suspended all communion between the Church of the East and the Church of the West. To the end of the eighteenth century, limited incidents of intercommunion between the two Churches are innumerable. Not only (as a general rule) were all baptized and communicating members of one received in the other on the same basis, without abjuration, but priests and even bishops passed from one to the other or, more exactly, occasionally "moved through" both without encountering major difficulties. However violent and acrimonious the polemics, they were only disputes of particularly spirited schools, and not necessarily more spirited than those that occasionally arose among Easterners or Westerners themselves, without a break in communion as the result. The policy among the great sees of Christendom, despite spasmodic outbursts of violent reproaches (though not one of them seemed to justify a schism), was to ignore one another in mutual embarrasment, rather than to condemn one another absolutely. In fact, at least *per conniventiam,* Rome—like Constantinople and Moscow—did not concern itself with preventing communion, which remained the rule where there was untroubled opportunity to meet and cooperate.

Not until the beginning of the nineteenth century did Latin missionaries, moved by unfortunate zeal, take it into their heads to apply to Orientals the canons decreed by Trent against Protestants, and, through a regrettable but understandable twist, that Orientals (particularly Greeks, in permanent conflict with Latins in the islands of the Peloponnesus or elsewhere) did the same. On both sides, then, people developed outrageous practices, such as repetition of baptism or ordination, in certain cases of contact. Also on both sides, theologians for the first time treated not only bishops or theologians of the other side as schismatics, but the totality of the two blocs, accusing each other of heresies with a systematization unknown until then (except in brief and local flushes of intolerance).

To all of these procedures and to those responsible for them we must apply

Christ's prayer: "Father, forgive them, for they know not what they do!" If their sly maneuvers made any sense, it could only be rejection of the Church they defended, as well as the one they attacked, as schismatic or heretical. For all these wretched polemics suppose, on both sides, a confusion of tradition, whether Catholic or Orthodox, with an artificial partisanship that, for this very reason, is adulterated, which is precisely the process whereby people normally go from schism into formal heresy. The primary question, then, is: How did we arrive at a situation as deplorable as it is absurd? Obviously, once this question has been answered, the complementary question can be broached: How are we to get out of it?

What is primarily responsible for preventing the East from returning to full and lasting communion with the Christian West is this hypertrophy and, consequently, this deformation of authority we have analyzed, whose consequences we gave in the preceding section. However, what obliges us to acknowledge that responsibilities for the division are shared on both sides is the undeniable fact that Church authority in the West involved itself in a near-fatal evolution from a healthy and originally necessary reaction against encroachments of the supposedly Christian empire on the Church, of the secular authority on the ecclesiastical authority, to which, on the whole, the East became too easily resigned. On the other hand, it is only right to acknowledge that if the endeavors of ancient popes, such as St. Leo and St. Gregory the Great, to regain or defend the independence of the Church, were in principle unassailable and, in fact, were never assailed in the East, bishops of the East, such as St. Basil and St. John Chrysostom, were never less clear or less courageous for the same cause. Consequently, in this conflict the *de facto* failings (in the opposing sense) of both East and West were never improperly canonized. At the time when the first conflicts threatened, the Byzantine doctrine of the *Epanagoge* was firmly articulated (as we have seen) with the doctrine uttered by Pope Gelasius. Even long after the apparently consummated division, the episcopate of the East, even when subjugated by basileus or tsar, never made a dogma of this situation—any more than Boniface VIII dared do with the more than doubtful vision that the famous bull, *Unam Sanctam,* proposed for relations between the two authorities. For a stronger reason, the Christian West, in its totality, was far from making such a view its own.

It is true, however, that alienation of the apostolic authority in the East, in contrast with its cancerous development in the West, permitted the liturgical function, more than the function of the magisterium (threatened with coemption, along with authority itself, by the secular power), an autonomous development which was not entirely beneficial. Orthodoxy became, or aspired to become, "heaven on earth"—above all, if not exclusively, in liturgical and sacramental celebration. Without doubt, this celebration retained substantial richness, and even had lasting and fecund developments, which had scarcely any equivalents in the West, where, as we have seen, the aggrandizement of authority tended to reduce worship to a court ceremonial. Tending to develop more and more outside real life (monastic life apart), the liturgy in the East, instead of remaining in this sacramental world (which should be intermediary between the eschatological world of the risen Christ and the concrete universe of our daily life), would always be tempted to become a world in itself—a dream world enclosed within itself—wishing to substitute itself for the real world but without the power to do so; indeed, concealing its reality, which has remained in great part pagan. Undoubtedly, as their best modern thinkers are the first to acknowledge, this was the major sin of the Orthodox, just as the major sin of Catholics of the West was their clerical imperialism.

Thus a twofold orbit was accentuated in the life of the Church and determined, over the course of centuries, a *de facto* separation, tending more and more to opposition in principle between Christian realities that should be conjoined in unity.

Confusing the papal function with its exercise or its more or less excessive theoretical justifications, the East, unlike the West, never developed its whole significance, implied in the deeds and texts of the New Testament and the early Church. What is worse, the East tends, if not to reduce its import unduly, to forget the attestations of its own past. Reciprocally, the West neglected and more and more misunderstood the irreplaceable value of the traditions it received from the fathers and the Church of the East; and in believing it could build itself independently of this heritage, it unconsciously risked cutting itself off from its roots.

Thus, on both sides, undue identification of the truth as Catholic and Orthodox became dangerously confused with partial form of its expression and with cultural nationalism: Orthodoxy and Byzantinism, Catholicism and Latinism (or, later, Romanism).

Today, the first remedy to this situation, now that sufficient historical awareness of these errors (which are above all, moral faults) has been assumed or is in process of being assumed on both sides, is escape from religious nationalism and the unilateralism it crystallized. Finally, it would be necessary to deny the obvious negation of "catholicity," of *sobornost* (to use a term the modern Orthodox have developed, often fortuitously). Beginning with this, rediscovery and reestablishment of full unity would become possible on both sides, or rather in common.

Recuperation of doctrinal harmony in the apostolic ministry, between its function of pastoral authority and its liturgical function, would come about in common renewal of its magisterium. However, renewal of the two inseparable units of the Church, finally coming together, could happen only in symphony with a common rebirth of living witness to the truth of love by the entire (now fraternal) life of all Christians, Orthodox and Catholic. Then, the unity of the Church, Catholic and Orthodox—which we believe has never ceased, though many clouds have obscured it—would reappear. Reappearing, she would immediately flourish and fructify in the special manifestation of charity and holiness that the modern world expects from the Church of Christ, which she will never bring it so long as this basic reunion is not effected.

## B. Protestants and the Church

The situation between the Catholic Church and Protestantism is quite different, though it presents certain analogies with what we have just examined. If schism has always threatened between Eastern Orthodoxy and Roman Catholicism (though never been consummated), schism was indeed the case with Protestantism, and early on. It was immediately extended among the different Protestant communities, which were its result, so that they are not only outside Catholic unity but, as a foreseeable consequence of this fact, they have hardly more unity among themselves, on the level of church community, than they have kept with the *una sancta catholica*.

Beyond that, the Protestant schism and its inevitable proliferation *within* Protestantism, though not the consequence of another proliferating accumulation of diverse and contradictory heresies, was accompanied by heresies. Short of abandoning the traditional notion of Church, evolving from the New Testament, which the Church of the Fathers unanimously developed and which, even in reciprocal tension, Catholics and Orthodox continue to uphold, we must acknowledge that Protestants are not in the one and only Church—which also comes down to what we have seen of the local church and the universal Church: their communities are not *local churches* in the traditional sense. To believe that we would facilitate *rapprochement* by dissimulating or suppressing *de facto* truths is to make it impossible, by creating ambiguity from the outset—a formal misunderstanding, which could very soon end in a renewal of disputes.[19]

Either one maintains the vision of the Church and her unity that our whole volume has tried to deduce from Scripture and tradition (though it is evident that it cannot be applied to Protestantism and its communities) or we must speak of the one Church as subsisting in disunited communities, so that local churches would have the right to this title without concern for being local epiphanies of one, universal Church. In the latter case, we must abandon the unanimous ensemble of Catholic (and Orthodox) tradition, and with it, whether we want to or not, the heart of the New Testament's teaching on the Church.

Indeed, the inseparable unity and unicity of the Church come from continuity in its legitimate successors of the apostolic ministry, always preaching one faith, the same faith that was entrusted, once and for all, to the apostles; always celebrating the same sacraments, instituted by Christ himself (or in the line of his teaching and his practice by these same apostles or their successors), and thus, through all times and places, bringing the faithful together in local communities, not only conscious of being the local manifestations of one universal Church but, *de facto,* all in communion with one another. Now on one hand the totality of these elements, which command each other mutually, is obviously not common to the Catholic and Orthodox Church and the Protestant churches, and, on the other hand, the latter do not have any community among themselves which presents an analogy with Catholic and Orthodox unity.

Strictly speaking, without abandoning what is most essential in the traditional view of the Catholic and Orthodox Church, we cannot say either that the Protestant churches are *churches* in the traditional sense or maintain that they are part of the *one Church.* Yet this is quite different from asserting that Protestants do not in general belong to the People of God or that their communities contain nothing of the Church. Indeed, identification between the People of God and the Church is not total at present;[20] it will be so only in the eschatological Church. On the other hand, if the Church cannot be said to be manifestly present except where all her inseparable elements (which constitute her indivisible existence) are present, it does not follow that she is totally absent in communities or, more exactly, assemblies where something of these elements remains or has been retained.

In other words, we should say: The authentic Church is always the People of God, in all possible fullness of its actual existence. But the People of God can also subsist where the authentic Church of the New Testament is incapable of coming together—just as it existed before she came together—and it subsists in particular, we believe, in indubitable fashion (though imperfectly, in a positively deficient fashion), where any assembly strives to maintain or recover some authentic vestige of what constitutes the Church of Christ: apostolic ministry, preaching the faith received from the apostles, and celebration of the sacraments of this faith.

The People of God are destined to find their unity by becoming the body of Christ in all truth, by the ministry that Christ established for this (more precisely, the ministers to whom he promised to be with until the end of the world for this purpose), insofar as this ministry authentically proclaims the evangelical faith and faithfully celebrates its sacraments. Because all this is realized in the Catholic Church—that is, in the assembly of the eucharistic celebration such as Christ willed and the apostles inaugurated—the Church is in the strongest sense—even the Church *in via,* with all her woes—the People of God in their fullness. It is for this reason that the People of God, as the Second Vatican Council said, subsist *fully* only in the Catholic Church.[21]

But in every man who docilely receives (to the extent that he depends on it) the truth of the Gospel, who endeavors, insofar as he discerns it, to appeal to the ministry established by Christ to communicate and maintain this truth, and, insofar as they are knowable by and accessible to him, to receive its sacraments, it is certain that the People of God are there—or, if you prefer, that such a man belongs to the People of God. When he comes together with his brothers—even in defective continuity with the apostolic ministry; even though the ministry that presides at their assembly cannot strictly be called a ministry sent by Christ and following the apostles; even if, through a defect in correct preaching and, consequently, reception of the evangelical truth, the faith that they confess in common is not rigorously authentic; even if, as a consequence of these defects of the ministry and the faith, the "sacraments" they receive are not the true signs in which Christ remains present to communicate his mystery—to the extent that this assembly is constituted on a vestige of all this and (still more) honestly seeks the authentic, full reality of all this—again, without being *a* church, an actual part and faithful manifestation of the *one* Church—it preserves something of it, and especially (which is perhaps even more important) it tends, obscurely, to regain its fullness.

In such Christians, however, and *a fortiori* in the assemblies in which they maintain their faith and charity—which, if it is not through personal fault that they are not inscribed in God's revealed and accomplished plan in Christ, can be just as (or even more) substantial as the faith and charity of many Catholics or Orthodox—we must deplore a fundamental, objective lack of correspondence with the divine plan. This lack paralyzes or at least burdens subjective development of faith and charity in individuals, and especially it makes their assemblies little more than a palliative for their lack of the authentic Church—a *de facto* obstacle to the missionary spread and growth of the Church. Yet the fault may be less in these Christians than in their ancestors, who, while remaining within the true and unique Church, furnished the cause or the pretext of their separation. Indeed, this consideration is more important because it is more practical in its effects upon Christians and, especially, the responsible leaders of the Catholic Church today—to the extent that, through incapacity or infidelity, they make her more difficult to recognize in their separated brothers in good faith.

Only in this way can we understand something that seems beyond question: God not only continues to communicate himself to many Christians who are separated from the one Church, he seems to use their ecclesiastical assemblies—radically defective though they may be; indeed, detrimental, in a sense, by their very existence, to the subsistence and work of the Catholic Church—to maintain with those who do not actually belong to this Church an obscure, imperfect desire for the common life in charity, which can only be (or tend to be) life in the *una sancta*.[22]

We shall not say, therefore, that these Christians are members of the Catholic Church, nor even that their communities are churches in the Catholic sense, in which the unique Church of Jesus Christ is locally present. Even if these Christians have been validly baptized, the fact of living in heresy and schism, even though they are not directly responsible, can only make residual or potential (or both at the same time) their belonging by right to the Catholic Church. Although they preserve or have recovered their communities from the Catholic Church, although they maintain some memory and perhaps revive some nostalgia and even sustain a presentiment of it (whether they want to or not), they form a screen to her presence and an obstacle to her action to unite all scattered children of God.

From the point of view of the only authentic Christianity, of the only Church that can be called the Church of God (the one he willed: the Body of Christ, which he provided for himself by his redemptive work; the Temple of the Spirit: he who never ceases to consecrate himself as the tabernacle of his presence in the midst of men until the end of time), there can therefore be no question of recognizing Protestant churches as satisfactory, of encouraging them (without restriction) to maintain and develop themselves as they are, and, for a stronger reason, to accept that they perpetually retain authentic Christians within themselves.

On the other hand, Christians who have the privilege of being in the one Church of Christ, and especially their lawful leaders, must recognize that the continued presence in other communities of faithful Christians—indeed, the use that God unquestionably makes of these communities (though, insufficient in themselves) to develop something in them (so much!) of this life of charity which must be life within the one Church—attests to the unsatisfactory character of past *and present* testimony of Catholic Christians, to the still more unsatisfactory manner in which pastors of the Catholic Church discharge their mission.

At this point, it is fitting to ask ourselves more precisely in what this fault of

Catholics consisted, and persists, that contributes to making the one true Church practically inaccessible to many Christians who ought to be within her and, at the same time, makes inevitable (regrettable as this may be) the separate subsistence of vestiges or sketches of churches in which they maintain their faith and develop their charity. Only in this recognition can the fault of the first Protestants be recognizable and reparable by their descendants. In giving up the separated existence of their provisional and unsatisfactory communities, without legitimate fear of abandoning anything of the eternal Christian truth that God had their forefathers rediscover, they will finally be able to rejoin the Catholic Church, who herself would recuperate (by reunion with them) an essential part of her *de facto* catholicity, which even today she lacks.

If our foregoing analyses are valid, we must say—again and always—that this hypertrophy of authority in the Catholic Church, and especially this incurvation of authority upon itself, is the primary origin of Protestant schisms and heresies and, on our part, the chief factor in the unhappy division between the Christian East and West.

In the reformation which was to become Protestant, the refusal or at least the slowness of authority to recognize its dependence on the divine Word, as well as its essential character of service of evangelical truth and, therefore, Christ's ministry in the service of personal faith, to develop in and through each faithful individual, was the source of the evil. Hence, as a reaction, the confusion in which the first Protestants were unfortunately incited to involve themselves: between the necessarily personal development of this faith, in direct contact with the Word of God, and the rejection of an authority that was confused and deformed in its exercise and more or less forgetful of its basic reason for being: to bring the Word of God, the Word of Christ himself, the Word who is Christ, to every man. Hence at a later period, the Word as the content of faith, finding itself isolated from the Word as historical fact—as a personal intervention of Christ himself throughout history, following the succession of the ministry he provided for himself and the whole, living tradition of truth of which this succession was the organ—the "Word," among Protestants, slipped into intellectualism, to a simple "teaching." Instead of becoming a living reality in the sacrament in which God himself seals the communication of the mystery of his Son, not only in words or concepts but in fact, the Word reabsorbed the sacrament into a *verbum visible,* in the devitalized sense of a simple teaching, an image. Thus as the historicity of the Church, her historical connection and continuity with Christ, seemed to disappear, her perpetually renewed actuality in an experience of the Spirit (which, always the same, is unceasingly renewed), seemed to become disincarnate.

In Latin Catholicism, forgetful of the fullness and unity of its tradition, authority set itself up as its own end and thereby adulterated itself; at the same time, it adulterated the truth of preaching with the reality of the sacramental liturgy. Thus it ended by stifling the life of faith and charity that it ought to have fomented in the whole body of the Church. In Eastern Orthodoxy, the sacramental liturgy, yielding to the secular authority the regulation of the whole of community life, and thereby ceasing to be the heart of human life, renewed in all its actuality, tended to become a life of anticipation (more dreamt of than lived) of the reign of God outside true life, and its doctrine, consequently, pure speculation of a Platonist kind. In Protestantism, subjective faith, detaching itself from historical realization of the Church through a ministry in which Christ, in person, invades history in a liturgical celebration which introduces into the heart of the world (in which we have to live) the mystery of his redemption, and its churches are merely human communities, like the rest, in which men, on their own initiative, try to help their brothers realize the Gospel. The "one Church," in this case, is a purely ideal, disincarnate reality, where divine grace, the gift of the Spirit, no longer introduces us—today, on earth, and throughout history—into the eschatological reign by the ways willed by Christ. She is reduced to a simple projection, by our thought, into a very internal world of a reign of Christ, on the scale of our pious desires.

What Protestants must therefore recover, but cannot recover except by reuniting with Catholics and Orthodox, is the Church—not an abstraction or a simply human organization, but a living being: the Betrothed of Christ, born of his torn body on the cross and associating, on the foundation of the apostles, in the communion of his risen body, all men who receive the Gospel from them as his Word. On the other hand, for this to be possible, Catholics first of all, but also the Orthodox, to a large extent, must recover within the one Church that respect, that efficacious love of the Word of God, that sense of pure, divine grace which is revealed there as our salvation—that exigency of Christian life which is first a life of personal faith, which distinguishes Protestants. In effect, to the extent that we fail to do this, that we more or less ban this from the Church, we continue to keep Protestants outside the Church.

We must add that Protestants, even though they remain in separation outside the Church, despite all bonds that attach them to her, still have, and continue to have, many intuitions of essential and complementary aspects of the life of the Church, of which Catholics are often too forgetful. Let us mention once again the Lutheran vision of the Church, as first and above all a community of living faith—the sense, so alive among Presbyterians, that ministers must represent the whole body of the faithful to be able to exercise their ministry among them, and that the Church, on all levels of her life, can be led only in an exercise of synodal collegiality—the no less remarkable sense with Congregationalists, that the Church exists concretely only in local churches and that, necessary though ministers be, each faithful member must be fully active and, therefore, associated with the life of the whole—and finally Wesley's intuition, the legacy of Methodism: in the Church, all Christians must not be thought "perfect" from the outset but tend, without respite, to perfect sanctification, and for this purpose, the most advanced must become the trainers of others. All these intuitions, though developed outside the Catholic Church, and too often in regrettable conflict among themselves, are essential to a just vision and healthy development of the Catholic Church. It is *in* her that they should be reconciled, producing not only a reformation but an *awakening,* in the strongest, most authentic sense of the word.

Protestant communities, moved by these glimpses of true life in the authentic Church, ought not think that their reconciliation in the one Church would signify their disappearance, if they adhere to her in joint rediscovery, with Catholics, of the essential catholicism of the Protestant movement. These communities would not only preserve everything which makes up their authentic value (though it is imperfect and transitory), but would provide the possibility of a new and unexpected flowering by reconciling and harmonizing the gifts of each Protestant church with all the others in the renewed fullness of the *una sancta* herself.

One last question pertaining to the hoped-for reunion cannot be avoided. Is it necessary that reunion between Catholics and Orthodox come first, for Protestants to be reconciled with the traditional Church? Or, as many Orthodox have maintained (following Khomiakov), is it first necessary for the Christian West to become reconciled in itself, before posing the problem of reunion between East and West?

Thus posed, the alternatives seem to be purely abstract. It is certain, we say, that the division between Catholics and Orthodox is of primordial gravity, because it constitutes a division that affects the Church from within. There is, then, for Catholics and Orthodox, a primordial duty of recognizing one another, forgiving one another, and reuniting. Among Catholics, on the other hand, it is unquestionable that a rebirth of authentic liturgical life, and thereby rediscovery of tradition at its living source, could not be conceived without *rapprochement* with Orthodoxy. Such a rebirth also is necessary for reincorporating in the Church that common life of personal faith, drawn from the living Word of God, which is the fundamental charism of Protestantism. It is, consequently, the *sine qua non* condition of a reconciliation of Protestants with the Church.

However, to come together, Catholics and Orthodox need an awakening of personal faith in the grace of Christ, recognized in living acceptance of the Word of God, such as Protestantism was on the way to producing in the West, had it not been spurned from without by the authorities and the mass of the faithful and vitiated from within by its own ferments of error and division.

Although the problems are different and demand different treatments, the ecumenical task is one. Indeed, it is rediscovery by all of the Church of the unity of Christianity in its fullness, and this fullness is indivisible, just as this unity is catholic. We cannot work toward reestablishing union on one point without working for its reestablishment on all points.

## VI. The Church and the Jewish People

The division between Christian East and West, the subsistence of Protestantism outside the Church, are weaknesses which have appeared over the course of her history and should be overcome as soon as possible. There is, however, another and perhaps even greater imperfection that the Lamb's Betrothed must surmount to be worthy of the wedding. It is a quasi-congenital infirmity and, with the witness of Scripture, it does not seem that the Church can ever be healed of it, at least before the approach of the Parousia. This does not mean that the Church must accommodate herself to this deficiency; quite the contrary, she could not tend (as she should) toward the eschatological reign of God without addressing it, though it undoubtedly will persist until the approach of the end in a historic impasse. We speak here of the fact that the Christian Church has failed to win Israel to Christ and, what is more, has seen wither and disappear the original Judeo-Christian Church from which she came. The result is that the first chosen people and our *Ekklesia,* this assembly which should reunite all "the saints of the latter days," are strangers to one another. (Once again, we note, blessed are they when fratricidal hatreds do not rise up in their midst!)

Of this unresolved mystery of Israel and the Church, when in human eyes it could seem only a transient misunderstanding, St. Paul gave us a prophetic interpretation that is a highpoint of his teaching. It is nevertheless true that his prophecy, like all that await fulfillment, is not susceptible at this point to interpretation which would dispel all obscurities. We are speaking, obviously, of the Epistle to the Romans, chapters 9 to 11,[23] and without giving a complete exegesis (which would make a whole book), we must point out its most salient points.

The first is the statement that the Church of the Gentiles subsists only as a graft on the trunk of Israel. The second is the statement that "God did not reject his people," for he "foreknew them"; his promises are always kept.[24] The third is that just as the apparent rejection of Israel was the occasion for "Gentiles" to accede to the "sonship of Abraham," similarly, when the "fullness of the Gentiles" is gathered in by the Church in the People of God, "all Israel will be saved."[25]

In the first place, the Christian Church has been peopled for innumerable generations almost exclusively with "pagans" and has always been tempted to forget what she could not misunderstand without destroying herself: she is the definitive People of God, and she can subsist as such only by being, and remaining, grafted onto Israel. Indeed, the Church is the Body of Christ, but this body, which each eucharistic celebration asserts more profoundly, is the body of a Jew in whom all Israel finds its fulfillment. The blood whose communion is in us as the living source of eternal life, the "incorruptible love,"[26] is also the blood of David and Abraham.

Not only this, but the twelve apostles, in whom were founded forever the people who were to be the new Twelve Tribes, and St. Paul, who was aided by the most gratuitous act of grace of the risen Lord in introducing the Gentiles into this people, *all* were Jews. Christianity will always be the perfected legacy of Israel, which the Jews along could give to the whole of mankind.

But this is not all. Renewed as the People of God may be by the work accomplished by Jesus in the flesh, these people, after the risen Lord sent his apostles on mission, live in the substance of their institutions, in the Word whose bearers they are, in the sacraments that communicate the mystery of this Word in all its reality, as St. Paul himself did, "Hebrew, born of Hebrews,"[27] despite all progressively universalizing adaptations. Better, the principle of the universalization of the People of God in the Church is not in denial by Christ of his Jewishness, but in its transfiguring fulfillment. In Jesus, we may say, all of Judaism was crucified; but Jesus' wounds were necessary for the divine blood to flow and to communicate, to the whole of mankind, the power of participation in resurrection, which was first that of the preeminent, the perfect Jew: Jesus of Nazareth. We are grafted to the death of Jesus by baptism; also when all is said and done, we are grafted on the tree of Jesse.

Pius XII's statement that "we are all spiritual Semites" goes much further than one ordinarily thinks. Again, there is nothing in the fundamental, permanent, constitutive institutions of the Church which is not Jewish in its source. Just as the Christian "apostle" comes directly from the Jewish *shaliah*, the Christian "bishop" is heir of the *meqaber* of Qumran and Jerusalem's "high priest." The Christian "presbyter" comes from the Jewish *presbyter* (elder), the Christian "deacon" from the "levite" and *hyperetes* of the synagogues, and the Christian "layman" himself from the Aaronic "priesthood."

Similarly, the Word of the Gospel, as Christ uttered it, as the apostles elucidated it, is woven entirely of the written Word of the Old Testament and its living commentary in Jewish tradition. To uproot them from the New Testament would make it not only incomprehensible but dumb and empty, for all its notions, images, and vocabulary, like all the realities to which this totality applies, proceeds from the Old Testament, and from the unwritten as well as the written Torah.

Finally, the Christian sacraments, beginning with the Eucharist (which proceeds directly from the Jewish *berakoth* of the meals and the synagogue service, so that it would be impossible to detach them), are a derived evolution of what we may call, after the fathers, the "Jewish sacraments."

Hence this profound and little-noticed truth that subtends the Christian allegory, even with St. Paul and the most apparently Hellenized fathers (e.g., Origen): the Old Testament has so influenced the New that every Christian, like the whole Church, can enter and progress in the mystery of Christ only by thinking of it as an abridgment of a series of transpositions throughout the history of Israel. As one says in biology, that ontogenesis reproduces phylogenesis, it was necessary that the Jewish Passover be reproduced and transfigured to be fulfilled in the death and resurrection of Jesus; and it is necessary that Christ's new Passover in the Eucharist become ours by expecting that the eschatological passover, toward which our faith and our hope tend and our love anticipates, introduces us forever into the definitive reign of God.[28]

If all this is true—and there is no doubt that it is—Judeo-Christianity cannot be considered a transitory phase of abolished Christianity, forever surpassed by pagano-Christianity, which would have triumphed over it. The Christian synthesis, on one hand, is always renewed but will not be completed until the Parousia, and, on the other hand, must always be renewed by renewing its contact with the primary and, in a sense, definitive expression of the Gospel, in the categories and forms of Judaism, for this is the only expression that Christians can consider inspired in the strictest sense.

It follows that if Judeo-Christianity, as Paul recognized and proclaimed and as St. Peter undoubtedly felt before him, cannot be the only form of Christianity, it remains forever its mother form, to which all other forms must always have recourse. It is therefore a weakness for the Church that Judeo-Christianity, from which it was born and from which it cannot free itself, no longer subsists in her except in tracings. It can be believed that she will not reach the ultimate stage of her development except by rediscovering it, fully living in her but finally unburdened of its narrowness and exclusiveness-ready, in other words, to bring together in final unity all the developments which have come from it.

If only because it reserves this possibility to the end of time, the religious survival of Judaism ought to appear providential to Christians. As experience has shown, since Origen and St. Jerome and Andrew of Saint Victor and down to our own day, throughout the unfolding of history, Christians have unceasingly felt the need for recourse to the surviving tradition of Judaism. To renew themselves in understanding the Gospel and the whole of Christian tradition, it is necessary that they be continually refreshed in their perception of its primary source.

Only naive pride (though we fall into it all the time) can persuade Christians that only the branch subsists in God's plan, rather than the trunk and the branch which was grafted onto it. As St. Paul said: "It is not you who bear the stock of the vine, it is the stock which bears you." "The promises are firm." Even if Israel has been surpassed by pagans in recognition and acceptance of what should be Israel's fullness, it remains forever destined that the pagans' entry into the Church will find its fullness only in the final salvation of the Jews.

We can perhaps get a glimpse of how that will happen by observing how the prophecy of the Old Covenant culminated in the Apocalypse, where it is completed and made open to the New, after accepting and remolding pagan wisdom. Similarly, we think, Israel's fidelity to the Torah, which today seems closed on itself but is still directed by invincible hope, will finally open itself—when all the empires and cultures of the Gentiles have brought their transitory interpretations and unfulfillable realizations to the Gospel—to their witness in order to be part of a new form of Judeo-Christianity. This will not be a premature halt of Christian flowering in its first principle, but the last fruit of the great tree of all the sons of Abraham, before the harvest of the Son of Man and his angels is gathered in for all time.

Thus the Church of the latter days would be neither a Jewish Church, in which Gentiles would blend in (as the first Judeo-Christian Church tried to be) nor a Church of Gentiles, in which only a few converted and uprooted Jews would survive, but "the assembly of the firstborn who are enrolled in heaven."[29] It would be in "the bosom of Abraham," broadened to gather in the only-begotten Son, in whose Father are fulfilled "all the children of God who are scattered abroad."[30]

But, once again, we must resist the temptation to read too explicitly what may be looked upon as the last prophecy, before the time of its fulfillment has come. On the other hand, if there is one point which all Christians must repent, it is not having yielded so many times to pandemic anti-semitism; it is having forgotten that the ultimate objective of their witness must be to win Israel to Christ, as the Messiah of the Jews. Gentiles will not be completely his until they accept all lessons that the first chosen people have to give them.

## VII. The Church and Anonymous People of God

As St. Paul said, "If their rejection [i.e., the apparent and temporary rejection of Israel] means the reconciliation of the world, what will their acceptance [of the grace of the Gospel] mean but life from the dead?"[31] Again, reconciliation of the pagan world is necessary for this acceptance to take place, as the immediate preamble to the resurrection of the dead. This is why the primary motif of the Apostle's zeal in his mission to the pagans was not disdain for his brothers in Judaism but the hope of hastening the moment of their conversion. Hence his cry: "Woe to me if I do not preach the Gospel!"[32]

This ought to be the cry of the Church unceasingly, beginning with her leaders, for what has been called the "delay of the Parousia" is the consequence of delay in preaching the Gospel. When the "fullness of the Gentiles" enters the Church, Israel will take its place there. Then the Christ of Israel will appear as Lord of the Church, finally completed in the ingathering of the "last chosen" with the first. The Betrothed of Christ, as we have said, cannot become the worthy bride of the wedding except by struggling without respite—by virtue of the cross—against the power of sin, both in her and outside her, in the world and in herself. But now, perhaps, the greatest sin of the Church, in her members and her leaders, is that she has ceased to struggle against the primary sin of unbelief in order to save the world, along with herself. And perhaps the entire Church, of any age in history, has never been more deeply averse to this responsibility than today!

Indeed the modern Church, despite the brilliant and ingenious formulas with which she cloaks avoidance of her responsibility, is less missionary than she has ever been before, as she seems to turn her back on Christ's cross more decidedly than ever. These aberrations go hand in hand. Indeed, as the Apostle said, "In my flesh I complete what is lacking in Christ's afflictions for the sake of his body, that is, the church."[33] Christians, even successors of the apostles, who think only of avoiding the cross (of their "human fulfillment," as they say), are unconcerned about evangelization, even though they try to hide it from themselves with lofty words. (Indeed, they may even pursue an opposite course.) It is natural—unavoidable—for example, that a Church whose priests and religious think only of getting married, "being a man (or woman) like everybody else," and whose "militants" they aspire to lead, who lose themselves in the contemporary mass of mankind through complete mimicry (under the guise of "adaptation"), have leaders who proclaim that their "mission" is no longer to win men for the Church but "to help men become more aware of the supernatural values they already possess."

The ambiguity of "win over" is a good indication of this, for it touches on the evil after effect of the clerical imperialism of the Church of yesterday, in the missionary defeatism of the Church of today. For too long, under the guise of "winning the world for Christ," of "making Christ reign" (as people used to say with derisive, sacrilegious fatuousness), we were especially concerned with setting up, if not sacristy dictatorships (though we grasped at any opportunity to do so), an insidious subservience of all human activities to a clerical authority that confuses itself with the reign of Christ. The reflex that must follow, when this scandalous confusion has been avowed and denounced (which does not suffice to dispel it, now that it has got into the marrow), is to deemphasize the Gospel. This gift of God, entrusted to this authority—about which it concerned itself, only to be choked by it—is forcefully abandoned as excessive, even idolatrous.

People are made by God, of Christ and his mysteries, and the prime possession of man, the *homo ecclesiasticus,* voluntarily forfeits his pride, believing he can "fulfill" himself by belittling the pledges entrusted to him, which he attributes to himself, like so many guarantees of his prestige. Then everything that justifies genuine authority—the apostolic authority, conferred as the service of divine truth; ministry of the Word and the mysteries of Christ to our human brothers—is excessively confused by perverted authority, is belittled with it, even *by* it, and is swept away in waves of false resignation and contestation.

The Church no longer dares to speak of converting the world: she thinks only of converting herself to the world. An admirable plan indeed, if it were a matter of turning toward the world in order to understand it, in its inextricable mixture of greatness and weakness, wherein its fall is revealed—in order to love it in the persistent love of its Creator and, therefore, work to convert it to this Creator, making him its Savior and sending ourselves as ministers and witnesses of his saving cross! On the other hand, we are an abomination if we become the blind leading the blind—if it is simply a question (as is often the case) of adhering to the world as such, in its decadence, and forgetting the "winning" claims of yesterday—by flattering and acclaiming the world, and prostituting the divine Name in order to disguise the world's faults: to help it gain possession of this Name and divinize *itself* in place of the only true God!

When such confusions are accepted, people arrive at extravagant theories, such as those that thrive today, according to which the Church need not be introduced in the world but would already be there. Through a fallacious reversal of things, we are no longer told that the same God is the Creator and the Savior, but that the Savior is "only" the Creator, and does not need to be anything else (as if the fall had not intervened between creation and salvation!). In this case, surely, the People of God would no longer have to be gathered into the Church, for it would already exist outside her. An "anonymous" Christianity is present, we are told, at least in potency, in every man, and the Church can only encourage it by acknowledging its presence. In the extreme, it will be said that the Church no longer has to concern herself with being implanted everywhere, since she is already everywhere, whether she knows it or not, whether her members are aware of it or not.

Thus we return to the Gnostic error, according to which no man needs to be saved but, at most, to *discover* that he is saved. Again, if he is saved, it is not necessary that he even be aware of it, since he is saved at all events!

Among Christians today, whose "generosity" is almost completely verbal, such nonsense seems nothing more than self-justification of the manner in which many have taken false possession of the Gospel and its proclamation, to which they were led by recognition of their guilt. In their behavior, they have made the Gospel an ordinary cultural good—indeed, a stepping stone for their exaltation. Later, without discerning that faith, truly reanimated, or authentic conversion would fortify "vessels of frailty" and preserve the priceless treasure entrusted to them, they totally confused, in the same disparagement, both themselves and their mission. They made the Gospel a pretext and a means to dominate the world; now, fallen from their pedestal, they naively think the Gospel has toppled with them. Because the world got along quite well without them, and abhorred their appetite for domination, they have concluded that the world does not need the Gospel, that it is saved without the Gospel—or that the only gospel that can be the object of preaching and testimony is that the world does not need salvation.

It follows that there is no reality in the vision of an anonymous "People of God" who are unaware of God and the Church. But the Church, of course, must accept all who are within her and everything that is human, for her mission is to make everyone a child of God on the conscious plane. This, certainly, is a profound truth, if properly understood. In this perspective, far from being satisfied with herself (as she is today), the Church ought not rest until she has made room within her for chosen but still invisible People of God. This must not be understood in the sense that anonymous, unaware chosen people are already in the Church, in such a way that they need only become aware of it, for such awareness would not be strictly necessary for their salvation. If they are already saved but do not know it, what need is there to know it? We mean in the sense that Jesus was sent, and sent his apostles: not for the righteous (if there are people in this world who do not need salvation) but *to save sinners*—that is, by converting them, by helping them pass from darkness to light, from death to life.[34]

The purpose of the Church and her mission in the world is not only to help the world become aware of salvation that is already fully or partially actual; *a fortiori,* the Church cannot limit herself or justify her inaction, through skillful reasoning, to awareness of salvation already realized without her. However powerless she may be—that is, the persons who compose her, from lowliest to most exalted—to "do something" for the salvation of fellow humans, even for "her own" on their own strength (through the Gospel entrusted to her, which, as the Apostle says, is "the power of God for the salvation of nations"), it is her right her duty to bring salvation to men by bringing them the possibility of conversion. This is the special mission of the apostles and their successors, and all their collaborators, which can be exercised only in close contact with the testimony of all believers.

If the Church should have doubts about this mission, so that she would deemphasize the obligation of accepting the cross, for all her members (without which she could not give witness to the salvation she must proclaim), she would doubt not only herself—what is purely human in her—but God and Christ. But a church that reaches this point is a sterile branch, condemned to be detached from the trunk which gave her life. "Woe to me if I do not preach the Gospel!" is as applicable to the whole Church as to the Apostle. Here, ultimately, is the proper characteristic of supernatural charity, of life in the Holy Spirit, of the Church community—of not being able to preserve oneself without communicating, of finding one's fulfillment in the Church by embracing the entire world, so that the complete and perfect Church of the last days may evolve from it.

This does not mean that we can misunderstand residual Christianity in the modern world, whether outside or even against the Church. If this is the case with schismatic and even heretical churches, we will not be surprised that they retain something, even a great deal, of truth, or even more than a particular part of the authentic Church—even perhaps, the "unchurched." This should inspire the deepest humility in members of the Church, beginning with her leaders. Again, we must not forget: Have not the homicidal wars and revolutions of the last generations demonstrated the precarious character of the residue?

We need not only salute every Christian remnant in this post-Christian

world, we must acknowledge the many sound aspirations, sketches, and out-
lines of Christianity among modern pagans (as among the ancients)—to the
extent that a theologian from antiquity dared speak of an *anima naturaliter
christiana,* even among the most intransigent! Again, we must not forget that
so much generosity among non-Christians, who may shame Christians for
their lukewarm charity, may have real anticipations of Christian charity. As
Cardinal Daniélou reminds us, it is not enough that we love our neighbor
sincerely, even generously; we must love him with the love of charity, as God
loves him; that is we must try to see him as God alone can see him. But how
can anyone be so loved, unless one already has Christian faith, however one
arrives at it?

None of this should mislead us. The Church, like Christ, is not sent to the
righteous, to rejoice with them in their righteousness, but to sinners, to save
them from their sins. Indeed, the world is immersed in sin, to the point that
the Church herself, as long as she remains in this world, will not be unharmed
by it. And the greatest sin that can be committed in the Church—the sin
against the Holy Spirit, we are tempted to say—is refusing to see sin in
oneself and in others and, therefore, refusing to use the means God gives us to
triumph over it in ourselves, by contributing to delivering others.

Whatever today's fine reasoning about the "salvation of nonbelievers,"
wherein the Church has no role, it turns into pure sophistry if it convinces us
that the Church could cease to be missionary in the sense defined by Christ
(according to St. Matthew): "Go, teach all nations, teaching them all I have
commanded you; baptizing them in the name of the Father and the Son and the
Holy Spirit. Whoever believes and is baptized will be saved; he who will not
believe will be condemned."

The world suffers as in childbirth in waiting to hear the Gospel, but a
Church which has ceased to be missionary would already be dead.[35]


## Notes


1. The theme of the Church as Bride appears in the New Testament, in
chapter 5 of the Epistle to the Ephesians and in the last chapters of Revelation,
the Johannine Apocalypse. It also appears in the whole of patristics. Origen
gave it very special development in his *Homilies on the Song of Solomon.* In
the Middle Ages, having never disappeared, the theme was applied to the
individual soul (*Commentary on the Song of Songs* had opened this path). M.
J. Scheeben, in particular, shed light on it in his *Mystères du christianisme*
(see above, p. 149). An Anglican writer, C. Chavasse, has published a re-

markable study, *The Bride of Christ, an Enquiry into the Nuptial Element in Early Christianity* (London, 1940). In twentieth-century Catholicism, we must point out the book of Dom A. Vonier, *L'Esprit et l'Epouse* (Paris, 1947). In the work of S. Tromp, *Corpus Christi quod est Ecclesia* (Rome, 1946), is a rich florilegium of traditional texts on this theme (pp. 26ff.). On the character of the incompleteness of the present Church, see the beginning of chapter 7 of *Lumen Gentium* (also chap. 5).

2. Cf. Gn 2:24 and Eph 5:22ff.

3. Rv 21:10.

4. *Adversus Haereses*, 1,1,5; P.G. 41, col. 181. The theme of the Church preexisting primitive Christianity comes from the Jewish apocalyptic theme of the heavenly Jerusalem. Cf. Cerfaux, *La Théologie de l'Eglise suivant saint Paul* (2d ed.; pp. 254ff.).

5. On the Church being born from the death of Christ on the cross, like Eve from Adam's slumber (cf. Gn 2:11-23), see the texts brought together by S. Tromp in his *Corpus Christi quod est Ecclesia,* pp. 35ff.

6. Rv 21 and 22.

7. 2 Cor 11:2.

8. Fr. Congar, again—more than anyone else—redirected our attention to the traditional character of this theme, first in *Vraie et fausse Réforme dans l'Eglise* (Paris, 1950). Since then, one of the most interesting endeavors in this direction has been that of Hans Küng, *The Church,* 1:50ff. and 2:452ff. Yet it seems to us that his reaction goes beyond the point of balance, for he tends to confuse the undeniable fact that the Church has no existence outside her members with the more or less implicit supposition that there is nothing more in her than what belongs to them on the phenomenal level. Cf. J. Ratzinger, *Das neue Volk Gottes,* pp. 249ff. On what follows, see the conciliar decree on ecumenism, *Unitatis redintegratio,* especially chap. 2.

9. Diadochus of Photice, "76th Chapter on Spiritual Perfection," in *Sources Chrétiennes* (no. 5 bis, p. 134).

10. Cf. 2 Cor 4:16.

11. Lk 18:8.

12. This question was earnestly disputed at the end of the Middle Ages. See O. de la Brosse, *Le Pape et le Concile, la comparaison de leurs pouvoirs à la veille de la Réforme* (Paris, 1965).

13. Lk 12:32. It will be noted that the same evangelist preserved the apparently opposite sentence in Luke 18:8.

14. Cf. above, pp. 357ff.

15. The formula seems to have been used for the first time by the theologian Voetius, at the synod of Dordrecht. Cf. Congar, *Sainte Eglise,* p. 142, and *Vraie et fausse Réforme*, pp. 461ff.

16. Cf. above, pp. 118ff.

17. This is why all attempts at Catholic ecumenism, however well intentioned, which are limited to proposing radical change in the Church's attitude

toward schisms and heresies, are irreconcilable with Catholic tradition, starting with the New Testament, and especially St. Paul and St. John. It must be said that ecumenists put aside the question and, despite their generous plans, misconstrue the positive value of Protestantism, to say nothing of Eastern Orthodoxy. Neither are the Orthodox in general schismatics, nor Protestants simple heretics, like Valentinus or Arius. To ignore this, while working (our purpose also) to make *rapprochement* easier, is not to see the real question. We are sorry to point out such an error, even with an author so open to Protestantism as H. Küng. Cf. *The Church,* 1:342ff.

18. The works of F. Dvornik have completely revised the question on the origins of the division between East and West: *Le schisme de Photius* (Paris, 1950) and *Byzance et la Primauté romaine* (Paris, 1964). For a short, critical history of the relations between the Church of the East and the Church of the West, see W. de Vries, *Orthodoxie et Catholicisme* (Paris, 1967). An explanation of present difficulties with Catholicism, by a friendly but critical Orthodox, will be found in the book of Jean Meyendorff (which has practically the same title), *Orthodoxie et Catholicité* (Paris, 1965). On this subject, see the beginning of chapter 3 of the decree on ecumenism.

19. See above, pp. 47ff.

20. See above, p. 241.

21. The constitution *Lumen Gentium,* par. 8 of chap. 1. Certain attempts since the council to reintroduce an idea of the one Church divided among the Christian churches, as among so many "branches," and in favor of the use of *subsistit* in this formula, rest on a complete misunderstanding of the intention with which it was proposed and ratified by the fathers.

22. On the problem posed by successive divisions in the Reformation, see pars. 19ff. in chapter 3 of the conciliar decree on ecumenism.

23. A critical explanation that sheds great light on recent discussions of the interpretation of this text is G. Fessard, *De l'actualité historique* (Paris, 1959), 1:215ff. See par. 4 in the declaration *Nostra aetate*.

24. Rom 11:2.

25. Gal 4:5. Cf. the prayer of Easter Even which accompanies the reading of Genesis 22.

26. A formula of Ignatius of Antioch on the eucharistic cup.

27. Phil 3:5.

28. See the book of H. de Lubac, *Ecriture et Tradition* (Paris, 1968).

29. Heb 12:23.

30. Jn 11:52.

31. Rom 11:15.

32. 1 Cor 9:16.

33. Col 1:24.

34. Cf. Mt 9:13.

35. The object of this whole section can also be seen in J. Ratzinger, *Das neue Volk Gottes* (pp. 325ff.), and J.-H. Walgrave, *Un salut aux dimensions du monde* (Paris, 1970).

# Chapter 12
# Ecclesia Mater

## I. *The Saints and the Church* in via

The last chapter showed us an aspect of the Church that is not only human but "too human," and it is all the more urgent that we consider it today since we have avoided it far too long! This aspect is the Church as *Ecclesia peccatorum,* composed of sinners, marked by their sin. Unceasingly, she needs to be forgiven because of this, and she needs the divine pardon that she is charged with proclaiming to the world. It is also, therefore, an aspect of the Church as *Ecclesia semper reformanda,* always in need of reforming herself—to the very day of the Parousia, when, the ever unworthy betrothed of her heavenly Bridegroom, she will be finally and forever purified and transfigured by his return and the definitive union in which he will establish her with himself, the bride "without stain or wrinkle," who from all eternity was predestined for him by his Father.[1]

Although we have established the point, it is time to return to it: the Church, even in her present reality, is in no way diminished by this view. This aspect, which must be brought to light (however painfully), is not, even today—in our age of expectation and therefore imperfection—her deepest aspect. However sinful her diverse members have been in the past, and still remain (often the most exalted, along with the most lowly), and despite the weaknesses, corruptions, and failings not only of individuals but of all the churches, in which she exists and is manifested, the Church, considered in her uni-totality, remains holy, as indefectible as she is one and catholic, despite everything that works within and outside her to break her up and disunite her.

She remains naturally holy, undoubtedly, because her Head never abandons her—neither in the apostolic ministry he sent her, assuring her he would be with her "all days, even until the end of time," nor in the divine Word, whose bearer this ministry is, nor in the divine reality of the communication of grace, which she proclaims and which is realized in the sacraments of the faith. Yet if there were only this aspect to her holiness, it would not, properly speaking, be the holiness of the Church but the presence in the sinful Church of the personal holiness of Christ. But if this were the case, would not this holiness of the Lord and Head of the Church seem ineffective, if it were powerless to communicate itself? What would a Savior be who is powerless to save? But the Church *is* holy, despite all the sin one sees in her, which is only too real.

In another sense, moreover, she would not truly be holy if she were without sin. If all her holiness proceeded from her Head, so that only this unique holiness were communicated, it would be communicated only to herself. It is not, however, only the holiness of the means of grace that makes her one body, it is also the personal holiness of the members of the Church, which, on the last day, will triumph forever over that power of sin with which the pilgrim Church never ceases to do battle. Undoubtedly, this struggle is unequal, inconsistent, and must always be renewed; but despite the still-subsisting power in the Church of the enemy of God and men, the victory of divine love in the eternal Son is already manifested in this Church, which is his body. This victory is the Spirit's, and the Spirit, as St. Thomas says, cannot be in the Church except as perfume in a porous vessel, which it penetrates entirely, little by little, with its own aroma and its own substance.[2] This victory signifies, therefore, since it is the characteristic of the Spirit and his presence in us, not the presence of a holiness that is in some way impersonal, nor even the personal holiness of the Son of God (who is God like his Father), but the presence of this new, holy personality in life in the Church: the life of the Spirit in us, life in communication, in the already effective community of the "love of God poured out into our hearts by the Holy Spirit," which mysteriously awakens in us.

In certain souls, in certain human lives, this life is not awakened only at the moment or hour that their earthly days are ended; it can be said that it consumed their lives or, at least, that in their death it consumes all the rest. Therefore, with the faithful preeminently, the perfect eschatological holiness that will be that of the whole Church at the end of her existence in this world is anticipated, so that it may be said that, in them, the wedding of the Lamb is accomplished in their membership in the Church, which no longer appears simply as the betrothed of the eternal Son, but as his bride.

This is why in the saints, as we call them, the Church in time may be called (is truly, in a sense, because she is the bride of the only Son) mother of all the adoptive sons whom he received from his Father.[3] More generally, to the extent that there is effective holiness (some gift of the Holy Spirit, some outline of the divine charity communicated in her members), the Church is not simply the material instrument of the communication of divine grace to men: she is also, by this communication, the mother, because to this extent she is associated with it. It is the characteristic of God's charity, poured out in us as it flows from him, to be life in the gift of self, to be possessed only by being given. In all who possess it—rather, in whom it lives, because the Holy Spirit has taken possession of their being—grace and charity, though received at each moment from God alone, are also there, and can only be actively communicated. It is exactly what constitutes, in them and in those we call "saints," the motherhood of the Church. She is the mother because she is not only the receptacle nor, even, the channel of grace, but because she receives an essential aspect of grace that makes her able to participate in the whole of divine life in communicating this life, whose communication is essential to this life because it is the life of the *agape*.

Thus light is shed on this very intimate union (which we have already pointed out) between the communication of grace and the means of grace, which may be called "objective," that is, established in the Church by the sole initiative of her Head, Christ, which functions only as a consequence of this initiative, and the "subjective" life of grace in us, which is properly the fruit of his Spirit, is communicated through it.

Let us repeat: in the pastoral function of the apostolic ministry in its exercise of authority in the name of Christ, who "sent" his ministers, this "objective" action of Christ is not discernible from their conscious and voluntary action—which comes down to saying that it is exercised (insofar as it is excercised) in and by what personal holiness is in them, what actual "faith, exercised by charity." The only assurance against deficiencies of this faith and this charity is given to us in the certainty that, in the long run, as insufficient as the correspondence to grace on the part of ministers may be, the divergence will never be such that they can precipitate the Church into a situation in which she would cease to be able to be Christ's instrument for the ingathering of his people.

In the function of the magisterium, it is not only the final indefectibility of the Church that constitutes the limit of what the personal infidelity of ministers could inflict on her. The positive inspiration which was granted the apostles (as it was the prophets) at the beginning of the Church, to preserve and illustrate the revelation of the Savior himself and then to fix its expression in the Scripture of the New Testament, is preserved from being obscured throughout successive ages by "negative infallibility," that is, certitude that never, no matter how deficient she may be, can any later definition of this truth, communicated once and for all, deform her or obscure her. Yet here again—and even in the original revelation and inspiration—communication of the divine gift, the truth that saves us, is entirely through the human intelligence and capacities of expression that are never dissociated from their human condition and its inevitable limitations.

In the sacraments alone, the presence of Christ and his personal action are in some way immediate, totally independent from what ministers may personally assimilate. And, as we have observed, the complement of this immediateness of the communication of grace in the sacraments is the mysterious obscurity in which it works, which renders it accessible only to pure faith.

On the other hand, even in the proclamation of truth by the Church, communication of this truth is not separable from its assimilation (which is more or less penetrating and intimate) by those who are its agents, assisted constantly by the divine Spirit, but capable of resisting him. Its opposite is a correlative fecundation of the human mind of those who learn from them by the Spirit of God, who receive the living teaching of the truth of life directly.

Finally, leadership of the People of God in the pastoral work of the apostolic ministers is in its very essence a work of love, a work of the "love of God poured out in their hearts by the Holy Spirit," as is testimony to the truth of this love by simple Christians. It is for this reason that this pastoral leadership and the witness it harmonizes, acting inseparably, communicate love by exercising it.

Only here, we must emphasize, is this truth susceptible of being clarified. Preaching the truth is not isolated from exercise of the pastoral function, but is associated with the witness of all, and the sacramental celebration itself could have no sense or content (since the sacraments are signs that effect what they signify, they would effect nothing if they did not signify something) independently of the truth proclaimed by the successors of the apostles, received in the hearts of all the faithful and fructifying their lives.

The result is that the whole of the Church's activity, as the "sacrament of Christ" (i.e., an instrument that is efficacious because it is created and used by him alone), is not separable from this communication of his Spirit in the hearts of his faithful, which accounts for the constant holiness of the Church. This makes the Church, despite all faults of her members (beginning with her leaders), his eschatological bride, which therefore associates her, in all truth, as a mother with the fatherly work of God the Father, who acts in him, who is but one with him.

If this were not the case, this association, which the Father willed of mankind for its salvation in the Church, as in Christ, would not be human. In effect, it would dehumanize the human intermediary, whom God uses in the Church to communicate himself, if this intermediary were used in a way that would not include his free cooperation, which would not make—for the Church as for God—the work of communicating the divine love a work of love, a work of this love "poured out in our hearts by the Holy Spirit."[4]

In each minister, undoubtedly, the communication of grace in the Church traverses many personal deficiencies as the instrument of Christ, and the witness of all the faithful, one by one—of the particular churches, their individual celebrations, their concrete, charitable actions—is not exempt from it. Yet grace, because it is the divine love itself, in the process of being communicated, can infinitely elicit, touch, and grasp each soul that it reaches by this way of the Church, beyond all her weaknesses—just as, served by the most constant and most transparent holiness, it would submerge the Church to the point of seeming to drown it in the infinite profusion of its immediate outpouring. Again, irruption of this love throughout the Church does not come about without first inflaming the Church with that fire that the Son of God came to cast upon the whole earth[5] and for whose spread he chose her. In the saints, this association of the Church with the gift she brings to the world becomes palpable, even if it is barely or not at all manifest with others. But all together, each for his own part, the members of the Church (who are not dead members) unceasingly participate, beyond what they can recognize, in a new, collective awareness of mankind, which is the ever-present community of charity. It is in and through this community that every gift of grace, of the *agape* of God in the Church, is at the same time, in all reality, a gift that the Church, together with her divine Head, makes to whoever receives it. Thereby, she is already a spouse, by having become the mother of the children of God, who are, within her, the fruit of his grace.

This is true of the whole body of Christians in whom this grace abides by faith and love, and is eminently true of the saints, and is not fully actual except in those saints, consummated in grace. They, of course, are no longer visibly with us. Having shed the flesh (even if not yet individually risen), they no longer live, except in the ever-glorious body of Christ, which is now, totally, the "life-giving Spirit."[6] But they are not separated from us. Those whom Christ has united to himself once and for all, in completing in their sanctified death their anticipated union with his resurrection, who from now on are inseparable from him, approach us, dwell with us, and live in us, at the same time that Christ himself lives with him.

In each church which comes together to celebrate the Eucharist, they are present with Christ, invisibly but really. They constitute the full actuality, thanks to the communion of saints, of this already present union, which is more and more real: the Church, with Christ, in all his work, completing the number of the elect; making them enter, little by little and one after the other, with the help of others, into his body in his present reign, which foreshadows and prepares the eternal reign of the Father.[7] In this way, according to Revelation, the reign of God over and in the Church is also "the reign of the saints."[8]

The concert of their constant prayer, the radiance of their holiness, which is one with the ardor with which the charity of Christ has inflamed them forever, makes them—their consciousnesses working together in common illumination, their hearts now one in Christ—the maternal heart, so to speak, of this incipient collective awareness, created little by little throughout the Church on earth, progressing in time toward the Parousia, of all human consciousness in the process of regeneration. Thus the Church is the mother of this new personality, which rises from the depths of our most personal self, as the heart of the future world in the midst of the present world.

## II. *Ecclesia de Angelis*

Yet the Church—and particularly the Church considered in her motherhood—cannot be understood completely, even if one adds to all her weak members (rather, to those who walk haltingly) those radiant members, the saints, overflowing with the life they have received in fullness. We must also add the "first of the saints" (to whom the title belongs before it fell to men), who have not only entered before us into the realm of the invisible; for all time, they have been waiting for us. These preeminent saints, "these firstborn whose names are inscribed in heaven," are of course the angels.[9]

What the Word of God teaches us about angels is profoundly mysterious, as is the case with what it tells us about God. It describes them only through images that instruct us more by deficiencies we sense than by anything positive. Those who dispute these images, confusing them with the realities they conceal (more than they may reveal), have only themselves to blame for the difficulties they thereby make for themselves. In an age like ours, in a world whose material dimensions have been revealed to be ever more vast than we thought, it is more believable than ever that man is not the only emergence of the spirit, nor the highest or first.

What the divine Word teaches us about the angels, what the ancient Jewish and Christian traditions both evolved, is that they constitute a spiritual universe, or rather the primary and governing part of our universe, where the decision of creatures, for or against God, was made for the first time.[10] Man, as a number of fathers say, appeared on earth in the manner of a "substitute" angel. This is to say, the angels, to whom the material world, through its creation, was subjected as a projection (objectified by the Creator) of their thoughts, brought this world with them in their fall. But man appeared as a spiritual resurgence: a new redemptive opportunity, offered by the Creator of the world to his created freedom. The creation, tempted by the first fallen spirits, had turned from its Creator, and had fallen in turn, but the naturally non-incarnate Spirit freely incarnated himself in his progeny, as the Son of God. By his death and resurrection in this flesh of sin, he made his body the life-giving Spirit," at the same time restoring to God the tangible universe, with the human spirits who had become captive in it.

All this time, the faithful angels never ceased in their glorification of the divine Holiness, or interceding for their brothers, fallen men, or struggling spiritually (by the power of prayer and love) against the forces of demoniacal seduction. Thus the fathers describe them as the ninety-nine faithful sheep; and the Good Shepherd came to look in darkness for the lost sheep, waiting for it to return to the flock, so that the complete choir of God, which must forever glorify him, might be reshaped. This, according to the fathers, is the meaning of Michael's and his angels' struggle in heaven with the ancient serpent, described in Revelation.

In the Eucharist—just as the Jews before us believed and said in their *berakoth*, the *qahal*—the *ekklesia,* convoked by the Word of salvation to respond to him in exultant thanksgiving, is not only an assembly of men but a gathering of saved men and angels, the first ministers of man's salvation, as they are the first to have known the love of God and to respond to it in praise. This, in effect, is the Church's vision, proposed by the Christian Apocalypse: the Eucharist of the earth completes itself, and transposes itself in heaven, by being caught up in the eucharist of the angels.[11]

The general meaning of these symbolic expressions is quite clear, even if the details elude us: it is a created spiritual world, or rather a spiritual surface or face of the created world, in which our precarious, barely emerged spirituality is threatened by shipwreck. This face of the world, since it is always turned toward its God (and ours), whom it sees face to face, does not cease supplicating and pleading that we might rejoin him, nor receiving messages of hope from him, impregnated by with graces of love, which it transmits to us. Thus the divine work of the Father for our salvation is accomplished in his only begotten Son, who has come down to us, and appears as seconded by the work of the angels, created spirits, who accompany us as they do the Father, and will not cease to accompany us, to the end of the divine Spirit's work, as an advocate and consoler, the Paraclete, who is one with this work. For the work of the Spirit is ultimately the motherly work of love, which always gives being by giving itself, the being received from God. This is why, again in Revelation, the Angel and the Spirit appear (if not confused) as inseparable, indistinguishable, in their common work: the action of the love that saves by communicating itself. And this is wh y, as if with one voice, the Spirit and the Bride speak, to answer the Bridegroom and say to him: "Come, Lord Jesus, come quickly!"[12]

The ancient Syriac fathers had a strong sense of the maternity of the Spirit, which is first of all exercised in the world of incorporeal spirits.[13] They emphasized that *Ruah* ("Spirit" in Hebrew) is feminine, not to introduce a sex differentiation in God, as in pagan religions, but quite the contrary: to establish that the Godhead, seen in this communication of the love which is its life and, at the same time, is the life of the saved world, transcends this opposition, as it does all others. As a Father, above all, from all eternity, in his love "poured out in our hearts by the Holy Spirit," God reveals himself in the motherhood that this Spirit communicates to creatures in raising them up to the Creator. But first in the angelic world, in the world of the first created spirits who remained faithful, with respect to our fallen world. Better, it is revealed in the never broken relationship, in this world of divine creation, between the always faithful spirits and the wavering, faltering, but finally exalted creatures that we hope to be. It is in the Church that this motherhood of grace is first manifested: the preeminent gift, in which the work of the Spirit in creation culminates.

Thus the Church is, first of all, the Church of the Angels; and through the primary participation of the angels in the Spirit, in the very love of God, we see her open and draw to herself the Church of Men, in such a way that there is now only one Church of divine praise, in which sin is abolished in love, while the earthly act of thanksgiving is accomplished in heavenly glorification. If this is the case, every prophetic and apostolic work is an association and participation in the primary work of the angels as the first "messengers" to us (this, in Greek, is the meaning of their name, *angelos*), because they are the first and primary adorers and prayers of the whole of creation.

A very practical consequence follows in traditional theological speculation on angels: one cannot be either a prophet or an authentic apostle if one is not first, like the angels themselves, a contemplative and an intercessor. In fact, on either the human or the angelic level, one cannot work efficaciously to transmit what one did not first endeavor to receive, and to make one's own in the deepest part of one's being. The mystery of God, revealed and communicated, must take possession of our whole being in order for the *agape*, which in us first, to spring forth, inseparably, in the prayer of praise and intercession. Only on this basis can God, if he wills, following the maternal grace he willed to give all his creation—to all his Church, in heaven and earth—bestow the gifts of prophetic witness or apostolic mission, exercised in the name of his Son. It is in this sense that the bishops must be, following an ancient interpretation of Revelation, the "Angels of the Church."[14]

Preeminently, not only in an exceptional but in a unique human personality, this association of men with the ministry of the angels (supposing the prior association with their innate condition as contemplatives and intercessors) is manifested. We speak now of John the Baptist, as he was understood by Christian antiquity, by an interpretation of the Gospel whose fidelity is quite other than literal. Indeed, it is neither by a simple play on words nor by naiveté that the fathers understood, as referring to John, the prophetic words from Malachi (Mt 11:10, quoting Mal 3:1):

> Behold I send my *angels*
> to prepare the way before me.[15]

Not only in the sense "I send my *messenger*" but in the sense "I send my *Angel*."

The context of the quote in St. Matthew shows that Jesus taught the superhuman character of John, at least in the sense of humanity raised so high that only the eschatological "Son of Man" would be above him.[16] And the narrative with which St. Luke opens leaves no doubt. John was "sanctified" from the womb of his mother, not only in the sense in which that could be said of the prophets of the Old Covenant (i.e., their vocation by God was prior to their birth) but in this very precise sense: the divine Spirit had taken total possession of him from that time.[17] This is exactly what makes John more (and better) than the angels—an angel made man, we might say. For him as for them, the first awakening of consciousness coincided with the awakening of his being; it was an unreserved handing over of himself to the divine Spirit, who called him.[18] In this way he became the prophet *par excellence*, "sent" to Israel before the apostles themselves.

Nothing is more revealing of the effects of *agape* in those who give themselves to it. Far from exalting himself because of this gift, which was unique among men, the Baptist not only placed himself in the service of his brothers in mankind, he abased himself before the preeminent Servant the moment he recognized him in Jesus of Nazareth. "I am not worthy to untie the strap of his sandals," he said, and again: "He must increase, but I must decrease."[20]

Although he was the last and the greatest of the prophets, the "Apostle before the Apostles" (the text which allows everything that is said of the angels to be applied to the Baptist also applies the characteristics of the apostolate to him)—all this, before the being and mission of Christ, becomes nothing, or can only subsist by melting, so to speak, into the glory of Jesus. This was also the case with the angels and their ministry. When Christ came, they no longer seem to have a function, nor even to exist, except in total dependence on him, as a halo of the divine presence in the midst of men or as servants of his servants.

This teaches us that the greatest holiness in the greatest gifts of the Spirit— even if they could appear and be recognized as superhuman, and even *when* they appear, as did the angels and the Baptist, prior to the appearance of Christ and independent of his historical work—are as nothing before him, and can subsist, once he appears, only in total submission to him and to the work of his life and death, and even to the work which, from then on, will be *his* apostles, in *his* earthly Church. For this work alone—from now on, in all the universe—can be called *his own,* and only by cooperating with it can the holiness of both the Angels and the greatest "saints" of the Old Covenant— even those who equal the angels in the holiness of "the Church of the firstborn, whose names are written in heaven"—participate in the birth in the New and Eternal Covenant of the "Church of the Latter Day Saints."

## III. The Virgin Mary and Mother Church

What we have just said is especially true of a still higher holiness, a higher vocation—fully realized and followed from the outset—than even the vocation of the angels or the Baptist. We speak, obviously, of the Blessed Virgin Mary, who is indeed the noteworthy example (as Dionysius saw her) of this truth, which transfigures the frameworks of thought he borrowed from Neoplatonism. Whatever the original hierarchy by which the gifts of God are transmitted to humblest creatures by the most exalted and, among humans, by those whom Christ first consecrated, a gift of God is given by God himself to the one who receives it, if he to whom God communicates gives a fitting answer. Whatever one's status in the hierarchical order, he is susceptible of being raised as high as the highest in this order, and even transcending it.

In the order of holiness, Mary is not only higher than all the "martyrs," the witnesses of God—even higher than the prophets and the apostles—she surpasses the highest angels. To say that is, in effect, to say an unquestionable ruth: she is the Mother in the supernatural order, in the order of the *agape,* the order of the Spirit—in a supreme sense, unique. This means, if we reflect on it, one and the same thing. The motherhood of the Church is actual because the Church has found her anticipated perfection: the supreme created holiness, a unique communication of the holiness of Christ to her, who is not only our Mother, as the saints or angels could never be, but first of all *his* Mother.

It is true, however, that the holiness and motherhood of the Virgin are only the flower and fruit of the holiness and the motherhood of grace of Israel, which themselves were the product of the incubation of the Spirit, of the "Angel of the Lord," showing himself on earth under the face of the angels, who contemplate, night and day, the face of God in heaven. Like the Church, Mary comes from the earth, from its desert, which flowers again beneath the showers of the sky, and yet comes down from God as the gift of the grace incorporated in mankind, in fallen creatures in the process of being saved. Indeed, Mary heralds the supreme moment of human and cosmic history, in which the saving Word is fully heard by perfect faith, its supreme creation, and elicits that response which gave birth not only to all those saved in grace but, first of all, to the Savior himself. Thus understood, according to the narrative of the incarnation in St. Luke, as interpreted by the tradition of all times (and this is the way it ought to be understood), the motherhood of the Virgin is not simply a physical miracle (is there even one miracle in the Bible that is only physical?) but the decisive association of mankind and the world with their salvation.

Indeed, expressing in her "Fiat" the consent of mankind to the redemptive incarnation, Mary gave herself to it and thereby to us, as well as to the coming and the work of Christ. At the same time, in this work of giving, in which the Only Begotten made himself the Firstborn, the innumerable children on fallen earth of the Father of Heaven find in Mary a motherly cooperation which is spiritual before it is physical. And the Spirit, which spread its wings like a dove over the first creation, so that, from its chaos, life might come forth, now covers Mary with his shadow, so that the life of the children of God, in the life of her Son, might be born in her—of the very flesh that sin had plunged into death.

In Mary, it can therefore be said, the spiritual motherhood of the Church is grafted to the perfection of physical motherhood that is natural to created mankind; or the perfection of spiritual motherhood, granted to a creature, reveals the full sense of what physical motherhood was capable. As St. Athanasius showed in a page of unforgettable profundity, God alone is the Father, properly speaking—that is, the primary source of life. Men never are, except through radically imperfect participation, for life is essentially derived, which is precisely contrary to the essence of fatherhood. This is why the more elevated and more spiritual the fatherhood that men exercise, the less it is theirs. The fatherhood of the priest, on the created plane, is the highest that can be conceived, since it engenders not only spiritual life but the life of the Spirit in us. For that very reason, it totally eludes the personality of the one who exercises it.

Motherhood, on the contrary,—the fact of being associated with the gift of life, even though one received it oneself—is absolutely proper to creatures. In this fact is our final vocation revealed: the vocation of exercising, in all truth, the divine love which created us. The high point of motherhood is thus the summit of a creature's possibilities as a creature: to live by a life received. Moreover, motherhood was exercised with regard to the Son, in whom the Fatherhood of God is realized so perfectly that God could not have other children, except in Him—and therefore the motherhood which embraces all the children of God, the children of his grace as the Only Begotten, who is forever God's by nature. This divine motherhood is realized, above all, in the communication of life, of the divine life, of the life which consists in loving as one has been loved by God. This communication is proper to the Spirit, as to the substantial, eternal gift of the *agape* of God, of the love which is his life.

Thus it is not only in Mary but in what is unique in Mary that this motherhood is realized essentially, to which the entire Church is called to associate herself, who is consecrated as the Eternal Bride of the Son, ever one with him. In the totality of the eschatological Church, of the Church in her perfection—when the last of the elect, angels and men, have been gathered into her—she will appear at the side of her Bridegroom in her definitive personality, as the one and perfect bride of the Only Begotten. To her also will belong, with the consummate holiness of the bride, the divine motherhood, which is but one with this holiness: motherhood with regard to God's own life, communicated in his Son by his Spirit, which today belongs in fullness only to Mary, in which her incomparable holiness as mother is revealed—the holiness of the one who was made the giver of God's very own love because the Spirit made her a pure offering of created faith in the uncreated Word.[21]

This is why Mary can be called Mother of God, Mother of Grace, and Mother of the Church, where this grace bears its fruit. And yet the whole Church of men and angels, destined to marry the Son of God, aspiring with the Spirit of God toward that blessed end, from now on, living in love, is also mother with Mary, *in* Mary, the daughter of God, in the one, beloved Son of the Father.

# Notes

1. Eph 5:27. On this whole chapter, see the end of *Lumen Gentium,* chaps. 7 and 8.

2. *Summa theologica,* IIIa, quaest. 72, art. 2.

3. This theme of the motherhood of the Church was recently studied throughout ancient Christian tradition by K. Delahaye, *Ecclesia Mater chez les Pères des trois premiers siècles* (Paris, 1964). Scheeben (see above, p. 149) was one of the first in the nineteenth century to rediscern all its importance.

4. Rom 5:5.

5. Lk 12:49.

6. 1 Cor 15:45.

7. *Lumen Gentium,* chap. 7, pars. 48 and 49.

8. Rv 5:10, 20:4 and 6, 22:5.

9. Heb 12:23.

10. See our study on the angelic world and the human world in *Initiation théologique,* mentioned above (p. 465). We plan a much more detailed examination of this traditional theme in our book (in preparation) on the Christian idea of the cosmos.

11. See chaps. 5 and 6 in particular.

12. Rv 22:17–20.

13. This is the case especially with Aphraates, *Demonstratio XVIII,* 10—p. 839 in vol. 1 of *Patrologia syriaca.*

14. Cf. the dedications of the seven epistles with that of the Johannine apocalypse.

15. Mal 3:1.

16. Mt 11:10ff.

17. Cf. Lk 1:5ff.

18. See the book (in Russian) by Serge Boulgakov, *The Friend of the Bridegroom.*

19. Jn 1:27.

20. Jn 3:30.

21. On all this, see our *Le Trône de la Sagesse* (2d ed.; Paris, 1961), especially pp. 135ff.

# Conclusion
# Domus Sapientiae

The Apostle, St. Paul, tells us that the divine Wisdom, which he calls *polypoikilos* (i.e., "shimmering with numberless lights"), is finally revealed to men and to the angels only in the Church.[1]

This Wisdom is nothing other than God's plan for all his work, which he bears within himself from all eternity and which is one with his Son, his Only Begotten, so that it is only by "marrying" this Only Begotten that everything created can bring about the eternal project, once the Son has become its accomplisher in time. Yet Wisdom is doubly distinct from the Son, in the sense, first of all, that it plans to draw from nothing in time the very image of the Father that he projects eternally from within himself, like the Son. And because of this, the divine love includes the possibility of a fall, of a falling back into the nothingness (loved by God) of a creature, and repairing this fall by the well-beloved Only Begotten of his love, who is the eternal Son.

Therefore, in the Spirit which unites the Son to the Father, as to his free goal, just as the Son remains eternally one with the Father, his origin, Wisdom is destined to be both bride and mother: mother of all the living, who will live forever in the Son, in the eternal life of the Father, and mother of the Son himself, in time, where he will come down to search for them—bride of the Only Begotten, with whom and in whom all will come together in fatherly love. Thus the divine Wisdom in Mary, by whose existence the whole history of creation must be rejoined in the eternal existence of the Son in the bosom of the Father, finds primary and primordial incarnation as mother. But it is in the Church, the eschatological Church, the completed Church, gathering in at the end of time—in the body that the Son received from Mary in time—all the elect, men and angels, that Wisdom will find its total and last incarnation as bride. In this way, the Church, in her completion, in her fullness, which is one with Christ's fullness (completing himself as everything in all), is the ultimate realization of everything in the world that preexisted in the eternal thought of God, which corresponds in created history to that eternal design.

In this way the Catholic Church is indeed, as the fathers said, the very principle of creation. Like Jerusalem—the definitive Jerusalem, which would spring forth, after many setbacks and destructions, into supreme victory and eternal reconstruction (already a theory with the Jews)—and like the reign of God, of which the Church is the created content, since its uncreated content is identified with the Son himself, the perfect Church will be the last word uttered in history of this primary and unique thought of God about all things. God engendered it eternally in his Son, and the history of men and the entire cosmos, starting with Mary, will not cease (until the end of time) giving birth to his thought by virtue of the same Spirit who perfects all created things, as he perfects the eternal existence of the Son *ad gloriam Patris*.

Thus Mary appears in the center of history as the Throne of Wisdom, and the Church, in her turn, as the abode that this Wisdom throughout history, from the bosom of the Father, constantly builds for itself, into which it invites all to enter, as into the Father's house:

> Come, eat of my bread
> and drink of the wine I have mixed.
> Leave simpleness, and live,
> and walk in the way of insight.[2]

The divine personality, we said, exists only in the eternal communion of the three persons, what Dionysius calls the *divine thearchy*. Similarly, the created personality, in its ultimate truth, will never exist except in our human persons, totally dedicated to sharing, through the *ecclesiastical hierarchy,* the communication in time of this thearchy of love and grace. Yet the divine personality has its primary origin, and the term in which it is entirely recapitulated, in the deity of the Father alone. Similarly, the created personality, in all its supernatural reality, originates in the divine motherhood of Mary and will have its historical end in the marriage of the Church with Christ, of Wisdom realized in time with the eternal Son, in whom and with whom the Spirit will ultimately recapitulate all created and uncreated things *in sinu Patris*.[3]

> To Him who can do beyond all that we ask and think, by the Power which acts in us, to Him be the glory in the Church and in Jesus Christ, for all the generations of age upon age. Amen.

ABBAYE DE LA LUCERNE

September 17, 1969
Feast of the Stigmata
of St. Francis of Assisi

## Notes

1. Eph 3:10.
2. Prv 9:5 and 6.
3. See the last chapter of *Trône de la Sagesse*. We propose to treat the theme of personified Wisdom in our works (in preparation) on the cosmos and Christ.

# Excursus

## I. Did Jesus Found the Church?

Formulated this way, the question has been the subject of the most impassioned debates (at the end of the nineteenth century and the beginning of the twentieth) between traditional Christians and liberal Protestants or agnostic critics. In the opinion of almost all exegetes today, it seems to be a prototype of a senseless question.

Whatever attitude (faith or unbelief) the contemporary exegete may adopt, two facts have become practically unquestionable:

1. For Jesus, as for the Jews of his time, the People of God were a reality that presented no problem: since they had existed since Abraham, and had evolved since then, they would subsist, one and the same, until the last day, despite all transformations in the future.

2. For Jesus especially, even if people still debate whether he proclaimed himself—indeed, quite simply believed himself—to be the Messiah, there is no doubt, according to even the most radical critics, that his mission, as he understood it, was addressed to this people and, more precisely, concerned the final conditions of belonging to it.

The choosing of the Twelve and their function appear to imply not a break with the old People of God but their radical renewal, an eschatological *qahal* or *ekklesia*.

Let us point out that modern exegesis has thereby joined hands with the fathers, for whom the Church had been founded since Abraham (if not since Abel or Adam), renewed at each covenant, and radically renewed (without break with the past) in Christ.

## 2. Which Councils Are Ecumenical?

The position we have adopted in this book, according to which the Catholic Church of the West and the Orthodox Church of the East have never ceased being *one* Church, inevitably brings up a question: Can the general councils that have met in the West since the eleventh century be considered ecumenical in the full sense of the word? In fact, the Latin Middle Ages, which held a position on the unity of the Church corresponding to the one we have merely reverted to in order to draw from it all the consequences, never placed these general councils of the West on the level of the seven ecumenical councils of antiquity. Only since Bellarmine (and those who followed him) have people come to a different position. The matter was set down in a manner that might be judged definitive by Vittorio Peri, in his book *Concilii e Chiese* (Rome, 1965).

It does not follow that the dogmatic decisions of the later general councils (later than the separation) are not of very high authority. Indeed, we have established that the Church has always admitted that partial councils (in certain cases) could definitively express the *mens ecclesiae*. This must be the case, to a certain point, with all the councils called by the pope and confirmed by him, after having brought together a considerable representation of bishops.

It is no less true that their decisions, even when they can be considered infallible and therefore irreformable, by the fact that they were made in the absence of a considerable portion of the episcopate, which would have represented one of the most venerable theological traditions, can appeal later complements that would not have been necessitated in the case of an ecumenical council, in the most ancient and truly plenary sense of the word.

Furthermore, even councils of this latter type (such as Chalcedon after Ephesus or the Council of the Three Chapters) were able to treat only one aspect of a complex question, so that their definitions had to be clarified by later definitions, perhaps without the process having yet come to its term (cf. Th. Sagi-Bunic, *Problemata christologiae chalcedonensis* [Rome, 1969]). *A fortiori*, we must admit that this may be the situation in the present case. This comes down to saying that pure and simple acceptance, without discussion, of the general councils of the West and their definitions cannot be a prerequisite to reunion between East and West. All that the West can and must ask of the East is that the work of these councils be accepted provisionally, with favorable prejudgment, as an essential, positive element for a broader and more profound common examination of the questions. At the same time, the West ought to offer the East the same consideration of the dogmatic councils and decisions that this other part of the Church is unanimous in judging equally important.

## 3. Presbyter et Sacerdos

If, as we have seen for Christian antiquity, the whole body of the Church, including the faithful laity, must be associated with the priesthood of Christ, particularly in the eucharistic celebration, what must be thought of the application to the pastoral ministry, first of the bishops and then of the "presbyters," their associates, of the sacerdotal expressions? In fact, today in the Catholic (or Orthodox) Church, when we say "priest," we think immediately of *sacerdos,* rather than *presbyter.*

We must point out that, since subapostolic times, we see assimilation between the function of the bishop, presiding over the eucharistic synaxis, and that of the "high priest" of the Old Covenant. As the simple presbyters, associated with the bishops, gradually replaced them in this function, this expression of a sacerdotal character *par excellence* was also applied to their own ministry. The matter must be considered perfectly legitimate if we observe that the pastoral function in the Church of the bishop and the presbyter, to the extent that the latter is called by the bishop to share in his function, is a ministry *of Christ,* of his presence as Head in the midst of his body, to all generations everywhere.

By union with and participation in Christ, all are priests in the Church in one sense, in the unity of their common attachment to Christ by the ministry that he instituted to this end in the apostles. The ecclesiastical ministry as a ministry of the Head—of his presence as Head in the midst of his body, to continue to gather it in this unity of the Spirit, of whom Jesus alone is the source, and thus allow it to participate in Christ's sacerdotal action—is therefore, properly, the ministry of the *priesthood of Jesus.* As with all the gifts of Jesus to his Church, the ministry of this priesthood exists only to permit everyone to participate in it in unity.

Separated from their legitimate pastors (i.e., those in the apostolic succession), as we have explained, the baptized faithful are incapable of being brought together in a Church which is that of Christ so as to exercise in it, as members of his body, the priesthood, which remains forever *his.*

This does not mean that God cannot occasionally make use of an irregular ministry to communicate his graces (just as he can, on occasion, dispense with every sacrament, even baptism). But this could not rescind the fact that a break with the apostolic succession implies that the Church of Christ can no longer be assembled locally, that his body, both mystical and eucharistic, has no longer any objective, real presence among us and, therefore, that his priesthood is no longer the object of common participation by the faithful in a eucharist which would be truly *his*. (We are sorry that Max Thurian's fine book, *Sacerdoce et ministère* [Taizé, 1970], which comes very close to the theses that we believe have to be maintained as essential to Catholic faith and tradition, is insufficiently sensitive to this aspect of things.)

The idea of a "presbyteral succession," which could palliate defect of the apostolic succession, seems to us in radical contradiction with the very nature of the presbyterate: this is, and can only be, representation of a local community of the Church to the ministry sent by Christ to his body, which alone, for this reason, can be the object of a succession. This succession is, in effect, only a *succession in the sending:* of the Father to the Son, of the Son to the preeminent apostles, of these apostles to the bishops, whom priests do not succeed (any more than they succeed one another) but are associated with in each generation.

## 4. *The False Decretals and the Donation of Constantine*

We have deliberately *not* introduced these two themes into our treatment, even in its historical section.

The false decretals, it is acknowledged today by all historians, did not emanate from Rome and did not have as their aim to uphold the papal primacy, but to rely on it, in order to guarantee the independence of episcopates versus temporal princes. Rome developed her own notion of her role, without recourse to them, and did not invoke them before the time of Gregory VII, that is, only when they were everywhere accepted.

As for the supposed Donation of Constantine, if indeed it was manufactured in the Curia (i.e., in its offices), it cannot be said that it ever served Rome to establish any theological thesis on the primacy. Quite the contrary. The theory of the two swords would, from its beginning, make any idea of a donation of this type superfluous, even contradictory. How could those who (in the supposition of Innocent III) received the temporal power from the spiritual power give the latter what was supposed to originate with it?

# Index
# Documents and Texts Relating to Vatican I and II

# Index
# Proper Names

# Subject Index